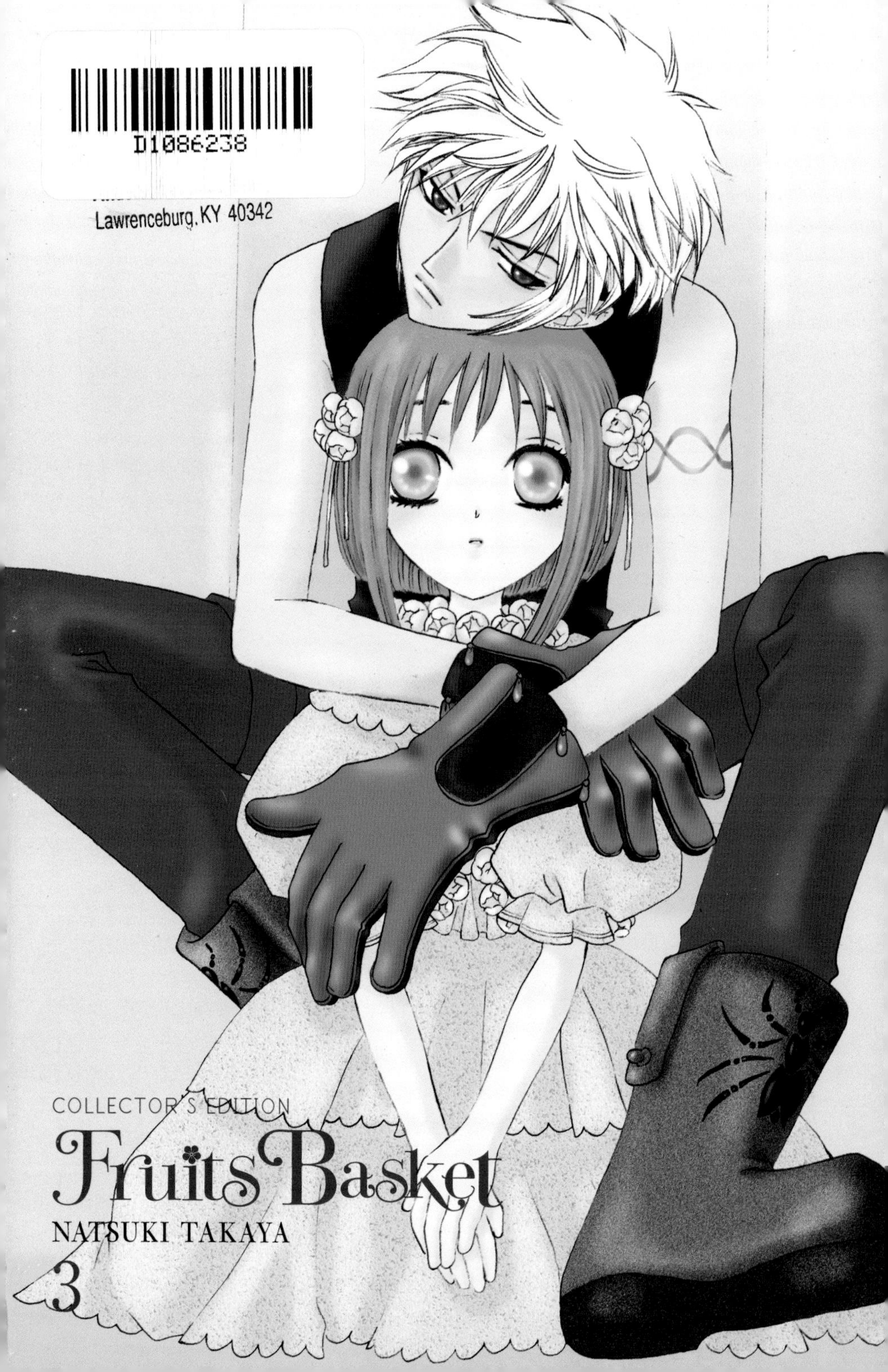

COLLECTOR'S EDITION

Fruits Basket

NATSUKI TAKAYA

3

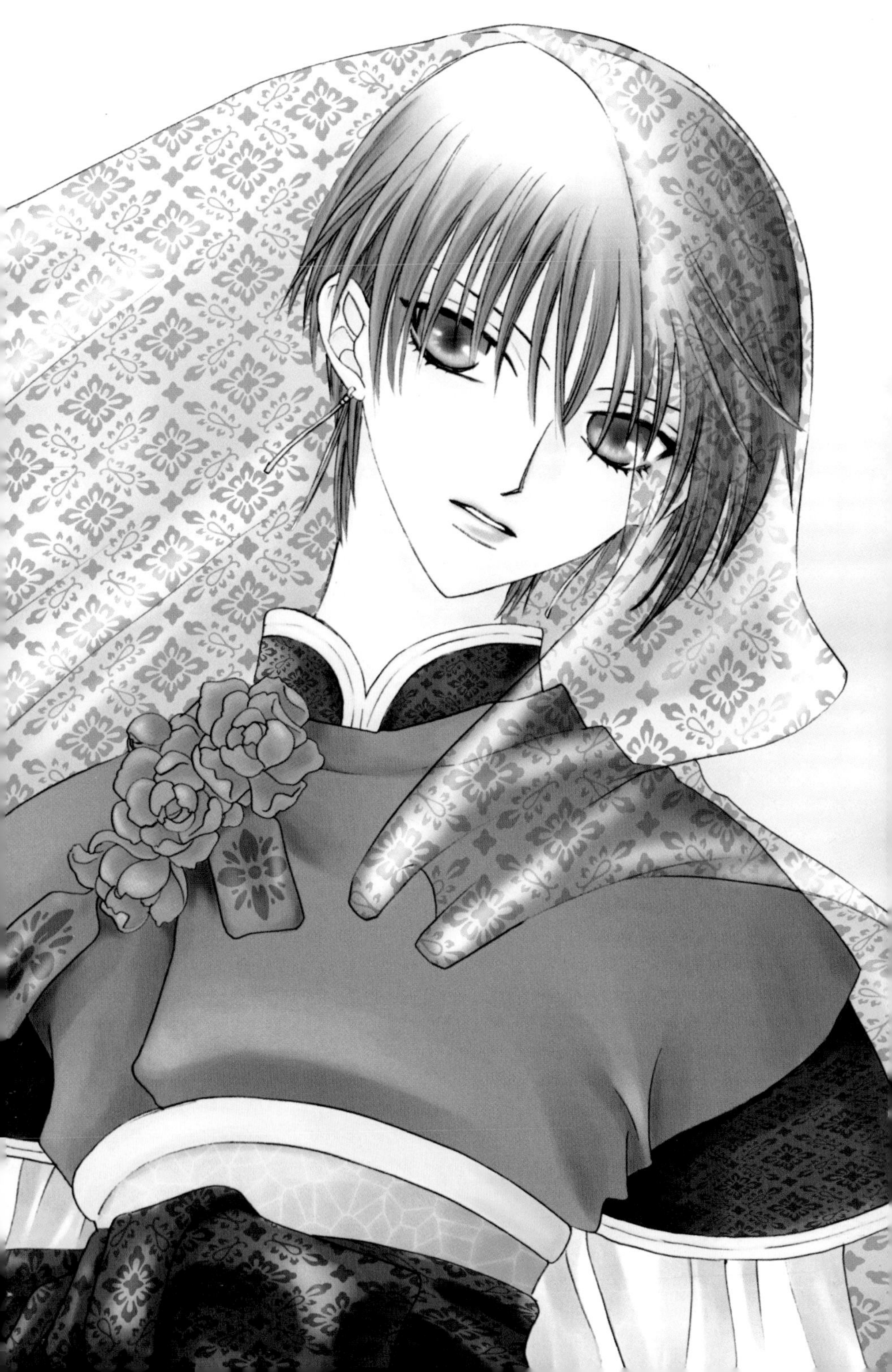

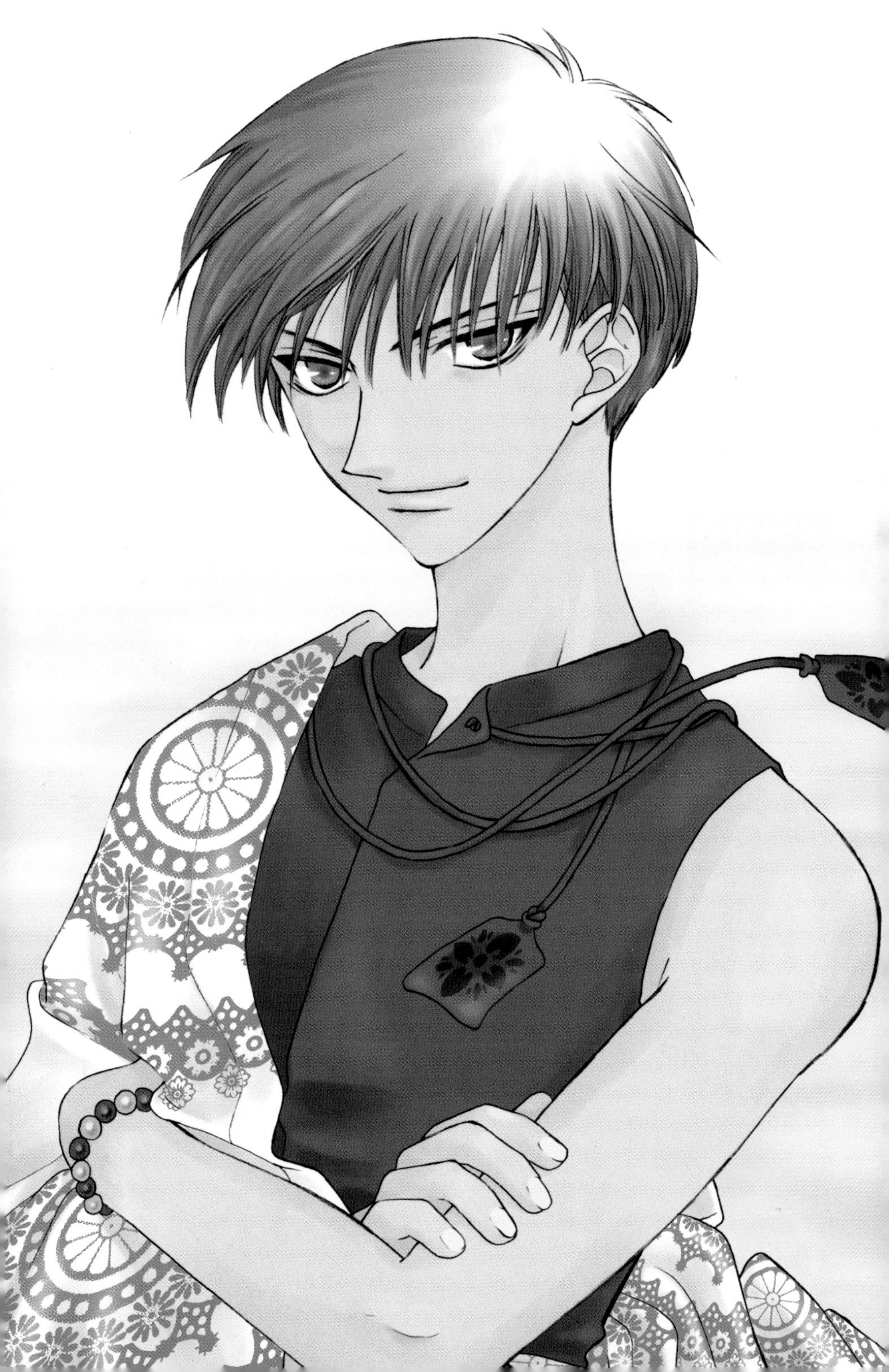

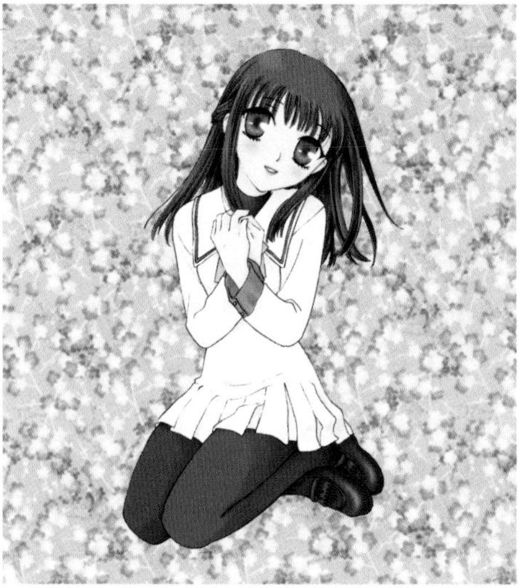

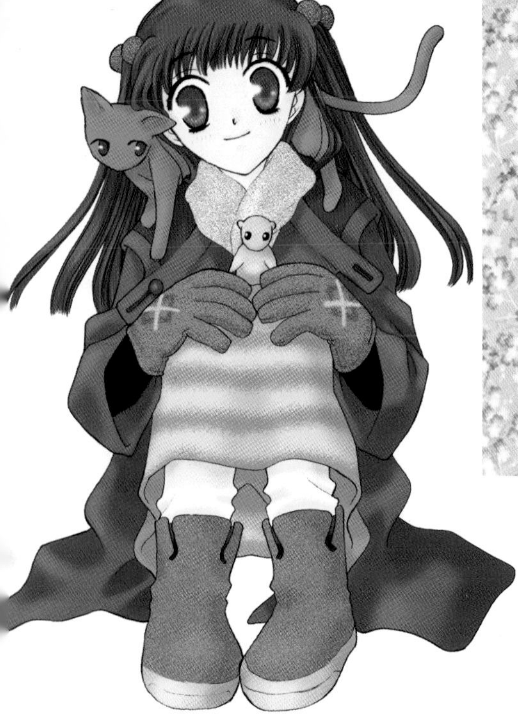

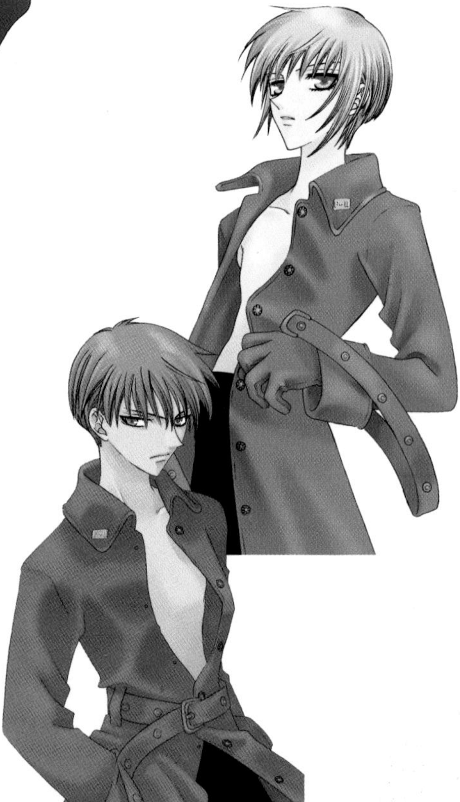

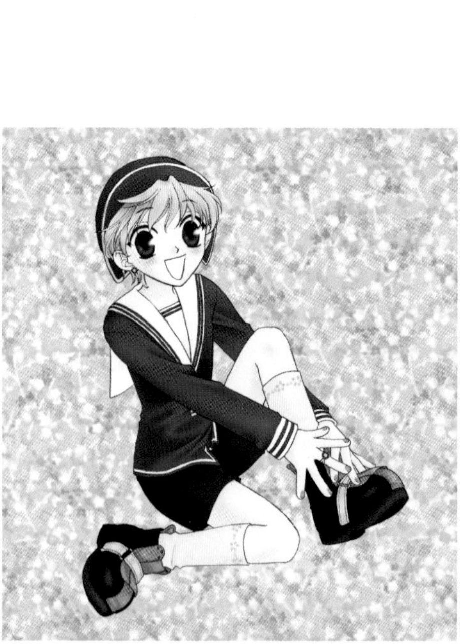

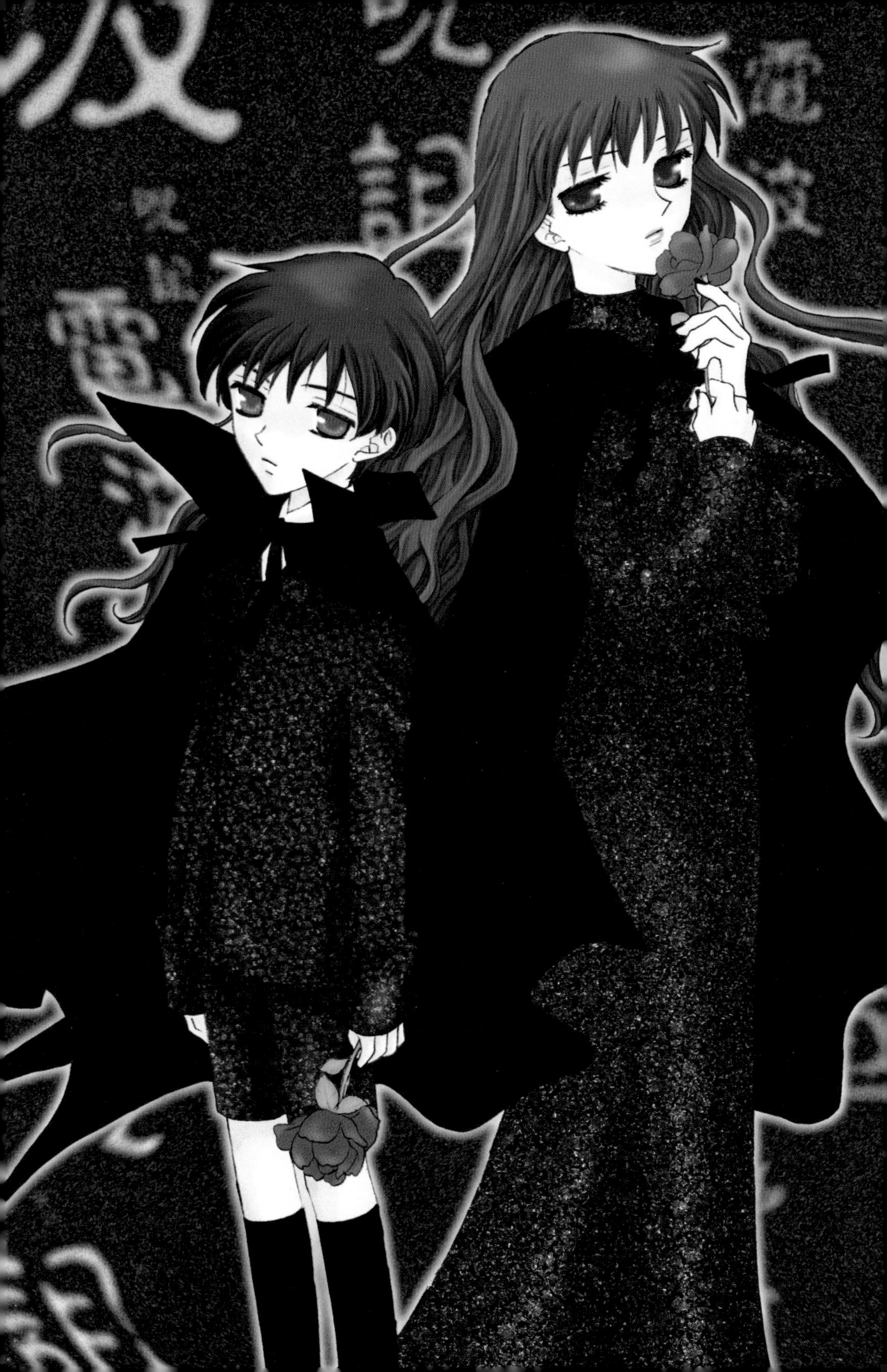

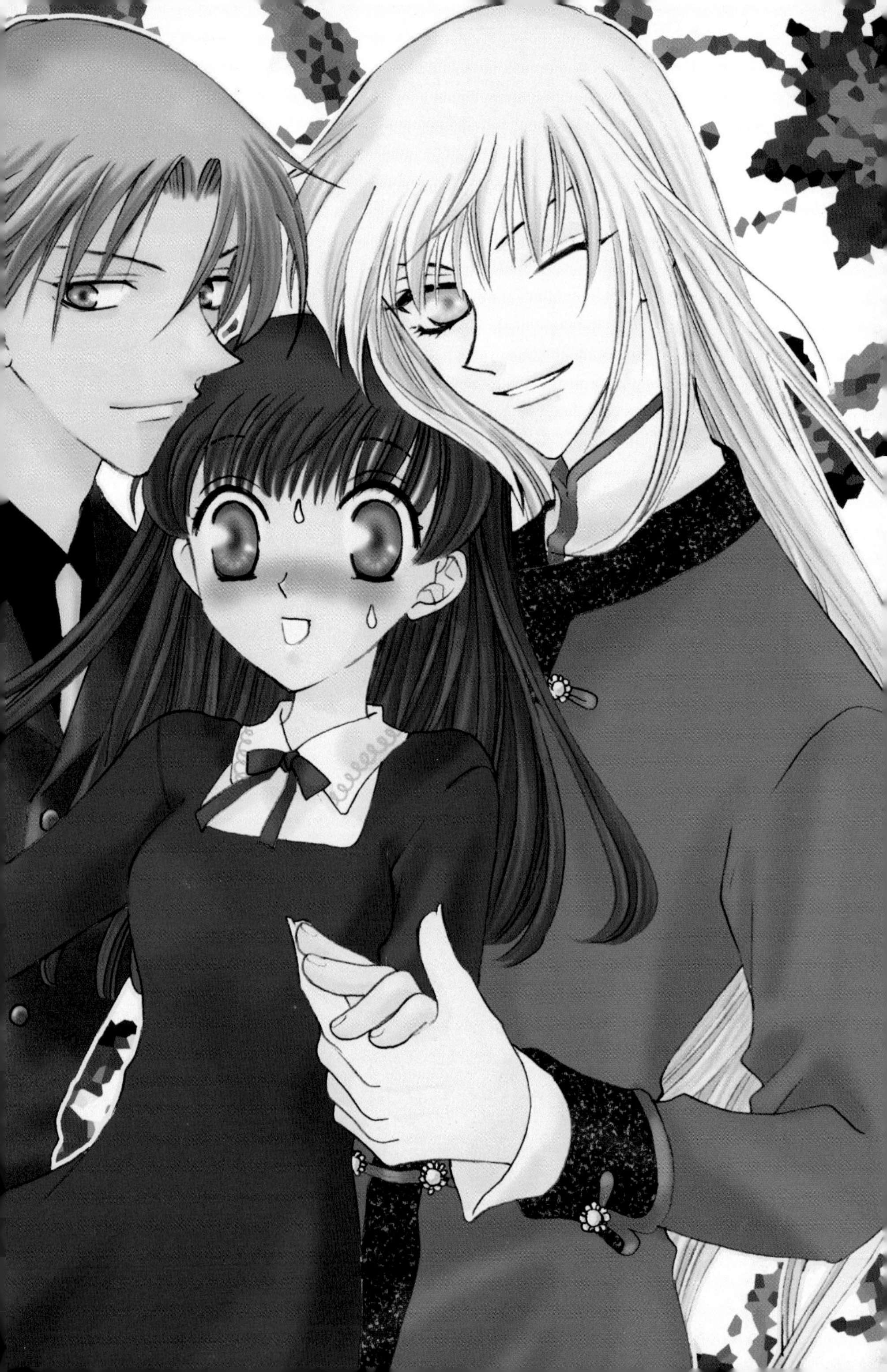

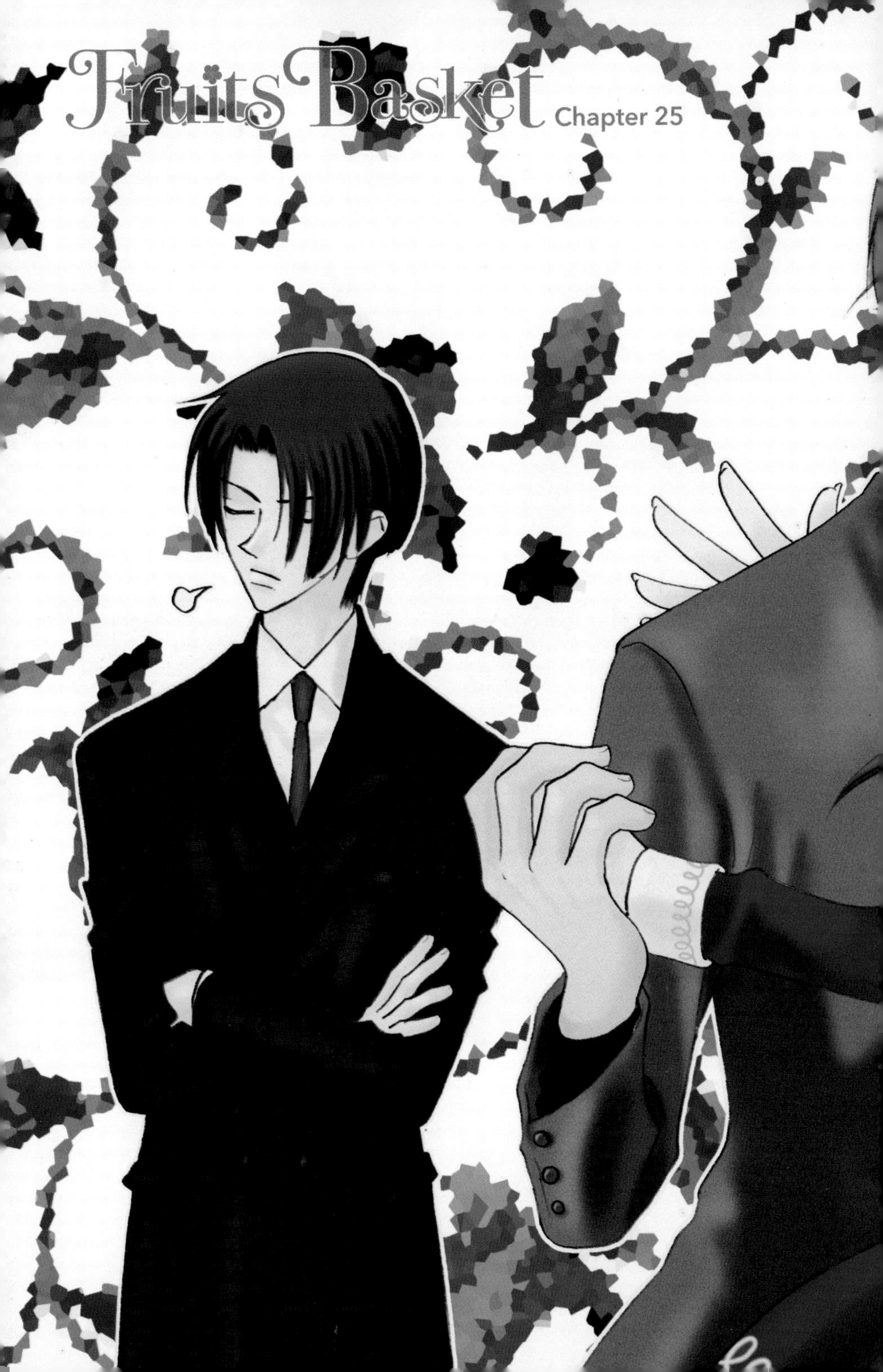
Fruits Basket
Chapter 25

TABLE OF CONTENTS
COLLECTOR'S EDITION

Fruits 3
Basket

Chapter 25 6
Chapter 26 39
Chapter 27 71
Chapter 28 101
Chapter 29 133
Chapter 30 165
Chapter 31 197
Chapter 32 229
Chapter 33 261
Chapter 34 293
Chapter 35 323
Chapter 36 355
Special Thanks
............387

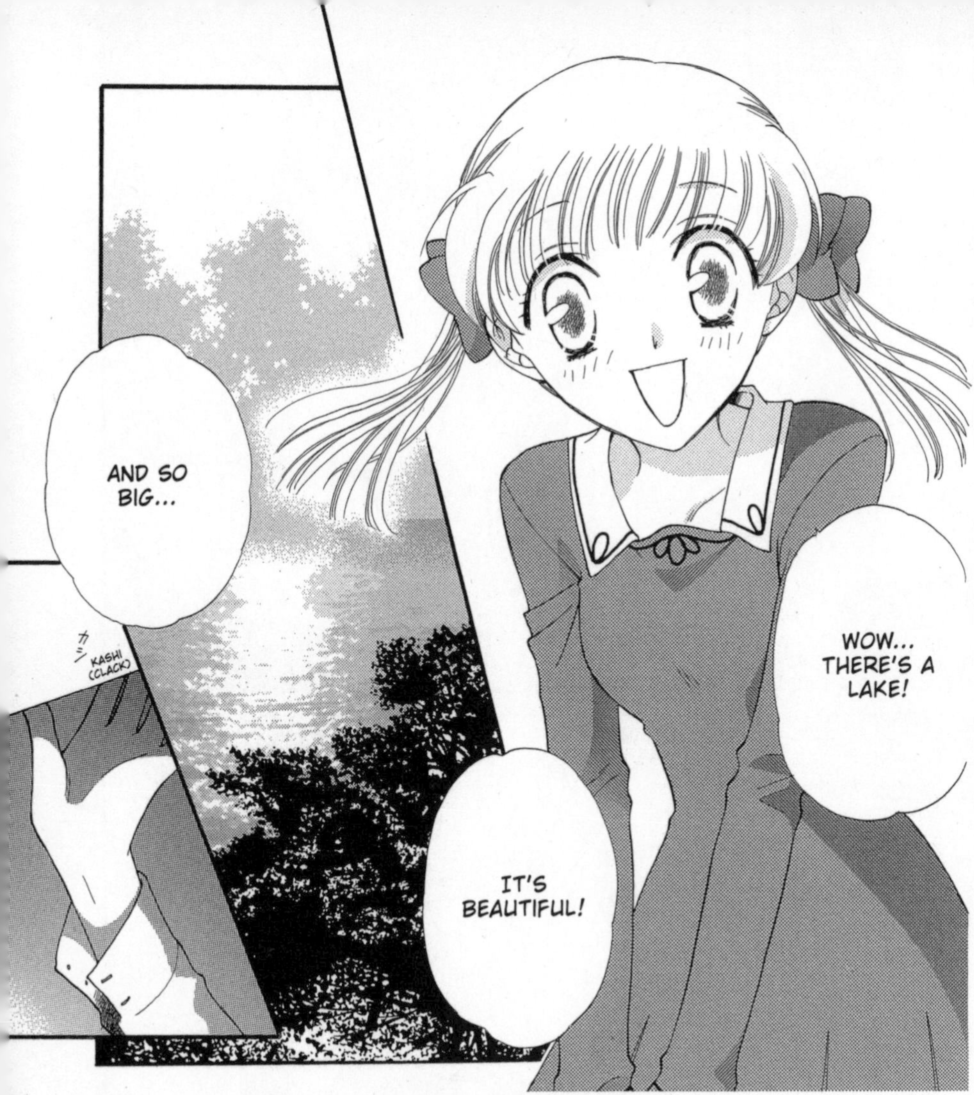
WOW... THERE'S A LAKE!
IT'S BEAUTIFUL!
AND SO BIG...
KASHI (CLACK)

tohru

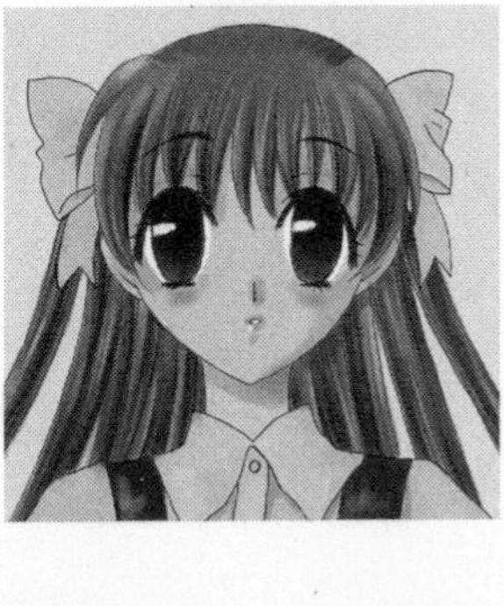

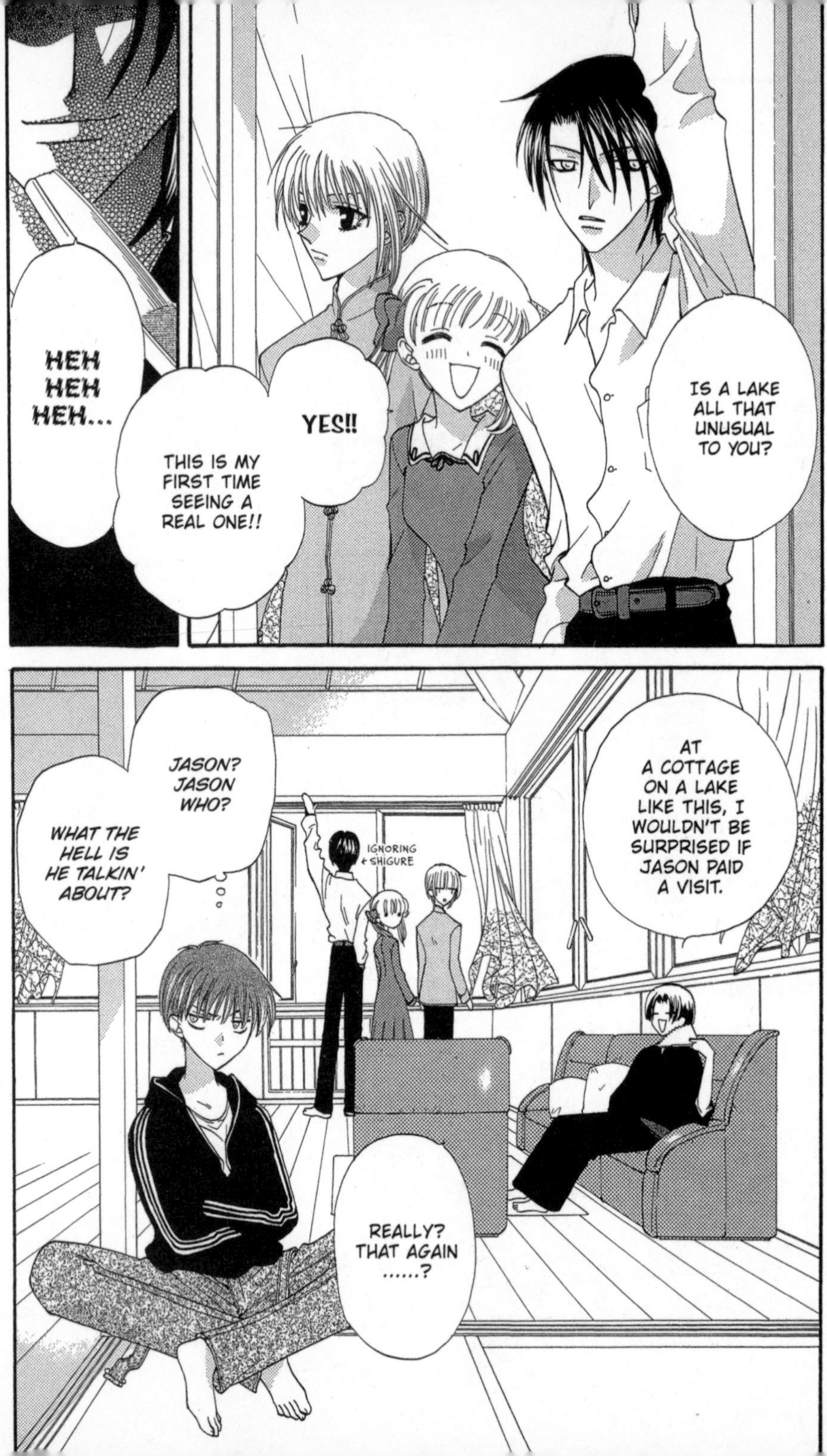
IS A LAKE ALL THAT UNUSUAL TO YOU?
YES!!
THIS IS MY FIRST TIME SEEING A REAL ONE!!
HEH HEH HEH...
AT A COTTAGE ON A LAKE LIKE THIS, I WOULDN'T BE SURPRISED IF JASON PAID A VISIT.
IGNORING SHIGURE
JASON? JASON WHO?
WHAT THE HELL IS HE TALKIN' ABOUT?
REALLY? THAT AGAIN ......?

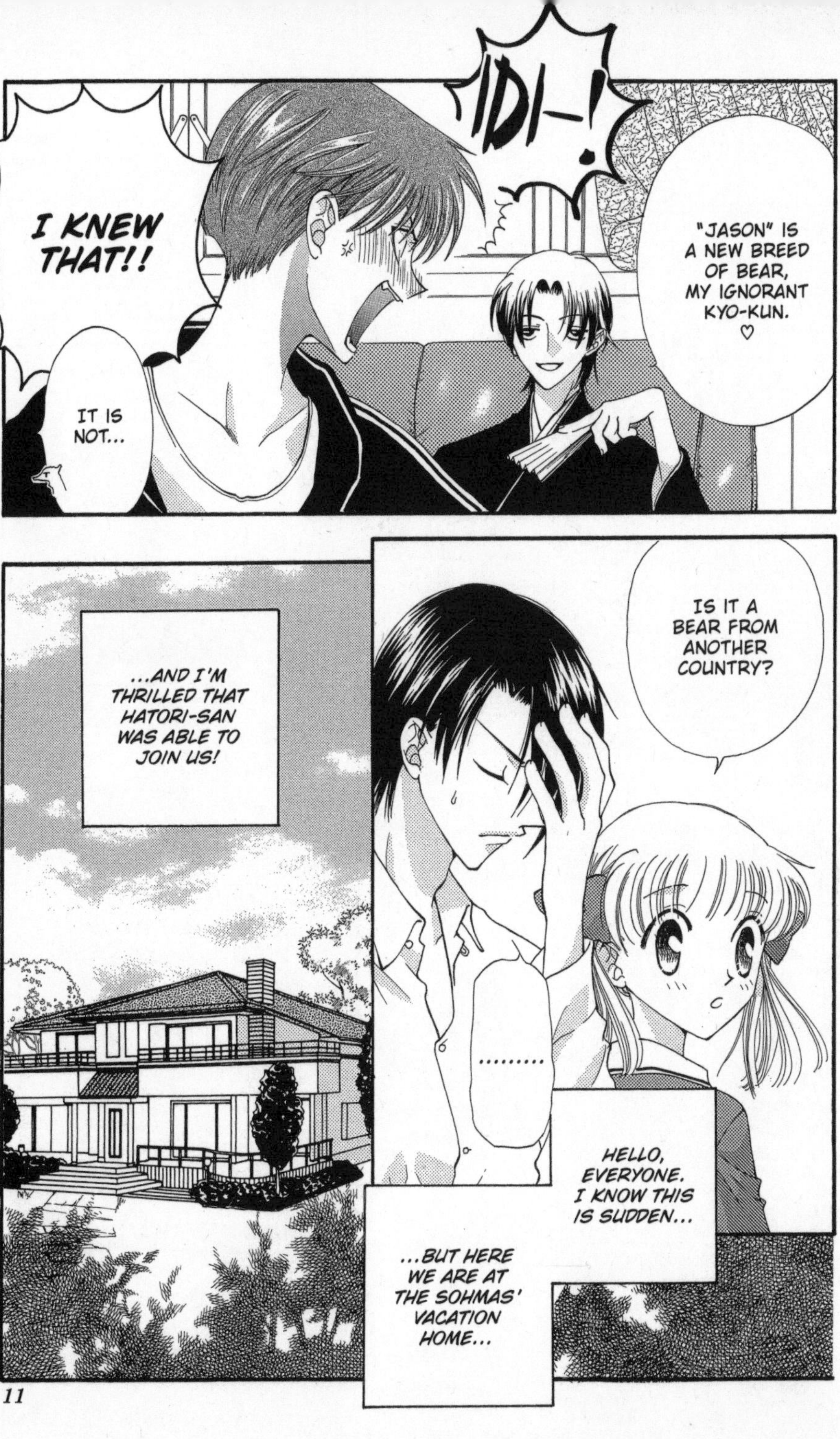
IDI—!
"JASON" IS A NEW BREED OF BEAR, MY IGNORANT KYO-KUN. ♡
I KNEW THAT!!
IT IS NOT...
IS IT A BEAR FROM ANOTHER COUNTRY?
....
HELLO, EVERYONE. I KNOW THIS IS SUDDEN...
...BUT HERE WE ARE AT THE SOHMAS' VACATION HOME...
...AND I'M THRILLED THAT HATORI-SAN WAS ABLE TO JOIN US!

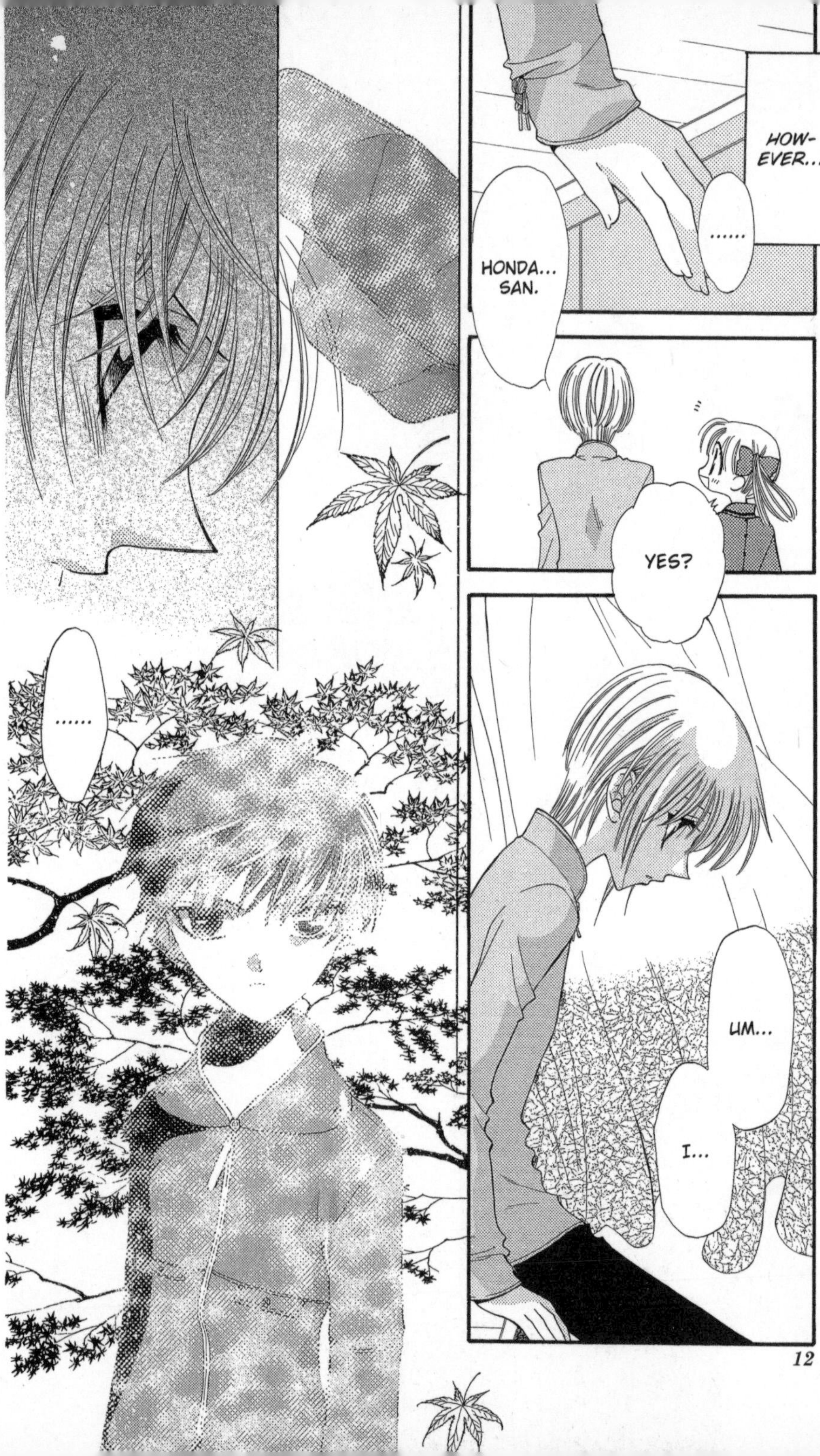
HOW-EVER...
......
HONDA... SAN.
YES?
UM...
I...
......

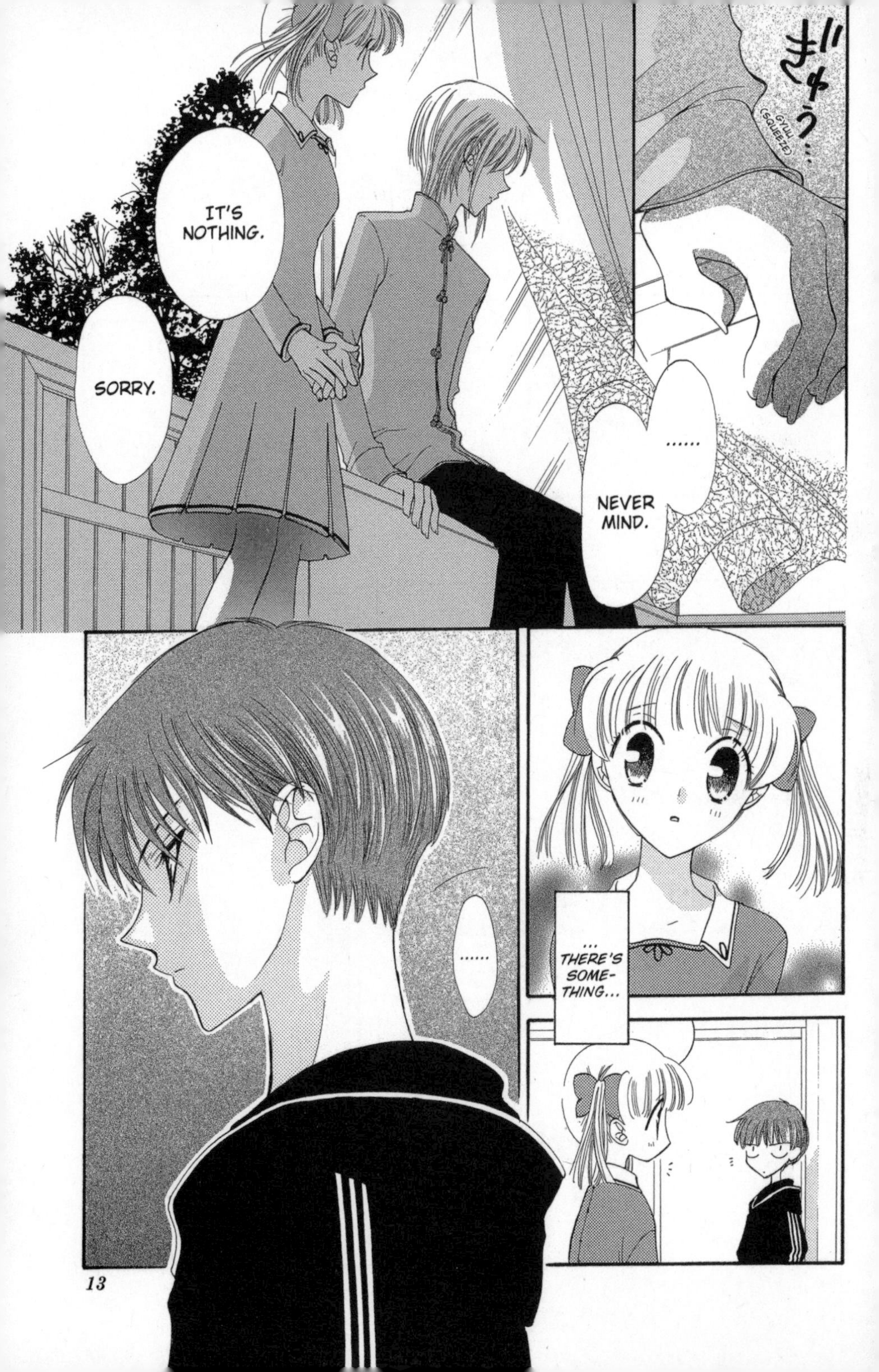
ぎゅう…
GYUU (SQUEEZE)
......
NEVER MIND.
IT'S NOTHING.
SORRY.
...THERE'S SOME-THING...
......

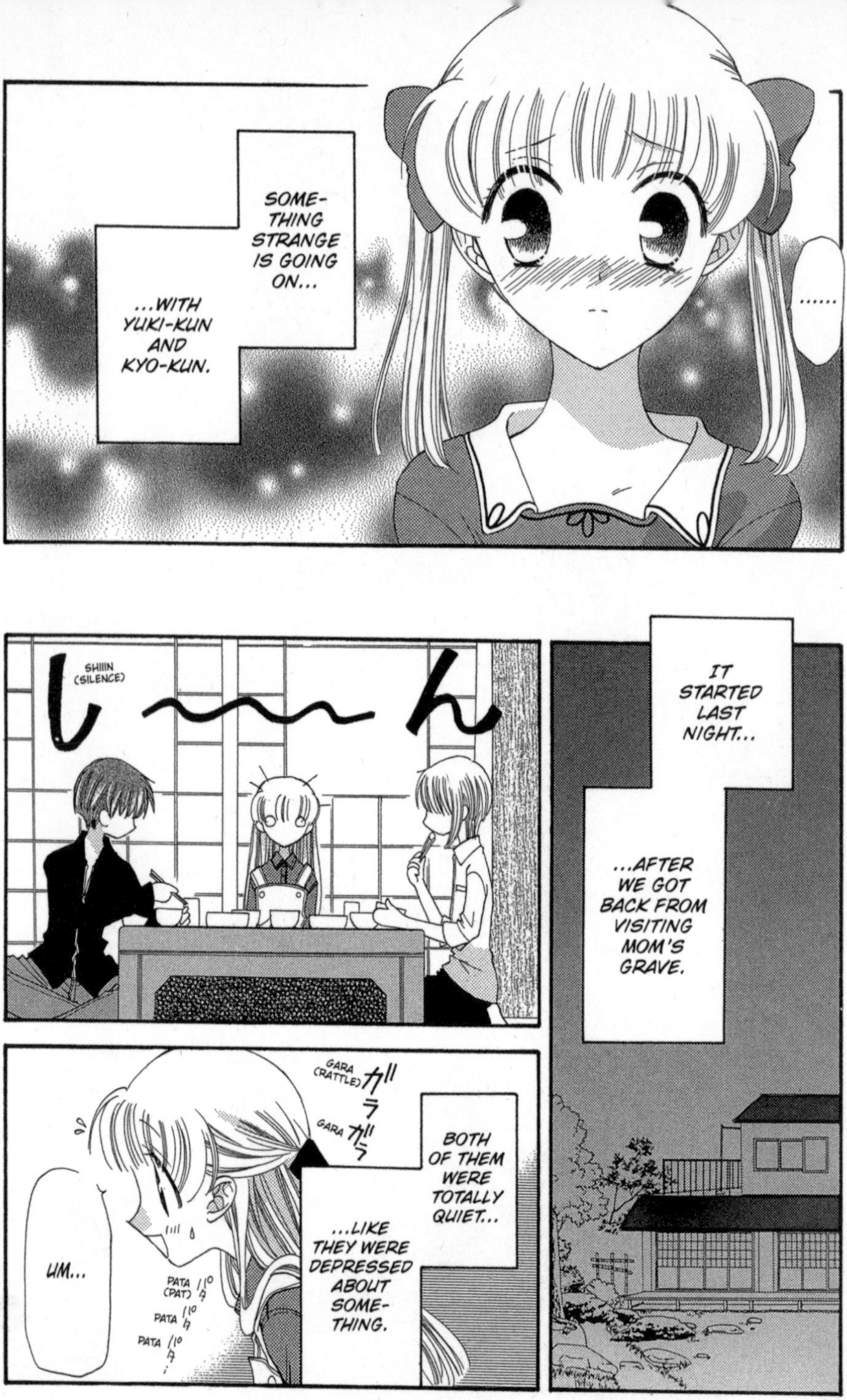
......
SOME-THING STRANGE IS GOING ON...
...WITH YUKI-KUN AND KYO-KUN.
IT STARTED LAST NIGHT...
...AFTER WE GOT BACK FROM VISITING MOM'S GRAVE.
しーーん
SHIIIN (SILENCE)
ガラ
GARA (RATTLE)
ガラ
GARA
BOTH OF THEM WERE TOTALLY QUIET...
...LIKE THEY WERE DEPRESSED ABOUT SOME-THING.
UM...
パタ
PATA (PAT)
パタ
PATA
パタ
PATA

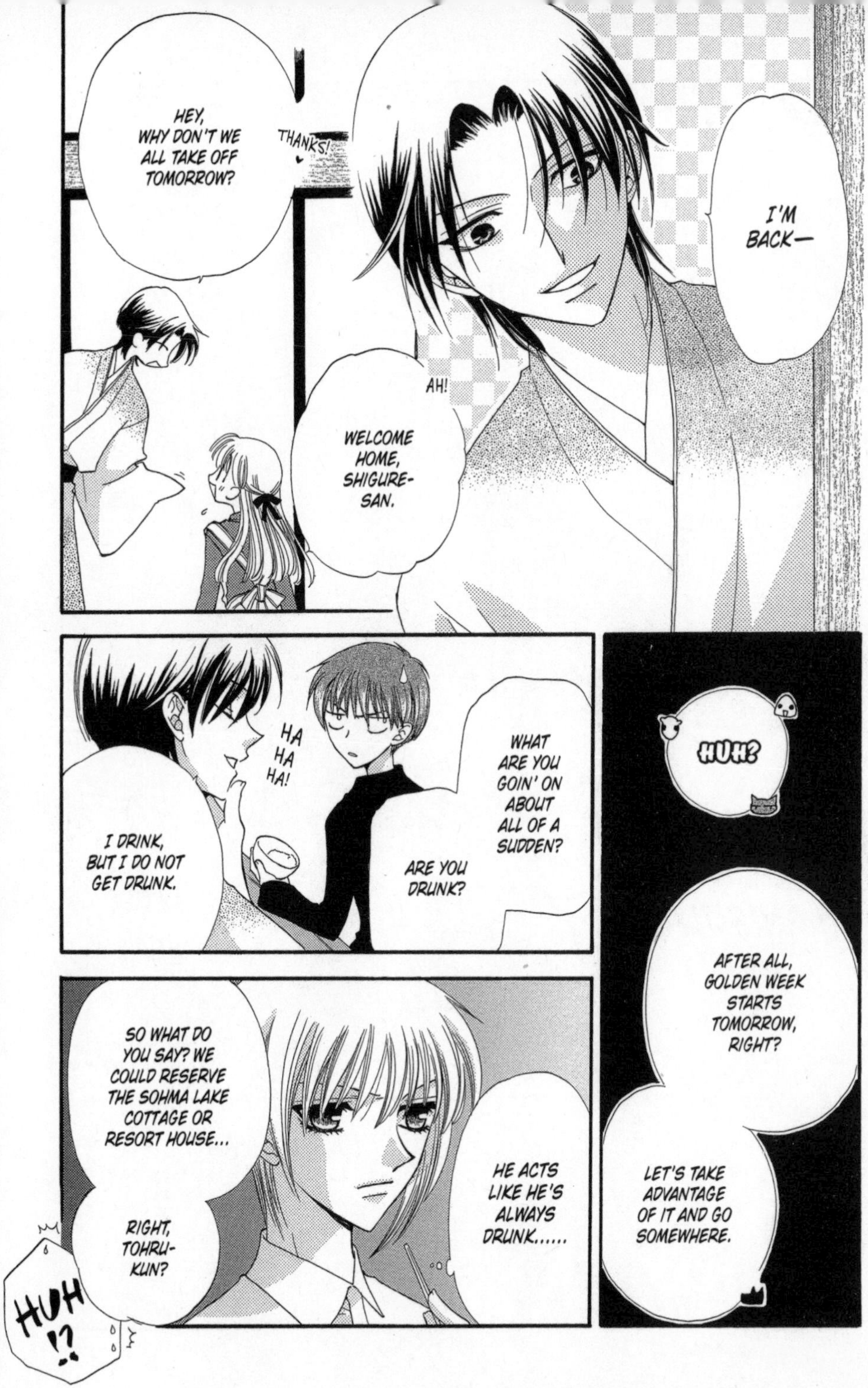
I'M BACK—
AH!
WELCOME HOME, SHIGURE-SAN.
THANKS!
HEY, WHY DON'T WE ALL TAKE OFF TOMORROW?
HUH?
AFTER ALL, GOLDEN WEEK STARTS TOMORROW, RIGHT?
LET'S TAKE ADVANTAGE OF IT AND GO SOMEWHERE.
WHAT ARE YOU GOIN' ON ABOUT ALL OF A SUDDEN?
ARE YOU DRUNK?
HA HA HA!
I DRINK, BUT I DO NOT GET DRUNK.
HE ACTS LIKE HE'S ALWAYS DRUNK......
SO WHAT DO YOU SAY? WE COULD RESERVE THE SOHMA LAKE COTTAGE OR RESORT HOUSE...
RIGHT, TOHRU-KUN?
HUH !?

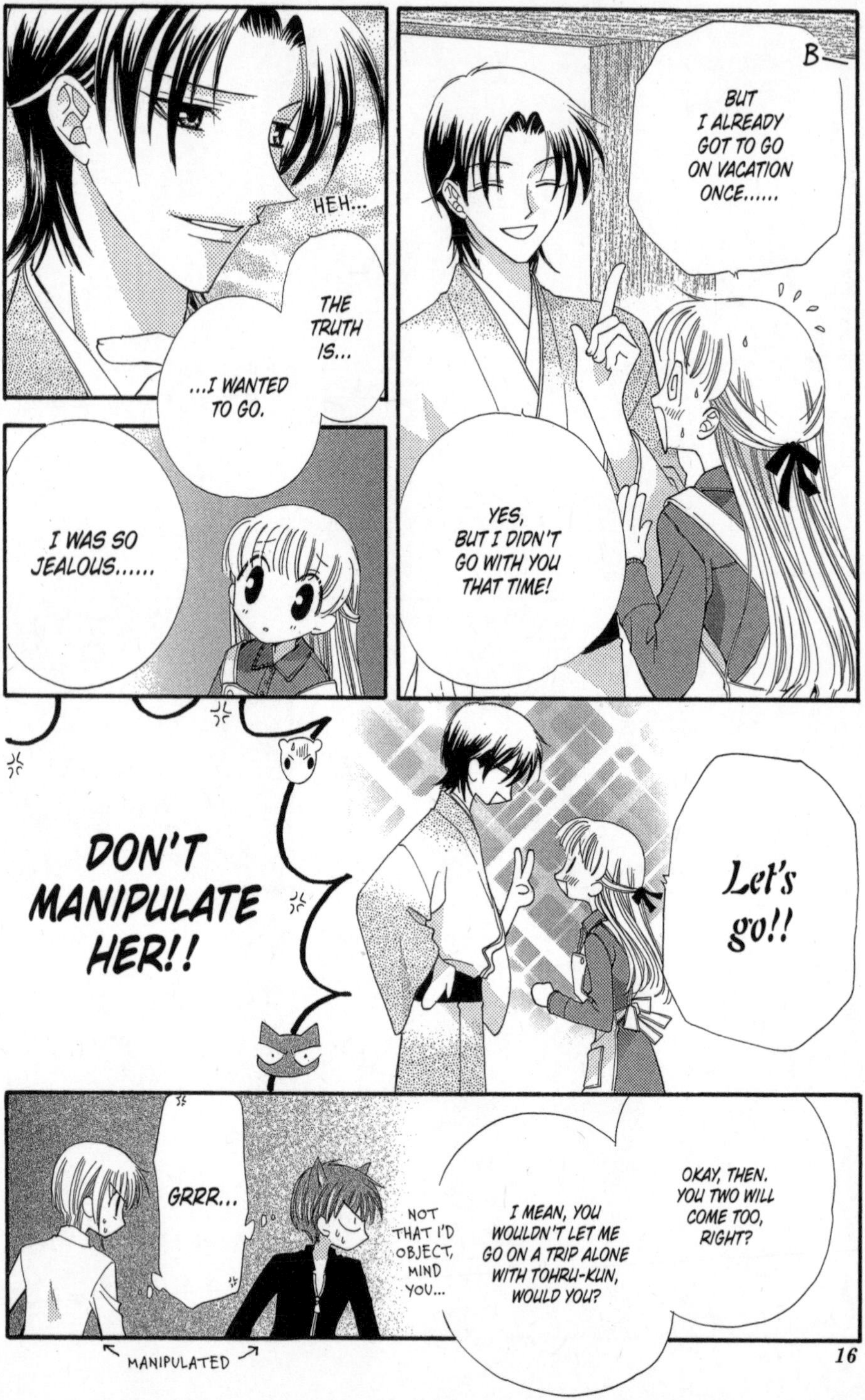
B—
BUT I ALREADY GOT TO GO ON VACATION ONCE......
YES, BUT I DIDN'T GO WITH YOU THAT TIME!
HEH...
THE TRUTH IS...
...I WANTED TO GO.
I WAS SO JEALOUS......
Let's go!!
DON'T MANIPULATE HER!!
OKAY, THEN. YOU TWO WILL COME TOO, RIGHT?
I MEAN, YOU WOULDN'T LET ME GO ON A TRIP ALONE WITH TOHRU-KUN, WOULD YOU?
NOT THAT I'D OBJECT, MIND YOU...
GRRR...
MANIPULATED

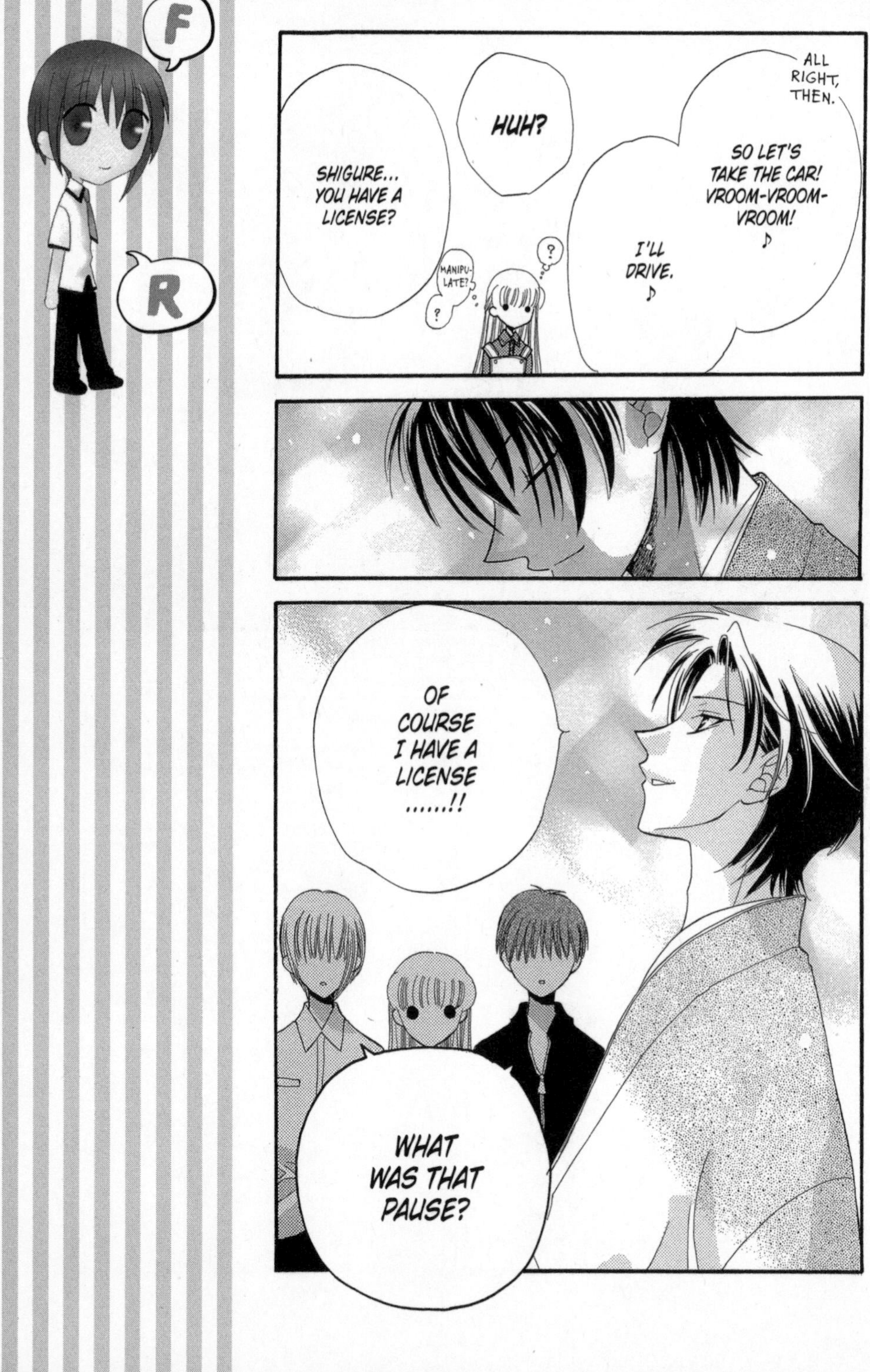
ALL RIGHT, THEN.
SO LET'S TAKE THE CAR! VROOM-VROOM-VROOM! ♪
I'LL DRIVE. ♪
HUH?
SHIGURE... YOU HAVE A LICENSE?
?
MANIPU-LATE?
?
OF COURSE I HAVE A LICENSE ......!!
WHAT WAS THAT PAUSE?
F
R

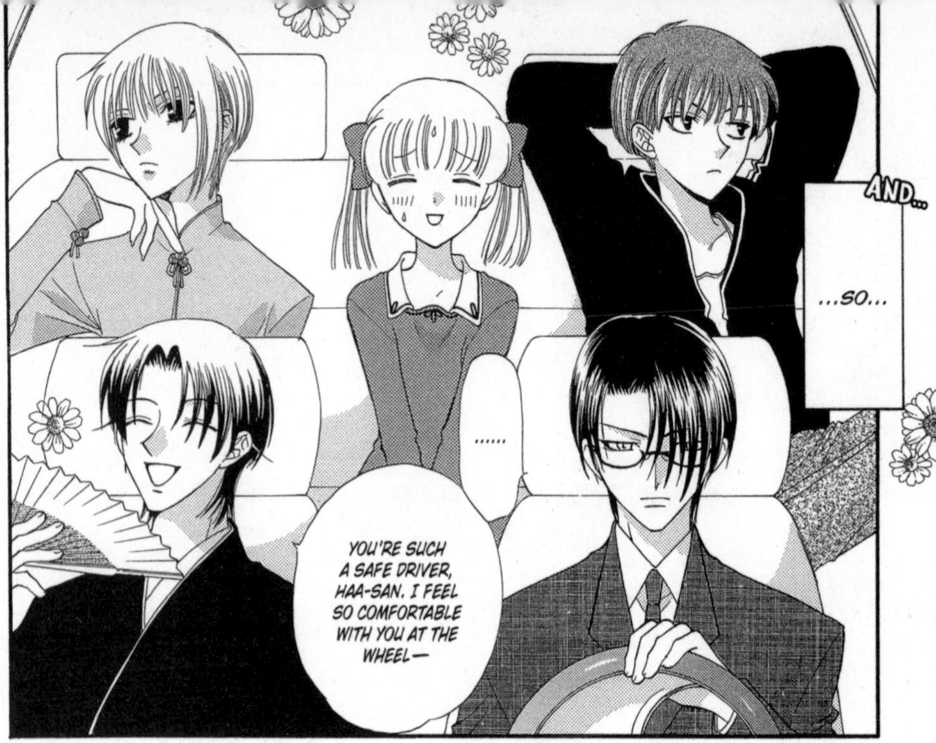
AND...
...SO...
......
YOU'RE SUCH A SAFE DRIVER, HAA-SAN. I FEEL SO COMFORTABLE WITH YOU AT THE WHEEL—

DRIVING A WESTERN CAR, STEERING WHEEL ON THE LEFT

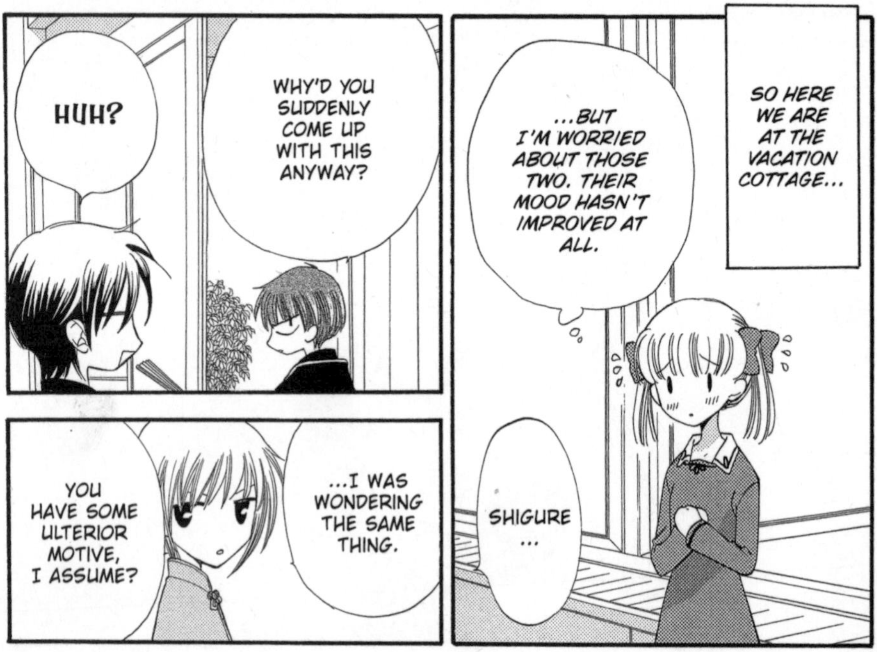
SO HERE WE ARE AT THE VACATION COTTAGE...
...BUT I'M WORRIED ABOUT THOSE TWO. THEIR MOOD HASN'T IMPROVED AT ALL.
SHIGURE ...
WHY'D YOU SUDDENLY COME UP WITH THIS ANYWAY?
HUH?
...I WAS WONDERING THE SAME THING.
YOU HAVE SOME ULTERIOR MOTIVE, I ASSUME?

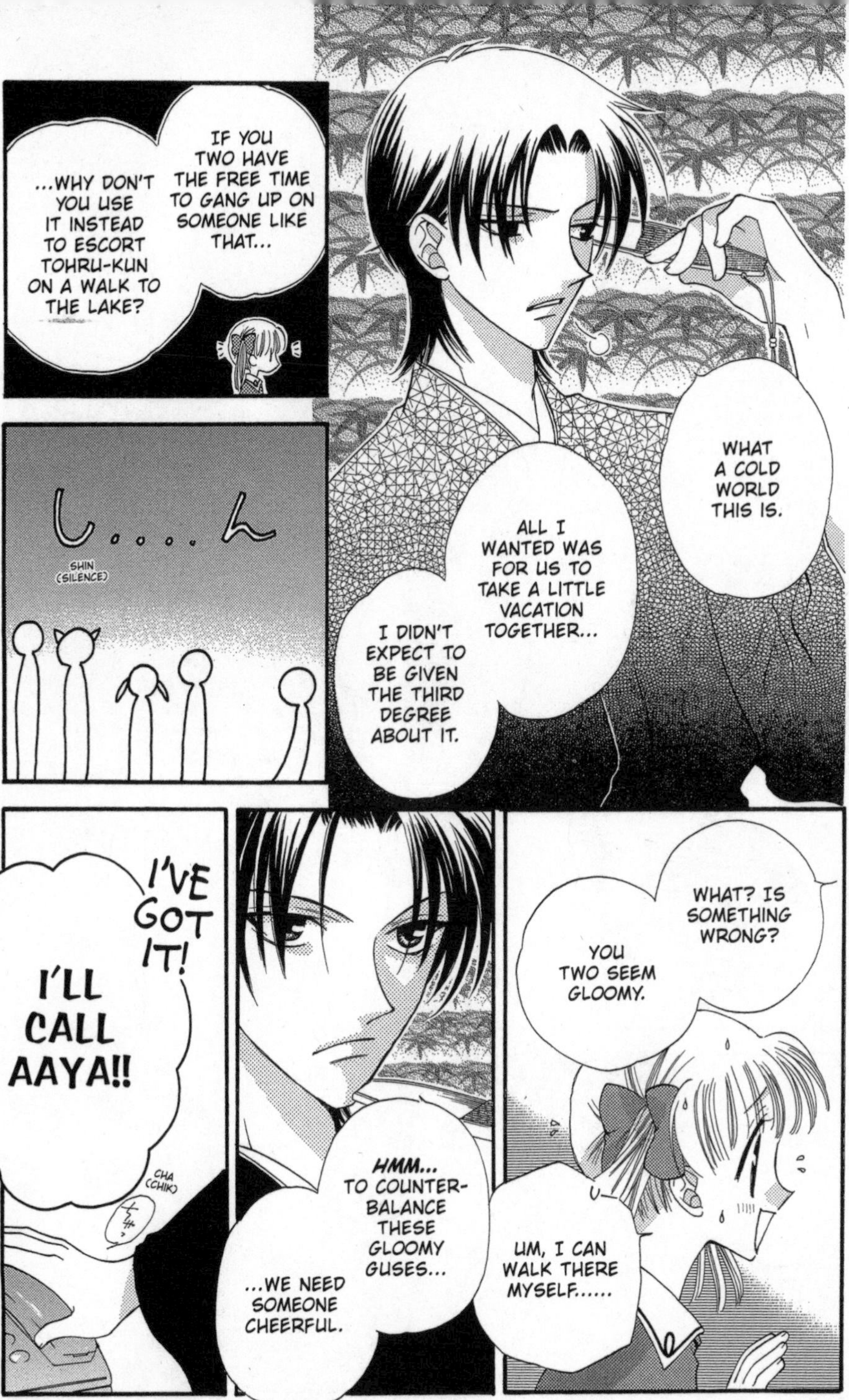
WHAT A COLD WORLD THIS IS.
ALL I WANTED WAS FOR US TO TAKE A LITTLE VACATION TOGETHER...
I DIDN'T EXPECT TO BE GIVEN THE THIRD DEGREE ABOUT IT.
IF YOU TWO HAVE THE FREE TIME TO GANG UP ON SOMEONE LIKE THAT...
...WHY DON'T YOU USE IT INSTEAD TO ESCORT TOHRU-KUN ON A WALK TO THE LAKE?
し...ん
SHIN (SILENCE)
WHAT? IS SOMETHING WRONG?
YOU TWO SEEM GLOOMY.
UM, I CAN WALK THERE MYSELF......
HMM... TO COUNTER-BALANCE THESE GLOOMY GUSES...
...WE NEED SOMEONE CHEERFUL.
I'VE GOT IT!
I'LL CALL AAYA!!
CHA (CHIK)

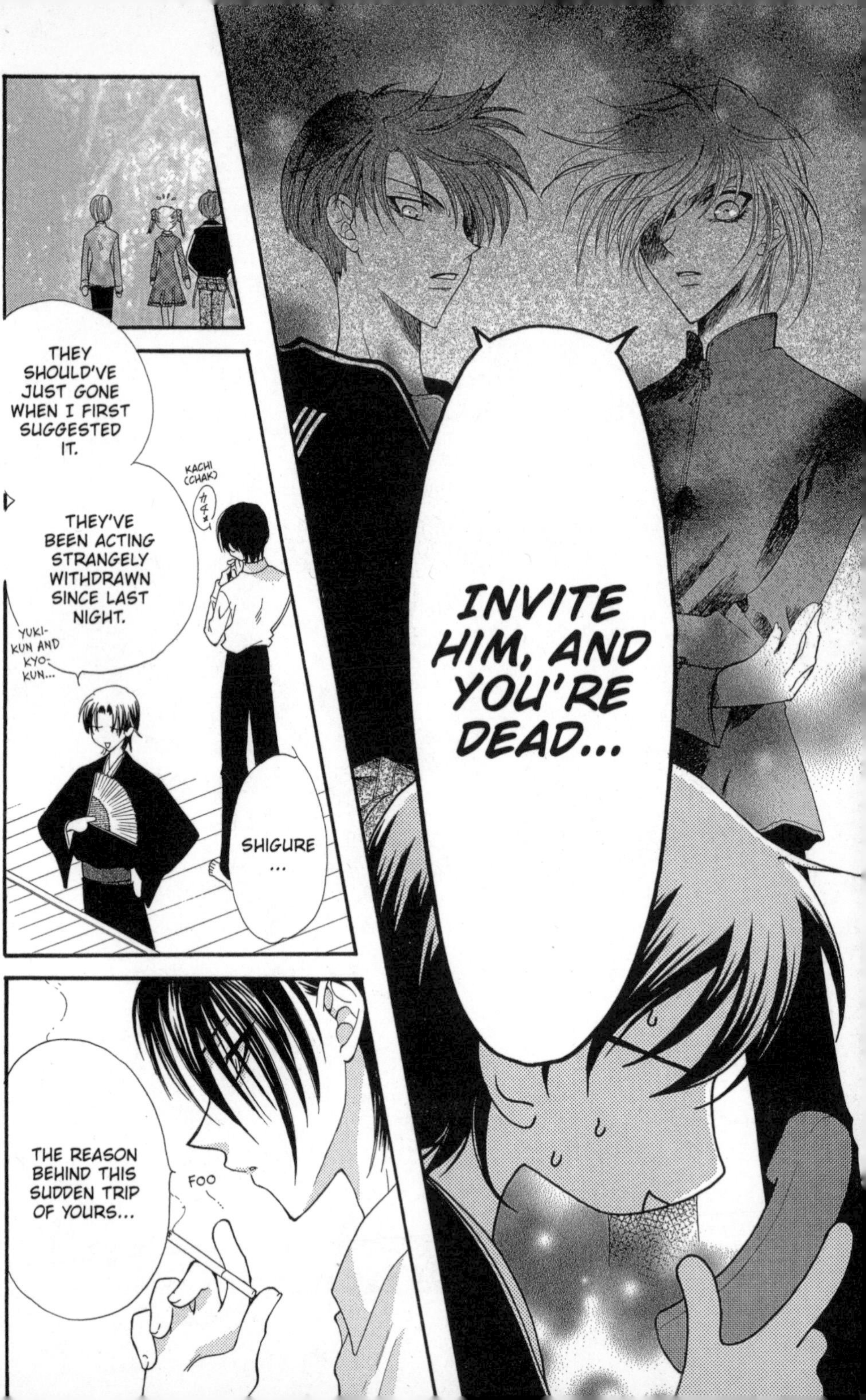
INVITE HIM, AND YOU'RE DEAD...
KACHI (CHAK)
SHIGURE...
THEY SHOULD'VE JUST GONE WHEN I FIRST SUGGESTED IT.
THEY'VE BEEN ACTING STRANGELY WITHDRAWN SINCE LAST NIGHT.
YUKI-KUN AND KYO-KUN...
FOO
THE REASON BEHIND THIS SUDDEN TRIP OF YOURS...

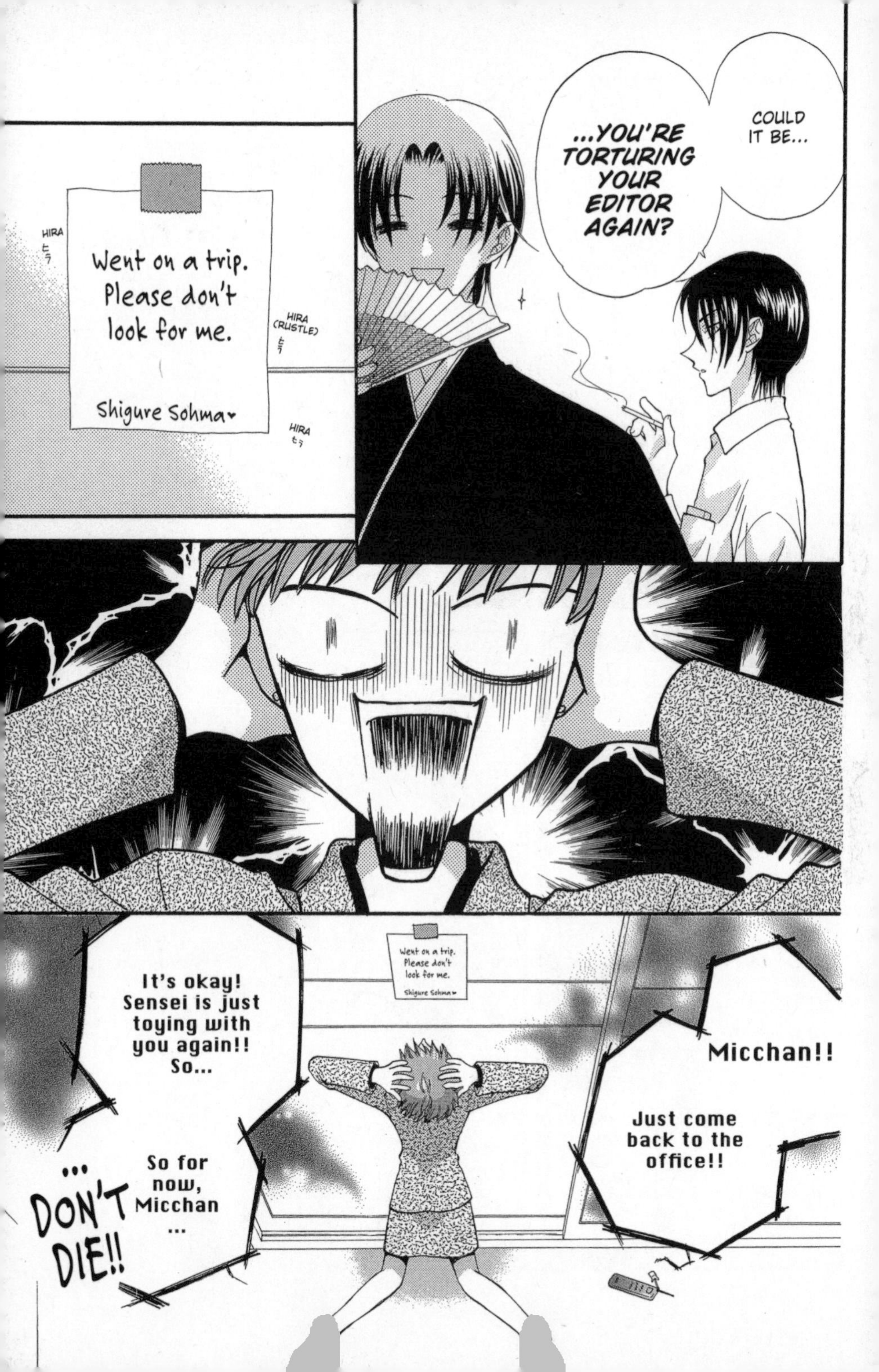
COULD IT BE...
...YOU'RE TORTURING YOUR EDITOR AGAIN?
HIRA
Went on a trip. Please don't look for me.
Shigure Sohma♥
HIRA (RUSTLE)
HIRA
Went on a trip. Please don't look for me.
Shigure Sohma♥
Micchan!!
Just come back to the office!!
It's okay! Sensei is just toying with you again!! So...
So for now, Micchan ...
... DON'T DIE!!

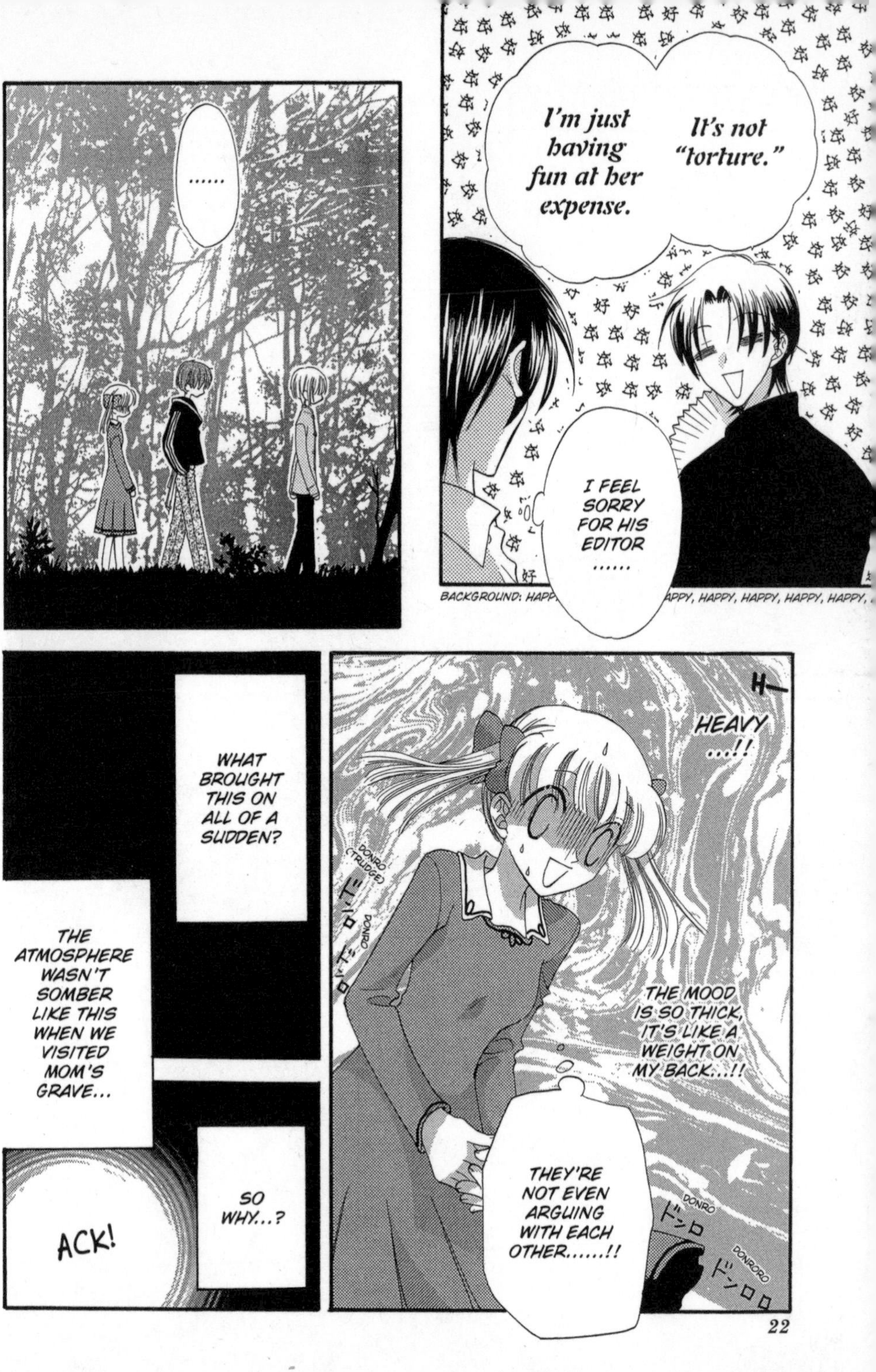

It's not "torture."
I'm just having fun at her expense.
I FEEL SORRY FOR HIS EDITOR ......
BACKGROUND: HAPP
APPY, HAPPY, HAPPY, HAPPY, HAPPY,
......
H—
HEAVY ...!!
DONRO (TRUDGE)
THE MOOD IS SO THICK, IT'S LIKE A WEIGHT ON MY BACK...!!
THEY'RE NOT EVEN ARGUING WITH EACH OTHER......!!
DONRO
DONRORO
WHAT BROUGHT THIS ON ALL OF A SUDDEN?
THE ATMOSPHERE WASN'T SOMBER LIKE THIS WHEN WE VISITED MOM'S GRAVE...
SO WHY...?
ACK!

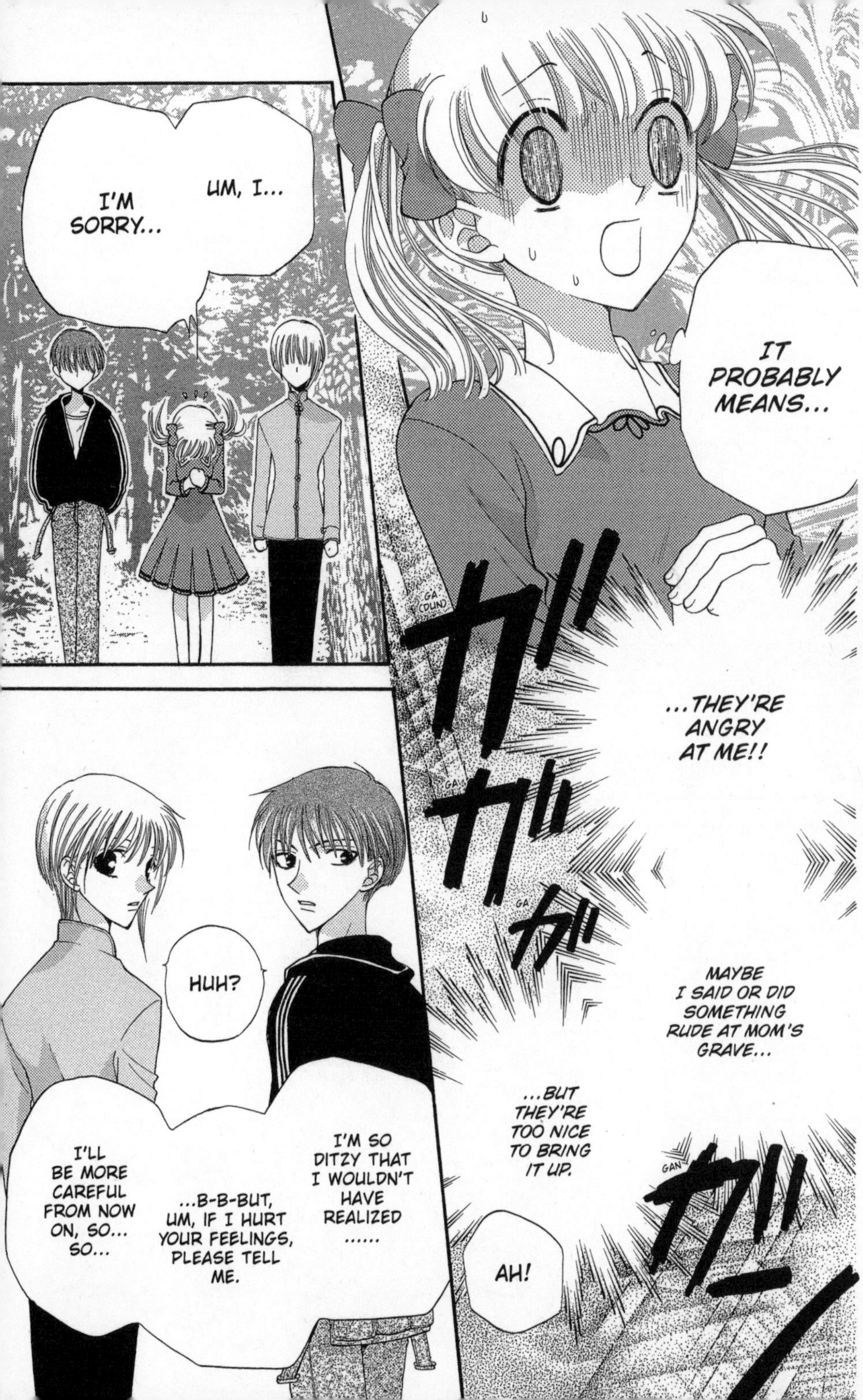
IT PROBABLY MEANS...
GA (DUN)
GA
...THEY'RE ANGRY AT ME!!
GA
MAYBE I SAID OR DID SOMETHING RUDE AT MOM'S GRAVE...
...BUT THEY'RE TOO NICE TO BRING IT UP.
GAN
AH!
UM, I...
I'M SORRY...
HUH?
I'M SO DITZY THAT I WOULDN'T HAVE REALIZED ......
...B-B-BUT, UM, IF I HURT YOUR FEELINGS, PLEASE TELL ME.
I'LL BE MORE CAREFUL FROM NOW ON, SO... SO...

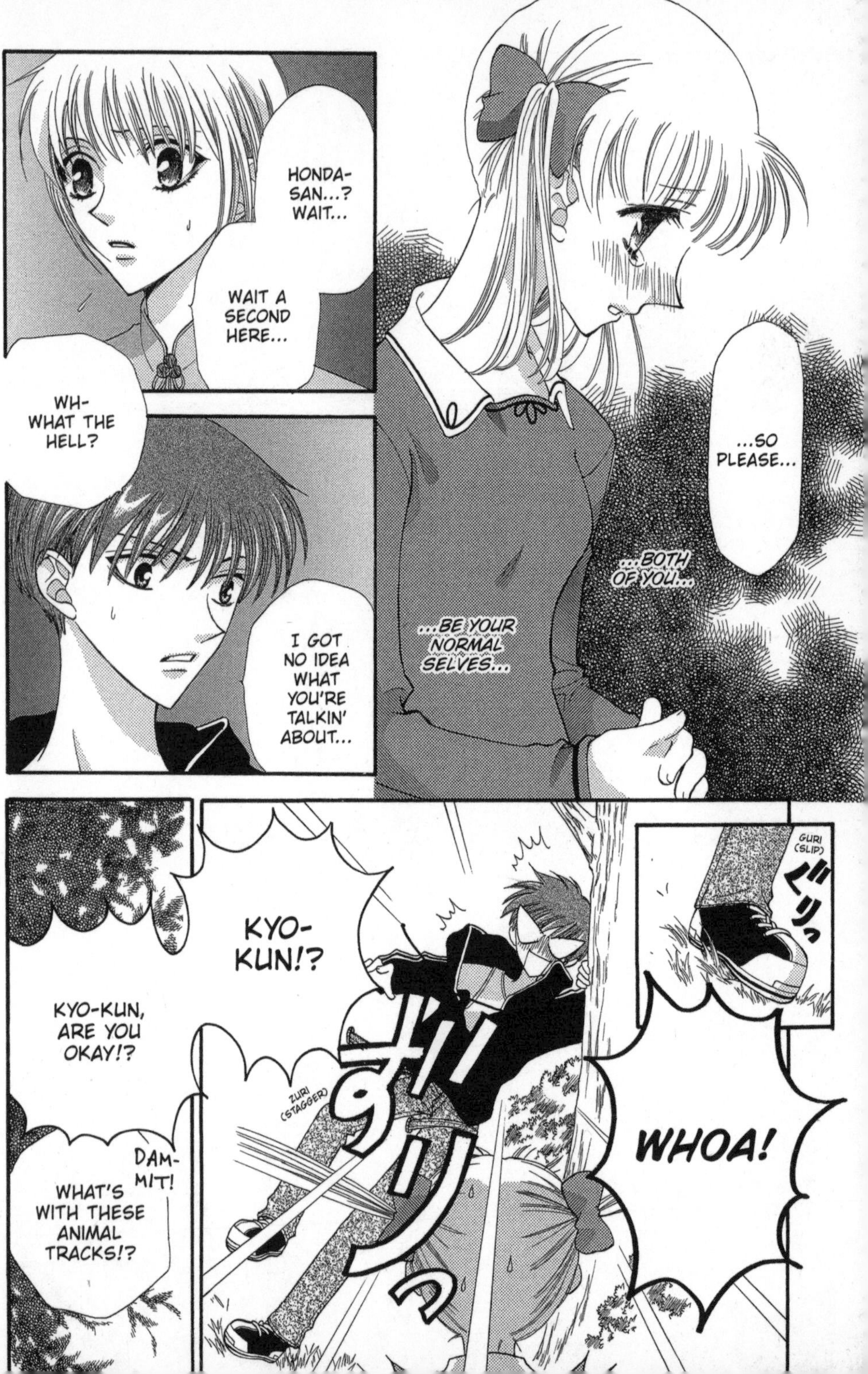
...SO PLEASE...
...BOTH OF YOU...
...BE YOUR NORMAL SELVES...
HONDA-SAN...? WAIT...
WAIT A SECOND HERE...
WH- WHAT THE HELL?
I GOT NO IDEA WHAT YOU'RE TALKIN' ABOUT...
GURI (SLIP)
ぐりっ
WHOA!
ずりっ
ZURI (STAGGER)
KYO-KUN!?
KYO-KUN, ARE YOU OKAY!?
DAM-MIT!
WHAT'S WITH THESE ANIMAL TRACKS!?

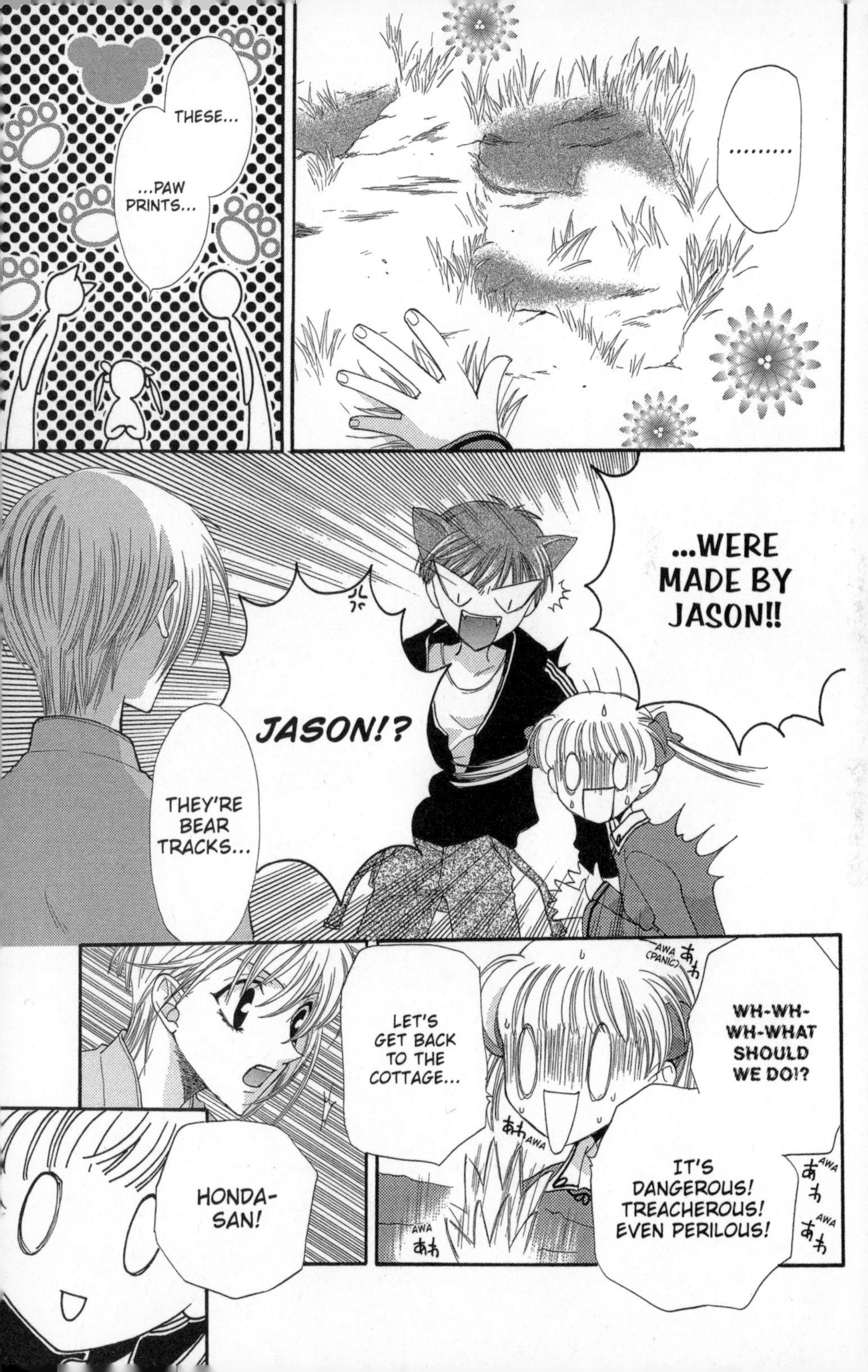
....
THESE...
...PAW PRINTS...
...WERE MADE BY JASON!!
JASON!?
THEY'RE BEAR TRACKS...
WH-WH-WH-WHAT SHOULD WE DO!?
あわ AWA (PANIC)
あわ AWA
IT'S DANGEROUS! TREACHEROUS! EVEN PERILOUS!
あわ AWA
あわ AWA
あわ AWA
LET'S GET BACK TO THE COTTAGE...
HONDA-SAN!

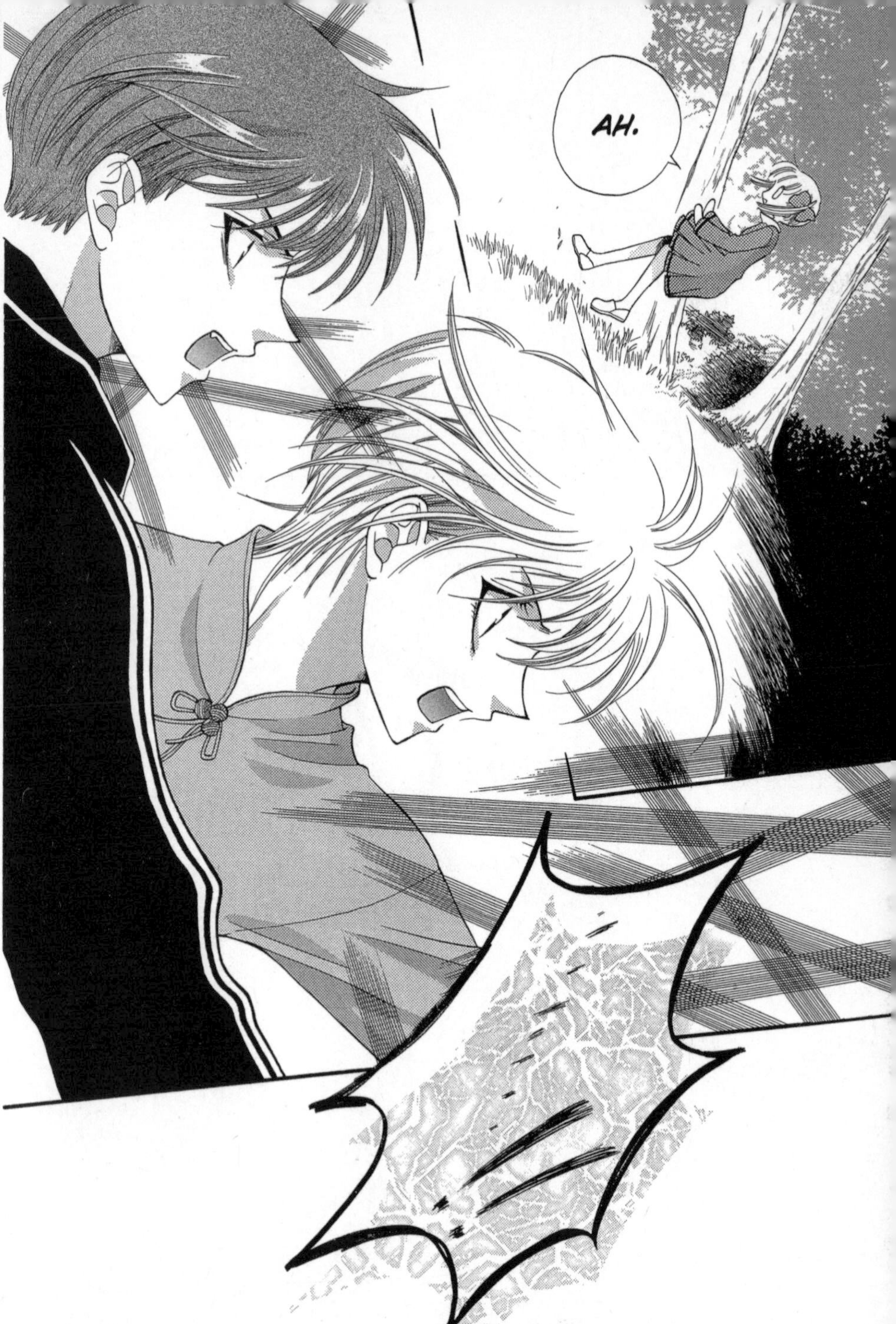
AH.

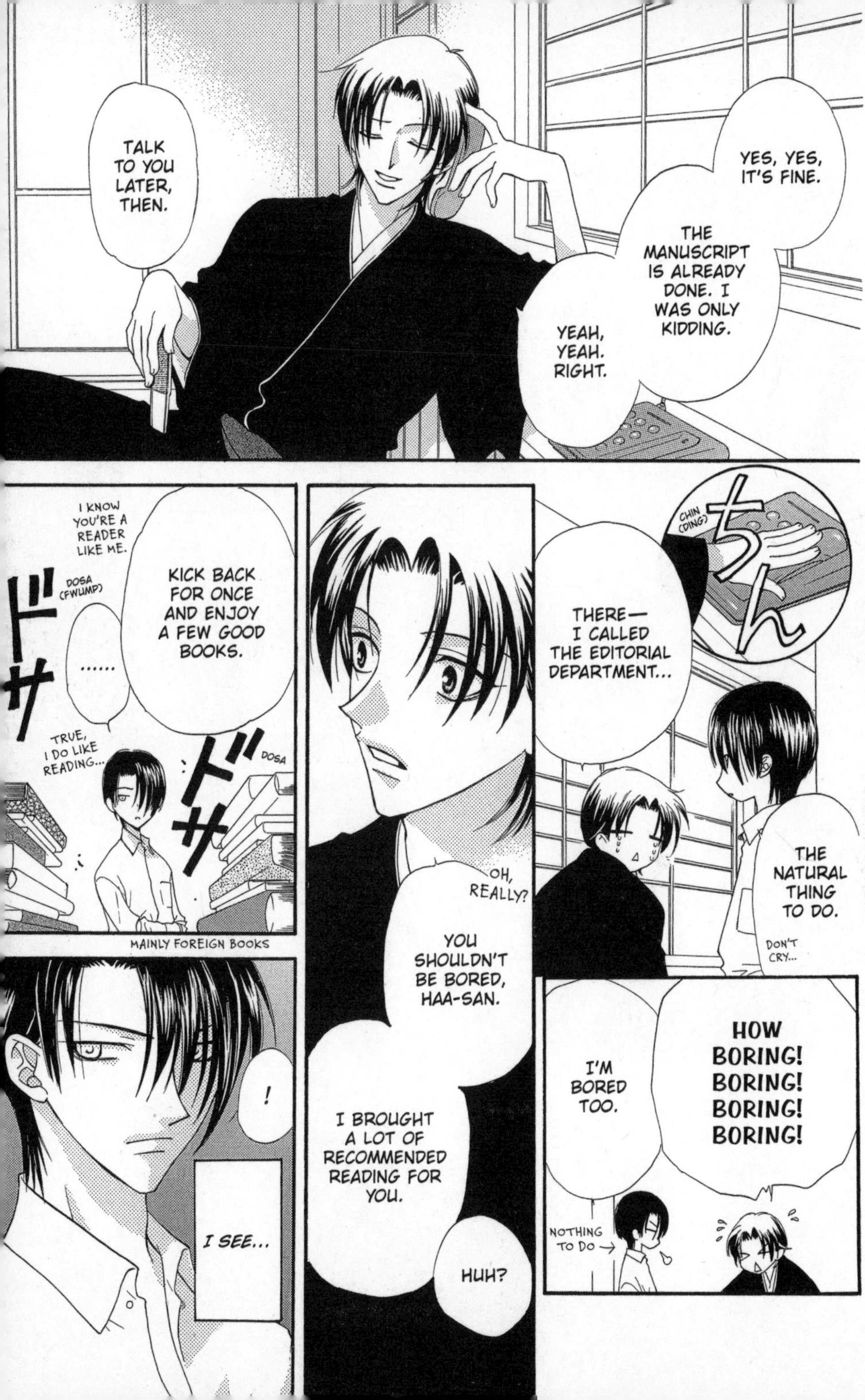
YES, YES, IT'S FINE.
THE MANUSCRIPT IS ALREADY DONE. I WAS ONLY KIDDING.
YEAH, YEAH. RIGHT.
TALK TO YOU LATER, THEN.
ちん
CHIN (DING)
THERE— I CALLED THE EDITORIAL DEPARTMENT...
THE NATURAL THING TO DO.
DON'T CRY...
HOW BORING! BORING! BORING! BORING!
I'M BORED TOO.
NOTHING TO DO
OH, REALLY?
YOU SHOULDN'T BE BORED, HAA-SAN.
I BROUGHT A LOT OF RECOMMENDED READING FOR YOU.
HUH?
KICK BACK FOR ONCE AND ENJOY A FEW GOOD BOOKS.
I KNOW YOU'RE A READER LIKE ME.
ドサ
DOSA (FWUMP)
......
ドサ
DOSA
TRUE, I DO LIKE READING...
MAINLY FOREIGN BOOKS
!
I SEE...

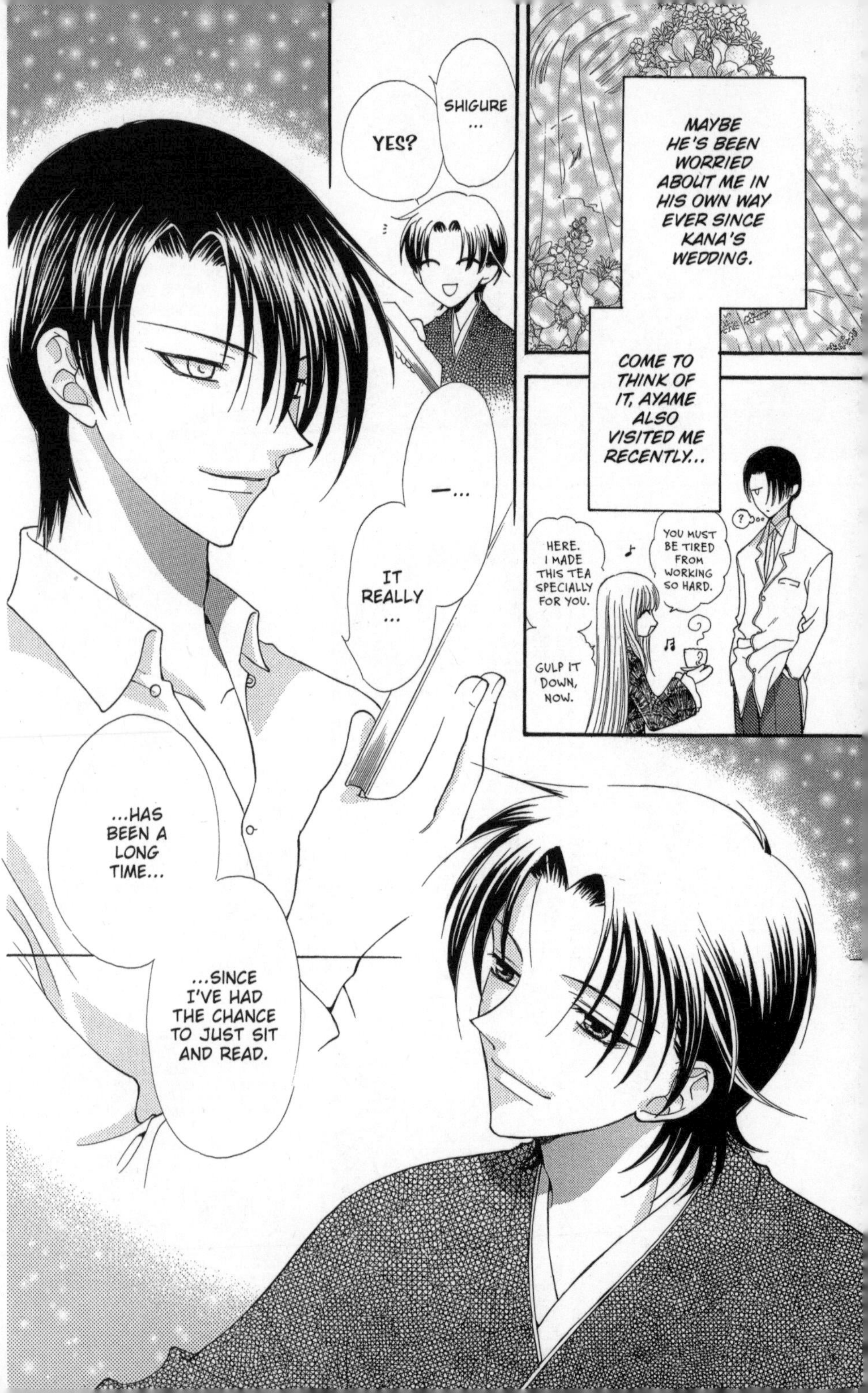
MAYBE HE'S BEEN WORRIED ABOUT ME IN HIS OWN WAY EVER SINCE KANA'S WEDDING.
COME TO THINK OF IT, AYAME ALSO VISITED ME RECENTLY...
YOU MUST BE TIRED FROM WORKING SO HARD.
HERE. I MADE THIS TEA SPECIALLY FOR YOU.
GULP IT DOWN, NOW.
SHIGURE...
YES?
—...
IT REALLY...
...HAS BEEN A LONG TIME...
...SINCE I'VE HAD THE CHANCE TO JUST SIT AND READ.

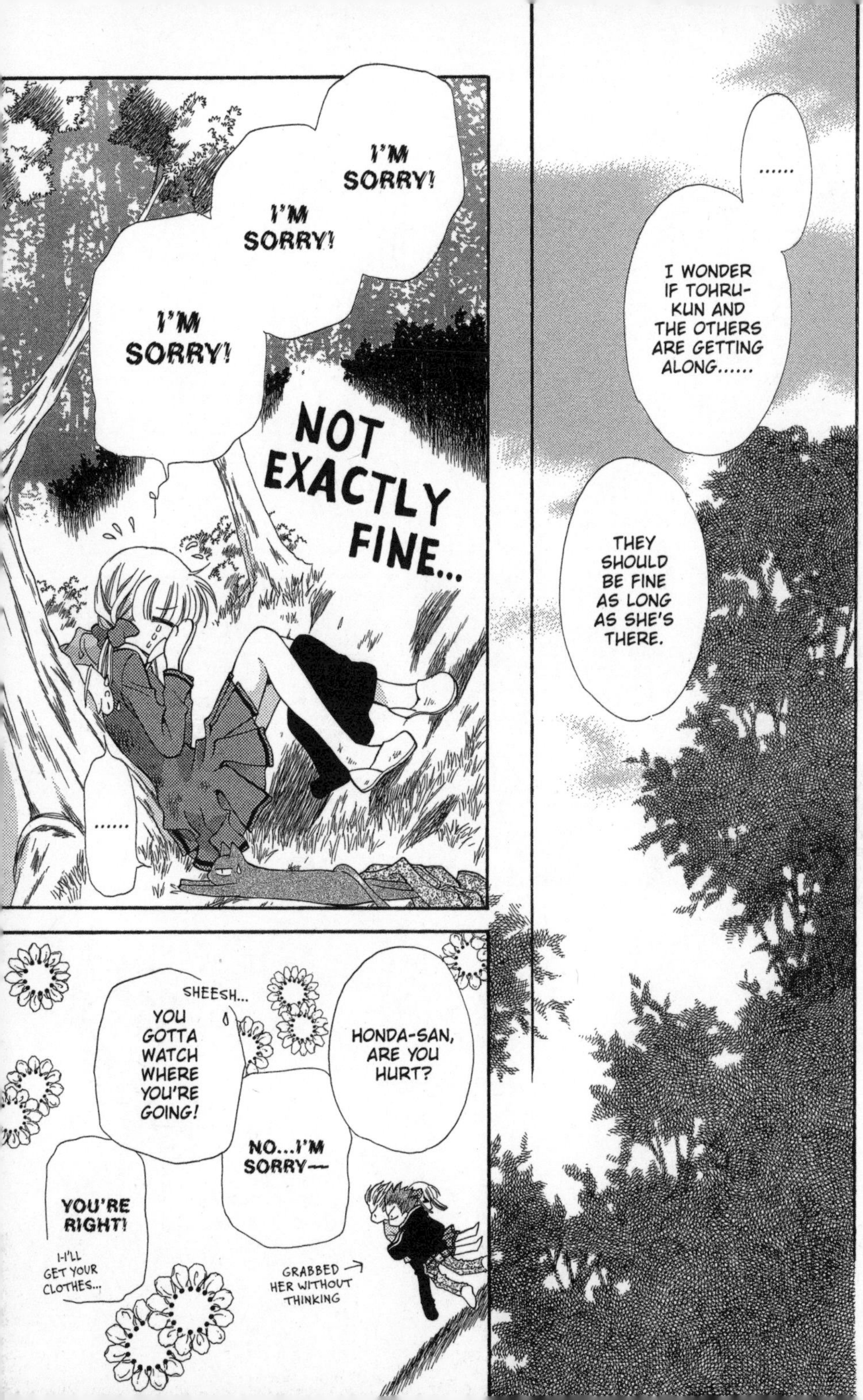
......
I WONDER IF TOHRU-KUN AND THE OTHERS ARE GETTING ALONG......
THEY SHOULD BE FINE AS LONG AS SHE'S THERE.
I'M SORRY!
I'M SORRY!
I'M SORRY!
NOT EXACTLY FINE...
......
HONDA-SAN, ARE YOU HURT?
SHEESH...
YOU GOTTA WATCH WHERE YOU'RE GOING!
NO...I'M SORRY—
GRABBED HER WITHOUT THINKING
YOU'RE RIGHT!
I-I'LL GET YOUR CLOTHES...

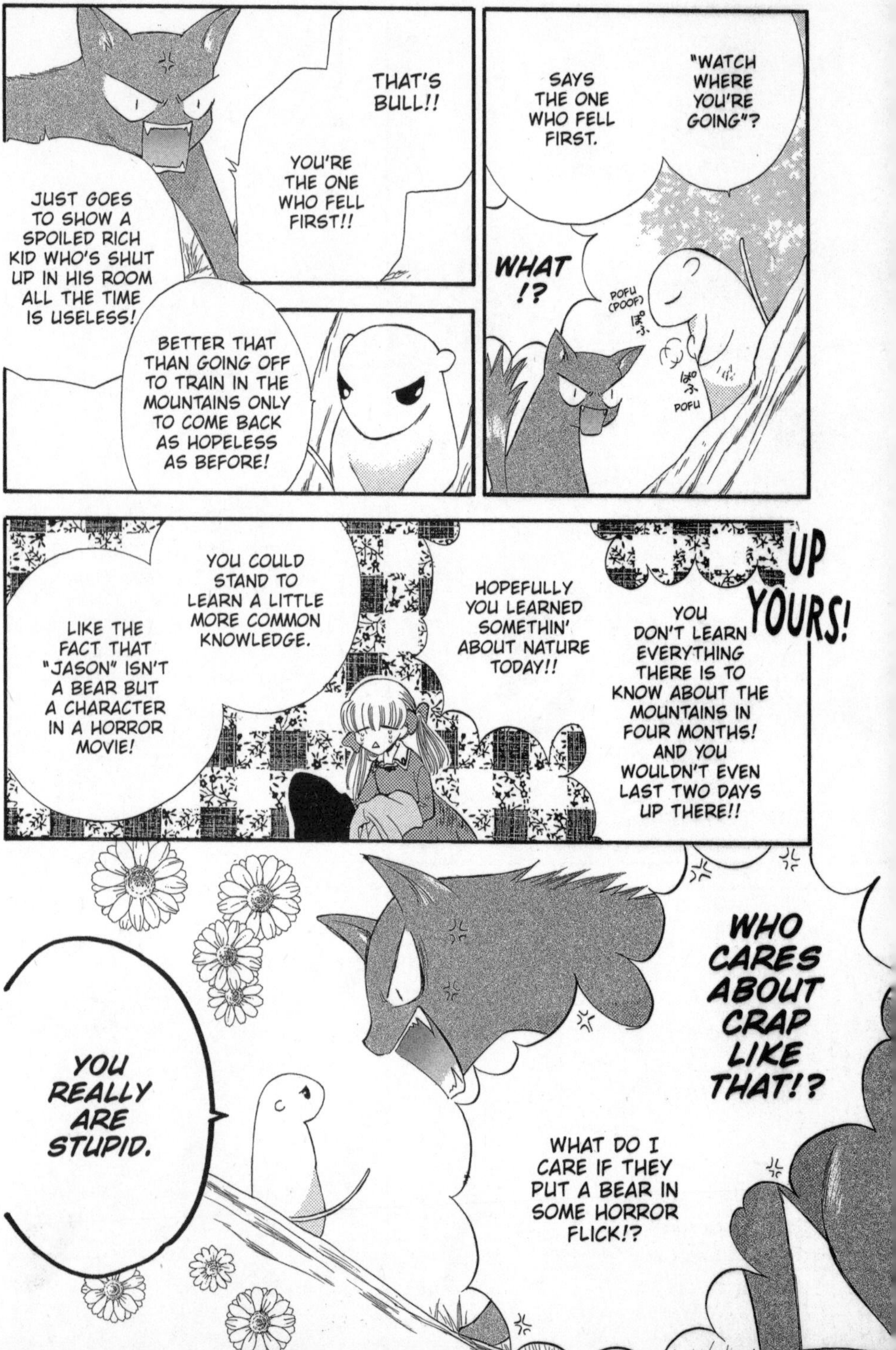
"WATCH WHERE YOU'RE GOING"?
SAYS THE ONE WHO FELL FIRST.
WHAT !?
POFU (POOF)
ぽふ
ぽふ
POFU
THAT'S BULL!!
YOU'RE THE ONE WHO FELL FIRST!!
JUST GOES TO SHOW A SPOILED RICH KID WHO'S SHUT UP IN HIS ROOM ALL THE TIME IS USELESS!
BETTER THAT THAN GOING OFF TO TRAIN IN THE MOUNTAINS ONLY TO COME BACK AS HOPELESS AS BEFORE!
UP YOURS!
YOU DON'T LEARN EVERYTHING THERE IS TO KNOW ABOUT THE MOUNTAINS IN FOUR MONTHS! AND YOU WOULDN'T EVEN LAST TWO DAYS UP THERE!!
HOPEFULLY YOU LEARNED SOMETHIN' ABOUT NATURE TODAY!!
YOU COULD STAND TO LEARN A LITTLE MORE COMMON KNOWLEDGE.
LIKE THE FACT THAT "JASON" ISN'T A BEAR BUT A CHARACTER IN A HORROR MOVIE!
WHO CARES ABOUT CRAP LIKE THAT!?
WHAT DO I CARE IF THEY PUT A BEAR IN SOME HORROR FLICK!?
YOU REALLY ARE STUPID.

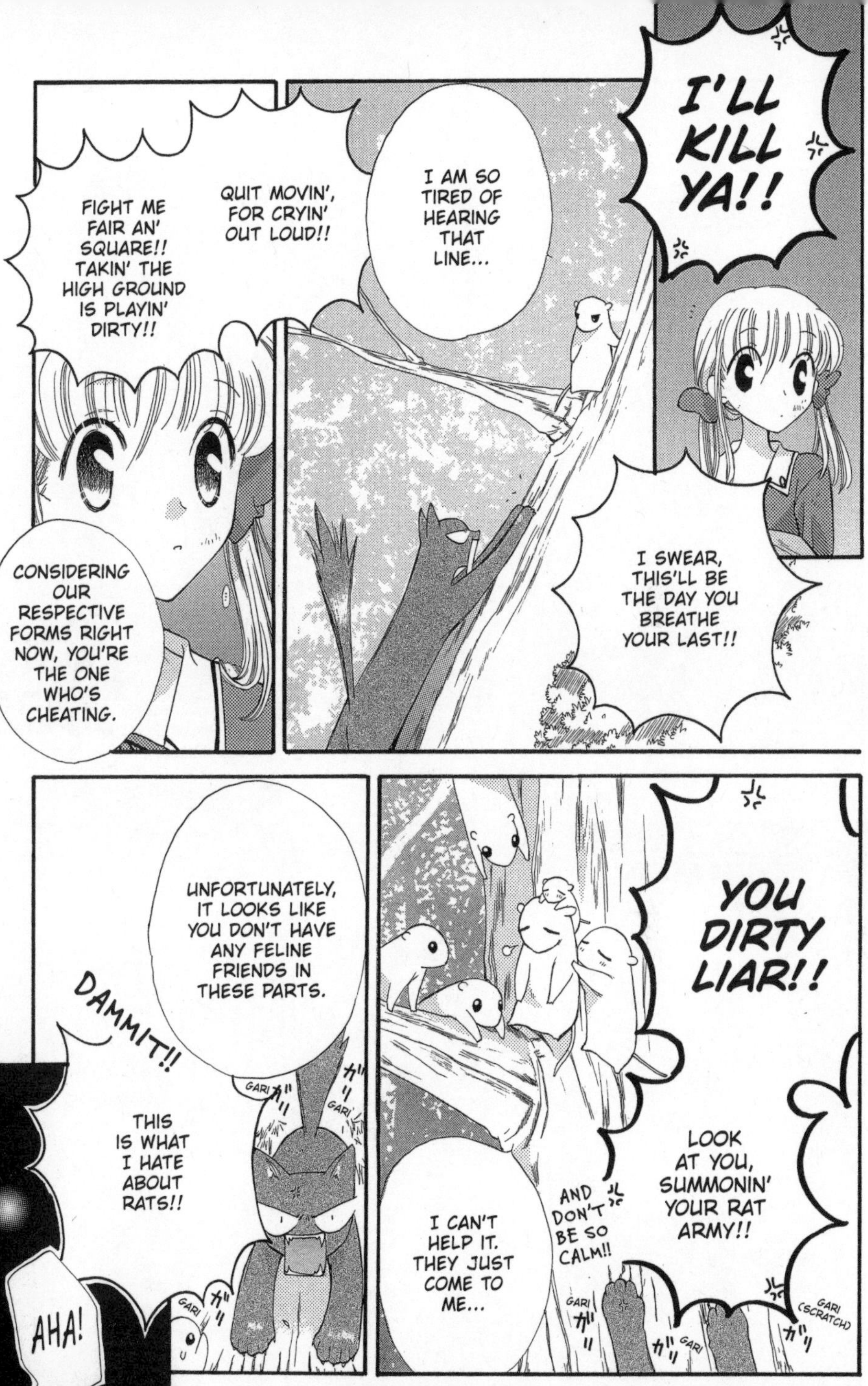
I'LL KILL YA!!
I AM SO TIRED OF HEARING THAT LINE...
I SWEAR, THIS'LL BE THE DAY YOU BREATHE YOUR LAST!!
QUIT MOVIN', FOR CRYIN' OUT LOUD!!
FIGHT ME FAIR AN' SQUARE!! TAKIN' THE HIGH GROUND IS PLAYIN' DIRTY!!
CONSIDERING OUR RESPECTIVE FORMS RIGHT NOW, YOU'RE THE ONE WHO'S CHEATING.
YOU DIRTY LIAR!!
LOOK AT YOU, SUMMONIN' YOUR RAT ARMY!!
AND DON'T BE SO CALM!!
I CAN'T HELP IT. THEY JUST COME TO ME...
GARI (SCRATCH)
GARI
GARI
UNFORTUNATELY, IT LOOKS LIKE YOU DON'T HAVE ANY FELINE FRIENDS IN THESE PARTS.
DAMMIT!!
GARI
GARI
THIS IS WHAT I HATE ABOUT RATS!!
GARI
AHA!

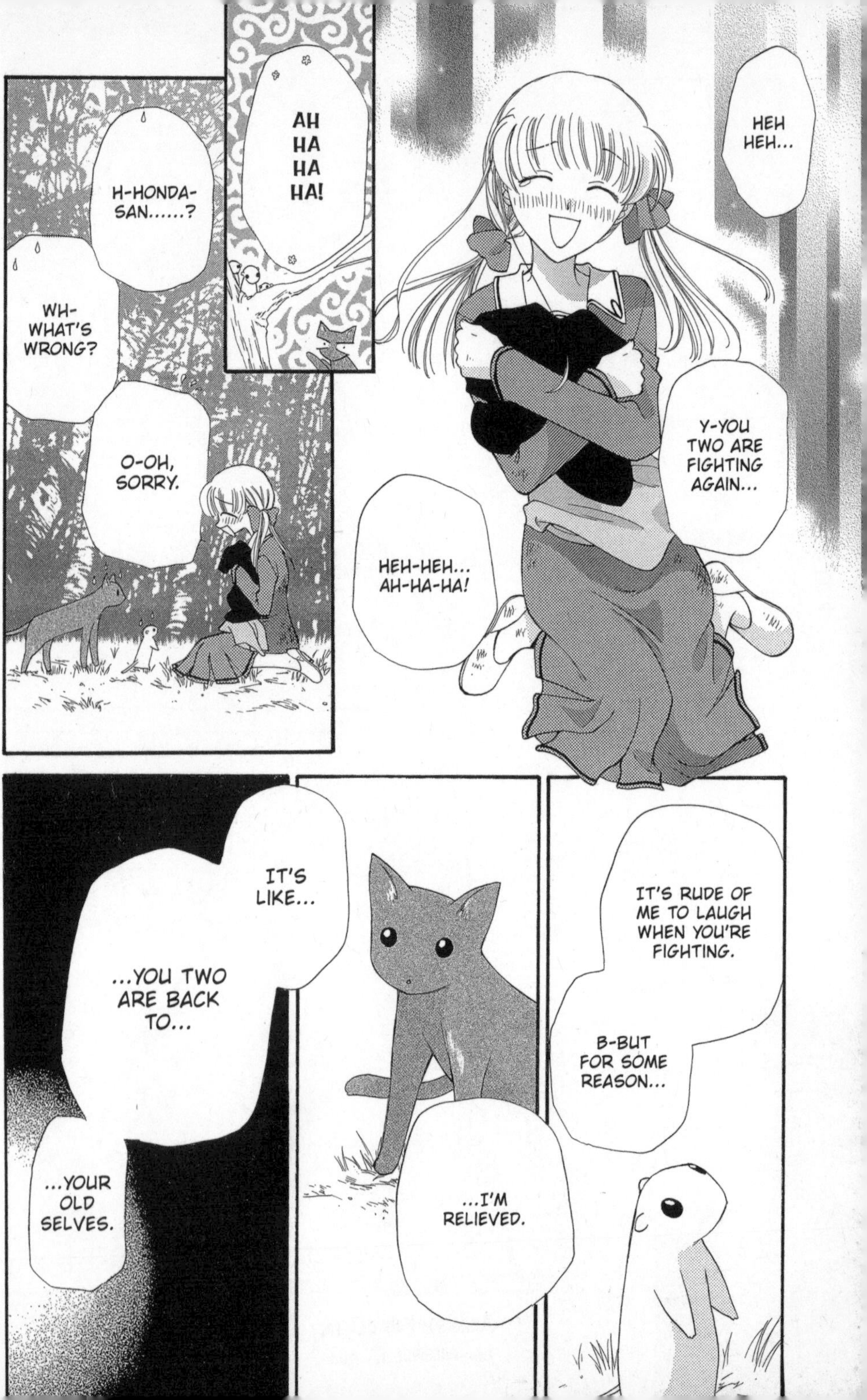
HEH HEH...
Y-YOU TWO ARE FIGHTING AGAIN...
HEH-HEH... AH-HA-HA!
AH HA HA HA!
H-HONDA-SAN......?
WH-WHAT'S WRONG?
O-OH, SORRY.
IT'S RUDE OF ME TO LAUGH WHEN YOU'RE FIGHTING.
B-BUT FOR SOME REASON...
...I'M RELIEVED.
IT'S LIKE...
...YOU TWO ARE BACK TO...
...YOUR OLD SELVES.

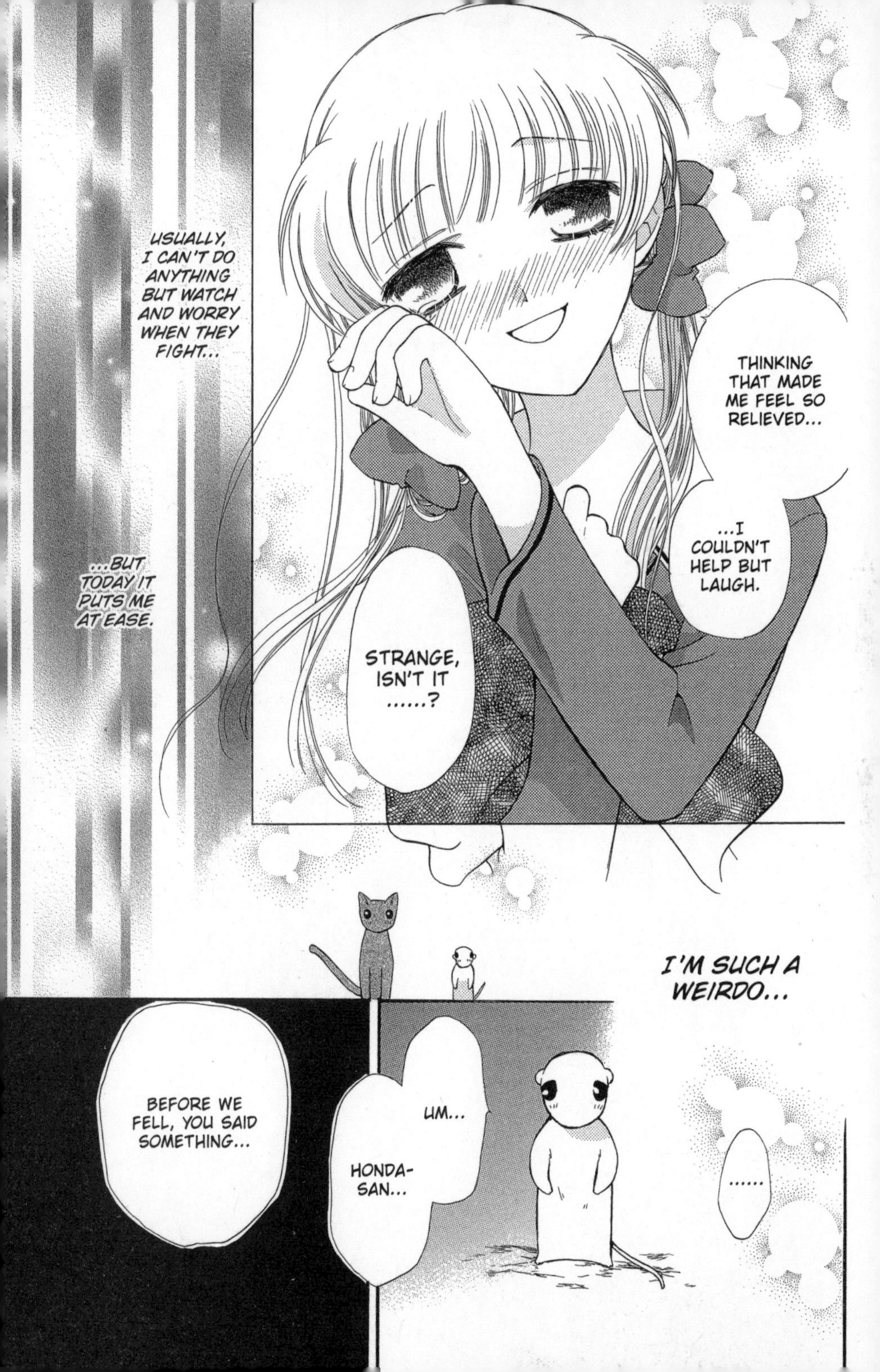

THINKING THAT MADE ME FEEL SO RELIEVED...
...I COULDN'T HELP BUT LAUGH.
STRANGE, ISN'T IT ......?
USUALLY, I CAN'T DO ANYTHING BUT WATCH AND WORRY WHEN THEY FIGHT...
...BUT TODAY IT PUTS ME AT EASE.
I'M SUCH A WEIRDO...
......
UM...
HONDA-SAN...
BEFORE WE FELL, YOU SAID SOMETHING...

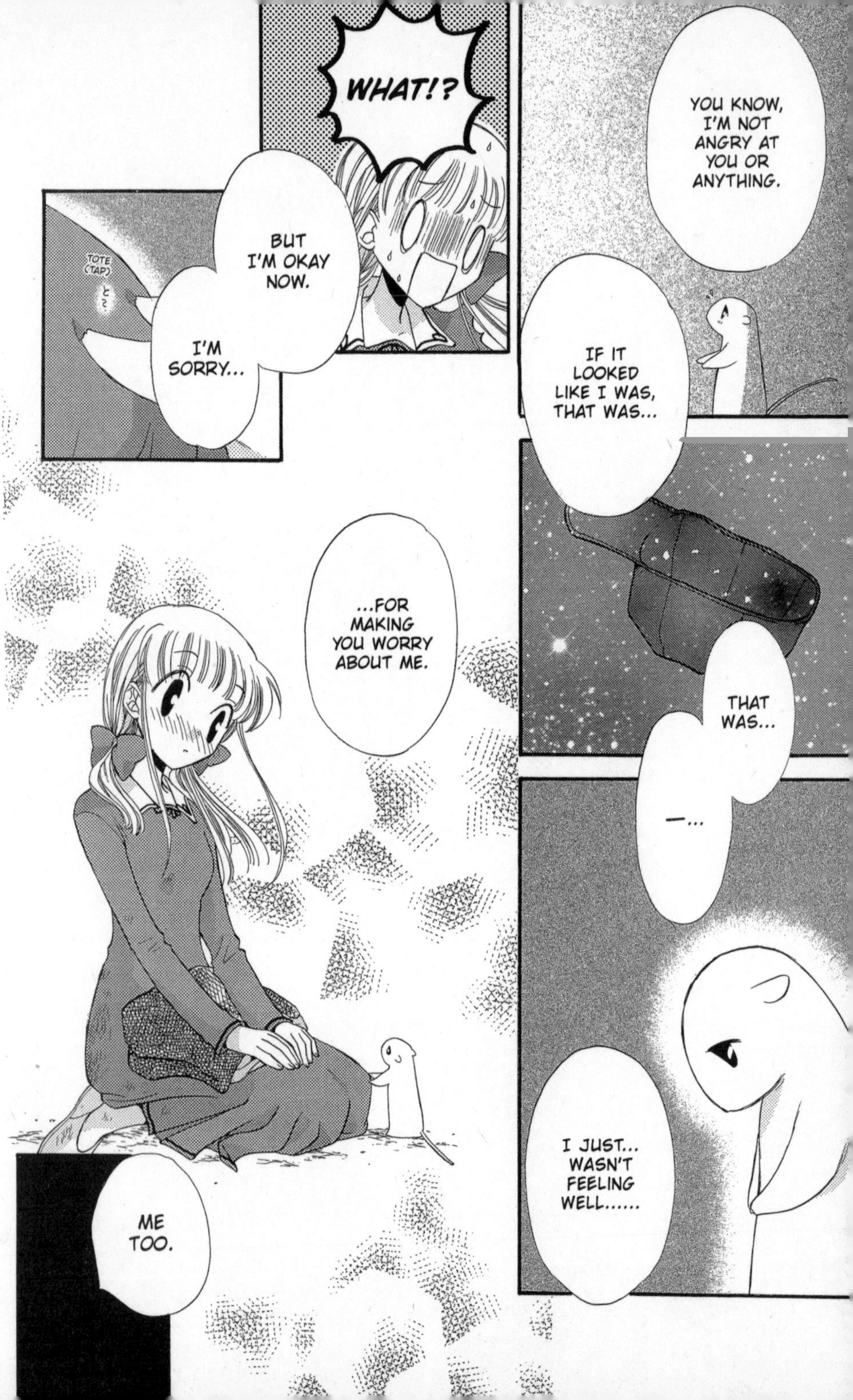

YOU KNOW, I'M NOT ANGRY AT YOU OR ANYTHING.
IF IT LOOKED LIKE I WAS, THAT WAS...
WHAT!?
BUT I'M OKAY NOW.
TOTE (TAP)
I'M SORRY...
THAT WAS...
—...
I JUST... WASN'T FEELING WELL......
...FOR MAKING YOU WORRY ABOUT ME.
ME TOO.

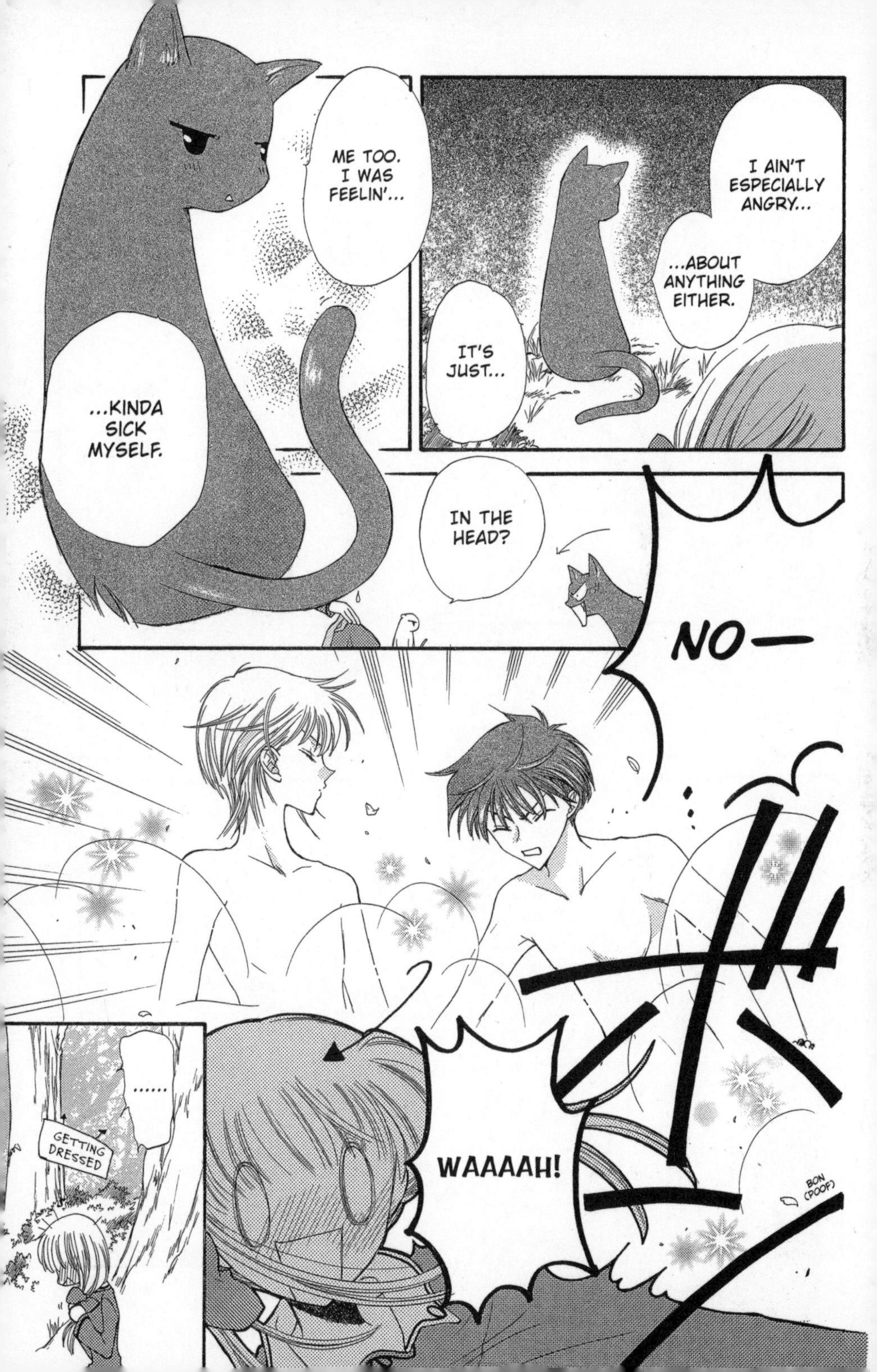
I AIN'T ESPECIALLY ANGRY...
...ABOUT ANYTHING EITHER.
IT'S JUST...
ME TOO. I WAS FEELIN'...
...KINDA SICK MYSELF.
IN THE HEAD?
NO—
WAAAAH!
BON (POOF)
......
GETTING DRESSED

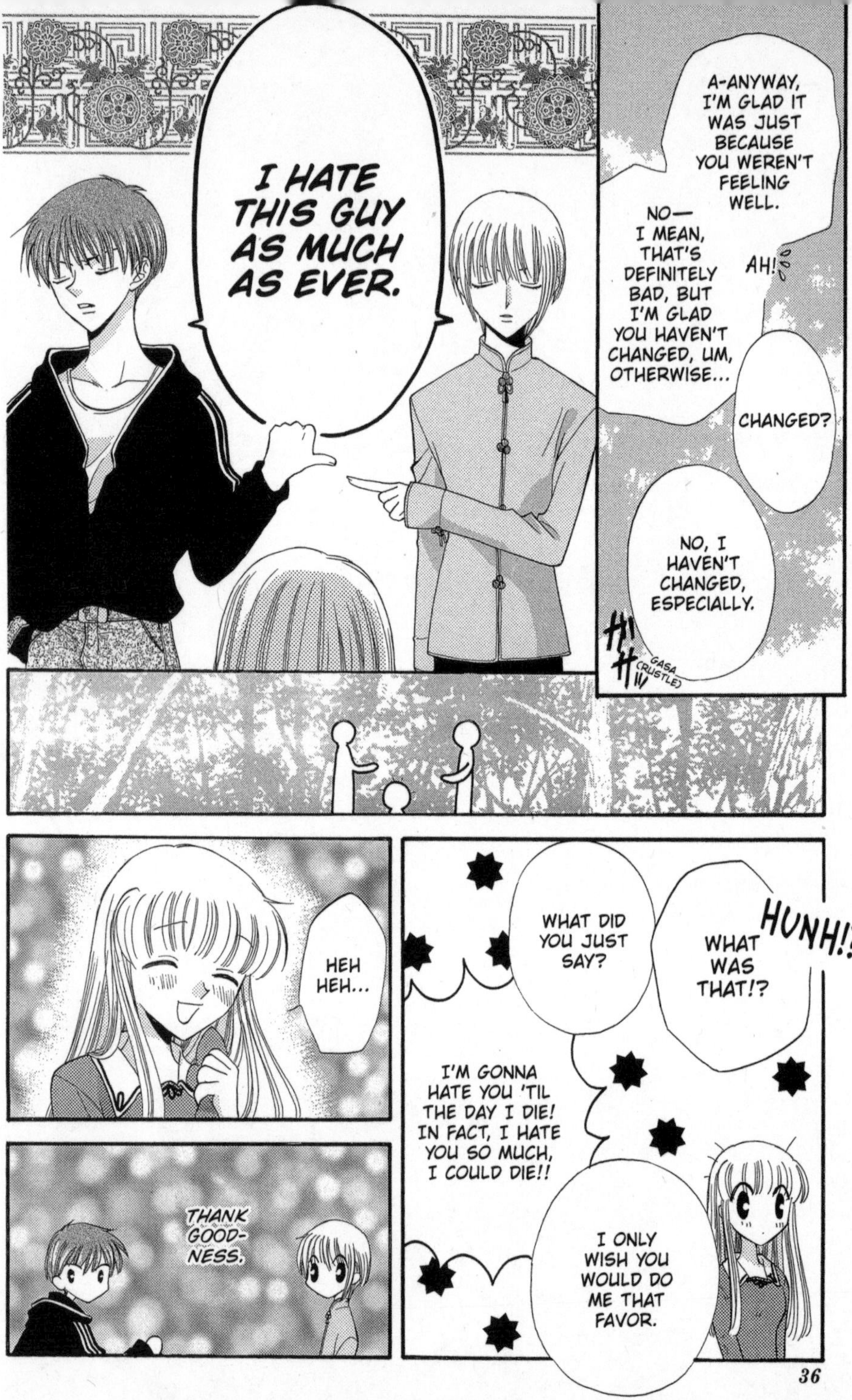
A-ANYWAY, I'M GLAD IT WAS JUST BECAUSE YOU WEREN'T FEELING WELL.
AH!
NO— I MEAN, THAT'S DEFINITELY BAD, BUT I'M GLAD YOU HAVEN'T CHANGED, UM, OTHERWISE...
CHANGED?
NO, I HAVEN'T CHANGED, ESPECIALLY.
GASA (RUSTLE)
I HATE THIS GUY AS MUCH AS EVER.
HUNH!?
WHAT WAS THAT!?
WHAT DID YOU JUST SAY?
I'M GONNA HATE YOU 'TIL THE DAY I DIE! IN FACT, I HATE YOU SO MUCH, I COULD DIE!!
I ONLY WISH YOU WOULD DO ME THAT FAVOR.
HEH HEH...
THANK GOOD-NESS.

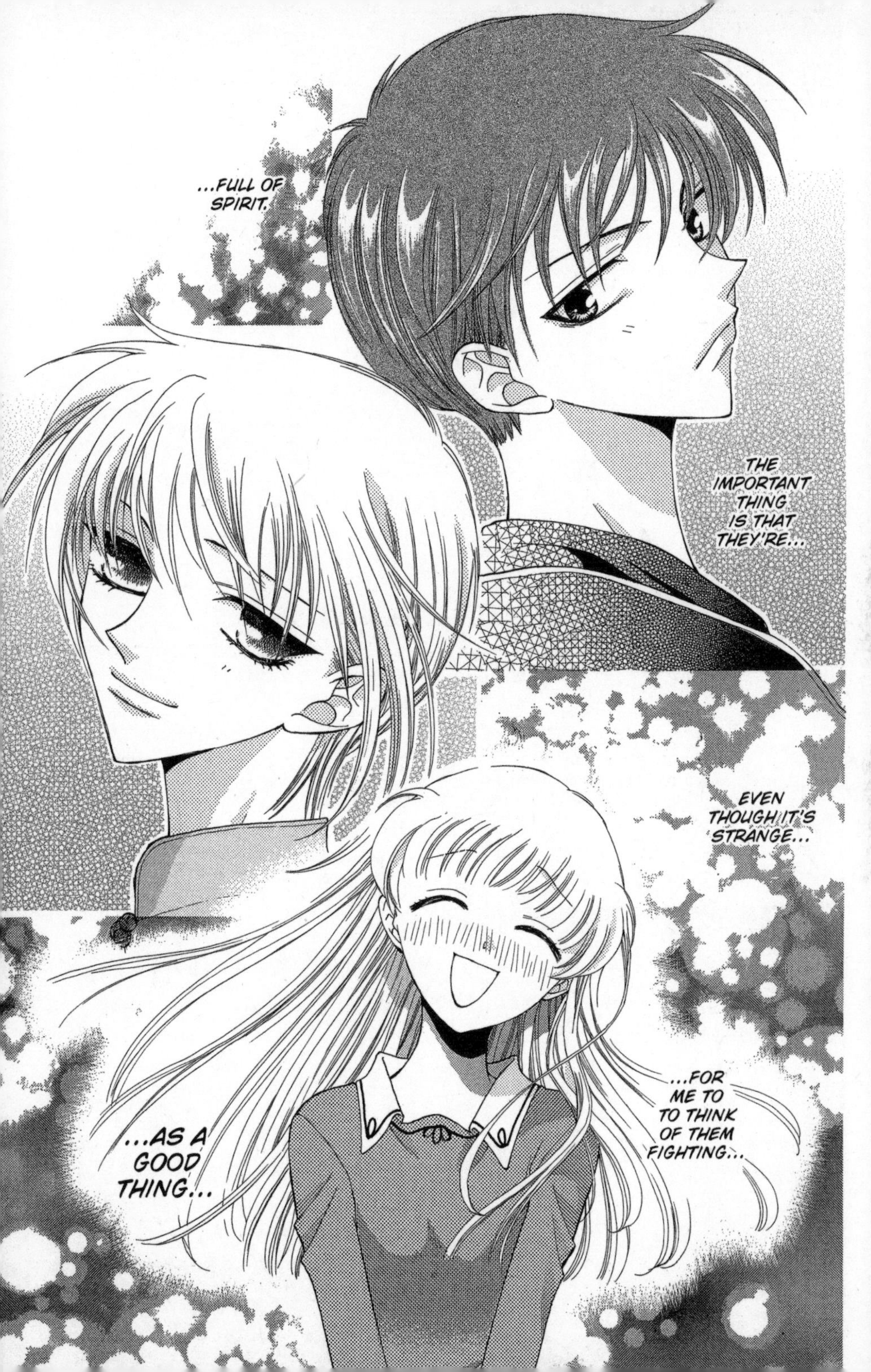
THE IMPORTANT THING IS THAT THEY'RE...
...FULL OF SPIRIT.
EVEN THOUGH IT'S STRANGE...
...FOR ME TO TO THINK OF THEM FIGHTING...
...AS A GOOD THING...

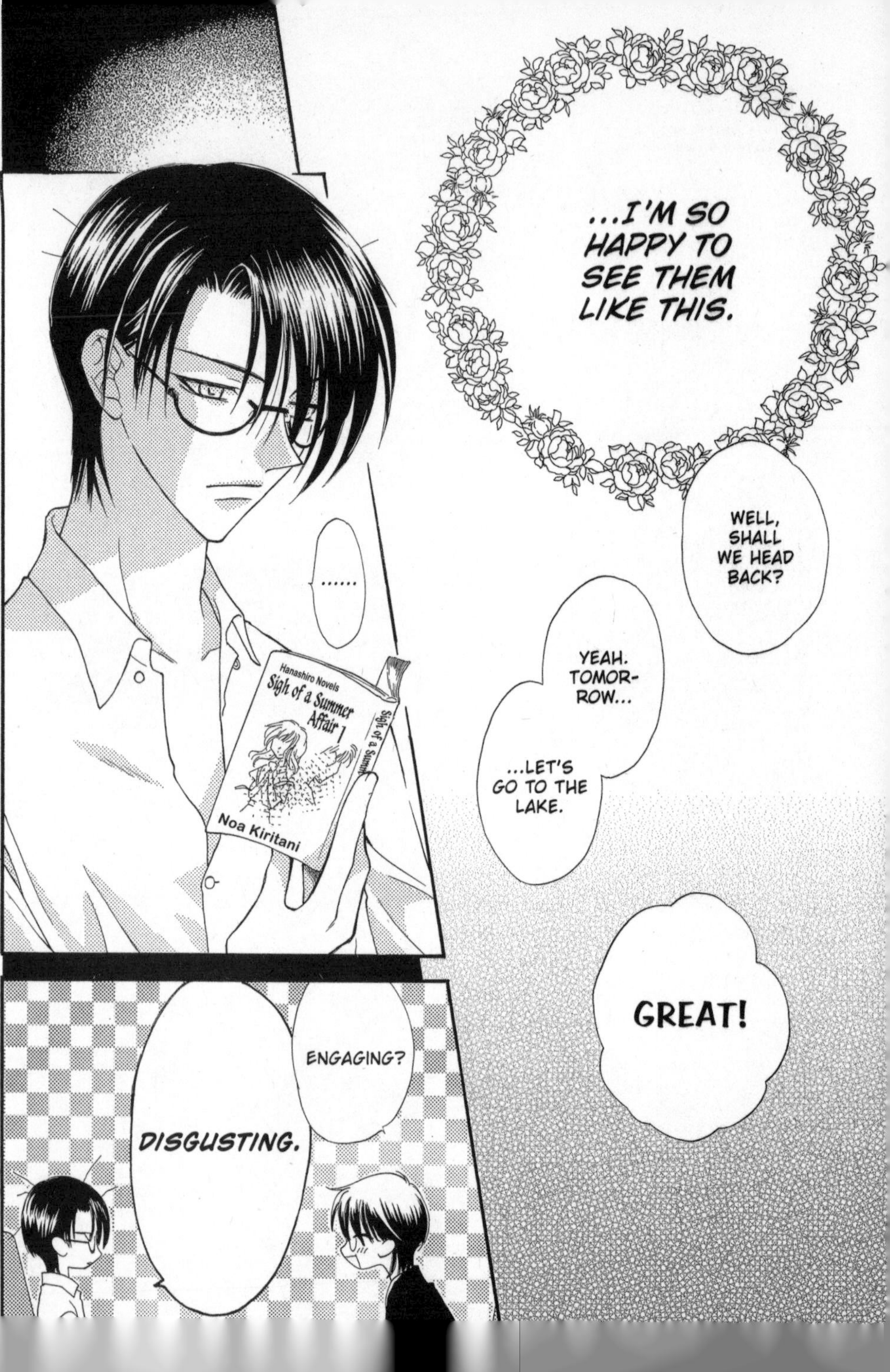
...I'M SO HAPPY TO SEE THEM LIKE THIS.
WELL, SHALL WE HEAD BACK?
YEAH. TOMOR-ROW...
...LET'S GO TO THE LAKE.
GREAT!
......
Hanashiro Novels
Sigh of a Summer Affair 1
Noa Kiritani
ENGAGING?
DISGUSTING.

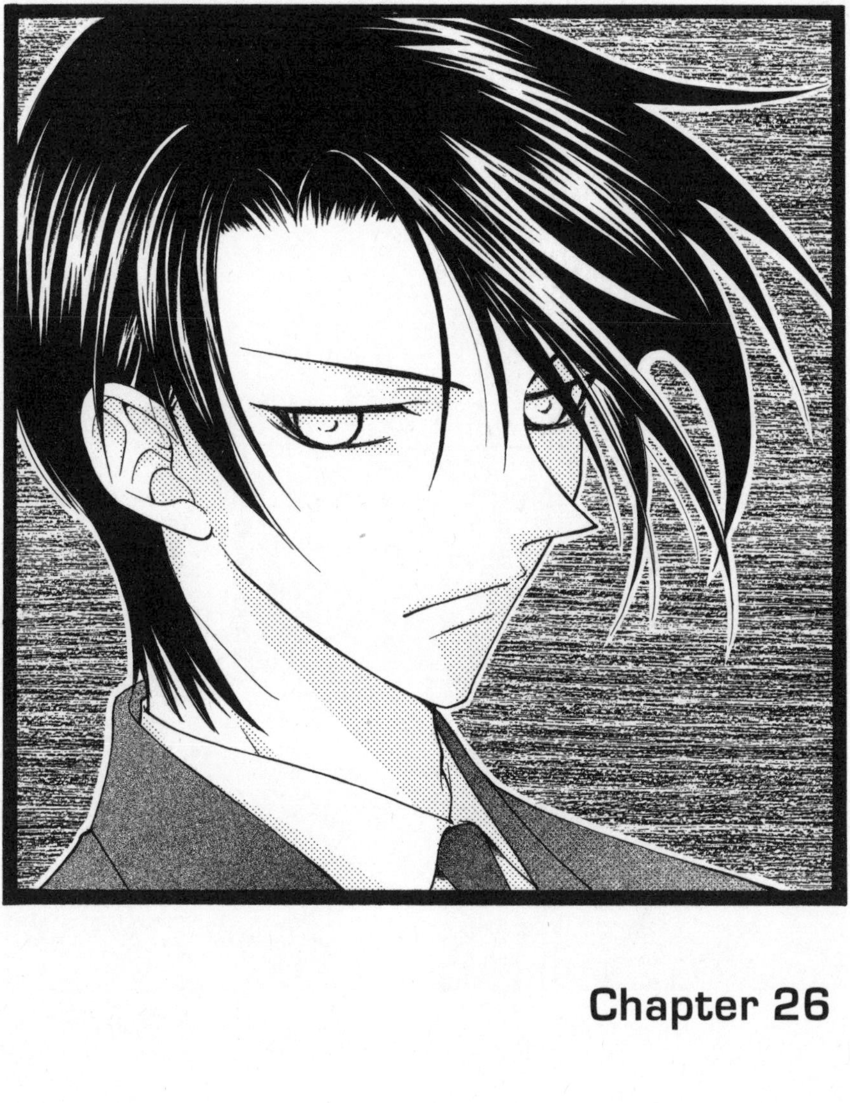

Chapter 26

HONDA-SAN, ARE YOU READY?
YES! I'VE GOT EVERYTHING.
YOU'RE GOING TO THE LAKE?
DON'T DROWN, KYO-KUN.
I AIN'T GONNA DROWN!!
YES!
WE'RE STAYING AT THE SOHMA FAMILY'S LAKE COTTAGE.
I CAN IMAGINE HONDA-SAN DROWNING TOO...
AH HA HA HA!
I'LL KEEP A CLOSE EYE ON HER...

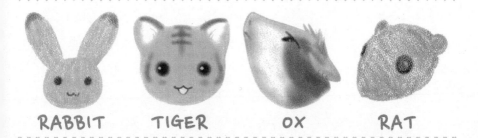

RABBIT
TIGER
OX
RAT

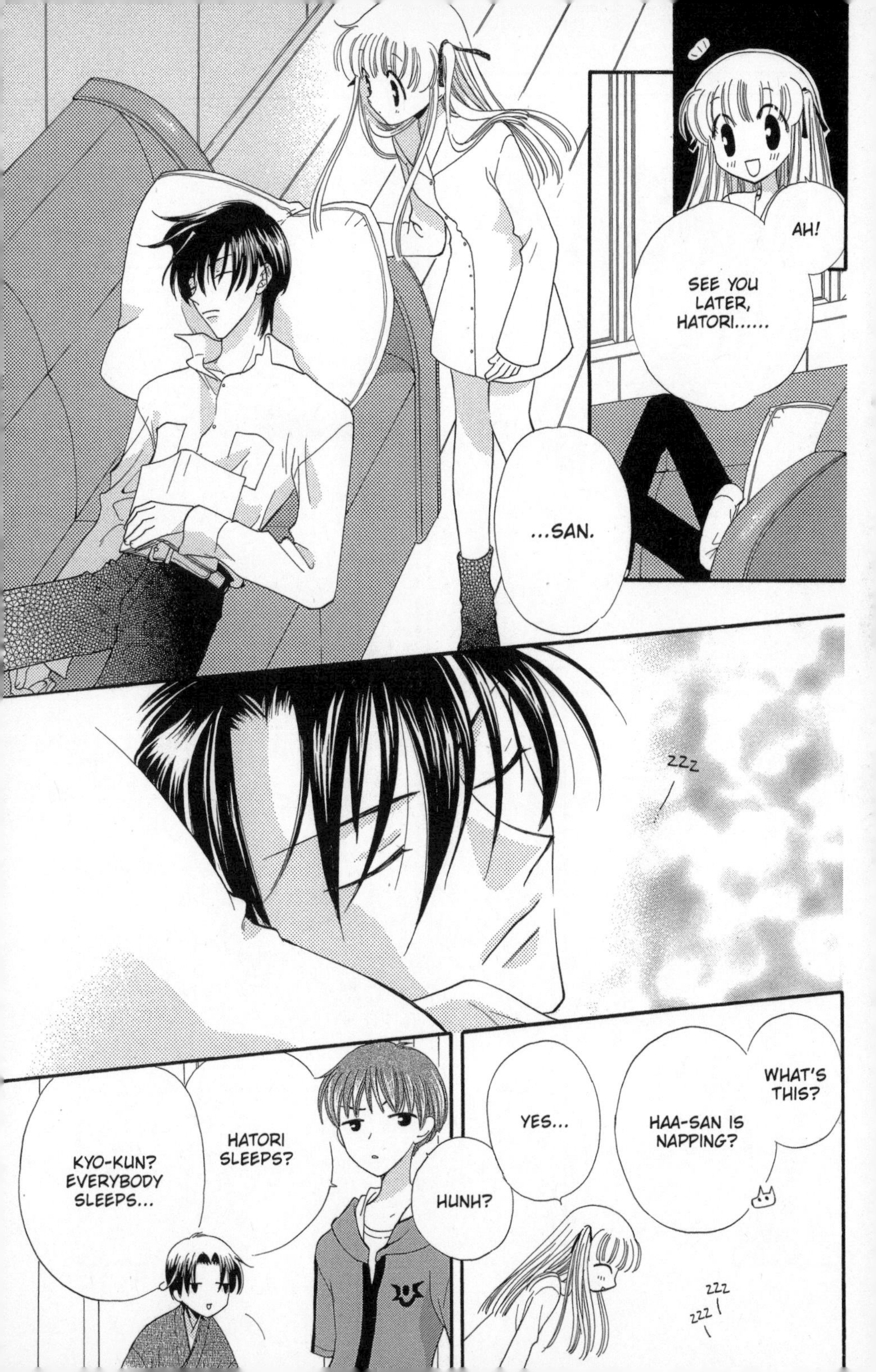
AH!
SEE YOU LATER, HATORI......
...SAN.
zzz
WHAT'S THIS?
HAA-SAN IS NAPPING?
YES...
zzz
zzz
HUNH?
HATORI SLEEPS?
KYO-KUN? EVERYBODY SLEEPS...

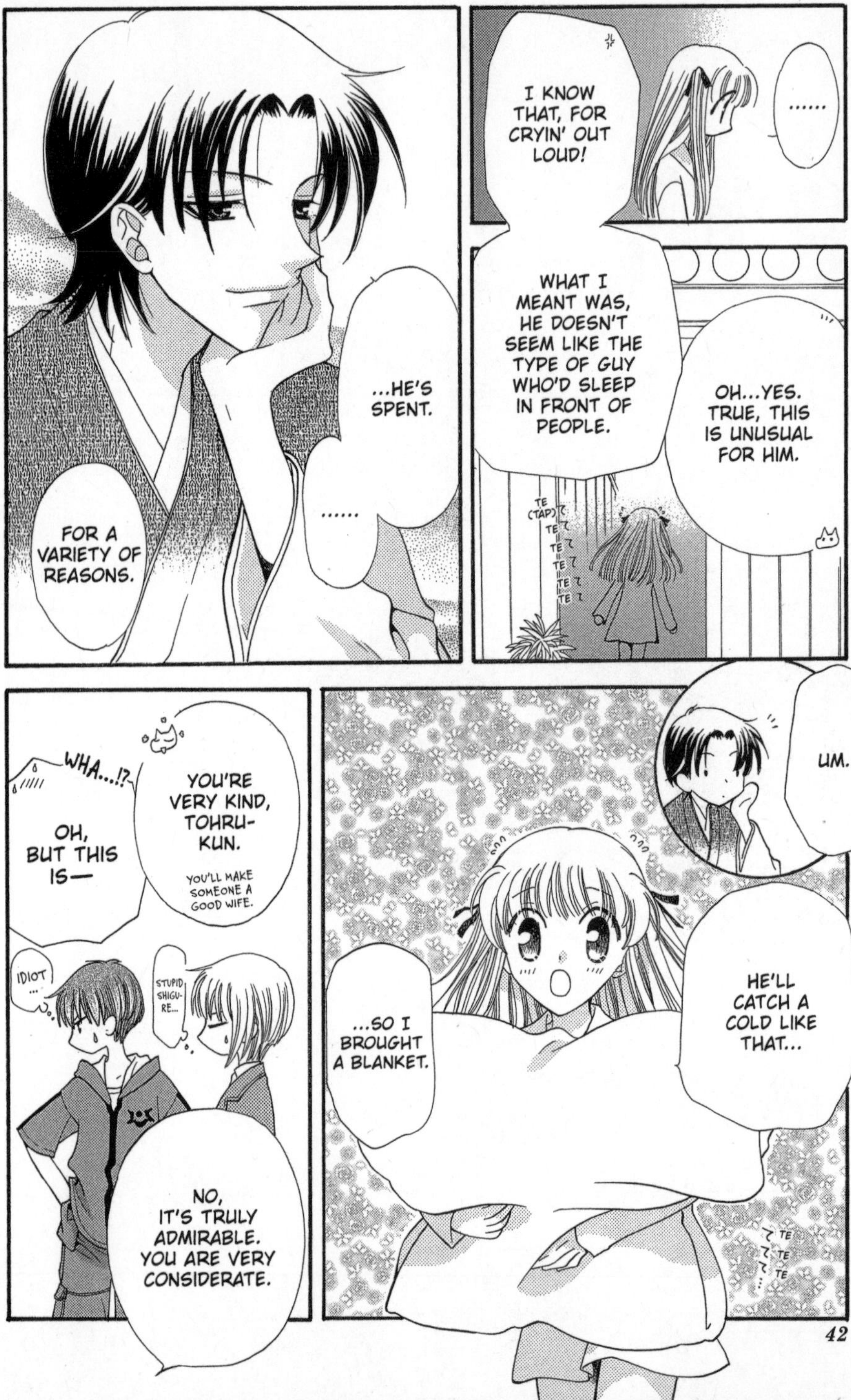

I KNOW THAT, FOR CRYIN' OUT LOUD!
......
WHAT I MEANT WAS, HE DOESN'T SEEM LIKE THE TYPE OF GUY WHO'D SLEEP IN FRONT OF PEOPLE.
OH...YES. TRUE, THIS IS UNUSUAL FOR HIM.
TE (TAP) TE TE TE TE TE
...HE'S SPENT.
......
FOR A VARIETY OF REASONS.
UM...
HE'LL CATCH A COLD LIKE THAT...
...SO I BROUGHT A BLANKET.
TE TE TE
YOU'RE VERY KIND, TOHRU-KUN.
YOU'LL MAKE SOMEONE A GOOD WIFE.
WHA...!?
OH, BUT THIS IS—
STUPID SHIGURE...
IDIOT...
NO, IT'S TRULY ADMIRABLE. YOU ARE VERY CONSIDERATE.

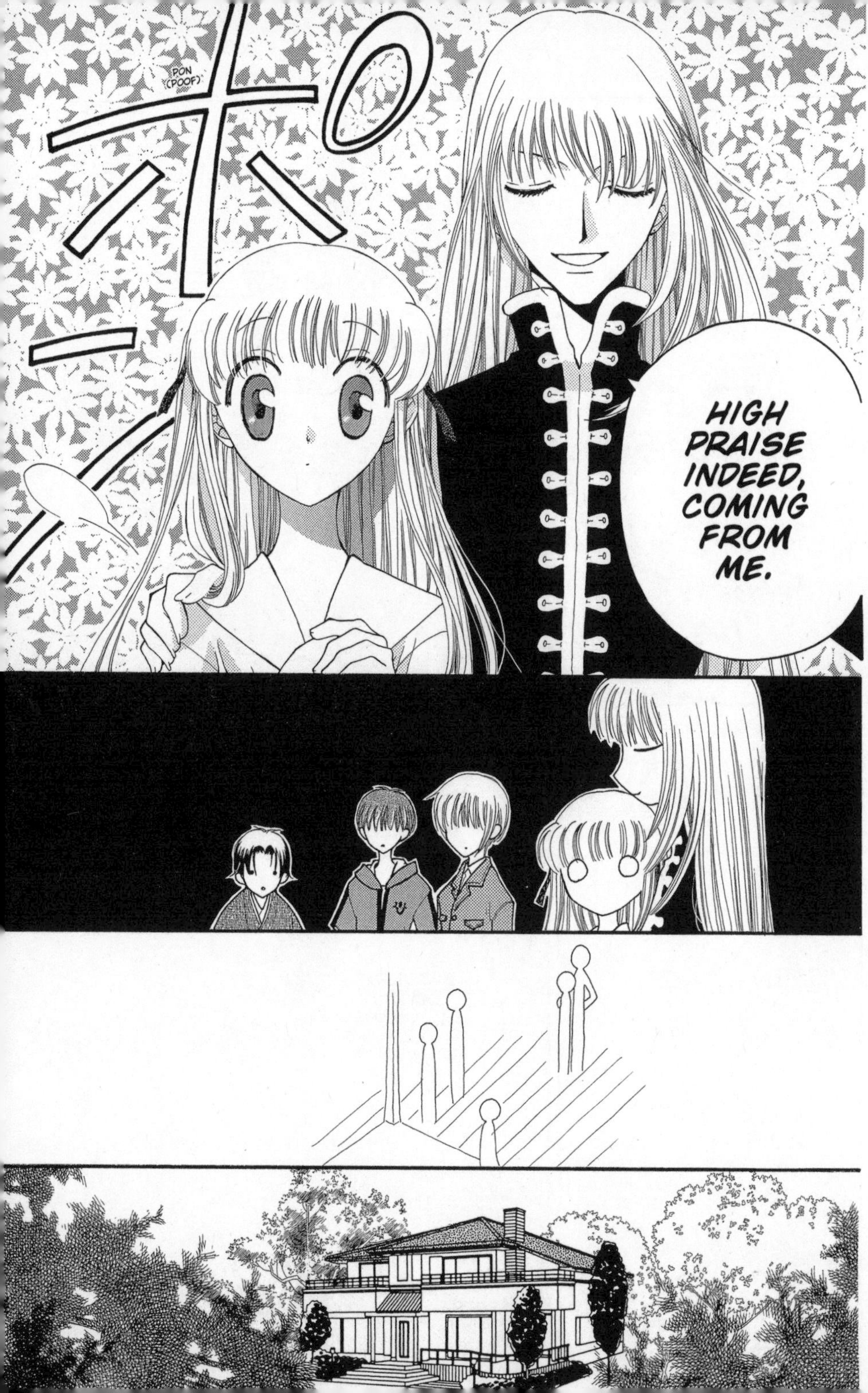
PON (POOF)
HIGH PRAISE INDEED, COMING FROM ME.

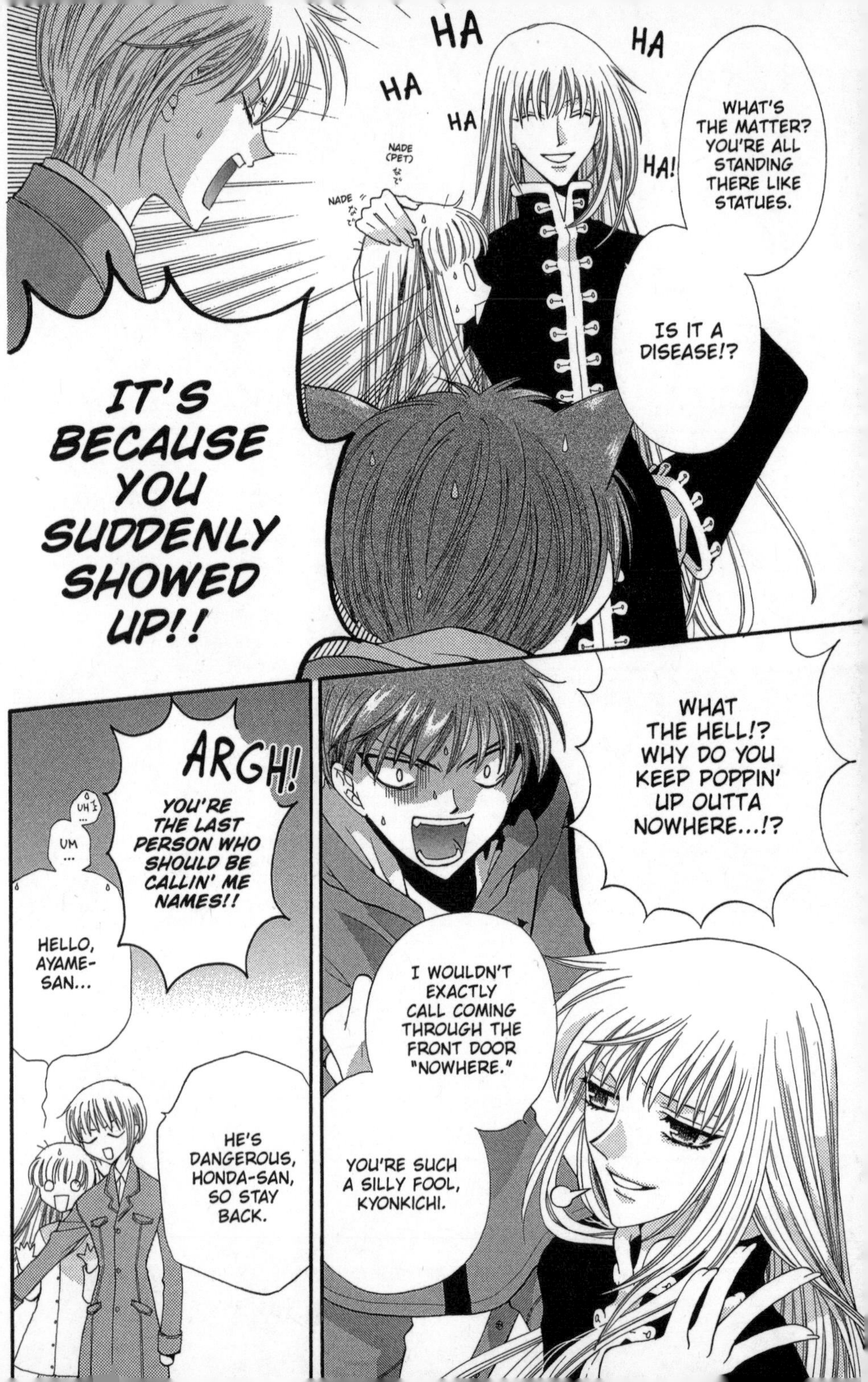
HA HA HA HA HA!
WHAT'S THE MATTER? YOU'RE ALL STANDING THERE LIKE STATUES.
NADE (PET) なで
NADE なで
IS IT A DISEASE!?
IT'S BECAUSE YOU SUDDENLY SHOWED UP!!
WHAT THE HELL!? WHY DO YOU KEEP POPPIN' UP OUTTA NOWHERE...!?
I WOULDN'T EXACTLY CALL COMING THROUGH THE FRONT DOOR "NOWHERE."
YOU'RE SUCH A SILLY FOOL, KYONKICHI.
ARGH!
YOU'RE THE LAST PERSON WHO SHOULD BE CALLIN' ME NAMES!!
UH...
UM...
HELLO, AYAME-SAN...
HE'S DANGEROUS, HONDA-SAN, SO STAY BACK.

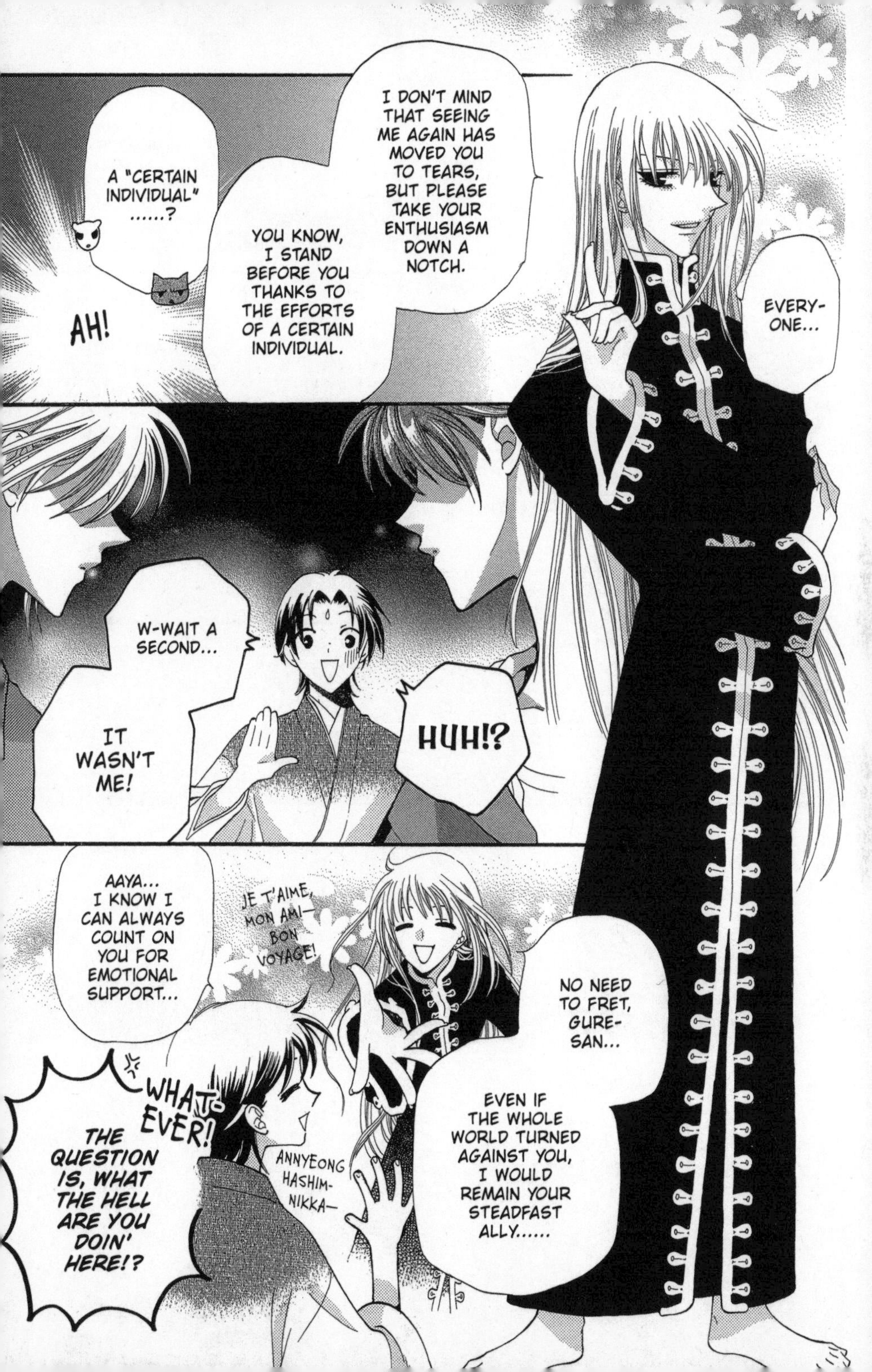
EVERY-ONE...
I DON'T MIND THAT SEEING ME AGAIN HAS MOVED YOU TO TEARS, BUT PLEASE TAKE YOUR ENTHUSIASM DOWN A NOTCH.
YOU KNOW, I STAND BEFORE YOU THANKS TO THE EFFORTS OF A CERTAIN INDIVIDUAL.
A "CERTAIN INDIVIDUAL" ......?
AH!
HUH!?
W-WAIT A SECOND...
IT WASN'T ME!
NO NEED TO FRET, GURE-SAN...
EVEN IF THE WHOLE WORLD TURNED AGAINST YOU, I WOULD REMAIN YOUR STEADFAST ALLY......
AAYA... I KNOW I CAN ALWAYS COUNT ON YOU FOR EMOTIONAL SUPPORT...
JE T'AIME, MON AMI— BON VOYAGE!
ANNYEONG HASHIM-NIKKA—
WHAT-EVER!
THE QUESTION IS, WHAT THE HELL ARE YOU DOIN' HERE!?

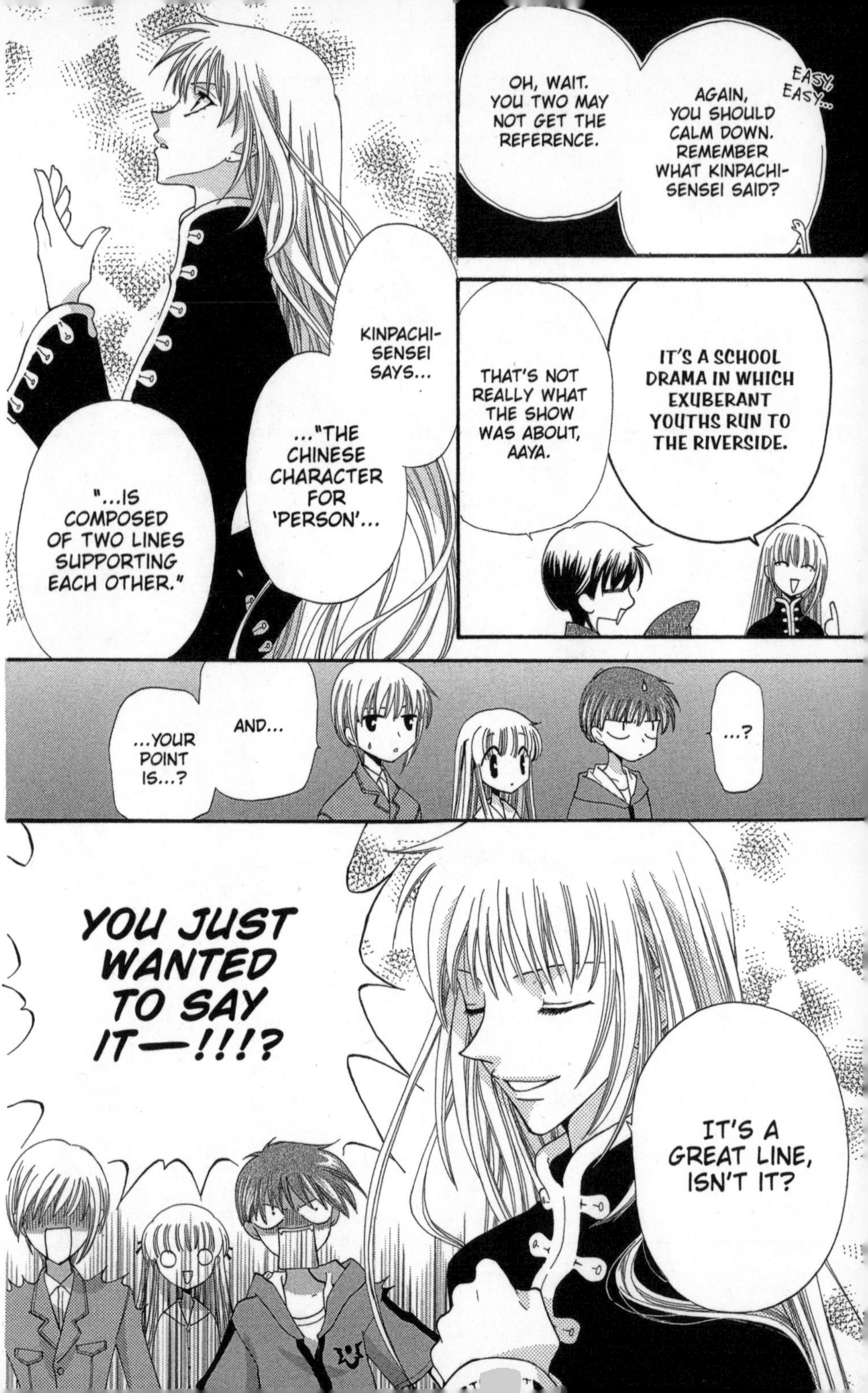
EASY, EASY...
AGAIN, YOU SHOULD CALM DOWN. REMEMBER WHAT KINPACHI-SENSEI SAID?
OH, WAIT. YOU TWO MAY NOT GET THE REFERENCE.
IT'S A SCHOOL DRAMA IN WHICH EXUBERANT YOUTHS RUN TO THE RIVERSIDE.
THAT'S NOT REALLY WHAT THE SHOW WAS ABOUT, AAYA.
KINPACHI-SENSEI SAYS...
..."THE CHINESE CHARACTER FOR 'PERSON'...
"...IS COMPOSED OF TWO LINES SUPPORTING EACH OTHER."
...?
AND...
...YOUR POINT IS...?
IT'S A GREAT LINE, ISN'T IT?
YOU JUST WANTED TO SAY IT—!!!?

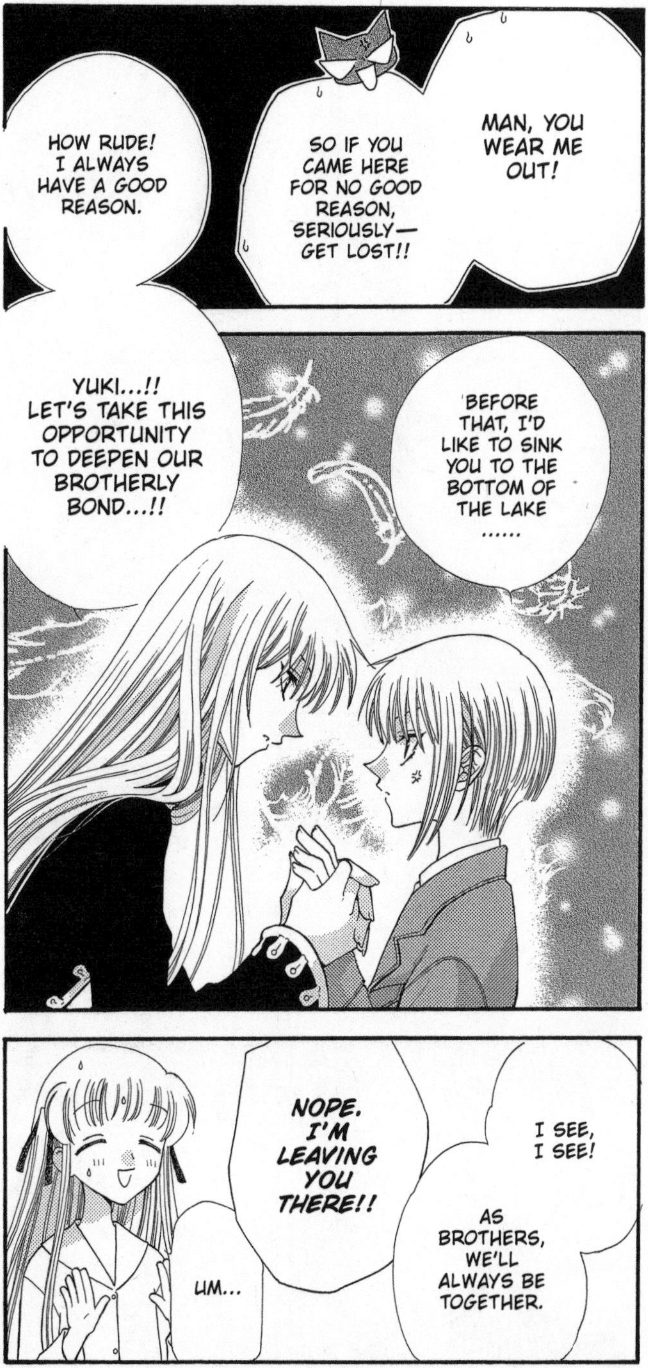
MAN, YOU WEAR ME OUT!
SO IF YOU CAME HERE FOR NO GOOD REASON, SERIOUSLY—GET LOST!!
HOW RUDE! I ALWAYS HAVE A GOOD REASON.
YUKI...!! LET'S TAKE THIS OPPORTUNITY TO DEEPEN OUR BROTHERLY BOND...!!
BEFORE THAT, I'D LIKE TO SINK YOU TO THE BOTTOM OF THE LAKE ......
I SEE, I SEE!
AS BROTHERS, WE'LL ALWAYS BE TOGETHER.
NOPE. I'M LEAVING YOU THERE!!
UM...
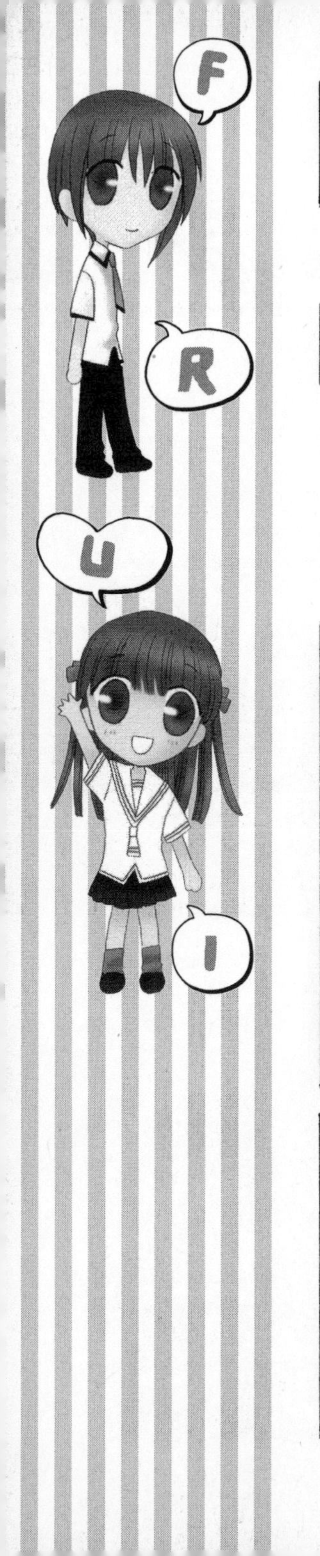
F
R
U
I

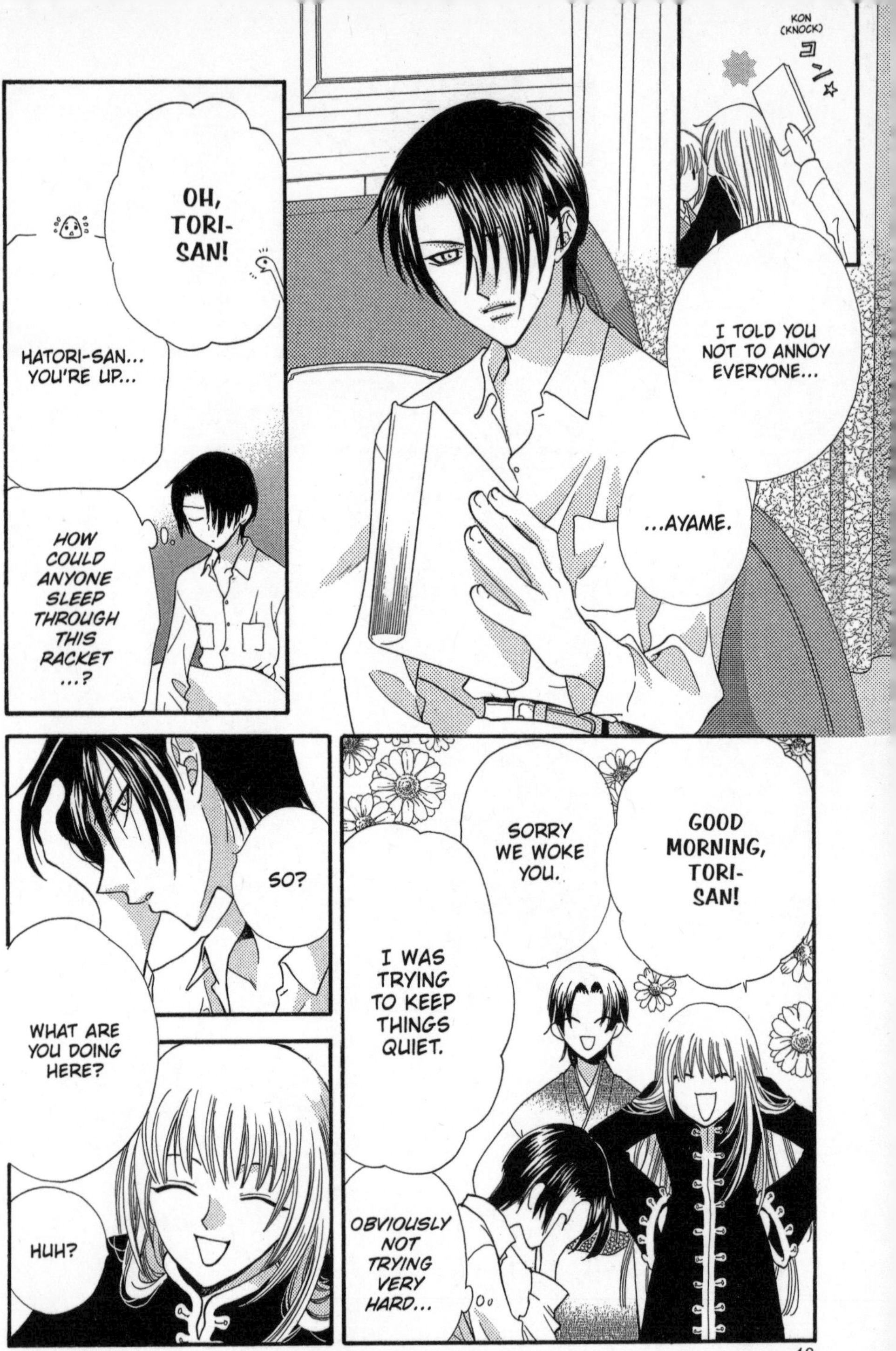
KON (KNOCK)
I TOLD YOU NOT TO ANNOY EVERYONE...
...AYAME.
OH, TORI-SAN!
HATORI-SAN... YOU'RE UP...
HOW COULD ANYONE SLEEP THROUGH THIS RACKET...?
GOOD MORNING, TORI-SAN!
SORRY WE WOKE YOU.
I WAS TRYING TO KEEP THINGS QUIET.
OBVIOUSLY NOT TRYING VERY HARD...
SO?
WHAT ARE YOU DOING HERE?
HUH?

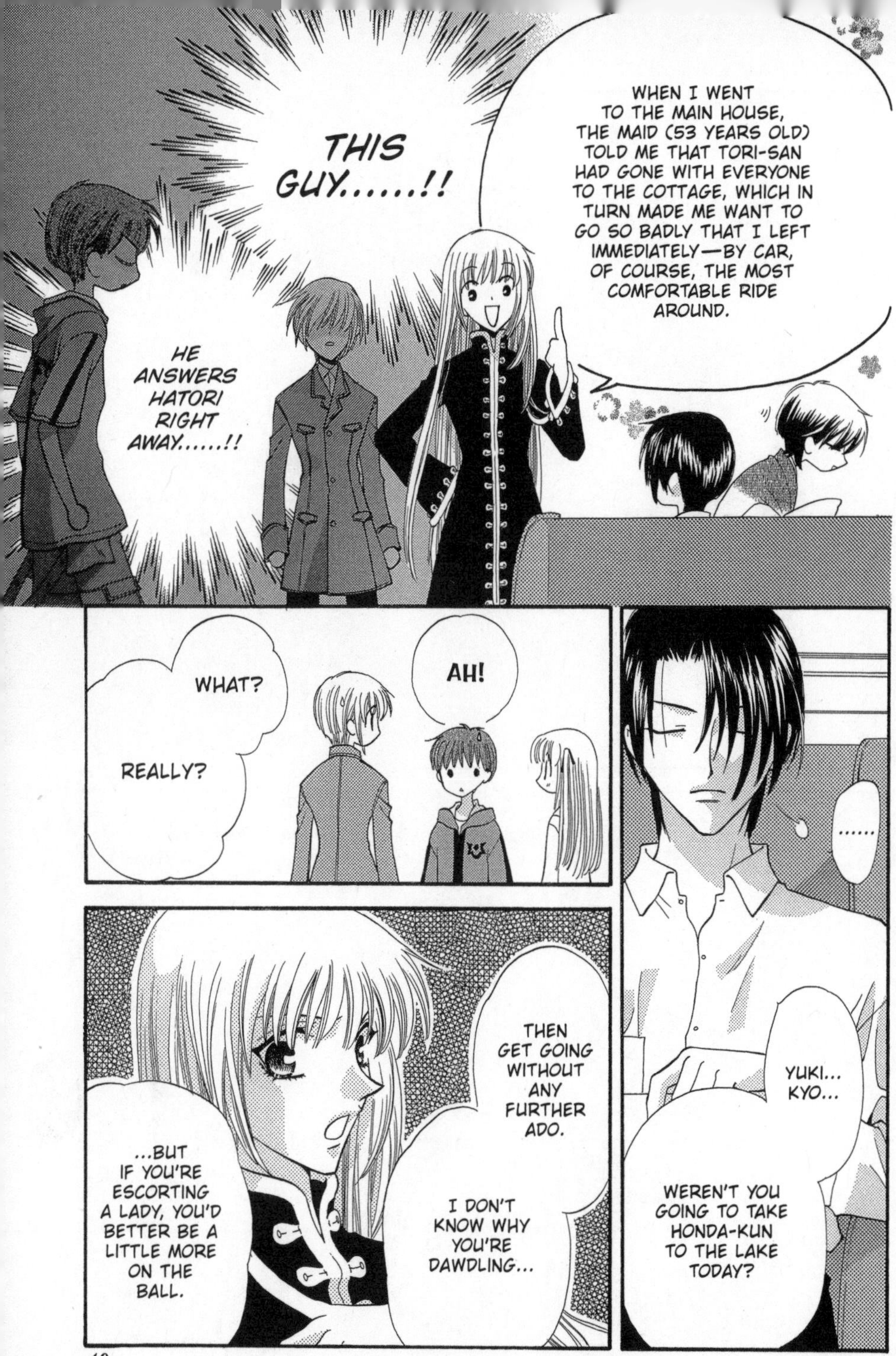
WHEN I WENT TO THE MAIN HOUSE, THE MAID (53 YEARS OLD) TOLD ME THAT TORI-SAN HAD GONE WITH EVERYONE TO THE COTTAGE, WHICH IN TURN MADE ME WANT TO GO SO BADLY THAT I LEFT IMMEDIATELY—BY CAR, OF COURSE, THE MOST COMFORTABLE RIDE AROUND.
THIS GUY......!!
HE ANSWERS HATORI RIGHT AWAY......!!
......
YUKI... KYO...
WEREN'T YOU GOING TO TAKE HONDA-KUN TO THE LAKE TODAY?
AH!
WHAT?
REALLY?
THEN GET GOING WITHOUT ANY FURTHER ADO.
I DON'T KNOW WHY YOU'RE DAWDLING...
...BUT IF YOU'RE ESCORTING A LADY, YOU'D BETTER BE A LITTLE MORE ON THE BALL.

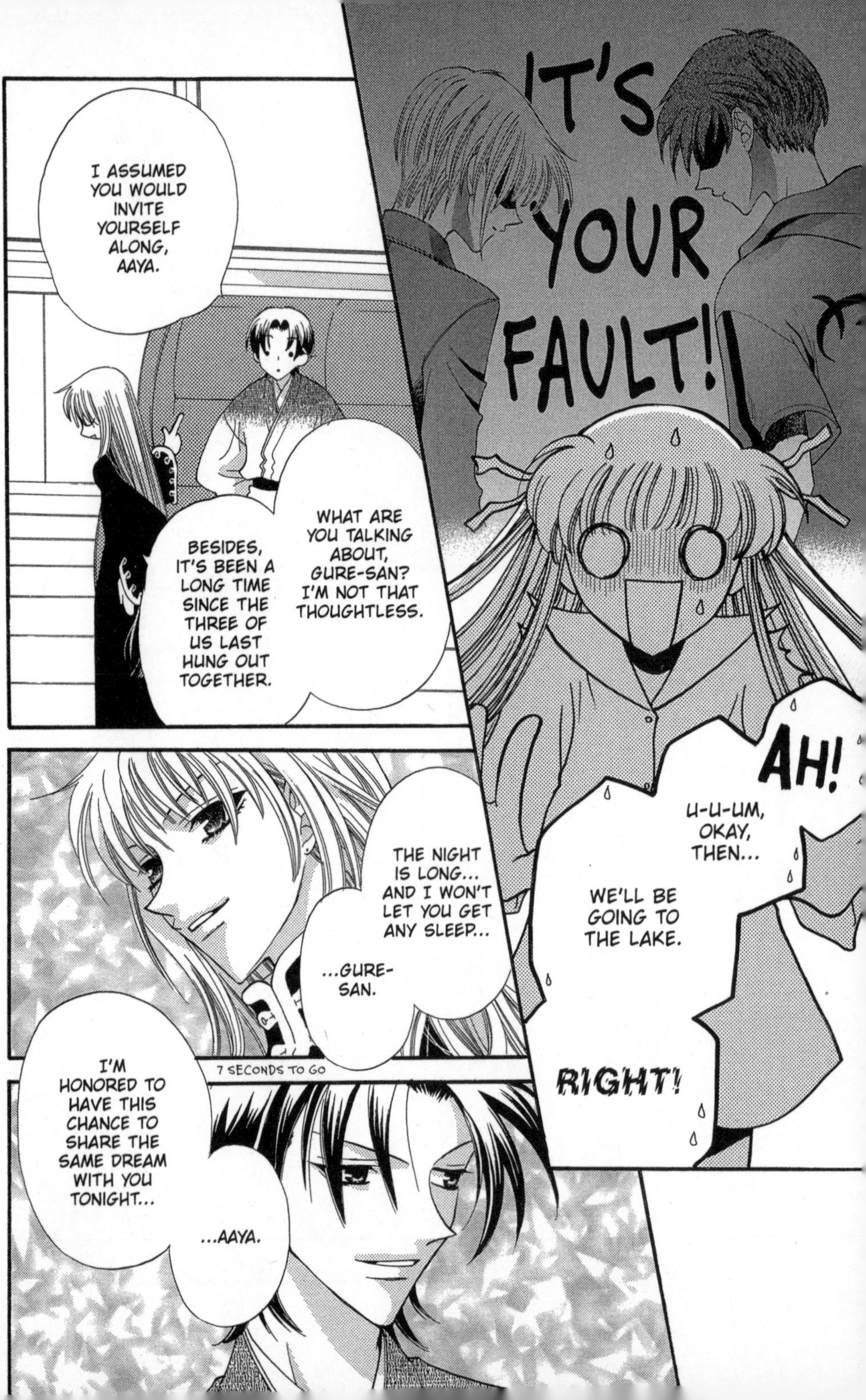
IT'S YOUR FAULT!!
AH!
U-U-UM, OKAY, THEN...
WE'LL BE GOING TO THE LAKE.
RIGHT!
I ASSUMED YOU WOULD INVITE YOURSELF ALONG, AAYA.
WHAT ARE YOU TALKING ABOUT, GURE-SAN? I'M NOT THAT THOUGHTLESS.
BESIDES, IT'S BEEN A LONG TIME SINCE THE THREE OF US LAST HUNG OUT TOGETHER.
THE NIGHT IS LONG... AND I WON'T LET YOU GET ANY SLEEP...
...GURE-SAN.
7 SECONDS TO GO
I'M HONORED TO HAVE THIS CHANCE TO SHARE THE SAME DREAM WITH YOU TONIGHT...
...AAYA.

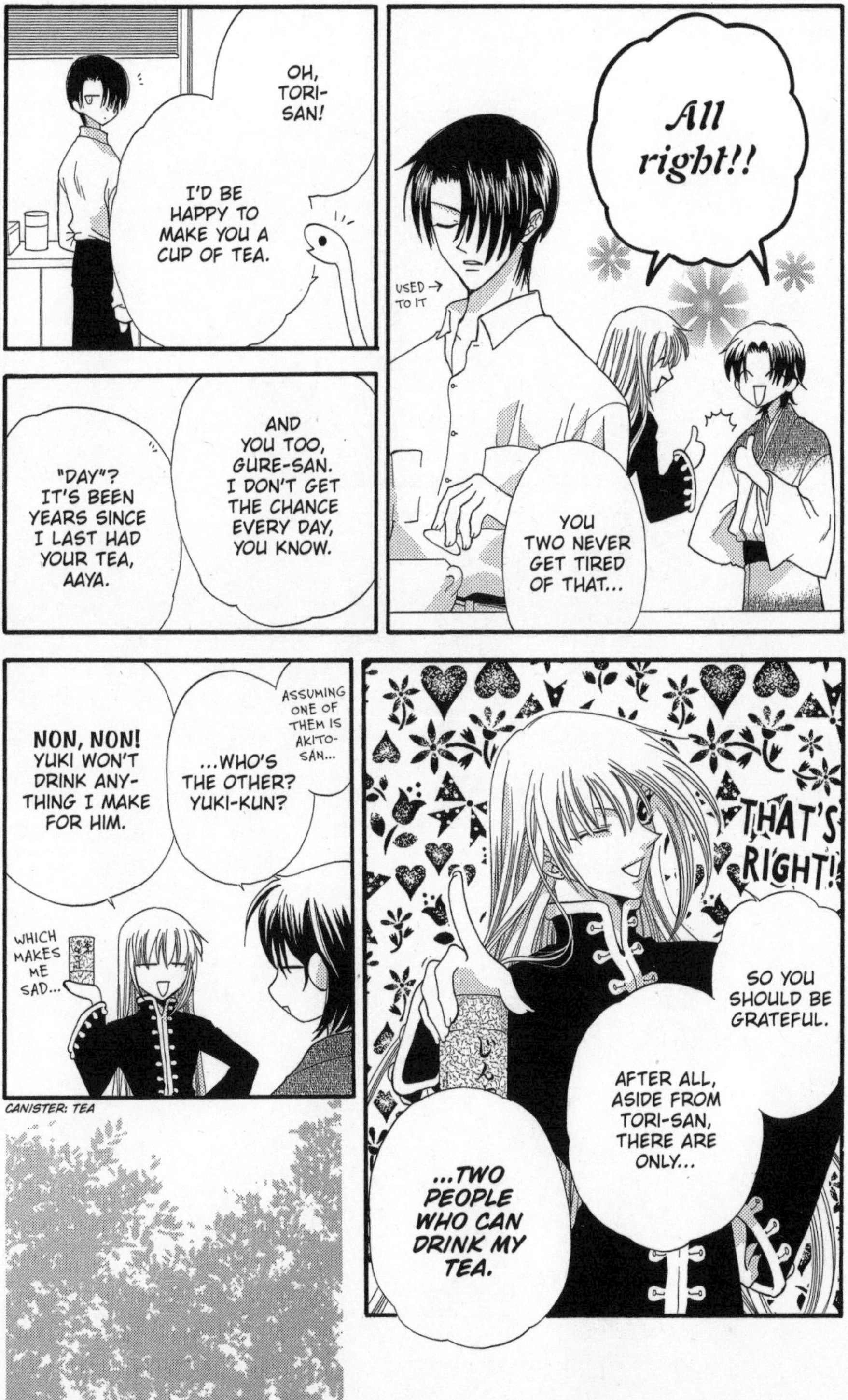
All right!!
USED TO IT
YOU TWO NEVER GET TIRED OF THAT...
OH, TORI-SAN!
I'D BE HAPPY TO MAKE YOU A CUP OF TEA.
AND YOU TOO, GURE-SAN. I DON'T GET THE CHANCE EVERY DAY, YOU KNOW.
"DAY"? IT'S BEEN YEARS SINCE I LAST HAD YOUR TEA, AAYA.
THAT'S RIGHT!
SO YOU SHOULD BE GRATEFUL.
AFTER ALL, ASIDE FROM TORI-SAN, THERE ARE ONLY...
...TWO PEOPLE WHO CAN DRINK MY TEA.
ASSUMING ONE OF THEM IS AKITO-SAN...
...WHO'S THE OTHER? YUKI-KUN?
NON, NON! YUKI WON'T DRINK ANYTHING I MAKE FOR HIM.
WHICH MAKES ME SAD...
CANISTER: TEA

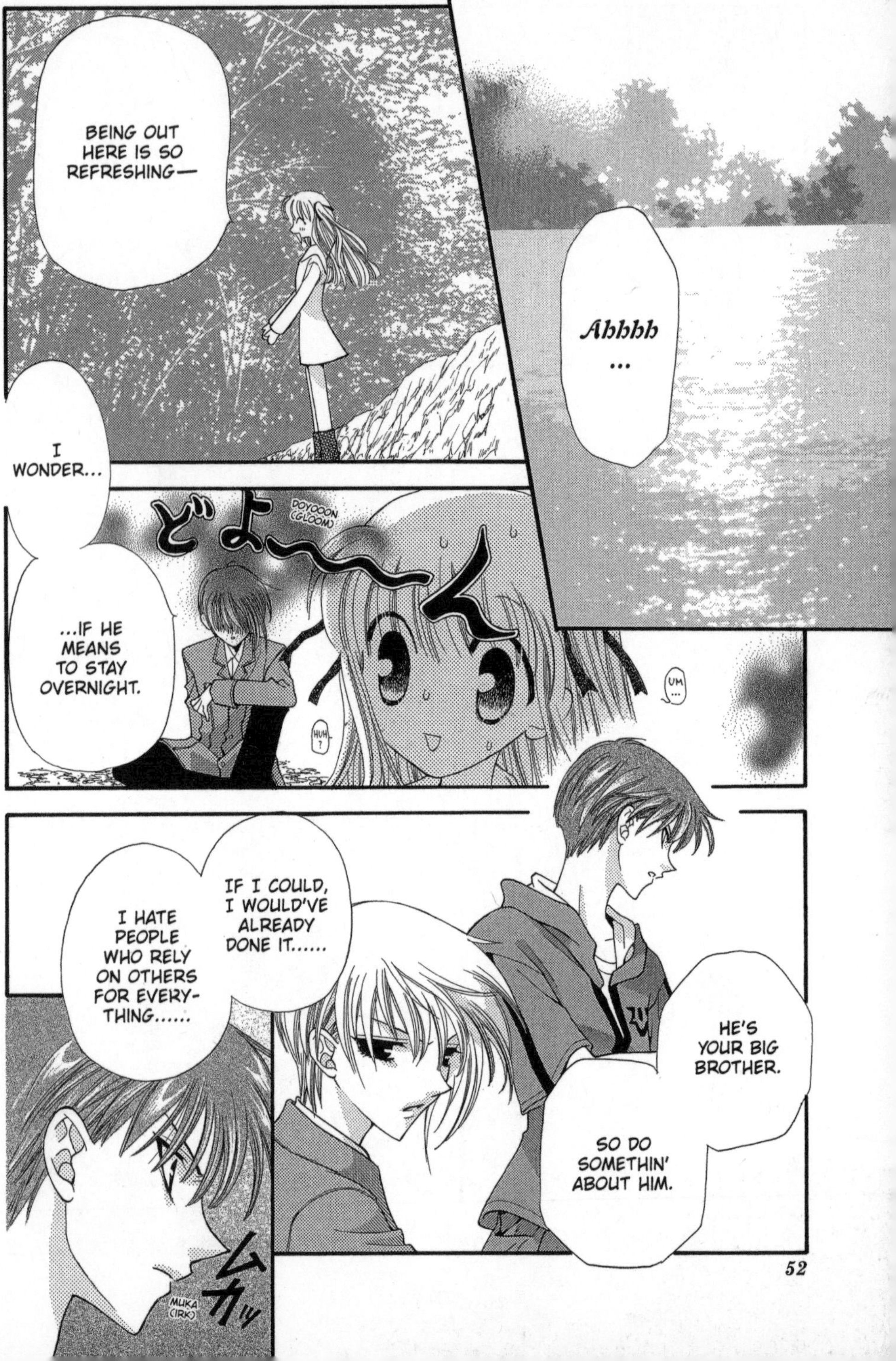
Ahhhh ...
BEING OUT HERE IS SO REFRESHING—
DOYOOON (GLOOM)
I WONDER...
...IF HE MEANS TO STAY OVERNIGHT.
HUH?
UM...
HE'S YOUR BIG BROTHER.
SO DO SOMETHIN' ABOUT HIM.
IF I COULD, I WOULD'VE ALREADY DONE IT......
I HATE PEOPLE WHO RELY ON OTHERS FOR EVERY-THING......
MUKA (IRK)

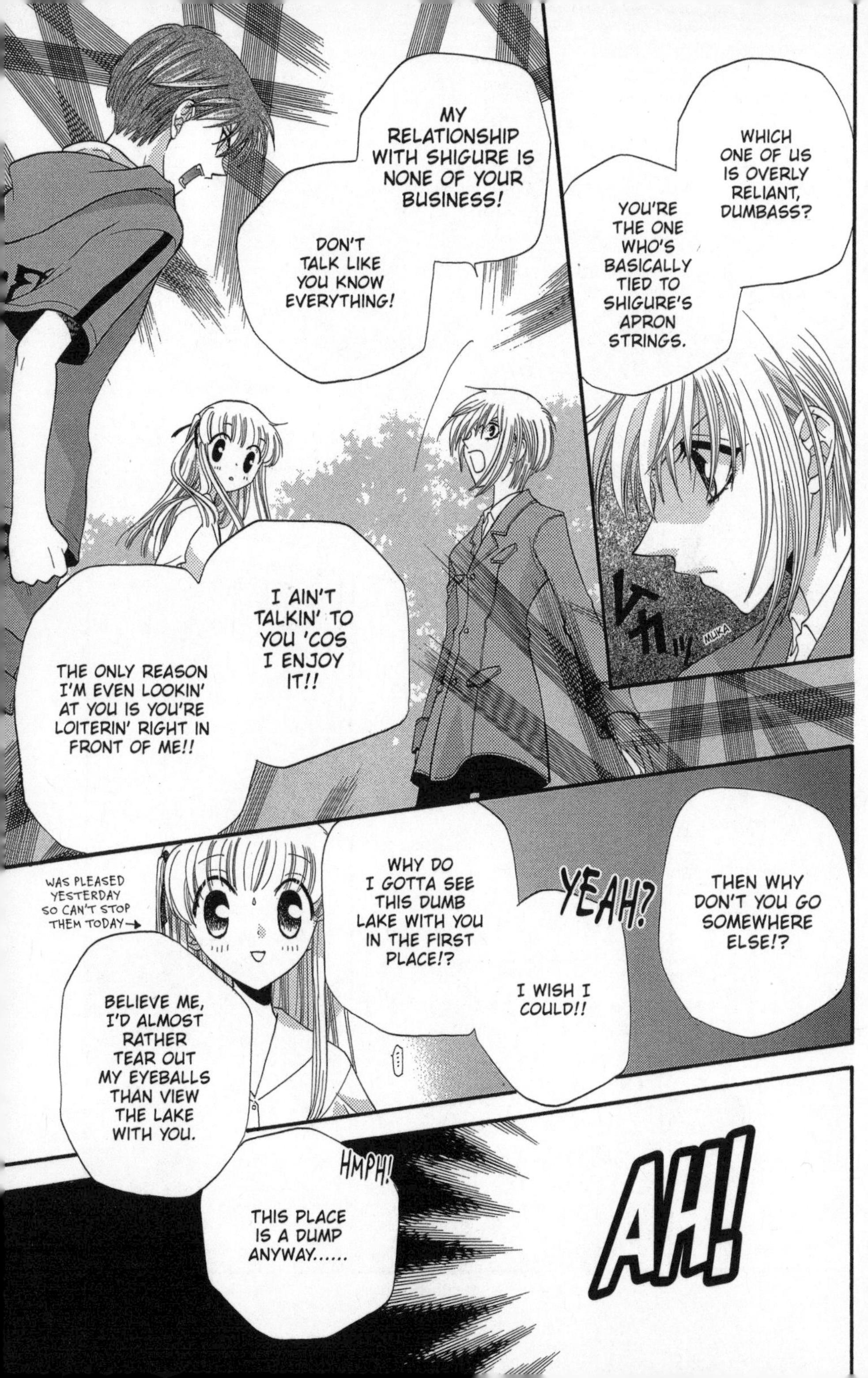
WHICH ONE OF US IS OVERLY RELIANT, DUMBASS?
YOU'RE THE ONE WHO'S BASICALLY TIED TO SHIGURE'S APRON STRINGS.
MUKA
MY RELATIONSHIP WITH SHIGURE IS NONE OF YOUR BUSINESS!
DON'T TALK LIKE YOU KNOW EVERYTHING!
I AIN'T TALKIN' TO YOU 'COS I ENJOY IT!!
THE ONLY REASON I'M EVEN LOOKIN' AT YOU IS YOU'RE LOITERIN' RIGHT IN FRONT OF ME!!
THEN WHY DON'T YOU GO SOMEWHERE ELSE!?
YEAH?
WHY DO I GOTTA SEE THIS DUMB LAKE WITH YOU IN THE FIRST PLACE!?
I WISH I COULD!!
WAS PLEASED YESTERDAY SO CAN'T STOP THEM TODAY →
BELIEVE ME, I'D ALMOST RATHER TEAR OUT MY EYEBALLS THAN VIEW THE LAKE WITH YOU.
AH!
HMPH!
THIS PLACE IS A DUMP ANYWAY......

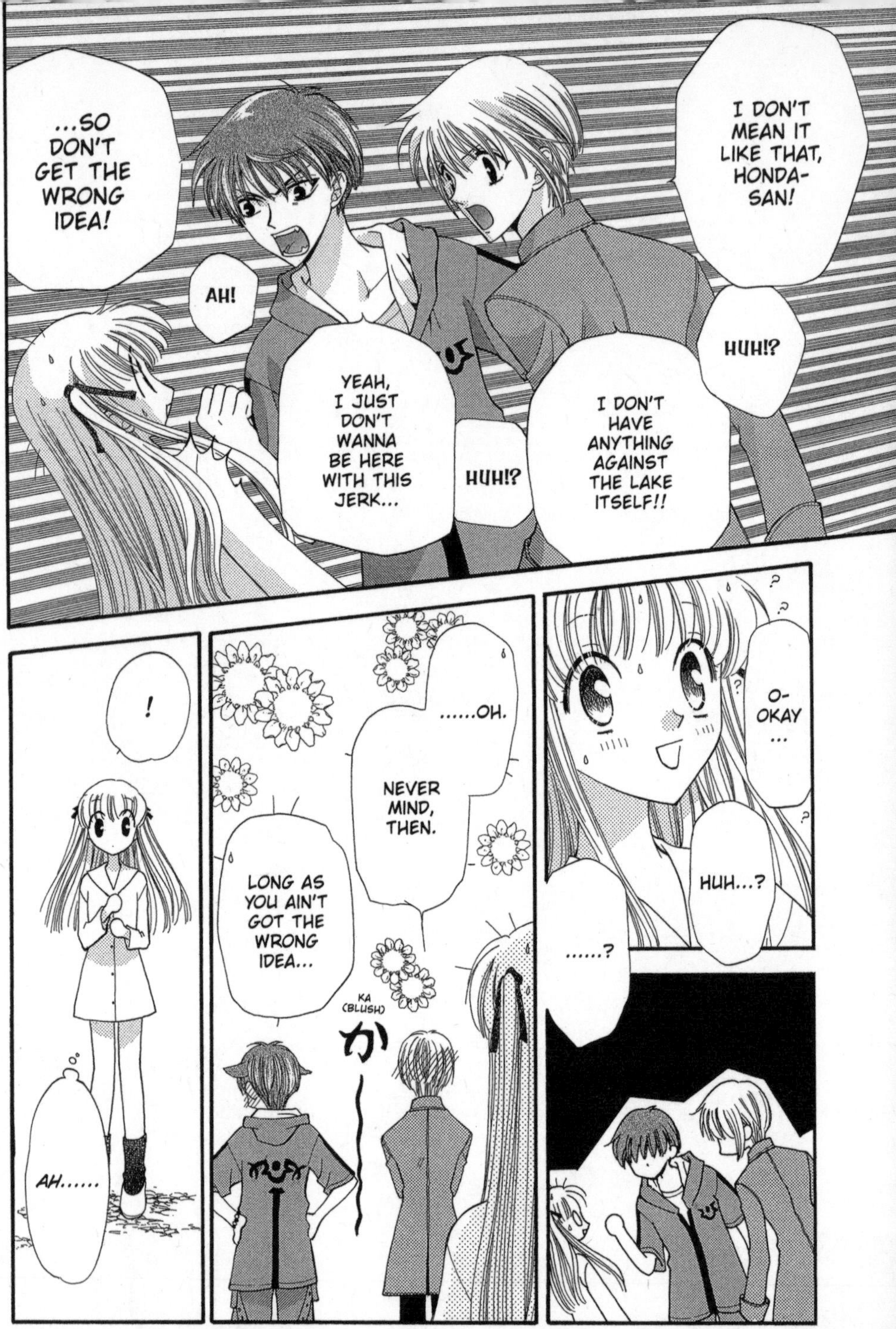
I DON'T MEAN IT LIKE THAT, HONDA-SAN!
...SO DON'T GET THE WRONG IDEA!
AH!
HUH!?
I DON'T HAVE ANYTHING AGAINST THE LAKE ITSELF!!
HUH!?
YEAH, I JUST DON'T WANNA BE HERE WITH THIS JERK...
O-OKAY ...
HUH...?
......?
......OH.
NEVER MIND, THEN.
LONG AS YOU AIN'T GOT THE WRONG IDEA...
KA (BLUSH)
か
!
AH......

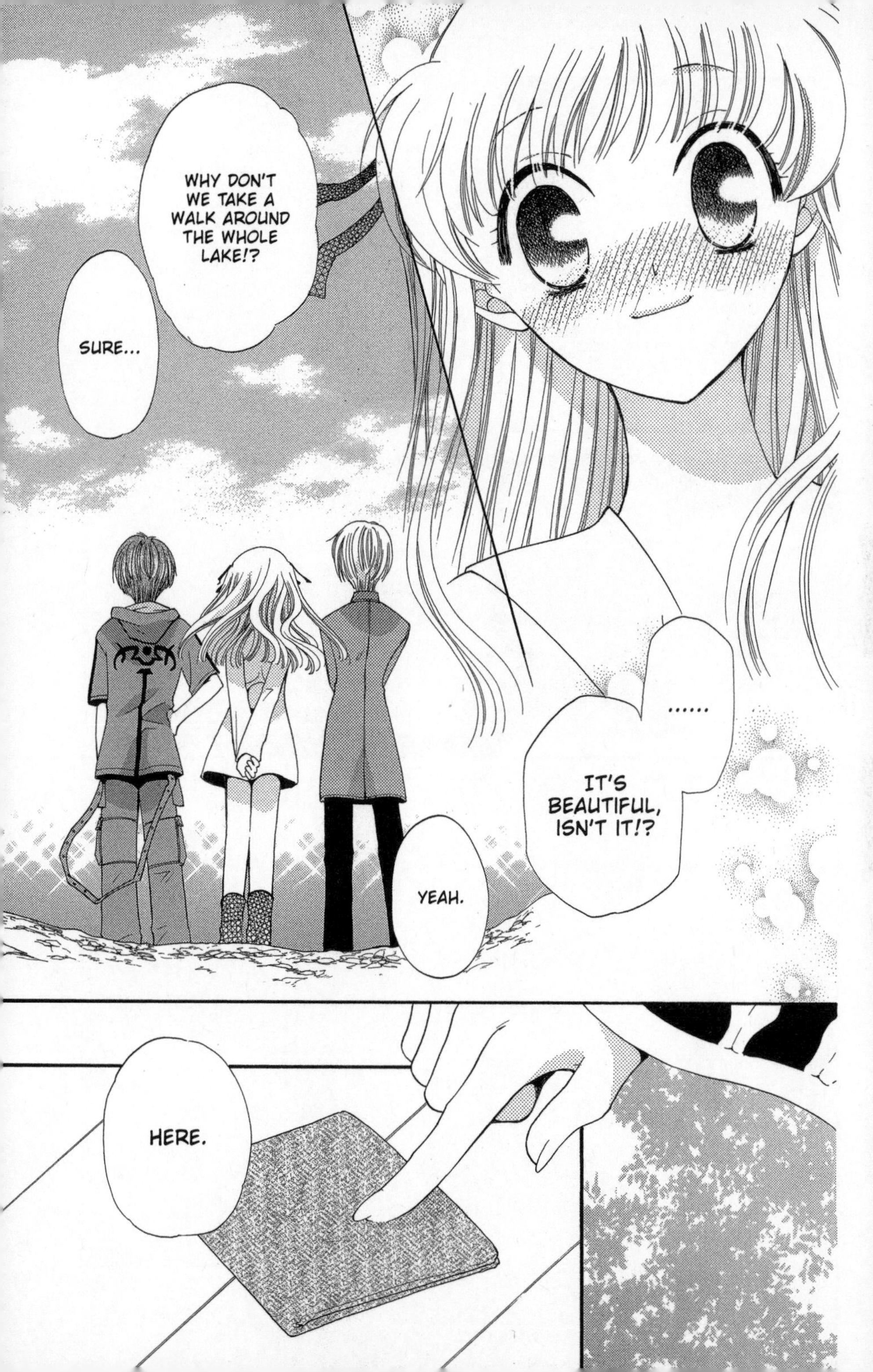
......
IT'S BEAUTIFUL, ISN'T IT!?
YEAH.
WHY DON'T WE TAKE A WALK AROUND THE WHOLE LAKE!?
SURE...
HERE.

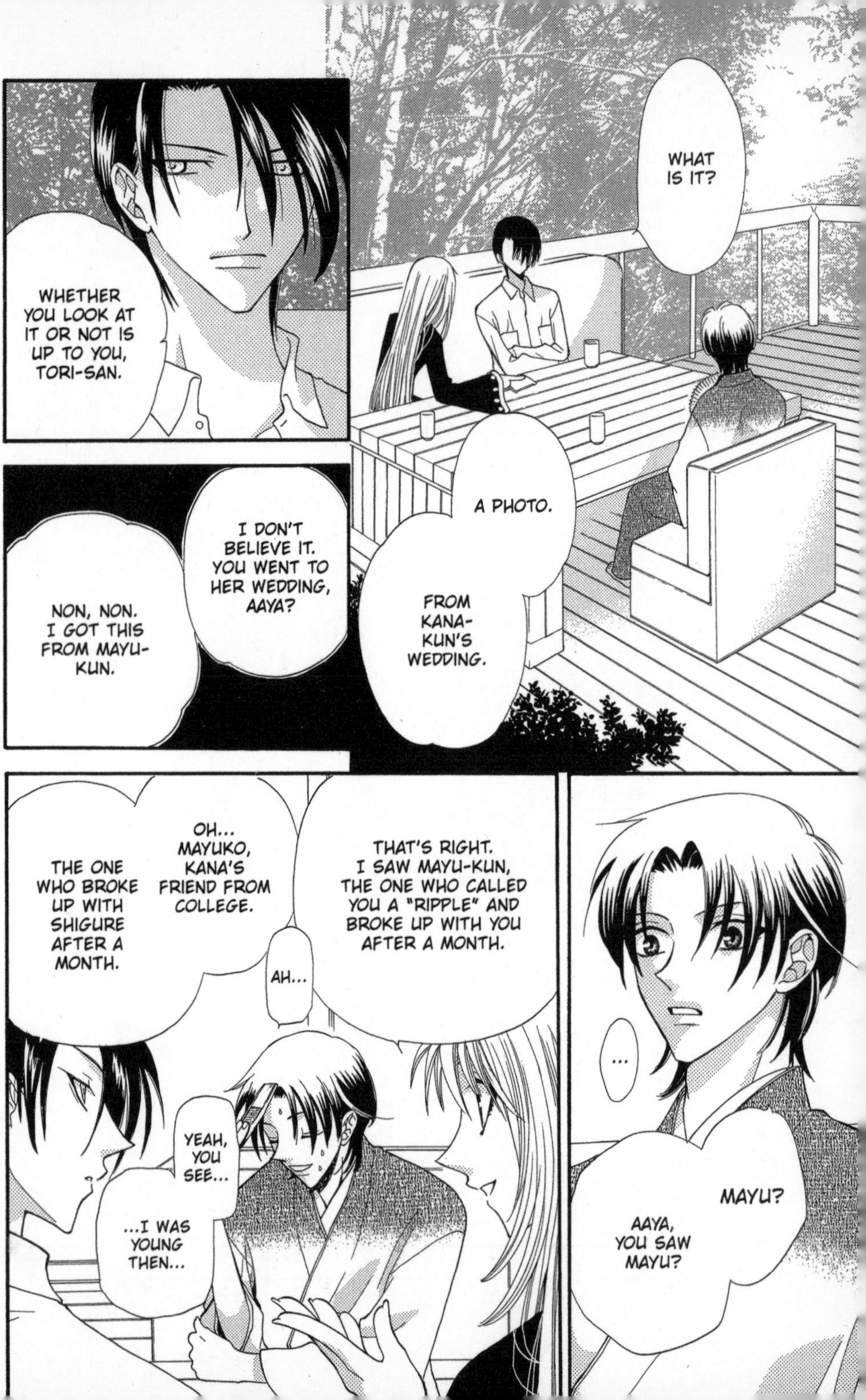
WHAT IS IT?
A PHOTO.
FROM KANA-KUN'S WEDDING.
WHETHER YOU LOOK AT IT OR NOT IS UP TO YOU, TORI-SAN.
I DON'T BELIEVE IT. YOU WENT TO HER WEDDING, AAYA?
NON, NON. I GOT THIS FROM MAYU-KUN.
...
MAYU?
AAYA, YOU SAW MAYU?
THAT'S RIGHT. I SAW MAYU-KUN, THE ONE WHO CALLED YOU A "RIPPLE" AND BROKE UP WITH YOU AFTER A MONTH.
OH... MAYUKO, KANA'S FRIEND FROM COLLEGE.
THE ONE WHO BROKE UP WITH SHIGURE AFTER A MONTH.
AH...
YEAH, YOU SEE...
...I WAS YOUNG THEN...

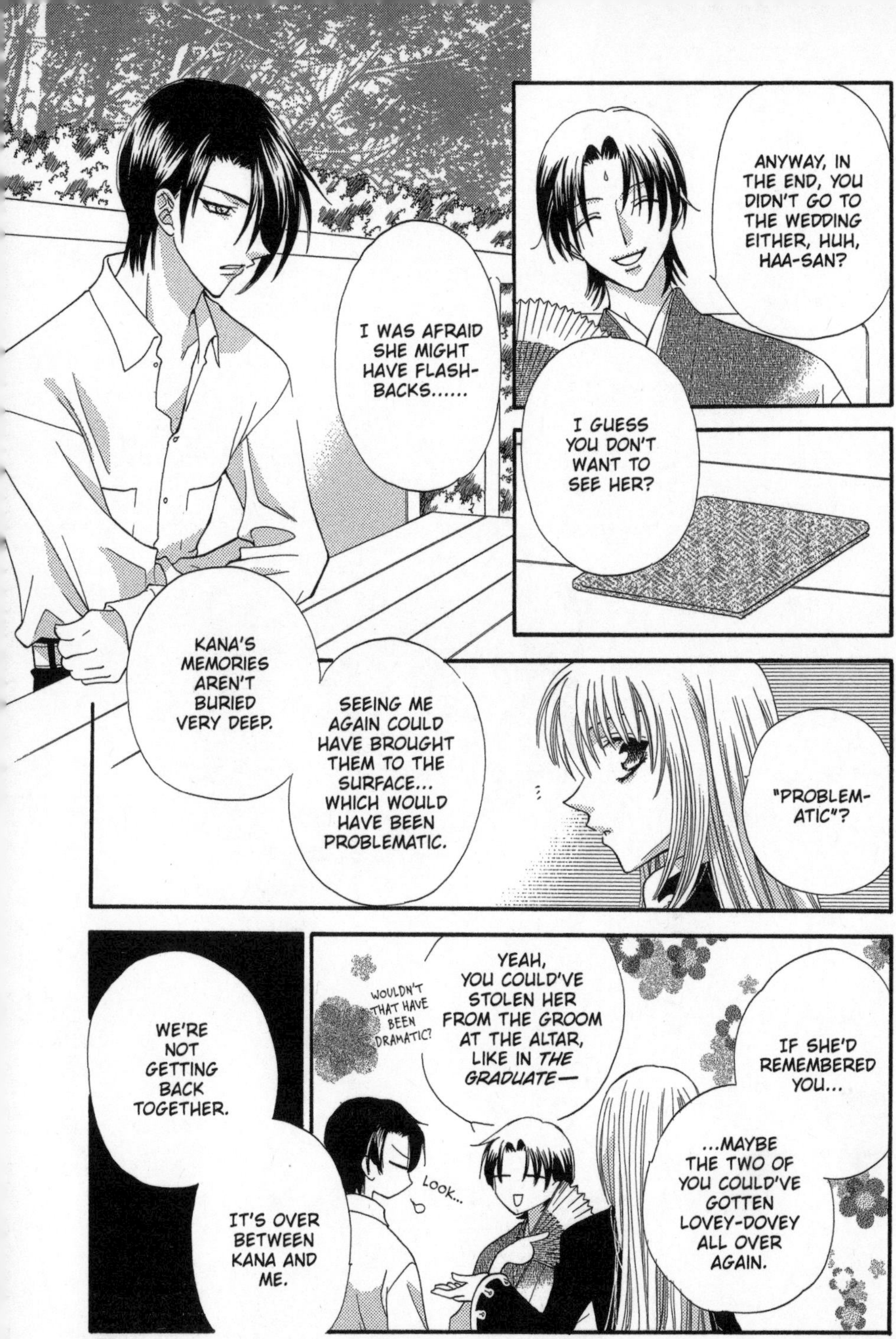
ANYWAY, IN THE END, YOU DIDN'T GO TO THE WEDDING EITHER, HUH, HAA-SAN?
I GUESS YOU DON'T WANT TO SEE HER?
I WAS AFRAID SHE MIGHT HAVE FLASH-BACKS......
KANA'S MEMORIES AREN'T BURIED VERY DEEP.
SEEING ME AGAIN COULD HAVE BROUGHT THEM TO THE SURFACE... WHICH WOULD HAVE BEEN PROBLEMATIC.
"PROBLEM-ATIC"?
IF SHE'D REMEMBERED YOU...
...MAYBE THE TWO OF YOU COULD'VE GOTTEN LOVEY-DOVEY ALL OVER AGAIN.
YEAH, YOU COULD'VE STOLEN HER FROM THE GROOM AT THE ALTAR, LIKE IN *THE GRADUATE*—
WOULDN'T THAT HAVE BEEN DRAMATIC?
LOOK...
WE'RE NOT GETTING BACK TOGETHER.
IT'S OVER BETWEEN KANA AND ME.

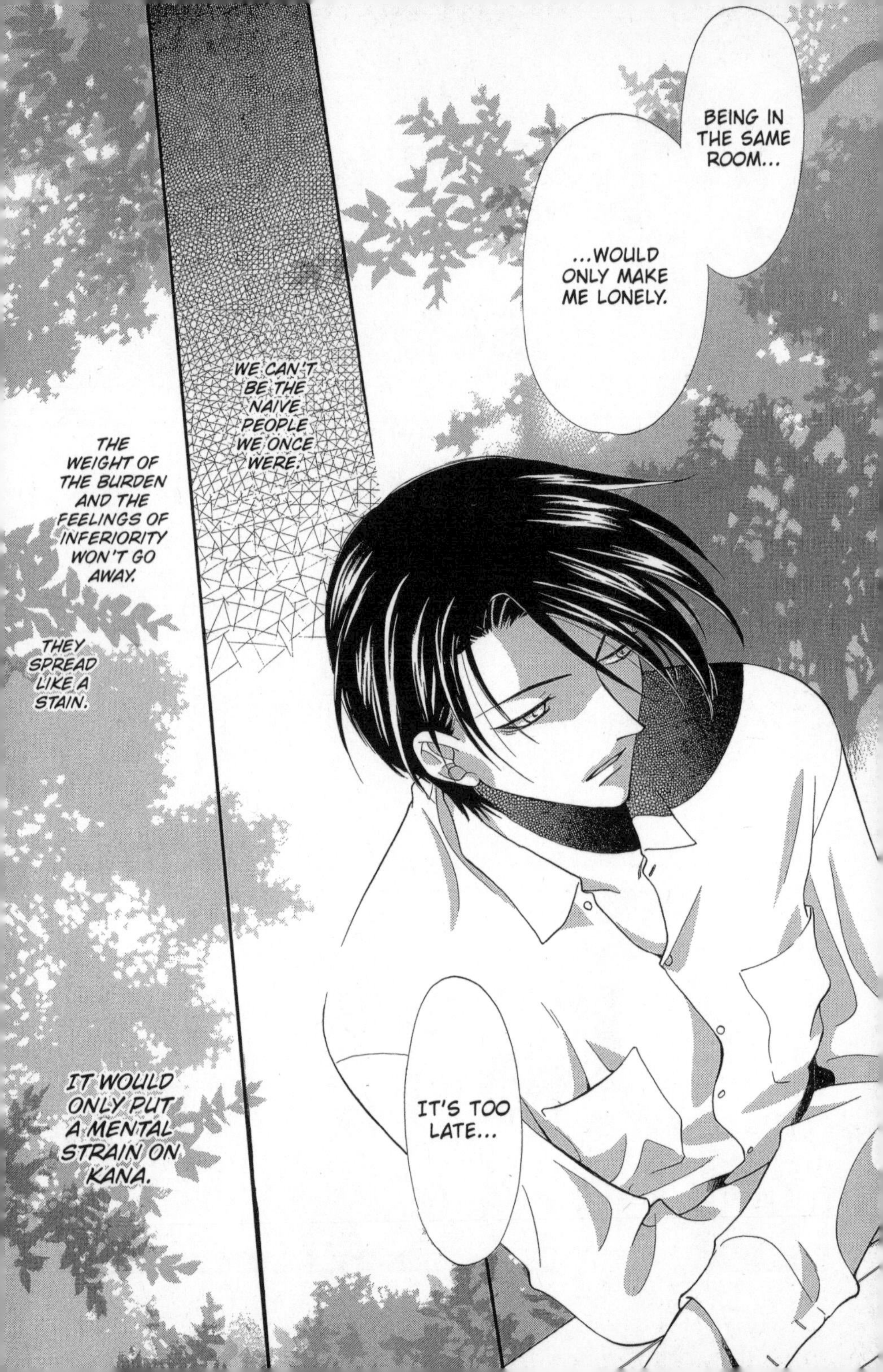
BEING IN THE SAME ROOM...
...WOULD ONLY MAKE ME LONELY.
IT'S TOO LATE...
WE CAN'T BE THE NAIVE PEOPLE WE ONCE WERE.
THE WEIGHT OF THE BURDEN AND THE FEELINGS OF INFERIORITY WON'T GO AWAY.
THEY SPREAD LIKE A STAIN.
IT WOULD ONLY PUT A MENTAL STRAIN ON KANA.

IT WOULD ONLY MAKE HER SAD...
...I DON'T WANT TO THINK...
...THAT OUR LOVE HAS BEEN ERASED...
...BUT...
...I DON'T WANT TO BE WITH HER EITHER.
I HAVE NO DESIRE TO SEE HER.
ALL THAT'S LEFT TO DO NOW...
...IS PRAY.
PLEASE LET HER BE HAPPY.

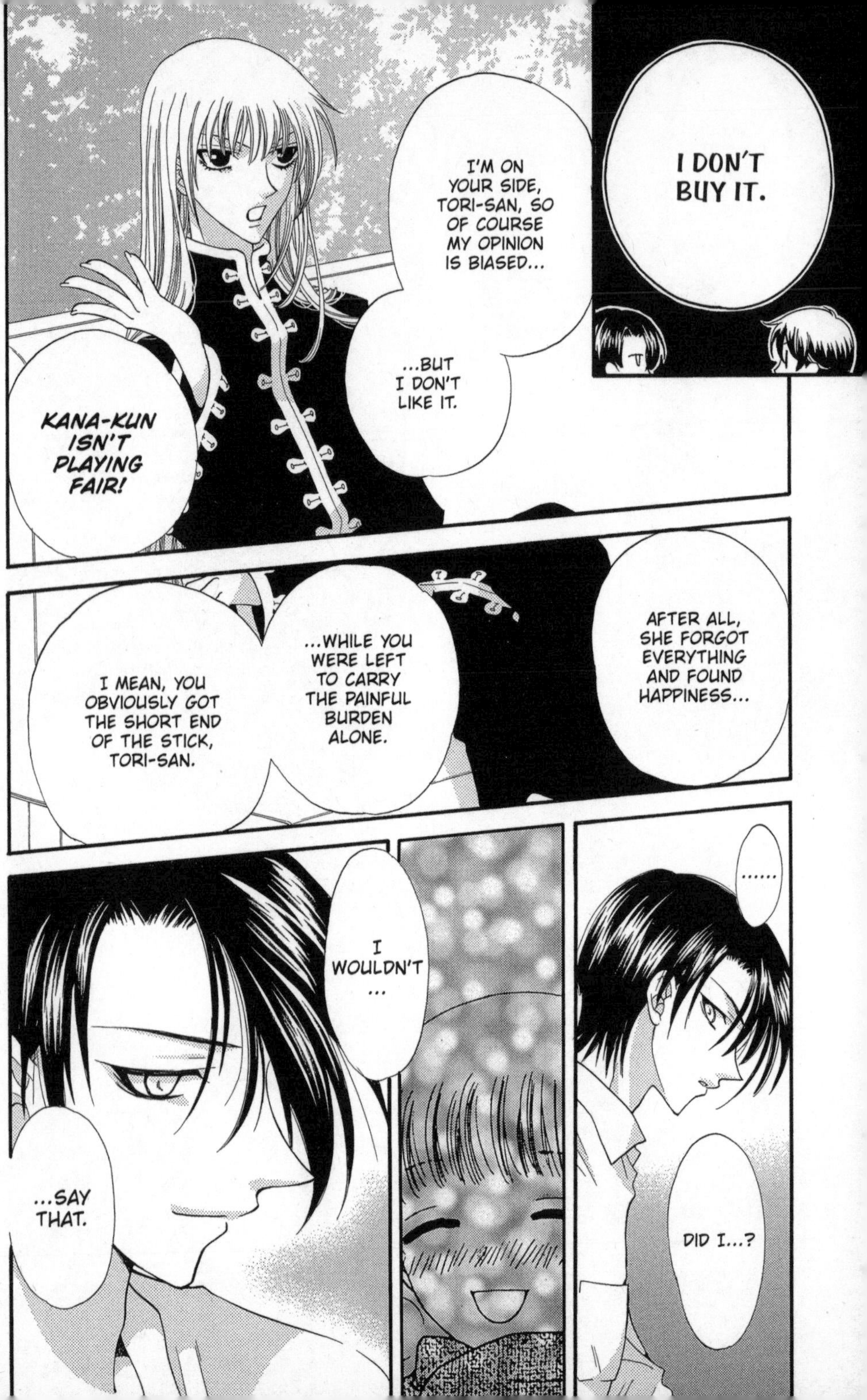
I DON'T BUY IT.
I'M ON YOUR SIDE, TORI-SAN, SO OF COURSE MY OPINION IS BIASED...
...BUT I DON'T LIKE IT.
KANA-KUN ISN'T PLAYING FAIR!
AFTER ALL, SHE FORGOT EVERYTHING AND FOUND HAPPINESS...
...WHILE YOU WERE LEFT TO CARRY THE PAINFUL BURDEN ALONE.
I MEAN, YOU OBVIOUSLY GOT THE SHORT END OF THE STICK, TORI-SAN.
......
DID I...?
I WOULDN'T ...
...SAY THAT.

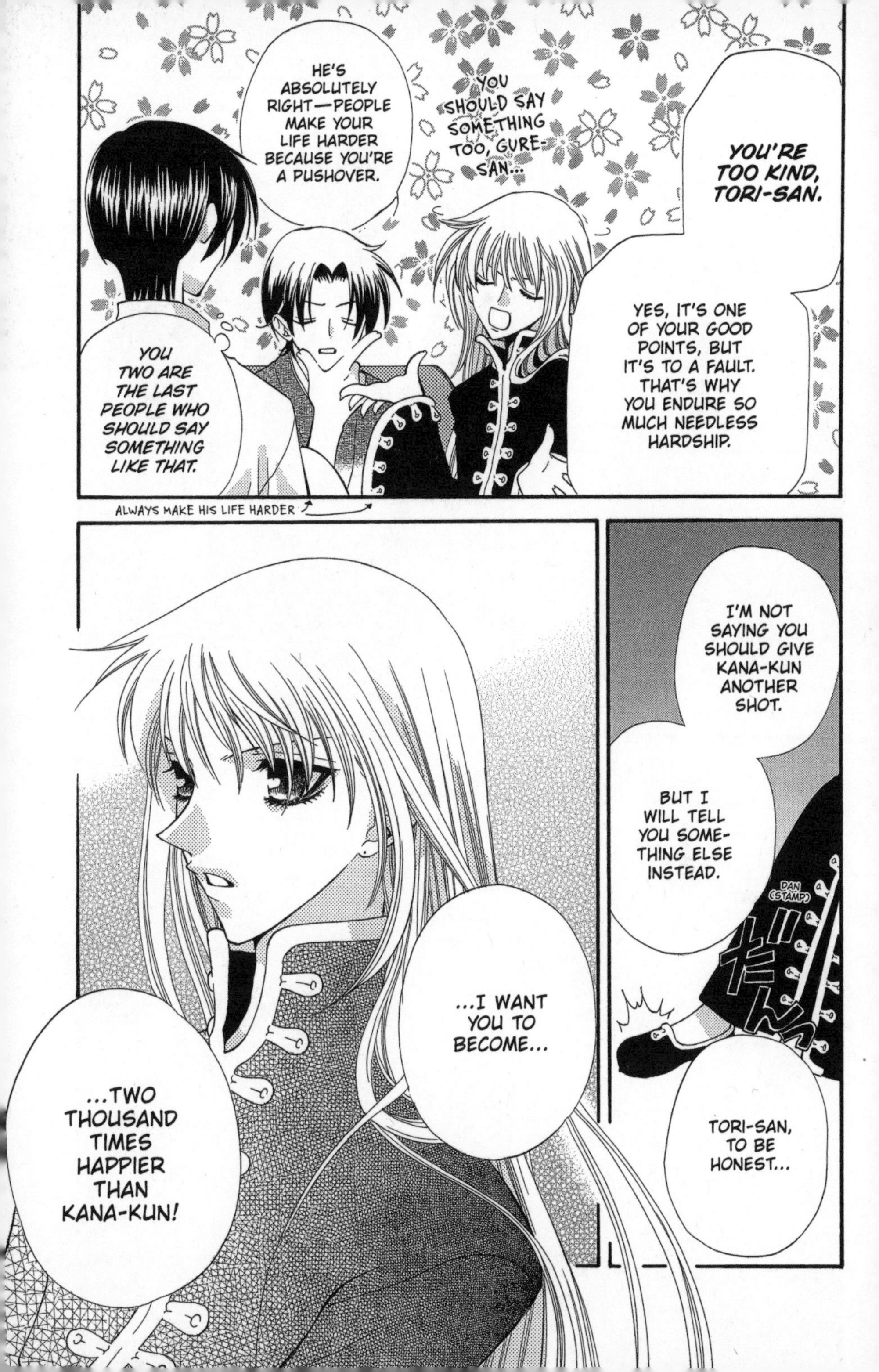
YOU'RE TOO KIND, TORI-SAN.
YES, IT'S ONE OF YOUR GOOD POINTS, BUT IT'S TO A FAULT. THAT'S WHY YOU ENDURE SO MUCH NEEDLESS HARDSHIP.
YOU SHOULD SAY SOMETHING TOO, GURE-SAN...
HE'S ABSOLUTELY RIGHT—PEOPLE MAKE YOUR LIFE HARDER BECAUSE YOU'RE A PUSHOVER.
YOU TWO ARE THE LAST PEOPLE WHO SHOULD SAY SOMETHING LIKE THAT.
ALWAYS MAKE HIS LIFE HARDER
I'M NOT SAYING YOU SHOULD GIVE KANA-KUN ANOTHER SHOT.
BUT I WILL TELL YOU SOMETHING ELSE INSTEAD.
DAN (STAMP)
TORI-SAN, TO BE HONEST...
...I WANT YOU TO BECOME...
...TWO THOUSAND TIMES HAPPIER THAN KANA-KUN!

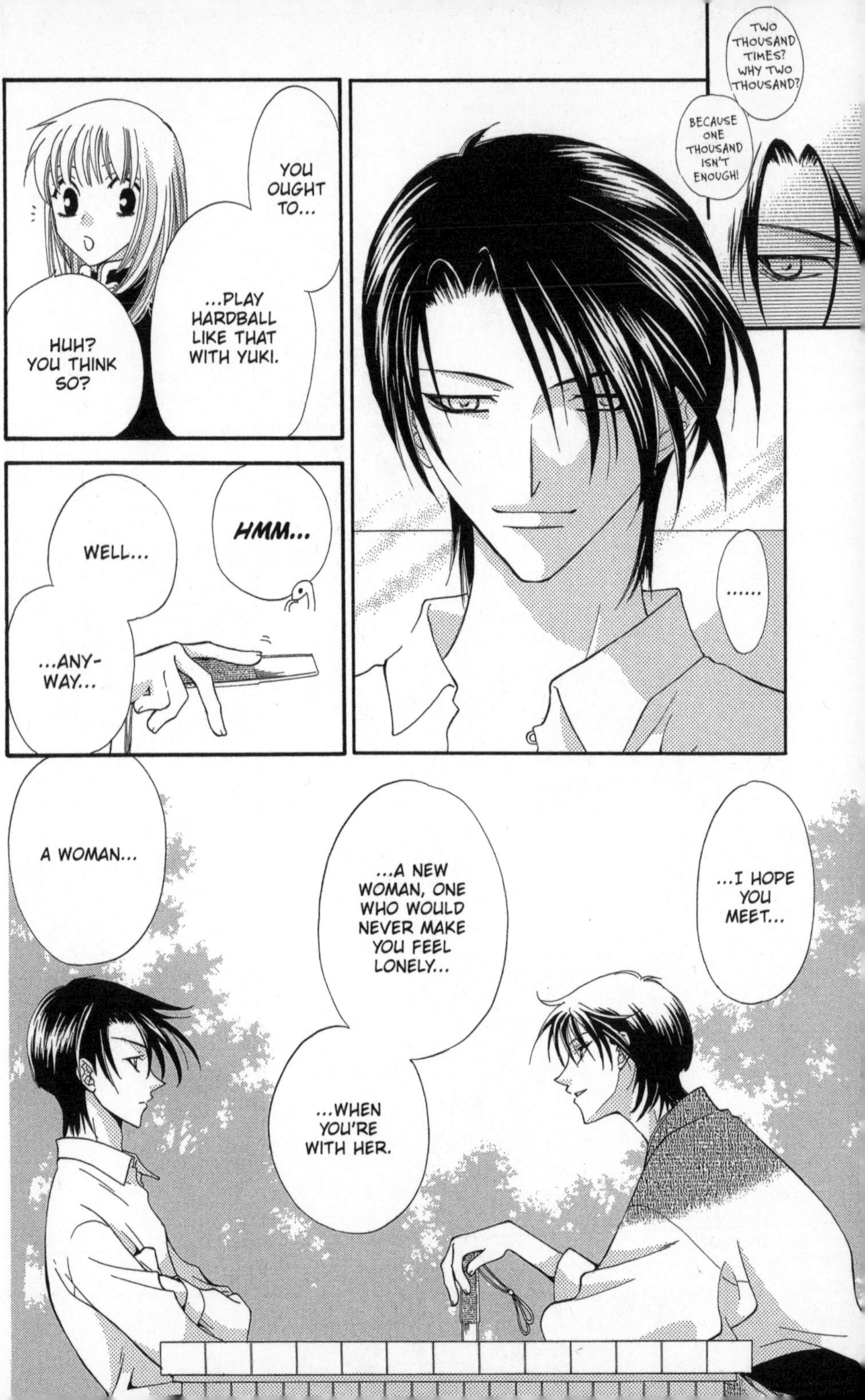

TWO THOUSAND TIMES? WHY TWO THOUSAND?
BECAUSE ONE THOUSAND ISN'T ENOUGH!
......
YOU OUGHT TO...
...PLAY HARDBALL LIKE THAT WITH YUKI.
HUH? YOU THINK SO?
HMM...
WELL...
...ANY-WAY...
...I HOPE YOU MEET...
...A NEW WOMAN, ONE WHO WOULD NEVER MAKE YOU FEEL LONELY...
...WHEN YOU'RE WITH HER.
A WOMAN...

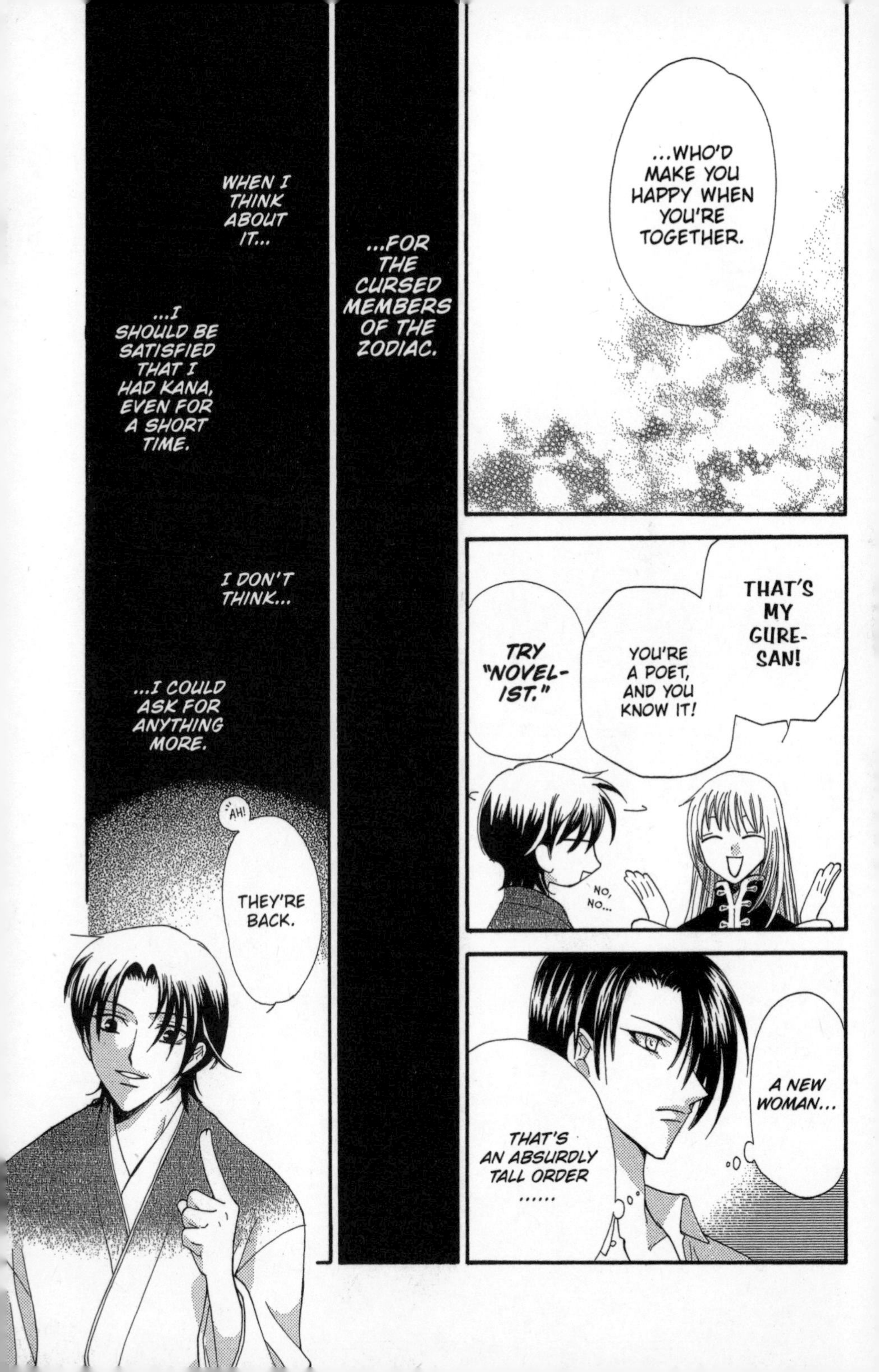
...WHO'D MAKE YOU HAPPY WHEN YOU'RE TOGETHER.
THAT'S MY GURE-SAN!
YOU'RE A POET, AND YOU KNOW IT!
TRY "NOVEL-IST."
NO, NO...
A NEW WOMAN...
THAT'S AN ABSURDLY TALL ORDER ......
...FOR THE CURSED MEMBERS OF THE ZODIAC.
WHEN I THINK ABOUT IT...
...I SHOULD BE SATISFIED THAT I HAD KANA, EVEN FOR A SHORT TIME.
I DON'T THINK...
...I COULD ASK FOR ANYTHING MORE.
AH!
THEY'RE BACK.

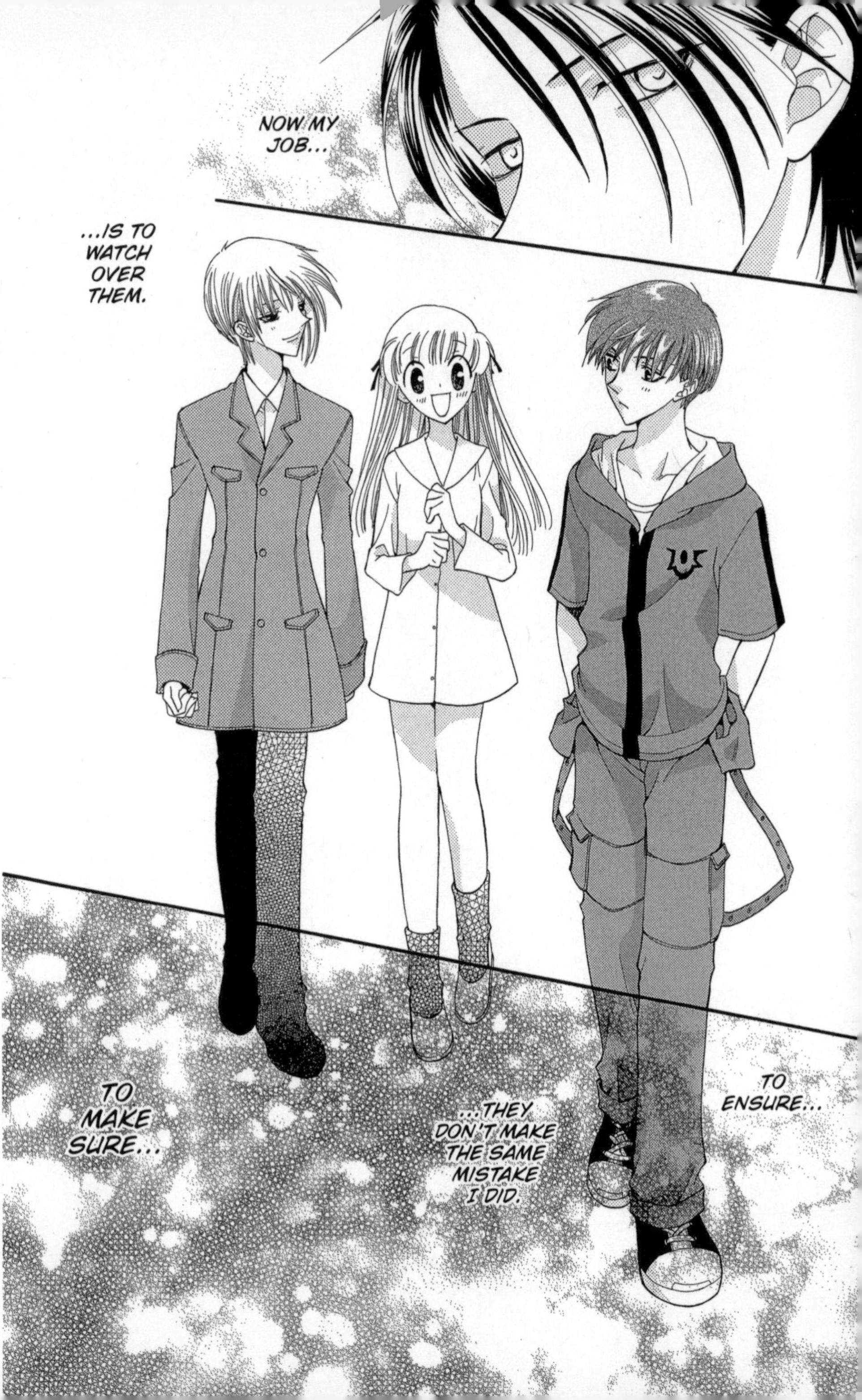
NOW MY JOB...
...IS TO WATCH OVER THEM.
TO ENSURE...
...THEY DON'T MAKE THE SAME MISTAKE I DID.
TO MAKE SURE...

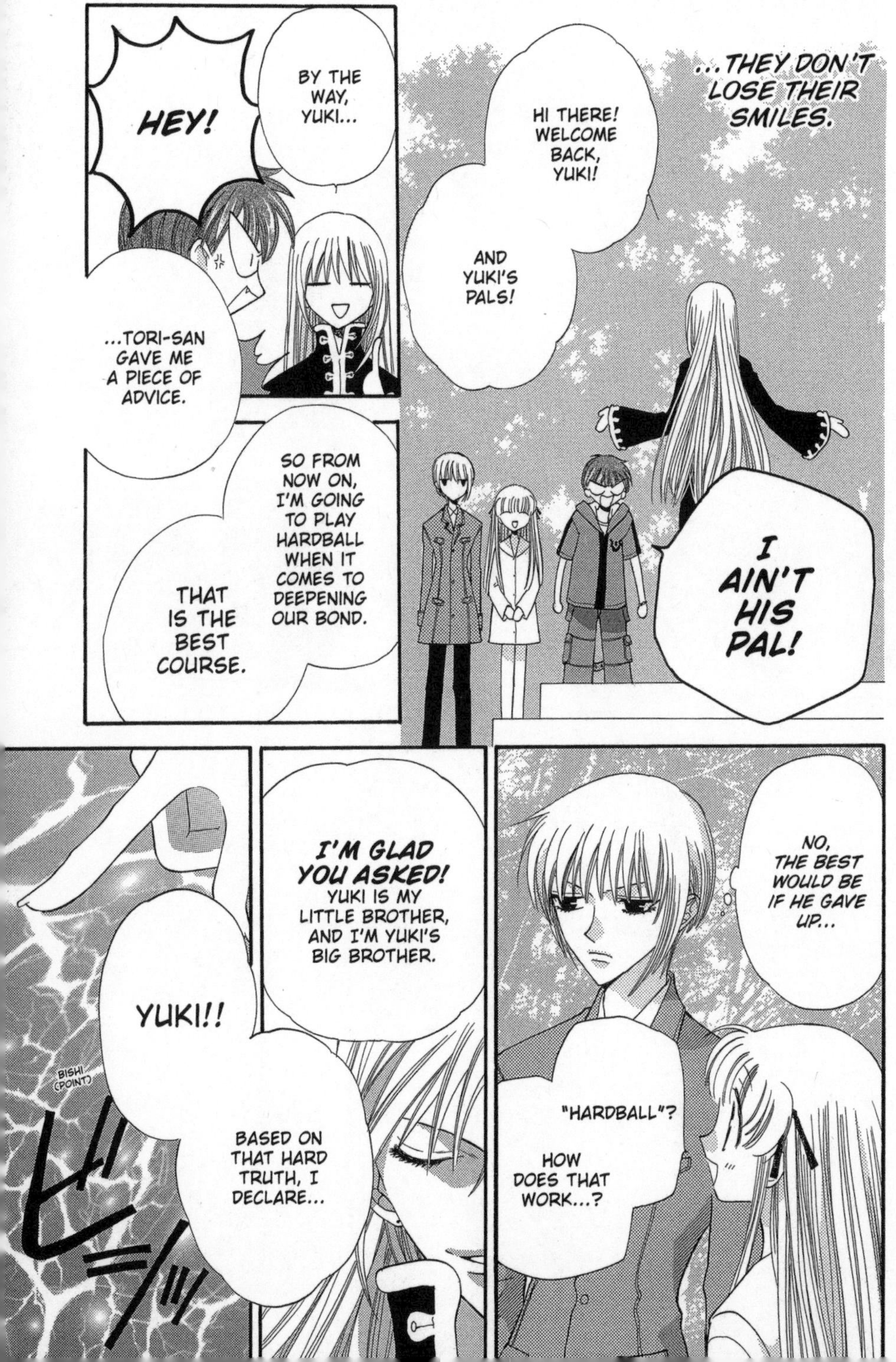
...THEY DON'T LOSE THEIR SMILES.
HI THERE! WELCOME BACK, YUKI!
AND YUKI'S PALS!
I AIN'T HIS PAL!
HEY!
BY THE WAY, YUKI...
...TORI-SAN GAVE ME A PIECE OF ADVICE.
SO FROM NOW ON, I'M GOING TO PLAY HARDBALL WHEN IT COMES TO DEEPENING OUR BOND.
THAT IS THE BEST COURSE.
NO, THE BEST WOULD BE IF HE GAVE UP...
"HARDBALL"?
HOW DOES THAT WORK...?
I'M GLAD YOU ASKED! YUKI IS MY LITTLE BROTHER, AND I'M YUKI'S BIG BROTHER.
BASED ON THAT HARD TRUTH, I DECLARE...
YUKI!!
BISHI (POINT)

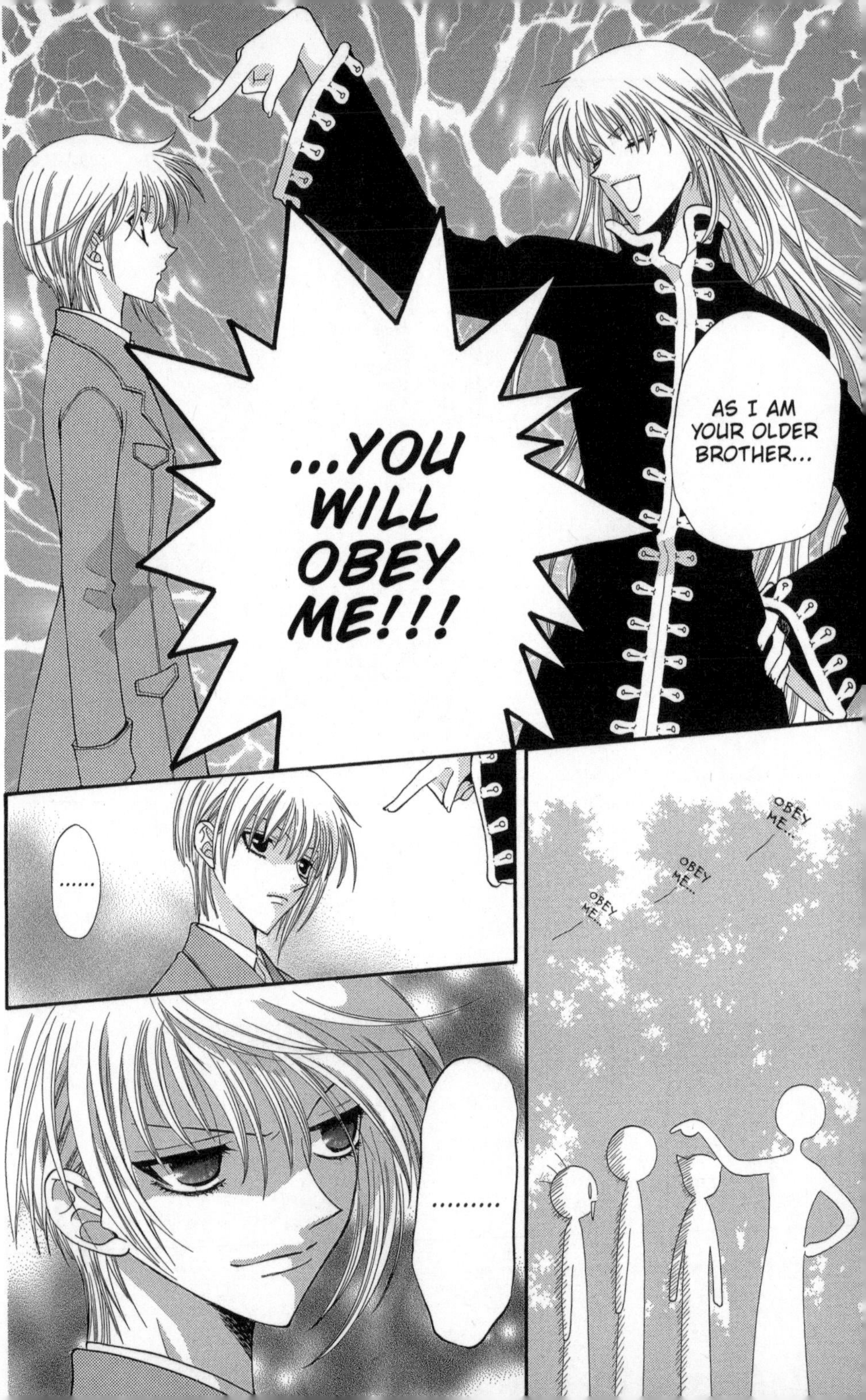
AS I AM YOUR OLDER BROTHER...
...YOU WILL OBEY ME!!!
OBEY ME...
OBEY ME...
OBEY ME...
......
....

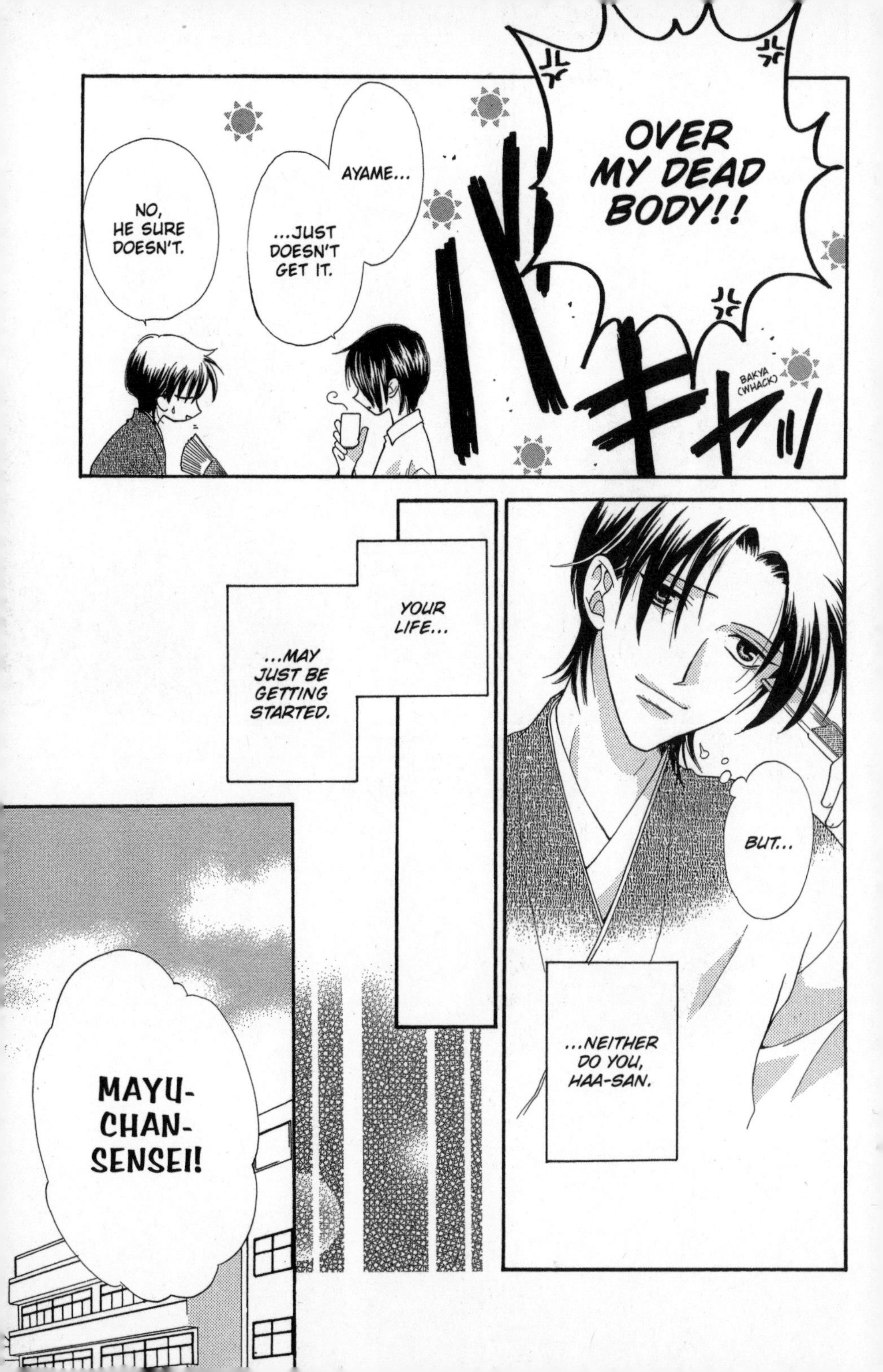
OVER MY DEAD BODY!!
BAKYA (WHACK)
AYAME...
...JUST DOESN'T GET IT.
NO, HE SURE DOESN'T.
BUT...
...NEITHER DO YOU, HAA-SAN.
YOUR LIFE...
...MAY JUST BE GETTING STARTED.
MAYU-CHAN-SENSEI!

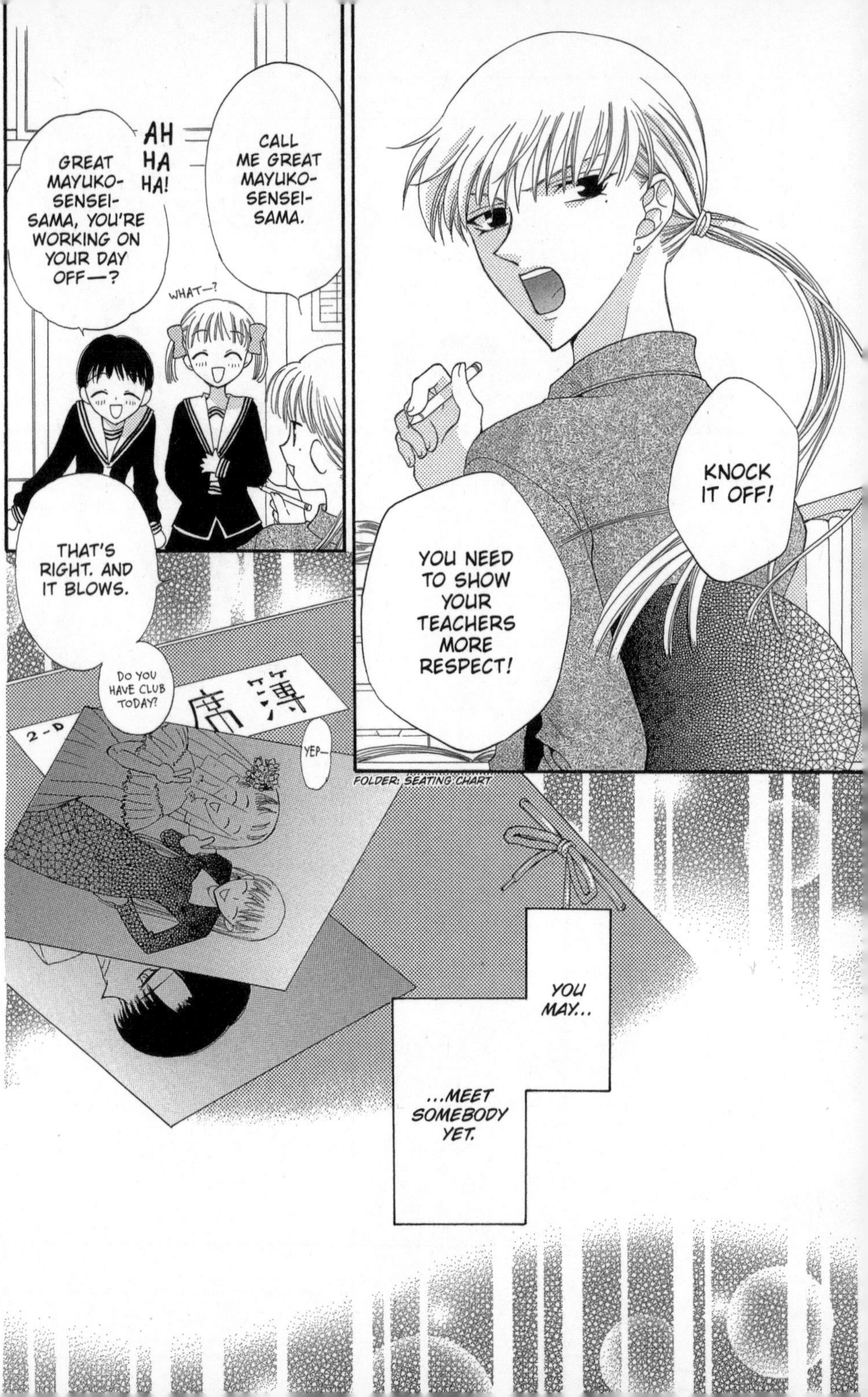
KNOCK IT OFF!
YOU NEED TO SHOW YOUR TEACHERS MORE RESPECT!
CALL ME GREAT MAYUKO-SENSEI-SAMA.
AH HA HA!
GREAT MAYUKO-SENSEI-SAMA, YOU'RE WORKING ON YOUR DAY OFF—?
WHAT—?
THAT'S RIGHT. AND IT BLOWS.
DO YOU HAVE CLUB TODAY?
YEP—
2-D
FOLDER: SEATING CHART
YOU MAY...
...MEET SOMEBODY YET.

COLLECTOR'S EDITION

Fruits Basket

COLLECTOR'S EDITION

Fruits
Basket

Chapter 27

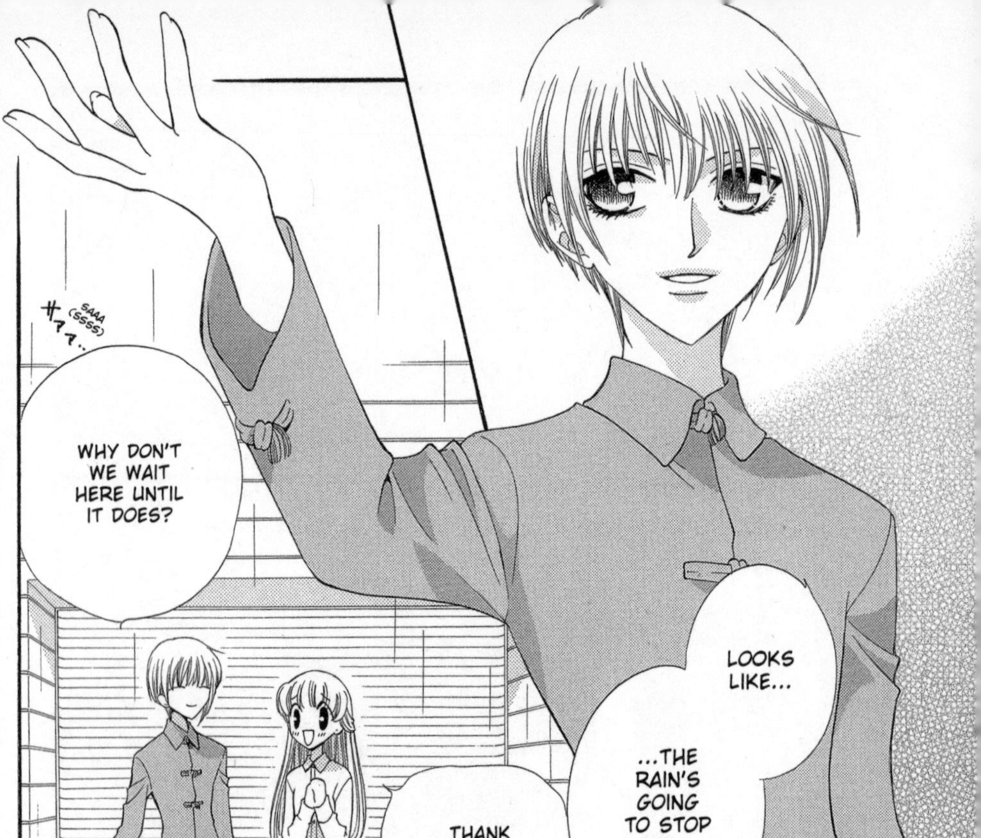
LOOKS LIKE...
...THE RAIN'S GOING TO STOP SOON.
THANK GOODNESS... FOR A WHILE THERE, I WASN'T SURE WHAT TO DO...
SAAA (SSSS)
WHY DON'T WE WAIT HERE UNTIL IT DOES?

ON THE WAY BACK FROM GROCERY SHOPPING

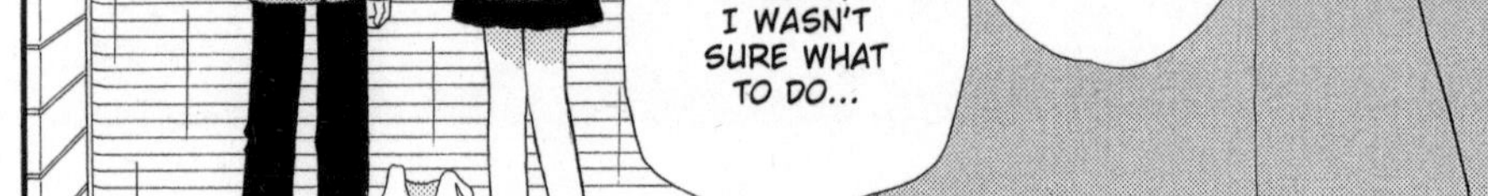
RAM
HORSE
SNAKE
DRAGON

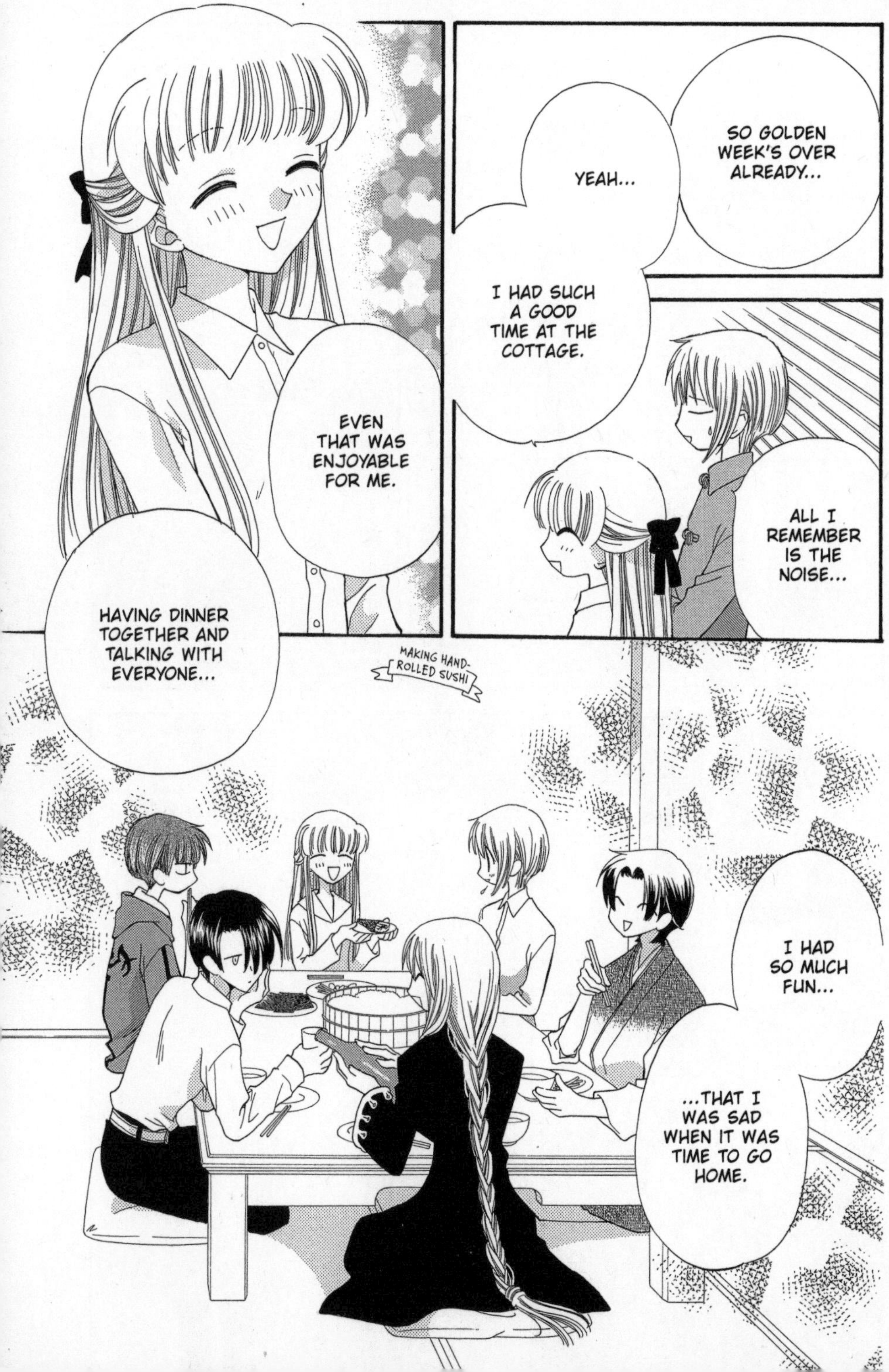
SO GOLDEN WEEK'S OVER ALREADY...
YEAH...
I HAD SUCH A GOOD TIME AT THE COTTAGE.
ALL I REMEMBER IS THE NOISE...
EVEN THAT WAS ENJOYABLE FOR ME.
HAVING DINNER TOGETHER AND TALKING WITH EVERYONE...
MAKING HAND-ROLLED SUSHI
I HAD SO MUCH FUN...
...THAT I WAS SAD WHEN IT WAS TIME TO GO HOME.

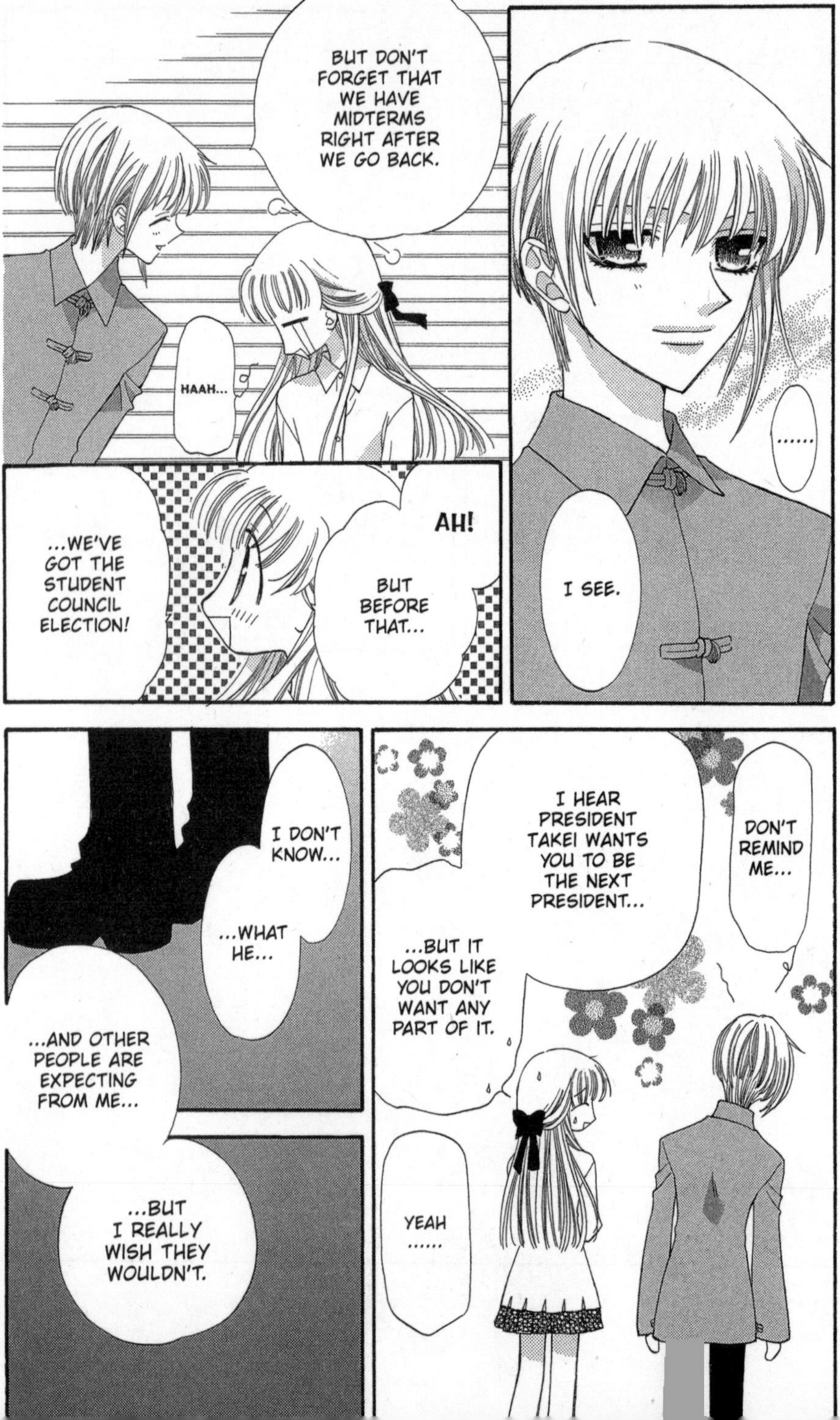
......
I SEE.
BUT DON'T FORGET THAT WE HAVE MIDTERMS RIGHT AFTER WE GO BACK.
HAAH...
AH!
BUT BEFORE THAT...
...WE'VE GOT THE STUDENT COUNCIL ELECTION!
I HEAR PRESIDENT TAKEI WANTS YOU TO BE THE NEXT PRESIDENT...
DON'T REMIND ME...
...BUT IT LOOKS LIKE YOU DON'T WANT ANY PART OF IT.
YEAH ......
I DON'T KNOW...
...WHAT HE...
...AND OTHER PEOPLE ARE EXPECTING FROM ME...
...BUT I REALLY WISH THEY WOULDN'T.

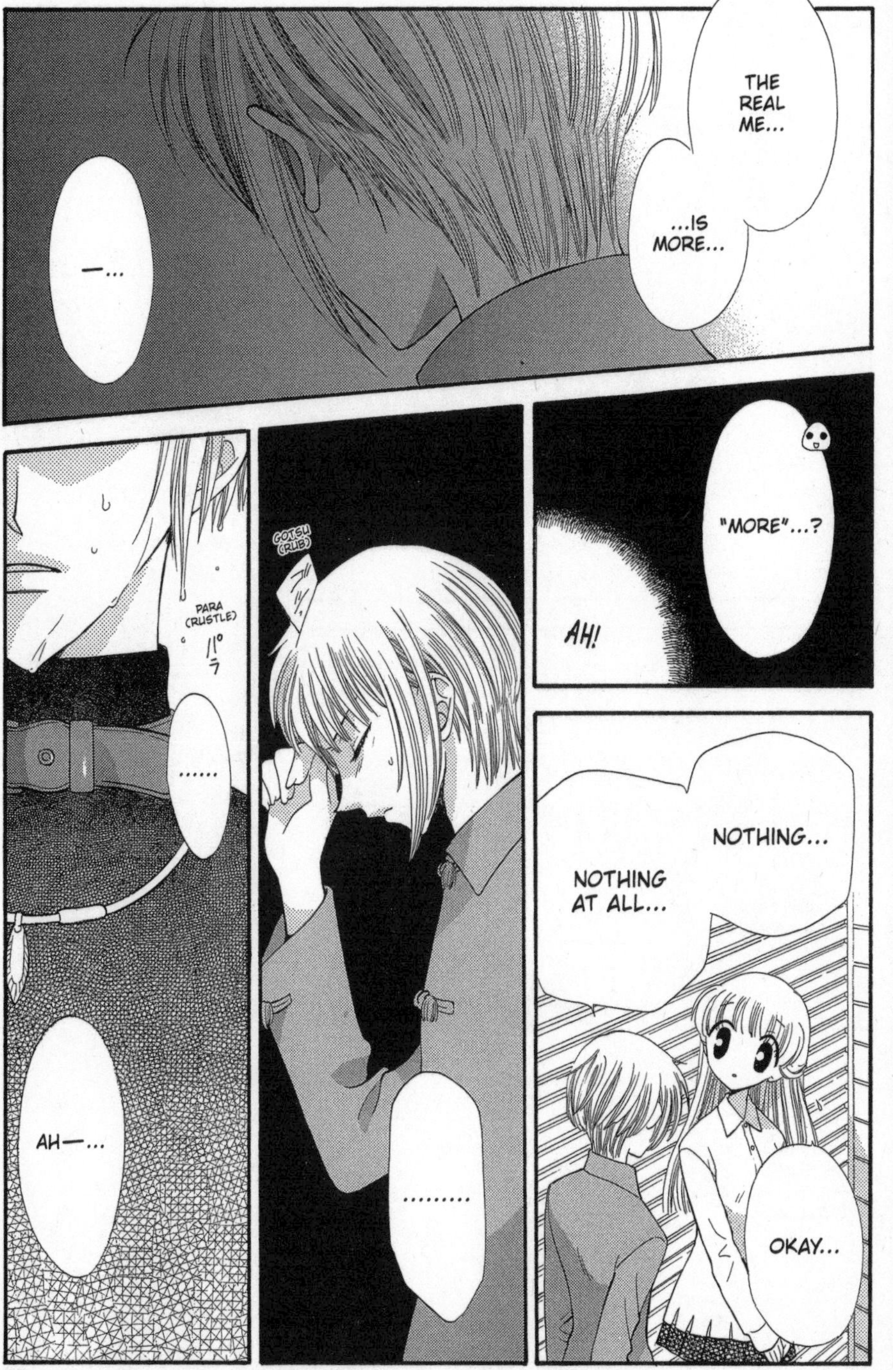
THE REAL ME...
...IS MORE...
—...
"MORE"...?
AH!
NOTHING...
NOTHING AT ALL...
OKAY...
GOTSU (RUB)
....
PARA (RUSTLE)
......
AH—...

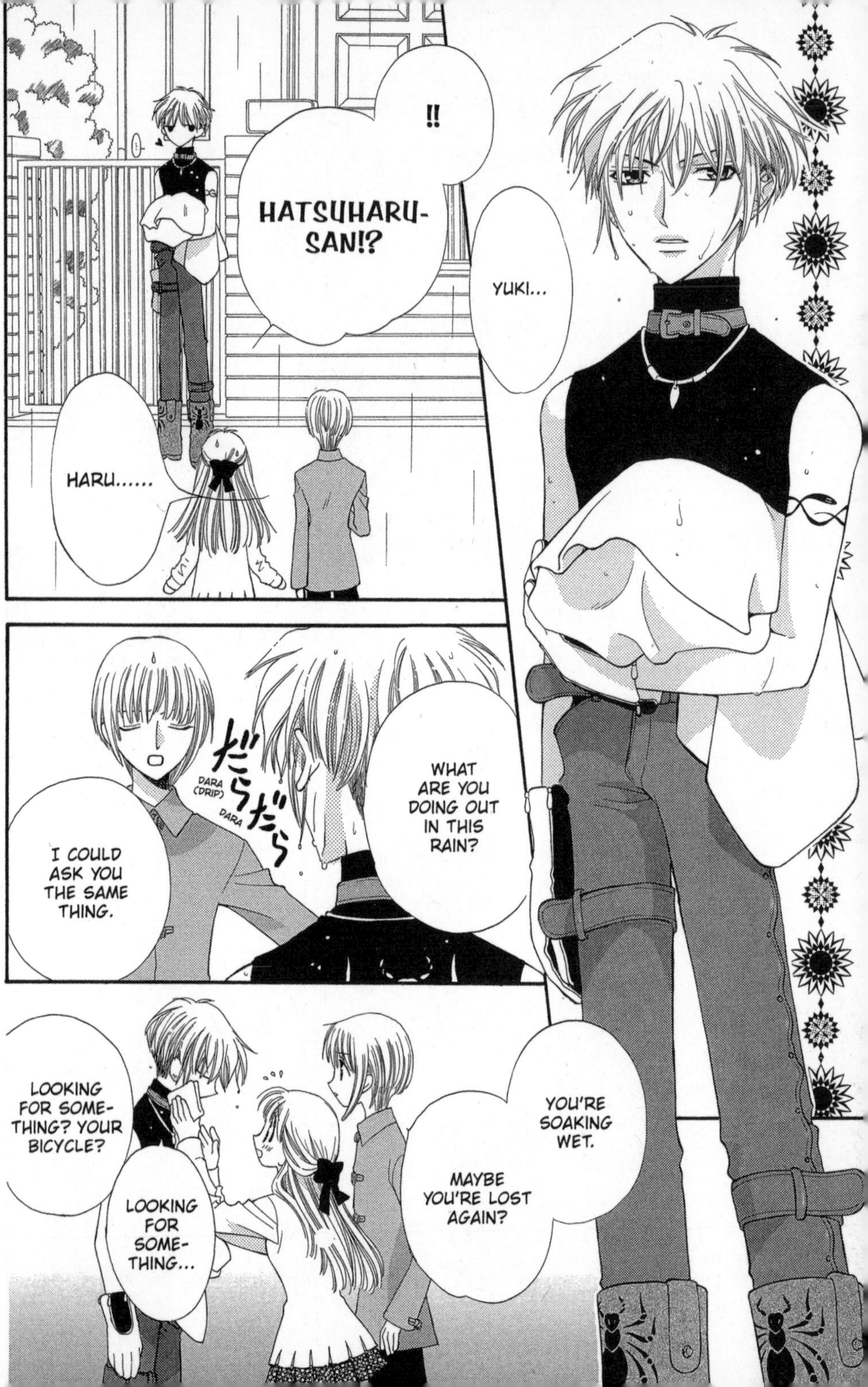
YUKI...
!!
HATSUHARU-SAN!?
HARU......
WHAT ARE YOU DOING OUT IN THIS RAIN?
だらだら
DARA (DRIP) DARA
I COULD ASK YOU THE SAME THING.
YOU'RE SOAKING WET.
MAYBE YOU'RE LOST AGAIN?
LOOKING FOR SOME-THING? YOUR BICYCLE?
LOOKING FOR SOME-THING...

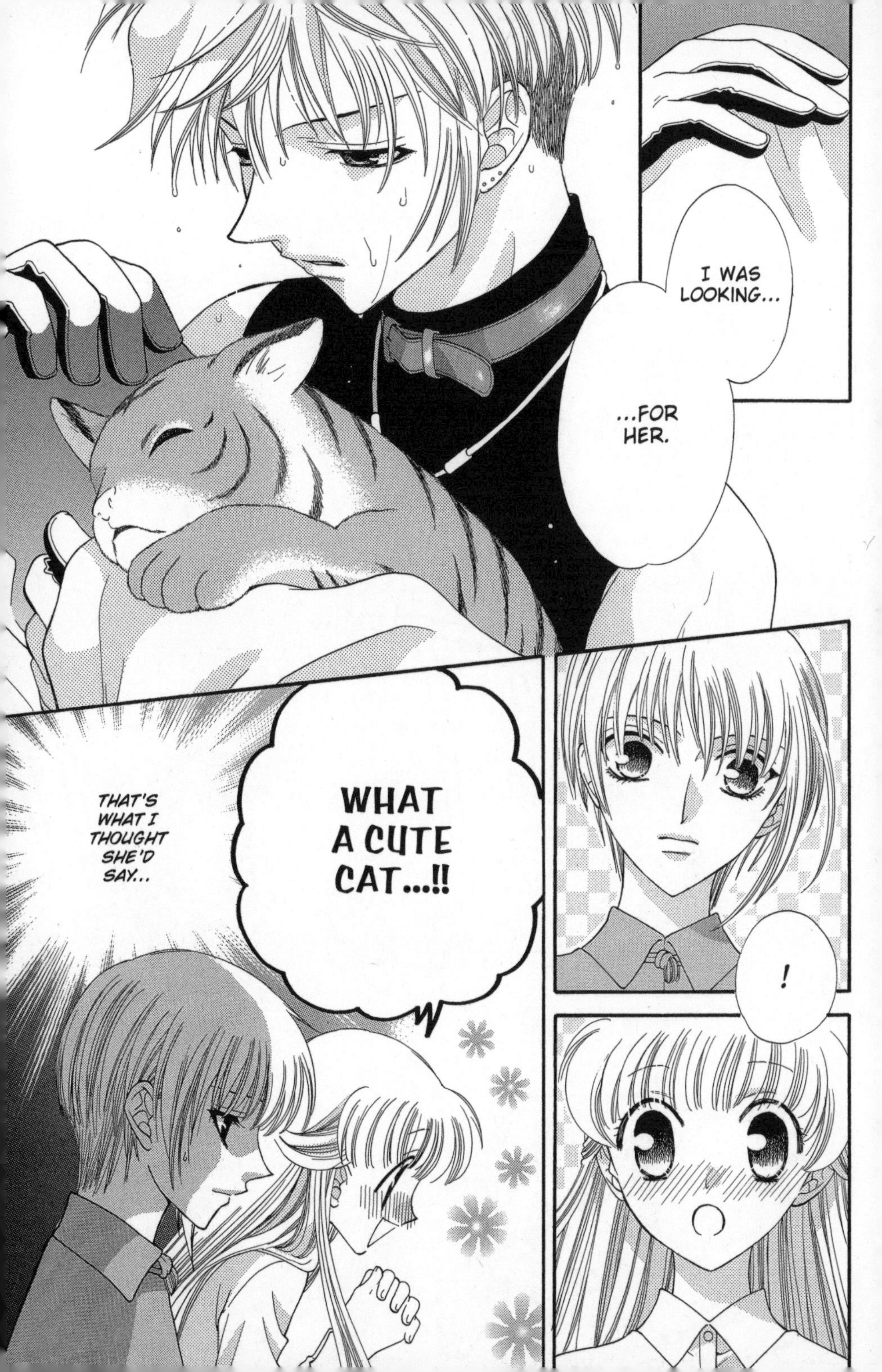
I WAS LOOKING...
...FOR HER.
!
WHAT A CUTE CAT...!!
THAT'S WHAT I THOUGHT SHE'D SAY...

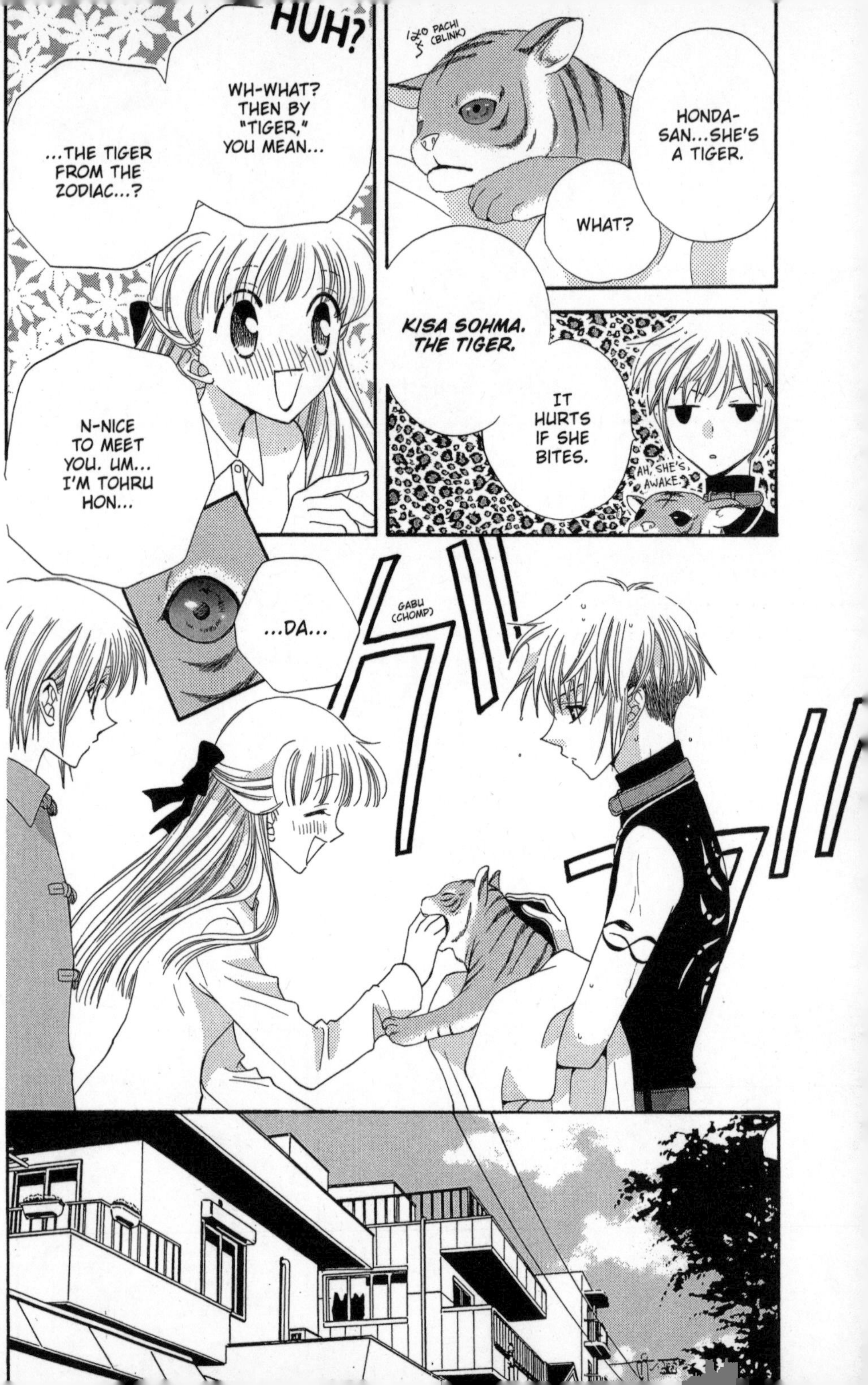
PACHI (BLINK)
HONDA-SAN...SHE'S A TIGER.
WHAT?
KISA SOHMA. THE TIGER.
IT HURTS IF SHE BITES.
AH, SHE'S AWAKE.
HUH?
WH-WHAT? THEN BY "TIGER," YOU MEAN...
...THE TIGER FROM THE ZODIAC...?
N-NICE TO MEET YOU. UM... I'M TOHRU HON...
...DA...
GABU (CHOMP)

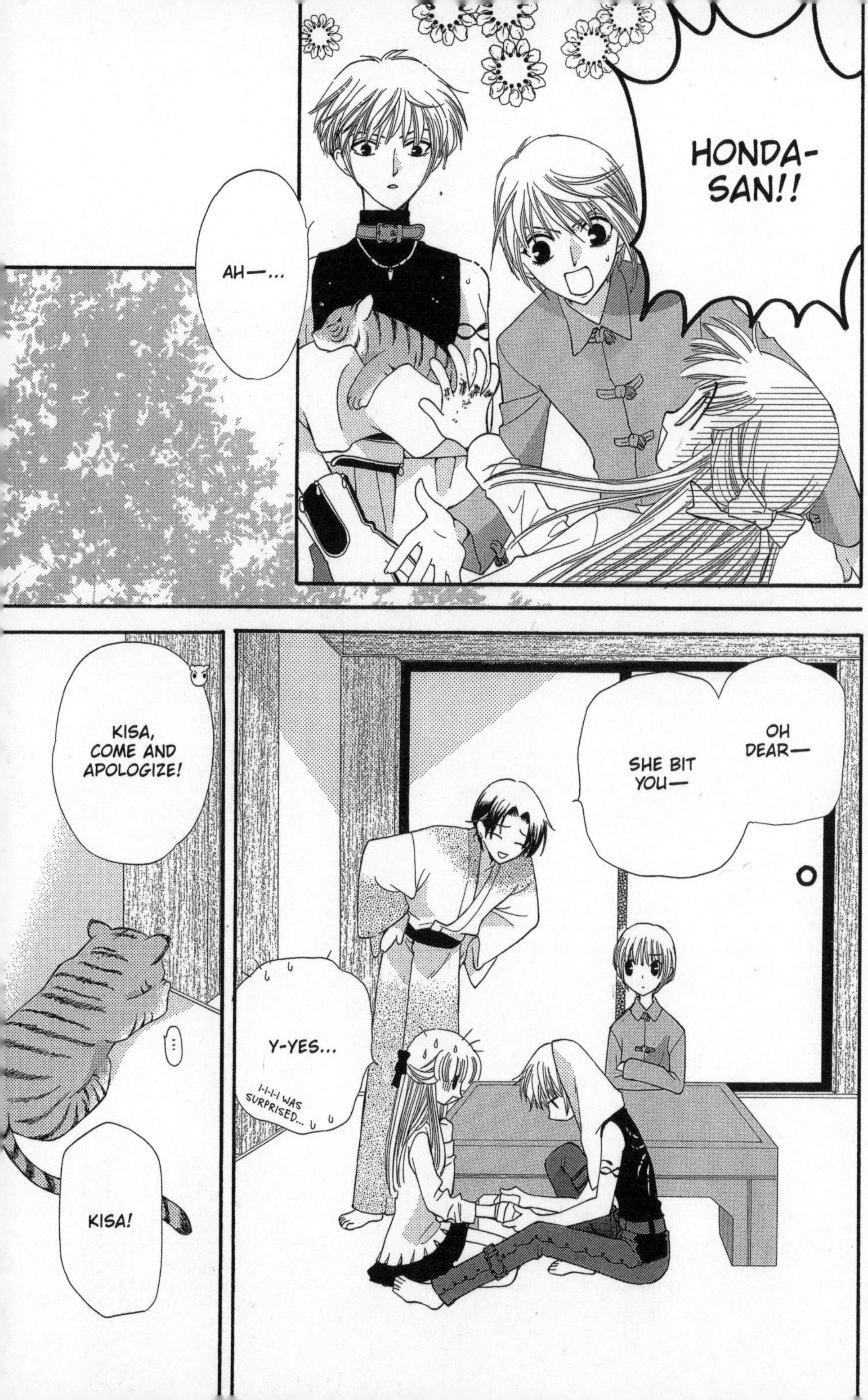
HONDA-SAN!!
AH—...
OH DEAR—
SHE BIT YOU—
Y-YES...
I-I-I-I WAS SURPRISED...
KISA, COME AND APOLOGIZE!
...
KISA!

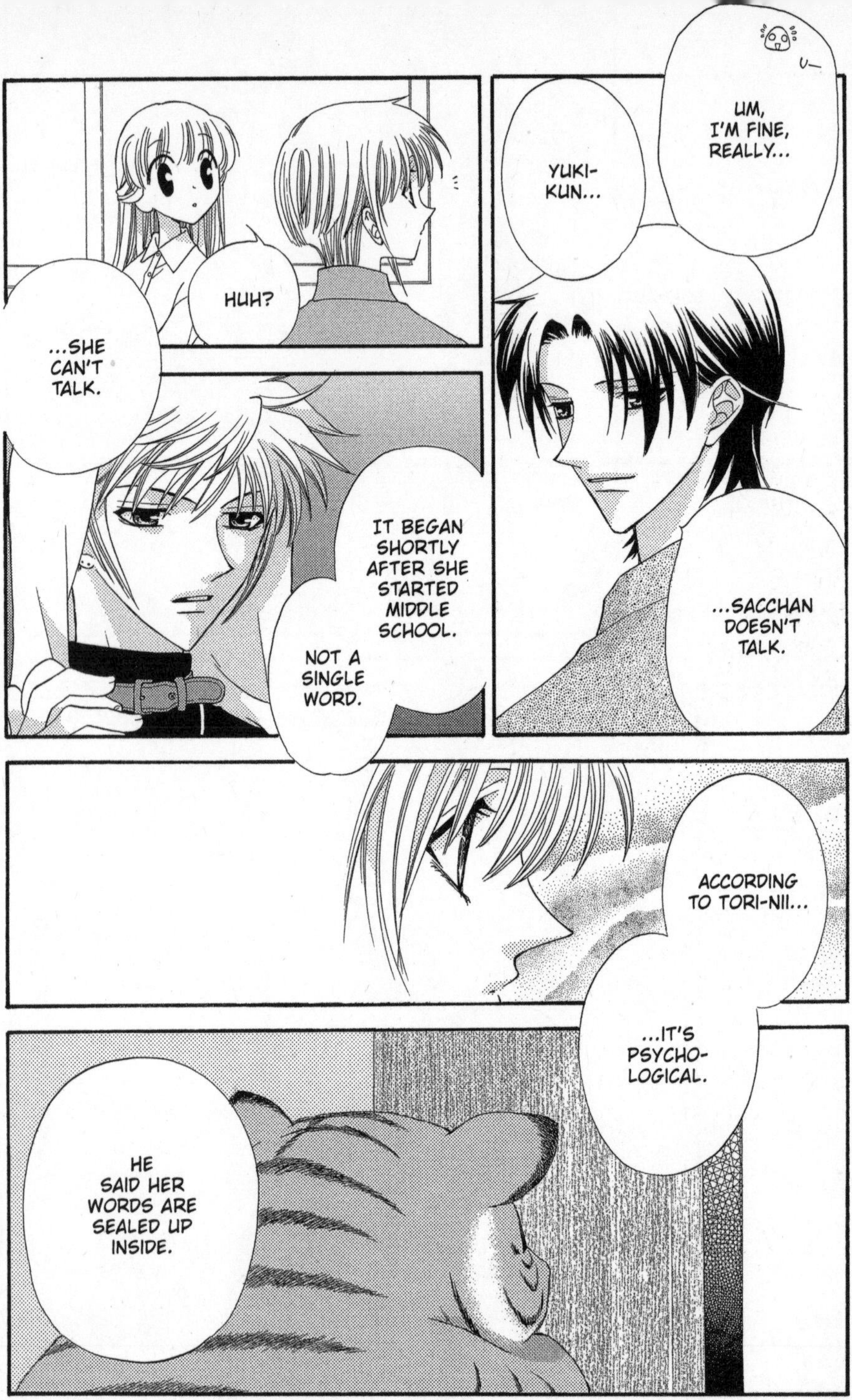
UM, I'M FINE, REALLY...
U—
YUKI-KUN...
...SACCHAN DOESN'T TALK.
HUH?
...SHE CAN'T TALK.
IT BEGAN SHORTLY AFTER SHE STARTED MIDDLE SCHOOL.
NOT A SINGLE WORD.
ACCORDING TO TORI-NII...
...IT'S PSYCHO-LOGICAL.
HE SAID HER WORDS ARE SEALED UP INSIDE.

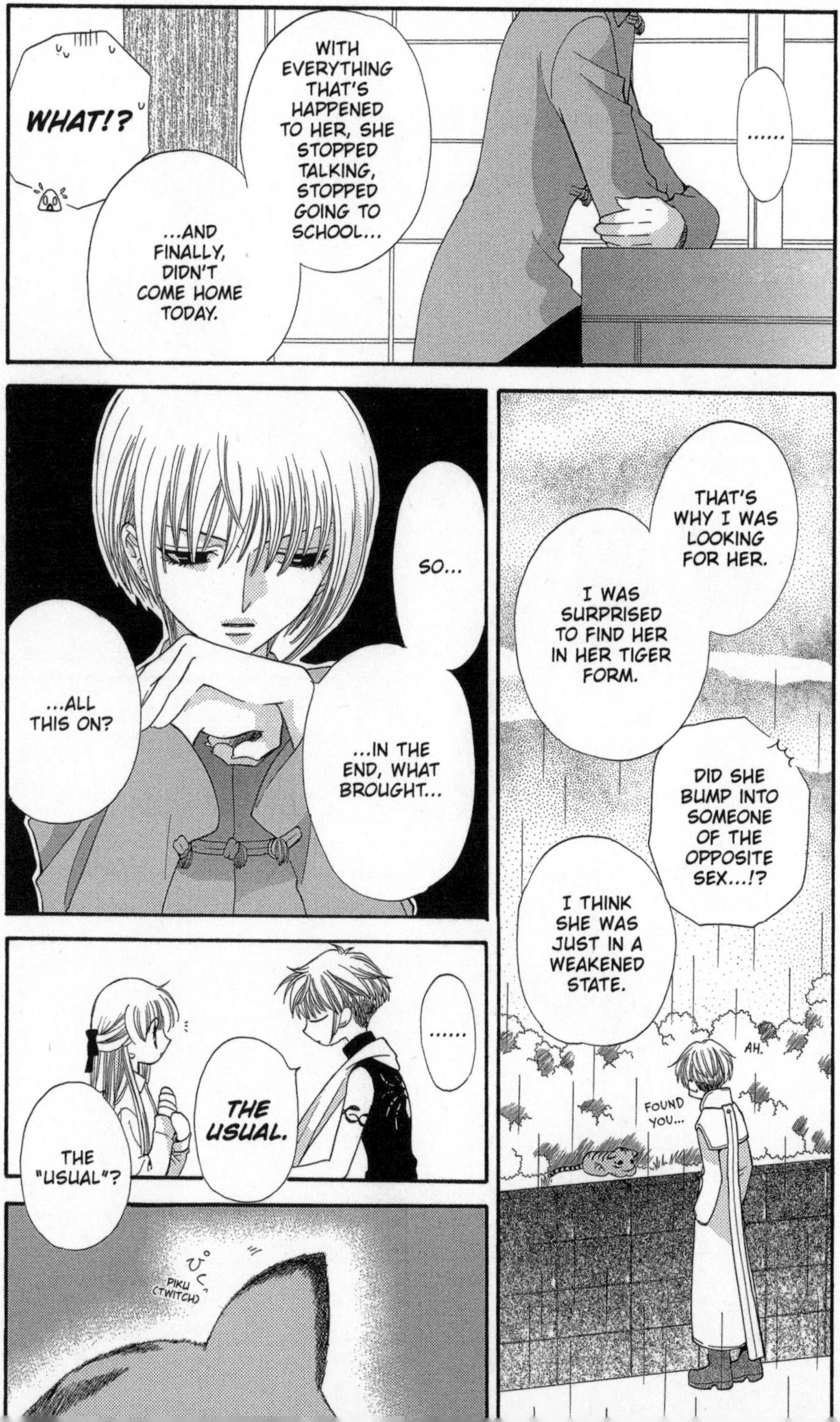
......
WITH EVERYTHING THAT'S HAPPENED TO HER, SHE STOPPED TALKING, STOPPED GOING TO SCHOOL...
...AND FINALLY, DIDN'T COME HOME TODAY.
WHAT!?
THAT'S WHY I WAS LOOKING FOR HER.
I WAS SURPRISED TO FIND HER IN HER TIGER FORM.
DID SHE BUMP INTO SOMEONE OF THE OPPOSITE SEX...!?
I THINK SHE WAS JUST IN A WEAKENED STATE.
AH.
FOUND YOU...
SO...
...IN THE END, WHAT BROUGHT...
...ALL THIS ON?
......
THE USUAL.
THE "USUAL"?
ぴく
PIKU (TWITCH)

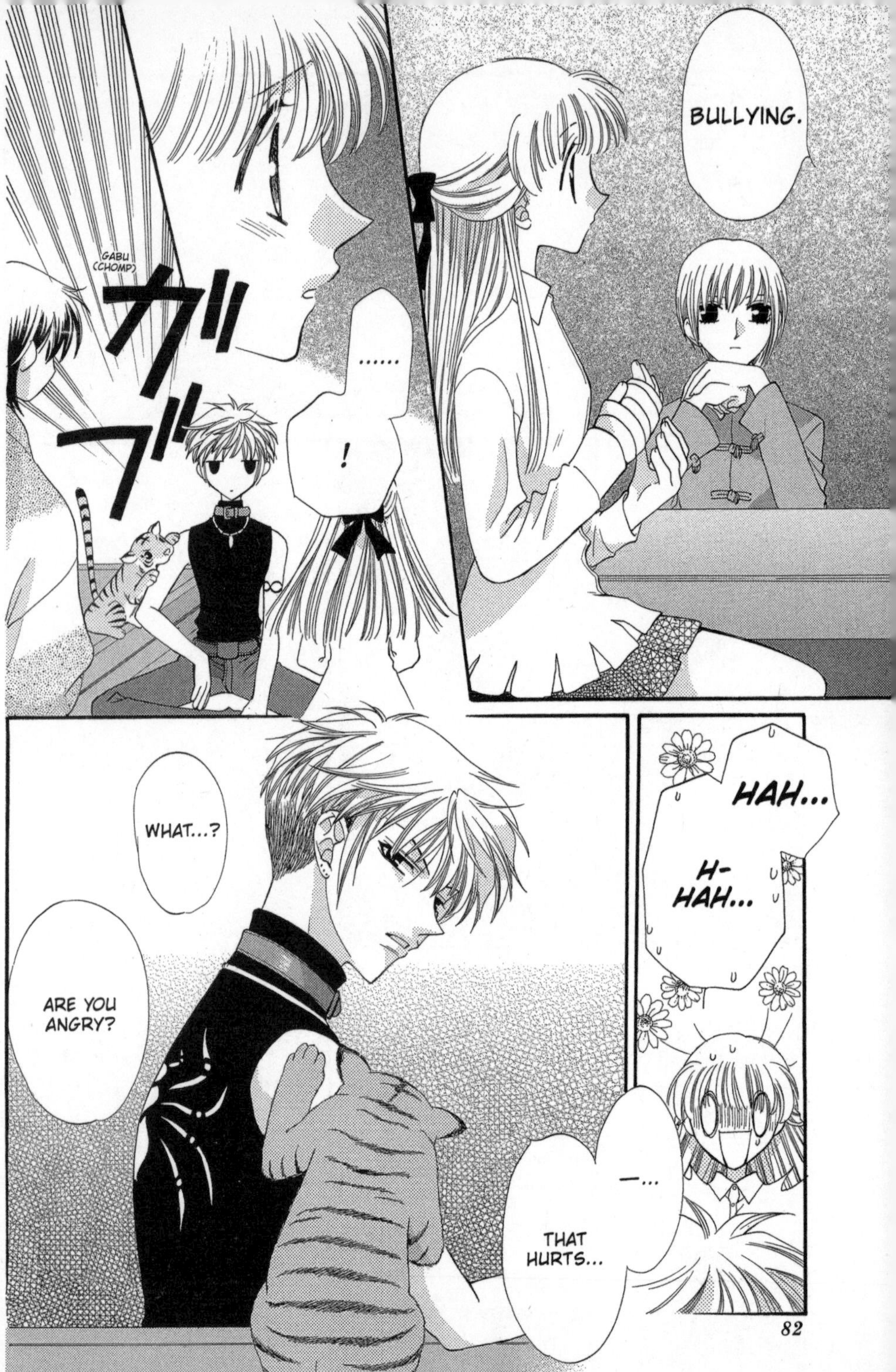
BULLYING.
......
!
GABU (CHOMP)
HAH...
H-HAH...
—...
THAT HURTS...
WHAT...?
ARE YOU ANGRY?

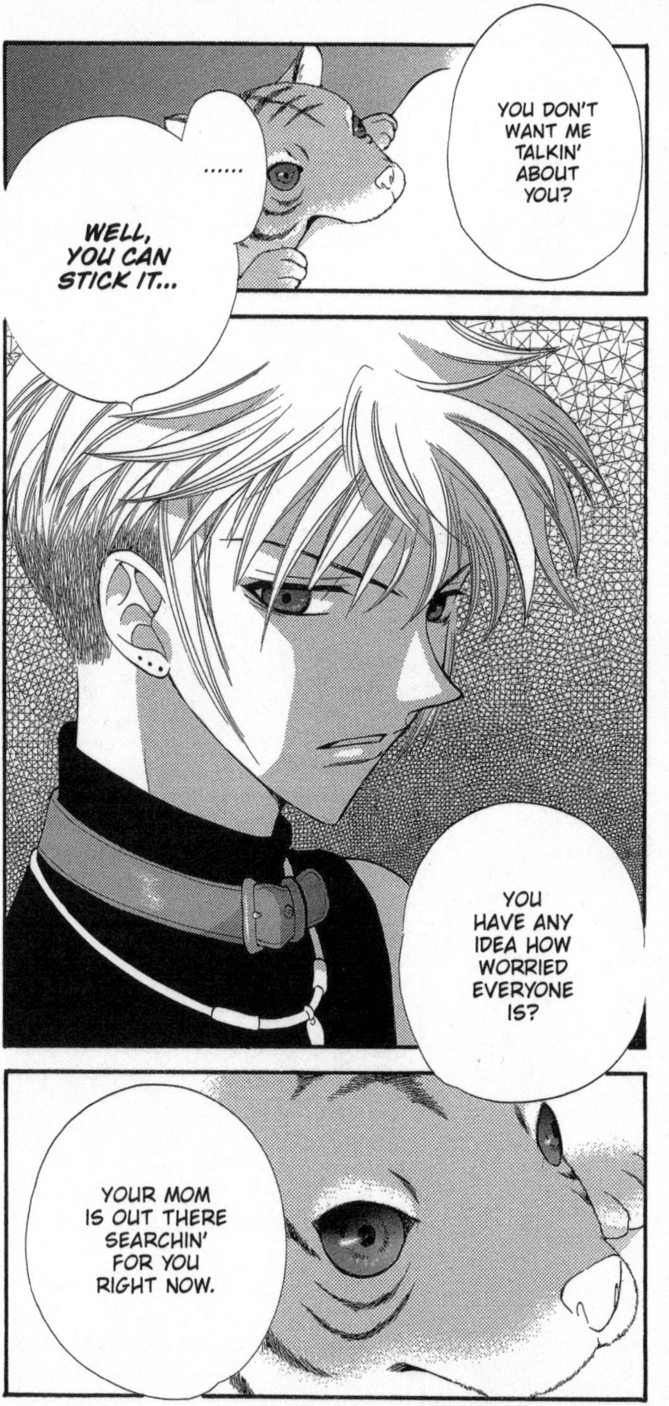
YOU DON'T WANT ME TALKIN' ABOUT YOU?
......
WELL, YOU CAN STICK IT...
YOU HAVE ANY IDEA HOW WORRIED EVERYONE IS?
YOUR MOM IS OUT THERE SEARCHIN' FOR YOU RIGHT NOW.

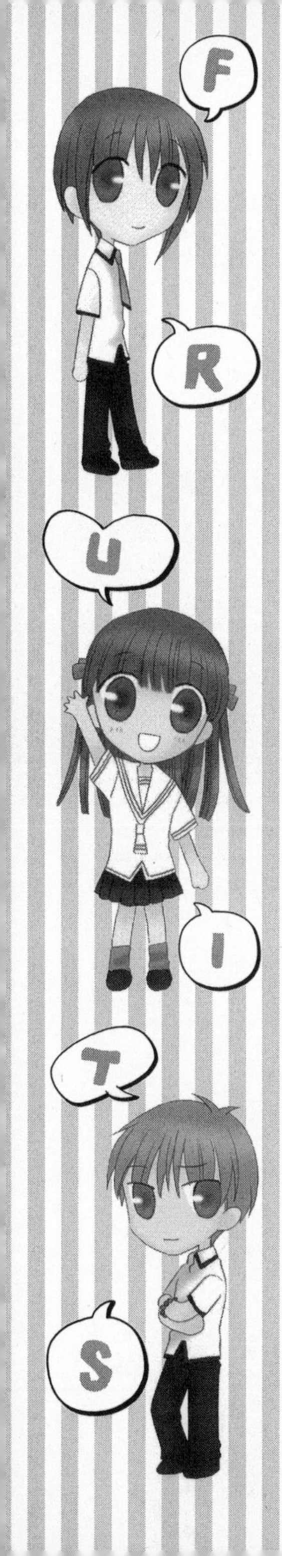
F
R
U
I
T
S

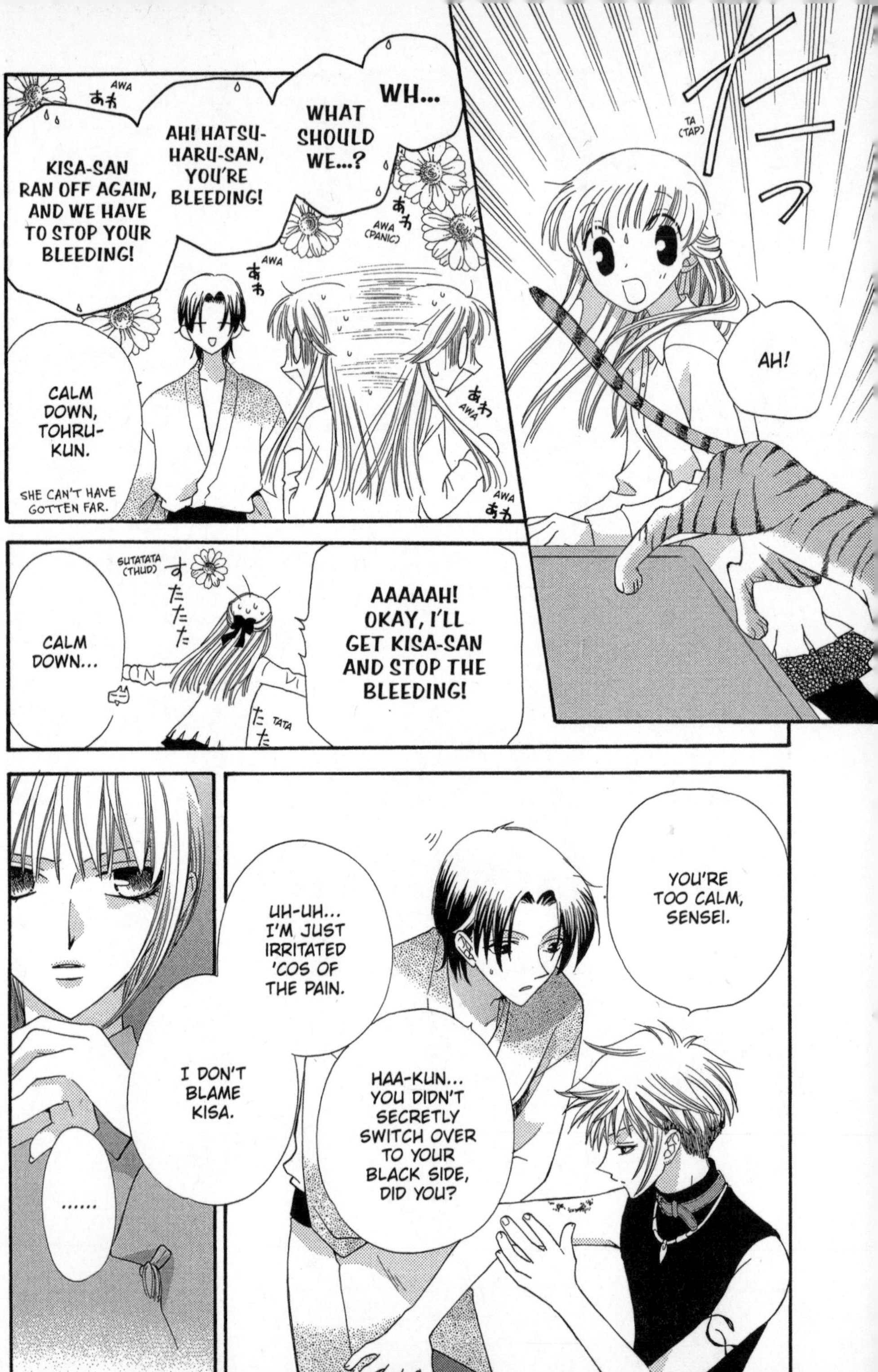

TA (TAP)
AH!
WH...
WHAT SHOULD WE...?
AH! HATSU-HARU-SAN, YOU'RE BLEEDING!
KISA-SAN RAN OFF AGAIN, AND WE HAVE TO STOP YOUR BLEEDING!
あわ AWA
あわ AWA (PANIC)
あわ AWA
あわ AWA
あわ AWA
CALM DOWN, TOHRU-KUN.
SHE CAN'T HAVE GOTTEN FAR.
AAAAAH! OKAY, I'LL GET KISA-SAN AND STOP THE BLEEDING!
すたたた SUTATATA (THUD)
たた TATA
CALM DOWN...
YOU'RE TOO CALM, SENSEI.
UH-UH... I'M JUST IRRITATED 'COS OF THE PAIN.
HAA-KUN... YOU DIDN'T SECRETLY SWITCH OVER TO YOUR BLACK SIDE, DID YOU?
I DON'T BLAME KISA.
......

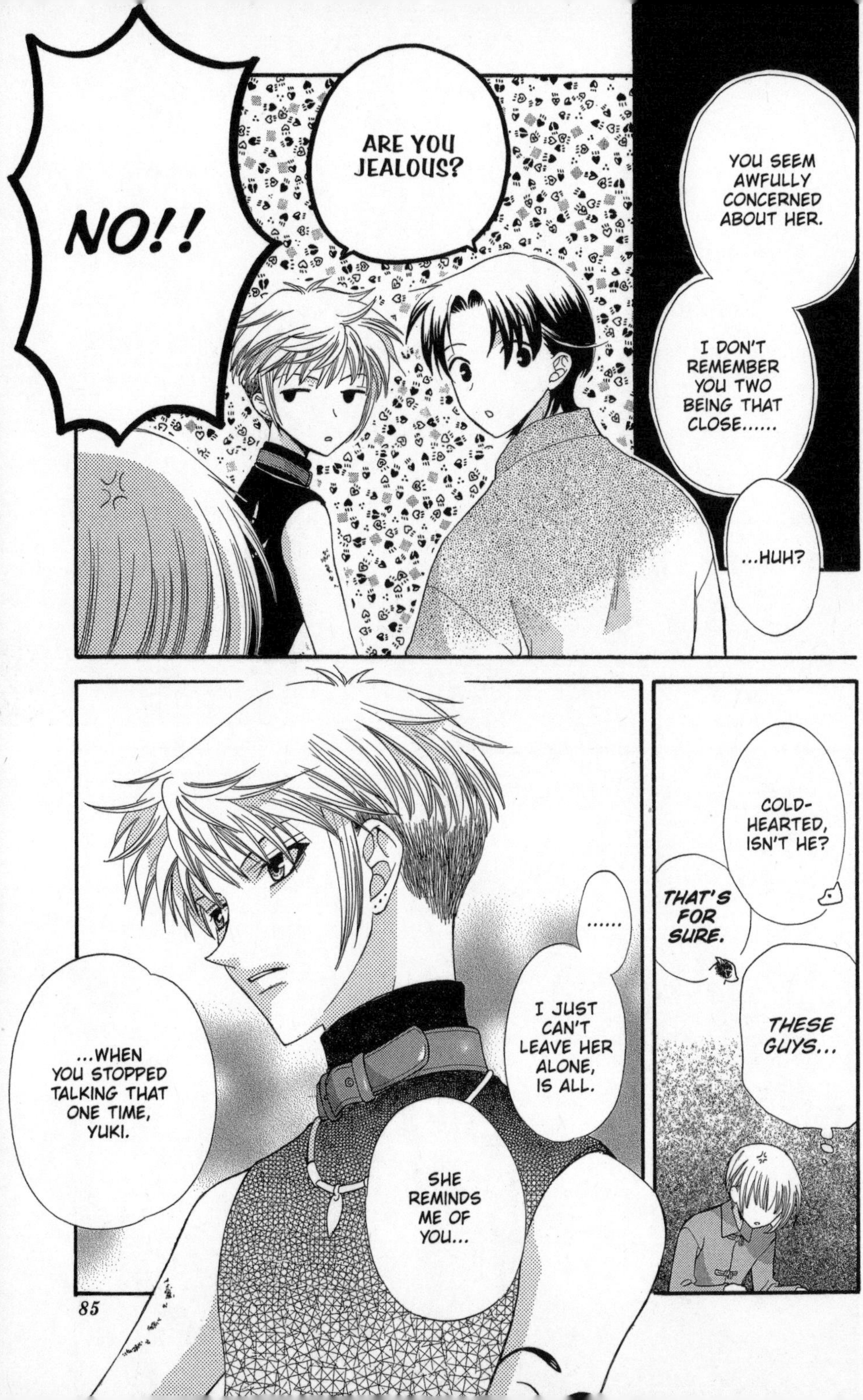
YOU SEEM AWFULLY CONCERNED ABOUT HER.
I DON'T REMEMBER YOU TWO BEING THAT CLOSE......
...HUH?
ARE YOU JEALOUS?
NO!!
COLD-HEARTED, ISN'T HE?
THAT'S FOR SURE.
THESE GUYS...
......
I JUST CAN'T LEAVE HER ALONE, IS ALL.
SHE REMINDS ME OF YOU...
...WHEN YOU STOPPED TALKING THAT ONE TIME, YUKI.

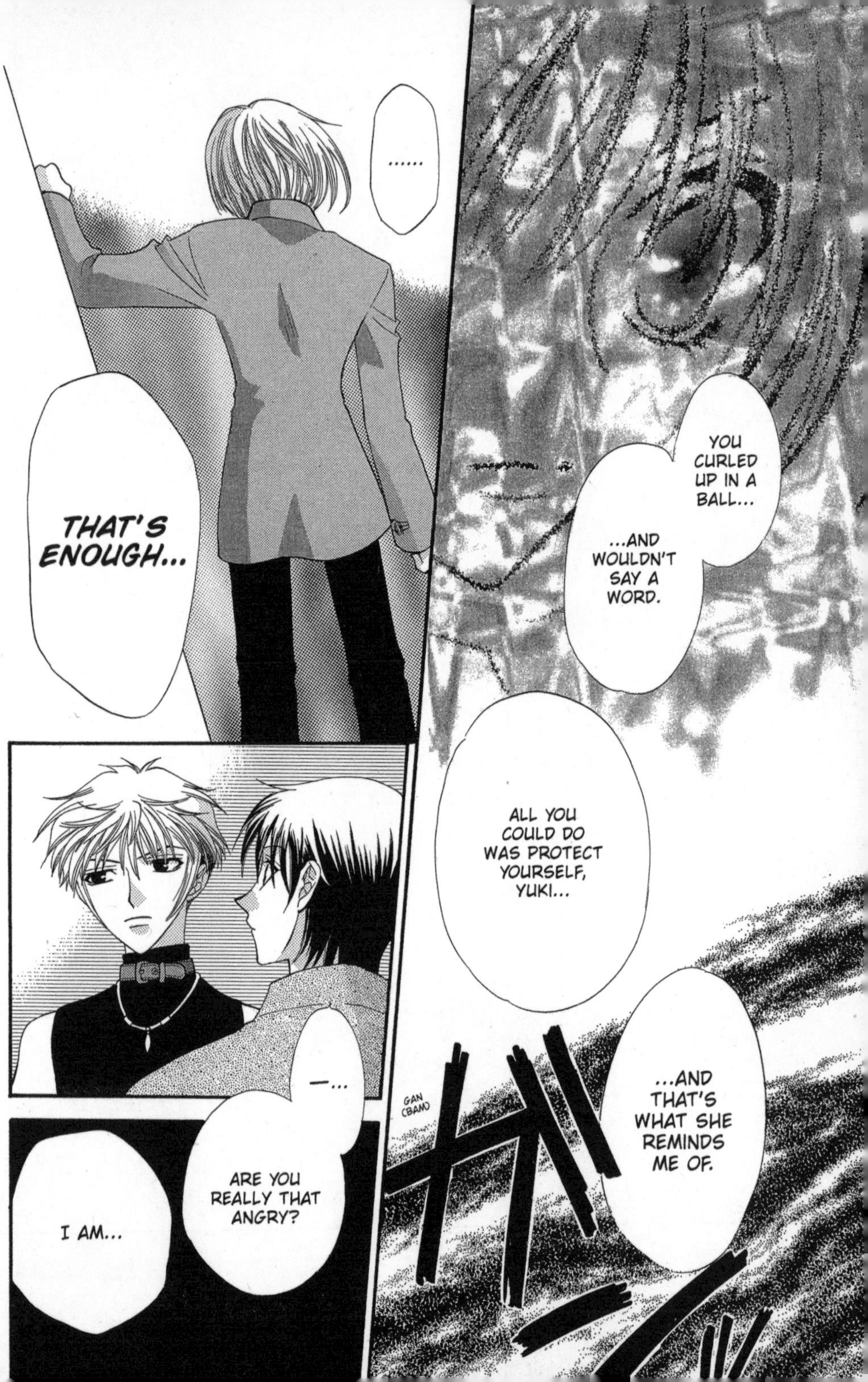
YOU CURLED UP IN A BALL...
...AND WOULDN'T SAY A WORD.
ALL YOU COULD DO WAS PROTECT YOURSELF, YUKI...
GAN (BAN)
...AND THAT'S WHAT SHE REMINDS ME OF.
......
THAT'S ENOUGH...
—...
ARE YOU REALLY THAT ANGRY?
I AM...

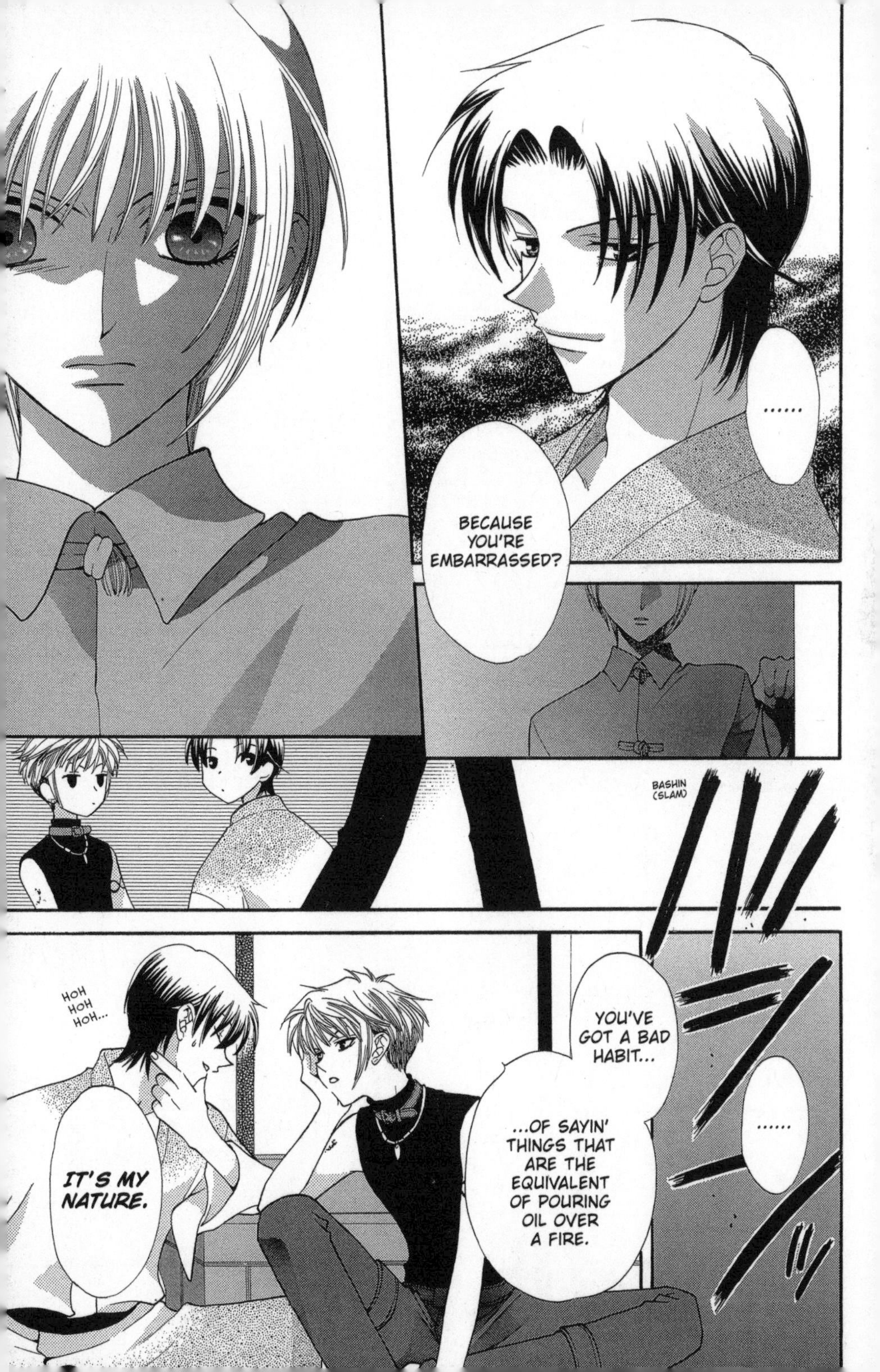

......
BECAUSE YOU'RE EMBARRASSED?
BASHIN (SLAM)
YOU'VE GOT A BAD HABIT...
......
...OF SAYIN' THINGS THAT ARE THE EQUIVALENT OF POURING OIL OVER A FIRE.
HOH HOH HOH...
IT'S MY NATURE.

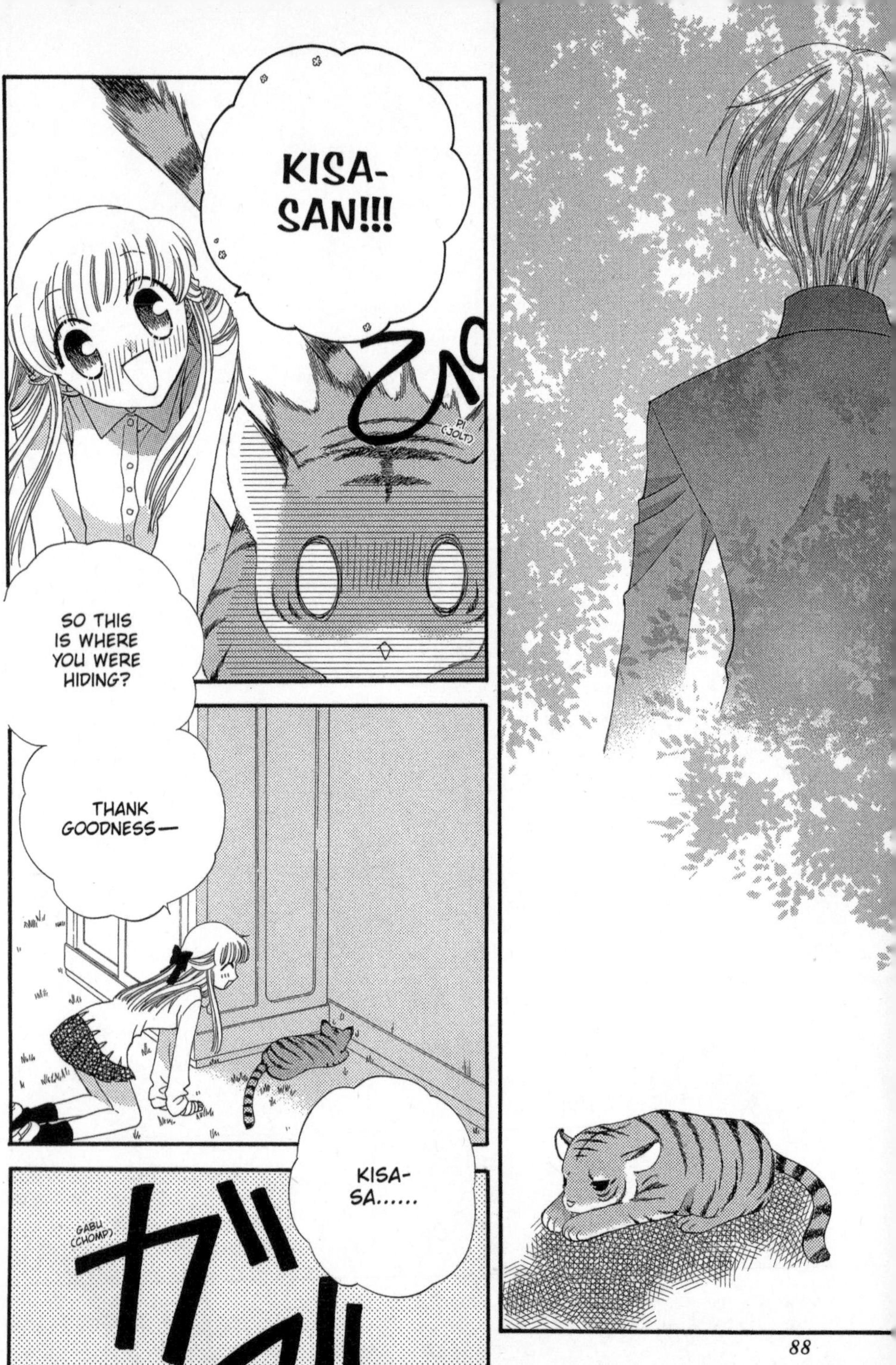
KISA-SAN!!!
PI (JOLT)
SO THIS IS WHERE YOU WERE HIDING?
THANK GOODNESS—
KISA-SA......
GABU (CHOMP)

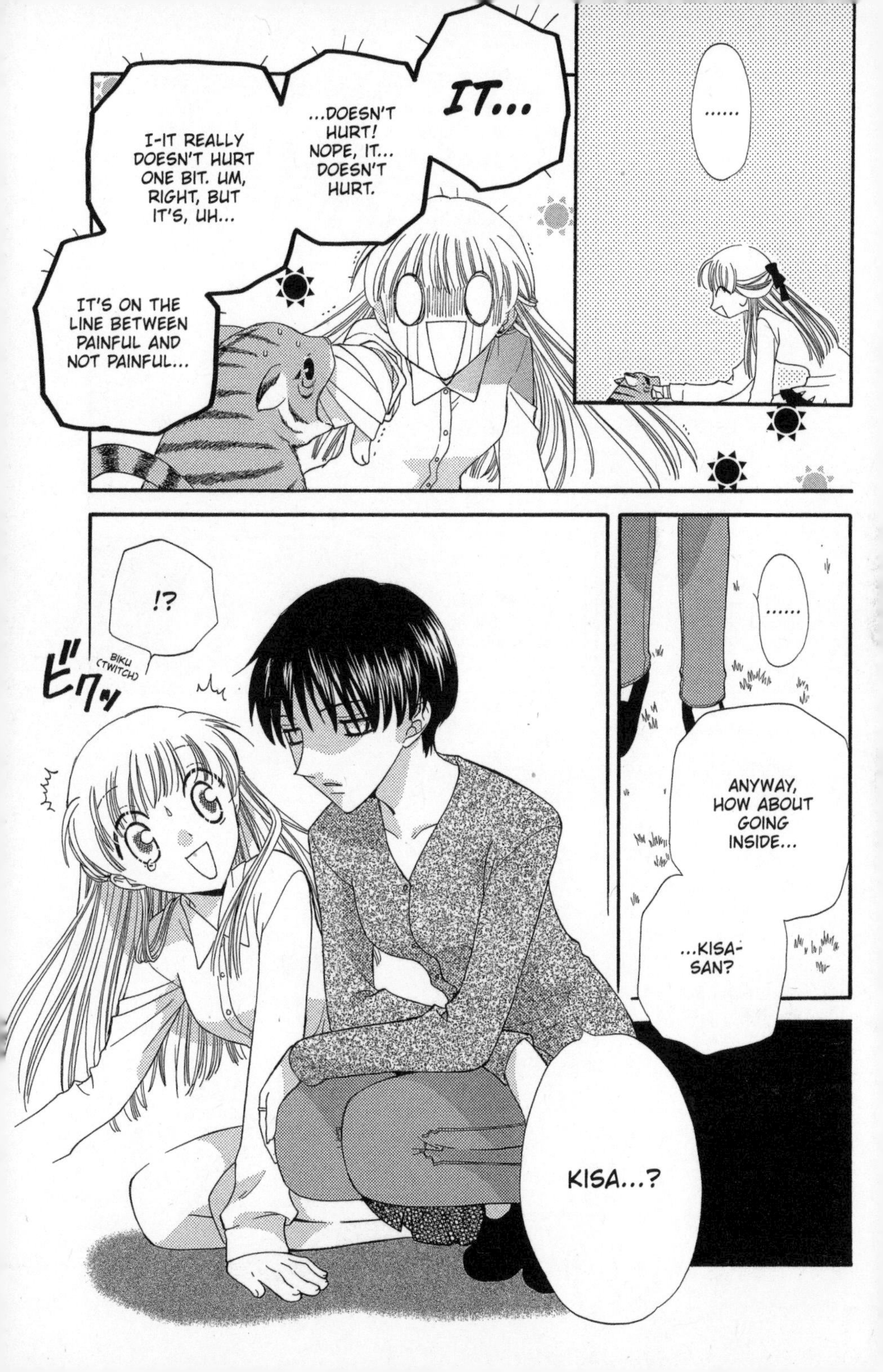
......
IT...
...DOESN'T HURT! NOPE, IT... DOESN'T HURT.
I-IT REALLY DOESN'T HURT ONE BIT. UM, RIGHT, BUT IT'S, UH...
IT'S ON THE LINE BETWEEN PAINFUL AND NOT PAINFUL...
......
ANYWAY, HOW ABOUT GOING INSIDE...
...KISA-SAN?
KISA...?
!?
ビクッ
BIKU (TWITCH)

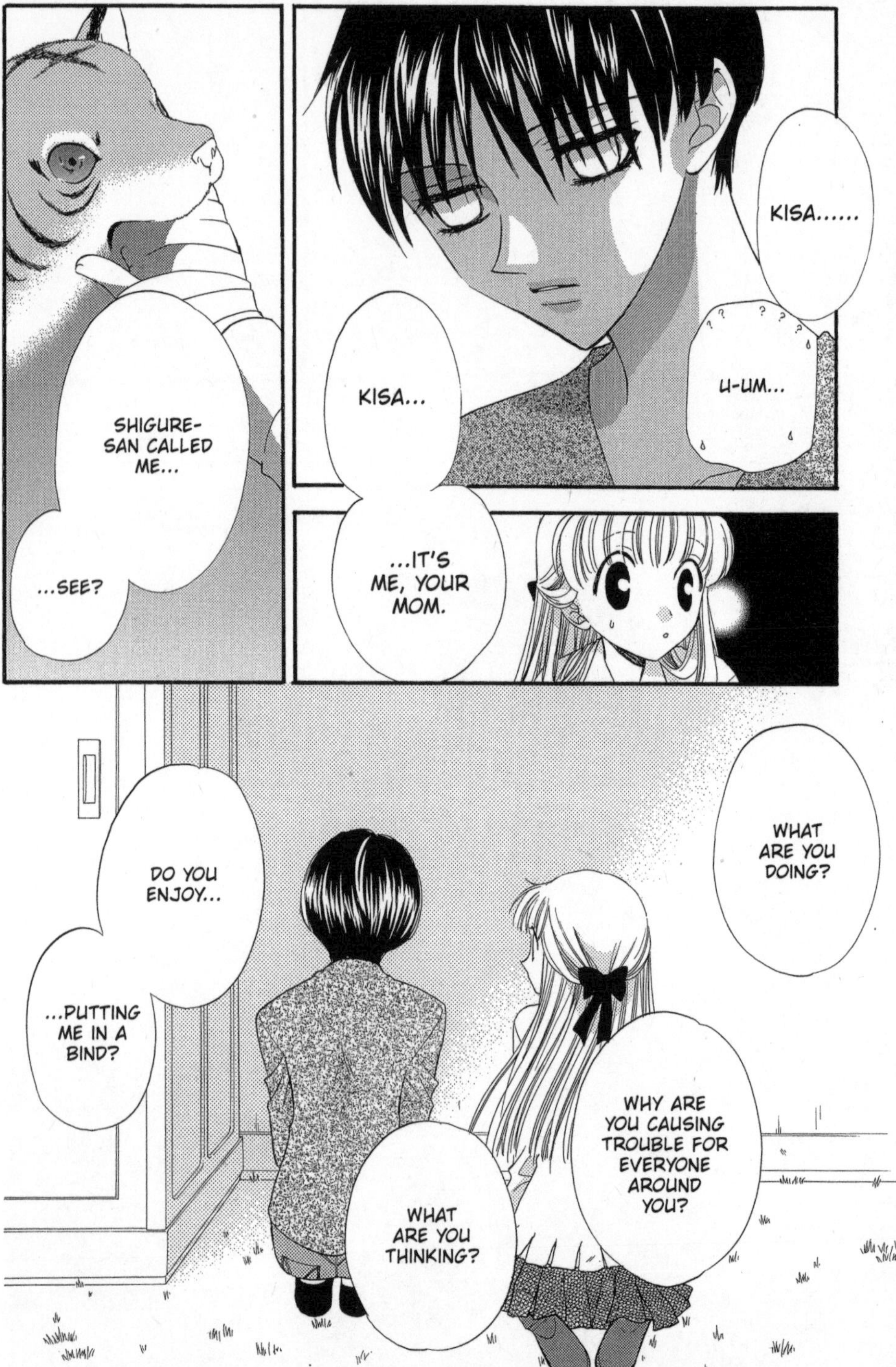
KISA......
U-UM...
KISA...
...IT'S ME, YOUR MOM.
SHIGURE-SAN CALLED ME...
...SEE?
WHAT ARE YOU DOING?
WHY ARE YOU CAUSING TROUBLE FOR EVERYONE AROUND YOU?
WHAT ARE YOU THINKING?
DO YOU ENJOY...
...PUTTING ME IN A BIND?

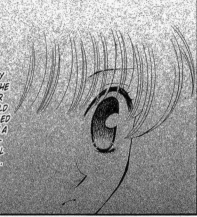

IN MANY CASES, THE MOTHER OF A CHILD POSSESSED BY SUCH A SUPERNATURAL BEING...

...EITHER BECOMES EXTREMELY OVERPROTECTIVE...

...OR REJECTS THEIR OFFSPRING.

TELL ME...

WHY DIDN'T YOU SAY ANYTHING ABOUT BEING BULLIED?

WHY DID YOU RUN AWAY FROM HOME?

......

YOU'VE...

WHY WON'T YOU TALK?

...WORN ME OUT.

I CAN'T...

...TAKE IT ANYMORE ......

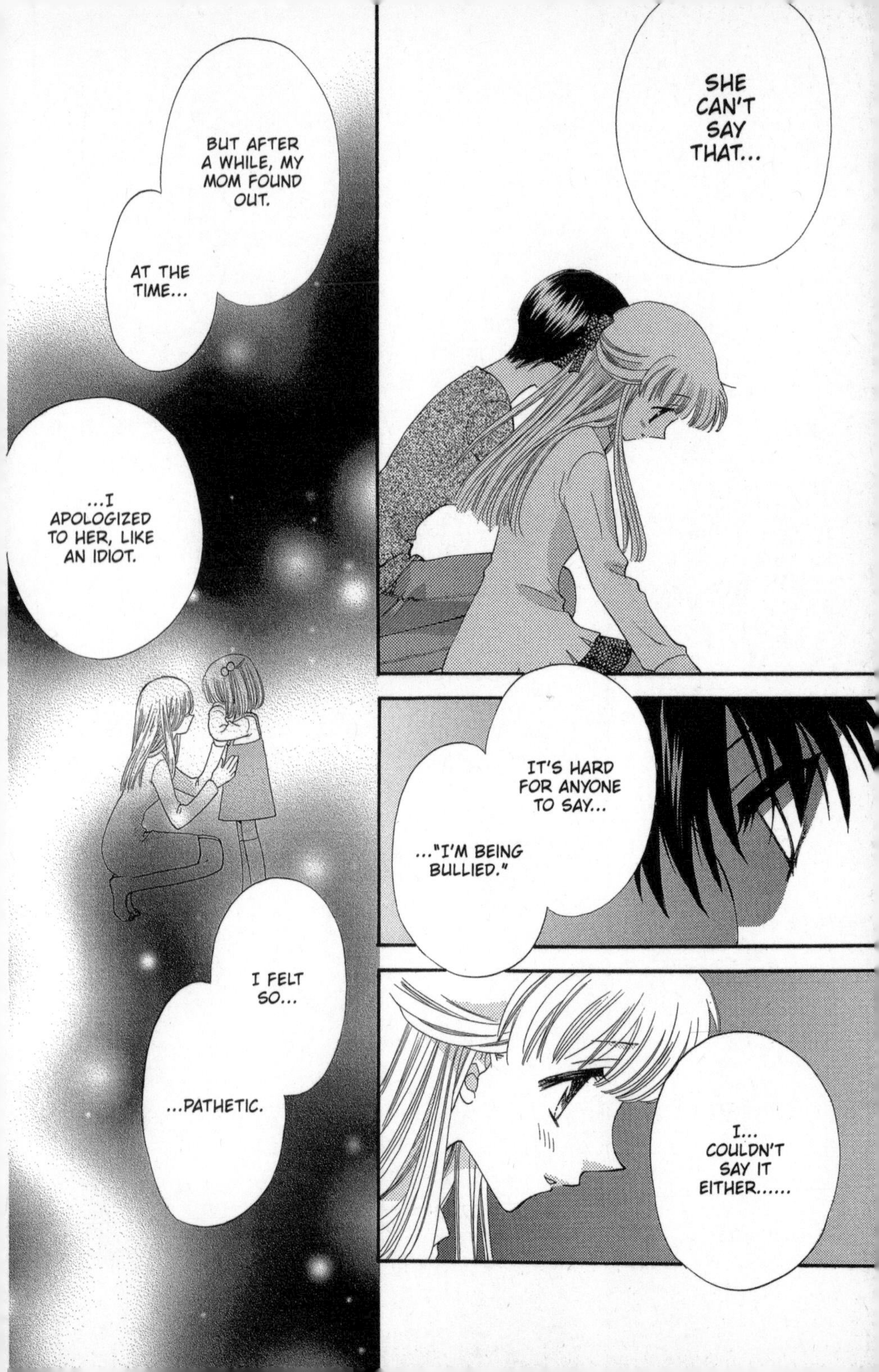
SHE CAN'T SAY THAT...
IT'S HARD FOR ANYONE TO SAY...
..."I'M BEING BULLIED."
I... COULDN'T SAY IT EITHER......
BUT AFTER A WHILE, MY MOM FOUND OUT.
AT THE TIME...
...I APOLOGIZED TO HER, LIKE AN IDIOT.
I FELT SO...
...PATHETIC.

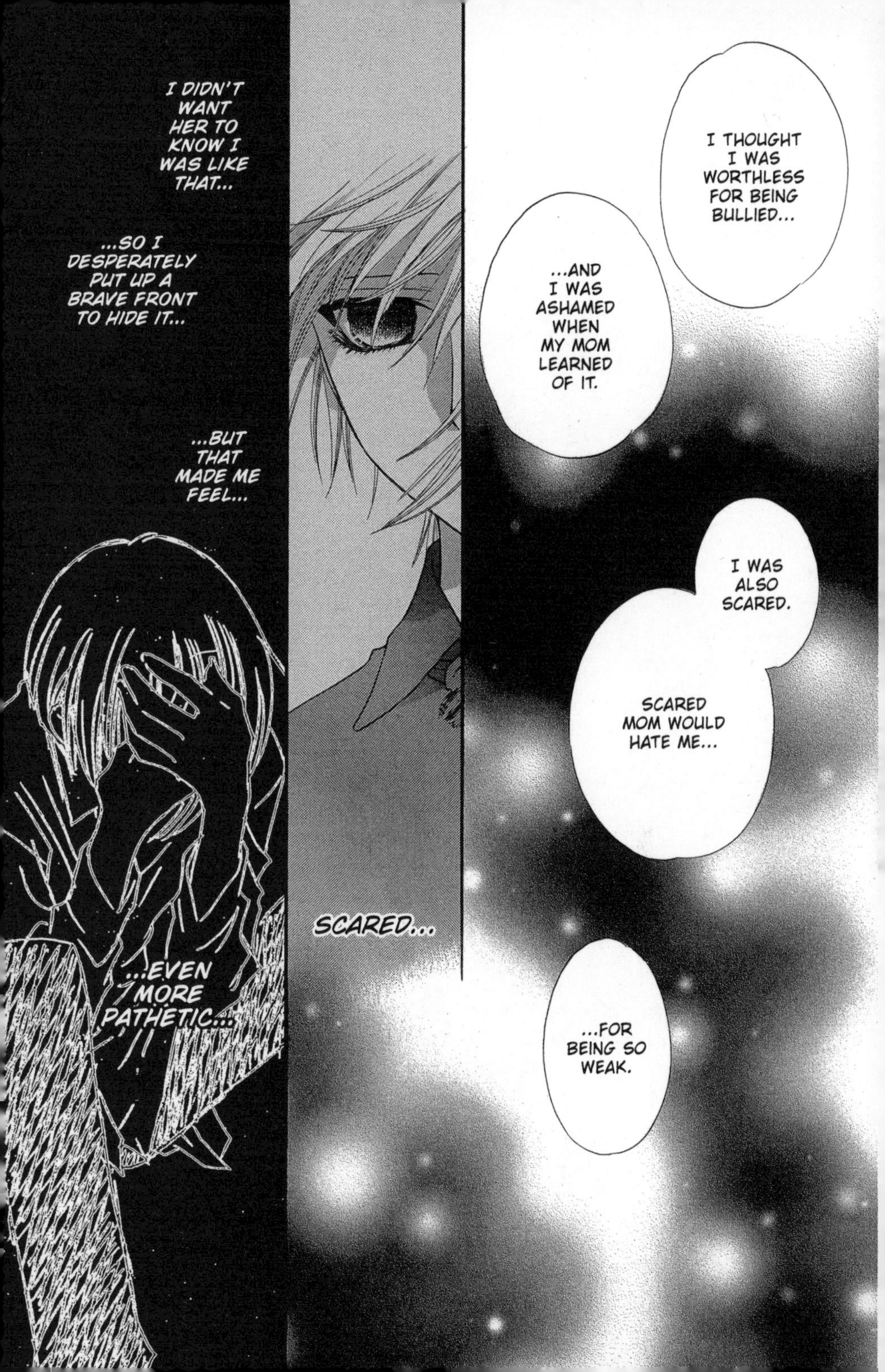
I THOUGHT I WAS WORTHLESS FOR BEING BULLIED...
...AND I WAS ASHAMED WHEN MY MOM LEARNED OF IT.
I WAS ALSO SCARED.
SCARED MOM WOULD HATE ME...
...FOR BEING SO WEAK.
SCARED...
I DIDN'T WANT HER TO KNOW I WAS LIKE THAT...
...SO I DESPERATELY PUT UP A BRAVE FRONT TO HIDE IT...
...BUT THAT MADE ME FEEL...
...EVEN MORE PATHETIC...

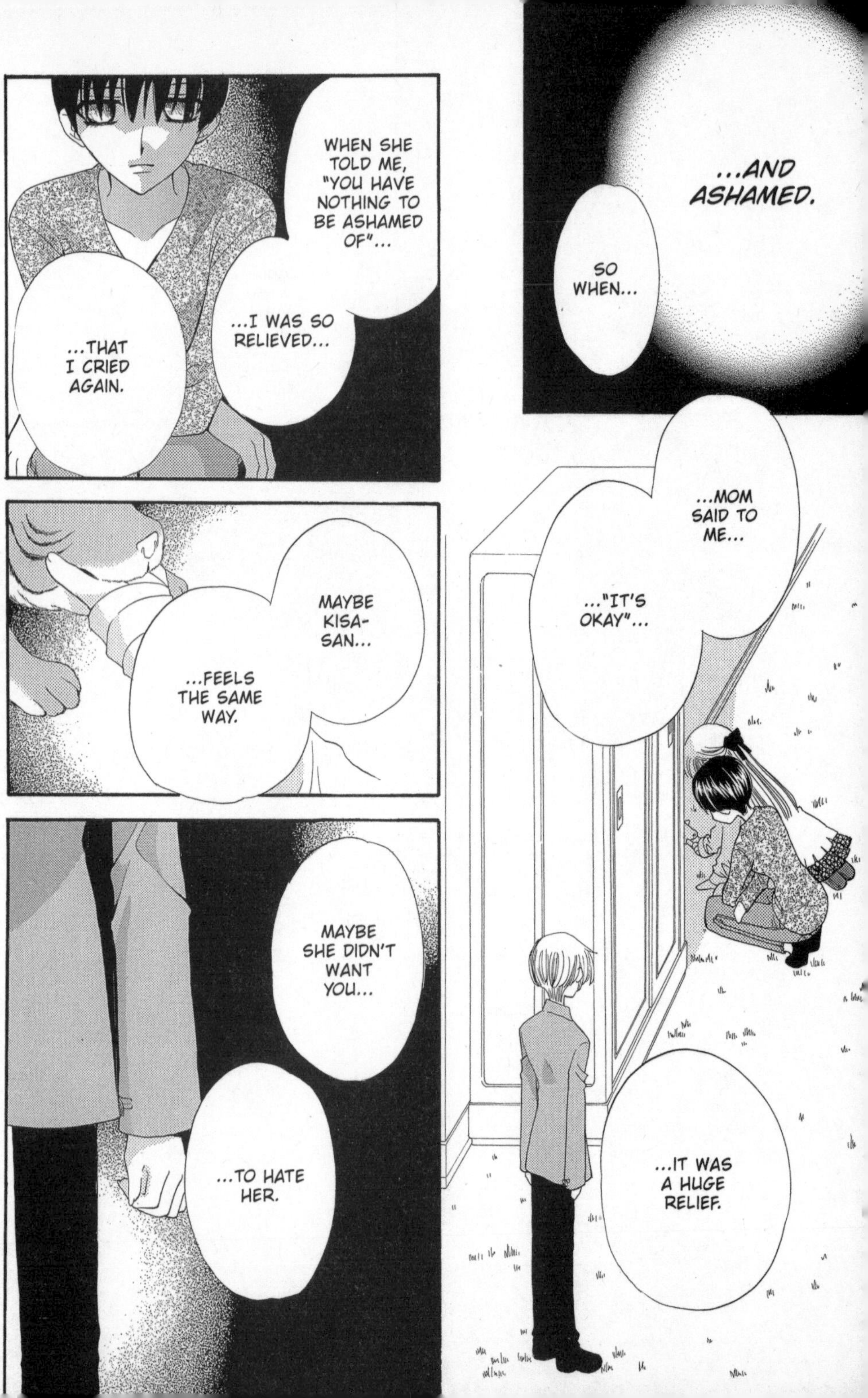
...AND ASHAMED.
SO WHEN...
...MOM SAID TO ME...
..."IT'S OKAY"...
...IT WAS A HUGE RELIEF.
WHEN SHE TOLD ME, "YOU HAVE NOTHING TO BE ASHAMED OF"...
...I WAS SO RELIEVED...
...THAT I CRIED AGAIN.
MAYBE KISA-SAN...
...FEELS THE SAME WAY.
MAYBE SHE DIDN'T WANT YOU...
...TO HATE HER.

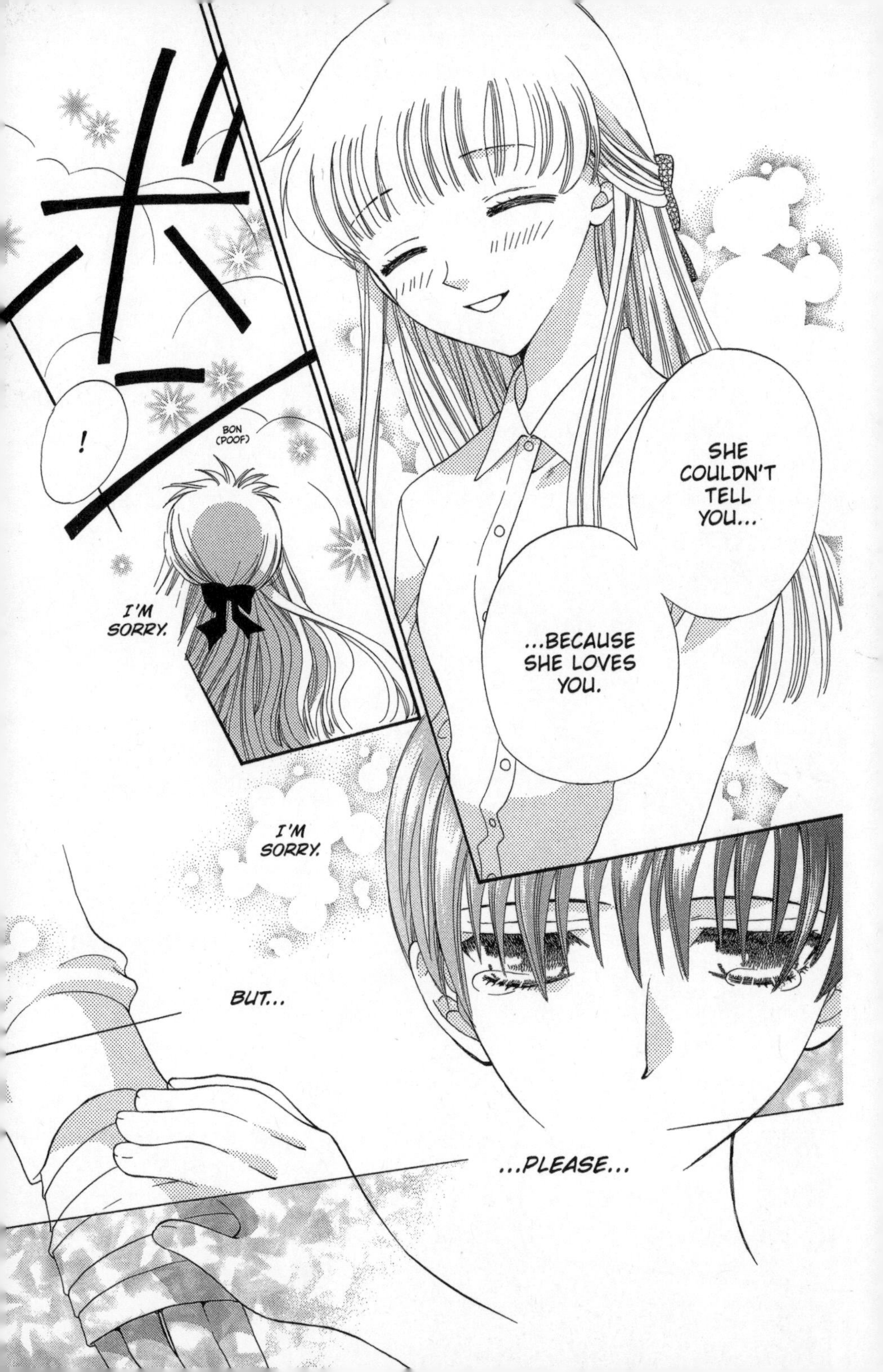
SHE COULDN'T TELL YOU...
...BECAUSE SHE LOVES YOU.
BON (POOF)
!
I'M SORRY.
I'M SORRY.
BUT...
...PLEASE...

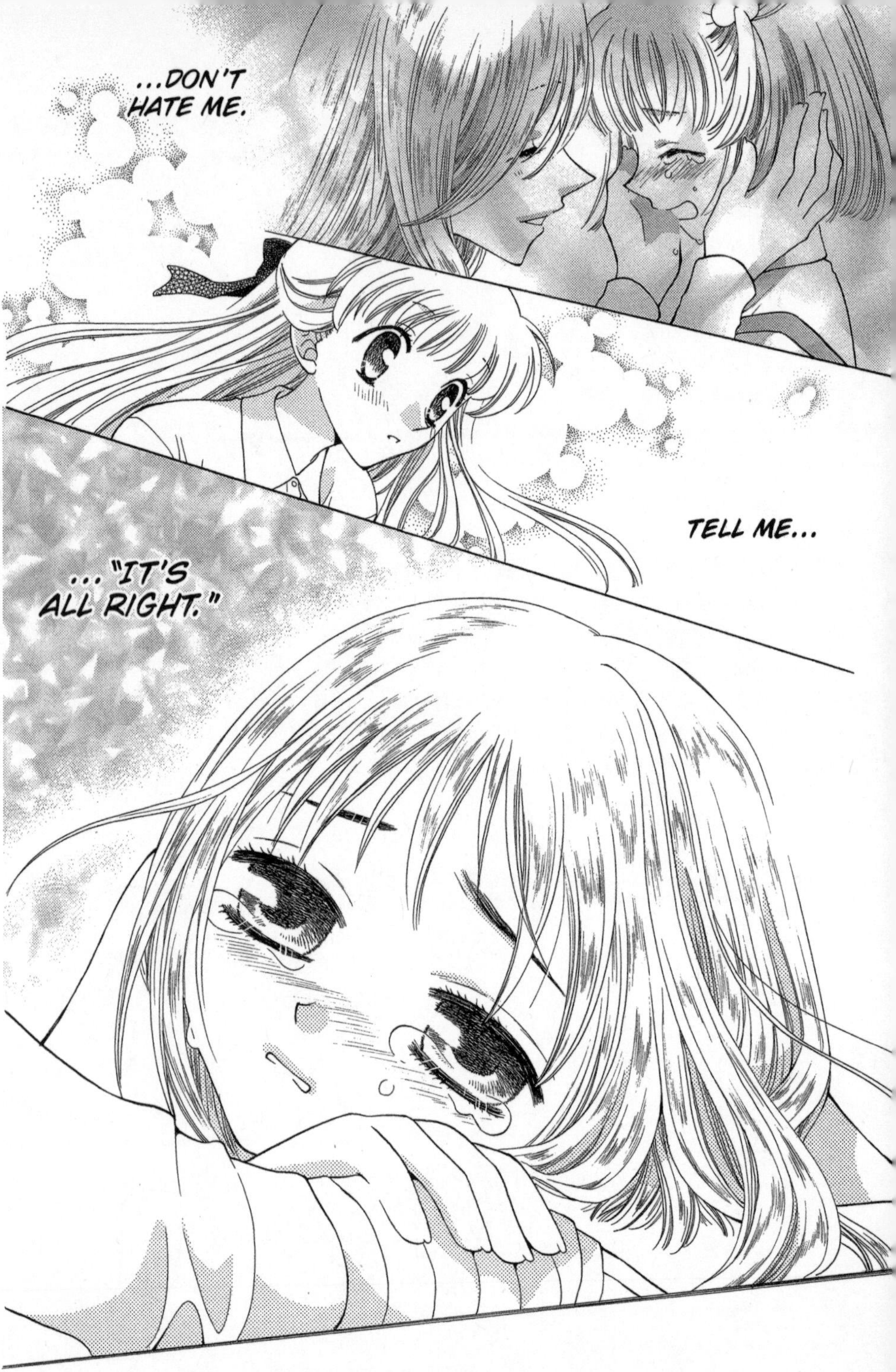
...DON'T HATE ME.
TELL ME...
..."IT'S ALL RIGHT."

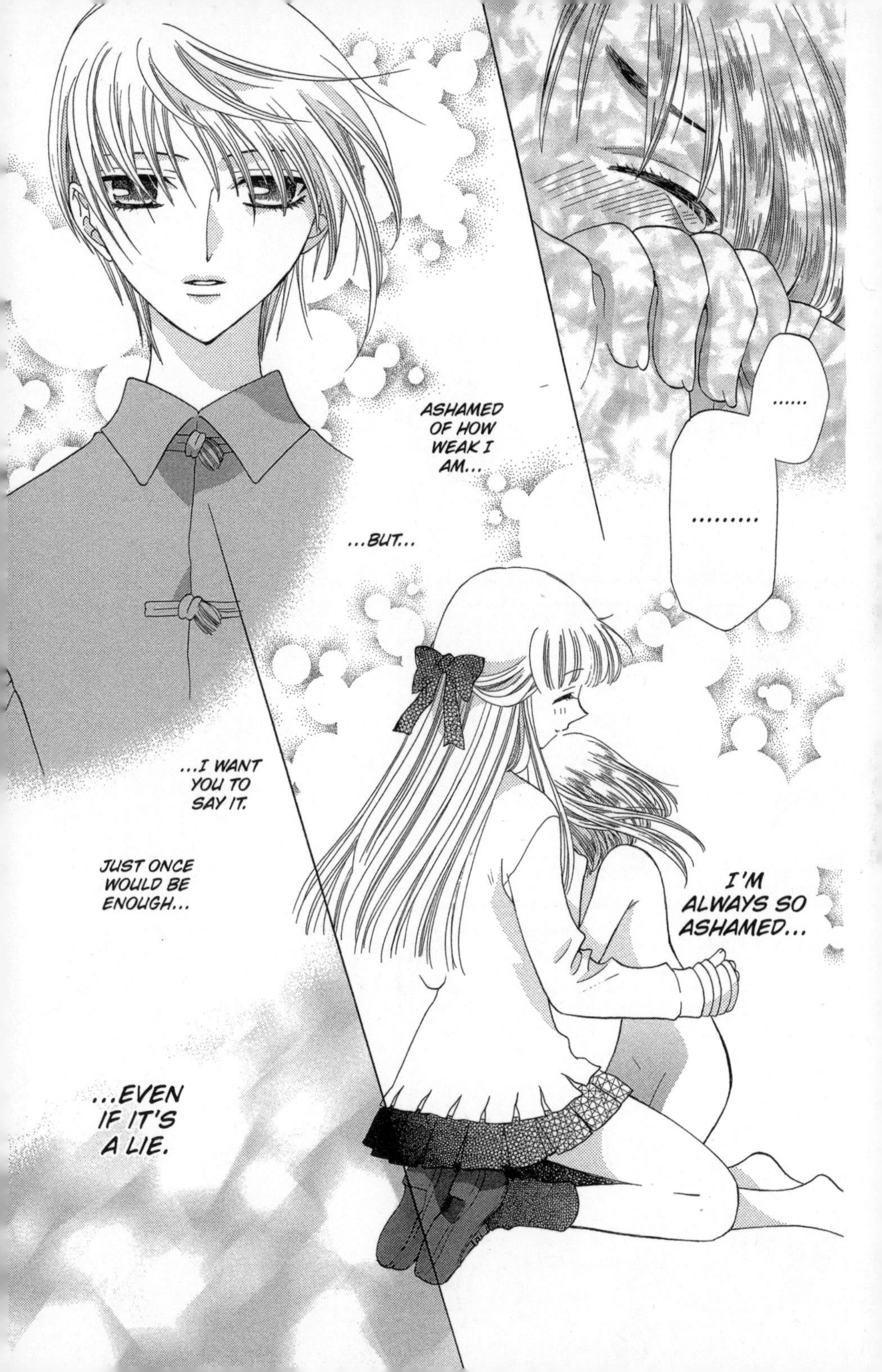
......
....
I'M ALWAYS SO ASHAMED...
ASHAMED OF HOW WEAK I AM...
...BUT...
...I WANT YOU TO SAY IT.
JUST ONCE WOULD BE ENOUGH...
...EVEN IF IT'S A LIE.

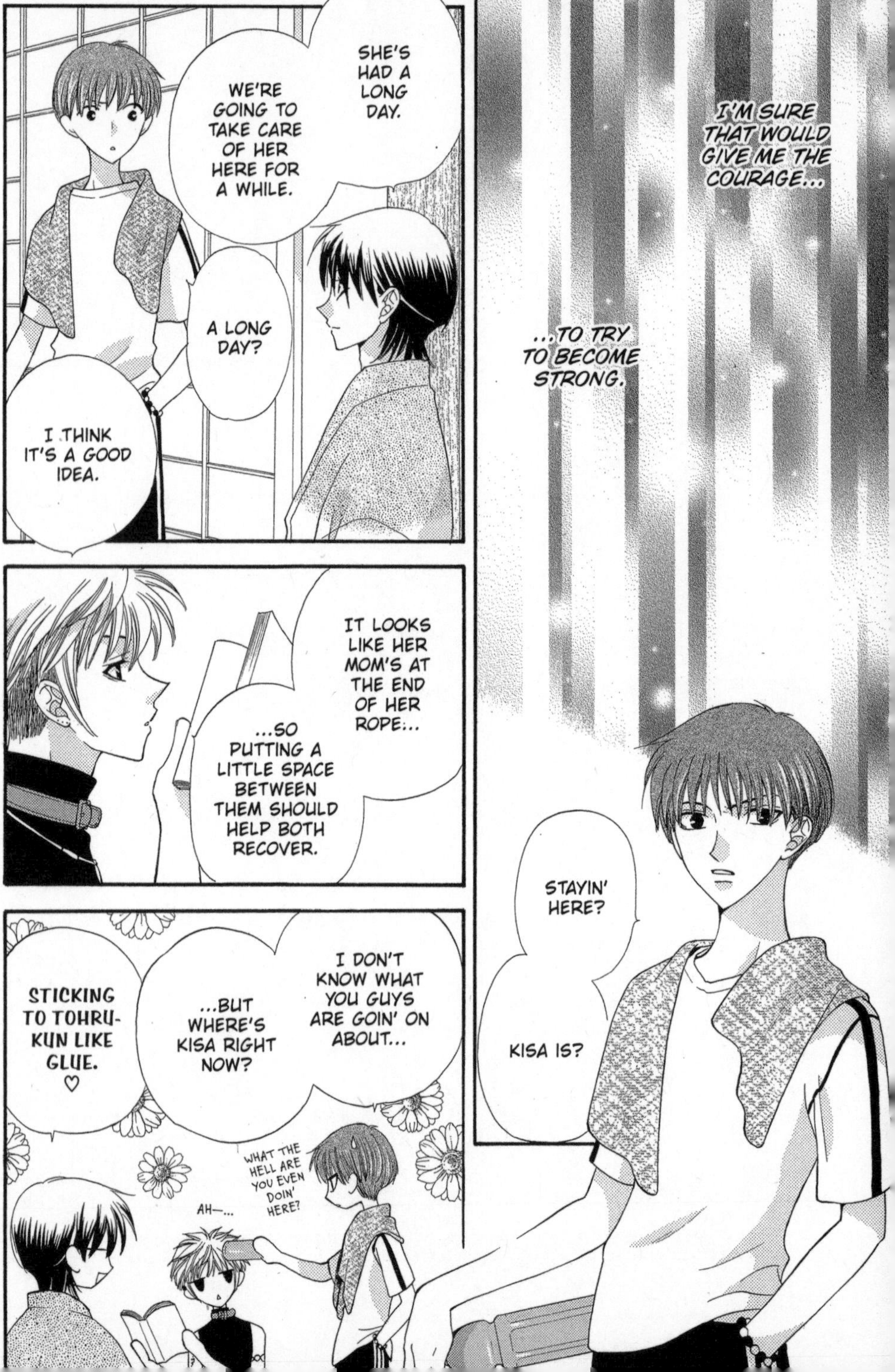
I'M SURE THAT WOULD GIVE ME THE COURAGE...
...TO TRY TO BECOME STRONG.
STAYIN' HERE?
KISA IS?
SHE'S HAD A LONG DAY.
WE'RE GOING TO TAKE CARE OF HER HERE FOR A WHILE.
A LONG DAY?
I THINK IT'S A GOOD IDEA.
IT LOOKS LIKE HER MOM'S AT THE END OF HER ROPE...
...SO PUTTING A LITTLE SPACE BETWEEN THEM SHOULD HELP BOTH RECOVER.
I DON'T KNOW WHAT YOU GUYS ARE GOIN' ON ABOUT...
...BUT WHERE'S KISA RIGHT NOW?
STICKING TO TOHRU-KUN LIKE GLUE. ♡
WHAT THE HELL ARE YOU EVEN DOIN' HERE?
AH—...

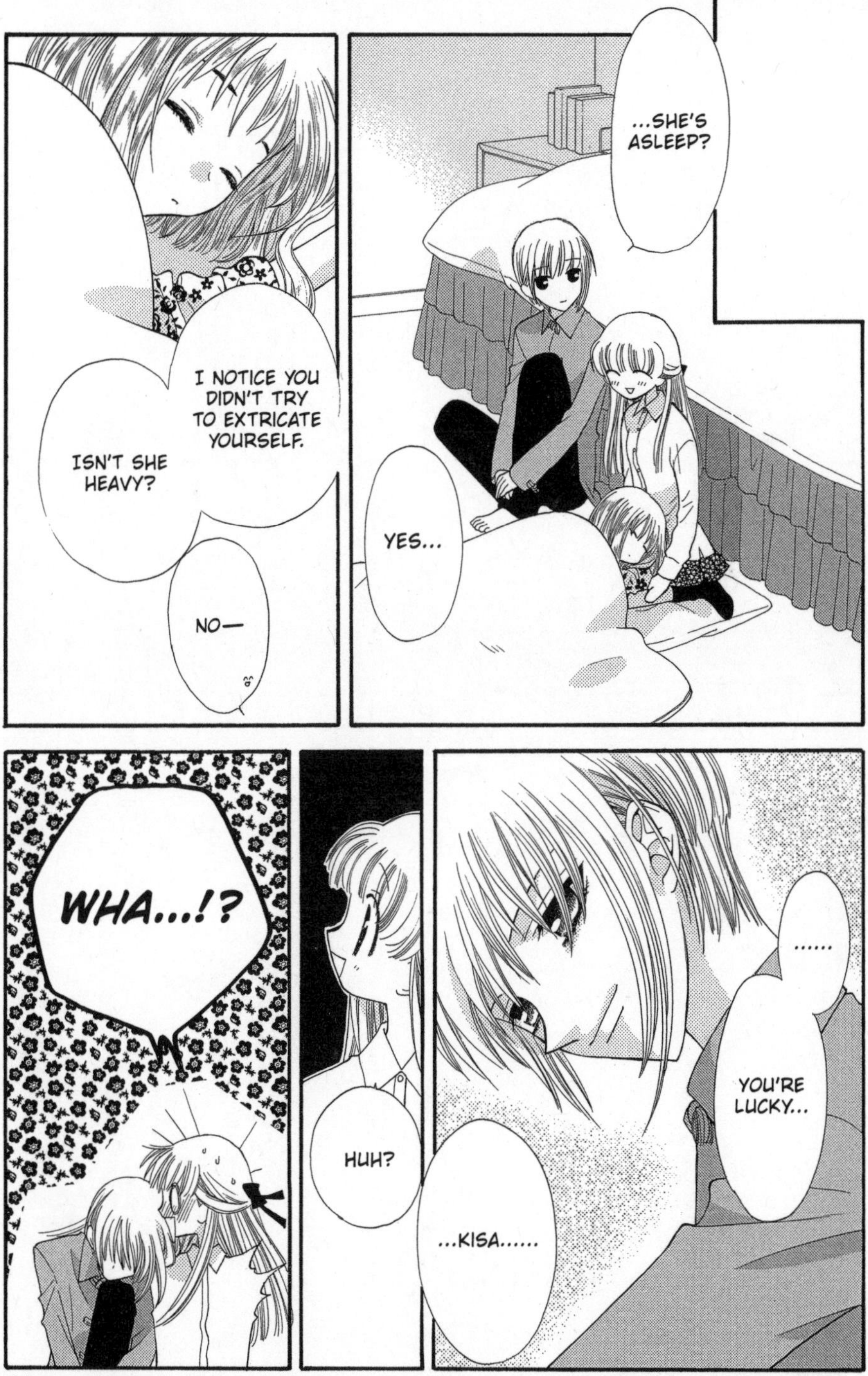
...SHE'S ASLEEP?
YES...
I NOTICE YOU DIDN'T TRY TO EXTRICATE YOURSELF.
ISN'T SHE HEAVY?
NO—
......
YOU'RE LUCKY...
...KISA......
HUH?
WHA...!?

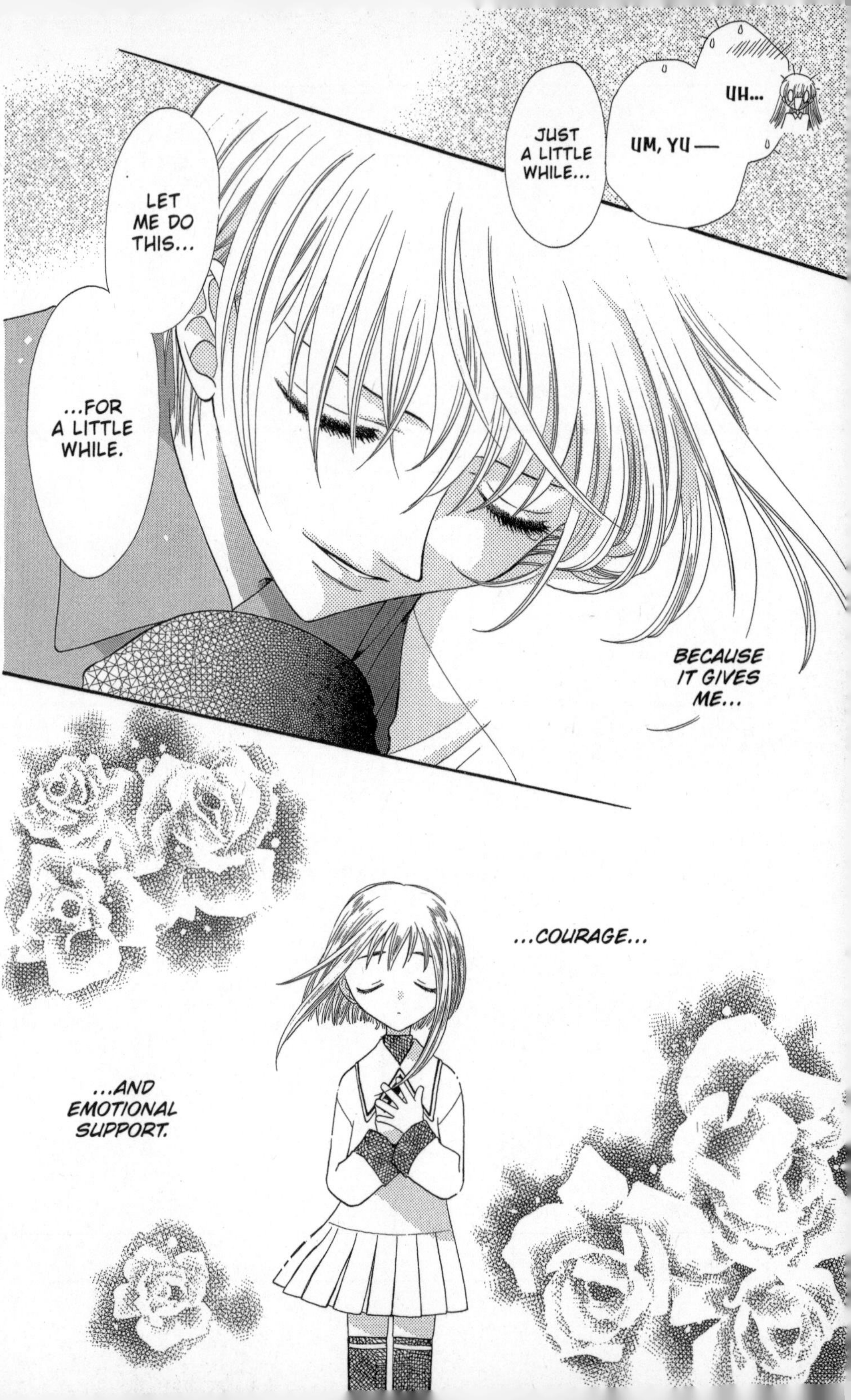
UH...
UM, YU —
JUST A LITTLE WHILE...
LET ME DO THIS...
...FOR A LITTLE WHILE.
BECAUSE IT GIVES ME...
...COURAGE...
...AND EMOTIONAL SUPPORT.

Chapter 28

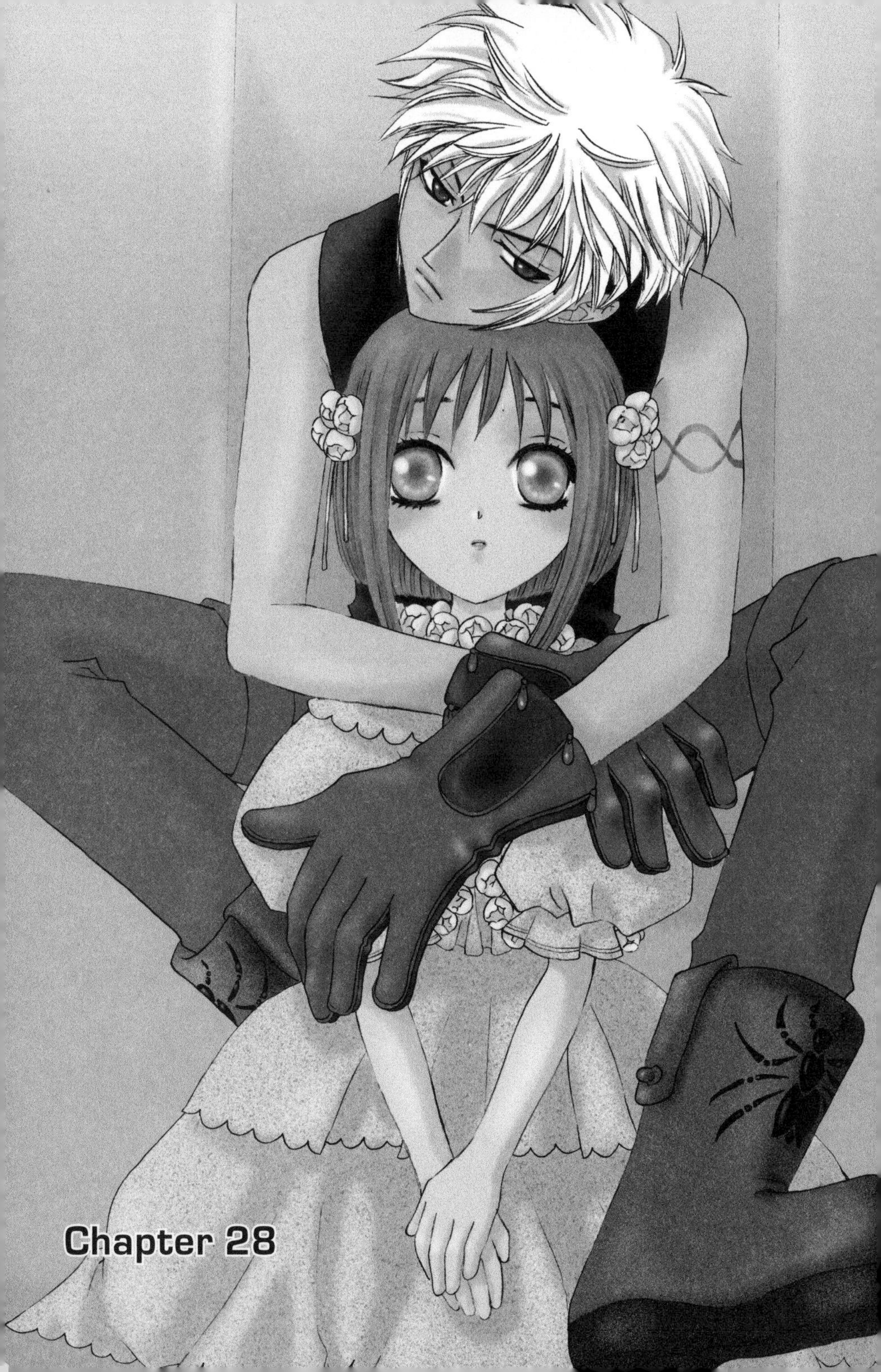

COLLECTOR'S EDITION

Fruits Basket

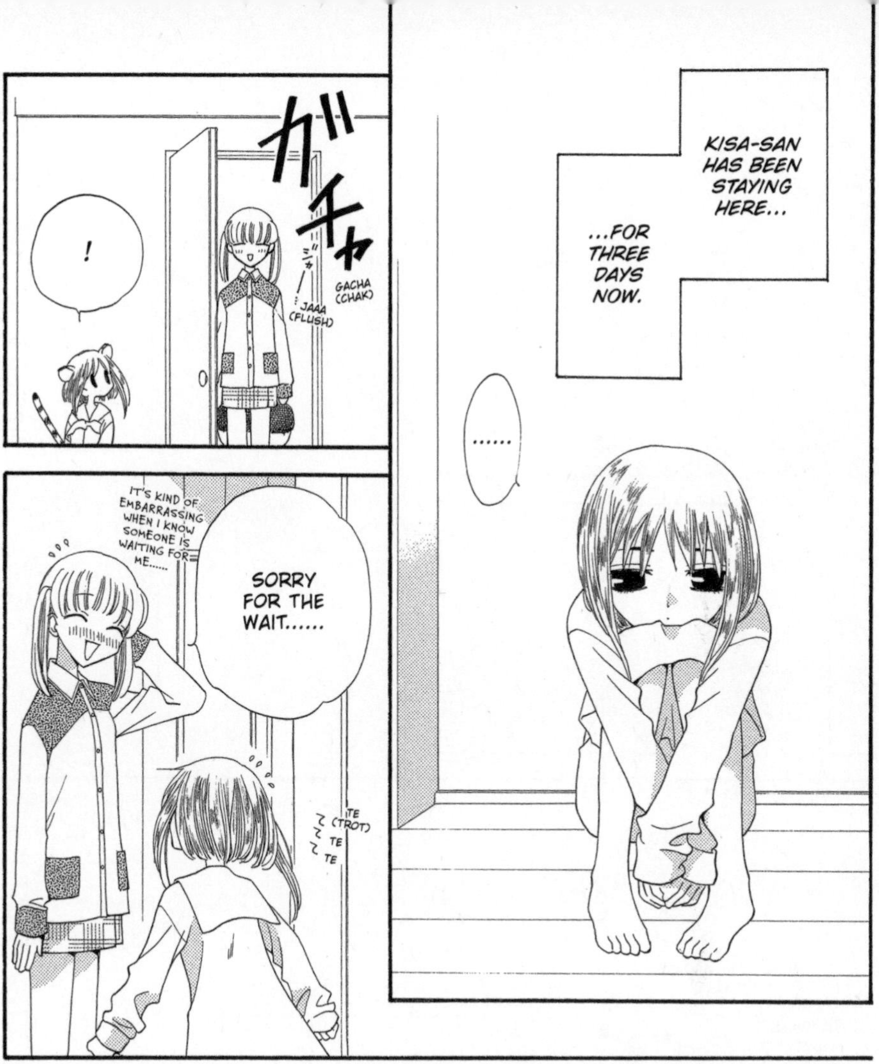
KISA-SAN HAS BEEN STAYING HERE...
...FOR THREE DAYS NOW.
......
ガチャ
GACHA (CHAK)
JAAA (FLUSH)
!
SORRY FOR THE WAIT......
IT'S KIND OF EMBARRASSING WHEN I KNOW SOMEONE IS WAITING FOR ME......
TE TE TE (TROT)

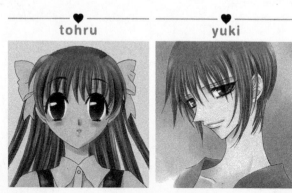

tohru

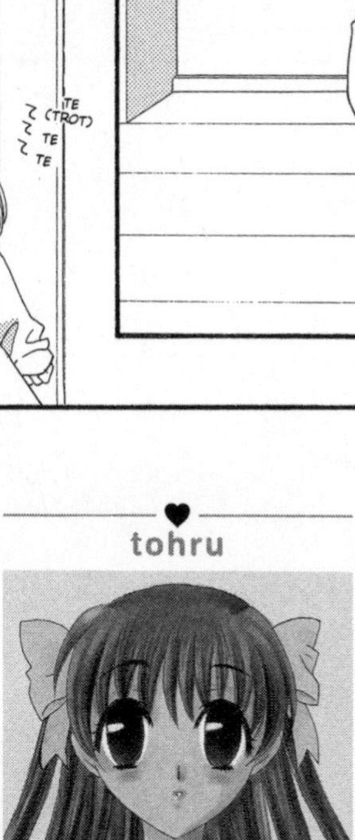

yuki

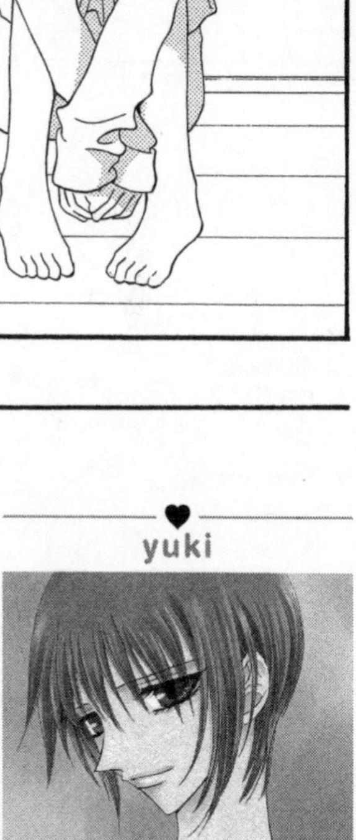

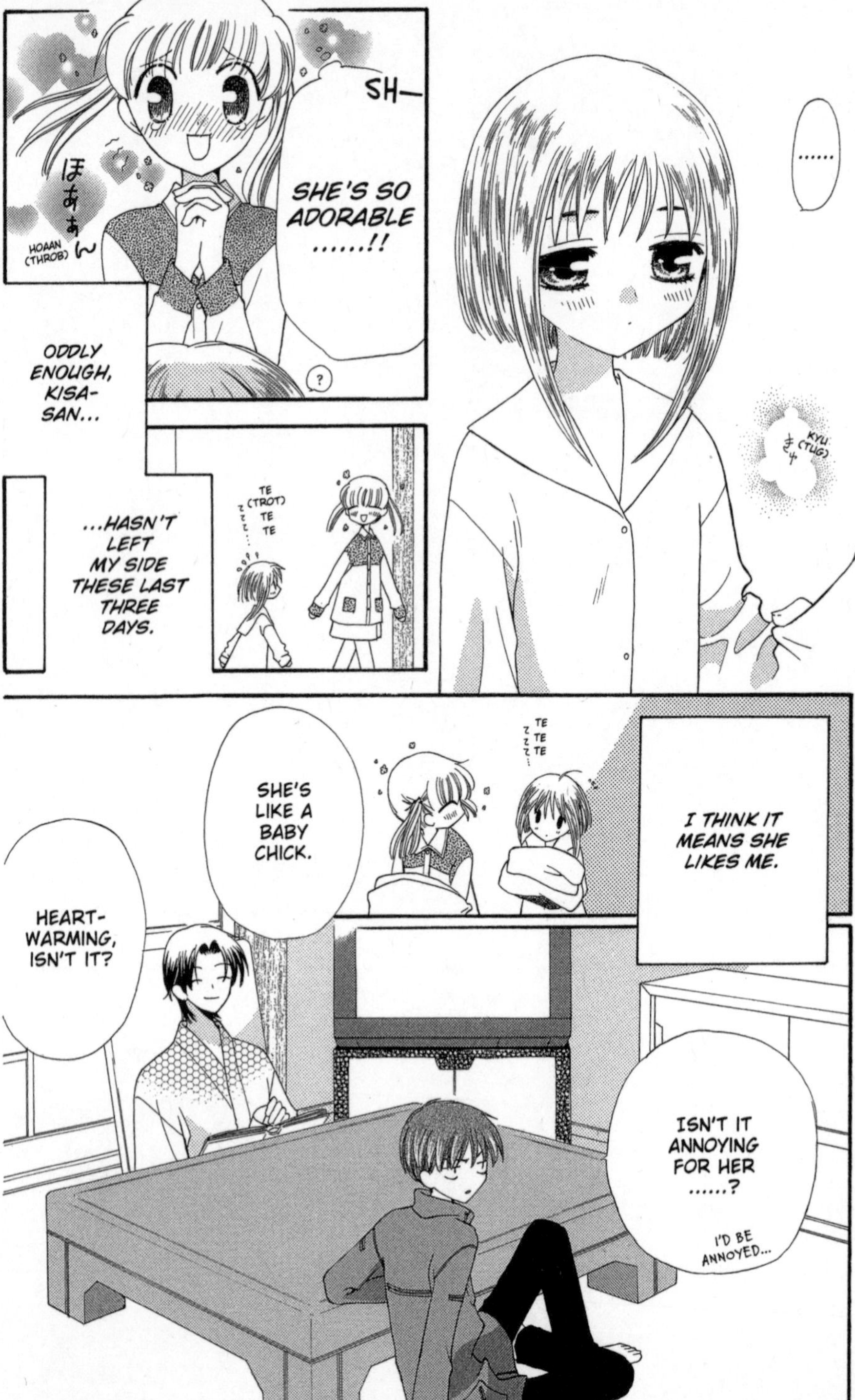
......
KYU (TUG)
きゅ
SH—
SHE'S SO ADORABLE ......!!
ほあぁん
HOAAN (THROB)
?
ODDLY ENOUGH, KISA-SAN...
...HASN'T LEFT MY SIDE THESE LAST THREE DAYS.
TE (TROT) TE TE
I THINK IT MEANS SHE LIKES ME.
TE TE TE
SHE'S LIKE A BABY CHICK.
HEART-WARMING, ISN'T IT?
ISN'T IT ANNOYING FOR HER ......?
I'D BE ANNOYED...

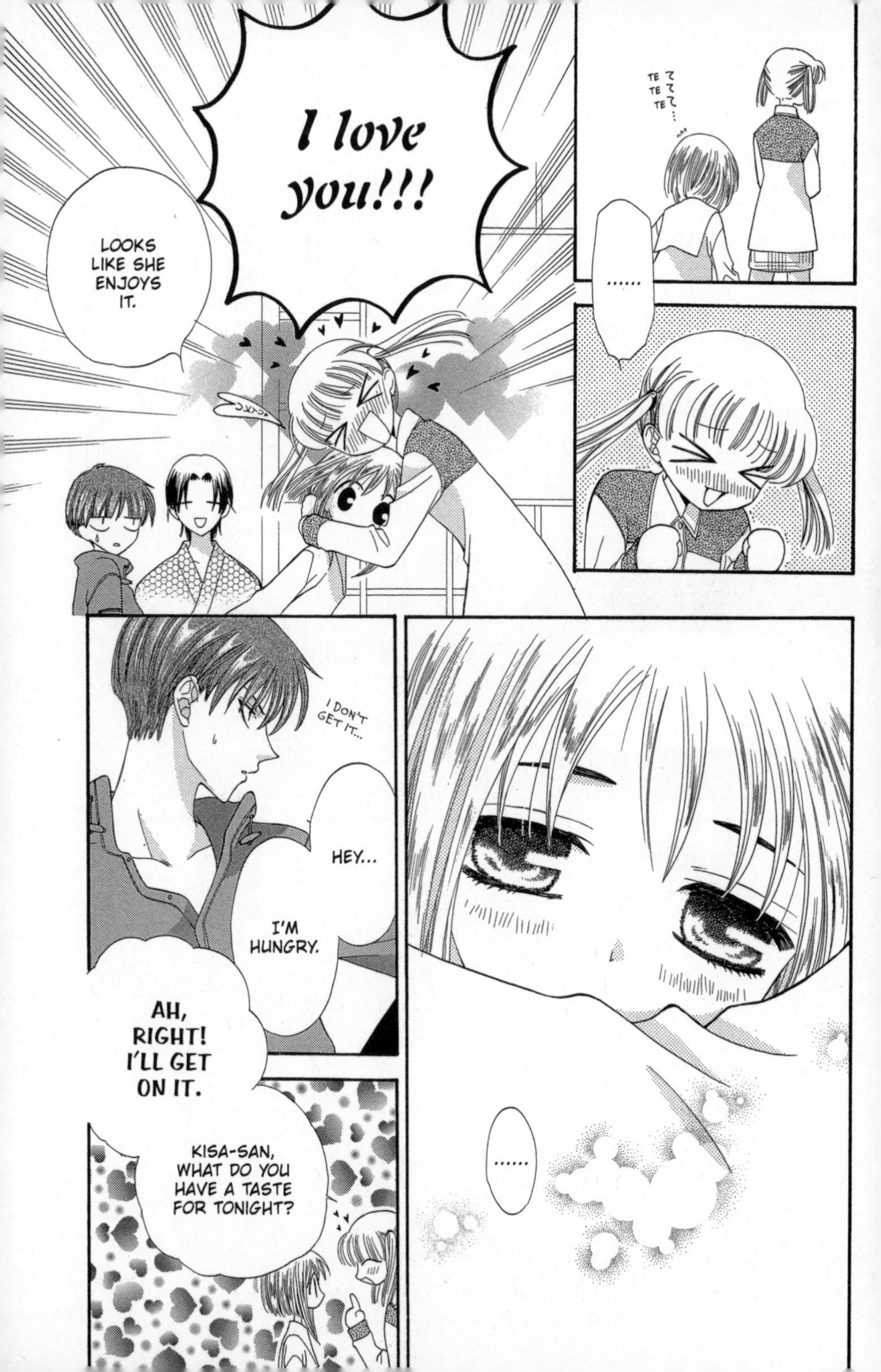
TE TE TE
ててて…
......
I love you!!!
LOOKS LIKE SHE ENJOYS IT.
......
I DON'T GET IT...
HEY...
I'M HUNGRY.
AH, RIGHT! I'LL GET ON IT.
KISA-SAN, WHAT DO YOU HAVE A TASTE FOR TONIGHT?

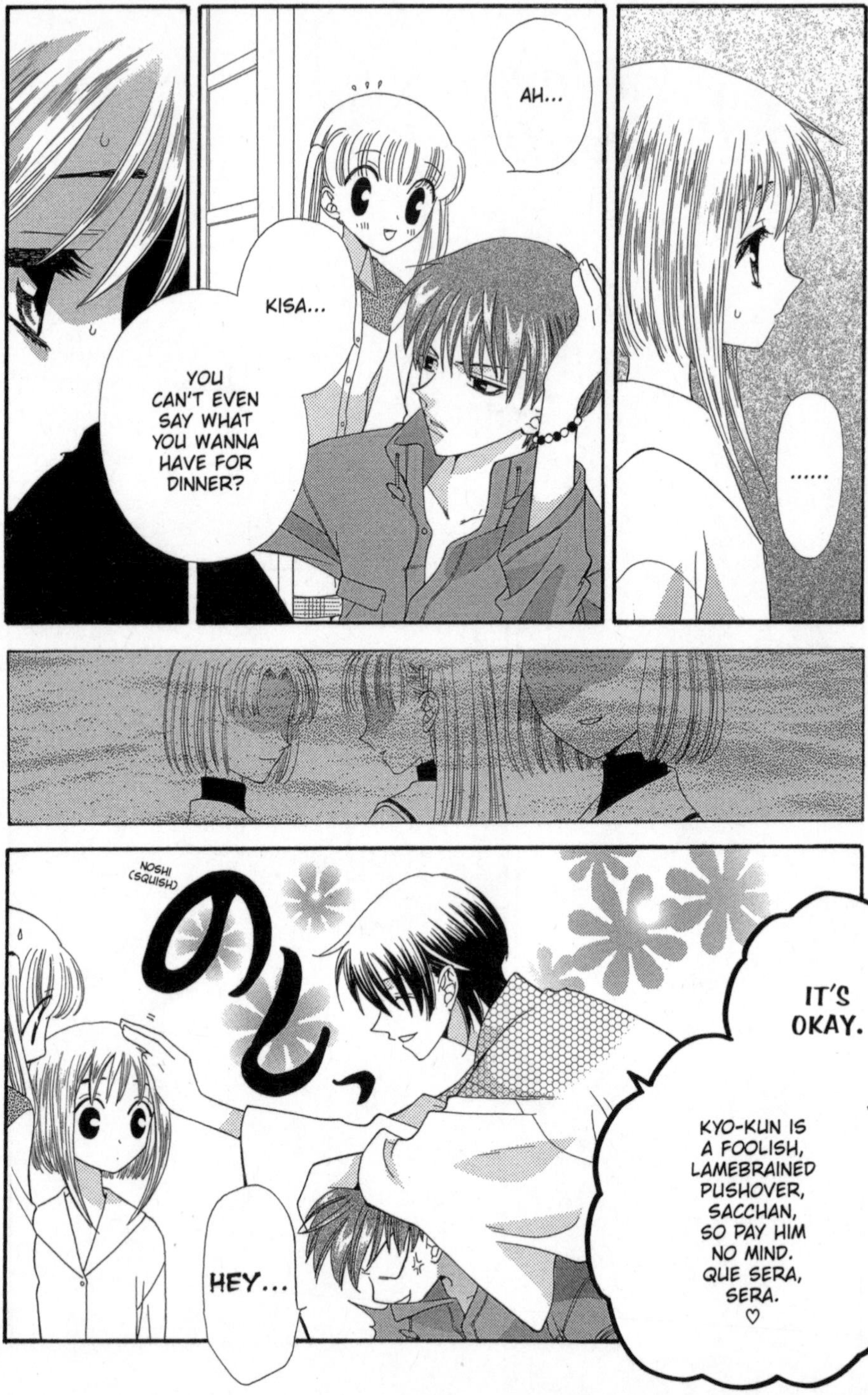
......
AH...
KISA...
YOU CAN'T EVEN SAY WHAT YOU WANNA HAVE FOR DINNER?
IT'S OKAY.
KYO-KUN IS A FOOLISH, LAMEBRAINED PUSHOVER, SACCHAN, SO PAY HIM NO MIND. QUE SERA, SERA. ♡
HEY...
のしっ
NOSHI (SQUISH)

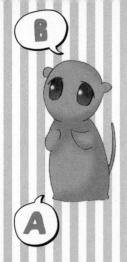

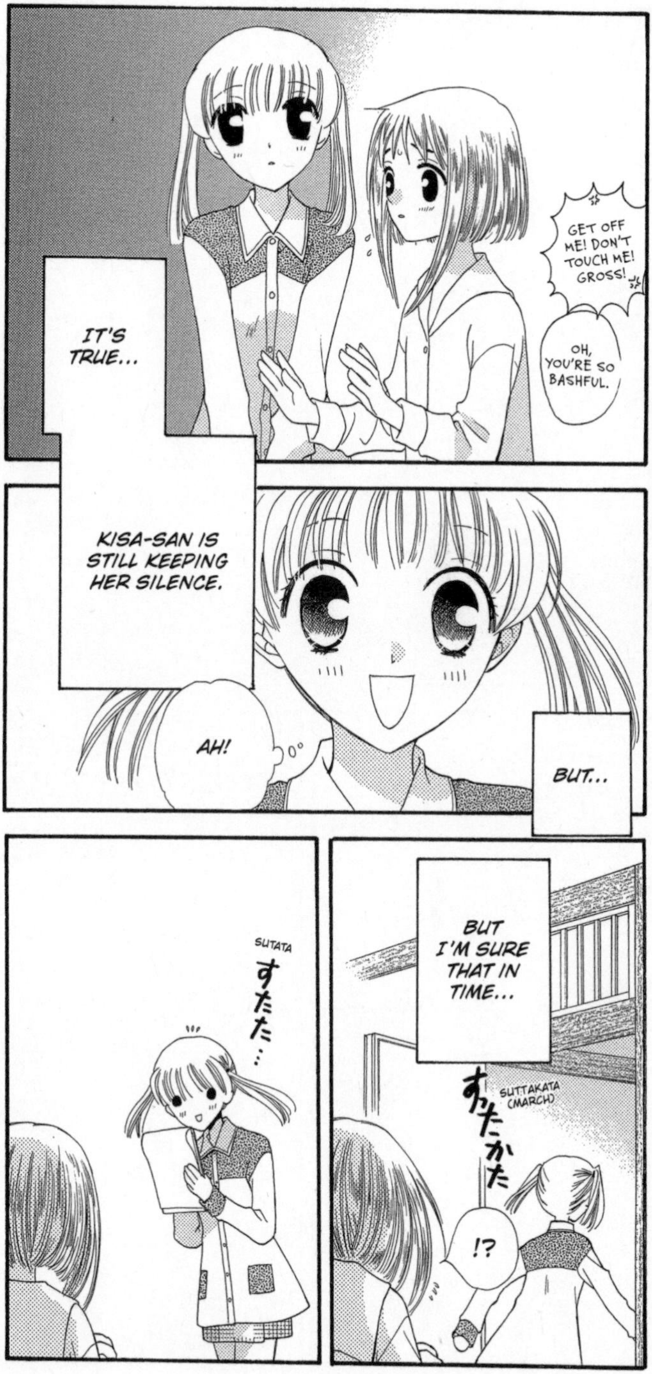
GET OFF ME! DON'T TOUCH ME! GROSS!
OH, YOU'RE SO BASHFUL.
IT'S TRUE...
KISA-SAN IS STILL KEEPING HER SILENCE.
BUT...
AH!
BUT I'M SURE THAT IN TIME...
すたかた
SUTTAKATA (MARCH)
!?
すたた…
SUTATA

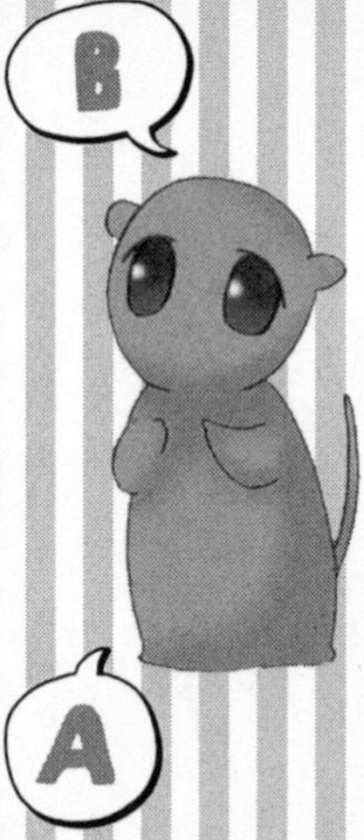
B
A

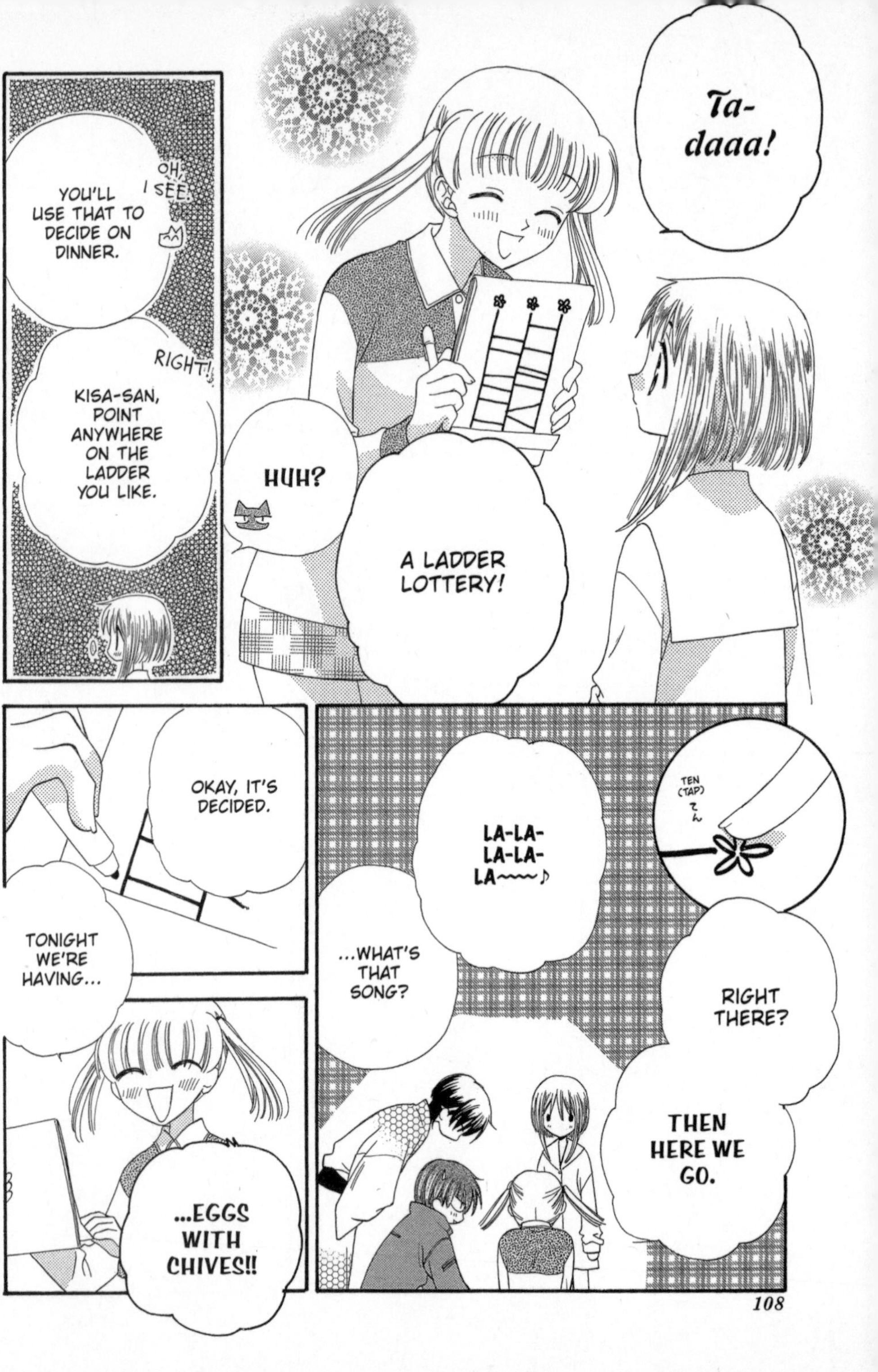
Ta-daaa!
A LADDER LOTTERY!
HUH?
OH, I SEE.
YOU'LL USE THAT TO DECIDE ON DINNER.
RIGHT!
KISA-SAN, POINT ANYWHERE ON THE LADDER YOU LIKE.
TEN (TAP)
てん
RIGHT THERE?
THEN HERE WE GO.
LA-LA-LA-LA-LA~~~♪
...WHAT'S THAT SONG?
OKAY, IT'S DECIDED.
TONIGHT WE'RE HAVING...
...EGGS WITH CHIVES!!

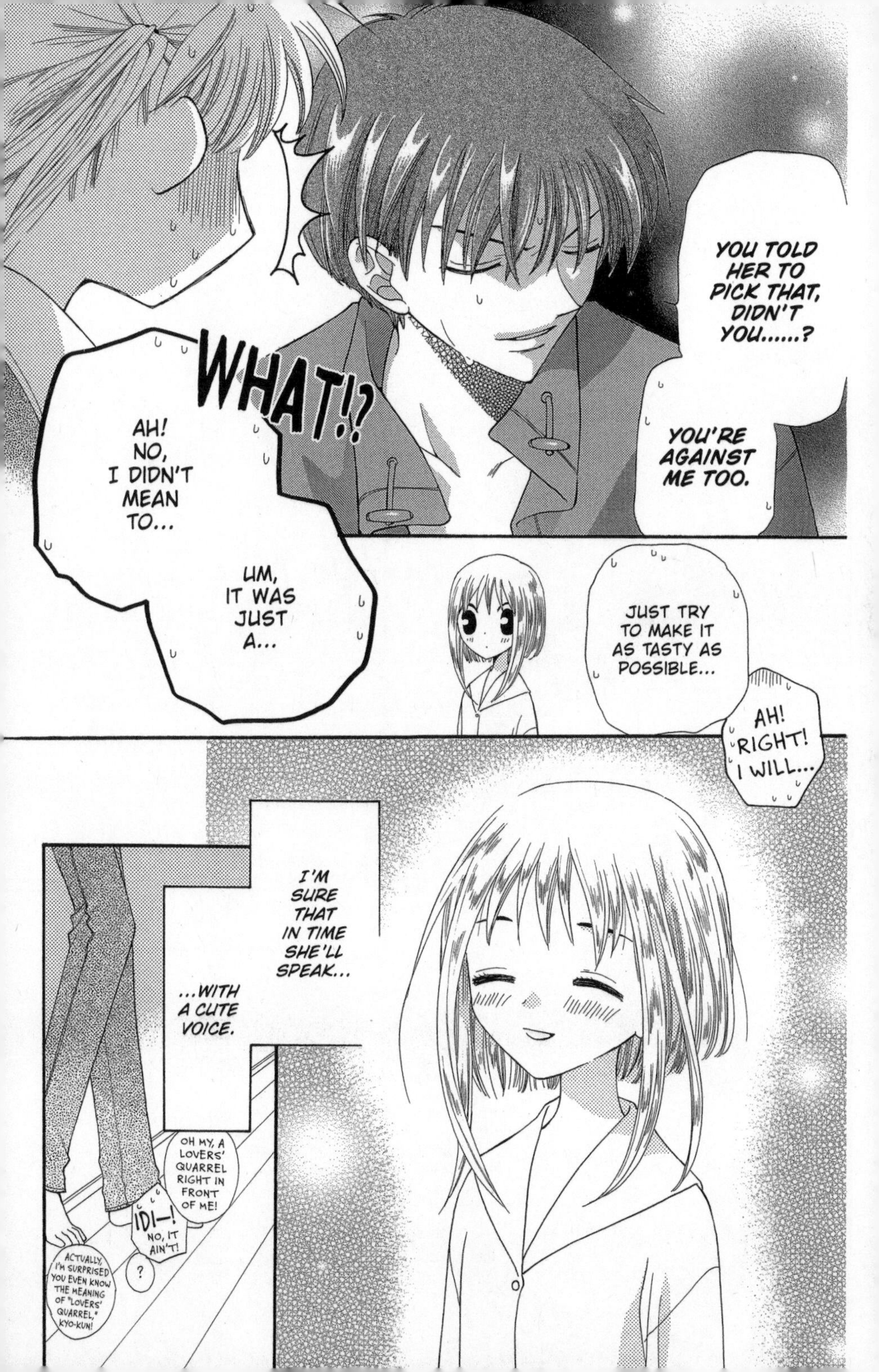
YOU TOLD HER TO PICK THAT, DIDN'T YOU......?
YOU'RE AGAINST ME TOO.
WHAT!?
AH! NO, I DIDN'T MEAN TO...
UM, IT WAS JUST A...
JUST TRY TO MAKE IT AS TASTY AS POSSIBLE...
AH! RIGHT! I WILL...
I'M SURE THAT IN TIME SHE'LL SPEAK...
...WITH A CUTE VOICE.
OH MY, A LOVERS' QUARREL RIGHT IN FRONT OF ME!
IDI—! NO, IT AIN'T!
?
ACTUALLY, I'M SURPRISED YOU EVEN KNOW THE MEANING OF "LOVERS' QUARREL," KYO-KUN!

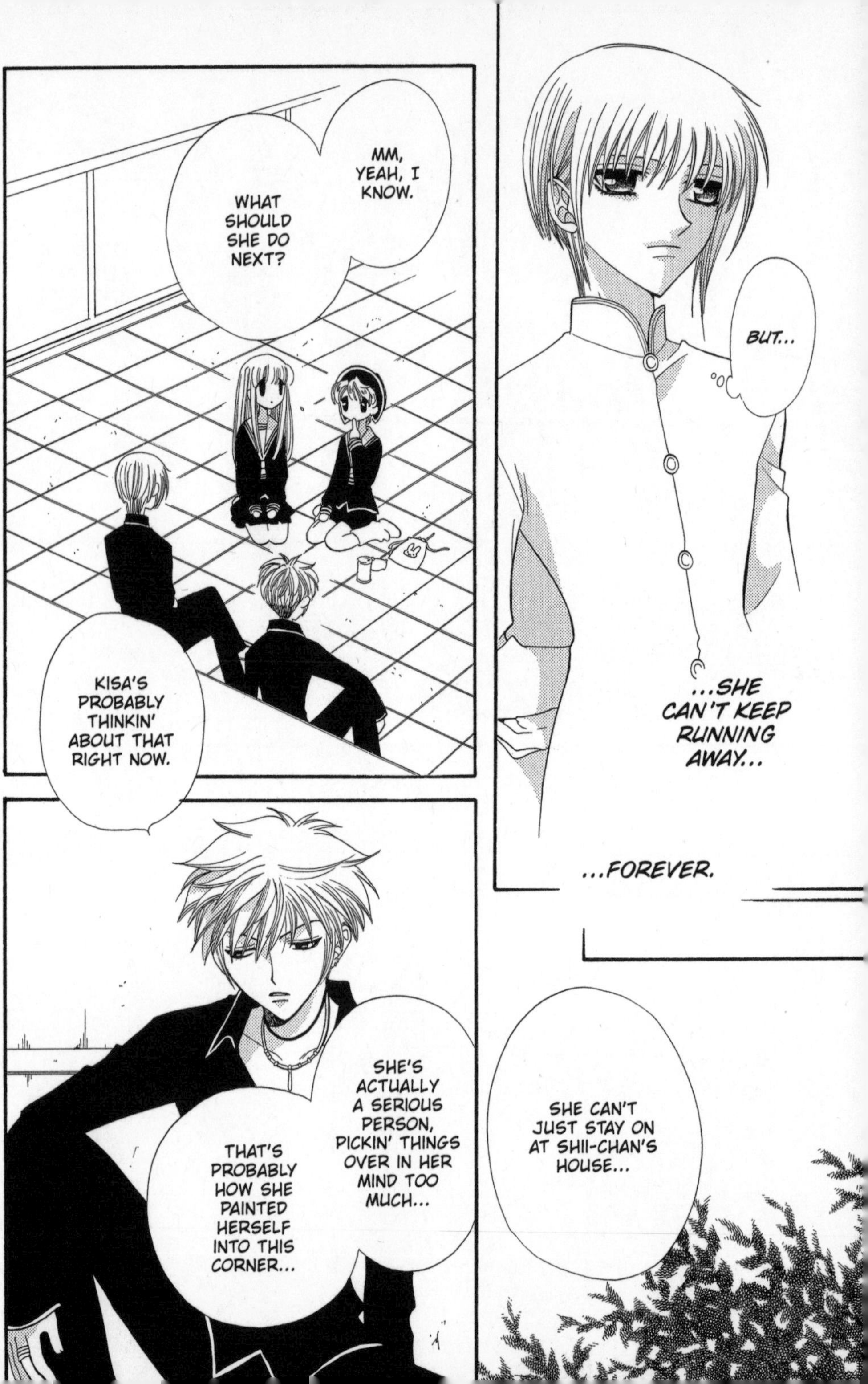
BUT...
...SHE CAN'T KEEP RUNNING AWAY...
...FOREVER.
MM, YEAH, I KNOW.
WHAT SHOULD SHE DO NEXT?
KISA'S PROBABLY THINKIN' ABOUT THAT RIGHT NOW.
SHE CAN'T JUST STAY ON AT SHII-CHAN'S HOUSE...
SHE'S ACTUALLY A SERIOUS PERSON, PICKIN' THINGS OVER IN HER MIND TOO MUCH...
THAT'S PROBABLY HOW SHE PAINTED HERSELF INTO THIS CORNER...

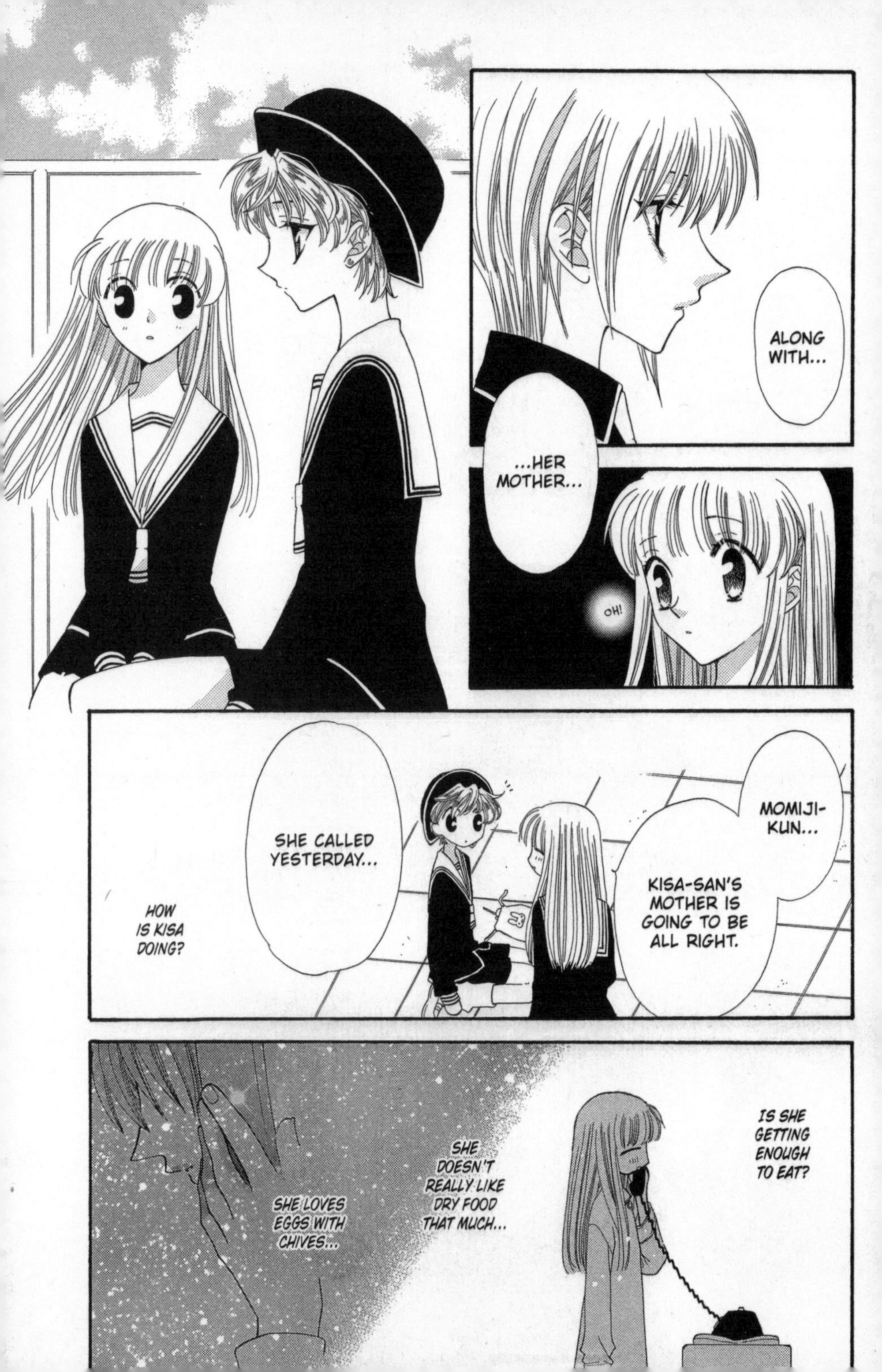
ALONG WITH...
...HER MOTHER...
OH!
MOMIJI-KUN...
KISA-SAN'S MOTHER IS GOING TO BE ALL RIGHT.
SHE CALLED YESTERDAY...
HOW IS KISA DOING?
IS SHE GETTING ENOUGH TO EAT?
SHE DOESN'T REALLY LIKE DRY FOOD THAT MUCH...
SHE LOVES EGGS WITH CHIVES...

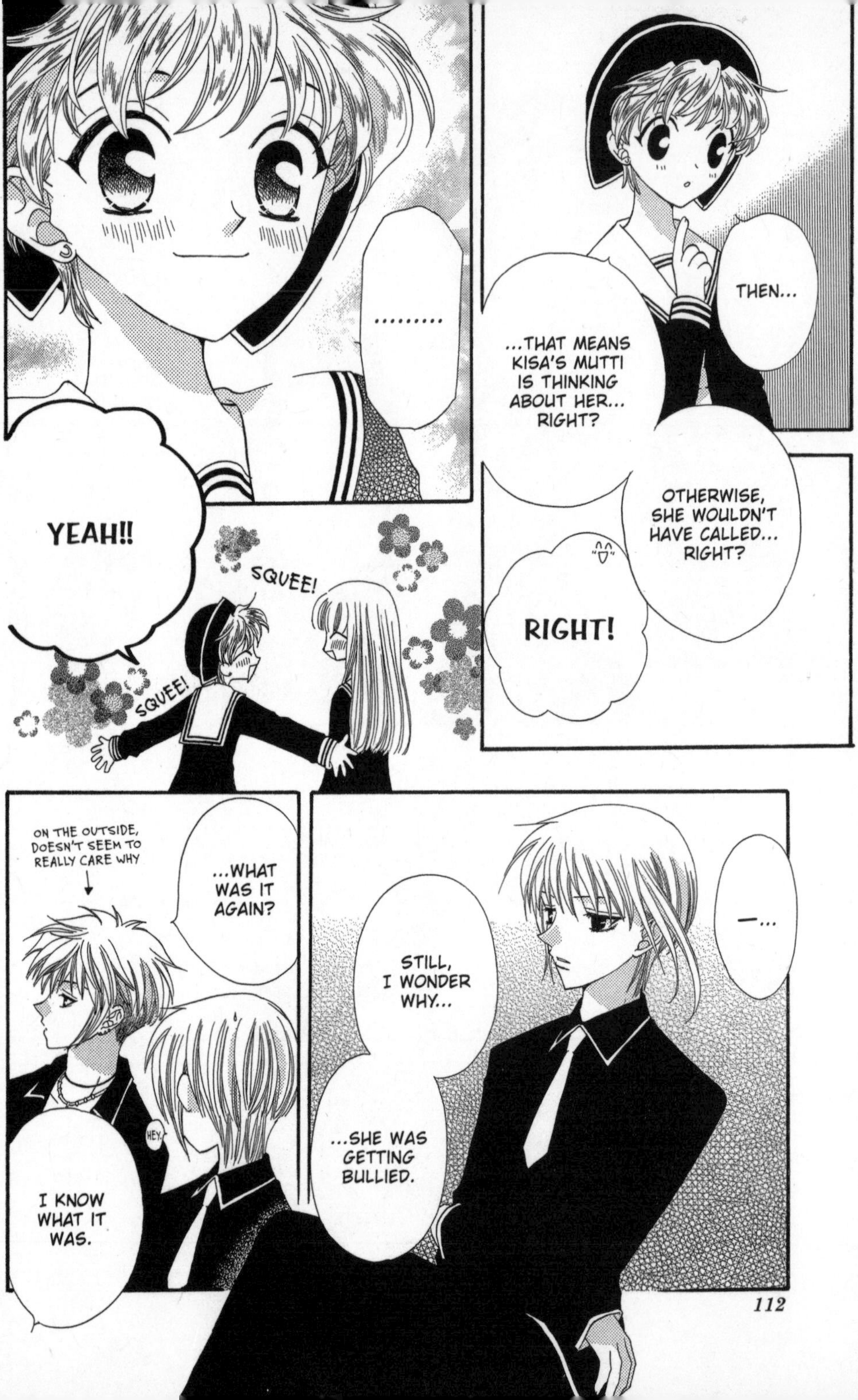
THEN...
...THAT MEANS KISA'S MUTTI IS THINKING ABOUT HER... RIGHT?
....
YEAH!!
OTHERWISE, SHE WOULDN'T HAVE CALLED... RIGHT?
RIGHT!
SQUEE!
SQUEE!
—...
STILL, I WONDER WHY...
...SHE WAS GETTING BULLIED.
...WHAT WAS IT AGAIN?
ON THE OUTSIDE, DOESN'T SEEM TO REALLY CARE WHY
HEY.
I KNOW WHAT IT WAS.

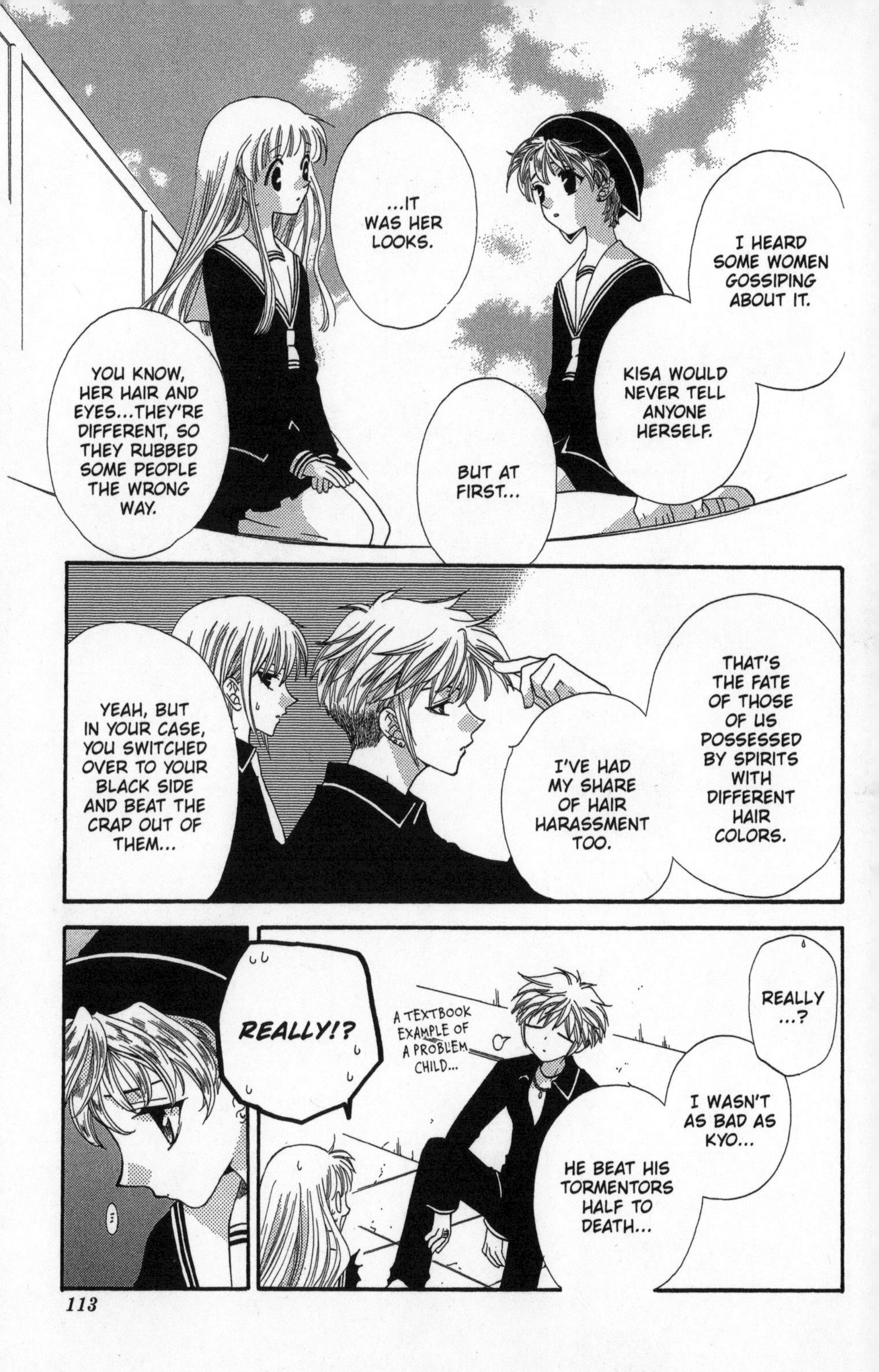
I HEARD SOME WOMEN GOSSIPING ABOUT IT.
KISA WOULD NEVER TELL ANYONE HERSELF.
BUT AT FIRST...
...IT WAS HER LOOKS.
YOU KNOW, HER HAIR AND EYES...THEY'RE DIFFERENT, SO THEY RUBBED SOME PEOPLE THE WRONG WAY.
THAT'S THE FATE OF THOSE OF US POSSESSED BY SPIRITS WITH DIFFERENT HAIR COLORS.
I'VE HAD MY SHARE OF HAIR HARASSMENT TOO.
YEAH, BUT IN YOUR CASE, YOU SWITCHED OVER TO YOUR BLACK SIDE AND BEAT THE CRAP OUT OF THEM...
REALLY ...?
I WASN'T AS BAD AS KYO...
HE BEAT HIS TORMENTORS HALF TO DEATH...
A TEXTBOOK EXAMPLE OF A PROBLEM CHILD...
REALLY!?
...

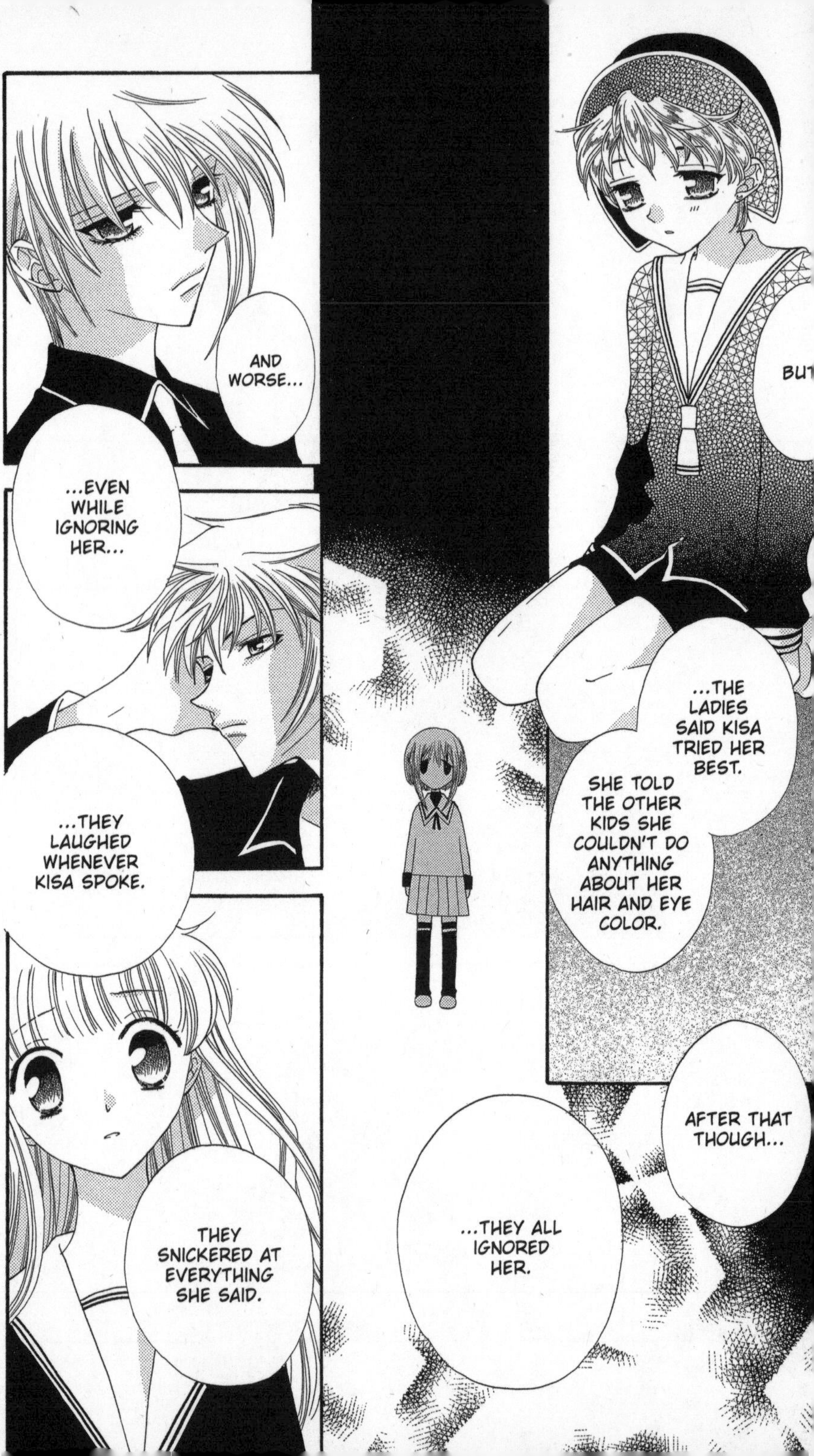
BUT
...THE LADIES SAID KISA TRIED HER BEST.
SHE TOLD THE OTHER KIDS SHE COULDN'T DO ANYTHING ABOUT HER HAIR AND EYE COLOR.
AFTER THAT THOUGH...
...THEY ALL IGNORED HER.
AND WORSE...
...EVEN WHILE IGNORING HER...
...THEY LAUGHED WHENEVER KISA SPOKE.
THEY SNICKERED AT EVERYTHING SHE SAID.

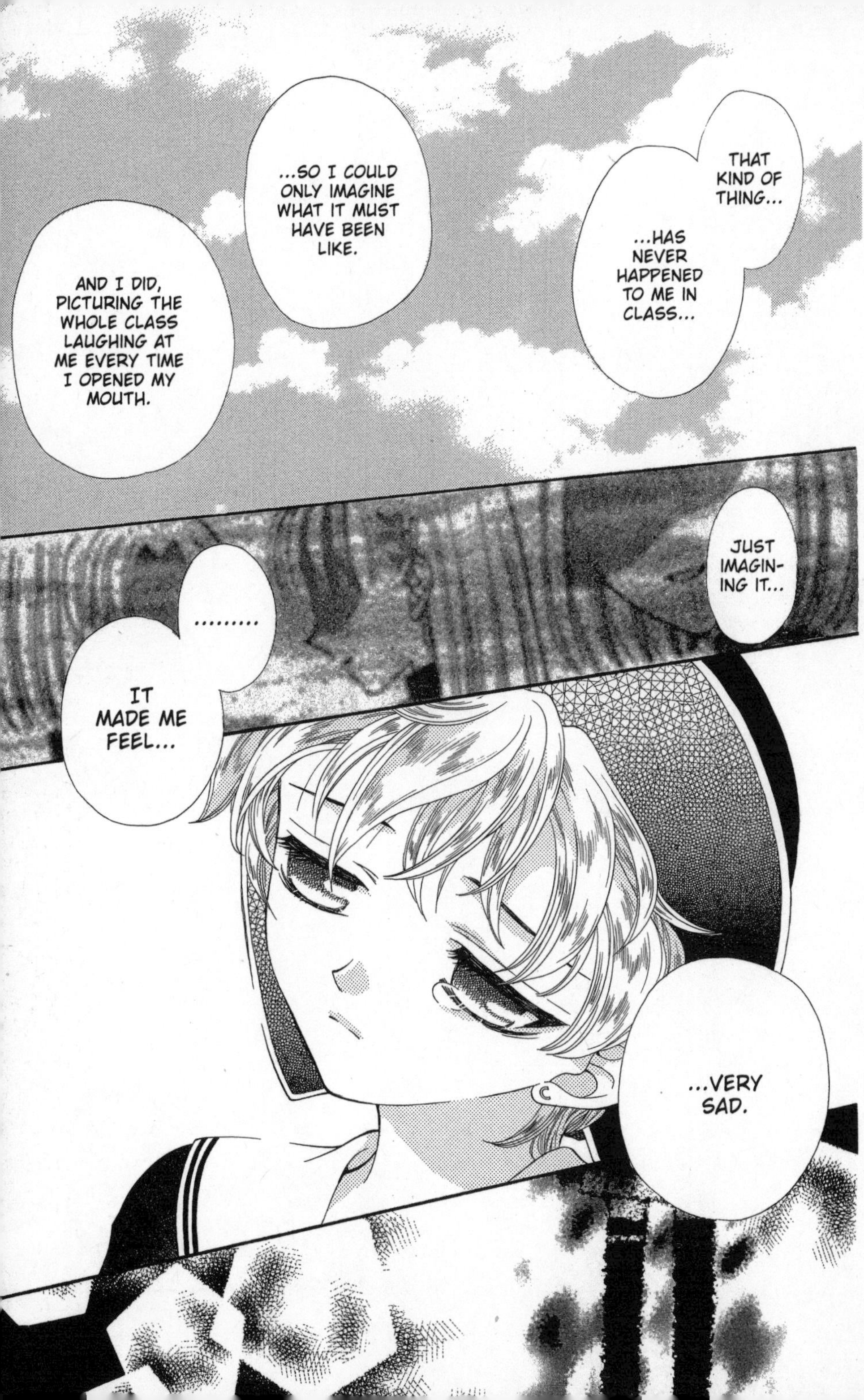
THAT KIND OF THING...
...HAS NEVER HAPPENED TO ME IN CLASS...
...SO I COULD ONLY IMAGINE WHAT IT MUST HAVE BEEN LIKE.
AND I DID, PICTURING THE WHOLE CLASS LAUGHING AT ME EVERY TIME I OPENED MY MOUTH.
JUST IMAGINING IT...
....
IT MADE ME FEEL...
...VERY SAD.

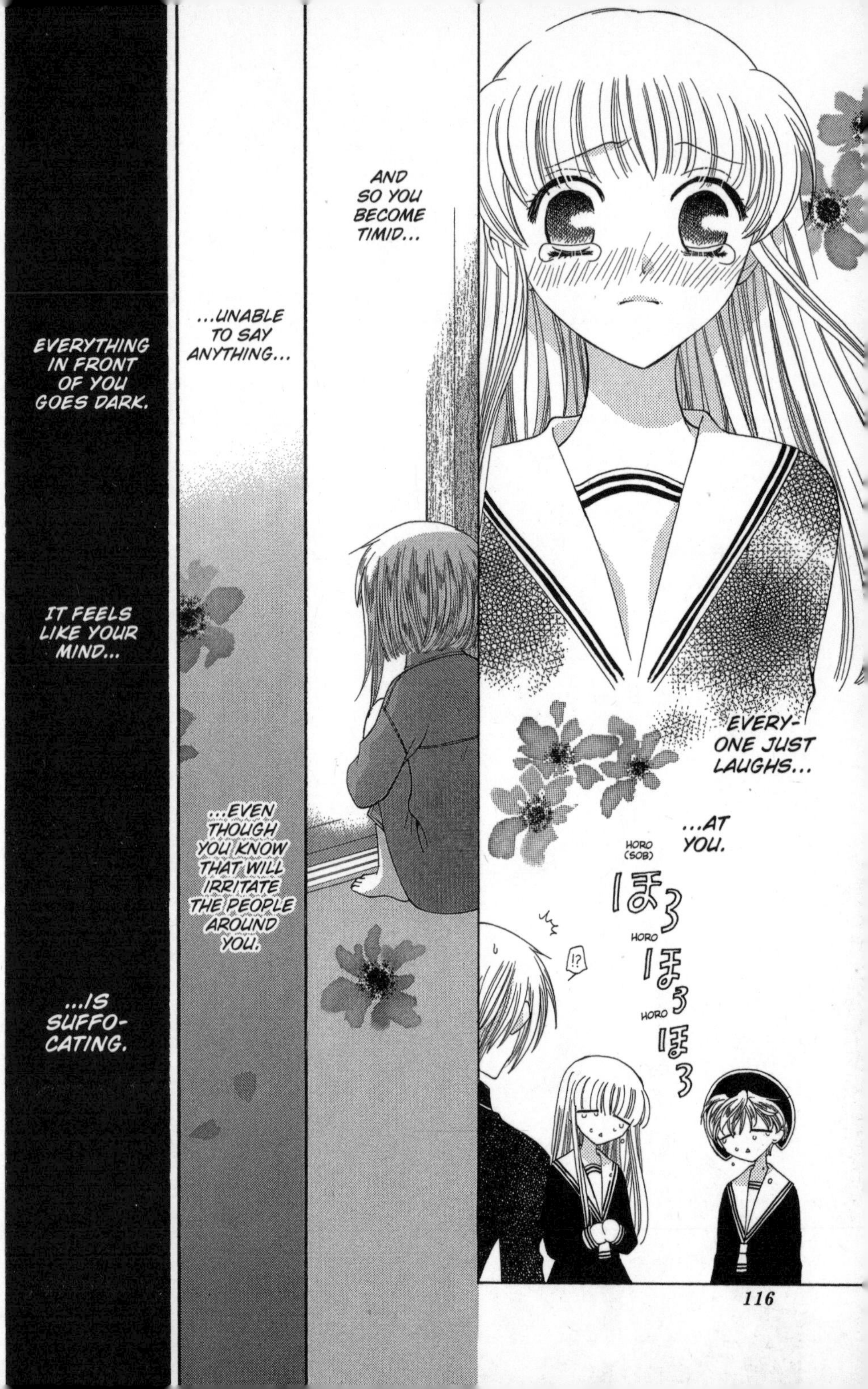
EVERY-ONE JUST LAUGHS...
...AT YOU.
HORO (SOB) ほろ
HORO ほろ
HORO ほろ
!?
AND SO YOU BECOME TIMID...
...UNABLE TO SAY ANYTHING...
...EVEN THOUGH YOU KNOW THAT WILL IRRITATE THE PEOPLE AROUND YOU.
EVERYTHING IN FRONT OF YOU GOES DARK.
IT FEELS LIKE YOUR MIND...
...IS SUFFO-CATING.

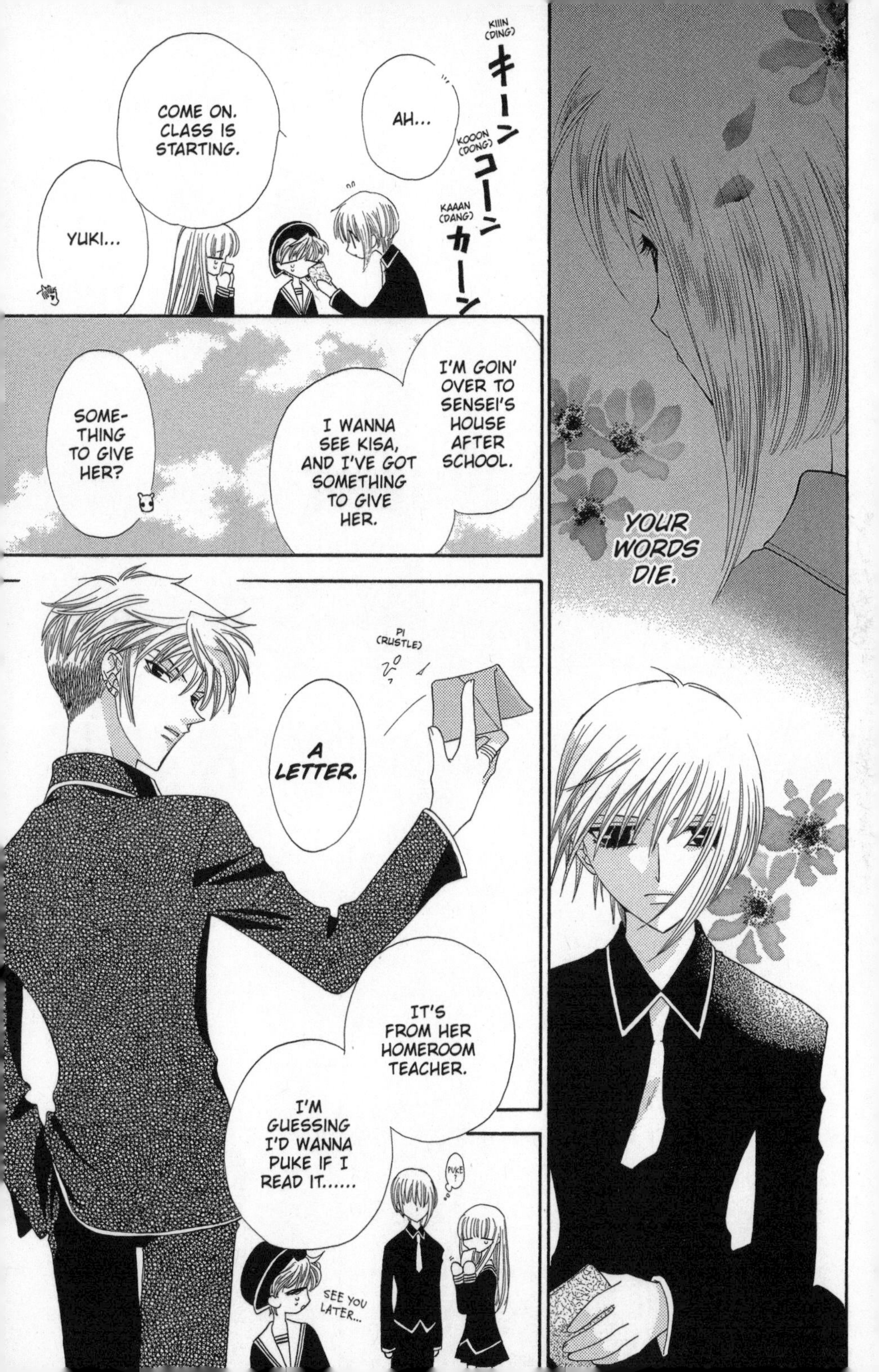
YOUR WORDS DIE.
キーン
KIIIN (DING)
コーン
KOOON (DONG)
カーン
KAAAN (DANG)
AH...
COME ON. CLASS IS STARTING.
YUKI...
I'M GOIN' OVER TO SENSEI'S HOUSE AFTER SCHOOL.
I WANNA SEE KISA, AND I'VE GOT SOMETHING TO GIVE HER.
SOME-THING TO GIVE HER?
PI (RUSTLE)
A LETTER.
IT'S FROM HER HOMEROOM TEACHER.
I'M GUESSING I'D WANNA PUKE IF I READ IT......
PUKE?
SEE YOU LATER...

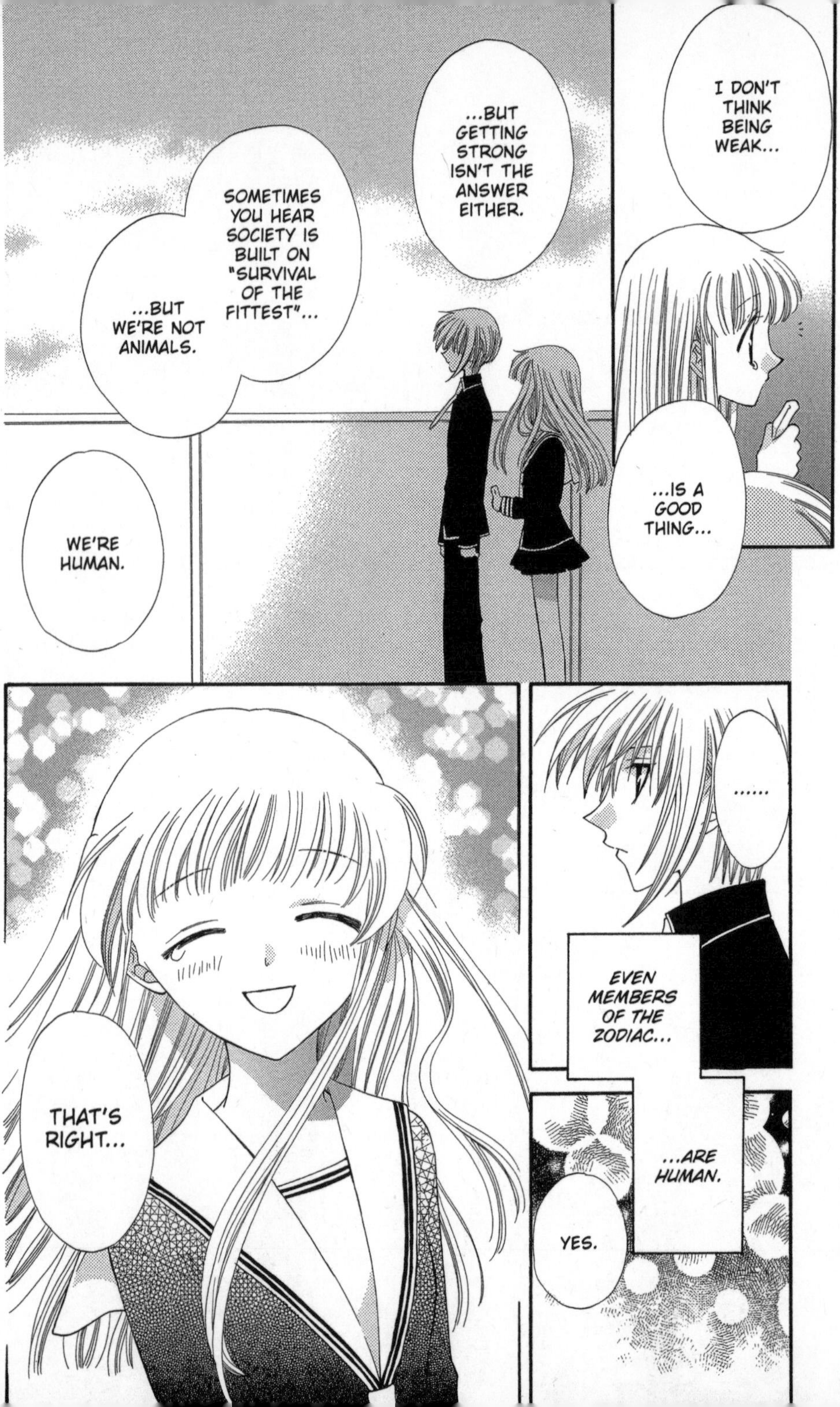
I DON'T THINK BEING WEAK...
...IS A GOOD THING...
...BUT GETTING STRONG ISN'T THE ANSWER EITHER.
SOMETIMES YOU HEAR SOCIETY IS BUILT ON "SURVIVAL OF THE FITTEST"...
...BUT WE'RE NOT ANIMALS.
WE'RE HUMAN.
......
EVEN MEMBERS OF THE ZODIAC...
...ARE HUMAN.
YES.
THAT'S RIGHT...

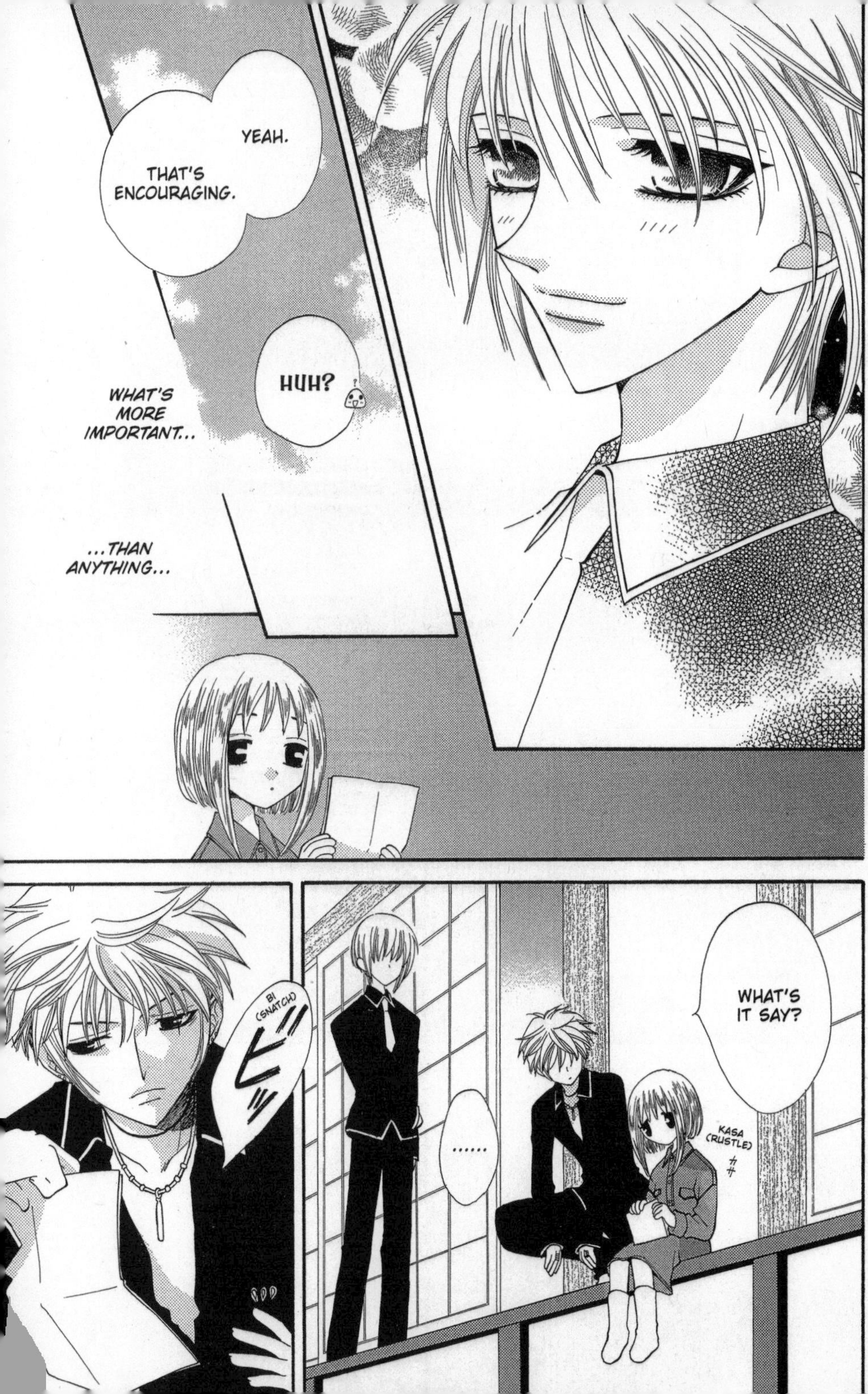
YEAH.
THAT'S ENCOURAGING.
HUH?
WHAT'S MORE IMPORTANT...
...THAN ANYTHING...
WHAT'S IT SAY?
KASA (RUSTLE)
......
BI (SNATCH)

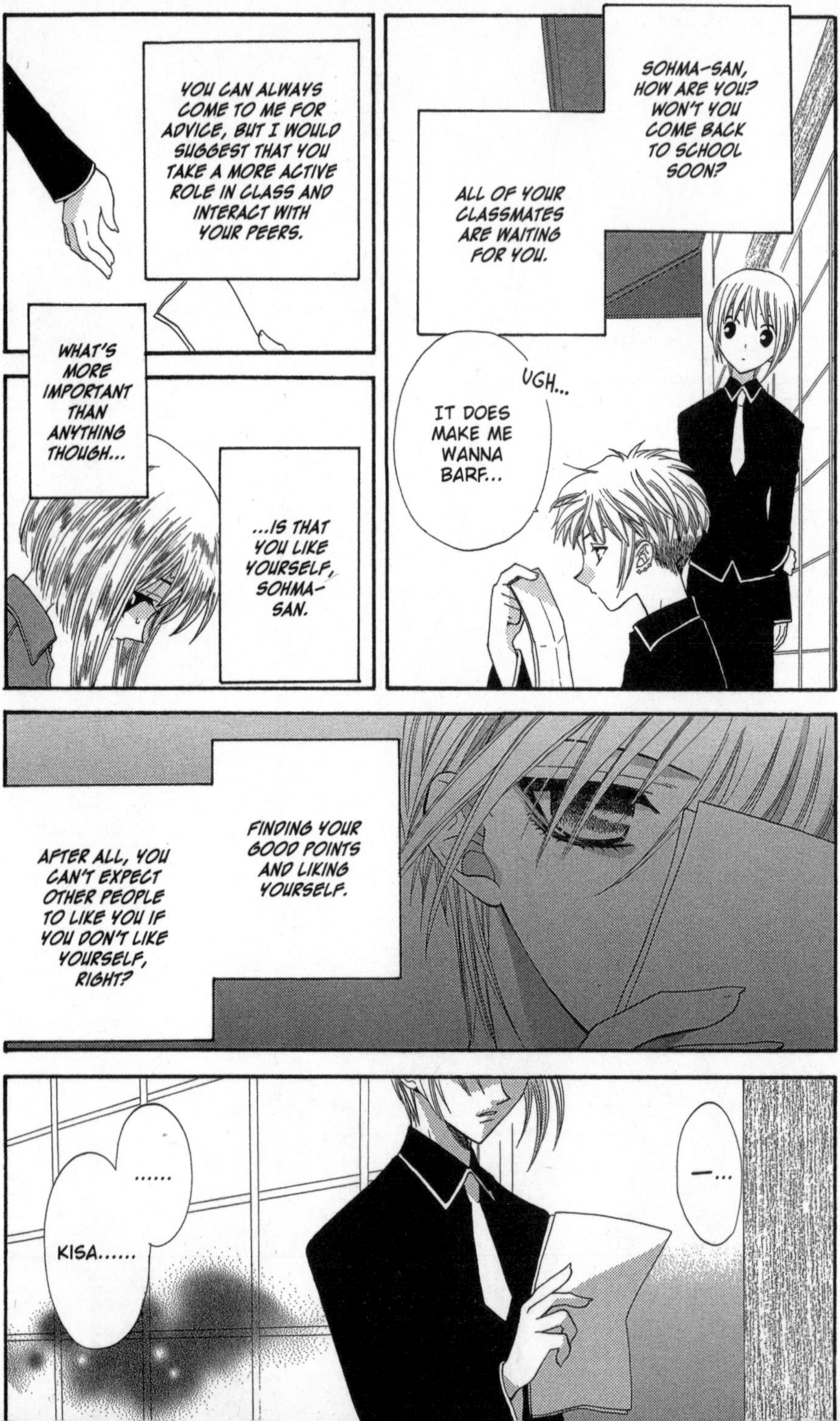
SOHMA-SAN, HOW ARE YOU? WON'T YOU COME BACK TO SCHOOL SOON?
ALL OF YOUR CLASSMATES ARE WAITING FOR YOU.
UGH...
IT DOES MAKE ME WANNA BARF...
YOU CAN ALWAYS COME TO ME FOR ADVICE, BUT I WOULD SUGGEST THAT YOU TAKE A MORE ACTIVE ROLE IN CLASS AND INTERACT WITH YOUR PEERS.
WHAT'S MORE IMPORTANT THAN ANYTHING THOUGH...
...IS THAT YOU LIKE YOURSELF, SOHMA-SAN.
FINDING YOUR GOOD POINTS AND LIKING YOURSELF.
AFTER ALL, YOU CAN'T EXPECT OTHER PEOPLE TO LIKE YOU IF YOU DON'T LIKE YOURSELF, RIGHT?
—...
......
KISA......

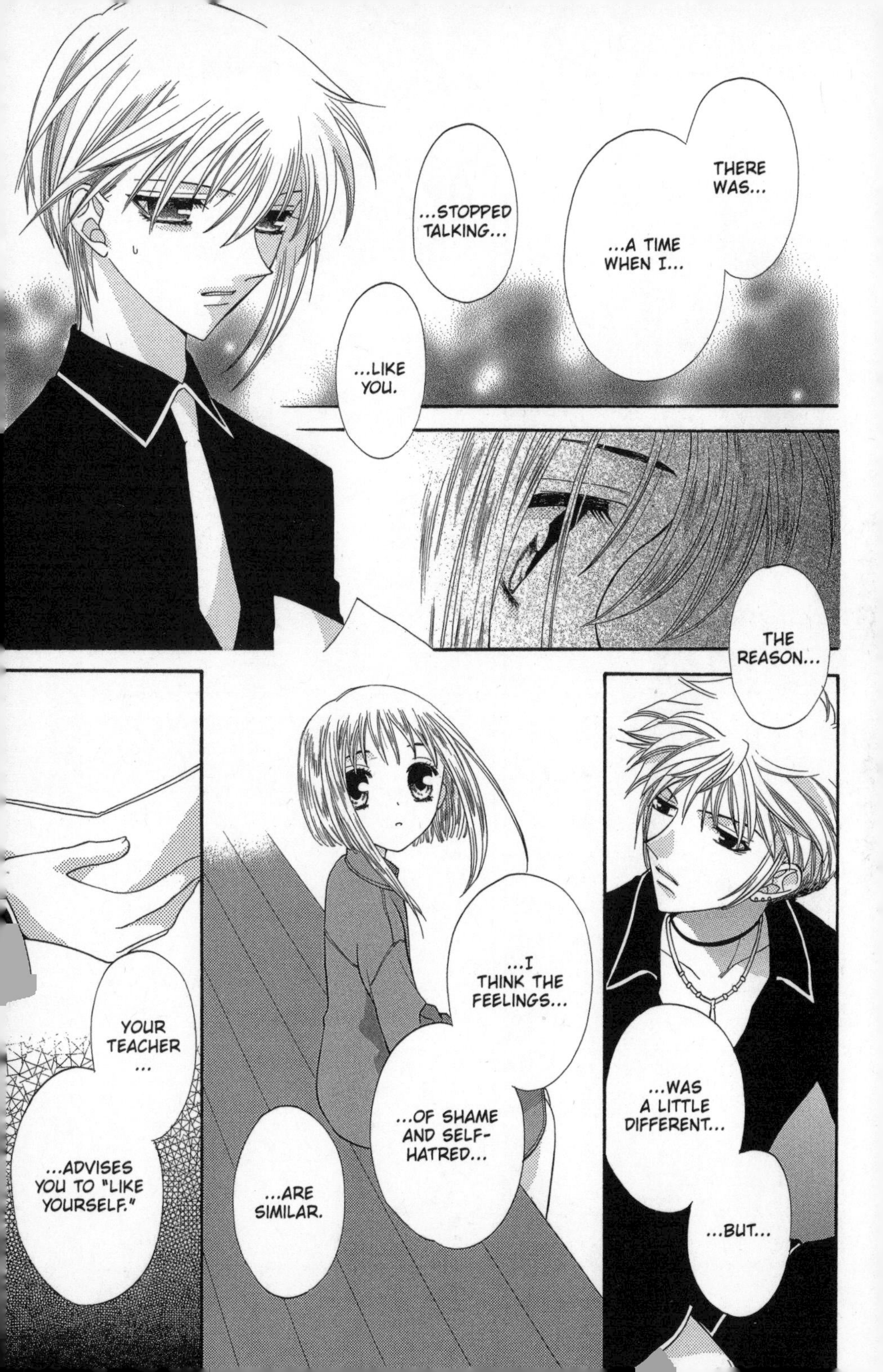
THERE WAS...
...A TIME WHEN I...
...STOPPED TALKING...
...LIKE YOU.
THE REASON...
...WAS A LITTLE DIFFERENT...
...BUT...
...I THINK THE FEELINGS...
...OF SHAME AND SELF-HATRED...
...ARE SIMILAR.
YOUR TEACHER ...
...ADVISES YOU TO "LIKE YOURSELF."

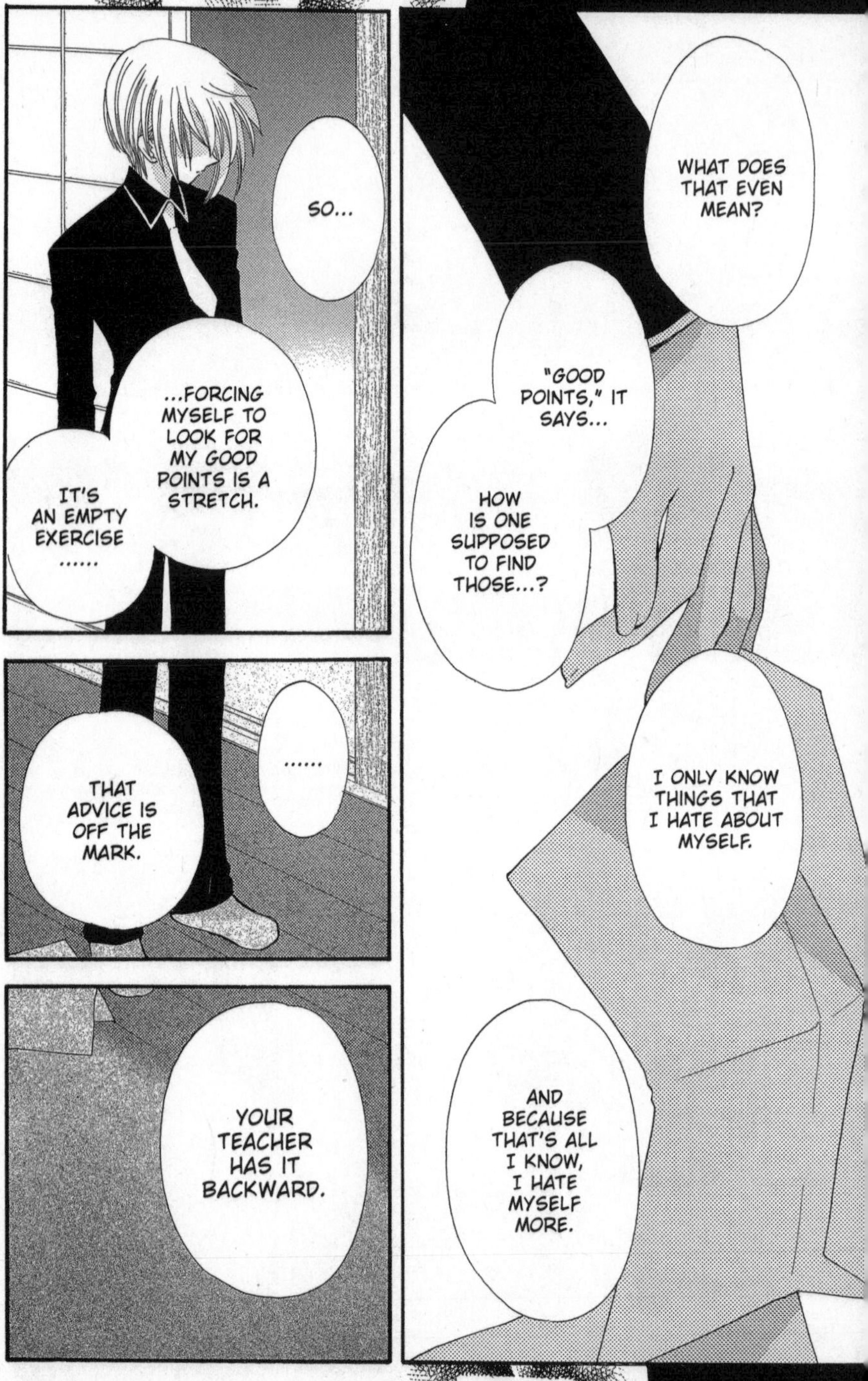
WHAT DOES THAT EVEN MEAN?
"GOOD POINTS," IT SAYS...
HOW IS ONE SUPPOSED TO FIND THOSE...?
I ONLY KNOW THINGS THAT I HATE ABOUT MYSELF.
AND BECAUSE THAT'S ALL I KNOW, I HATE MYSELF MORE.
SO...
...FORCING MYSELF TO LOOK FOR MY GOOD POINTS IS A STRETCH.
IT'S AN EMPTY EXERCISE ......
......
THAT ADVICE IS OFF THE MARK.
YOUR TEACHER HAS IT BACKWARD.

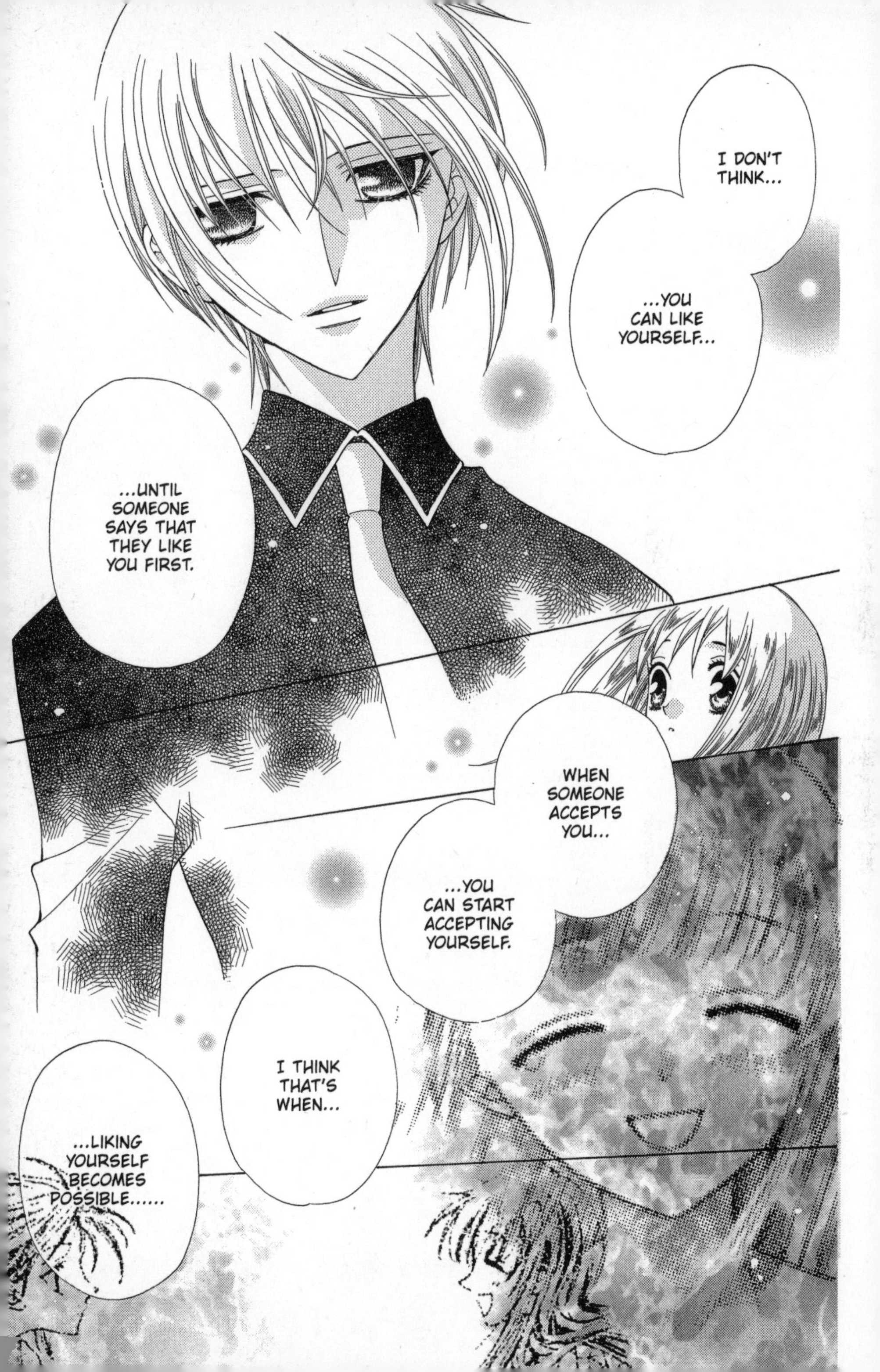
I DON'T THINK...
...YOU CAN LIKE YOURSELF...
...UNTIL SOMEONE SAYS THAT THEY LIKE YOU FIRST.
WHEN SOMEONE ACCEPTS YOU...
...YOU CAN START ACCEPTING YOURSELF.
I THINK THAT'S WHEN...
...LIKING YOURSELF BECOMES POSSIBLE......

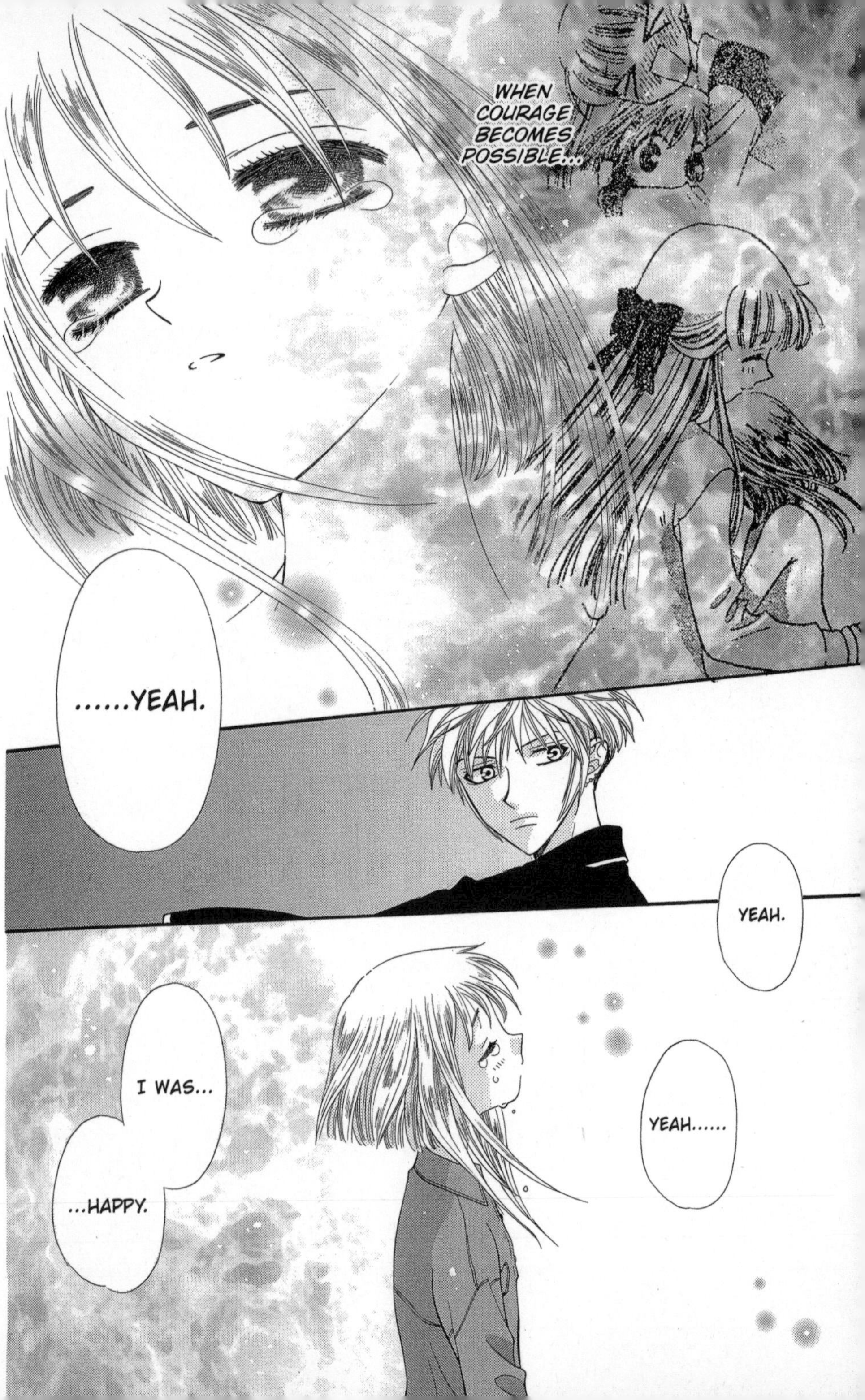
WHEN COURAGE BECOMES POSSIBLE...
......YEAH.
YEAH.
YEAH......
I WAS...
...HAPPY.

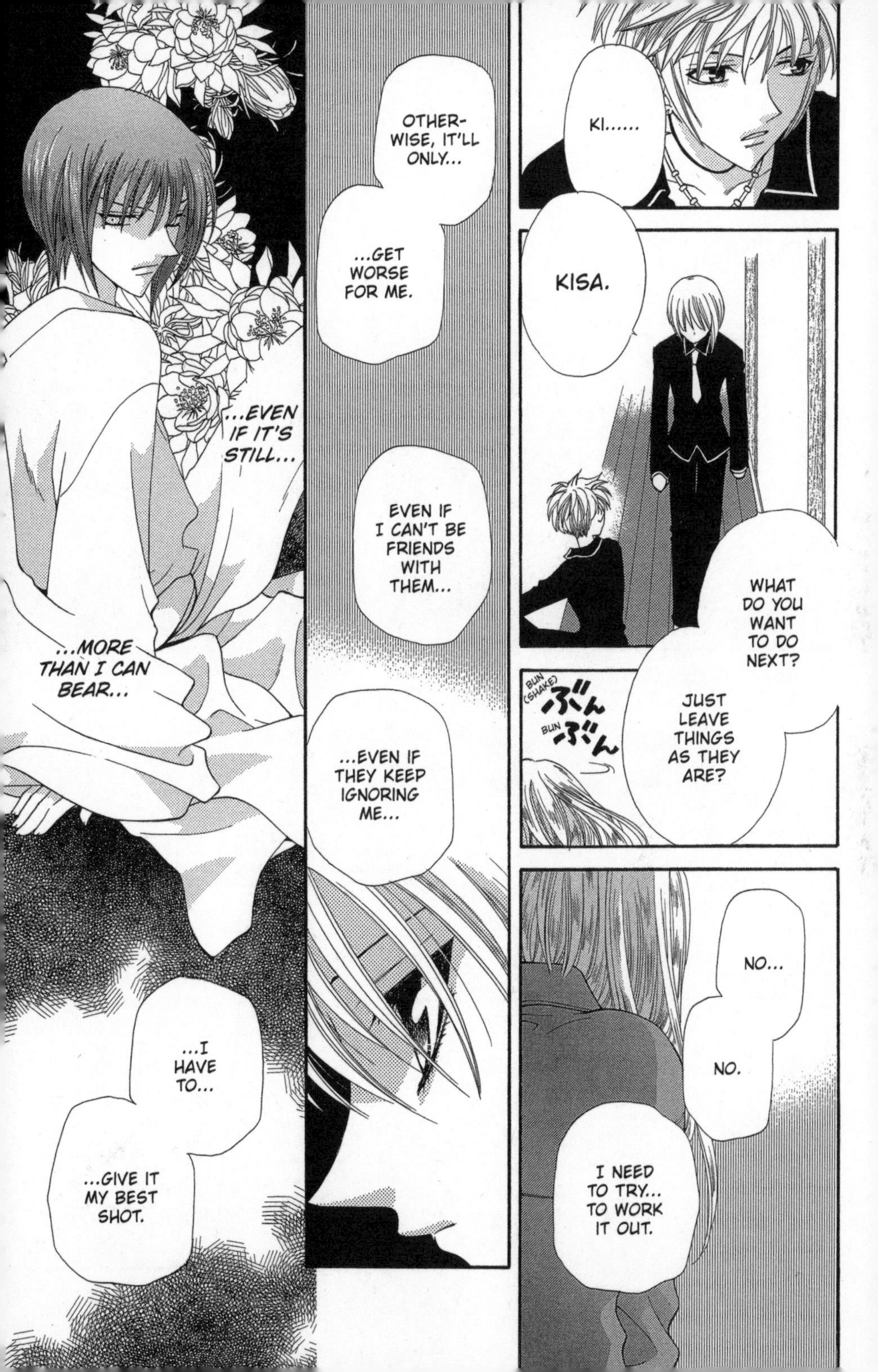
KI......
KISA.
WHAT DO YOU WANT TO DO NEXT?
ぶん BUN (SHAKE)
ぶん BUN
JUST LEAVE THINGS AS THEY ARE?
NO...
NO.
I NEED TO TRY... TO WORK IT OUT.
OTHER-WISE, IT'LL ONLY...
...GET WORSE FOR ME.
EVEN IF I CAN'T BE FRIENDS WITH THEM...
...EVEN IF THEY KEEP IGNORING ME...
...EVEN IF IT'S STILL...
...MORE THAN I CAN BEAR...
...I HAVE TO...
...GIVE IT MY BEST SHOT.

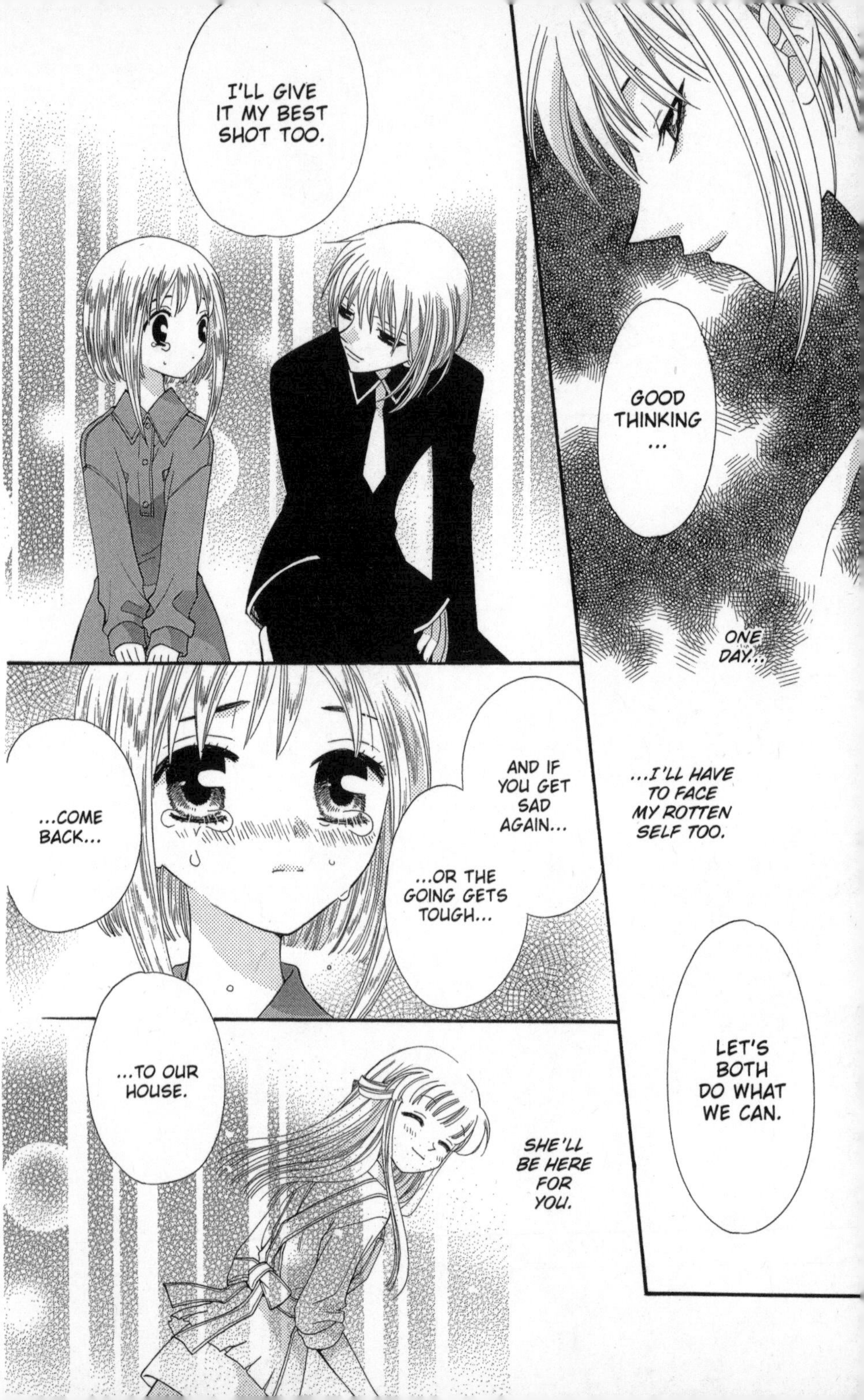
GOOD THINKING ...
ONE DAY...
...I'LL HAVE TO FACE MY ROTTEN SELF TOO.
LET'S BOTH DO WHAT WE CAN.
I'LL GIVE IT MY BEST SHOT TOO.
AND IF YOU GET SAD AGAIN...
...OR THE GOING GETS TOUGH...
...COME BACK...
...TO OUR HOUSE.
SHE'LL BE HERE FOR YOU.

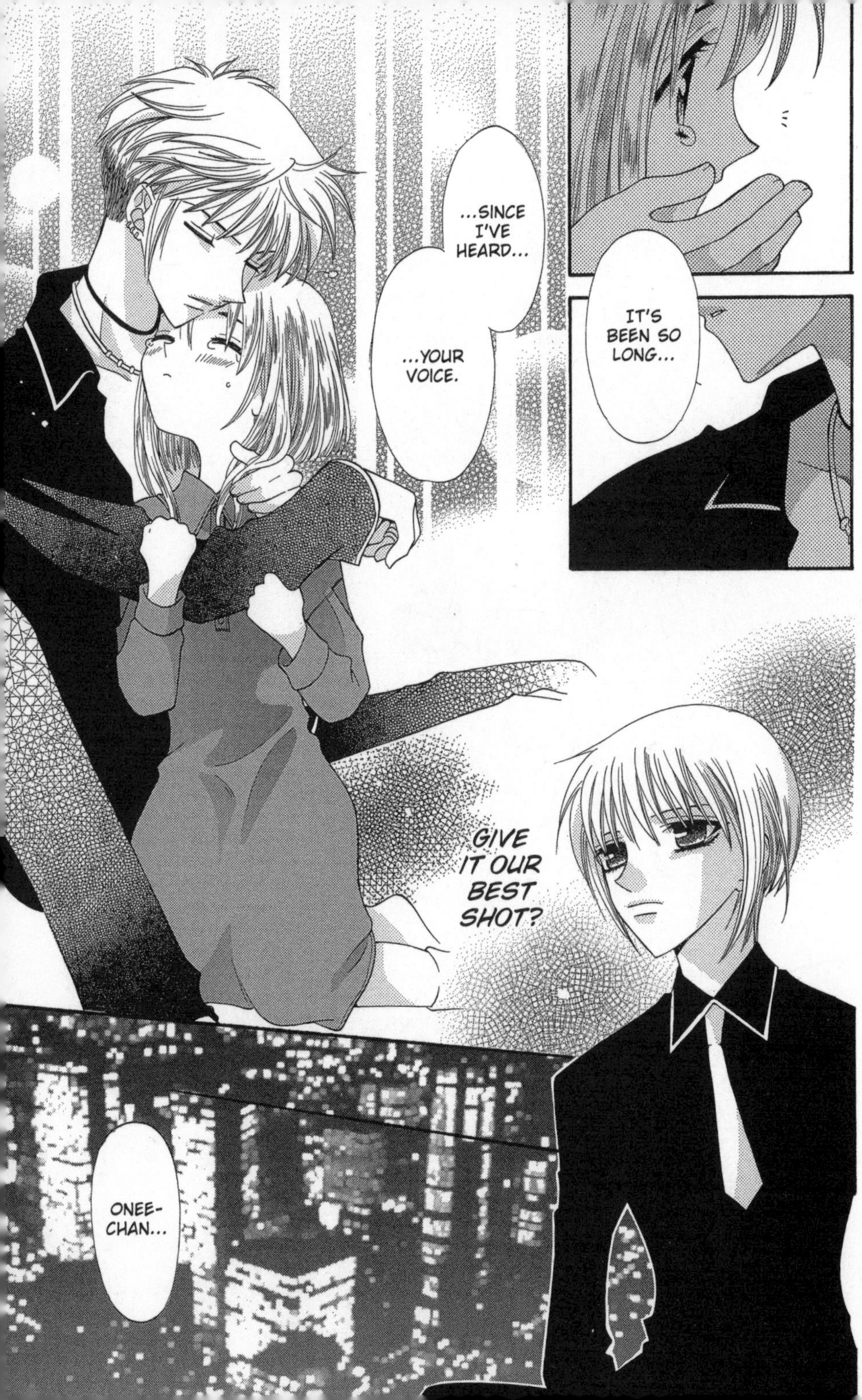
IT'S BEEN SO LONG...
...SINCE I'VE HEARD...
...YOUR VOICE.
GIVE IT OUR BEST SHOT?
ONEE-CHAN...

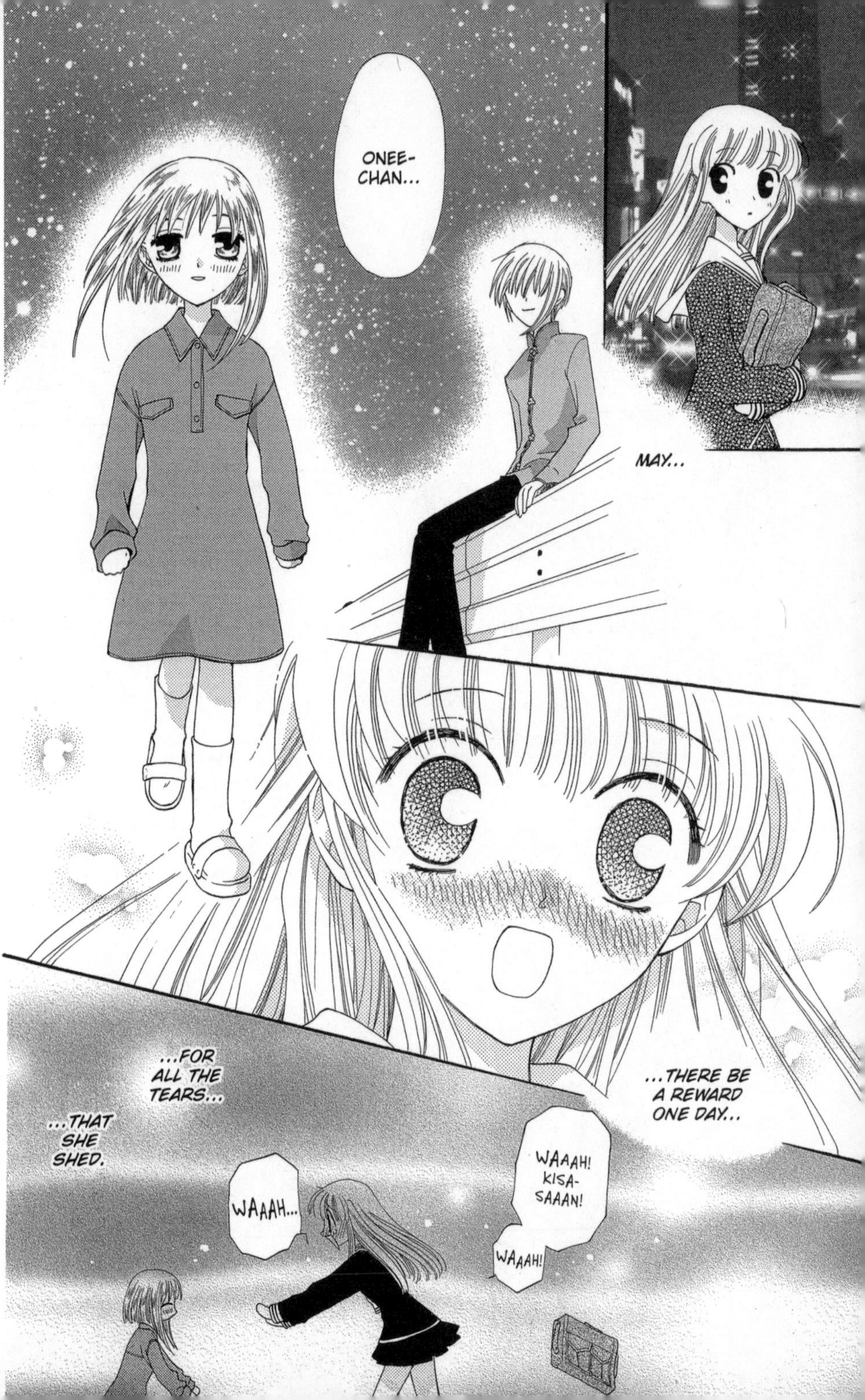
ONEE-CHAN...
MAY...
...THERE BE A REWARD ONE DAY...
...FOR ALL THE TEARS...
...THAT SHE SHED.
WAAAH! KISA-SAAAN!
WAAAH!
WAAAH...

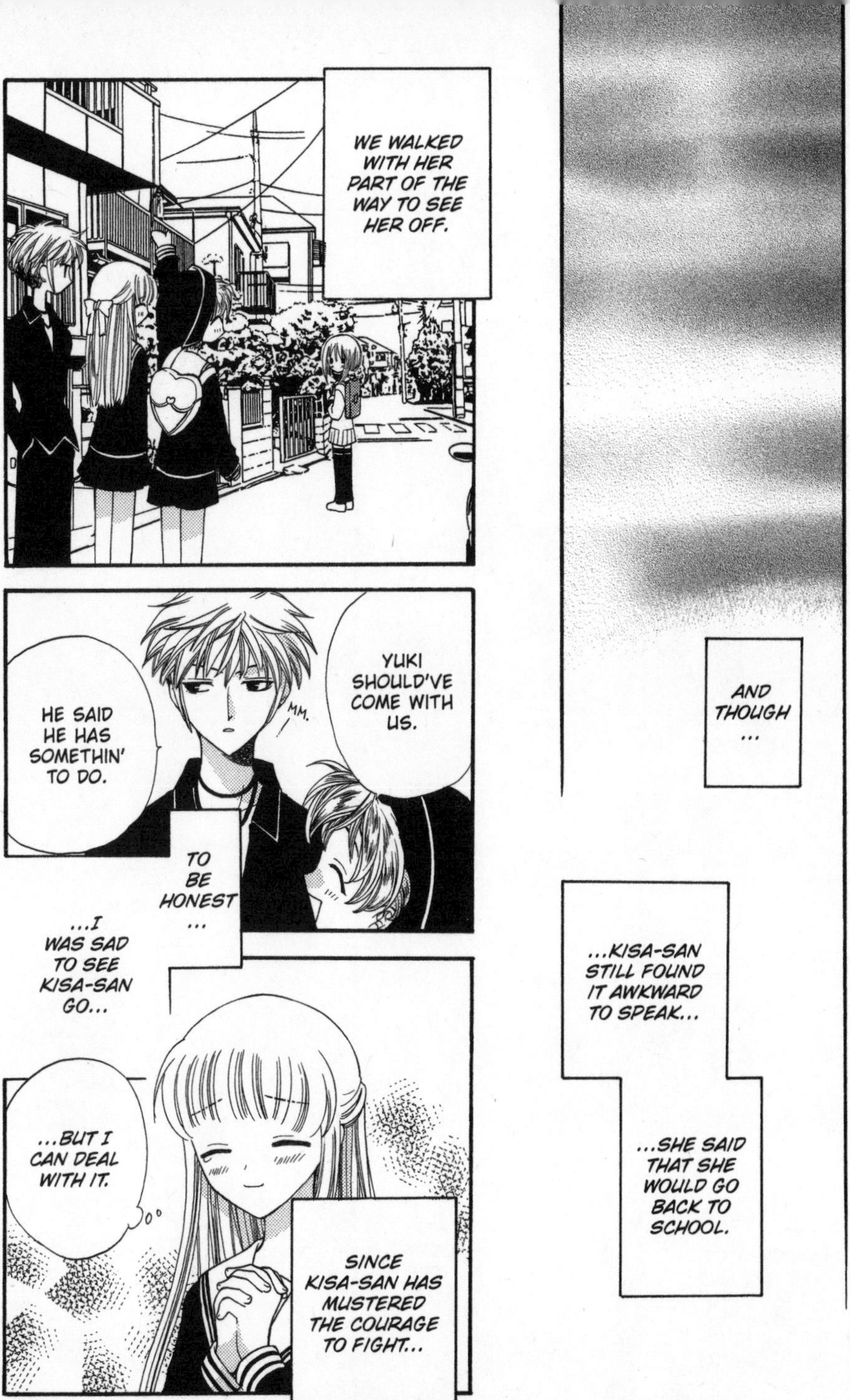
AND THOUGH ...
...KISA-SAN STILL FOUND IT AWKWARD TO SPEAK...
...SHE SAID THAT SHE WOULD GO BACK TO SCHOOL.
WE WALKED WITH HER PART OF THE WAY TO SEE HER OFF.
YUKI SHOULD'VE COME WITH US.
MM.
HE SAID HE HAS SOMETHIN' TO DO.
TO BE HONEST ...
...I WAS SAD TO SEE KISA-SAN GO...
...BUT I CAN DEAL WITH IT.
SINCE KISA-SAN HAS MUSTERED THE COURAGE TO FIGHT...

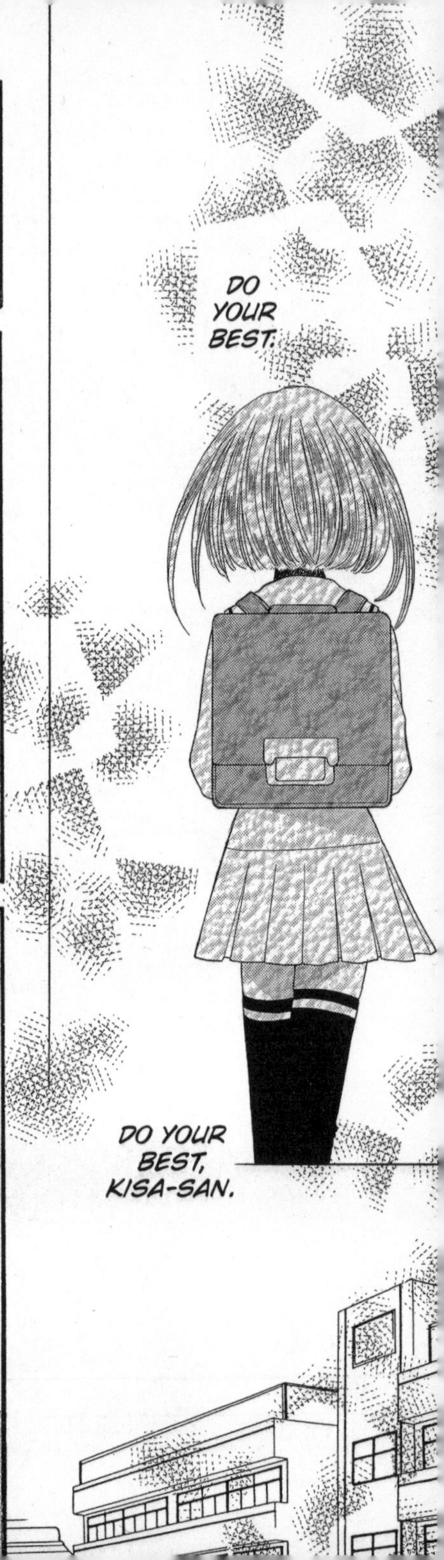
DO YOUR BEST.
DO YOUR BEST, KISA-SAN.

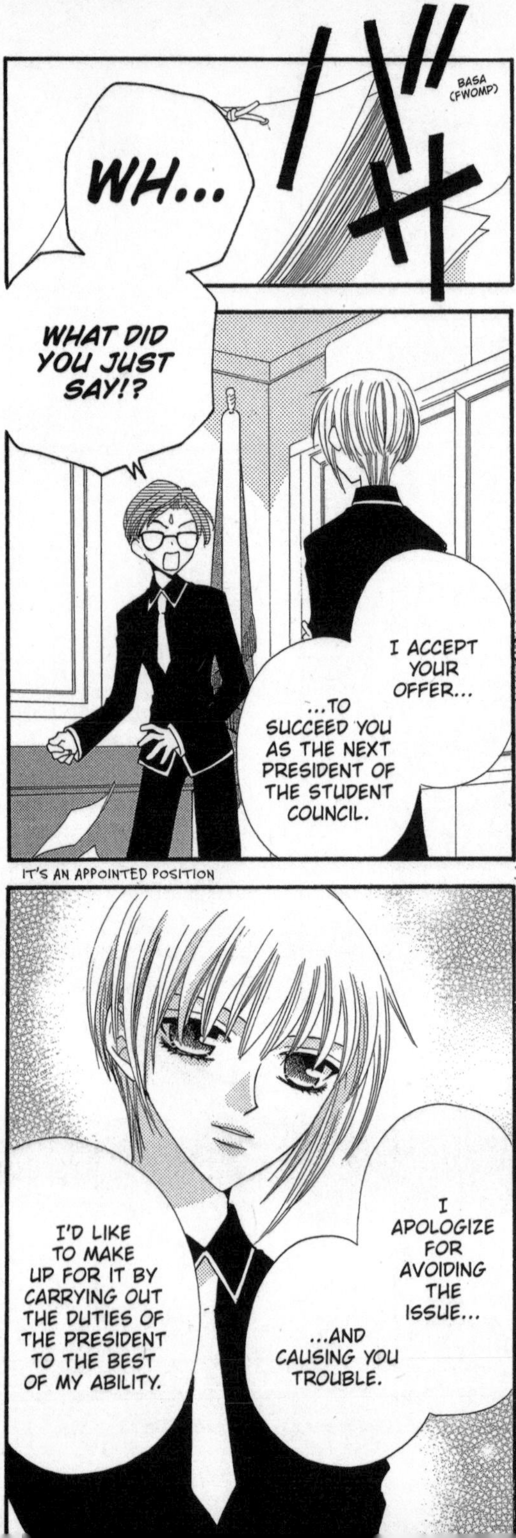
BASA (FWOMP)
WH...
WHAT DID YOU JUST SAY!?
I ACCEPT YOUR OFFER...
...TO SUCCEED YOU AS THE NEXT PRESIDENT OF THE STUDENT COUNCIL.
IT'S AN APPOINTED POSITION
I APOLOGIZE FOR AVOIDING THE ISSUE...
...AND CAUSING YOU TROUBLE.
I'D LIKE TO MAKE UP FOR IT BY CARRYING OUT THE DUTIES OF THE PRESIDENT TO THE BEST OF MY ABILITY.

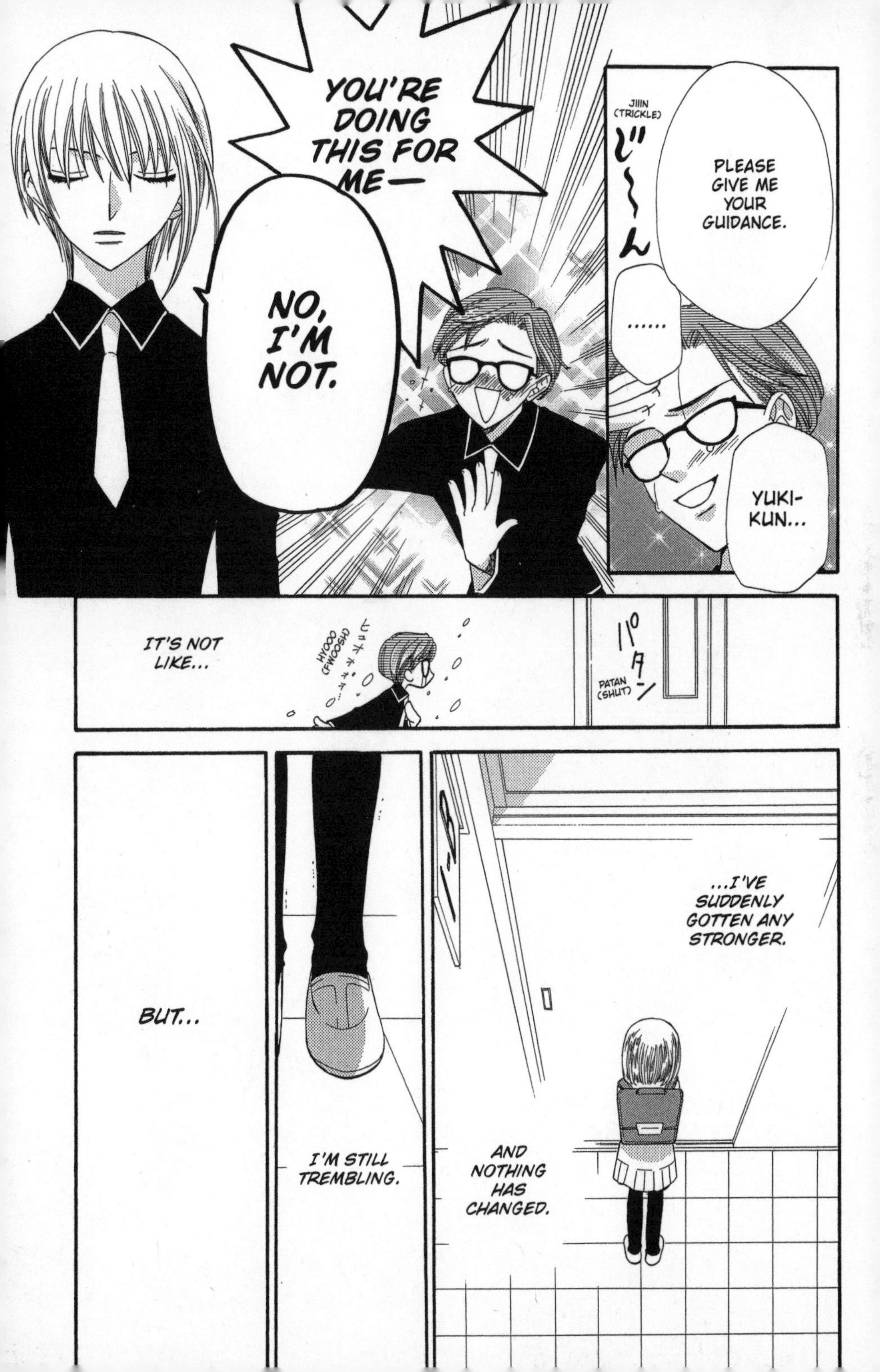
PLEASE GIVE ME YOUR GUIDANCE.
JIIIN (TRICKLE)
......
YUKI-KUN...
YOU'RE DOING THIS FOR ME—
NO, I'M NOT.
PATAN (SHUT)
HYOOO (FWOOSH)
IT'S NOT LIKE...
...I'VE SUDDENLY GOTTEN ANY STRONGER.
AND NOTHING HAS CHANGED.
I'M STILL TREMBLING.
BUT...

...LET'S STILL FACE OUR FEARS.

THE MOST IMPORTANT THING...

...IS THE DESIRE TO OVERCOME OUR WEAKNESSES.

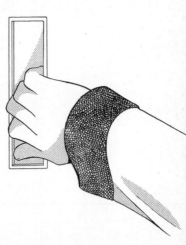

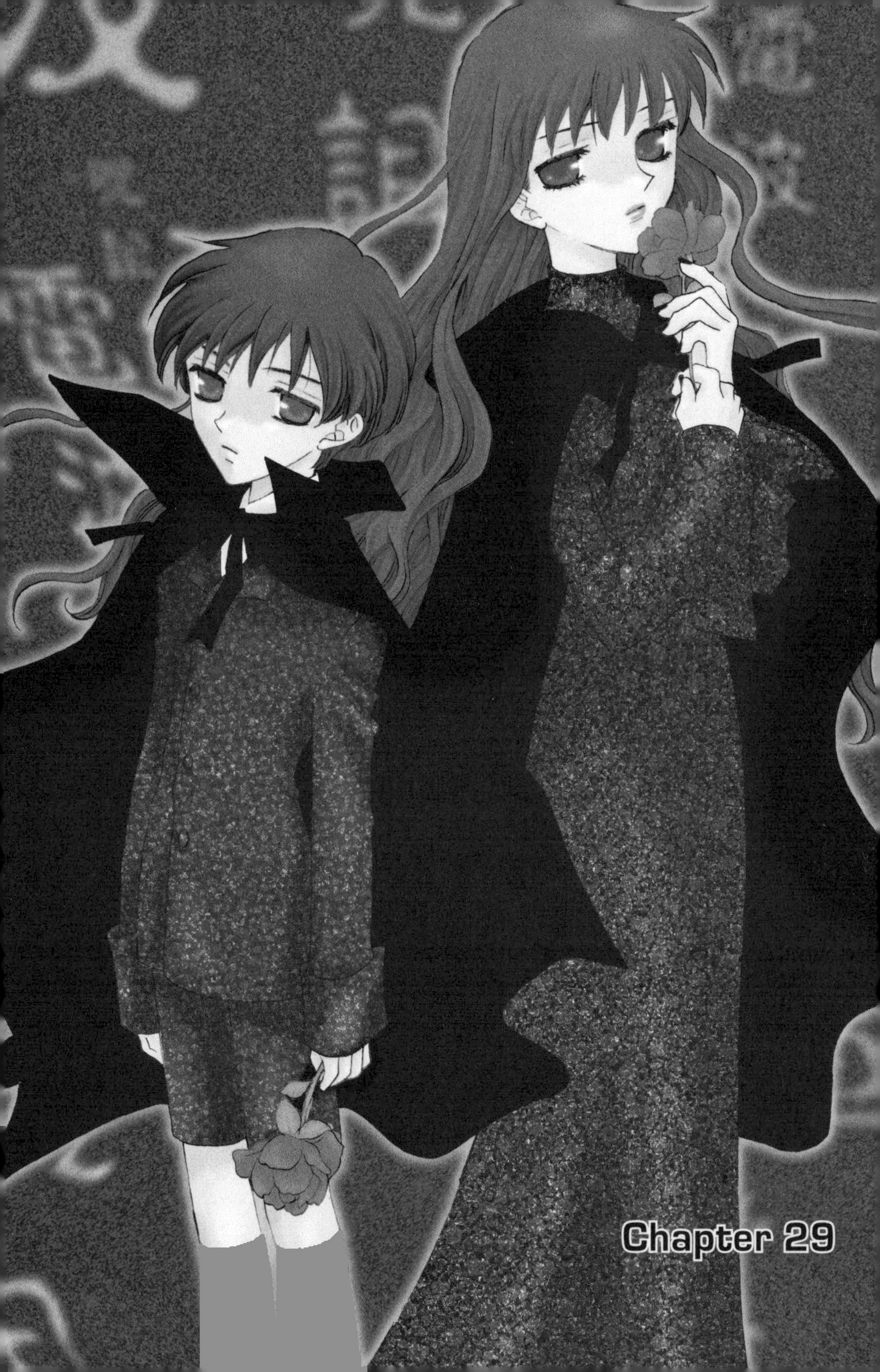

Chapter 29

COLLECTOR'S EDITION

Fruits Basket

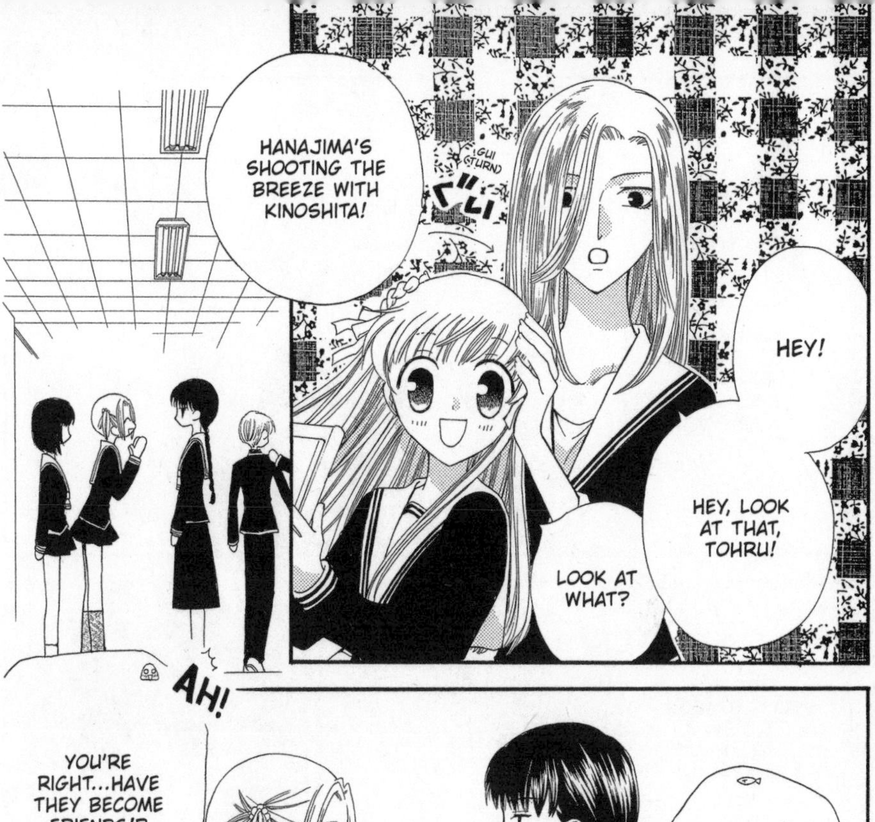
GUI (TURN)
HEY!
HEY, LOOK AT THAT, TOHRU!
LOOK AT WHAT?
HANAJIMA'S SHOOTING THE BREEZE WITH KINOSHITA!
AH!
YOU'RE RIGHT...HAVE THEY BECOME FRIENDS!?
NO WAY—HANAJIMA HATES HER TYPE.

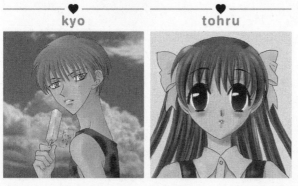

kyo

tohru

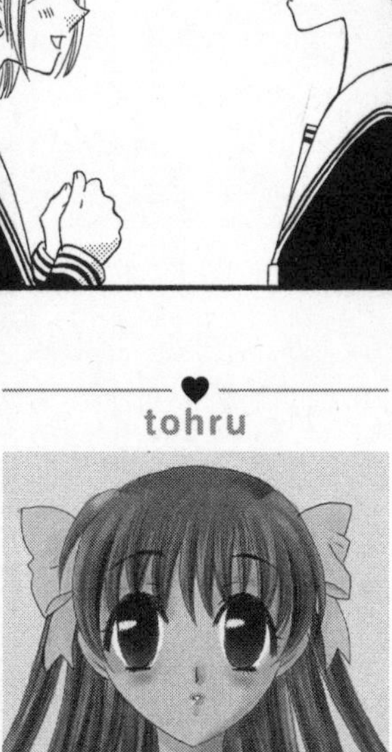

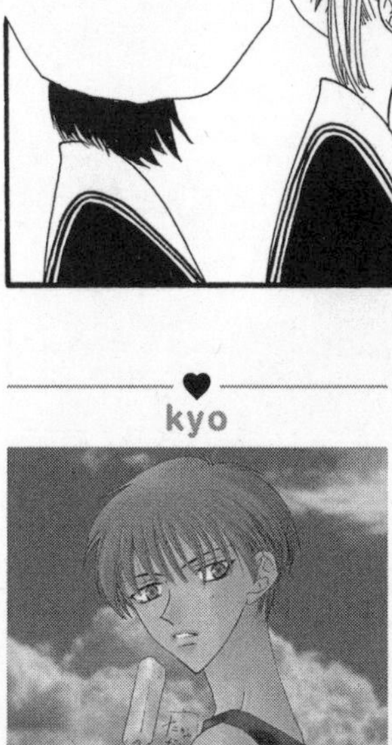

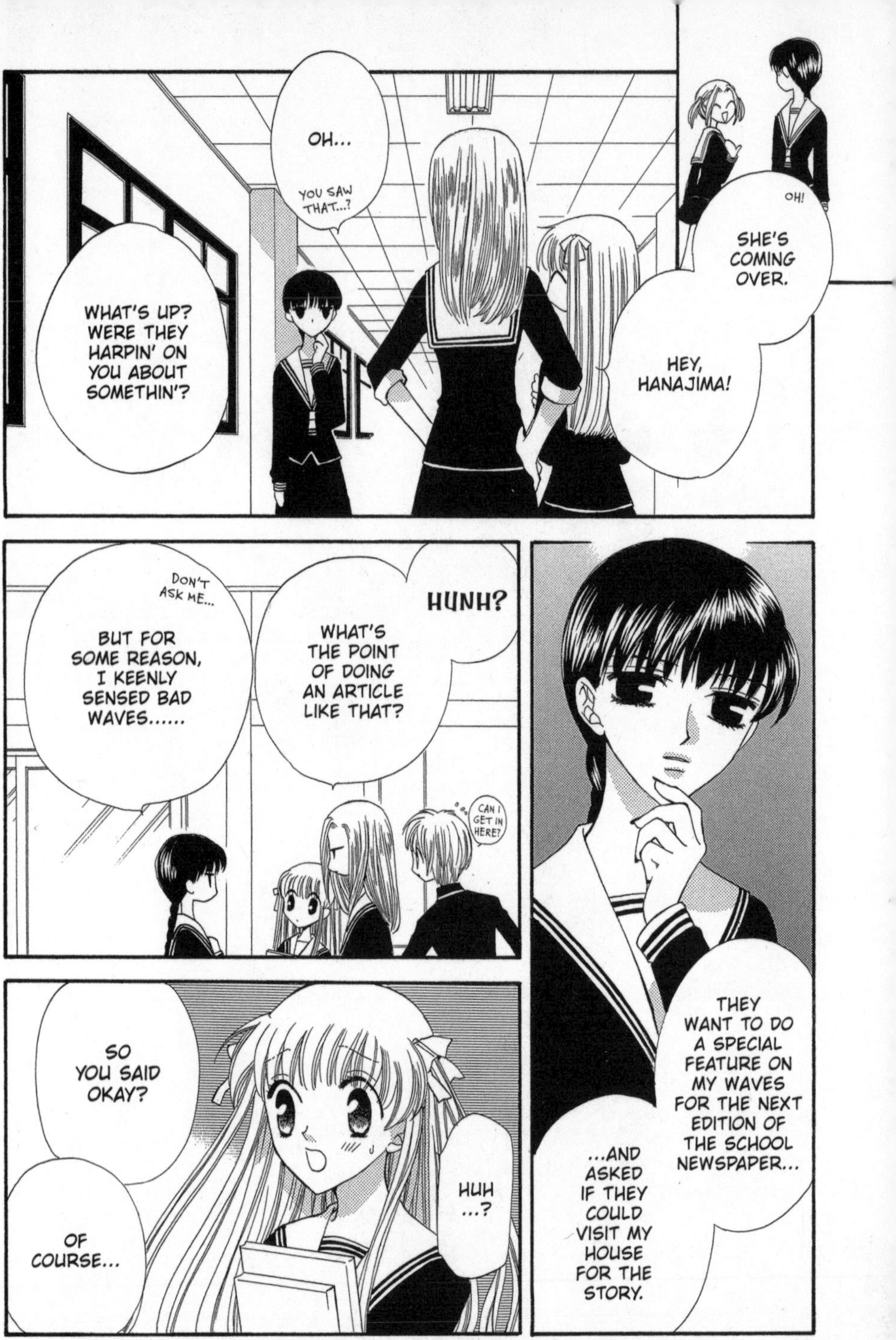
OH!
SHE'S COMING OVER.
HEY, HANAJIMA!
OH...
YOU SAW THAT...?
WHAT'S UP? WERE THEY HARPIN' ON YOU ABOUT SOMETHIN'?
THEY WANT TO DO A SPECIAL FEATURE ON MY WAVES FOR THE NEXT EDITION OF THE SCHOOL NEWSPAPER...
...AND ASKED IF THEY COULD VISIT MY HOUSE FOR THE STORY.
HUNH?
WHAT'S THE POINT OF DOING AN ARTICLE LIKE THAT?
CAN I GET IN HERE?
DON'T ASK ME...
BUT FOR SOME REASON, I KEENLY SENSED BAD WAVES......
HUH ...?
SO YOU SAID OKAY?
OF COURSE...

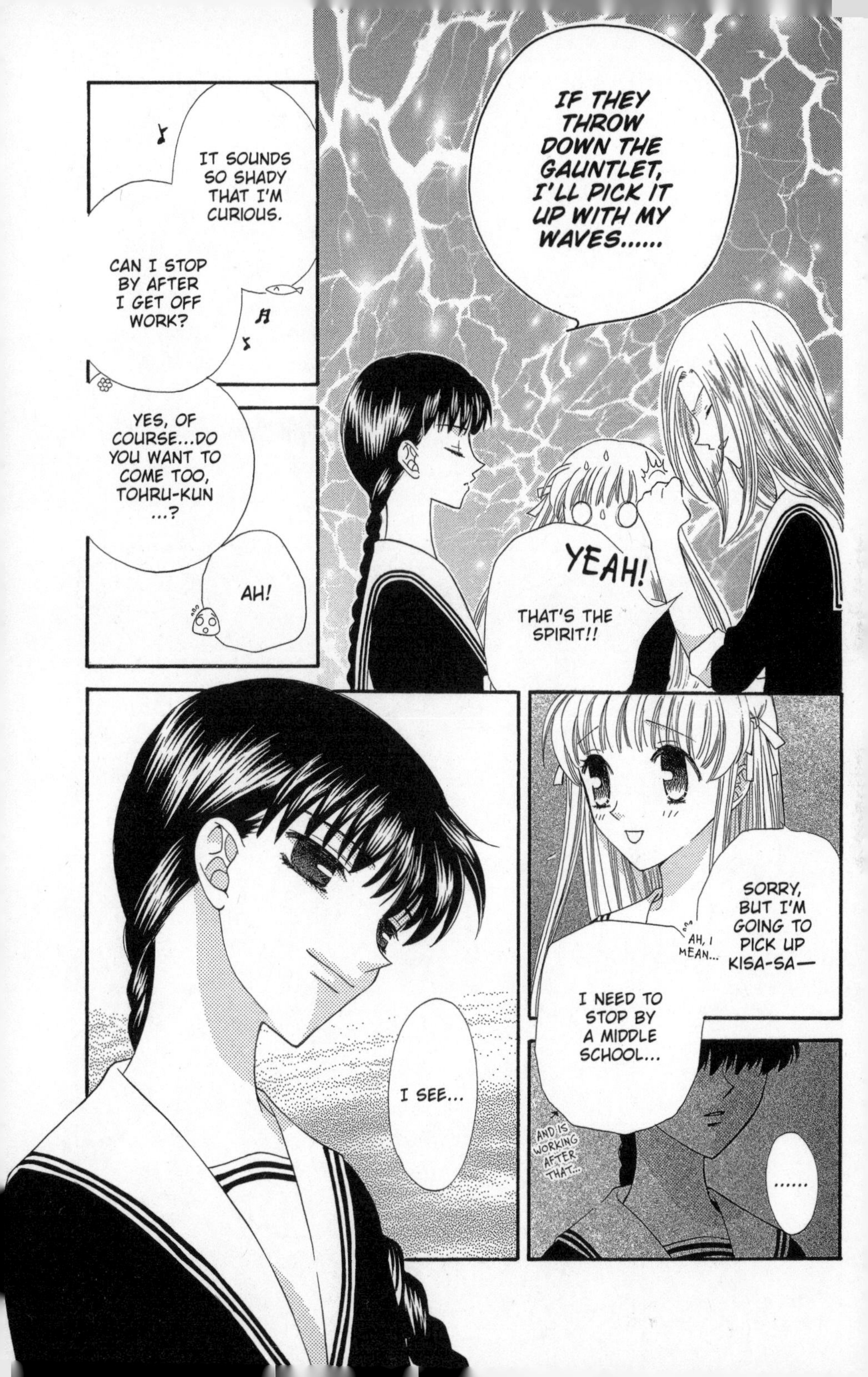
IF THEY THROW DOWN THE GAUNTLET, I'LL PICK IT UP WITH MY WAVES......
YEAH!
THAT'S THE SPIRIT!!
IT SOUNDS SO SHADY THAT I'M CURIOUS.
CAN I STOP BY AFTER I GET OFF WORK?
YES, OF COURSE...DO YOU WANT TO COME TOO, TOHRU-KUN...?
AH!
SORRY, BUT I'M GOING TO PICK UP KISA-SA—
AH, I MEAN...
I NEED TO STOP BY A MIDDLE SCHOOL...
......
AND IS WORKING AFTER THAT...
I SEE...

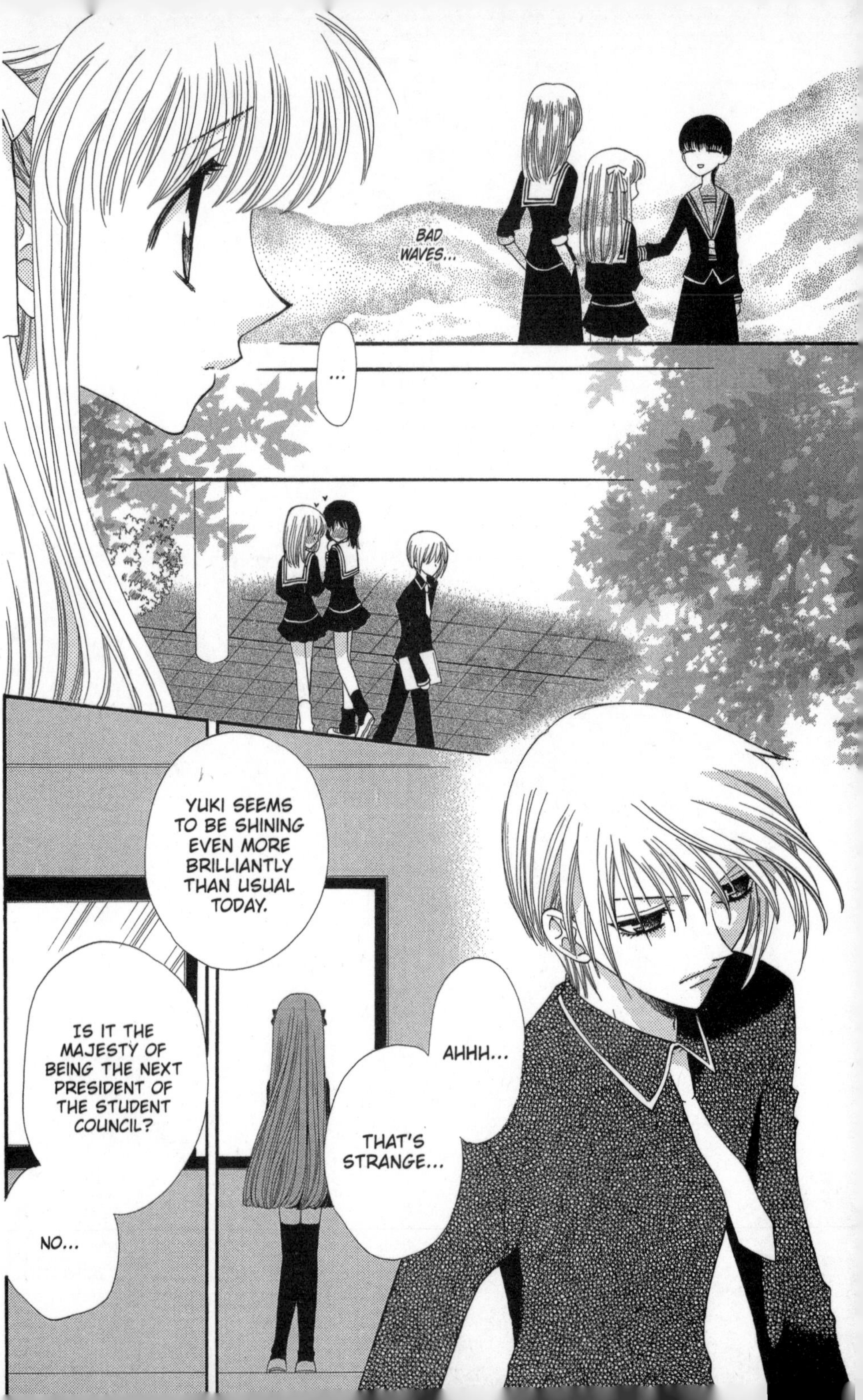
BAD WAVES...
...
YUKI SEEMS TO BE SHINING EVEN MORE BRILLIANTLY THAN USUAL TODAY.
AHHH...
THAT'S STRANGE...
IS IT THE MAJESTY OF BEING THE NEXT PRESIDENT OF THE STUDENT COUNCIL?
NO...

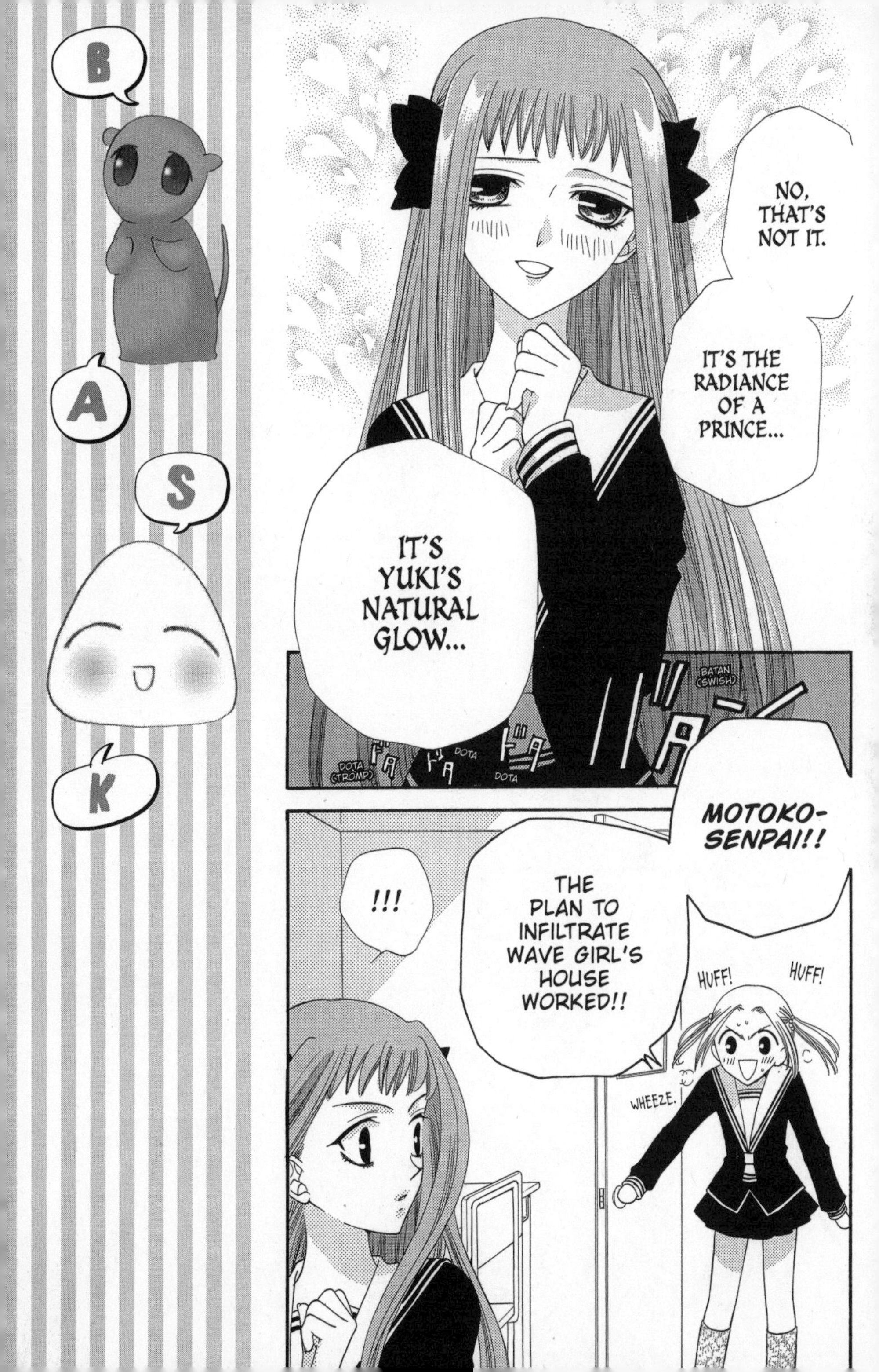
NO, THAT'S NOT IT.
IT'S THE RADIANCE OF A PRINCE...
IT'S YUKI'S NATURAL GLOW...
BATAN (SWISH)
DOTA
DOTA
DOTA
DOTA (TROMP)
MOTOKO-SENPAI!!
THE PLAN TO INFILTRATE WAVE GIRL'S HOUSE WORKED!!
HUFF!
HUFF!
WHEEZE.
!!!
B
A
S
K

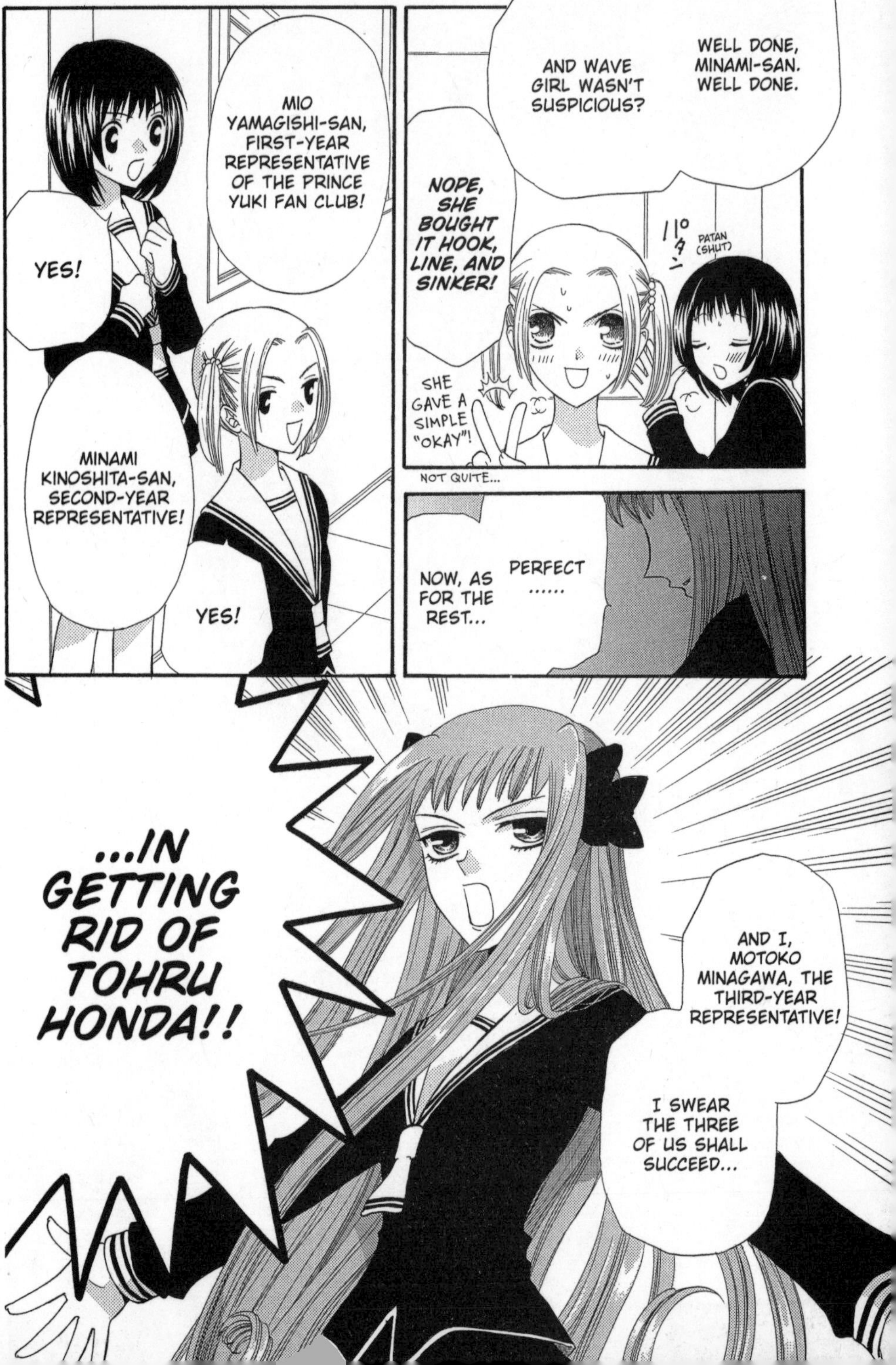
WELL DONE, MINAMI-SAN. WELL DONE.
AND WAVE GIRL WASN'T SUSPICIOUS?
NOPE, SHE BOUGHT IT HOOK, LINE, AND SINKER!
PATAN (SHUT)
SHE GAVE A SIMPLE "OKAY"!
NOT QUITE...
PERFECT ......
NOW, AS FOR THE REST...
MIO YAMAGISHI-SAN, FIRST-YEAR REPRESENTATIVE OF THE PRINCE YUKI FAN CLUB!
YES!
MINAMI KINOSHITA-SAN, SECOND-YEAR REPRESENTATIVE!
YES!
AND I, MOTOKO MINAGAWA, THE THIRD-YEAR REPRESENTATIVE!
I SWEAR THE THREE OF US SHALL SUCCEED...
...IN GETTING RID OF TOHRU HONDA!!

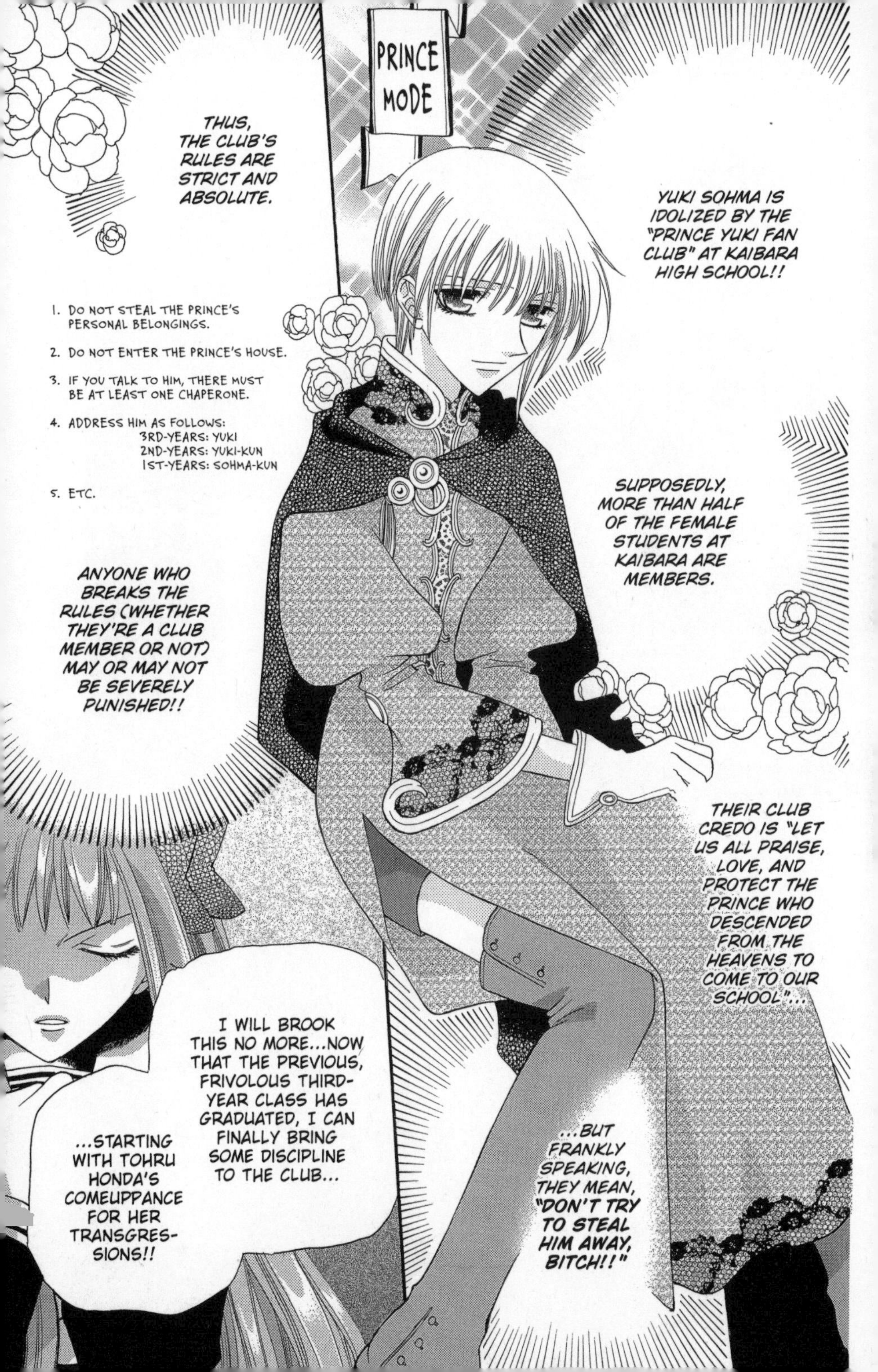
PRINCE MODE
YUKI SOHMA IS IDOLIZED BY THE "PRINCE YUKI FAN CLUB" AT KAIBARA HIGH SCHOOL!!
THUS, THE CLUB'S RULES ARE STRICT AND ABSOLUTE.
1. DO NOT STEAL THE PRINCE'S PERSONAL BELONGINGS.
2. DO NOT ENTER THE PRINCE'S HOUSE.
3. IF YOU TALK TO HIM, THERE MUST BE AT LEAST ONE CHAPERONE.
4. ADDRESS HIM AS FOLLOWS:
3RD-YEARS: YUKI
2ND-YEARS: YUKI-KUN
1ST-YEARS: SOHMA-KUN
5. ETC.
SUPPOSEDLY, MORE THAN HALF OF THE FEMALE STUDENTS AT KAIBARA ARE MEMBERS.
ANYONE WHO BREAKS THE RULES (WHETHER THEY'RE A CLUB MEMBER OR NOT) MAY OR MAY NOT BE SEVERELY PUNISHED!!
THEIR CLUB CREDO IS "LET US ALL PRAISE, LOVE, AND PROTECT THE PRINCE WHO DESCENDED FROM THE HEAVENS TO COME TO OUR SCHOOL"...
...BUT FRANKLY SPEAKING, THEY MEAN, "DON'T TRY TO STEAL HIM AWAY, BITCH!!"
I WILL BROOK THIS NO MORE...NOW THAT THE PREVIOUS, FRIVOLOUS THIRD-YEAR CLASS HAS GRADUATED, I CAN FINALLY BRING SOME DISCIPLINE TO THE CLUB...
...STARTING WITH TOHRU HONDA'S COMEUPPANCE FOR HER TRANSGRES-SIONS!!

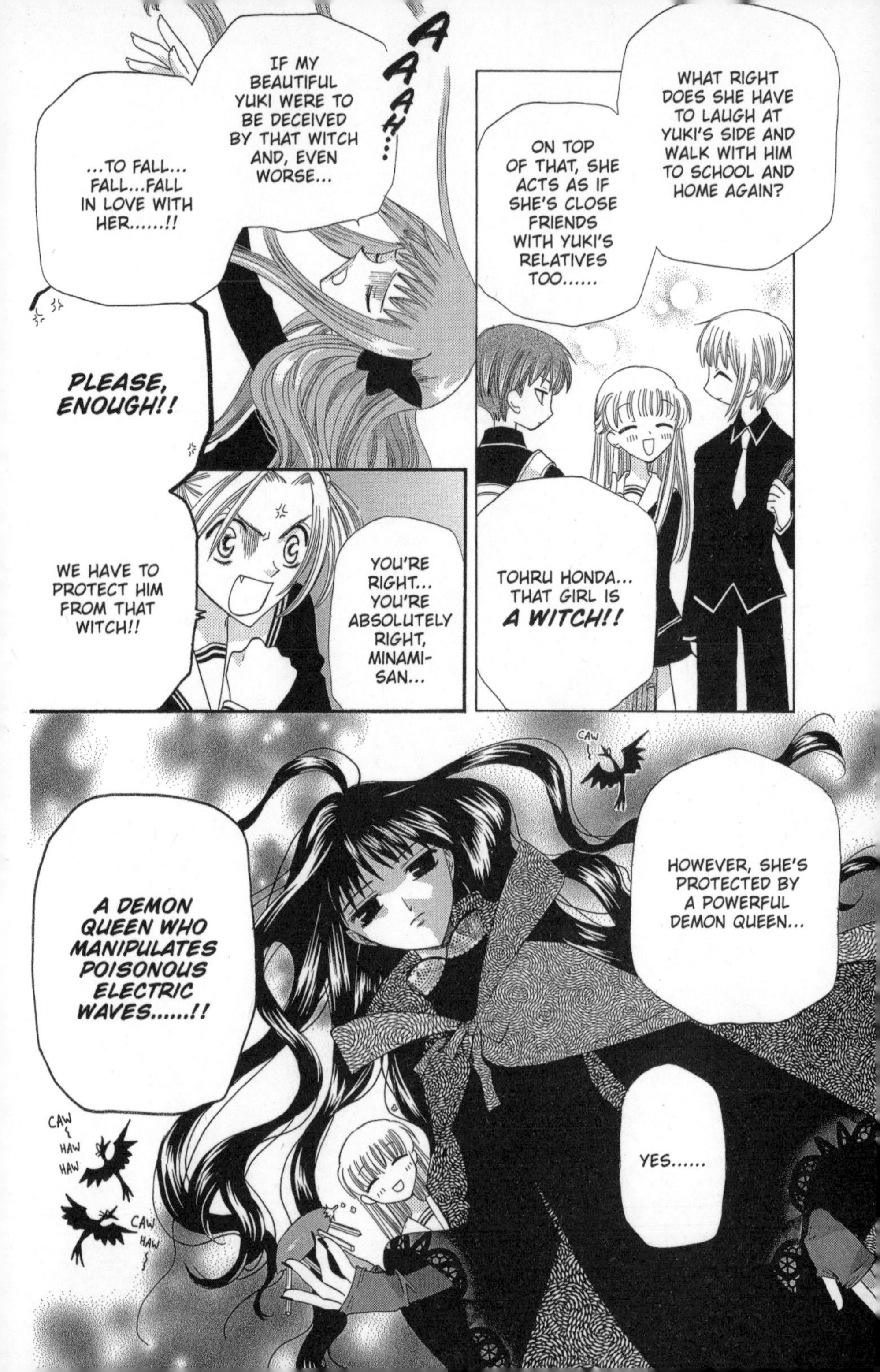
WHAT RIGHT DOES SHE HAVE TO LAUGH AT YUKI'S SIDE AND WALK WITH HIM TO SCHOOL AND HOME AGAIN?
ON TOP OF THAT, SHE ACTS AS IF SHE'S CLOSE FRIENDS WITH YUKI'S RELATIVES TOO......
TOHRU HONDA... THAT GIRL IS A WITCH!!
IF MY BEAUTIFUL YUKI WERE TO BE DECEIVED BY THAT WITCH AND, EVEN WORSE...
AAAAH...
...TO FALL... FALL...FALL IN LOVE WITH HER......!!
PLEASE, ENOUGH!!
YOU'RE RIGHT... YOU'RE ABSOLUTELY RIGHT, MINAMI-SAN...
WE HAVE TO PROTECT HIM FROM THAT WITCH!!
CAW
HOWEVER, SHE'S PROTECTED BY A POWERFUL DEMON QUEEN...
YES......
A DEMON QUEEN WHO MANIPULATES POISONOUS ELECTRIC WAVES......!!
CAW HAW HAW
CAW HAW

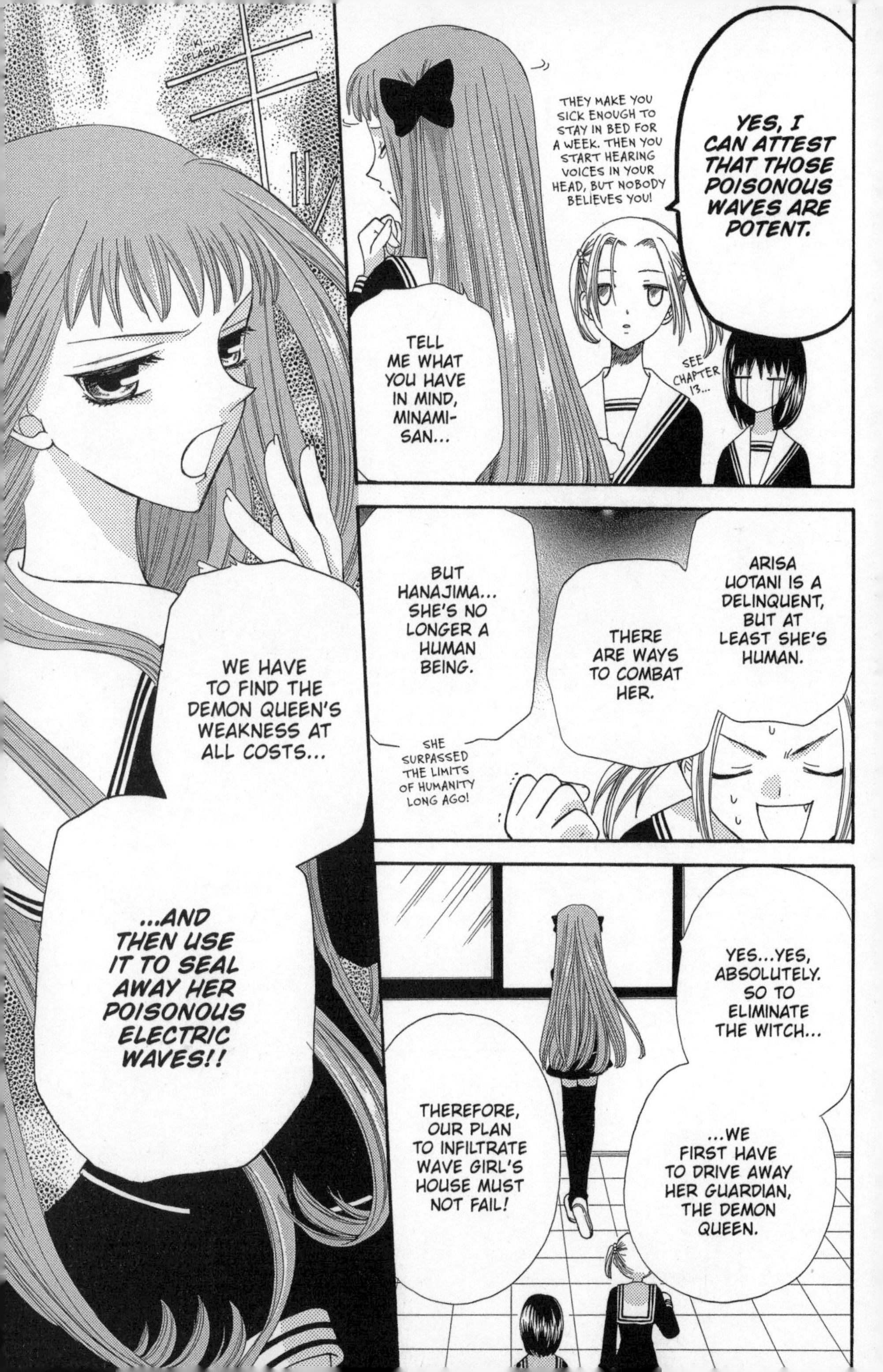

YES, I CAN ATTEST THAT THOSE POISONOUS WAVES ARE POTENT.
THEY MAKE YOU SICK ENOUGH TO STAY IN BED FOR A WEEK. THEN YOU START HEARING VOICES IN YOUR HEAD, BUT NOBODY BELIEVES YOU!
SEE CHAPTER 13...
TELL ME WHAT YOU HAVE IN MIND, MINAMI-SAN...
ARISA UOTANI IS A DELINQUENT, BUT AT LEAST SHE'S HUMAN.
THERE ARE WAYS TO COMBAT HER.
BUT HANAJIMA... SHE'S NO LONGER A HUMAN BEING.
SHE SURPASSED THE LIMITS OF HUMANITY LONG AGO!
YES...YES, ABSOLUTELY. SO TO ELIMINATE THE WITCH...
...WE FIRST HAVE TO DRIVE AWAY HER GUARDIAN, THE DEMON QUEEN.
THEREFORE, OUR PLAN TO INFILTRATE WAVE GIRL'S HOUSE MUST NOT FAIL!
KI (FLASH)
WE HAVE TO FIND THE DEMON QUEEN'S WEAKNESS AT ALL COSTS...
...AND THEN USE IT TO SEAL AWAY HER POISONOUS ELECTRIC WAVES!!

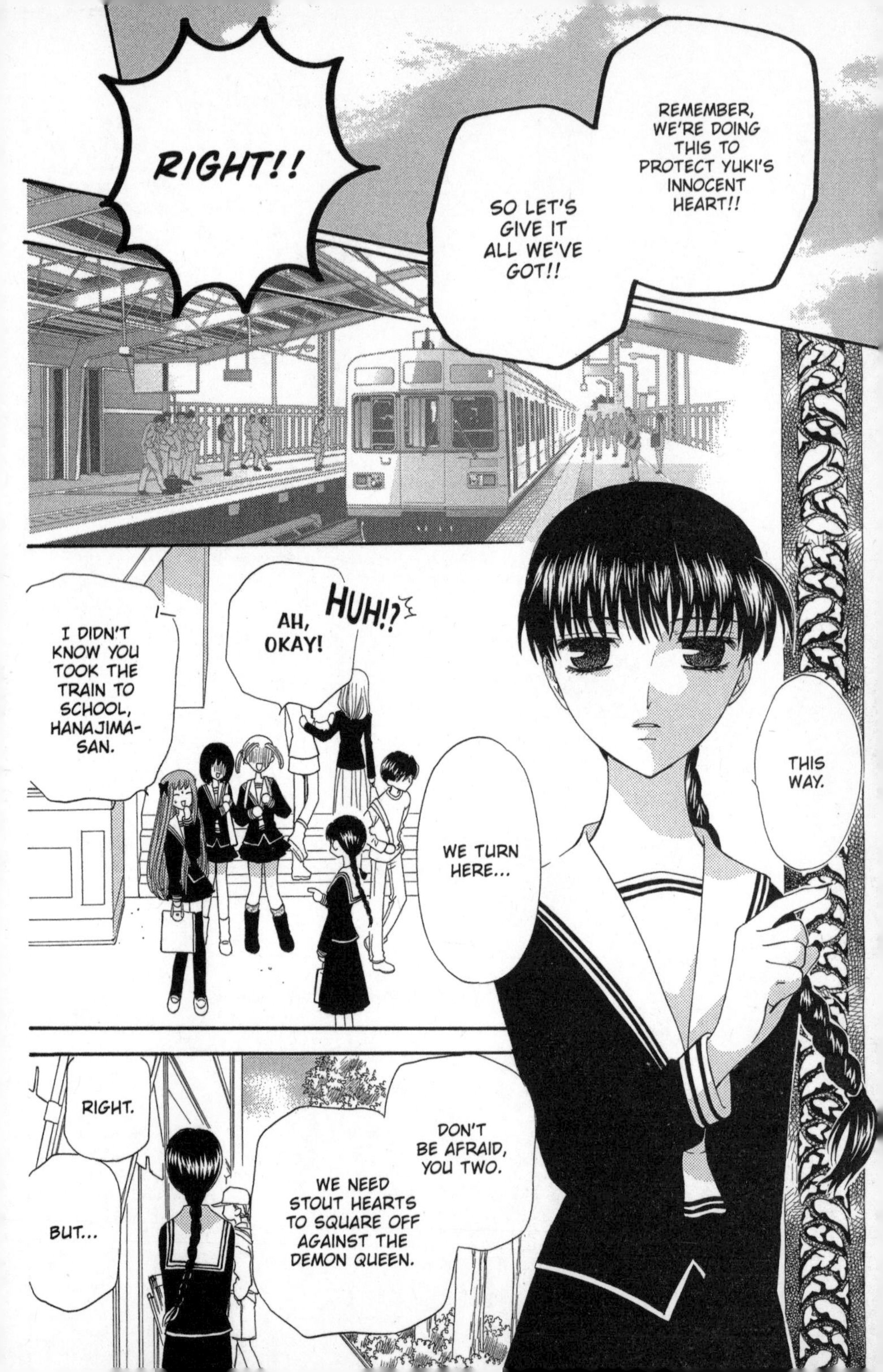
REMEMBER, WE'RE DOING THIS TO PROTECT YUKI'S INNOCENT HEART!!
SO LET'S GIVE IT ALL WE'VE GOT!!
RIGHT!!
THIS WAY.
WE TURN HERE...
HUH!?
AH, OKAY!
I DIDN'T KNOW YOU TOOK THE TRAIN TO SCHOOL, HANAJIMA-SAN.
DON'T BE AFRAID, YOU TWO.
WE NEED STOUT HEARTS TO SQUARE OFF AGAINST THE DEMON QUEEN.
RIGHT.
BUT...

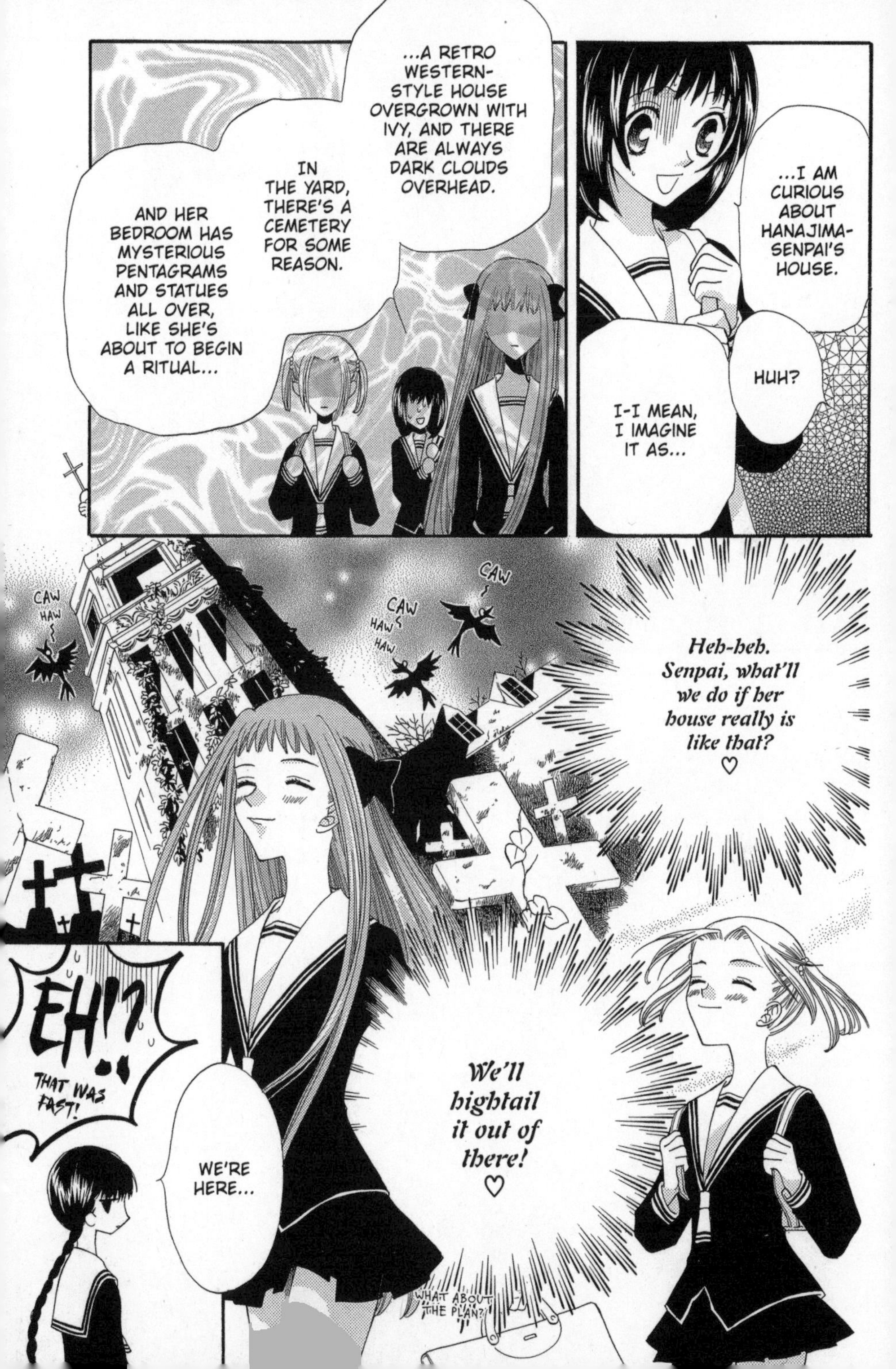
...I AM CURIOUS ABOUT HANAJIMA-SENPAI'S HOUSE.
HUH?
I-I MEAN, I IMAGINE IT AS...
...A RETRO WESTERN-STYLE HOUSE OVERGROWN WITH IVY, AND THERE ARE ALWAYS DARK CLOUDS OVERHEAD.
IN THE YARD, THERE'S A CEMETERY FOR SOME REASON.
AND HER BEDROOM HAS MYSTERIOUS PENTAGRAMS AND STATUES ALL OVER, LIKE SHE'S ABOUT TO BEGIN A RITUAL...
CAW
CAW HAW HAW
CAW HAW
Heh-heh. Senpai, what'll we do if her house really is like that? ♡
We'll hightail it out of there! ♡
WHAT ABOUT THE PLAN?
WE'RE HERE...
EH!?
THAT WAS FAST!

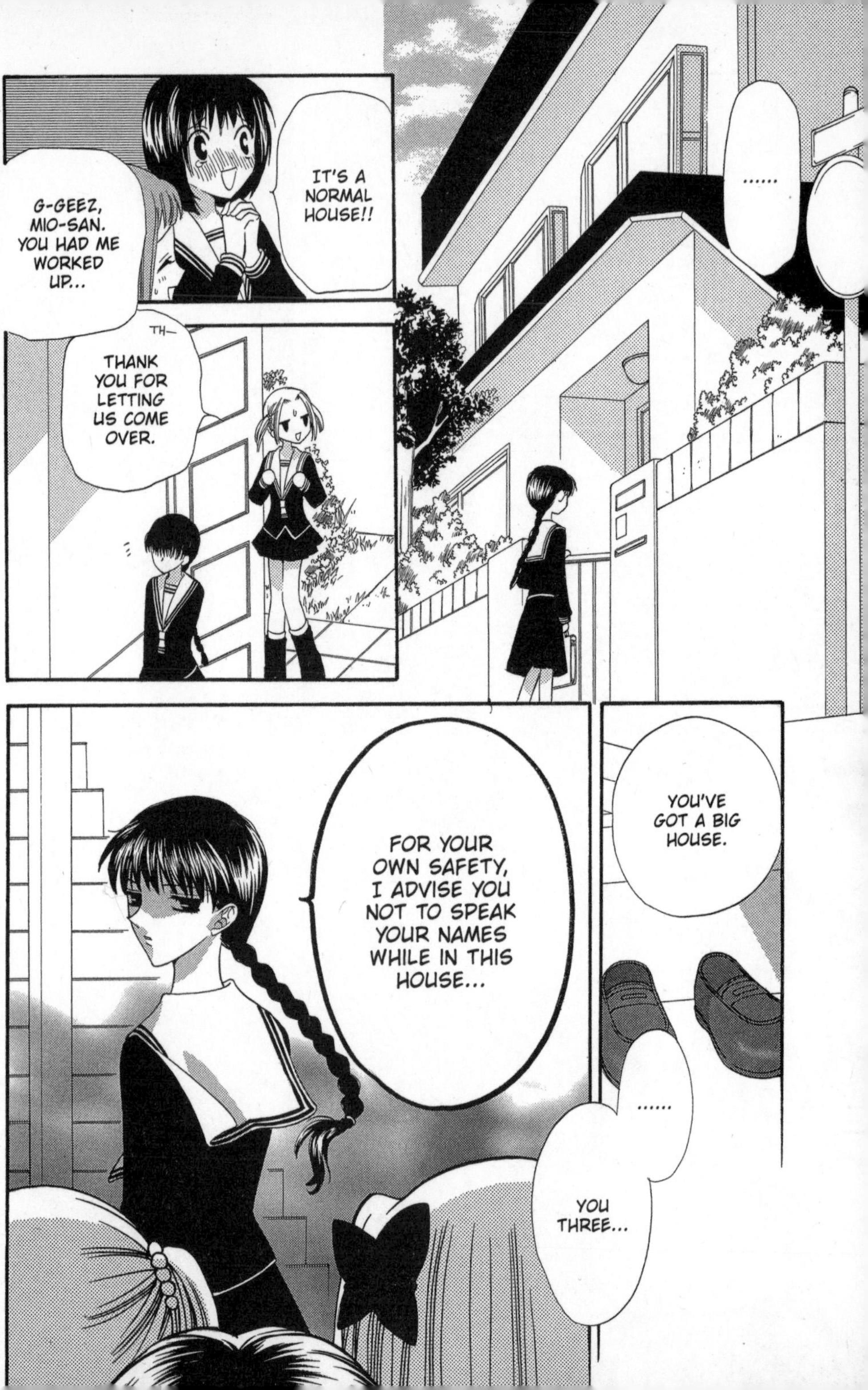
......
IT'S A NORMAL HOUSE!!
G-GEEZ, MIO-SAN. YOU HAD ME WORKED UP...
TH—
THANK YOU FOR LETTING US COME OVER.
YOU'VE GOT A BIG HOUSE.
......
YOU THREE...
FOR YOUR OWN SAFETY, I ADVISE YOU NOT TO SPEAK YOUR NAMES WHILE IN THIS HOUSE...

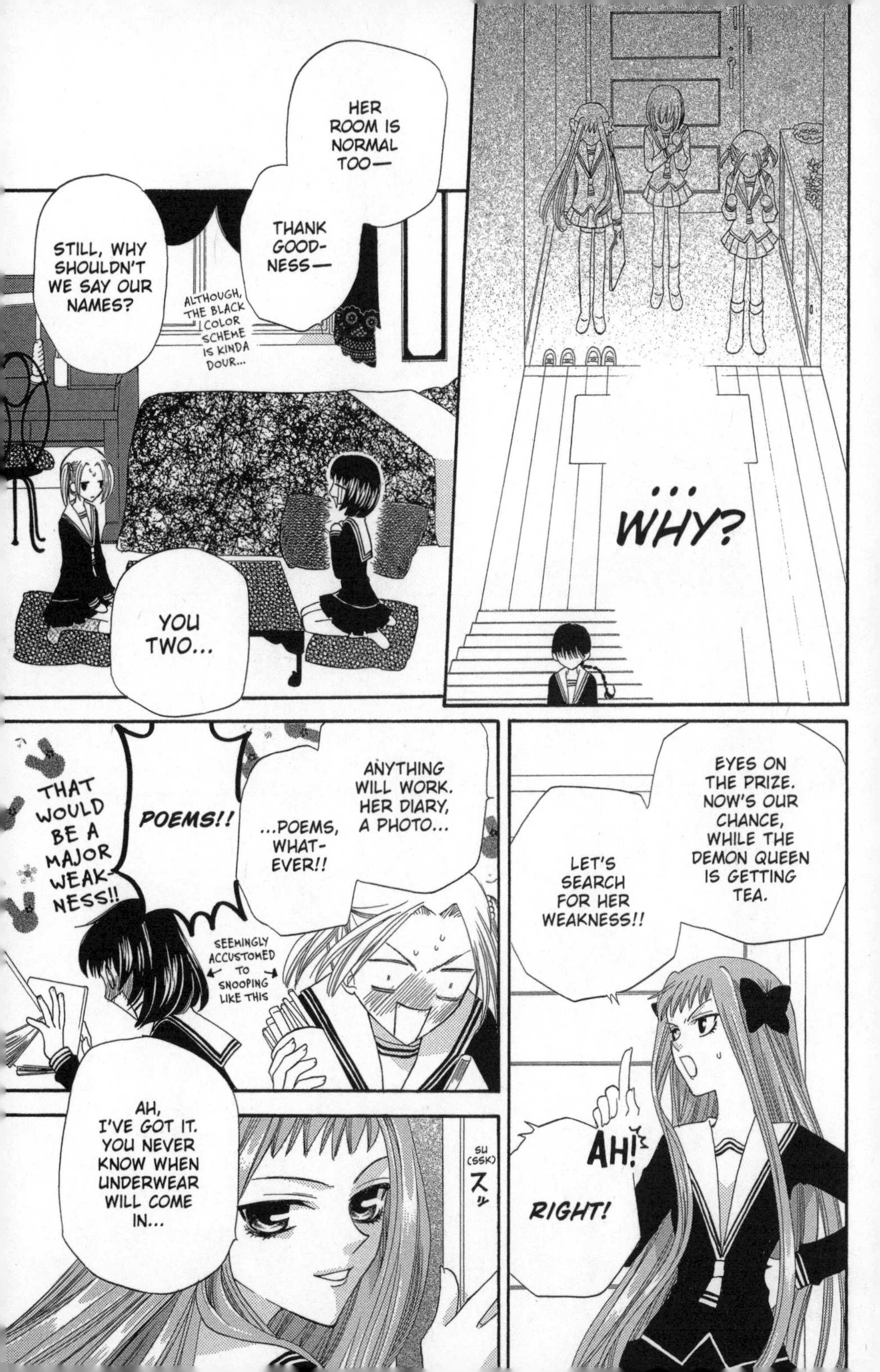
...WHY?
HER ROOM IS NORMAL TOO—
THANK GOODNESS—
ALTHOUGH, THE BLACK COLOR SCHEME IS KINDA DOUR...
STILL, WHY SHOULDN'T WE SAY OUR NAMES?
YOU TWO...
EYES ON THE PRIZE. NOW'S OUR CHANCE, WHILE THE DEMON QUEEN IS GETTING TEA.
LET'S SEARCH FOR HER WEAKNESS!!
AH!
RIGHT!
ANYTHING WILL WORK. HER DIARY, A PHOTO...
...POEMS, WHATEVER!!
POEMS!!
THAT WOULD BE A MAJOR WEAKNESS!!
SEEMINGLY ACCUSTOMED TO SNOOPING LIKE THIS
SU (SSK)
スッ
AH, I'VE GOT IT. YOU NEVER KNOW WHEN UNDERWEAR WILL COME IN...

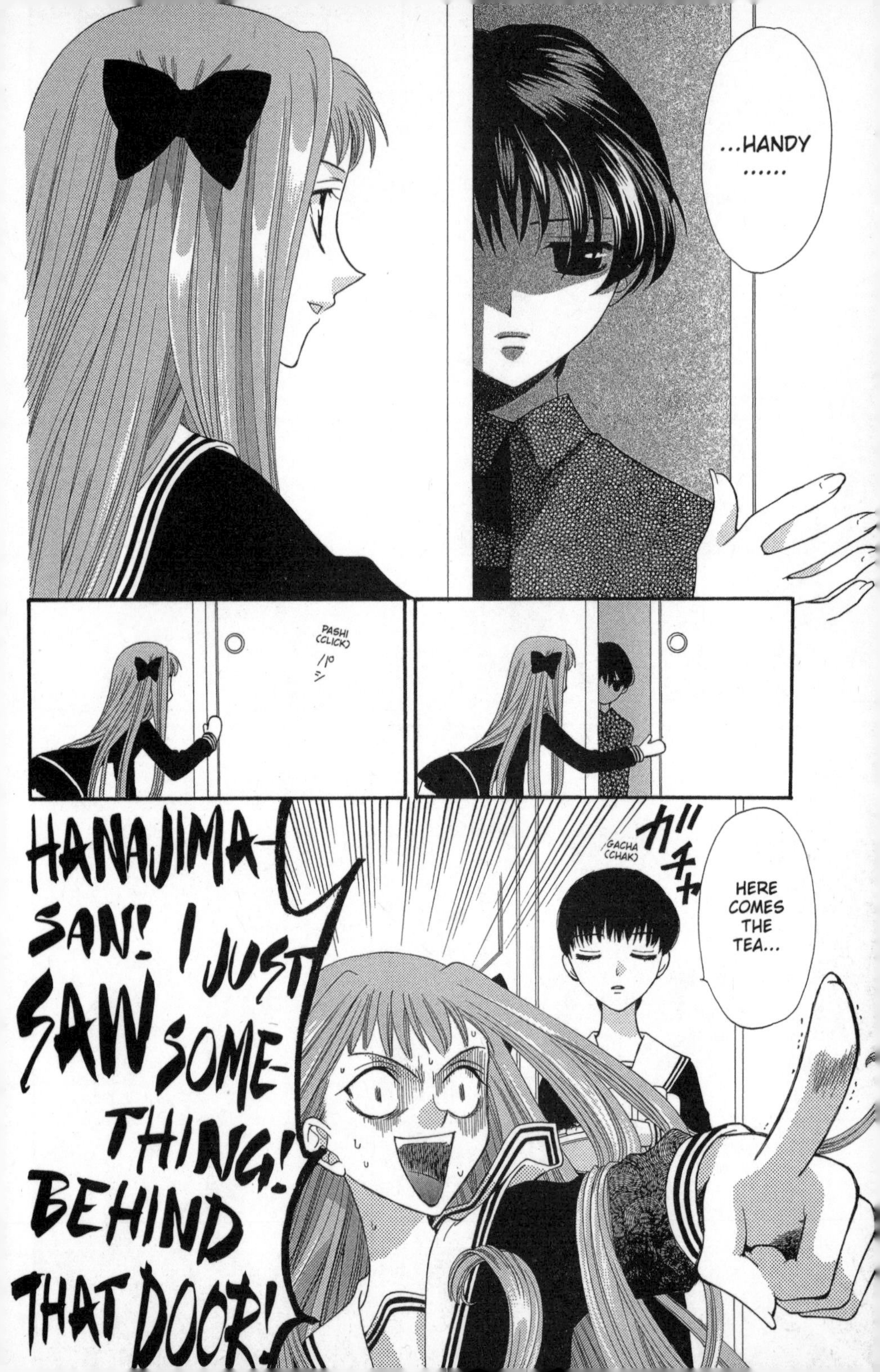

...HANDY ......
PASHI (CLICK)
パシ
ガチャ
GACHA (CHAK)
HERE COMES THE TEA...
HANAJIMA-SAN! I JUST SAW SOMETHING! BEHIND THAT DOOR!

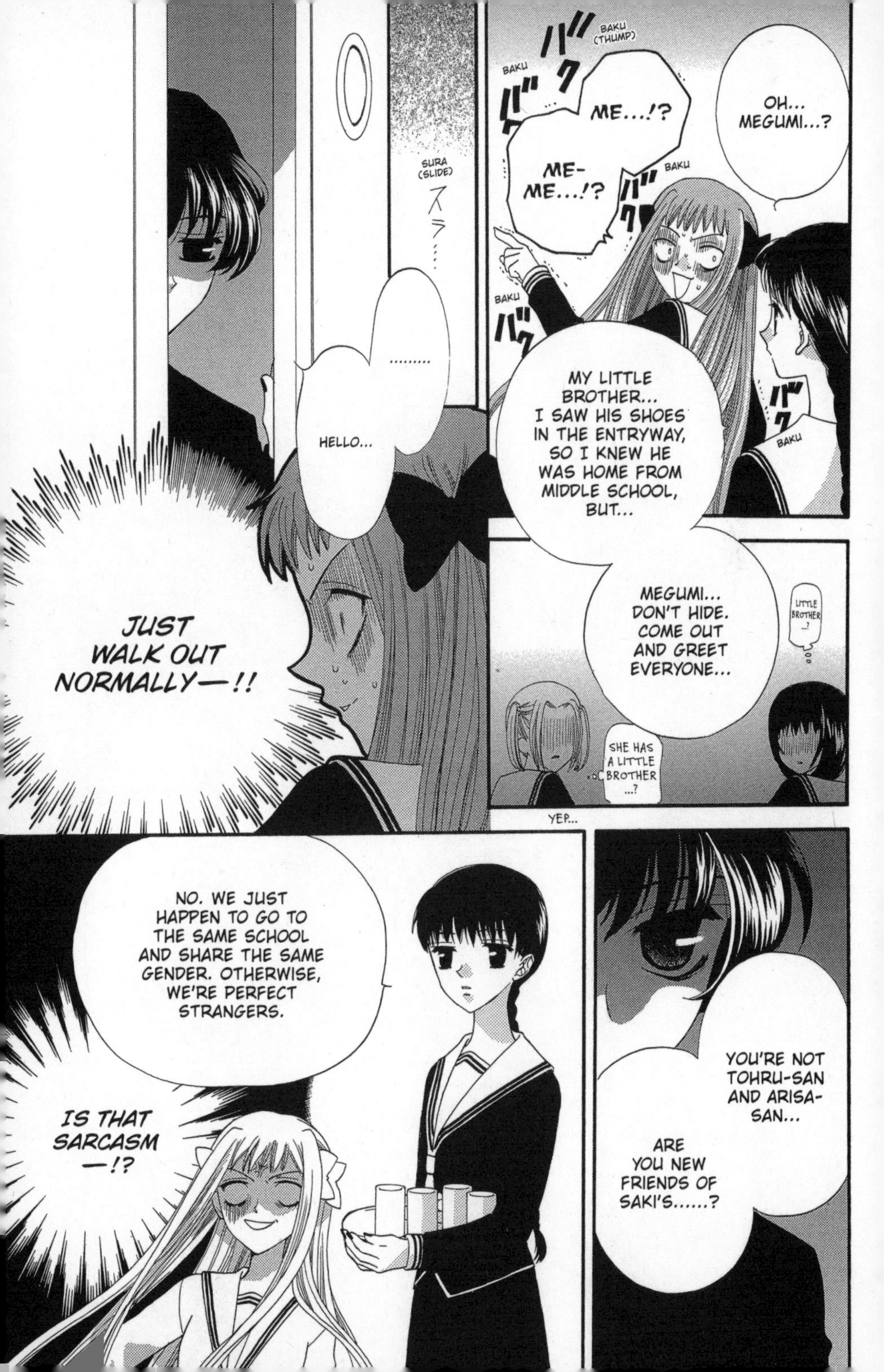
OH... MEGUMI...?
BAKU (THUMP)
ME...!?
ME-ME...!?
BAKU
BAKU
BAKU
BAKU
MY LITTLE BROTHER... I SAW HIS SHOES IN THE ENTRYWAY, SO I KNEW HE WAS HOME FROM MIDDLE SCHOOL, BUT...
MEGUMI... DON'T HIDE. COME OUT AND GREET EVERYONE...
LITTLE BROTHER ...?
SHE HAS A LITTLE BROTHER ...?
YEP...
SURA (SLIDE)
....
HELLO...
JUST WALK OUT NORMALLY—!!
YOU'RE NOT TOHRU-SAN AND ARISA-SAN...
ARE YOU NEW FRIENDS OF SAKI'S......?
NO. WE JUST HAPPEN TO GO TO THE SAME SCHOOL AND SHARE THE SAME GENDER. OTHERWISE, WE'RE PERFECT STRANGERS.
IS THAT SARCASM—!?

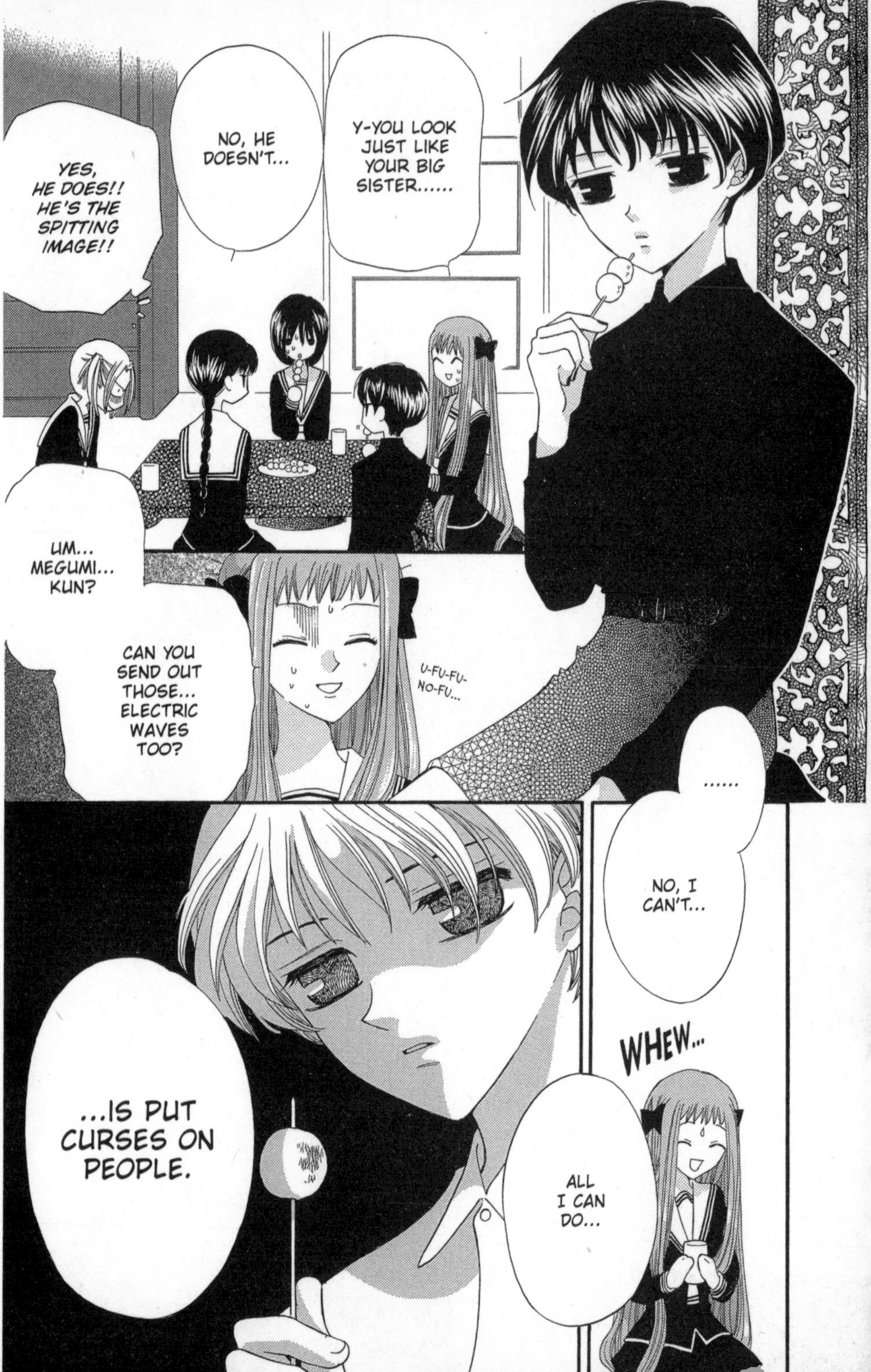
Y-YOU LOOK JUST LIKE YOUR BIG SISTER......
NO, HE DOESN'T...
YES, HE DOES!! HE'S THE SPITTING IMAGE!!
UM... MEGUMI... KUN?
CAN YOU SEND OUT THOSE... ELECTRIC WAVES TOO?
U-FU-FU-NO-FU...
......
NO, I CAN'T...
WHEW...
ALL I CAN DO...
...IS PUT CURSES ON PEOPLE.

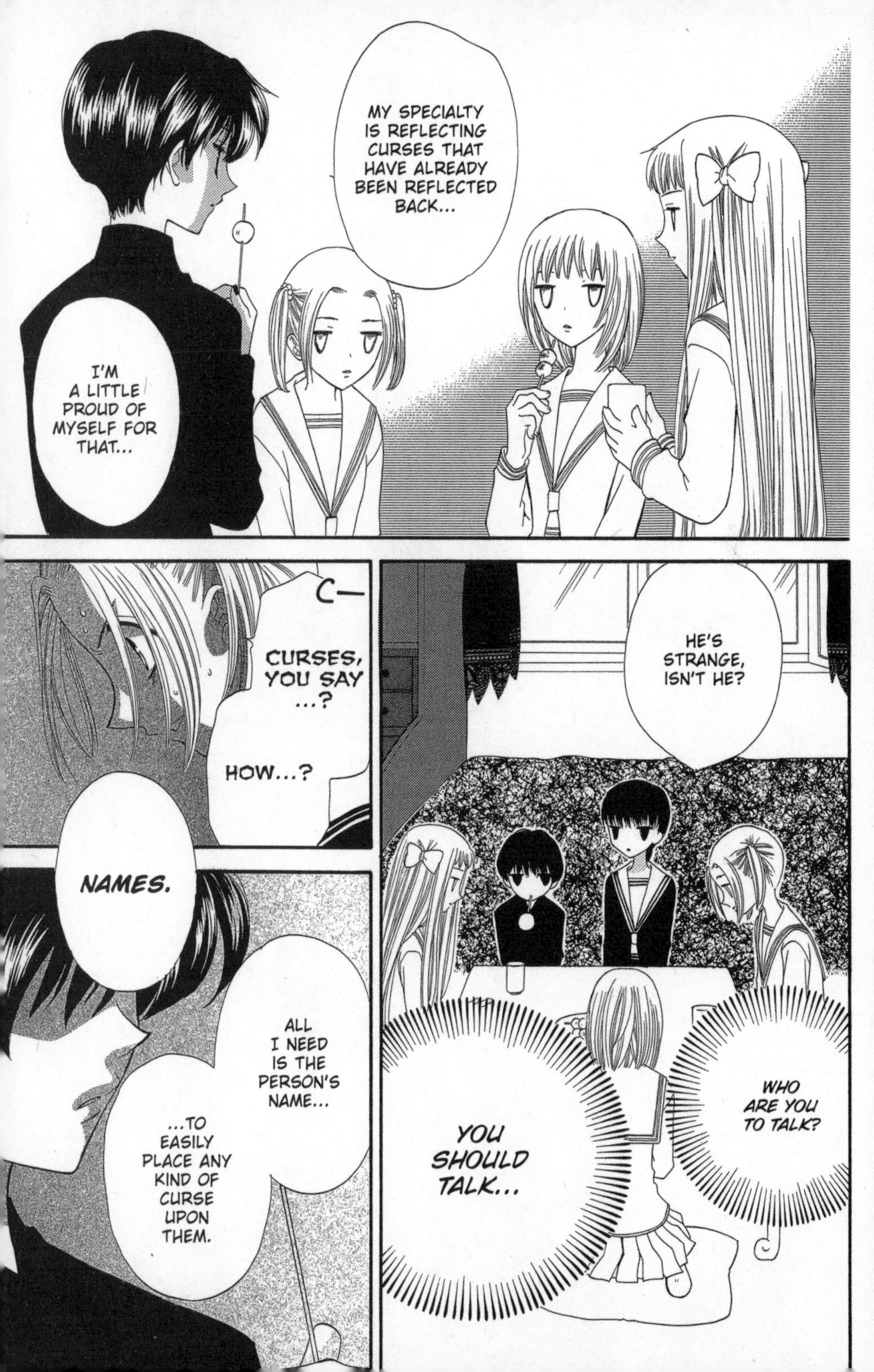
MY SPECIALTY IS REFLECTING CURSES THAT HAVE ALREADY BEEN REFLECTED BACK...
I'M A LITTLE PROUD OF MYSELF FOR THAT...
HE'S STRANGE, ISN'T HE?
WHO ARE YOU TO TALK?
YOU SHOULD TALK...
C—
CURSES, YOU SAY ...?
HOW...?
NAMES.
ALL I NEED IS THE PERSON'S NAME...
...TO EASILY PLACE ANY KIND OF CURSE UPON THEM.

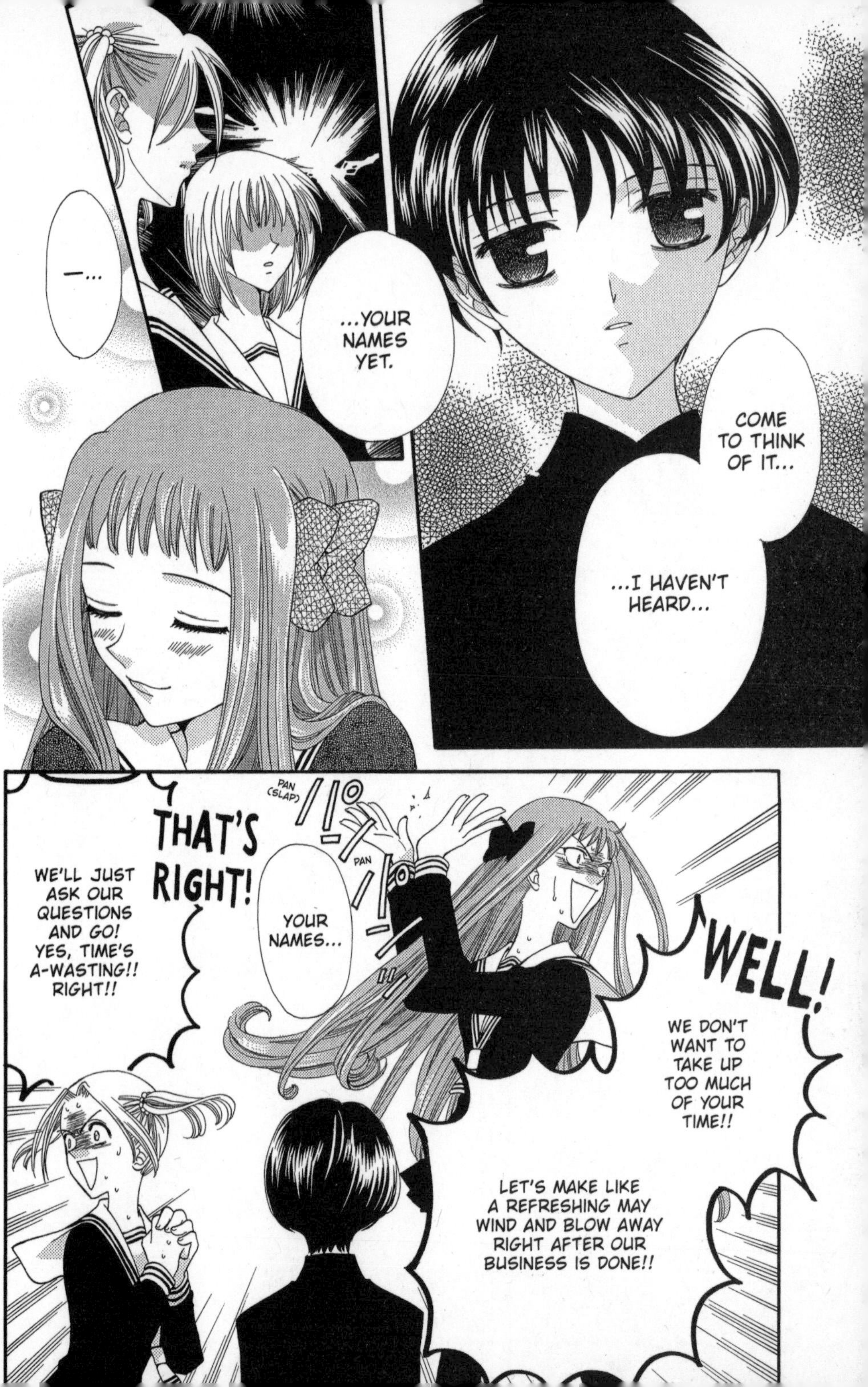
COME TO THINK OF IT...
...I HAVEN'T HEARD...
...YOUR NAMES YET.
—...
WELL!
WE DON'T WANT TO TAKE UP TOO MUCH OF YOUR TIME!!
LET'S MAKE LIKE A REFRESHING MAY WIND AND BLOW AWAY RIGHT AFTER OUR BUSINESS IS DONE!!
PAN (SLAP)
PAN
YOUR NAMES...
THAT'S RIGHT!
WE'LL JUST ASK OUR QUESTIONS AND GO! YES, TIME'S A-WASTING!! RIGHT!!

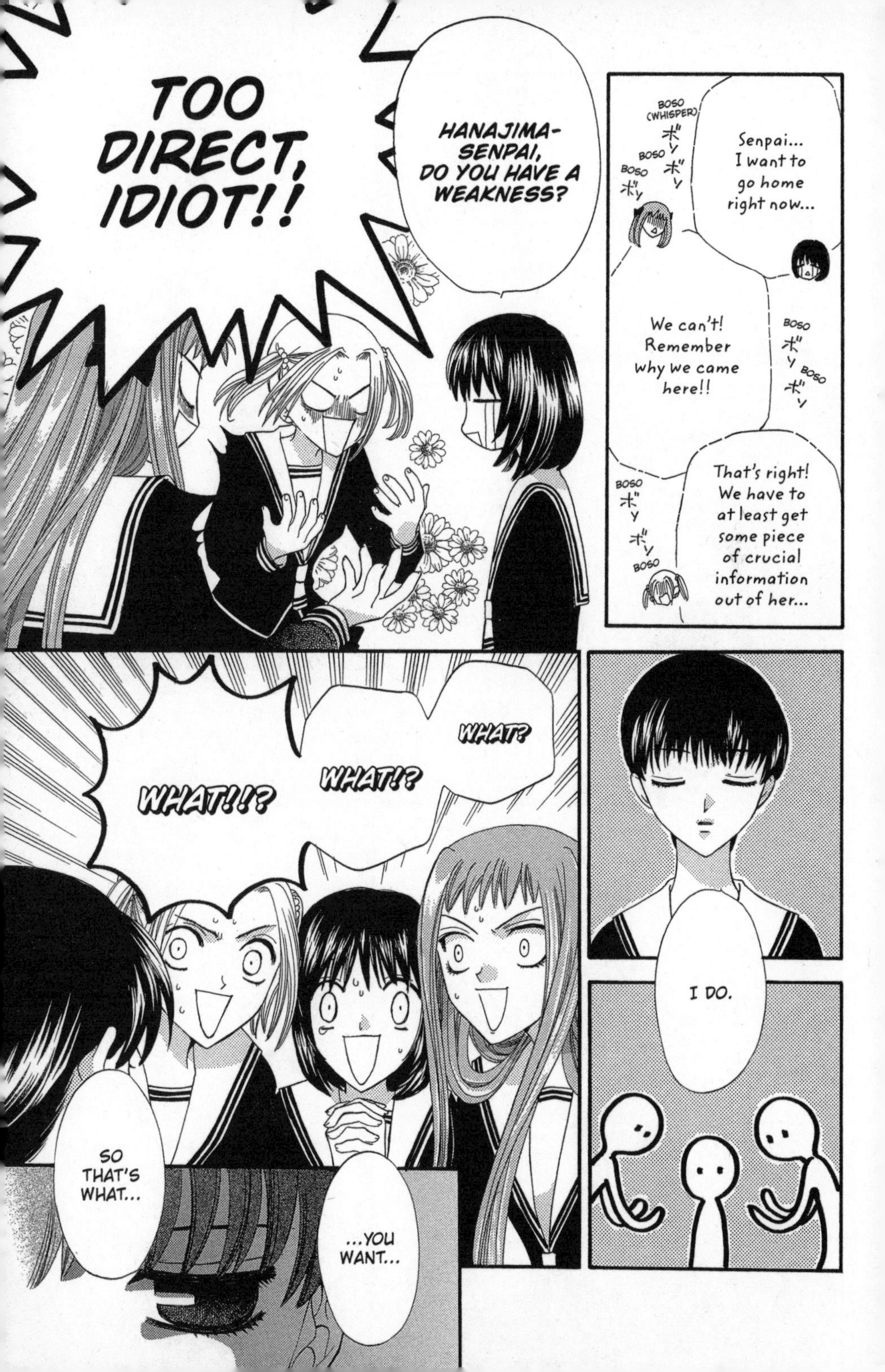
BOSO (WHISPER) ボソ
BOSO ボソ
BOSO ボソ
Senpai... I want to go home right now...
We can't! Remember why we came here!!
BOSO ボソ BOSO ボソ
That's right! We have to at least get some piece of crucial information out of her...
BOSO ボソ ボソ BOSO
HANAJIMA-SENPAI, DO YOU HAVE A WEAKNESS?
TOO DIRECT, IDIOT!!
I DO.
WHAT?
WHAT!?
WHAT!!?
SO THAT'S WHAT...
...YOU WANT...

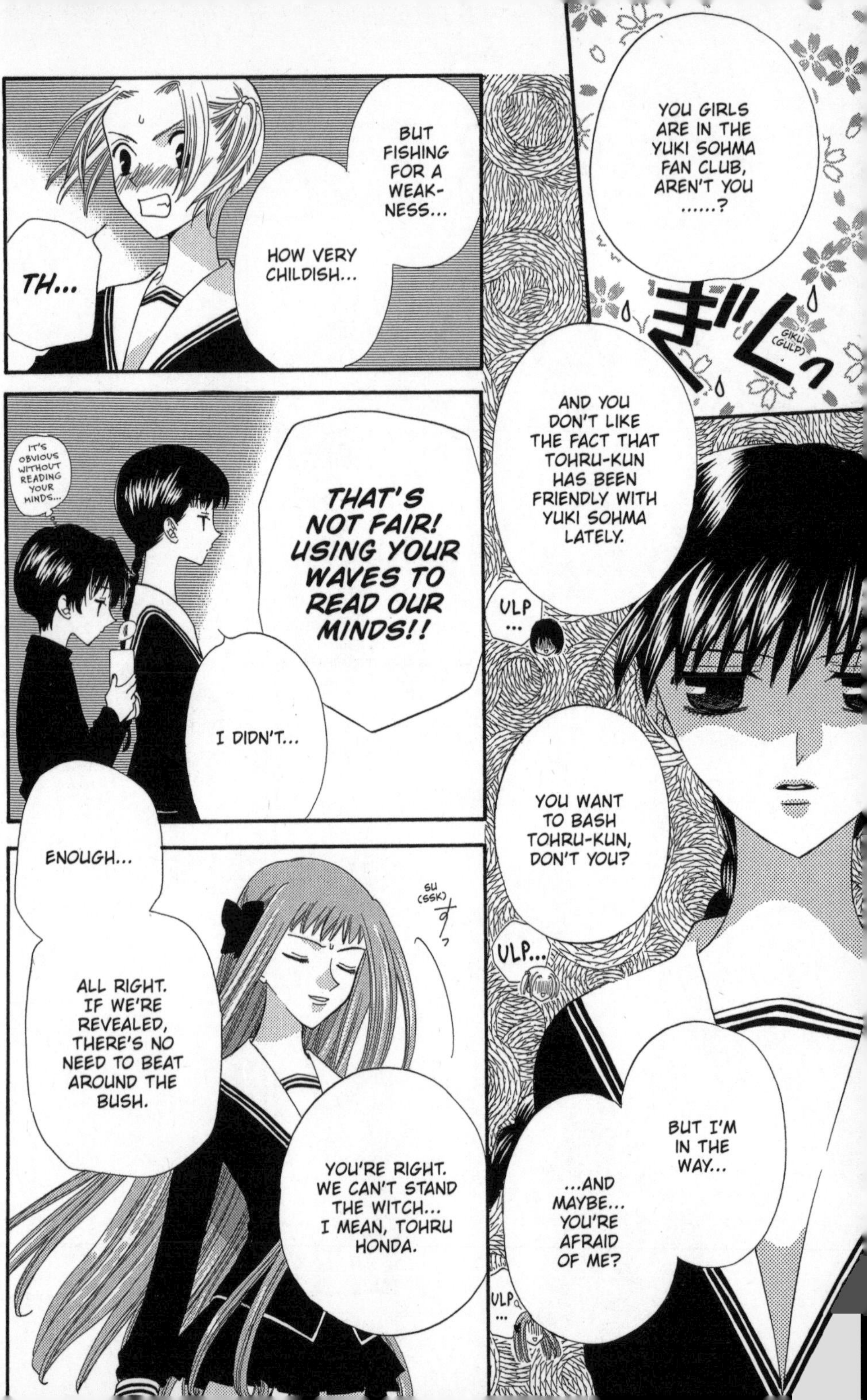
YOU GIRLS ARE IN THE YUKI SOHMA FAN CLUB, AREN'T YOU ......?
GIKU (GULP)
AND YOU DON'T LIKE THE FACT THAT TOHRU-KUN HAS BEEN FRIENDLY WITH YUKI SOHMA LATELY.
ULP ...
YOU WANT TO BASH TOHRU-KUN, DON'T YOU?
ULP...
BUT I'M IN THE WAY...
...AND MAYBE... YOU'RE AFRAID OF ME?
ULP ...
BUT FISHING FOR A WEAK-NESS...
HOW VERY CHILDISH...
TH...
THAT'S NOT FAIR! USING YOUR WAVES TO READ OUR MINDS!!
I DIDN'T...
IT'S OBVIOUS WITHOUT READING YOUR MINDS...
SU (SSK)
ENOUGH...
ALL RIGHT. IF WE'RE REVEALED, THERE'S NO NEED TO BEAT AROUND THE BUSH.
YOU'RE RIGHT. WE CAN'T STAND THE WITCH... I MEAN, TOHRU HONDA.

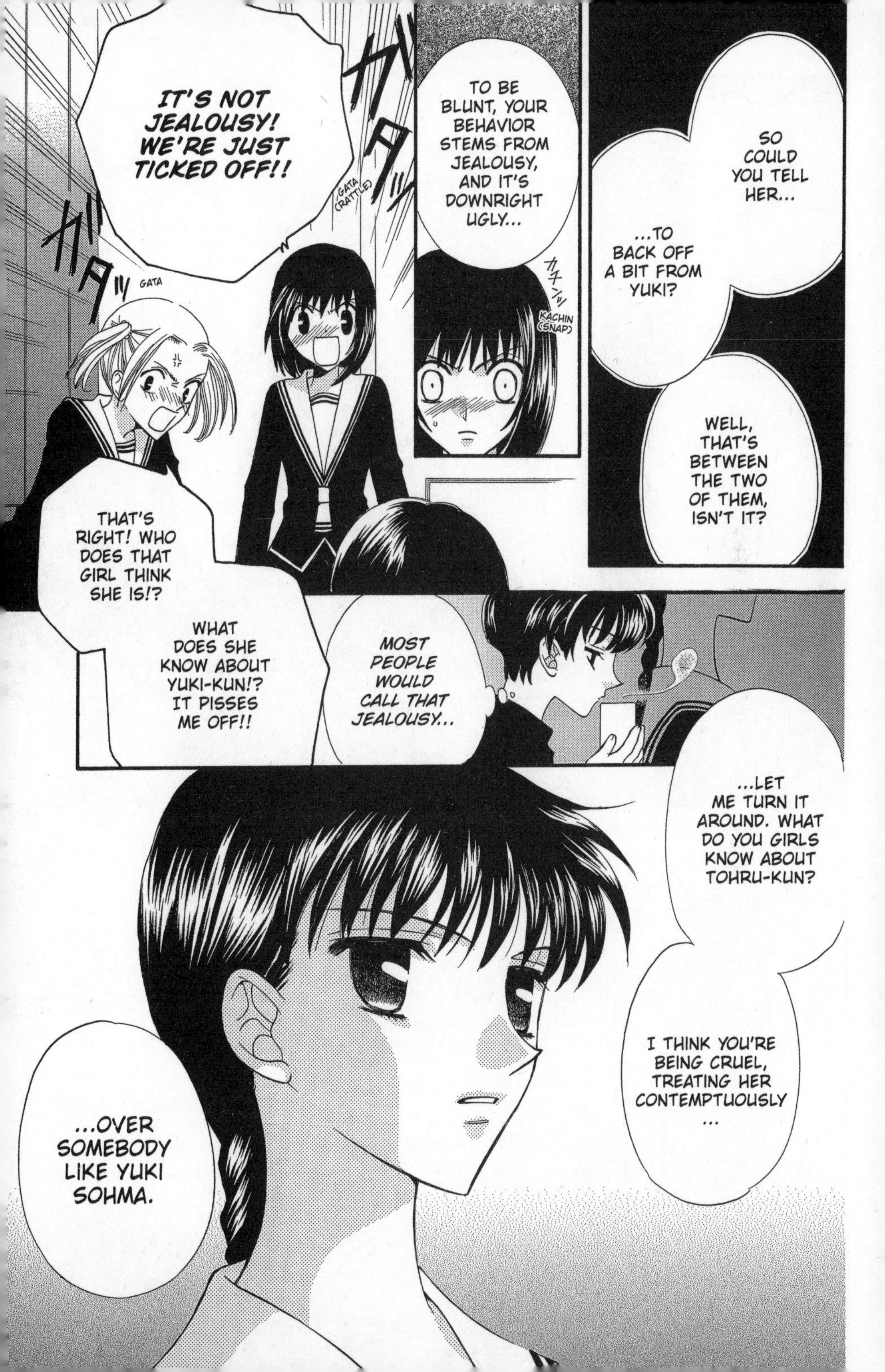
SO COULD YOU TELL HER...
...TO BACK OFF A BIT FROM YUKI?
WELL, THAT'S BETWEEN THE TWO OF THEM, ISN'T IT?
TO BE BLUNT, YOUR BEHAVIOR STEMS FROM JEALOUSY, AND IT'S DOWNRIGHT UGLY...
KACHIN (SNAP)
IT'S NOT JEALOUSY! WE'RE JUST TICKED OFF!!
GATA (RATTLE)
GATA
THAT'S RIGHT! WHO DOES THAT GIRL THINK SHE IS!?
MOST PEOPLE WOULD CALL THAT JEALOUSY...
WHAT DOES SHE KNOW ABOUT YUKI-KUN!? IT PISSES ME OFF!!
...LET ME TURN IT AROUND. WHAT DO YOU GIRLS KNOW ABOUT TOHRU-KUN?
I THINK YOU'RE BEING CRUEL, TREATING HER CONTEMPTUOUSLY ...
...OVER SOMEBODY LIKE YUKI SOHMA.

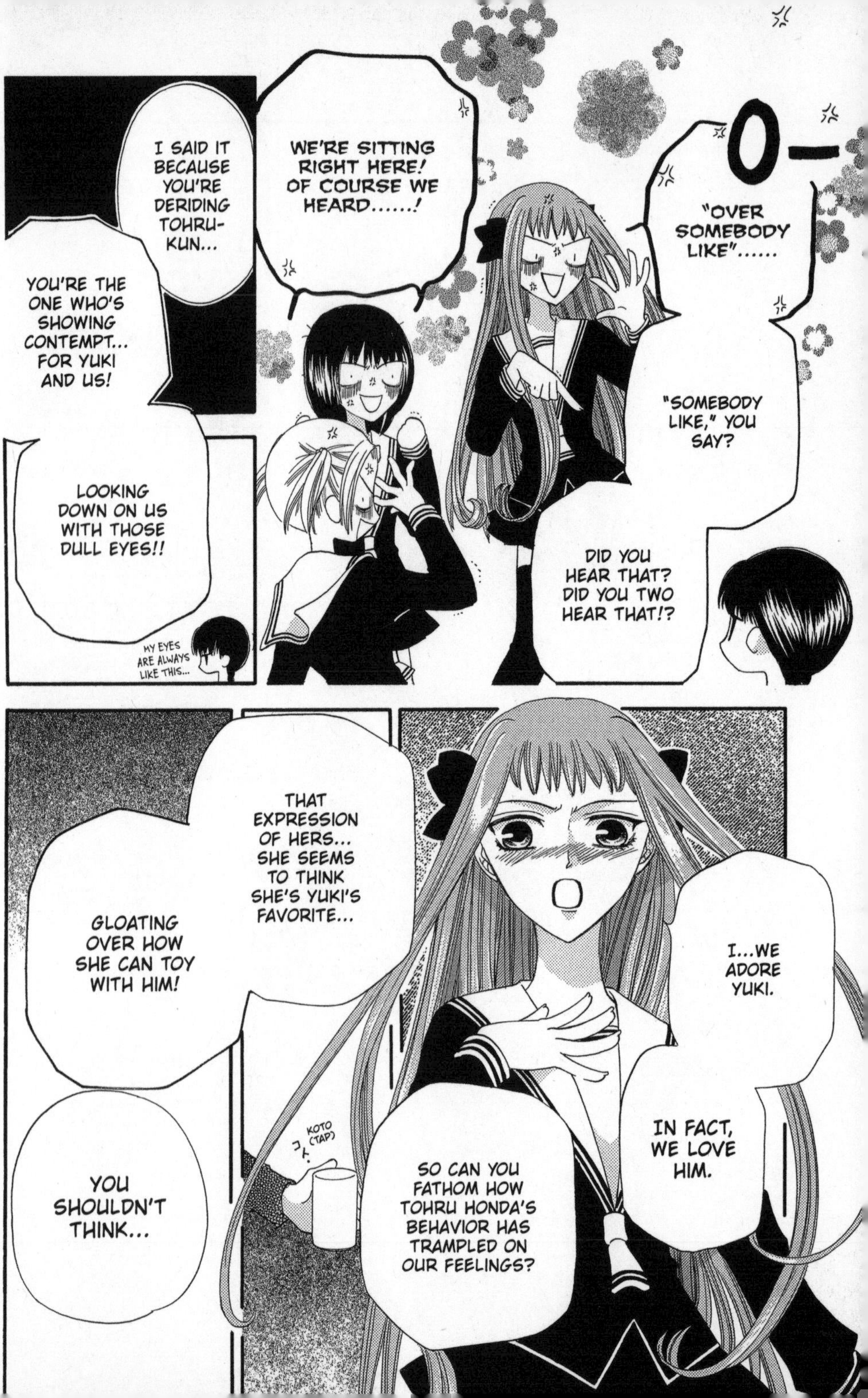
O—
"OVER SOMEBODY LIKE"......
"SOMEBODY LIKE," YOU SAY?
DID YOU HEAR THAT? DID YOU TWO HEAR THAT!?
WE'RE SITTING RIGHT HERE! OF COURSE WE HEARD......!
I SAID IT BECAUSE YOU'RE DERIDING TOHRU-KUN...
YOU'RE THE ONE WHO'S SHOWING CONTEMPT... FOR YUKI AND US!
LOOKING DOWN ON US WITH THOSE DULL EYES!!
MY EYES ARE ALWAYS LIKE THIS...
I...WE ADORE YUKI.
IN FACT, WE LOVE HIM.
SO CAN YOU FATHOM HOW TOHRU HONDA'S BEHAVIOR HAS TRAMPLED ON OUR FEELINGS?
THAT EXPRESSION OF HERS... SHE SEEMS TO THINK SHE'S YUKI'S FAVORITE...
GLOATING OVER HOW SHE CAN TOY WITH HIM!
KOTO (TAP)
YOU SHOULDN'T THINK...

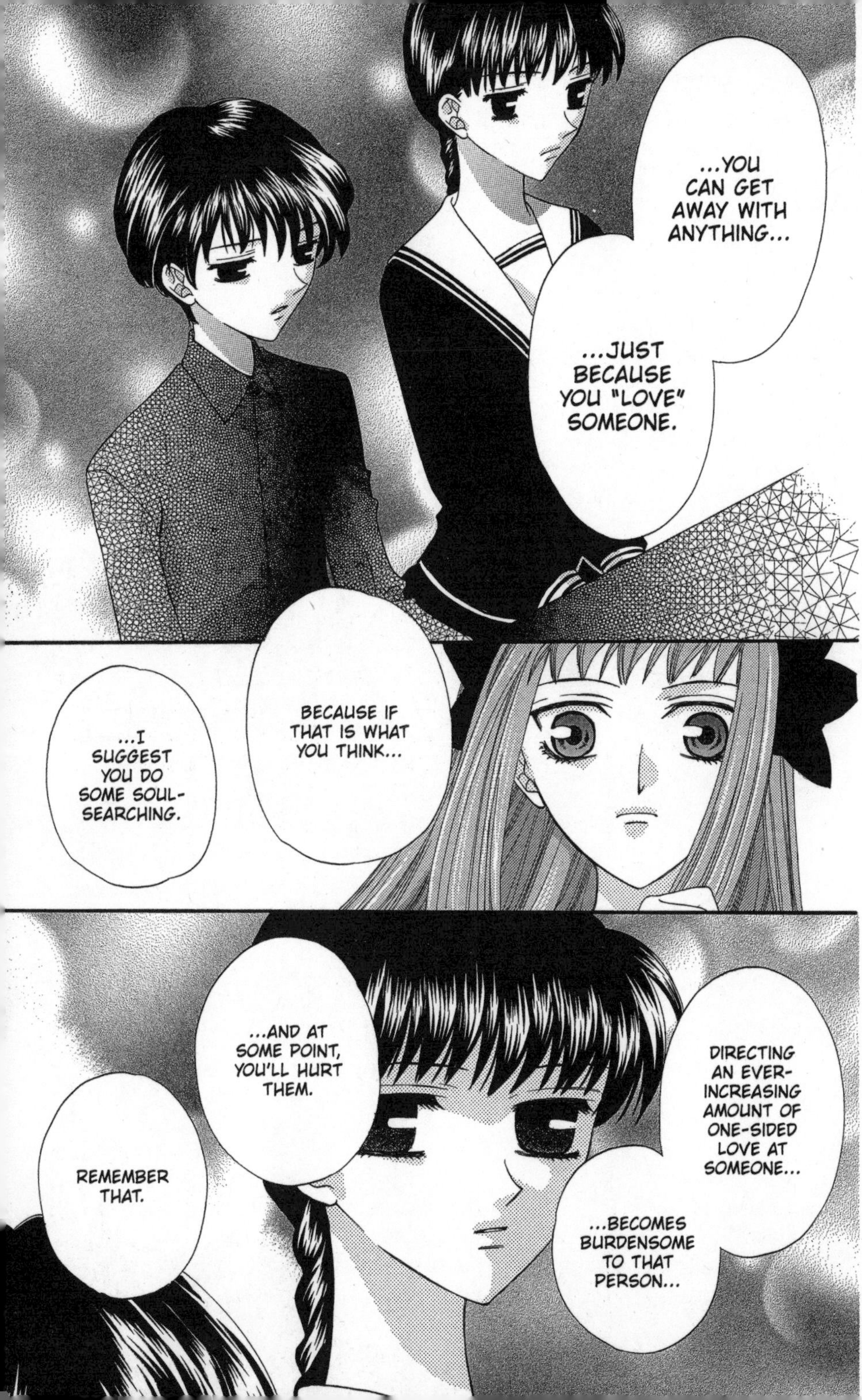
...YOU CAN GET AWAY WITH ANYTHING...
...JUST BECAUSE YOU "LOVE" SOMEONE.
BECAUSE IF THAT IS WHAT YOU THINK...
...I SUGGEST YOU DO SOME SOUL-SEARCHING.
DIRECTING AN EVER-INCREASING AMOUNT OF ONE-SIDED LOVE AT SOMEONE...
...BECOMES BURDENSOME TO THAT PERSON...
...AND AT SOME POINT, YOU'LL HURT THEM.
REMEMBER THAT.

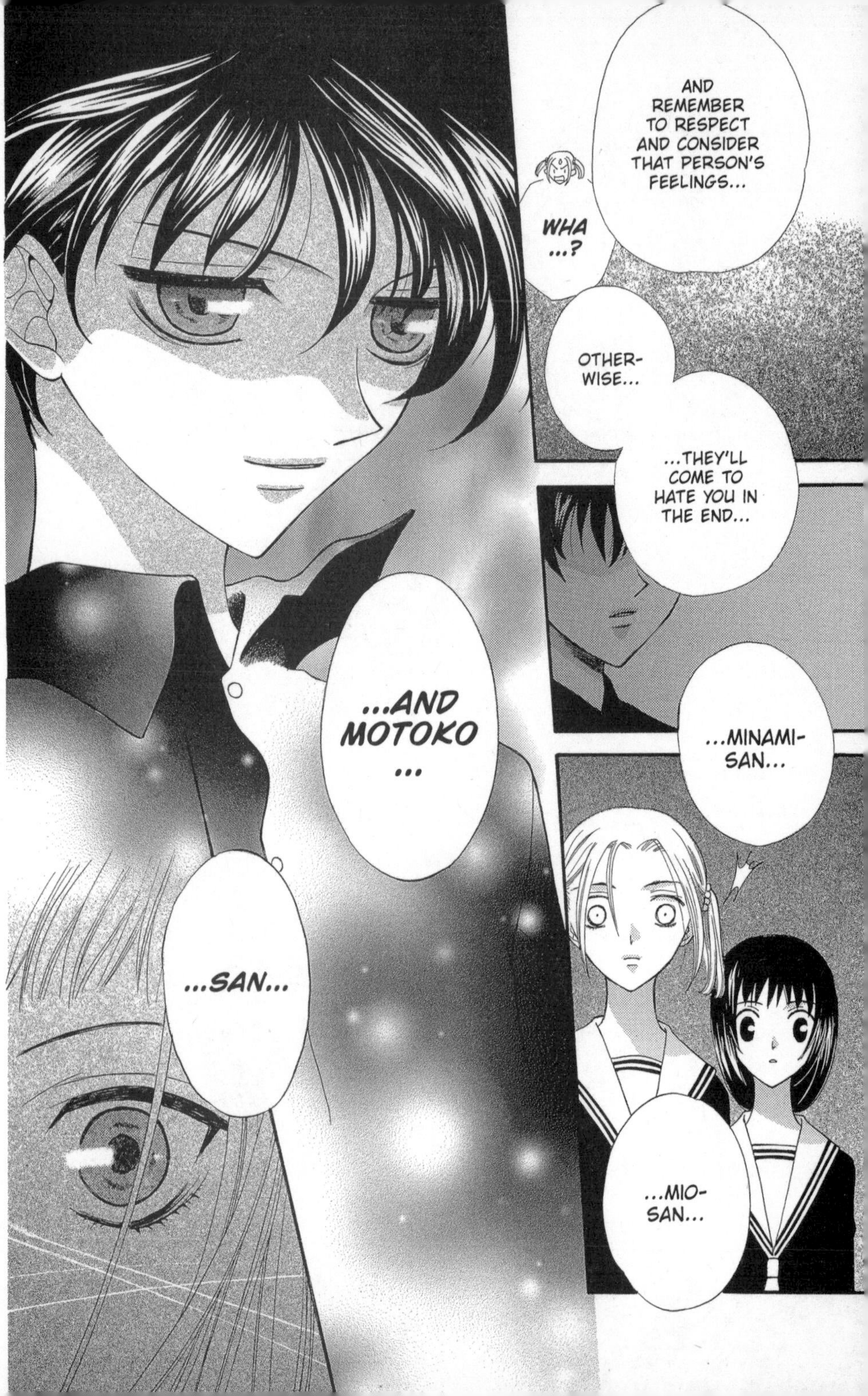
AND REMEMBER TO RESPECT AND CONSIDER THAT PERSON'S FEELINGS...
WHA ...?
OTHER-WISE...
...THEY'LL COME TO HATE YOU IN THE END...
...MINAMI-SAN...
...MIO-SAN...
...AND MOTOKO ...
...SAN...

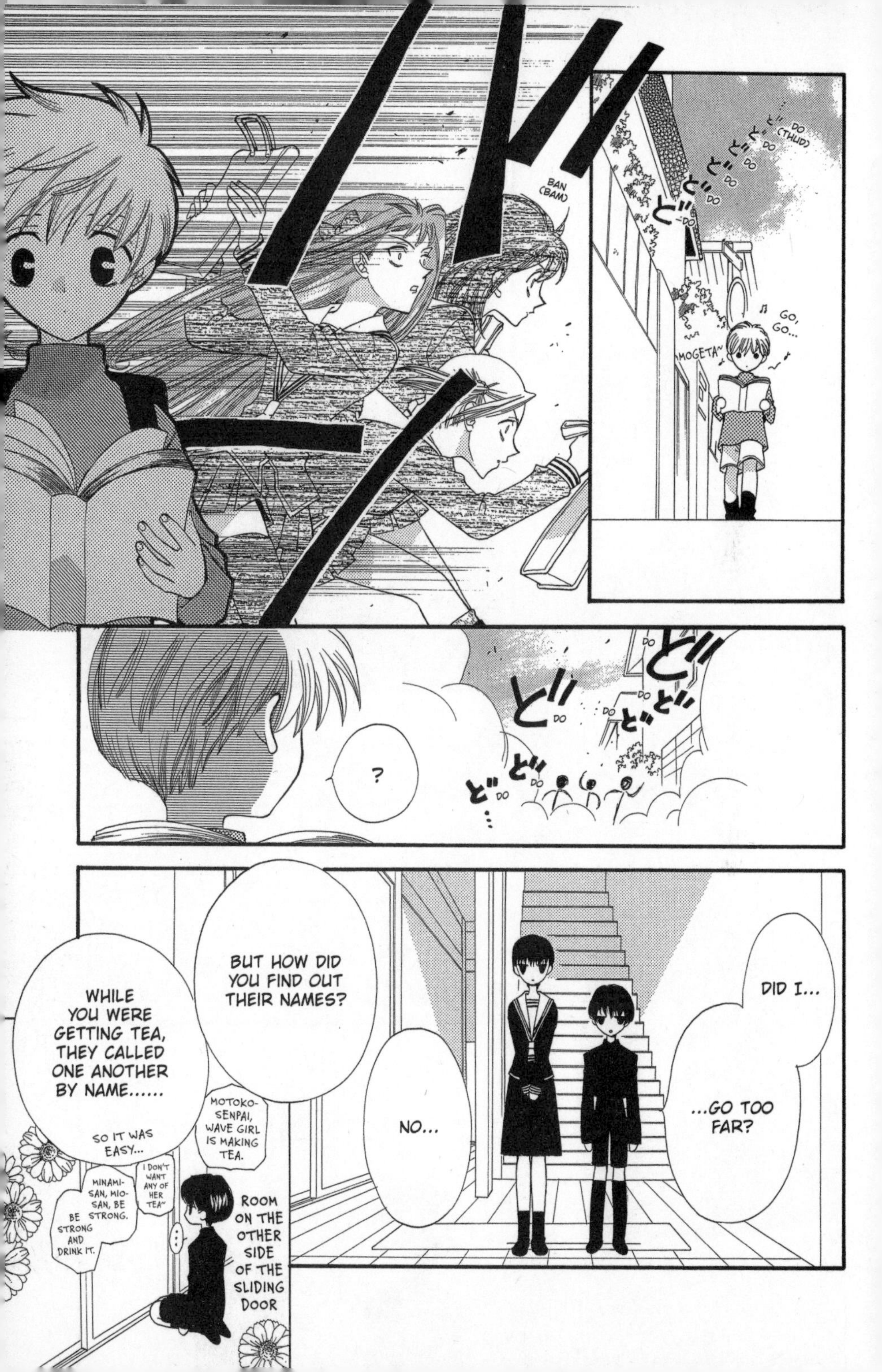

…ど DO (THUD)
ど DO
ど DO
ど DO
ど DO
ど DO
GO, GO…
MOGETA~
BAN (BAM)
ど DO
ど DO
ど DO
ど DO
ど DO
ど DO
?
DID I…
…GO TOO FAR?
NO…
BUT HOW DID YOU FIND OUT THEIR NAMES?
WHILE YOU WERE GETTING TEA, THEY CALLED ONE ANOTHER BY NAME……
SO IT WAS EASY…
ROOM ON THE OTHER SIDE OF THE SLIDING DOOR
MOTOKO-SENPAI, WAVE GIRL IS MAKING TEA.
I DON'T WANT ANY OF HER TEA~
MINAMI-SAN, MIO-SAN, BE STRONG.
BE STRONG AND DRINK IT.
…

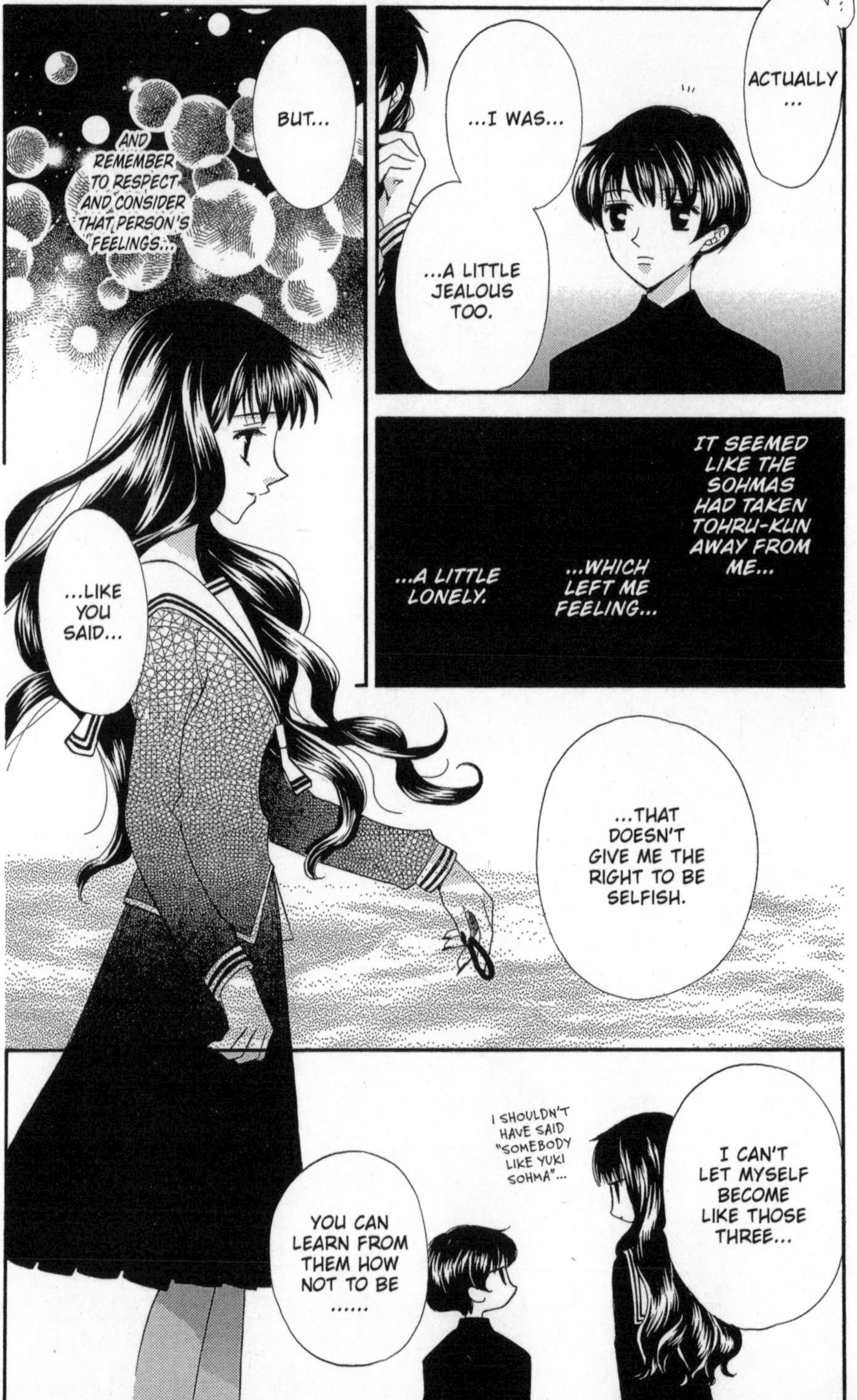

...
ACTUALLY ...
...I WAS...
...A LITTLE JEALOUS TOO.
IT SEEMED LIKE THE SOHMAS HAD TAKEN TOHRU-KUN AWAY FROM ME...
...WHICH LEFT ME FEELING...
...A LITTLE LONELY.
BUT...
AND REMEMBER TO RESPECT AND CONSIDER THAT PERSON'S FEELINGS...
...LIKE YOU SAID...
...THAT DOESN'T GIVE ME THE RIGHT TO BE SELFISH.
I CAN'T LET MYSELF BECOME LIKE THOSE THREE...
I SHOULDN'T HAVE SAID "SOMEBODY LIKE YUKI SOHMA"...
YOU CAN LEARN FROM THEM HOW NOT TO BE ......

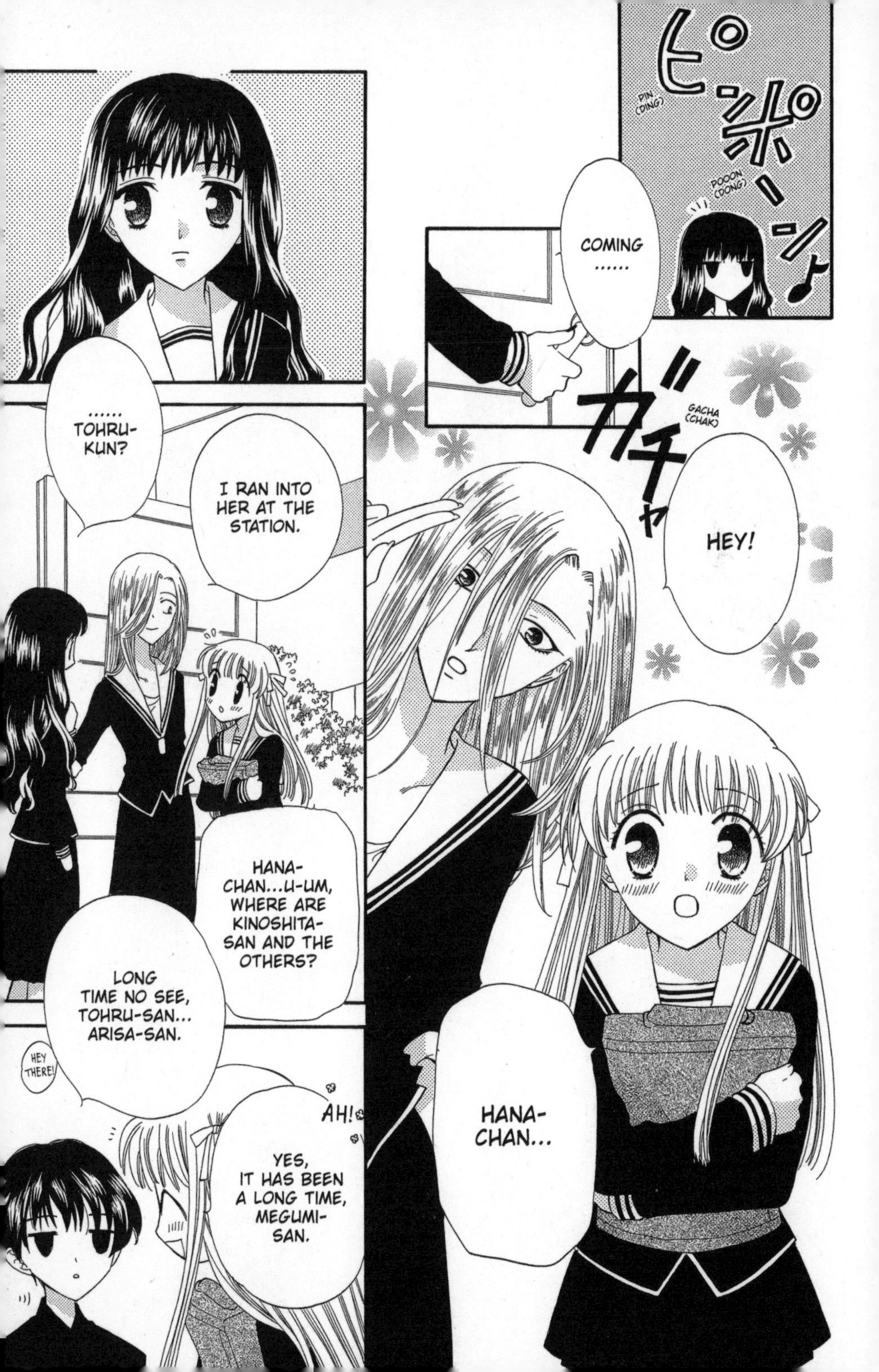
PIN (DING)
POOON (DONG)
COMING ......
GACHA (CHAK)
HEY!
HANA-CHAN...
...... TOHRU-KUN?
I RAN INTO HER AT THE STATION.
HANA-CHAN...U-UM, WHERE ARE KINOSHITA-SAN AND THE OTHERS?
LONG TIME NO SEE, TOHRU-SAN... ARISA-SAN.
HEY THERE!
AH!
YES, IT HAS BEEN A LONG TIME, MEGUMI-SAN.

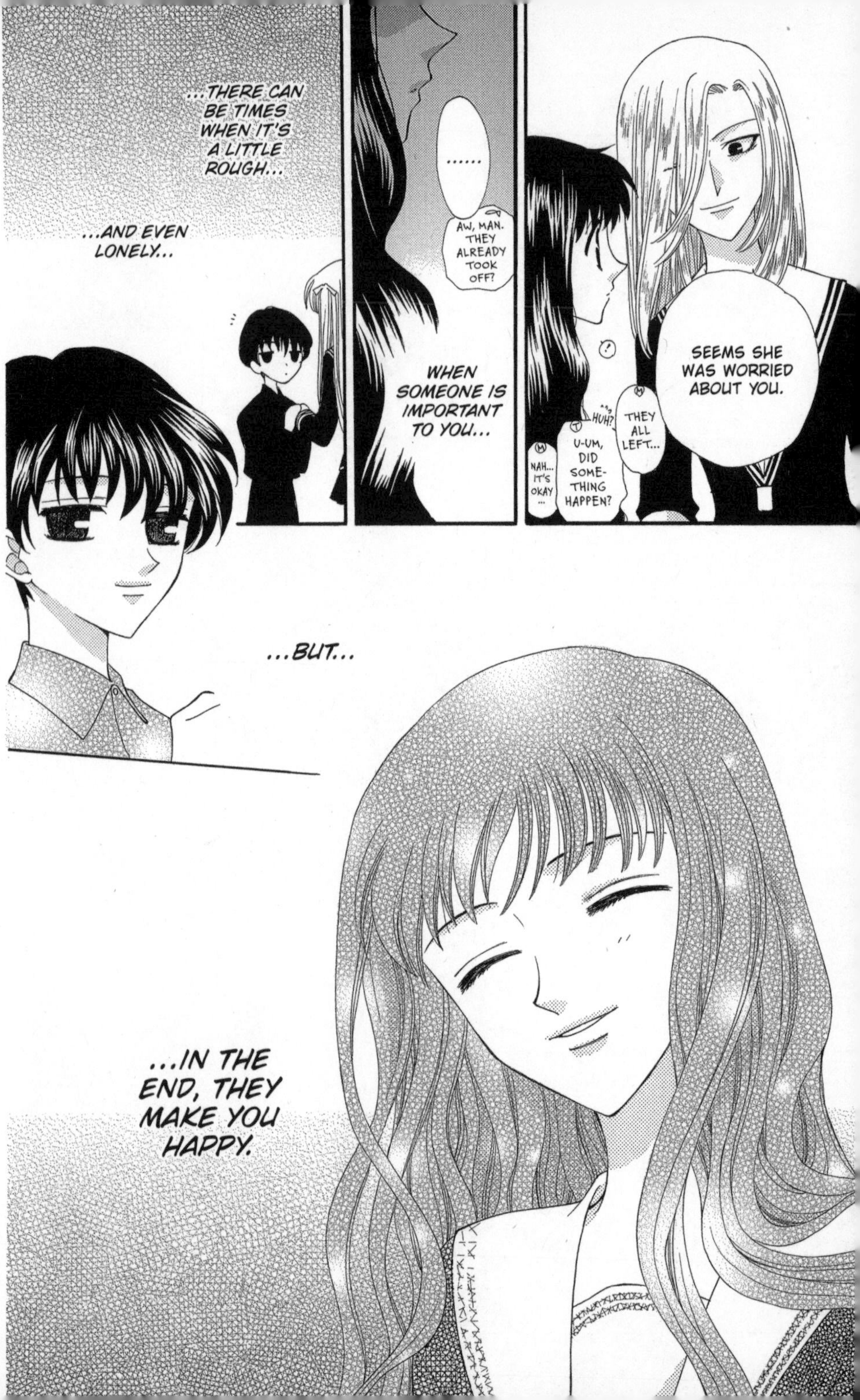

SEEMS SHE WAS WORRIED ABOUT YOU.
THEY ALL LEFT...
HUH?
U-UM, DID SOME-THING HAPPEN?
NAH... IT'S OKAY...
......
AW, MAN. THEY ALREADY TOOK OFF?
WHEN SOMEONE IS IMPORTANT TO YOU...
...THERE CAN BE TIMES WHEN IT'S A LITTLE ROUGH...
...AND EVEN LONELY...
...BUT...
...IN THE END, THEY MAKE YOU HAPPY.

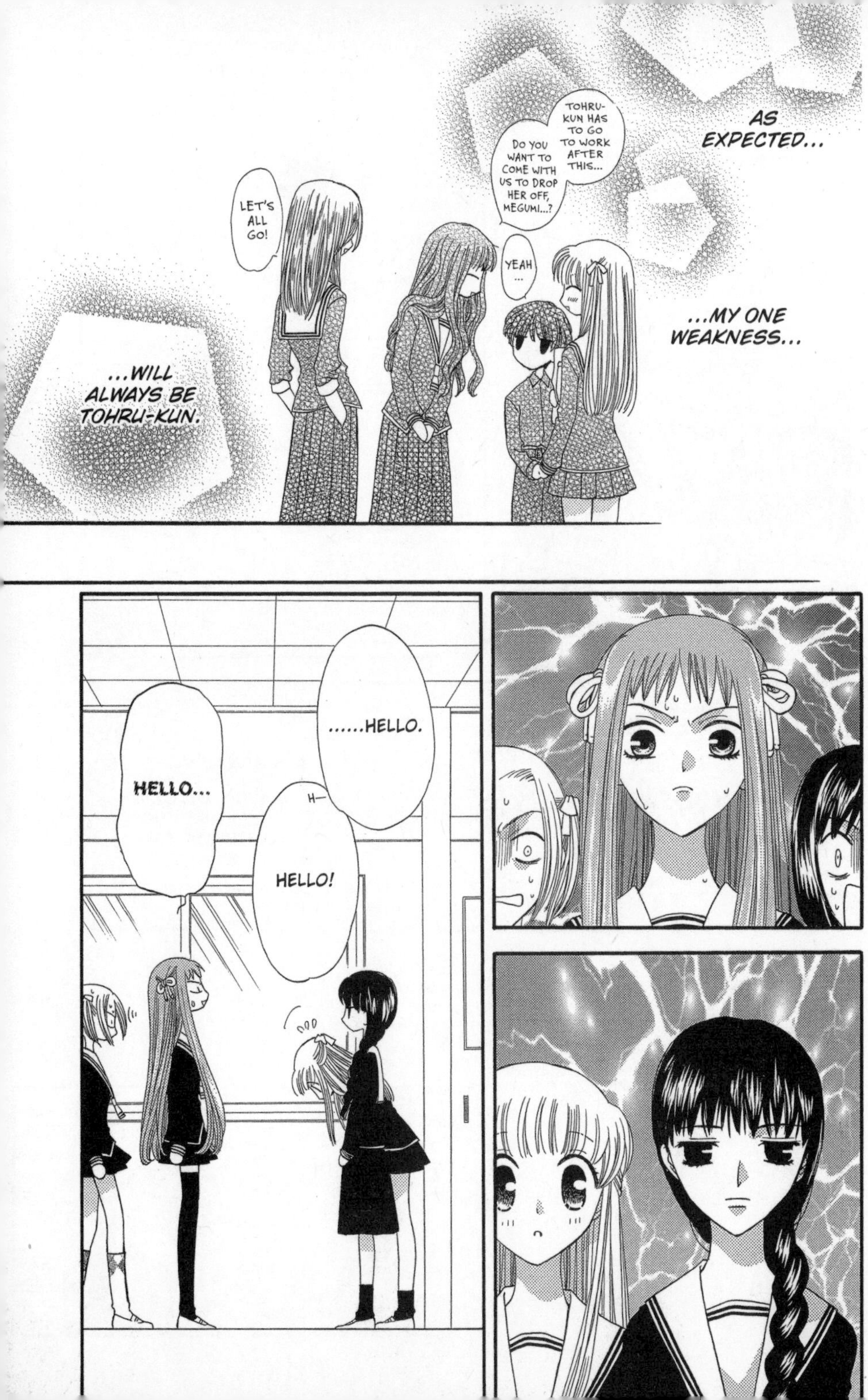
AS EXPECTED...
...MY ONE WEAKNESS...
TOHRU-KUN HAS TO GO TO WORK AFTER THIS...
DO YOU WANT TO COME WITH US TO DROP HER OFF, MEGUMI...?
YEAH...
LET'S ALL GO!
...WILL ALWAYS BE TOHRU-KUN.
......HELLO.
H—
HELLO!
HELLO...

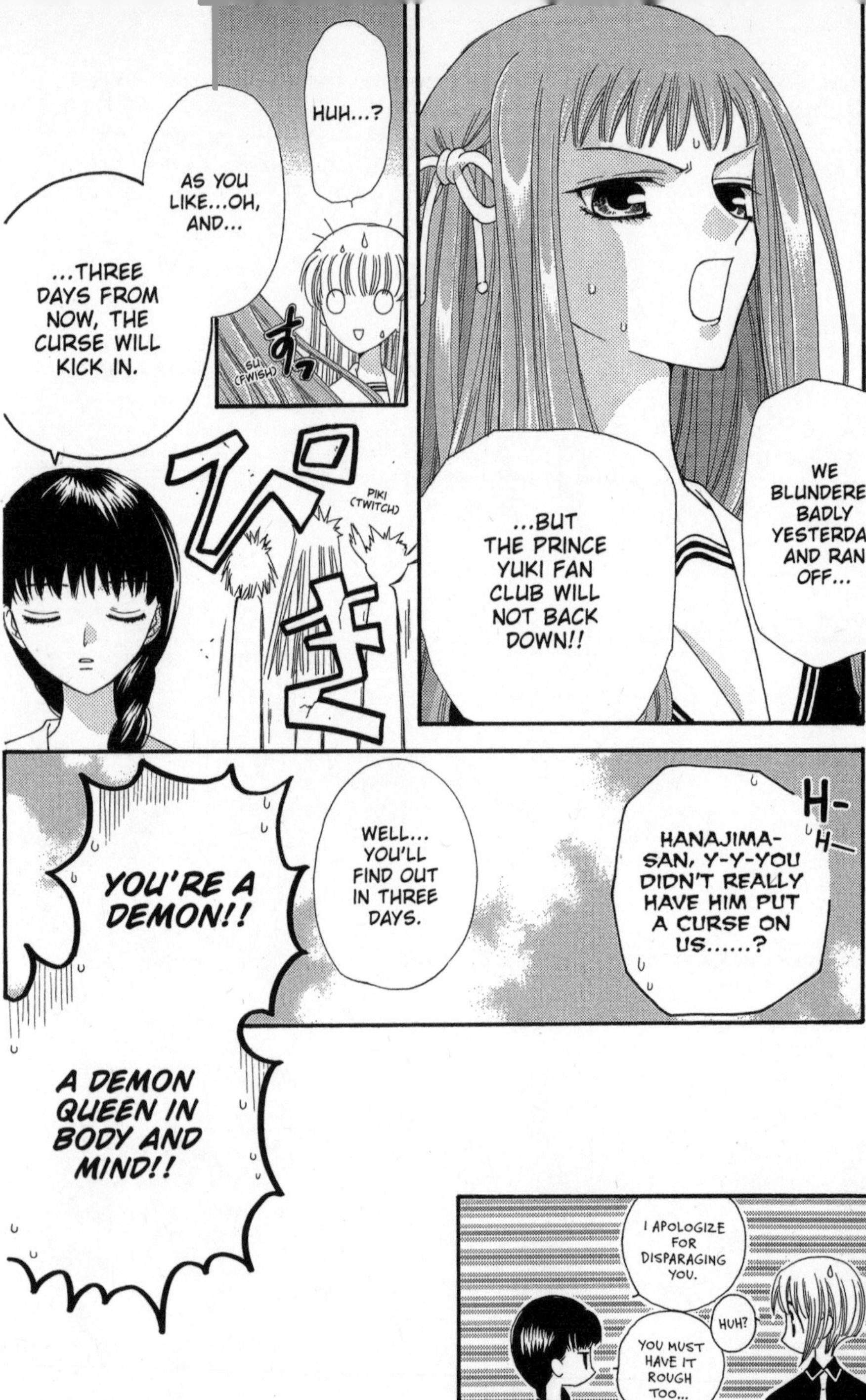
WE BLUNDERED BADLY YESTERDAY AND RAN OFF...
...BUT THE PRINCE YUKI FAN CLUB WILL NOT BACK DOWN!!
HUH...?
AS YOU LIKE...OH, AND...
...THREE DAYS FROM NOW, THE CURSE WILL KICK IN.
SU (FWISH)
PIKI (TWITCH)
H-H-
HANAJIMA-SAN, Y-Y-YOU DIDN'T REALLY HAVE HIM PUT A CURSE ON US......?
WELL... YOU'LL FIND OUT IN THREE DAYS.
YOU'RE A DEMON!!
A DEMON QUEEN IN BODY AND MIND!!
I APOLOGIZE FOR DISPARAGING YOU.
HUH?
YOU MUST HAVE IT ROUGH TOO...
WHAT?

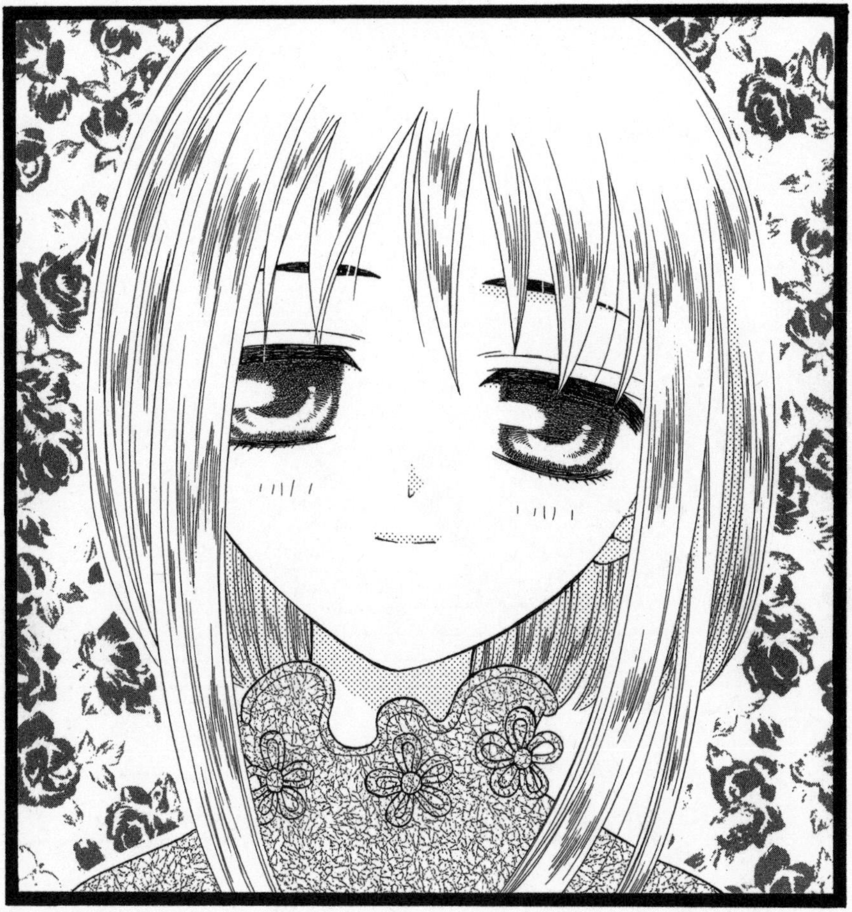

Chapter 30

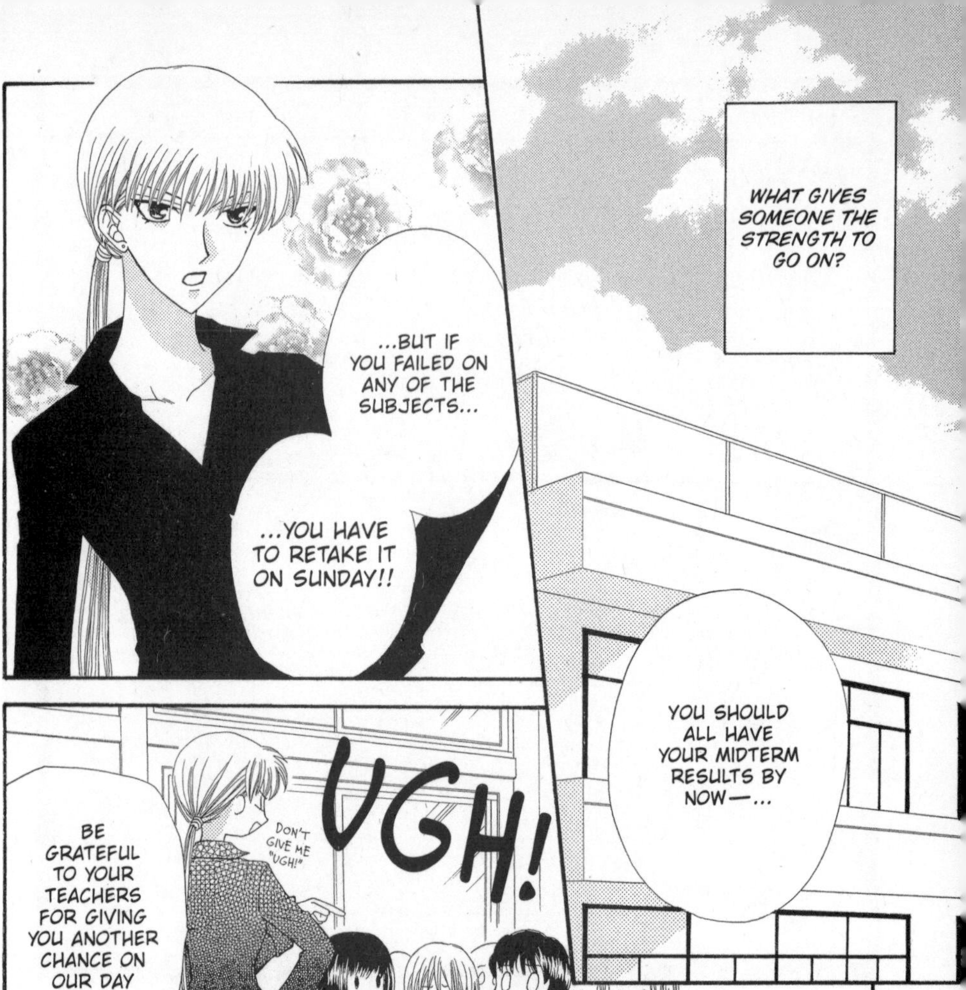
WHAT GIVES SOMEONE THE STRENGTH TO GO ON?
YOU SHOULD ALL HAVE YOUR MIDTERM RESULTS BY NOW—...
...BUT IF YOU FAILED ON ANY OF THE SUBJECTS...
...YOU HAVE TO RETAKE IT ON SUNDAY!!
UGH!
DON'T GIVE ME "UGH!"
BE GRATEFUL TO YOUR TEACHERS FOR GIVING YOU ANOTHER CHANCE ON OUR DAY OFF!

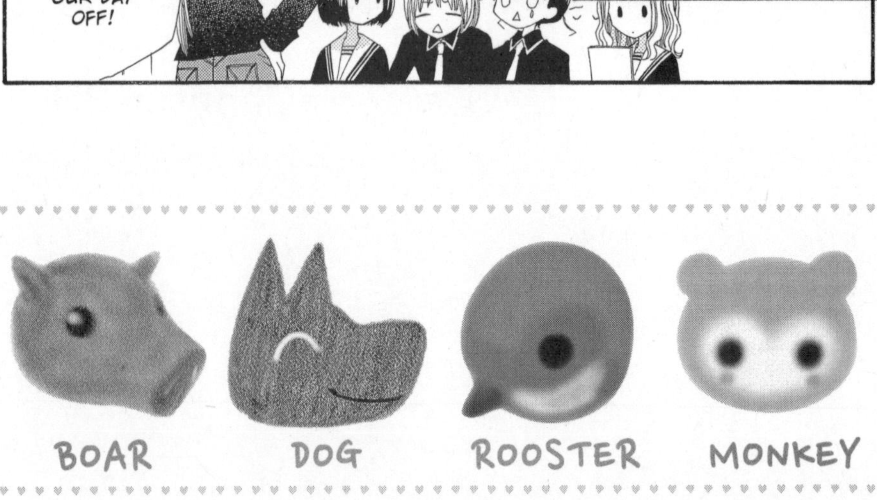
BOAR
DOG
ROOSTER
MONKEY

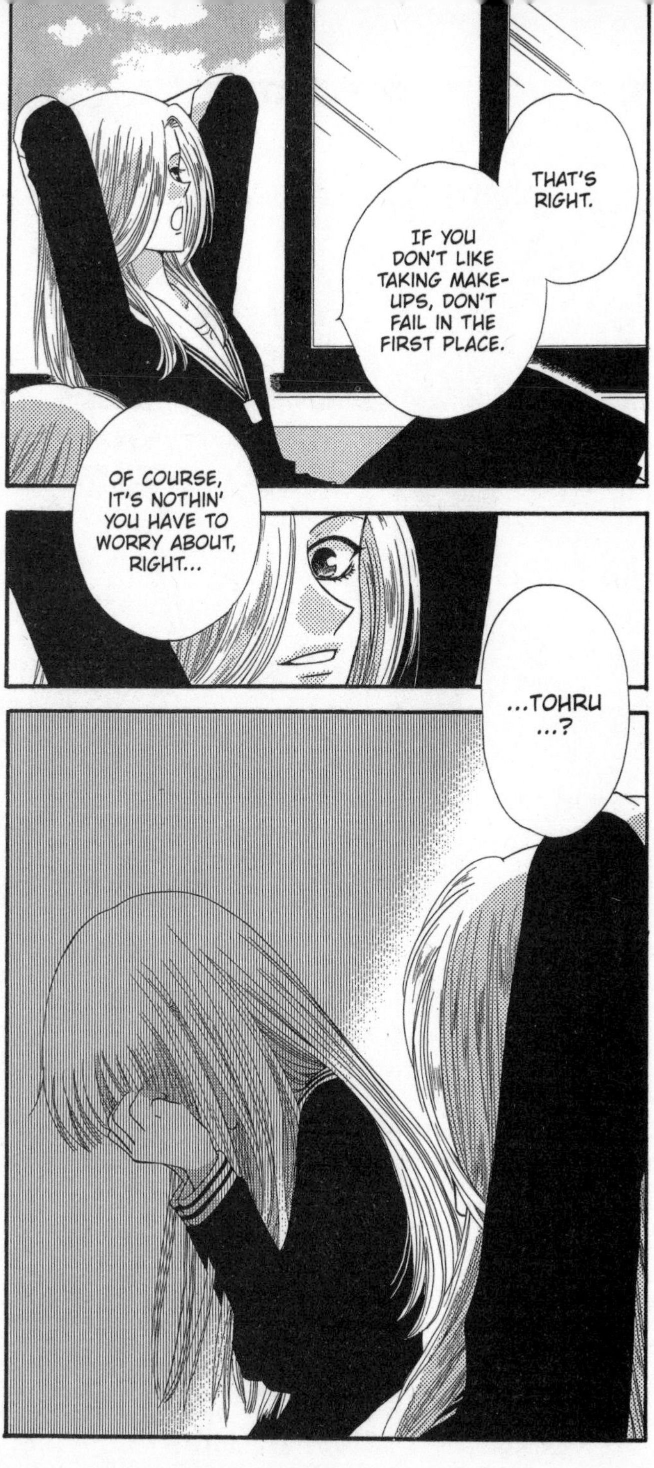
THAT'S RIGHT.
IF YOU DON'T LIKE TAKING MAKE-UPS, DON'T FAIL IN THE FIRST PLACE.
OF COURSE, IT'S NOTHIN' YOU HAVE TO WORRY ABOUT, RIGHT...
...TOHRU ...?
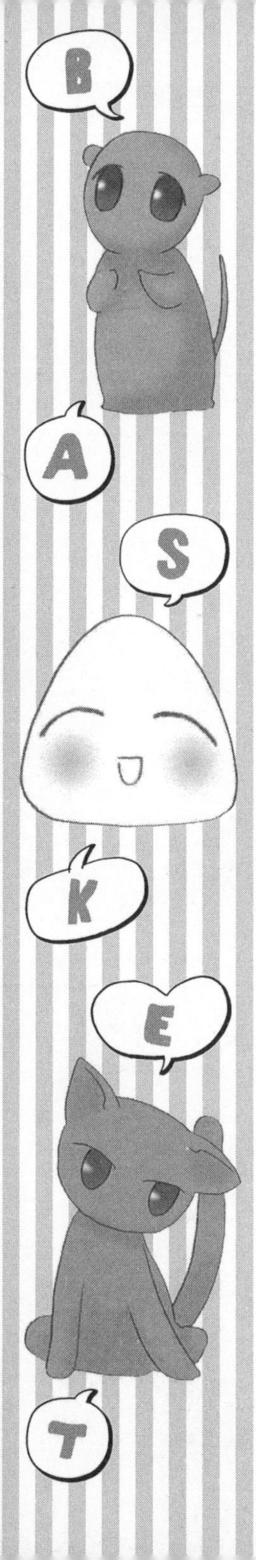
B
A
S
K
E
T

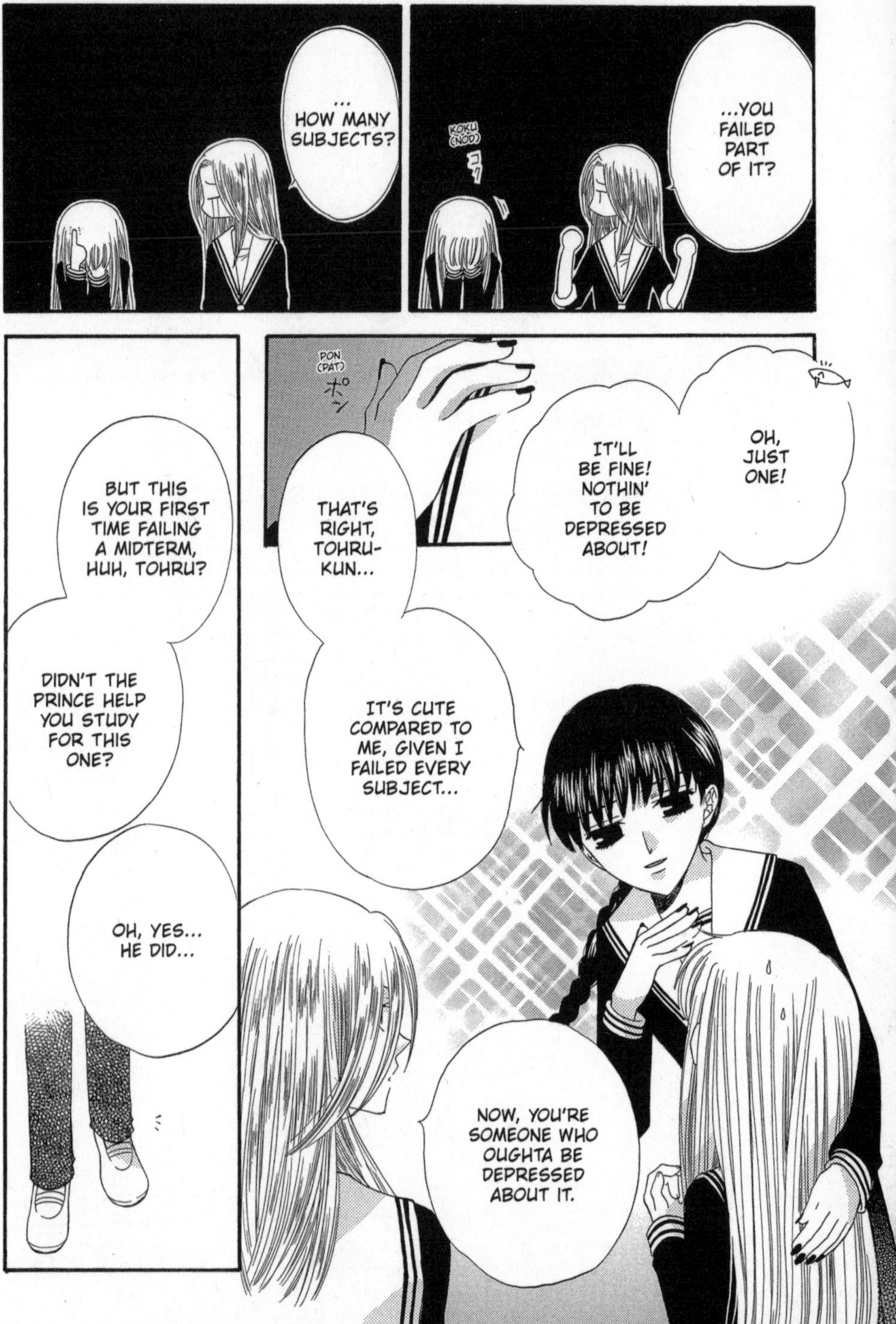
KOKU (NOD)
...YOU FAILED PART OF IT?
... HOW MANY SUBJECTS?
PON (PAT)
OH, JUST ONE!
IT'LL BE FINE! NOTHIN' TO BE DEPRESSED ABOUT!
THAT'S RIGHT, TOHRU-KUN...
IT'S CUTE COMPARED TO ME, GIVEN I FAILED EVERY SUBJECT...
NOW, YOU'RE SOMEONE WHO OUGHTA BE DEPRESSED ABOUT IT.
BUT THIS IS YOUR FIRST TIME FAILING A MIDTERM, HUH, TOHRU?
DIDN'T THE PRINCE HELP YOU STUDY FOR THIS ONE?
OH, YES... HE DID...

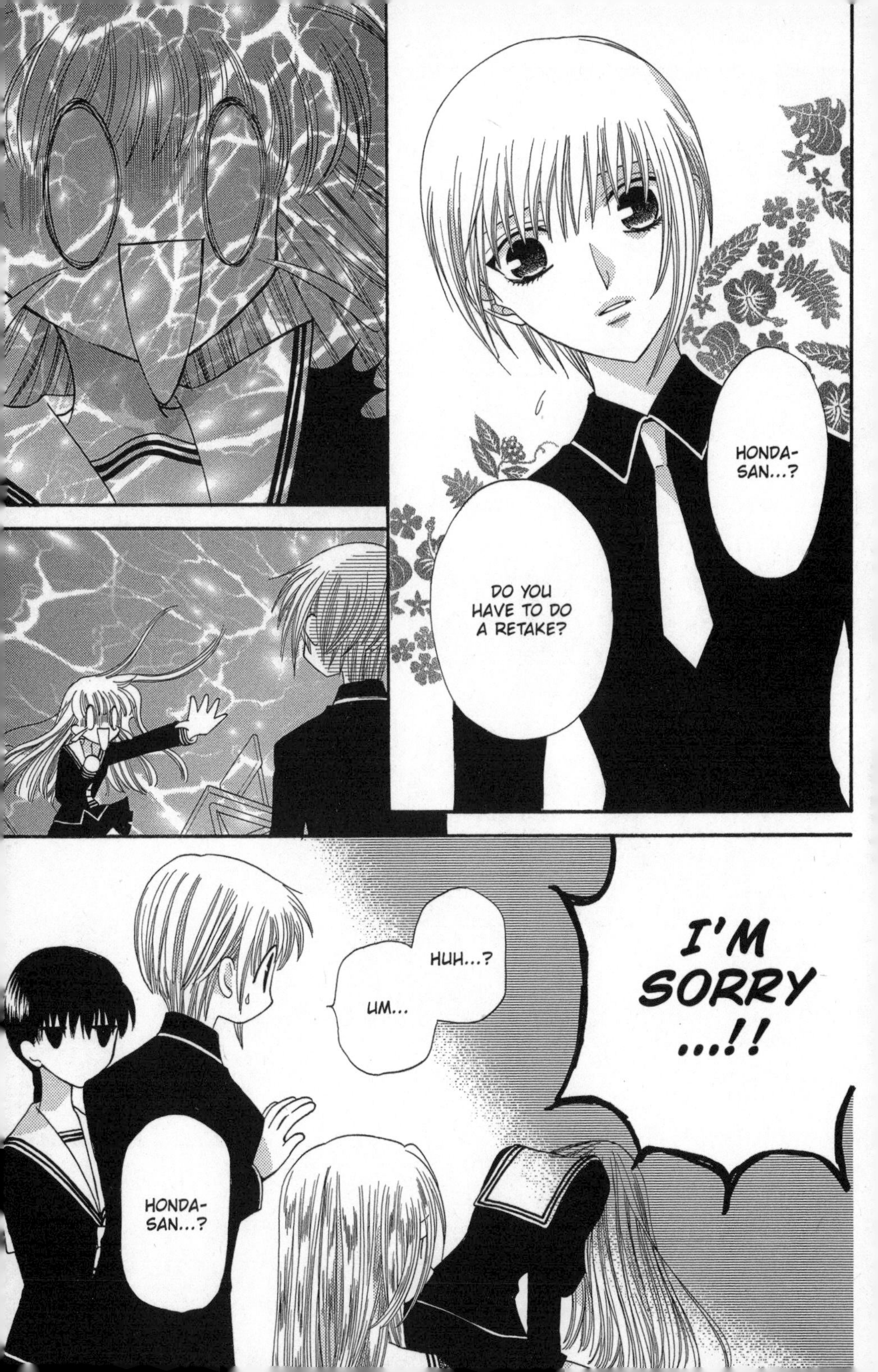
HONDA-SAN...?
DO YOU HAVE TO DO A RETAKE?
I'M SORRY ...!!
HUH...? UM...
HONDA-SAN...?

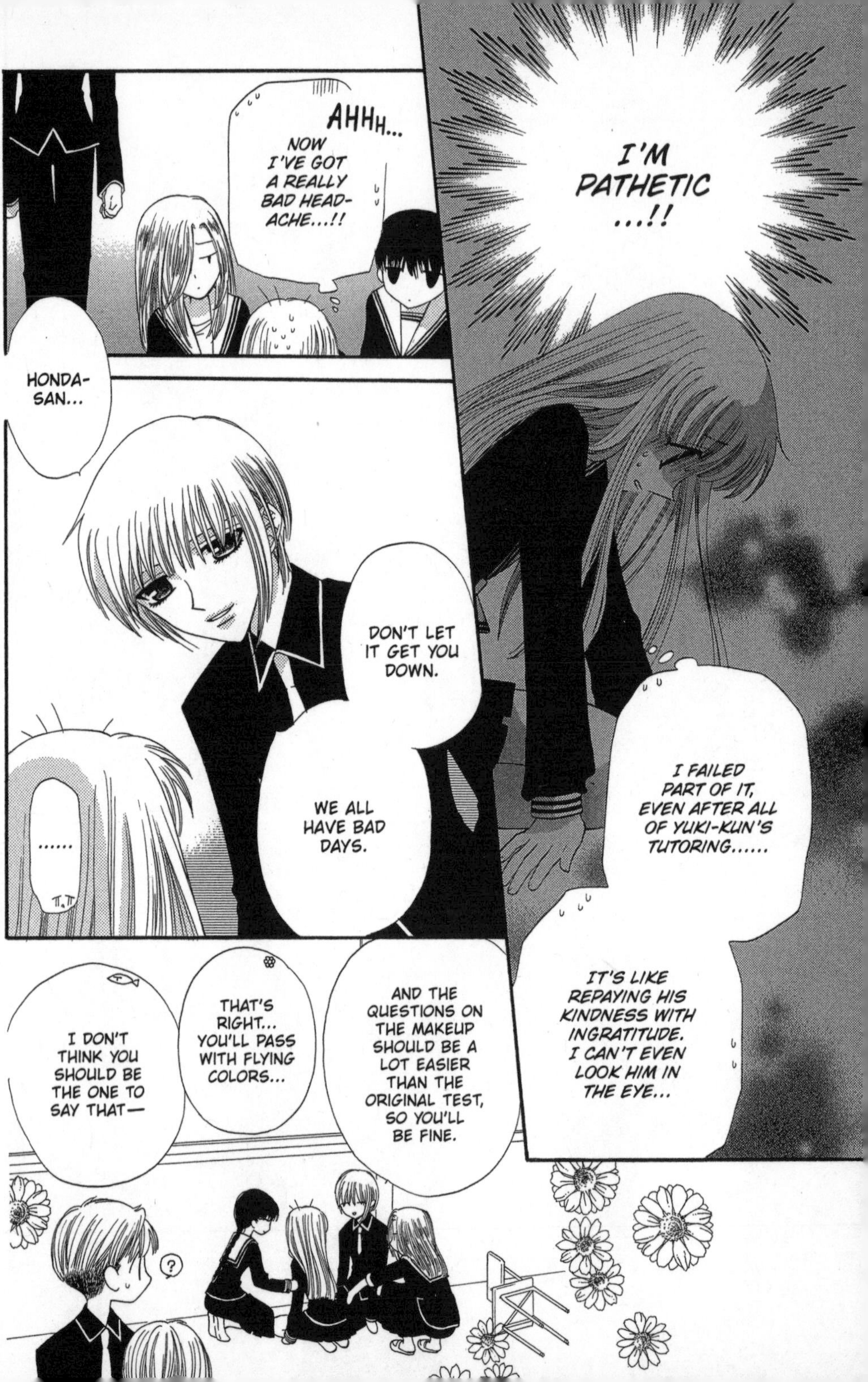
I'M PATHETIC ...!!
I FAILED PART OF IT, EVEN AFTER ALL OF YUKI-KUN'S TUTORING......
IT'S LIKE REPAYING HIS KINDNESS WITH INGRATITUDE. I CAN'T EVEN LOOK HIM IN THE EYE...
AHHH...
NOW I'VE GOT A REALLY BAD HEAD-ACHE...!!
HONDA-SAN...
DON'T LET IT GET YOU DOWN.
WE ALL HAVE BAD DAYS.
......
AND THE QUESTIONS ON THE MAKEUP SHOULD BE A LOT EASIER THAN THE ORIGINAL TEST, SO YOU'LL BE FINE.
THAT'S RIGHT... YOU'LL PASS WITH FLYING COLORS...
I DON'T THINK YOU SHOULD BE THE ONE TO SAY THAT—
?

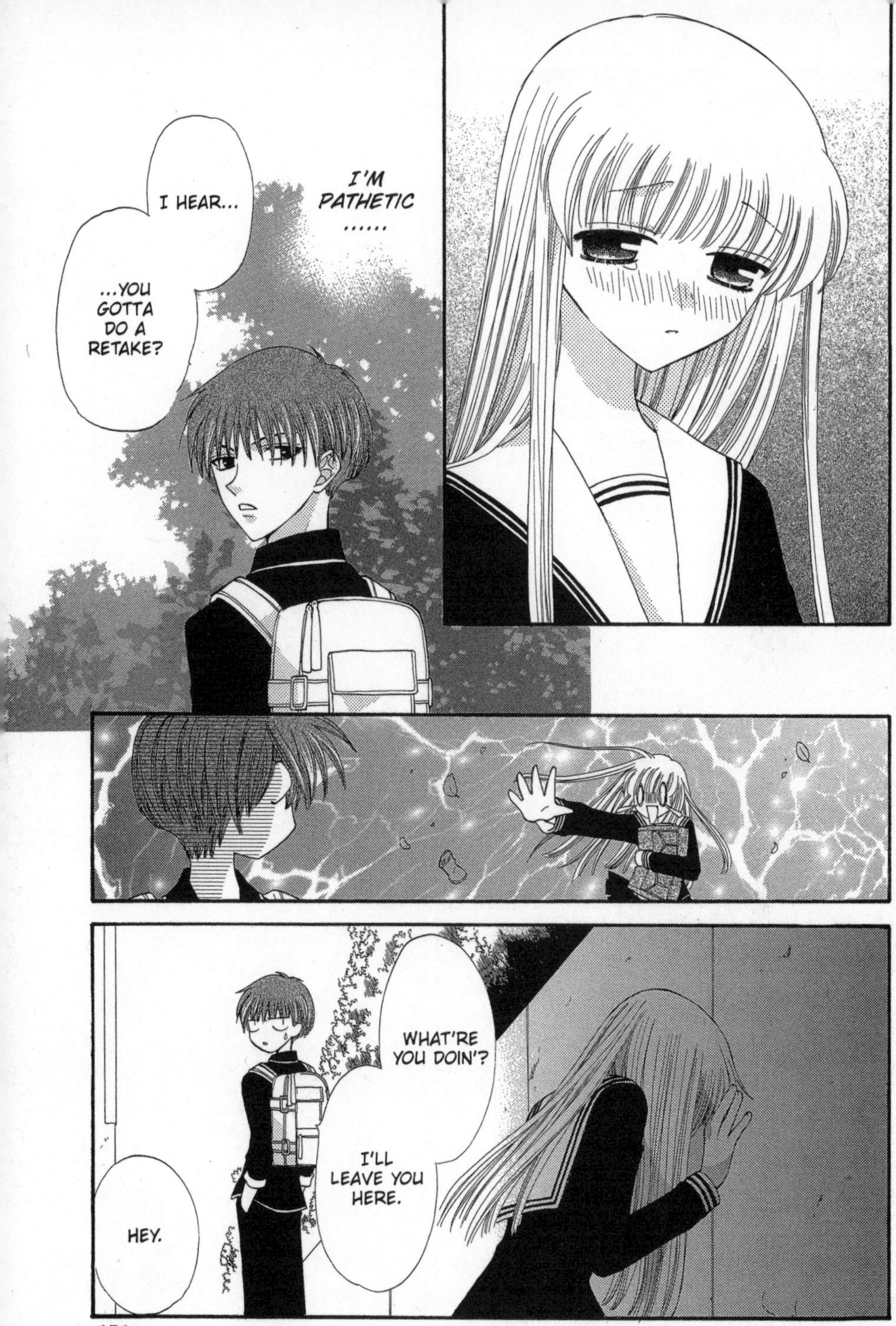
I'M PATHETIC ......
I HEAR...
...YOU GOTTA DO A RETAKE?
WHAT'RE YOU DOIN'?
I'LL LEAVE YOU HERE.
HEY.

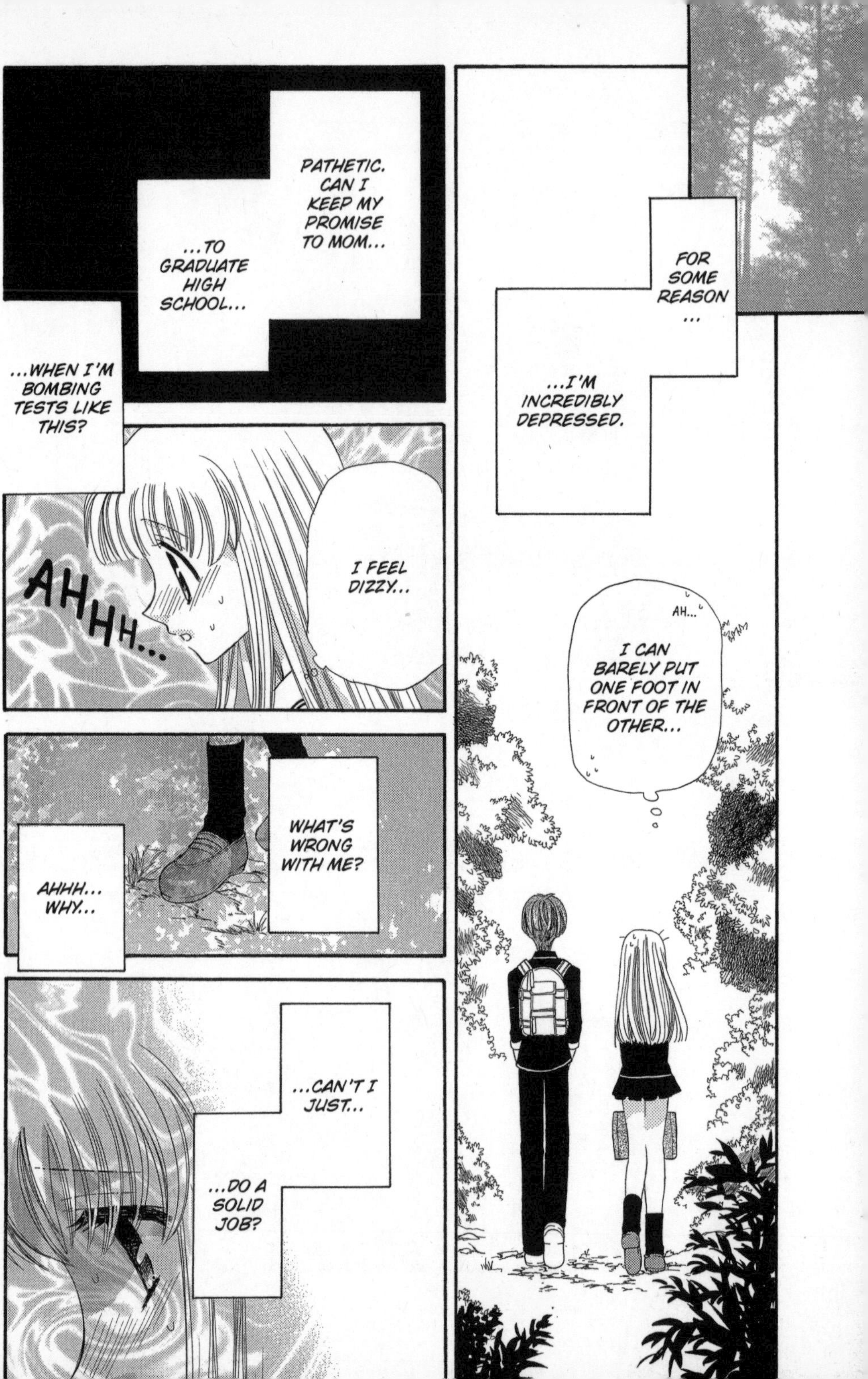
FOR SOME REASON...
...I'M INCREDIBLY DEPRESSED.
AH...
I CAN BARELY PUT ONE FOOT IN FRONT OF THE OTHER...
PATHETIC. CAN I KEEP MY PROMISE TO MOM...
...TO GRADUATE HIGH SCHOOL...
...WHEN I'M BOMBING TESTS LIKE THIS?
I FEEL DIZZY...
AHHH...
WHAT'S WRONG WITH ME?
AHHH... WHY...
...CAN'T I JUST...
...DO A SOLID JOB?

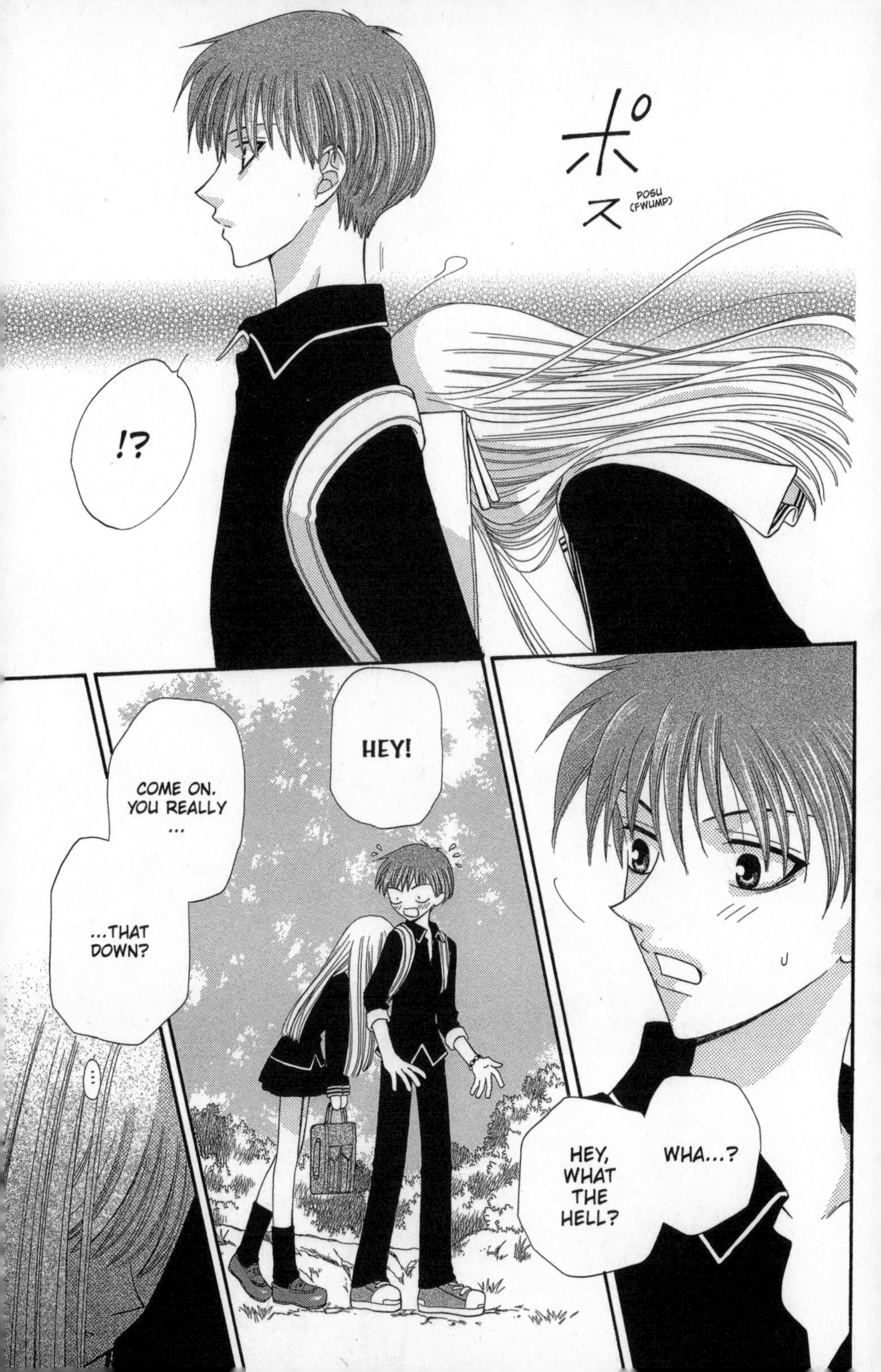
ポス
POSU (FWUMP)
!?
WHA...?
HEY, WHAT THE HELL?
HEY!
COME ON. YOU REALLY ...
...THAT DOWN?
...

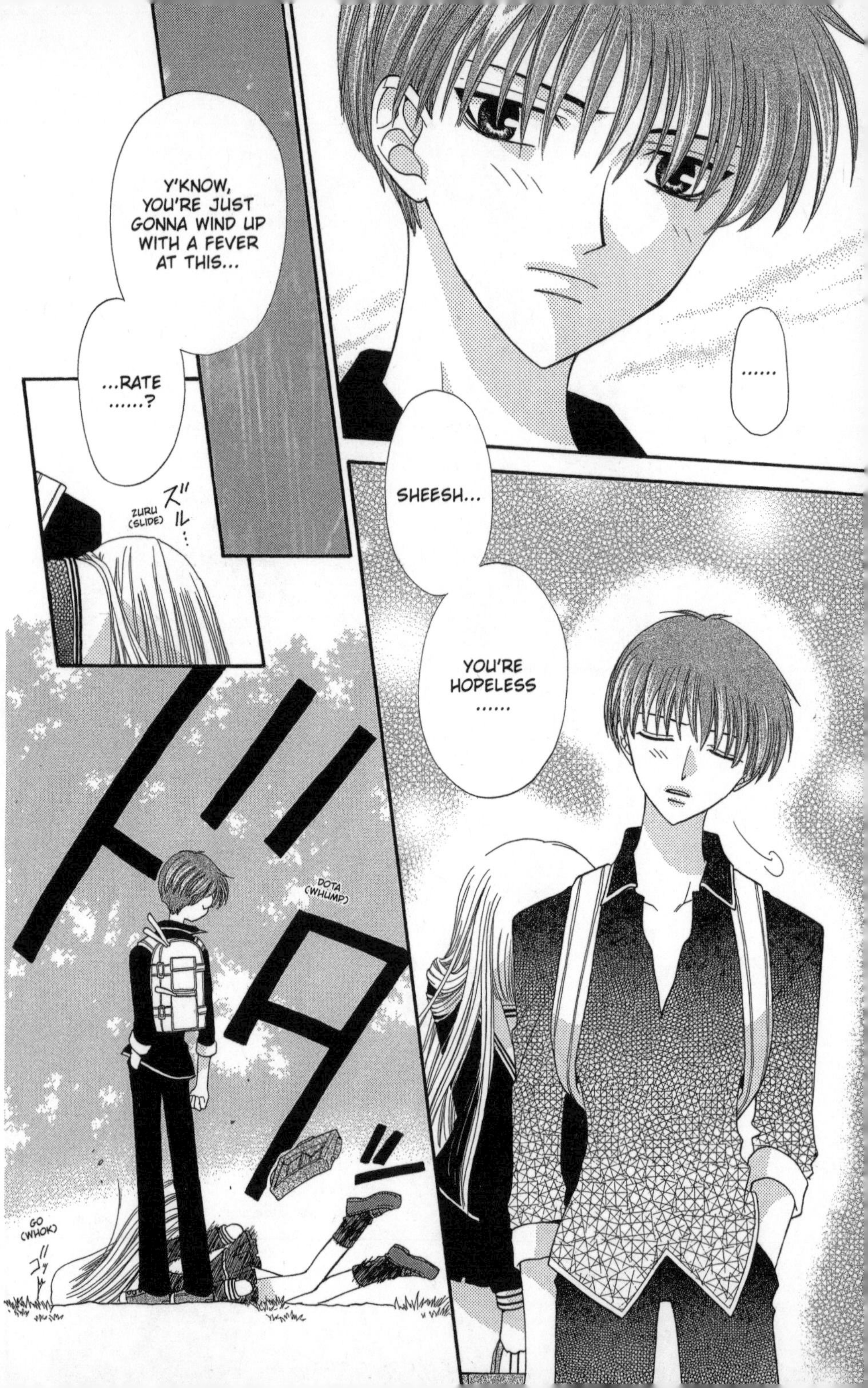
......
Y'KNOW, YOU'RE JUST GONNA WIND UP WITH A FEVER AT THIS...
...RATE ......?
ZURU (SLIDE) ズル…
SHEESH...
YOU'RE HOPELESS ......
ドタ
DOTA (WHUMP)
GO (WHOK) ゴッ

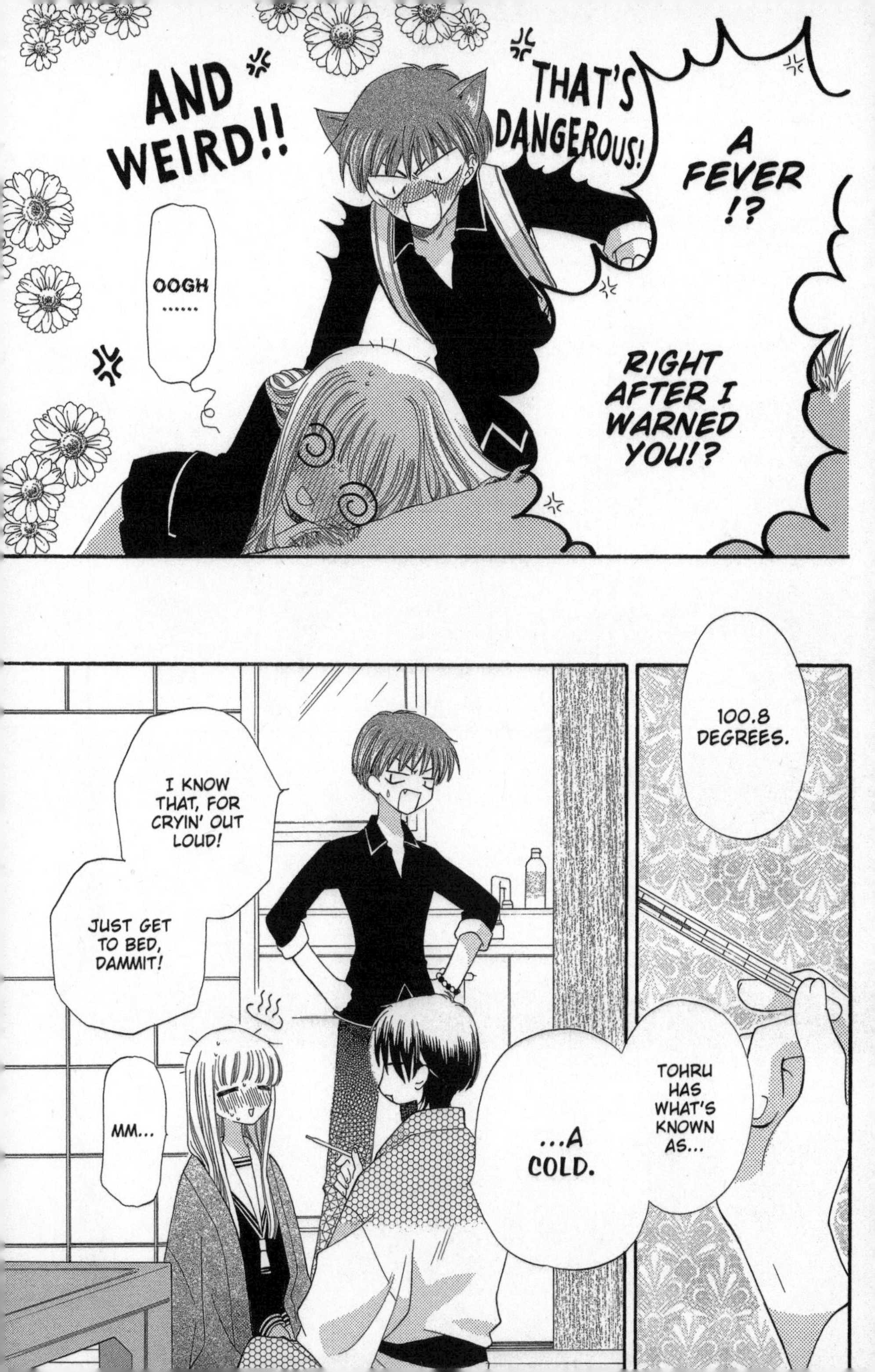
A FEVER!?
RIGHT AFTER I WARNED YOU!?
THAT'S DANGEROUS!
AND WEIRD!!
OOGH.......
100.8 DEGREES.
TOHRU HAS WHAT'S KNOWN AS...
...A COLD.
I KNOW THAT, FOR CRYIN' OUT LOUD!
JUST GET TO BED, DAMMIT!
MM...

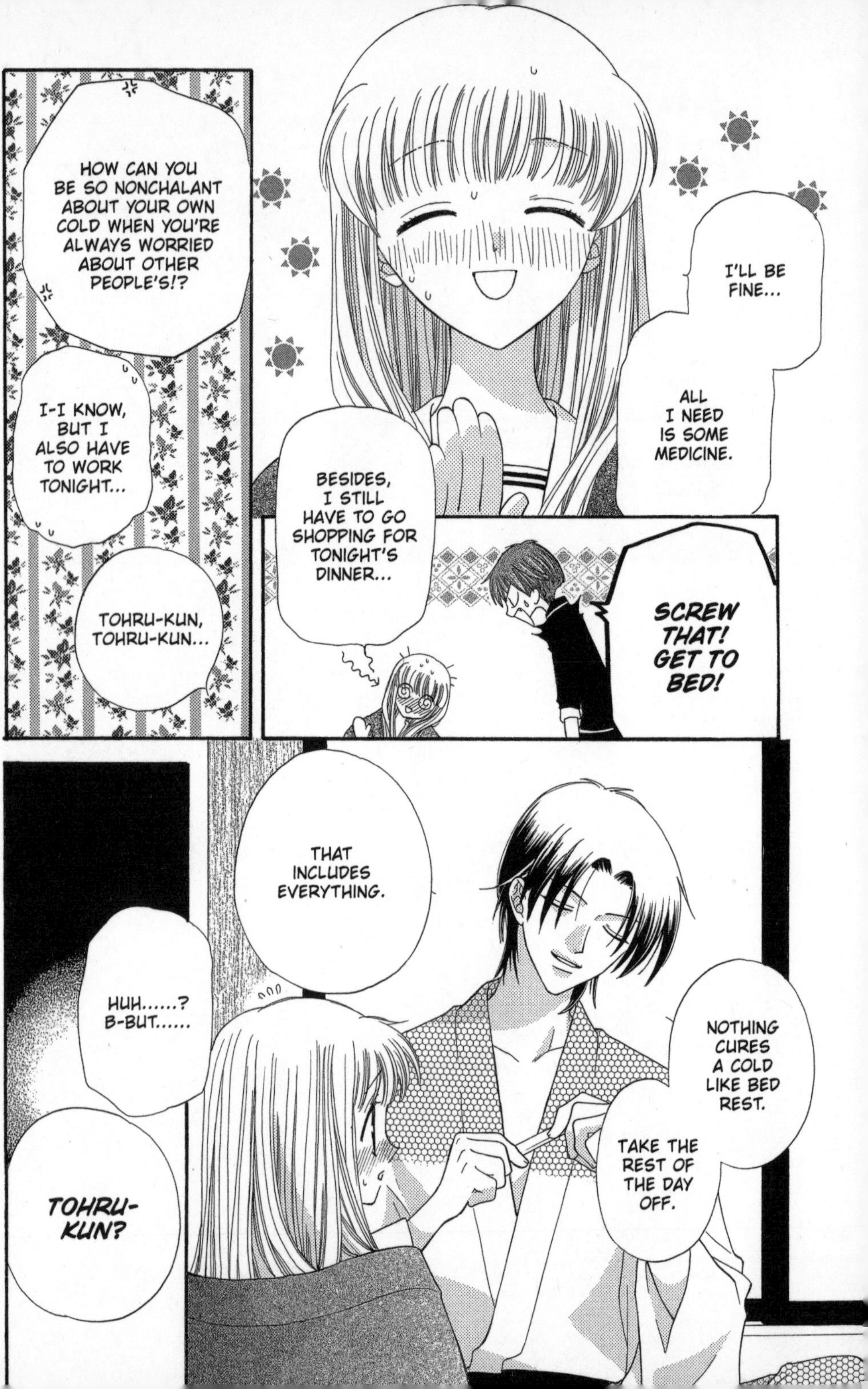
I'LL BE FINE...
ALL I NEED IS SOME MEDICINE.
BESIDES, I STILL HAVE TO GO SHOPPING FOR TONIGHT'S DINNER...
SCREW THAT! GET TO BED!
HOW CAN YOU BE SO NONCHALANT ABOUT YOUR OWN COLD WHEN YOU'RE ALWAYS WORRIED ABOUT OTHER PEOPLE'S!?
I-I KNOW, BUT I ALSO HAVE TO WORK TONIGHT...
TOHRU-KUN, TOHRU-KUN...
NOTHING CURES A COLD LIKE BED REST.
TAKE THE REST OF THE DAY OFF.
THAT INCLUDES EVERYTHING.
HUH......? B-BUT......
TOHRU-KUN?

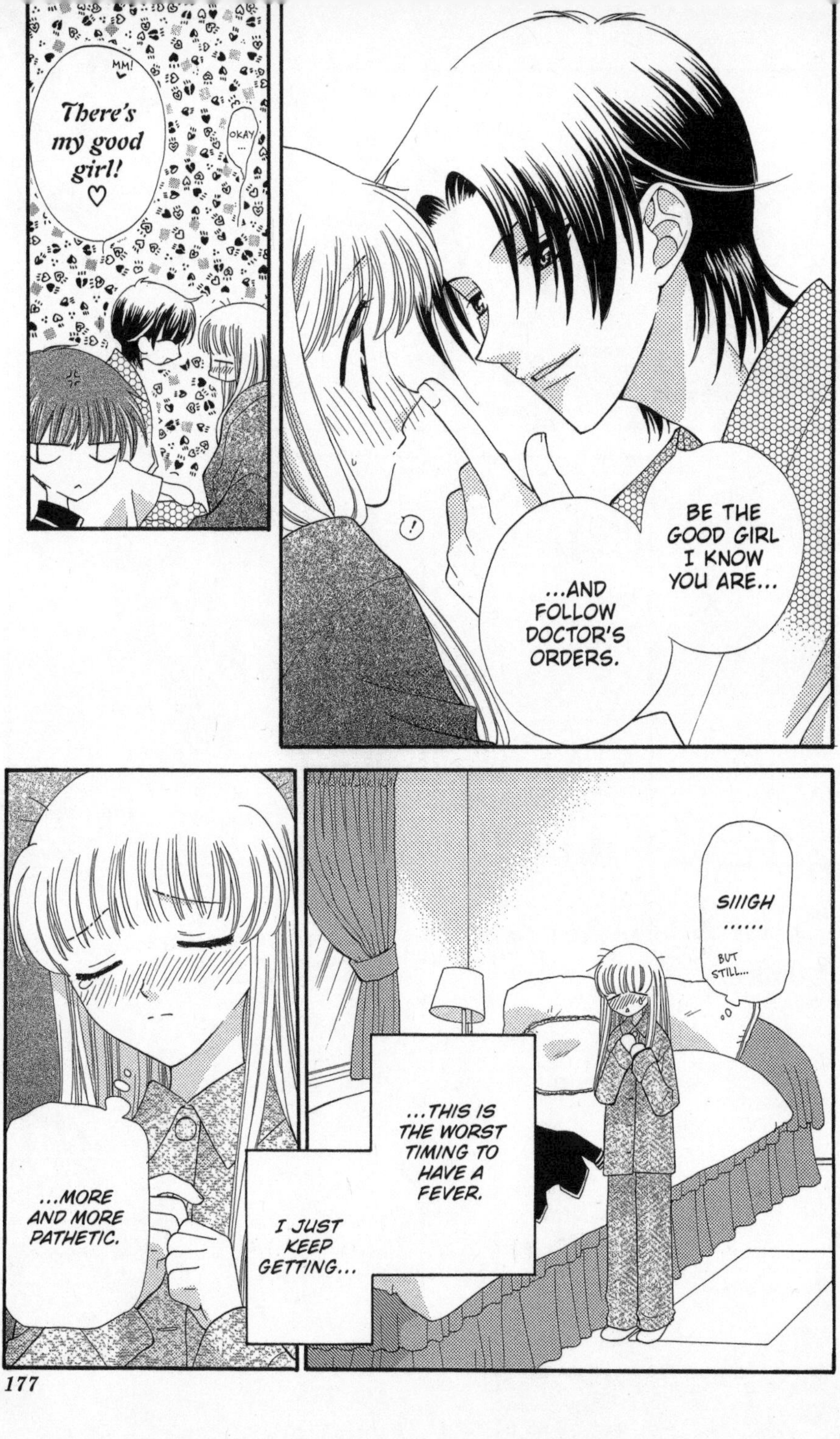
BE THE GOOD GIRL I KNOW YOU ARE...
...AND FOLLOW DOCTOR'S ORDERS.
!
OKAY...
There's my good girl! ♡
MM!
SIIIGH ......
BUT STILL...
...THIS IS THE WORST TIMING TO HAVE A FEVER.
I JUST KEEP GETTING...
...MORE AND MORE PATHETIC.

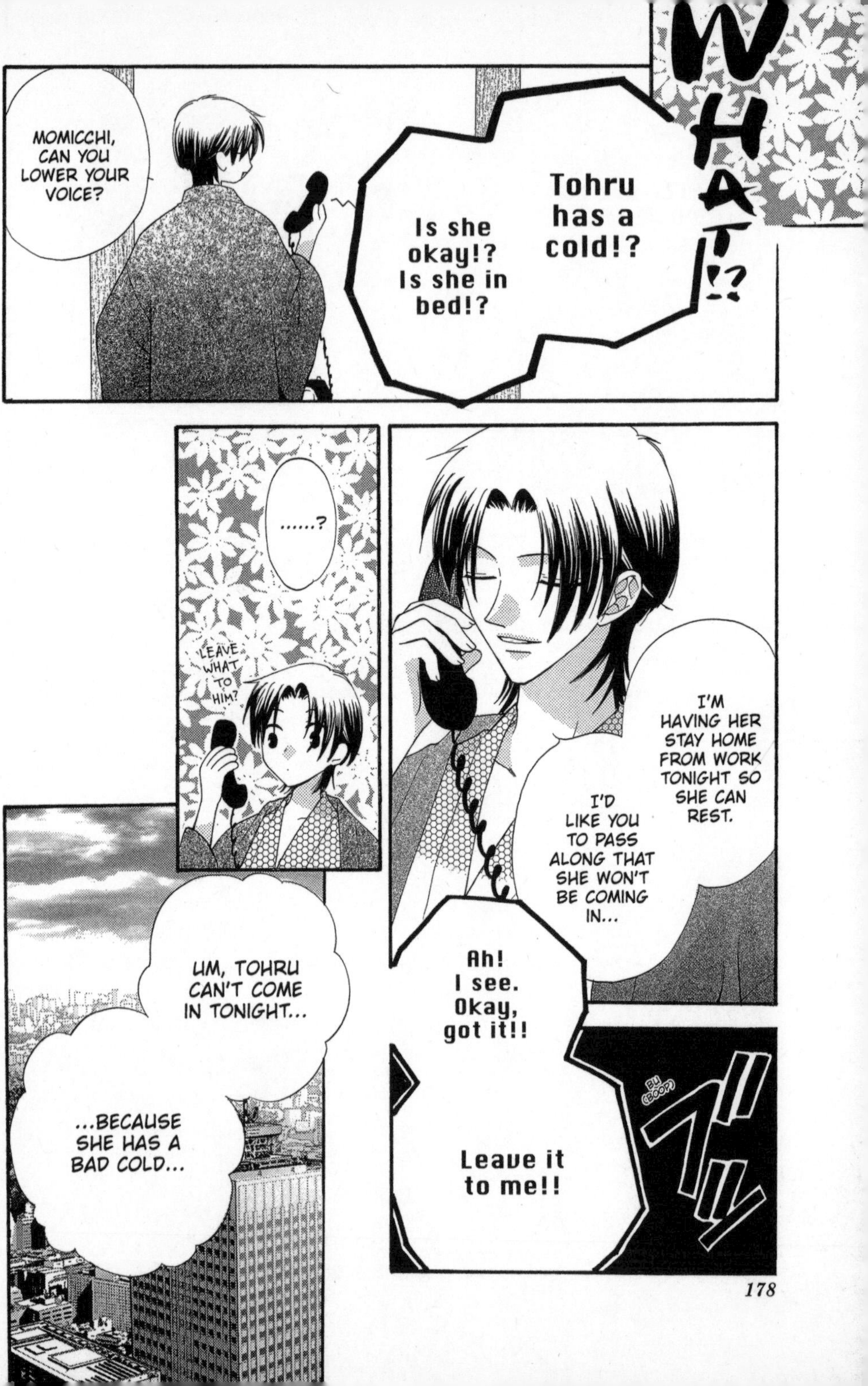
WHAT!?
Tohru has a cold!?
Is she okay!? Is she in bed!?
MOMICCHI, CAN YOU LOWER YOUR VOICE?
I'M HAVING HER STAY HOME FROM WORK TONIGHT SO SHE CAN REST.
I'D LIKE YOU TO PASS ALONG THAT SHE WON'T BE COMING IN...
......?
LEAVE WHAT TO HIM?
UM, TOHRU CAN'T COME IN TONIGHT...
...BECAUSE SHE HAS A BAD COLD...
Ah! I see. Okay, got it!!
Leave it to me!!
BU (BOOP)

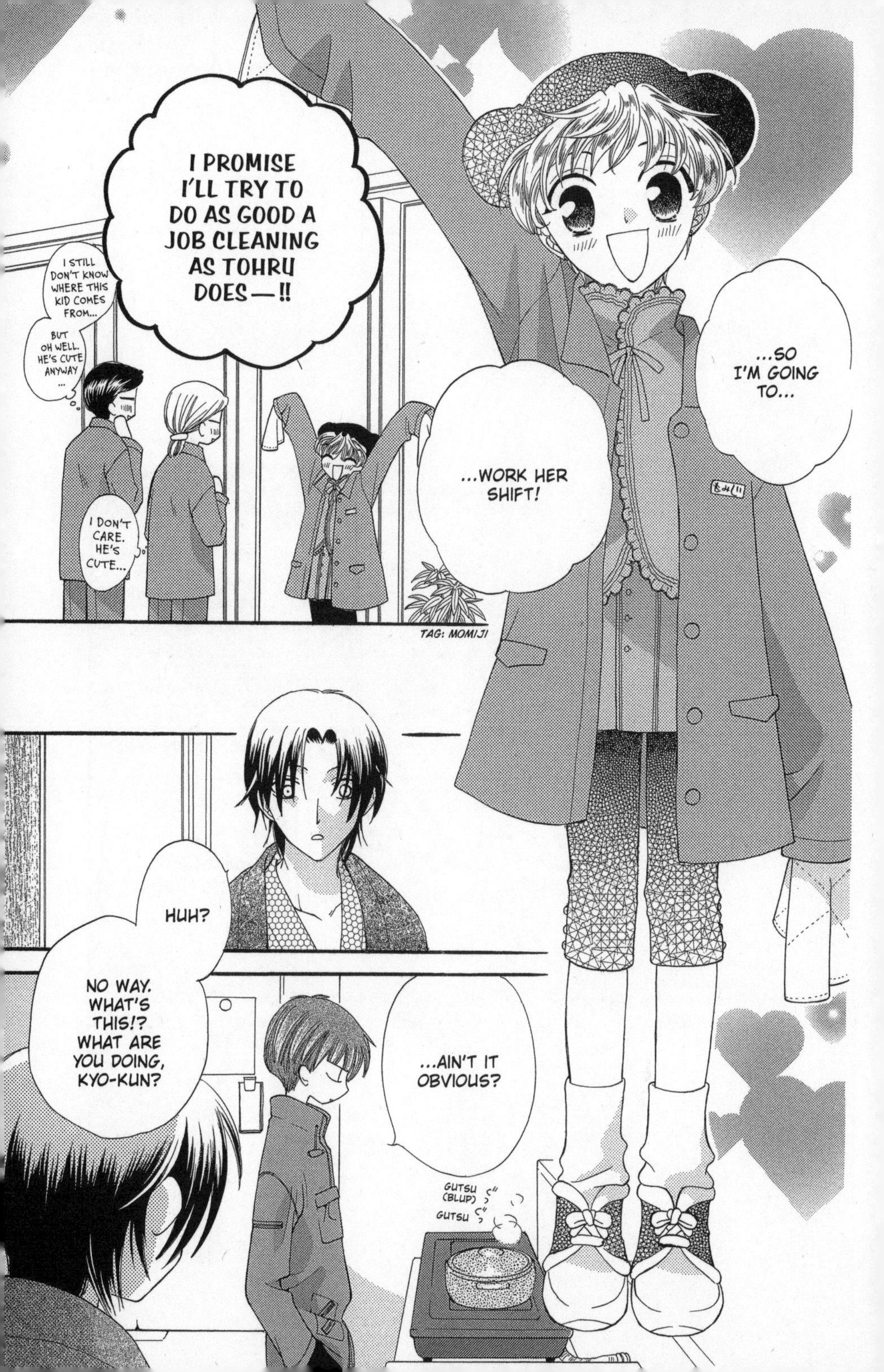
...SO I'M GOING TO...
...WORK HER SHIFT!
I PROMISE I'LL TRY TO DO AS GOOD A JOB CLEANING AS TOHRU DOES—!!
I STILL DON'T KNOW WHERE THIS KID COMES FROM...
BUT OH WELL. HE'S CUTE ANYWAY...
I DON'T CARE. HE'S CUTE...
TAG: MOMIJI
HUH?
...AIN'T IT OBVIOUS?
NO WAY. WHAT'S THIS!? WHAT ARE YOU DOING, KYO-KUN?
GUTSU (BLUP)
GUTSU

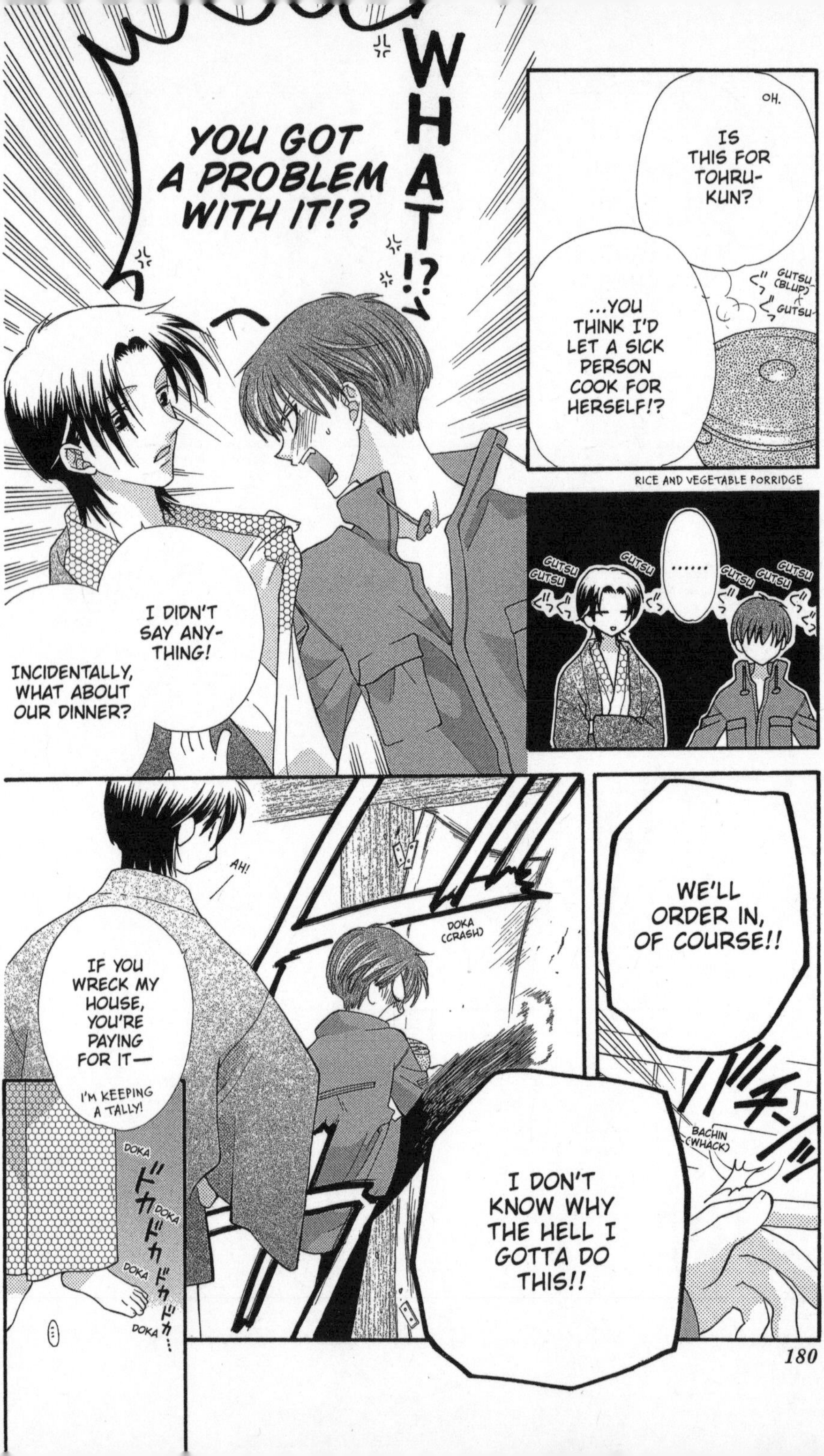
OH.
IS THIS FOR TOHRU-KUN?
...YOU THINK I'D LET A SICK PERSON COOK FOR HERSELF!?
GUTSU (BLUP) GUTSU
RICE AND VEGETABLE PORRIDGE
GUTSU GUTSU GUTSU GUTSU GUTSU GUTSU
......
WHAT!?
YOU GOT A PROBLEM WITH IT!?
I DIDN'T SAY ANY-THING!
INCIDENTALLY, WHAT ABOUT OUR DINNER?
WE'LL ORDER IN, OF COURSE!!
BACHIN (WHACK)
I DON'T KNOW WHY THE HELL I GOTTA DO THIS!!
DOKA (CRASH)
AH!
IF YOU WRECK MY HOUSE, YOU'RE PAYING FOR IT—
I'M KEEPING A TALLY!
DOKA DOKA DOKA DOKA
...

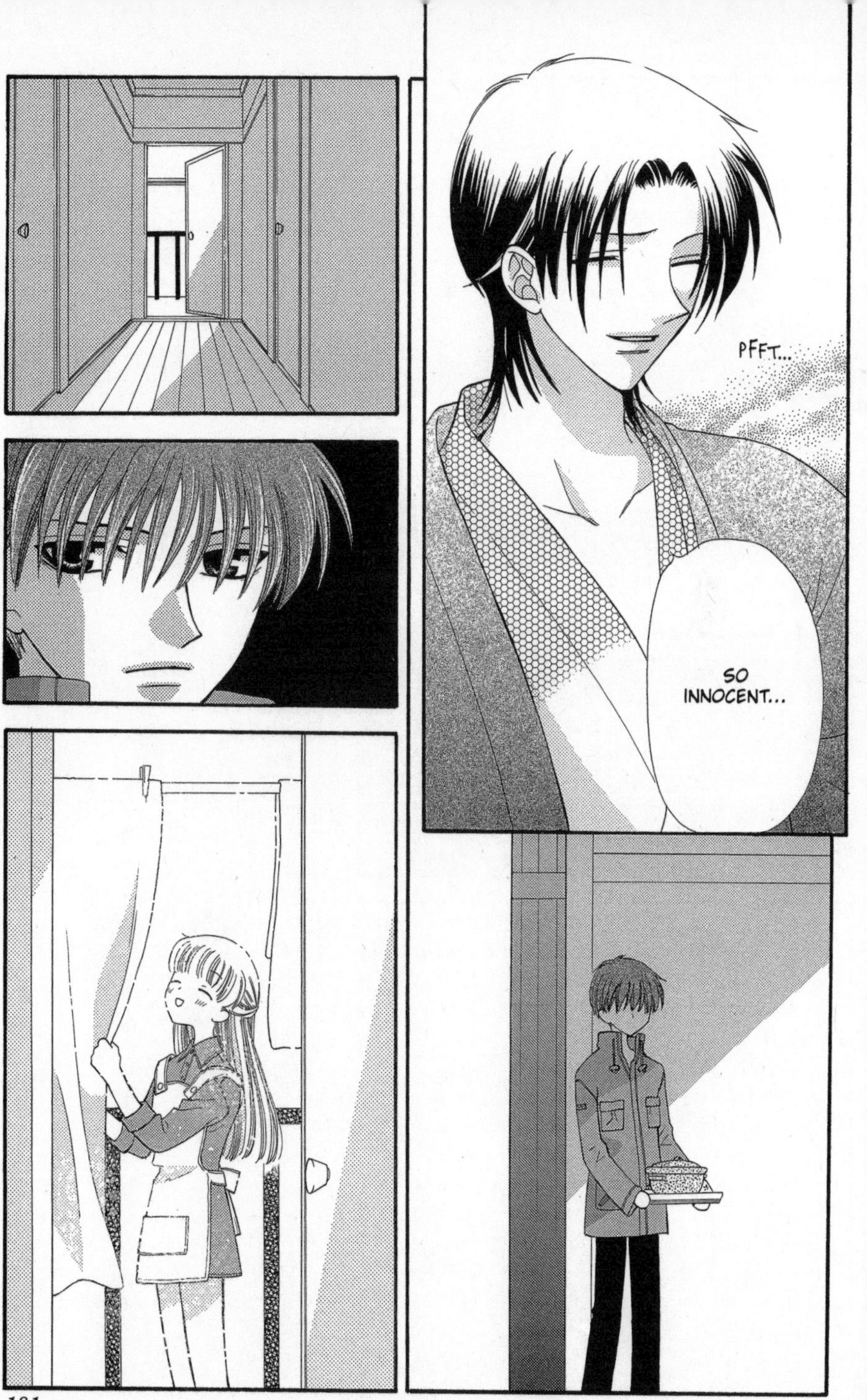
PFFT...
SO INNOCENT...

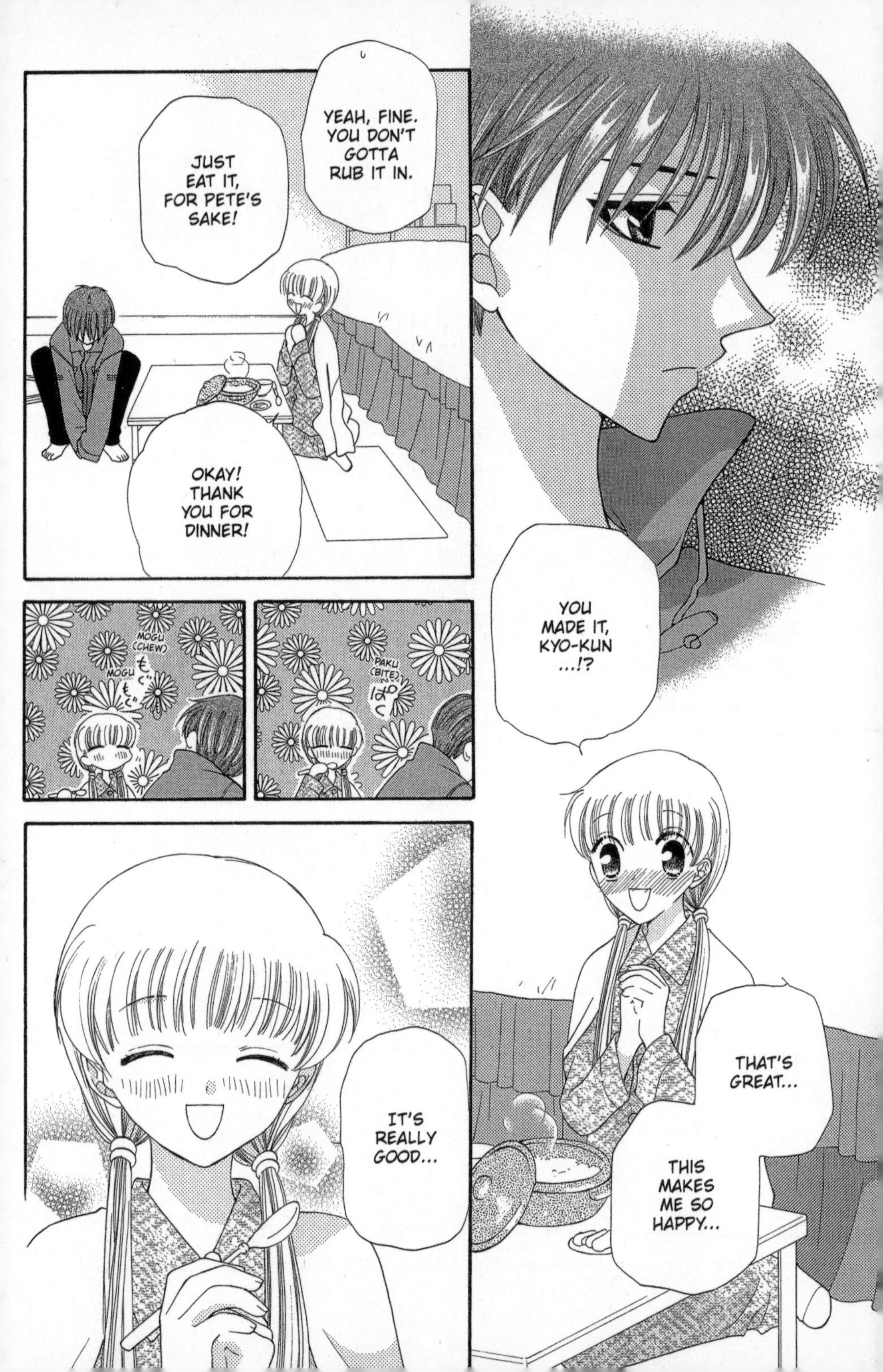
YOU MADE IT, KYO-KUN ...!?
THAT'S GREAT...
THIS MAKES ME SO HAPPY...
YEAH, FINE. YOU DON'T GOTTA RUB IT IN.
JUST EAT IT, FOR PETE'S SAKE!
OKAY! THANK YOU FOR DINNER!
PAKU (BITE)
ぱく
MOGU (CHEW)
MOGU
もぐ
もぐ
IT'S REALLY GOOD...

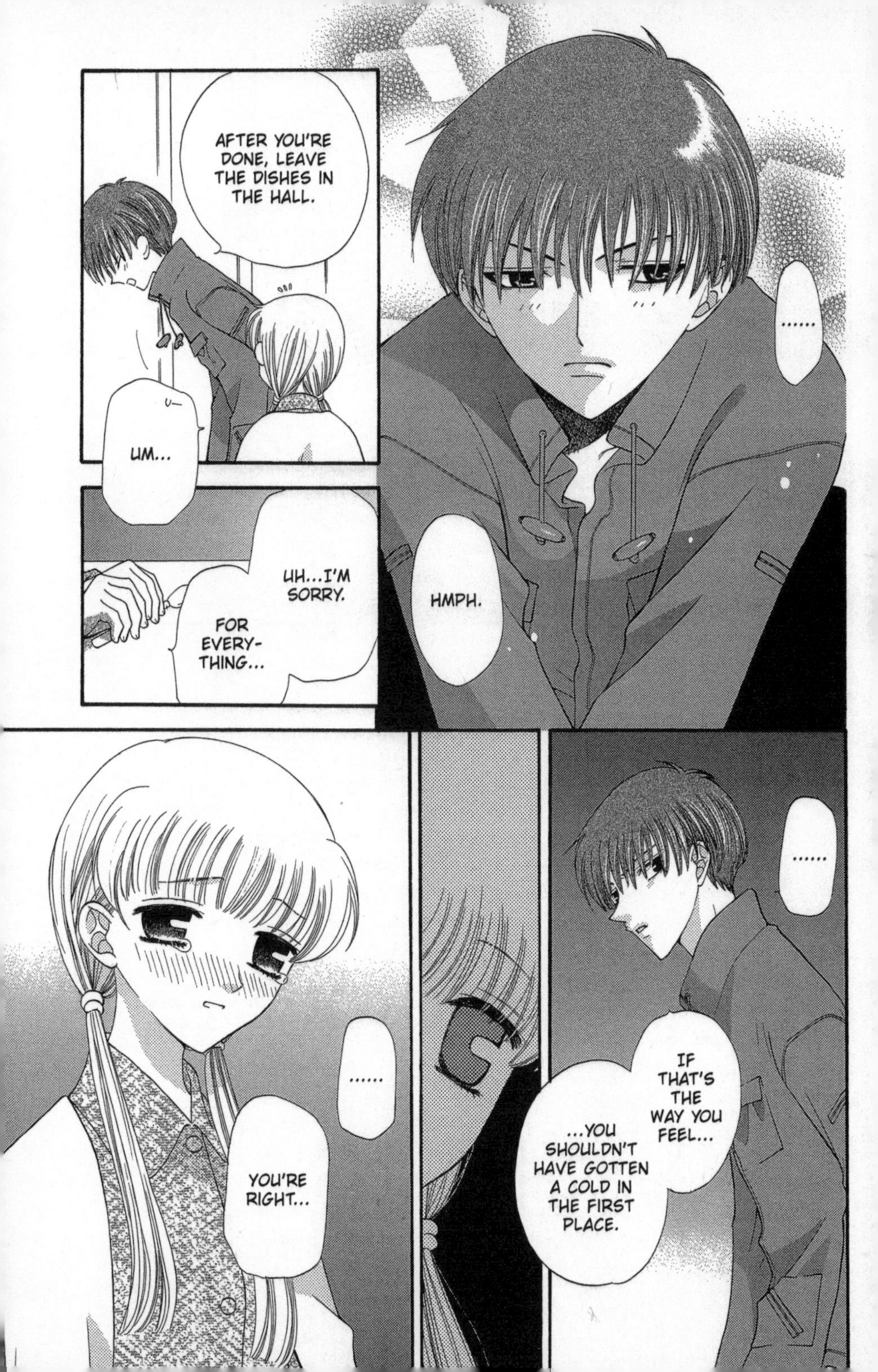
......
HMPH.
AFTER YOU'RE DONE, LEAVE THE DISHES IN THE HALL.
UM...
UH...I'M SORRY.
FOR EVERY-THING...
......
IF THAT'S THE WAY YOU FEEL...
...YOU SHOULDN'T HAVE GOTTEN A COLD IN THE FIRST PLACE.
......
YOU'RE RIGHT...

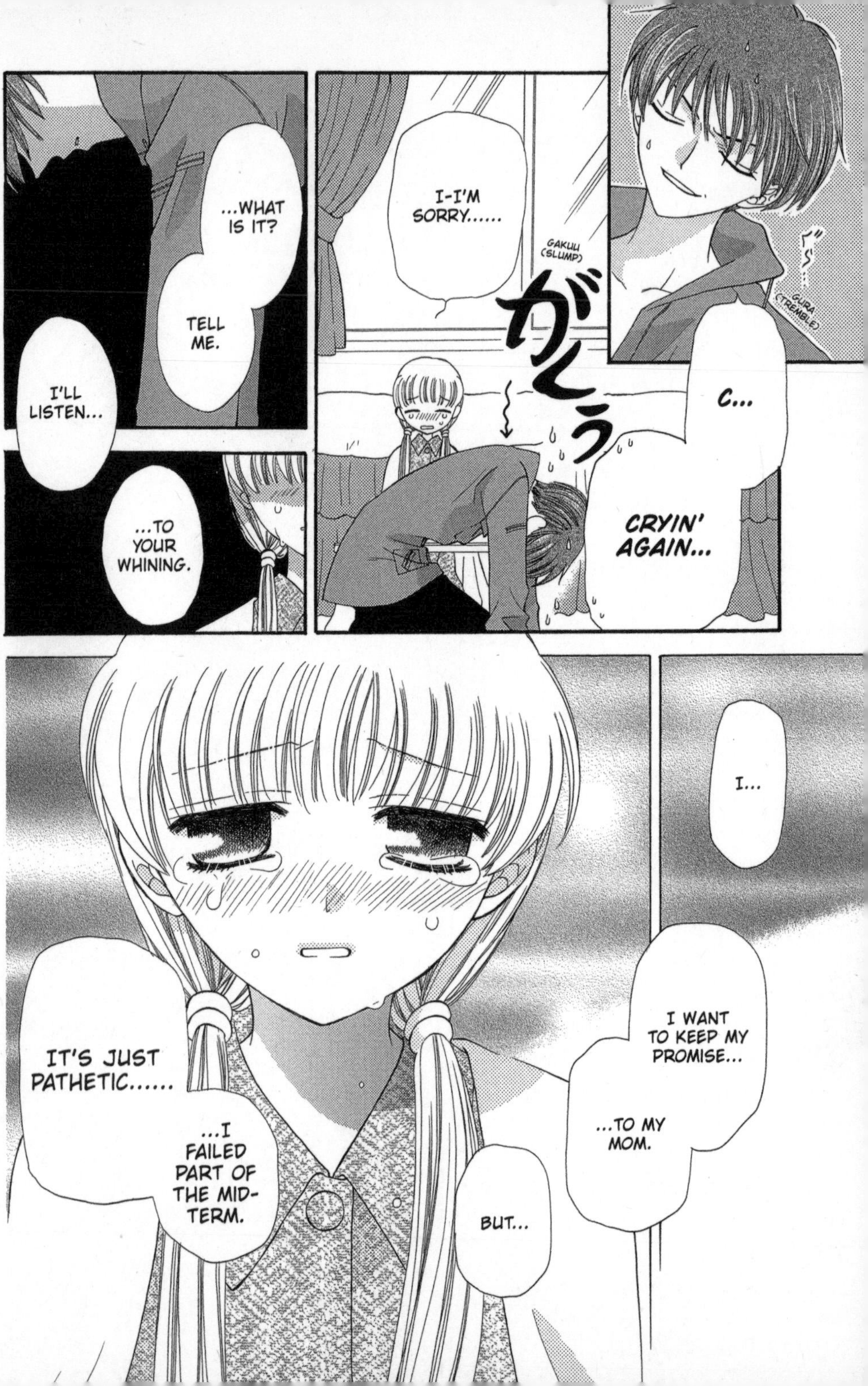
ぐら
GURA (TREMBLE)
I-I'M SORRY......
GAKUU (SLUMP)
がくう
C...
CRYIN' AGAIN...
...WHAT IS IT?
TELL ME.
I'LL LISTEN...
...TO YOUR WHINING.
I...
I WANT TO KEEP MY PROMISE...
...TO MY MOM.
BUT...
IT'S JUST PATHETIC......
...I FAILED PART OF THE MID-TERM.

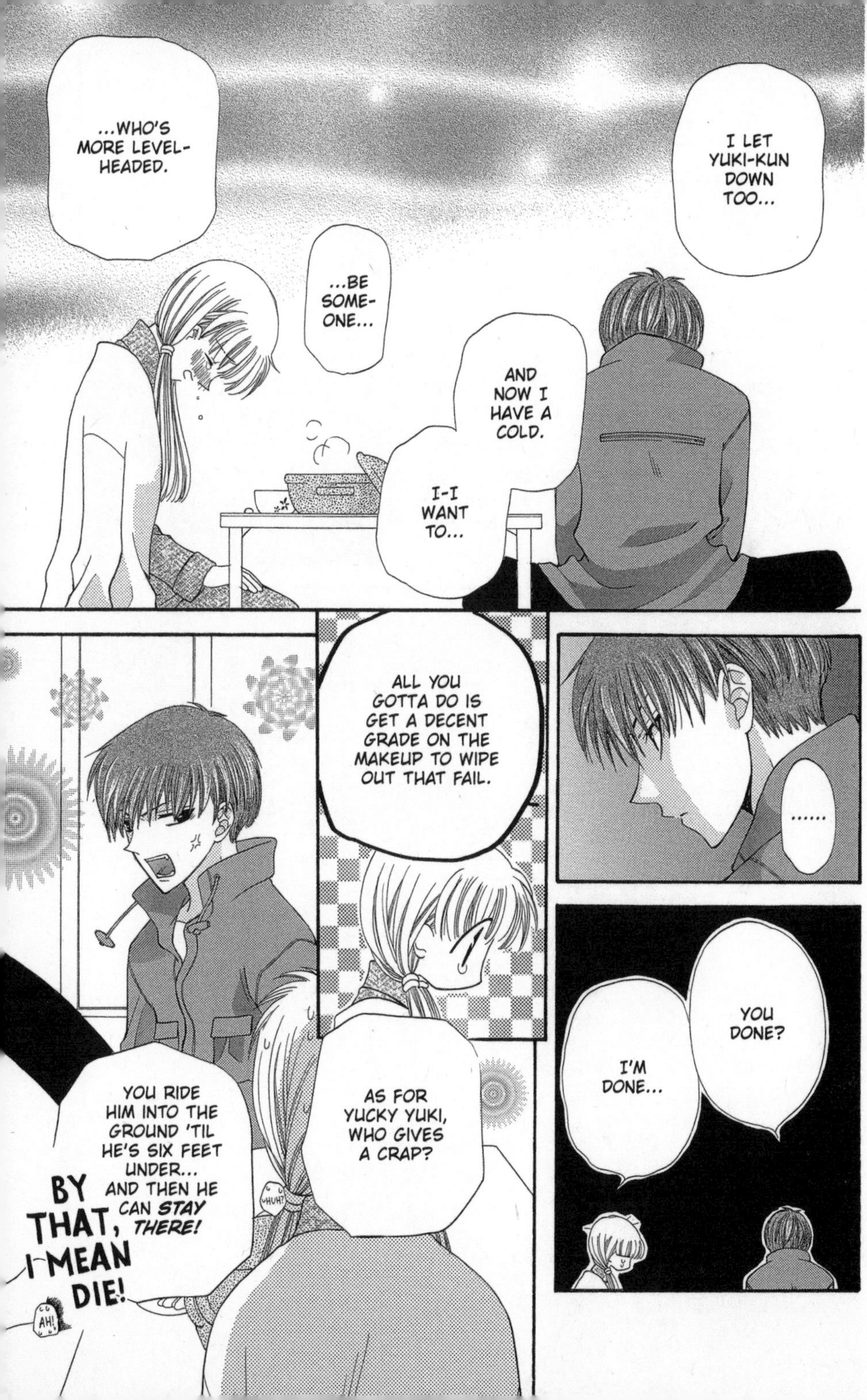
I LET YUKI-KUN DOWN TOO...
AND NOW I HAVE A COLD.
I-I WANT TO...
...BE SOME-ONE...
...WHO'S MORE LEVEL-HEADED.
......
YOU DONE?
I'M DONE...
ALL YOU GOTTA DO IS GET A DECENT GRADE ON THE MAKEUP TO WIPE OUT THAT FAIL.
AS FOR YUCKY YUKI, WHO GIVES A CRAP?
YOU RIDE HIM INTO THE GROUND 'TIL HE'S SIX FEET UNDER... AND THEN HE CAN STAY THERE!
HUH?
BY THAT, I MEAN DIE!
AH!

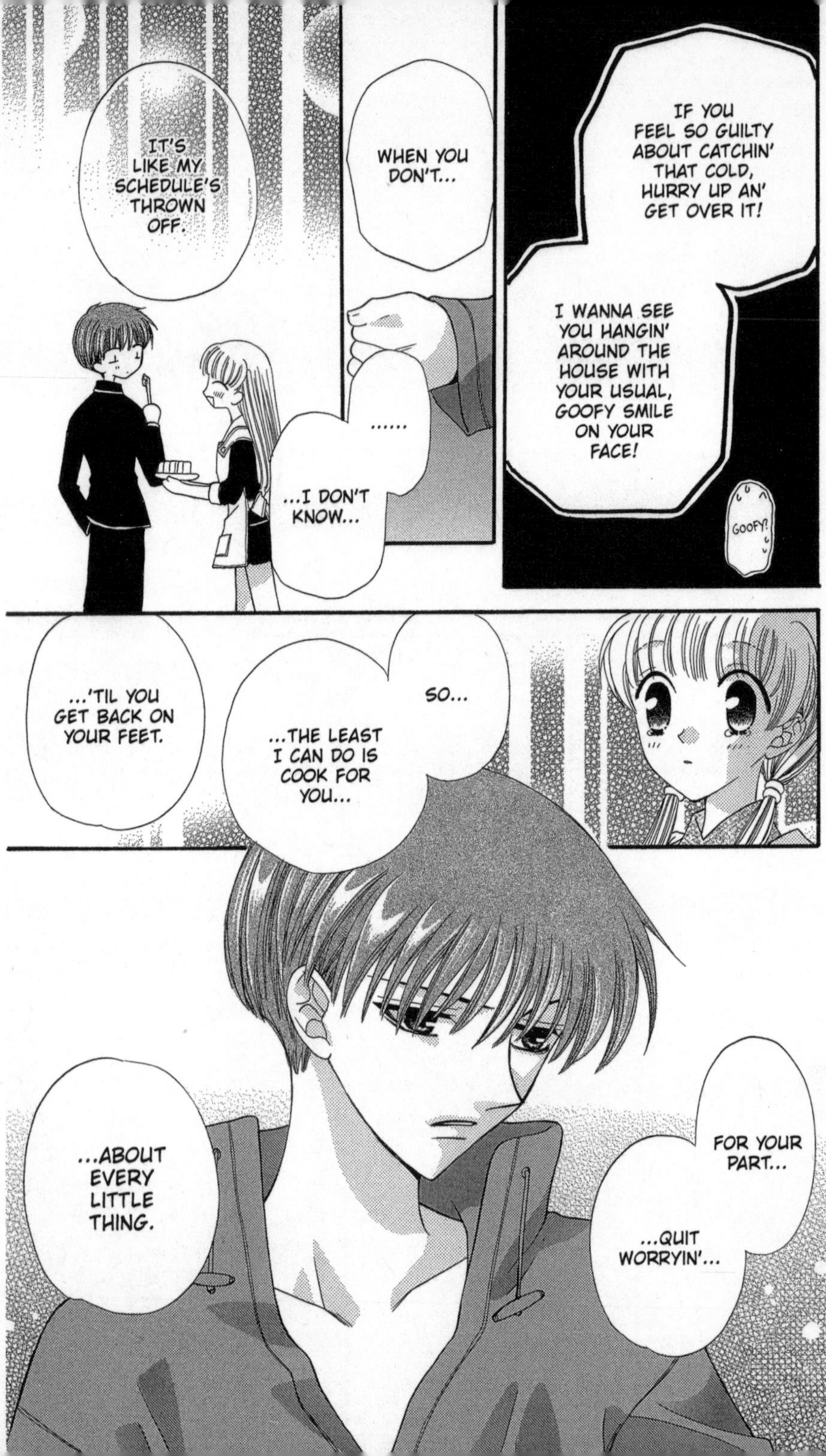
IF YOU FEEL SO GUILTY ABOUT CATCHIN' THAT COLD, HURRY UP AN' GET OVER IT!
I WANNA SEE YOU HANGIN' AROUND THE HOUSE WITH YOUR USUAL, GOOFY SMILE ON YOUR FACE!
GOOFY!
WHEN YOU DON'T...
......
...I DON'T KNOW...
IT'S LIKE MY SCHEDULE'S THROWN OFF.
SO...
...THE LEAST I CAN DO IS COOK FOR YOU...
...'TIL YOU GET BACK ON YOUR FEET.
FOR YOUR PART...
...QUIT WORRYIN'...
...ABOUT EVERY LITTLE THING.

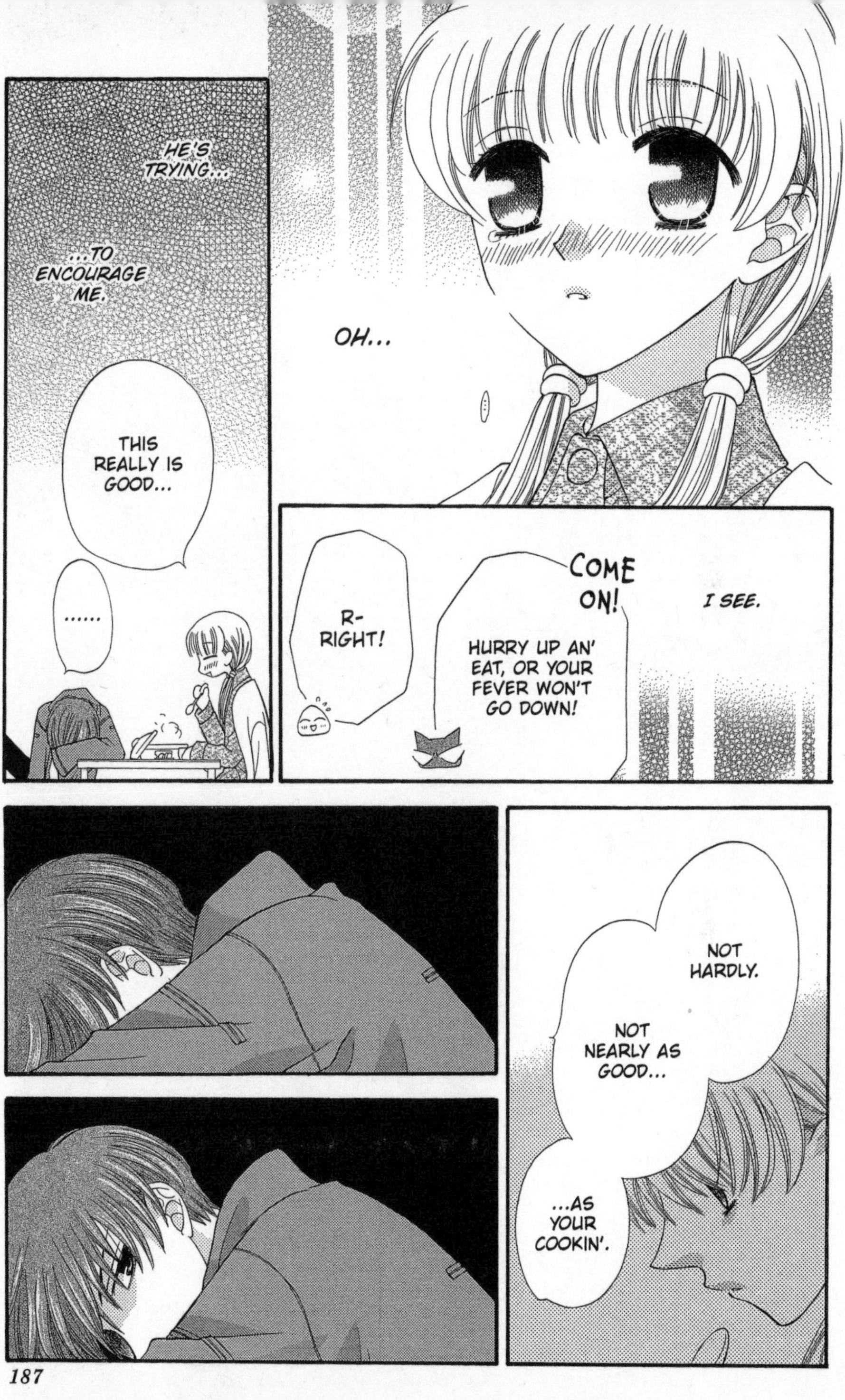
OH...
I SEE.
COME ON!
HURRY UP AN' EAT, OR YOUR FEVER WON'T GO DOWN!
R-RIGHT!
HE'S TRYING...
...TO ENCOURAGE ME.
THIS REALLY IS GOOD...
......
NOT HARDLY.
NOT NEARLY AS GOOD...
...AS YOUR COOKIN'.

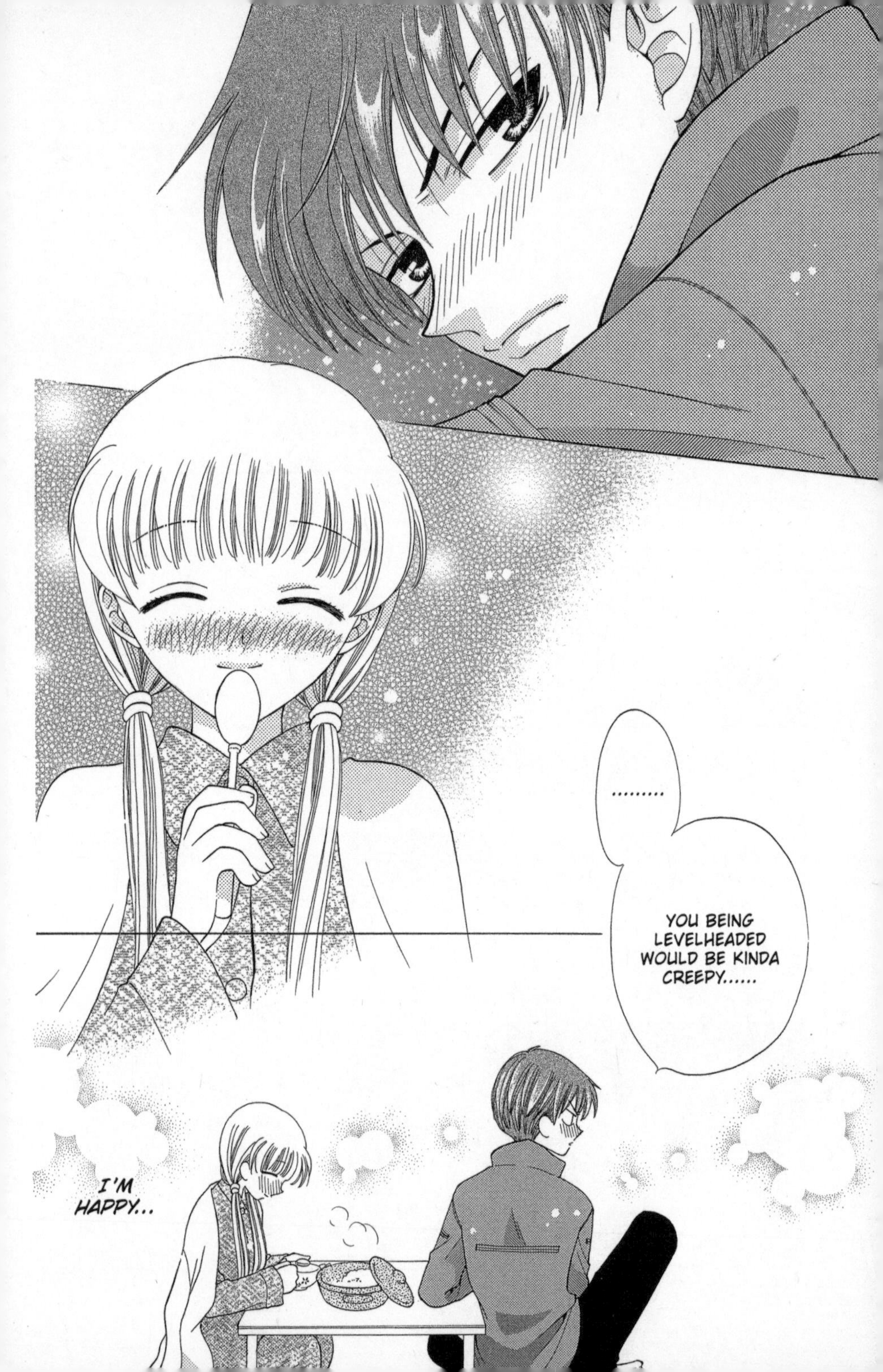
....
YOU BEING LEVELHEADED WOULD BE KINDA CREEPY......
I'M HAPPY...

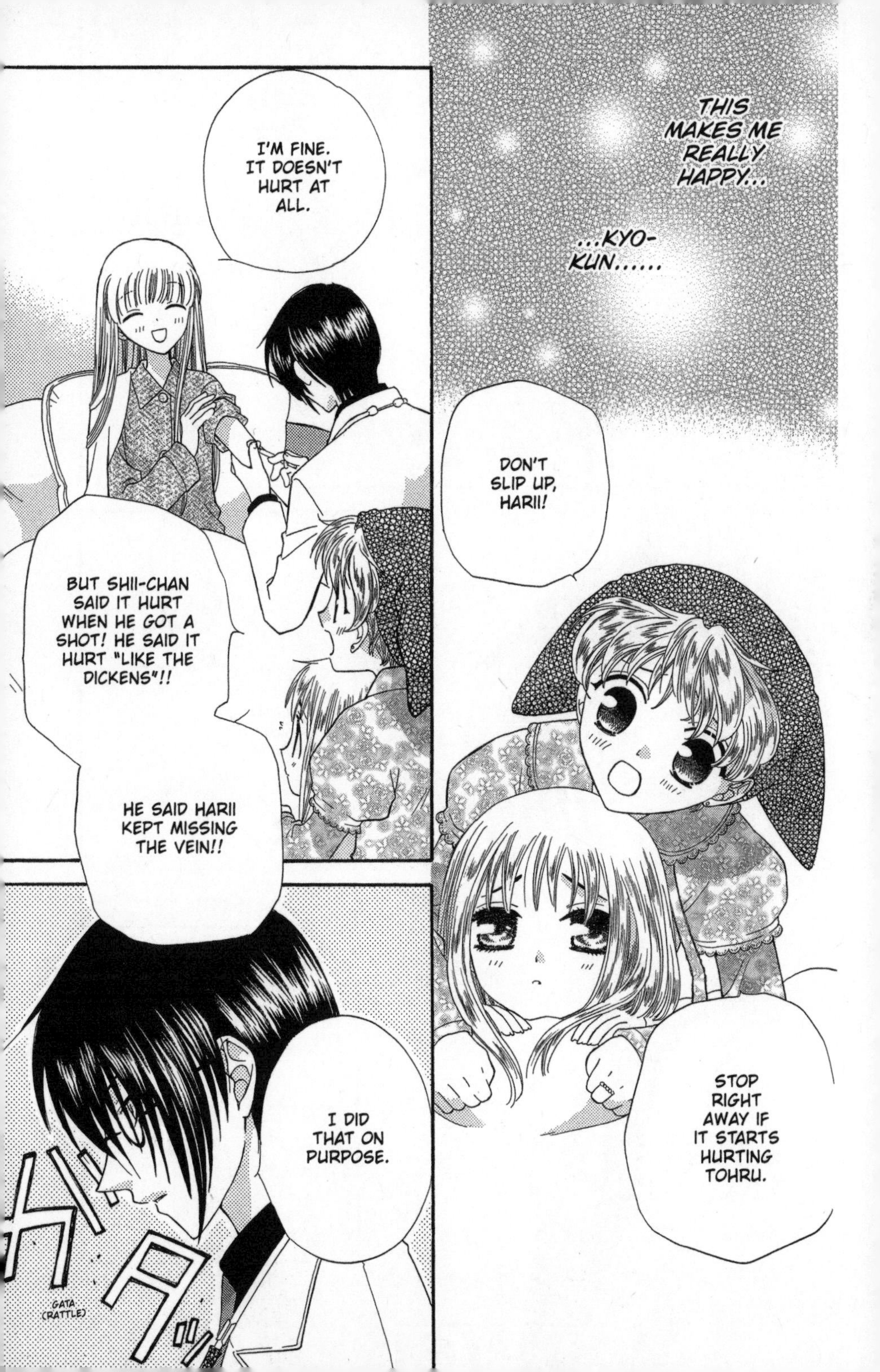
THIS MAKES ME REALLY HAPPY...
...KYO-KUN......
DON'T SLIP UP, HARII!
STOP RIGHT AWAY IF IT STARTS HURTING TOHRU.
I'M FINE. IT DOESN'T HURT AT ALL.
BUT SHII-CHAN SAID IT HURT WHEN HE GOT A SHOT! HE SAID IT HURT "LIKE THE DICKENS"!!
HE SAID HARII KEPT MISSING THE VEIN!!
I DID THAT ON PURPOSE.
GATA (RATTLE)

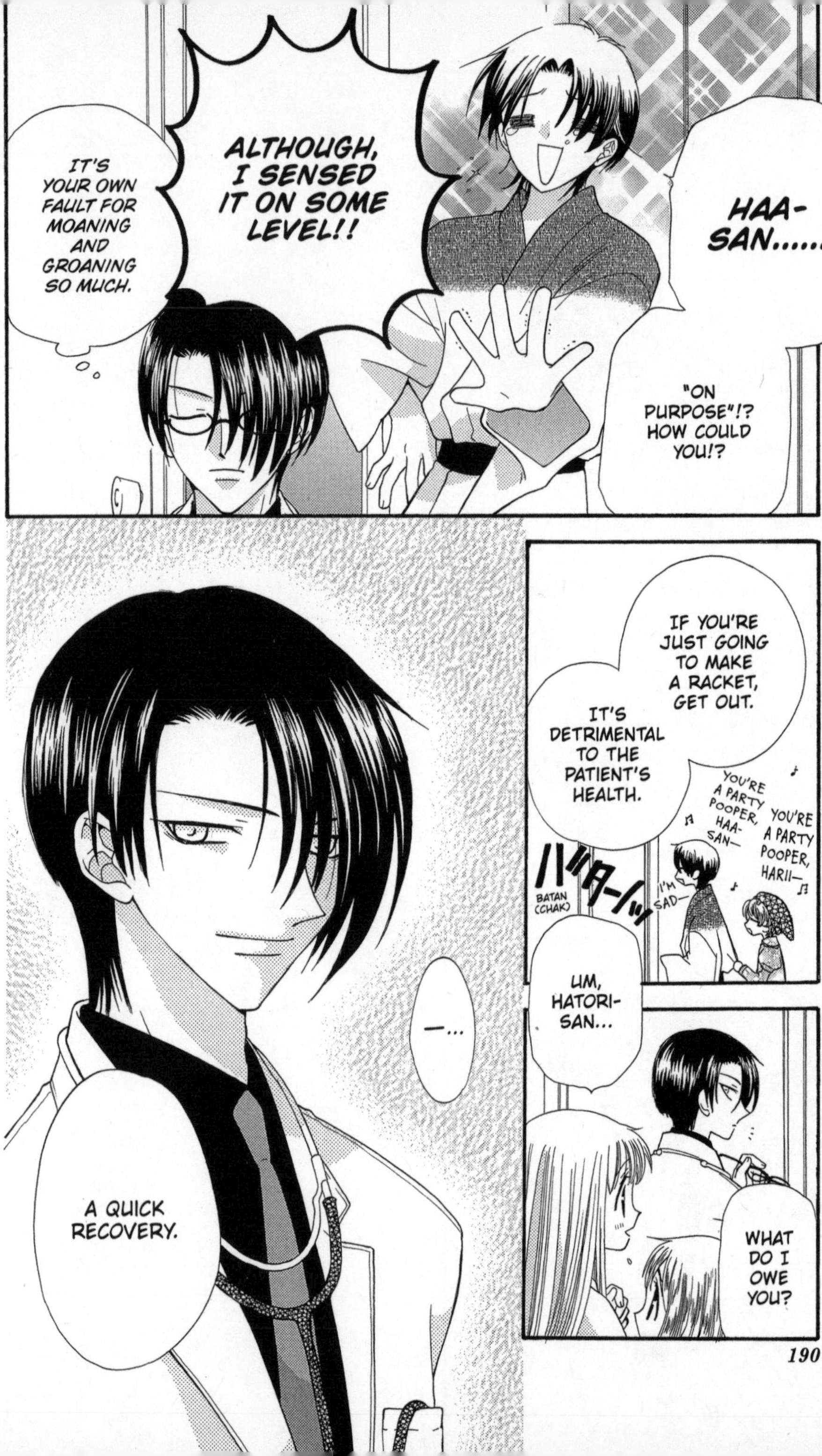
HAA-SAN......
"ON PURPOSE"!? HOW COULD YOU!?
ALTHOUGH, I SENSED IT ON SOME LEVEL!!
IT'S YOUR OWN FAULT FOR MOANING AND GROANING SO MUCH.
IF YOU'RE JUST GOING TO MAKE A RACKET, GET OUT.
IT'S DETRIMENTAL TO THE PATIENT'S HEALTH.
YOU'RE A PARTY POOPER, HARII—
YOU'RE A PARTY POOPER, HAA-SAN—
I'M SAD—
BATAN (CHAK)
UM, HATORI-SAN...
WHAT DO I OWE YOU?
—...
A QUICK RECOVERY.

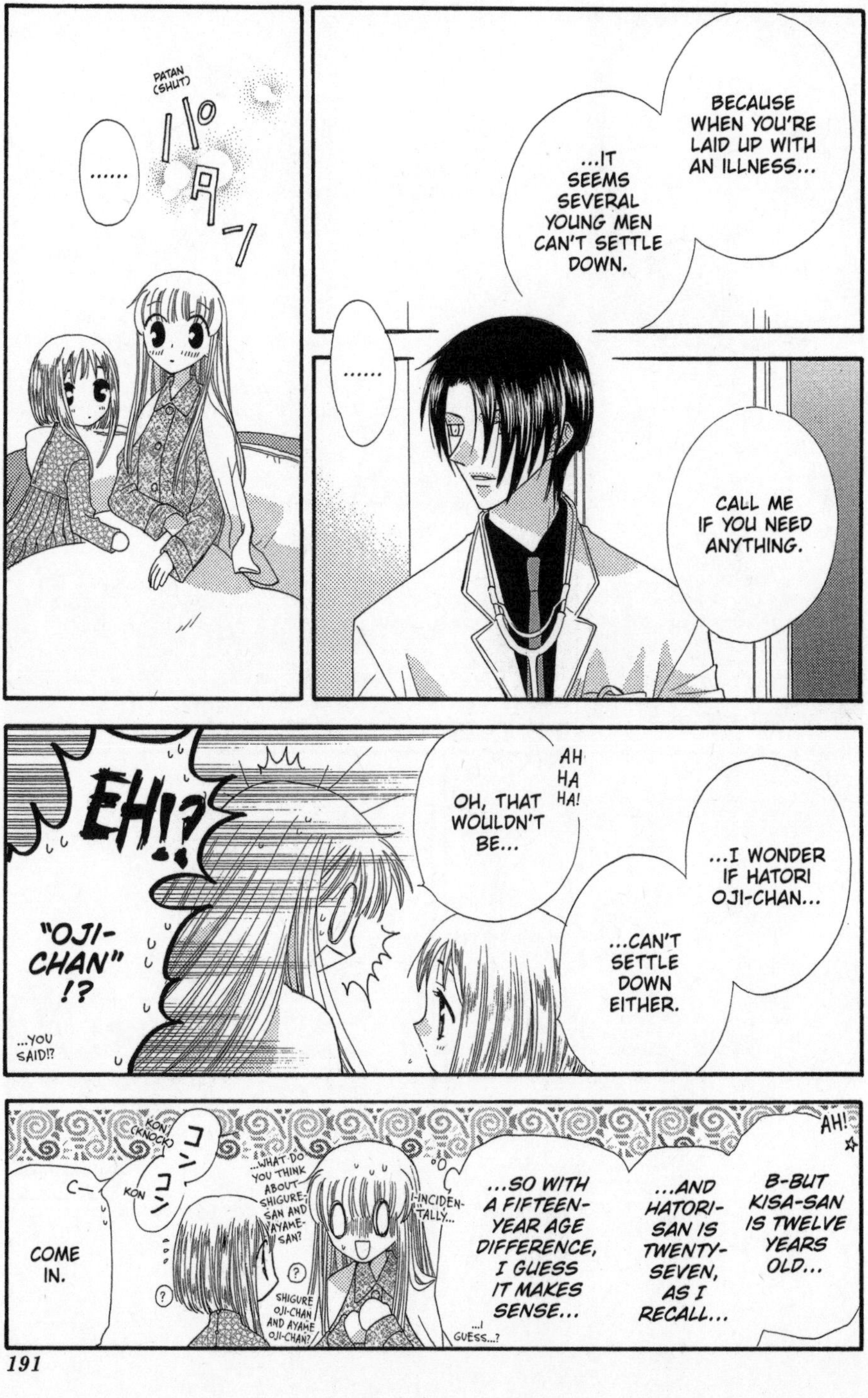
BECAUSE WHEN YOU'RE LAID UP WITH AN ILLNESS...
...IT SEEMS SEVERAL YOUNG MEN CAN'T SETTLE DOWN.
CALL ME IF YOU NEED ANYTHING.
......
PATAN (SHUT)
......
...I WONDER IF HATORI OJI-CHAN...
...CAN'T SETTLE DOWN EITHER.
AH HA HA!
OH, THAT WOULDN'T BE...
EH!?
"OJI-CHAN" !?
...YOU SAID!?
AH! ☆
B-BUT KISA-SAN IS TWELVE YEARS OLD...
...AND HATORI-SAN IS TWENTY-SEVEN, AS I RECALL...
...SO WITH A FIFTEEN-YEAR AGE DIFFERENCE, I GUESS IT MAKES SENSE...
...I GUESS...?
I-INCIDENTALLY...
...WHAT DO YOU THINK ABOUT SHIGURE-SAN AND AYAME-SAN?
SHIGURE OJI-CHAN AND AYAME OJI-CHAN?
KON (KNOCK) KON
C—
COME IN.

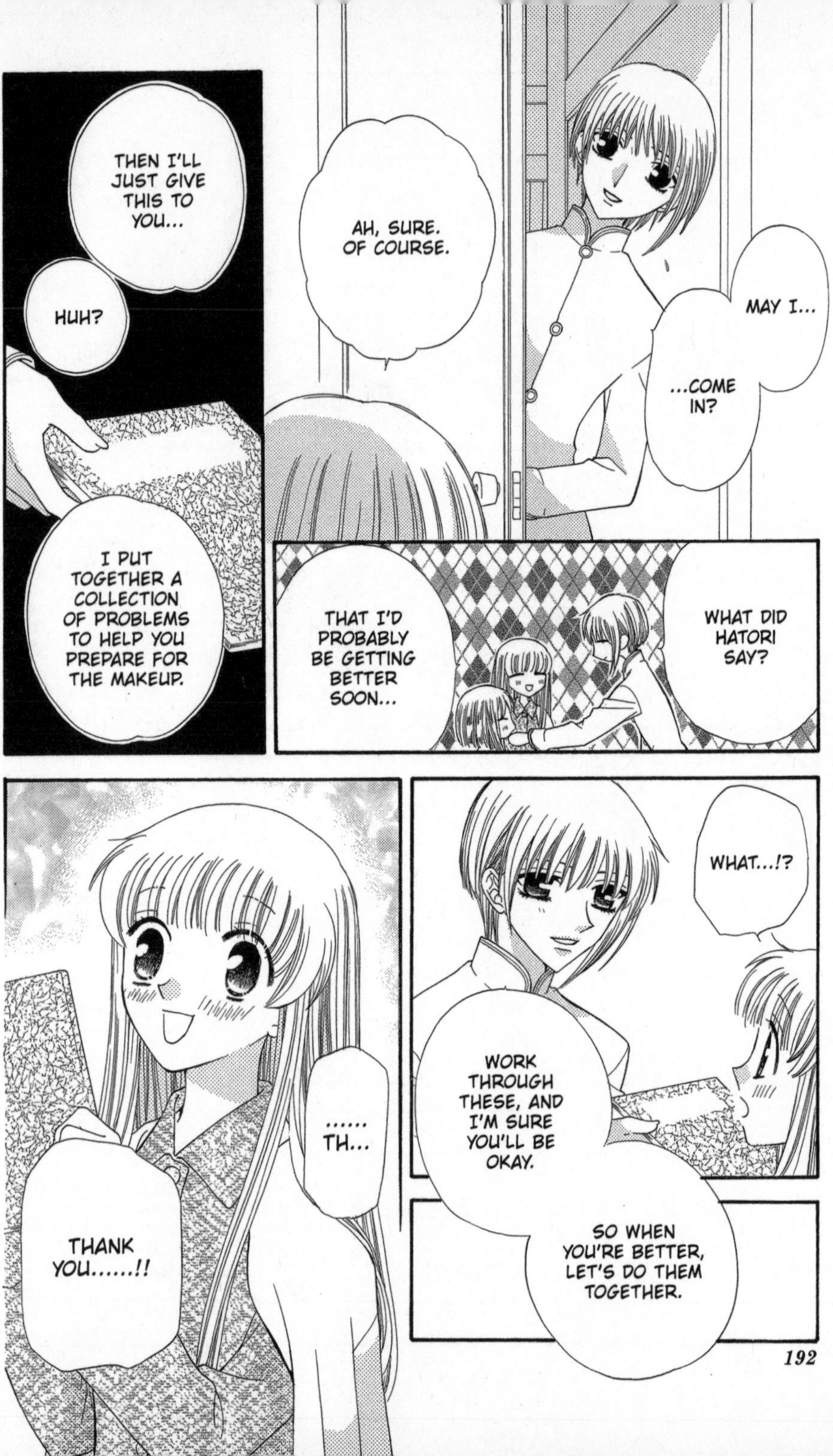
MAY I...
...COME IN?
AH, SURE. OF COURSE.
WHAT DID HATORI SAY?
THAT I'D PROBABLY BE GETTING BETTER SOON...
THEN I'LL JUST GIVE THIS TO YOU...
HUH?
I PUT TOGETHER A COLLECTION OF PROBLEMS TO HELP YOU PREPARE FOR THE MAKEUP.
WHAT...!?
WORK THROUGH THESE, AND I'M SURE YOU'LL BE OKAY.
SO WHEN YOU'RE BETTER, LET'S DO THEM TOGETHER.
...... TH...
THANK YOU......!!

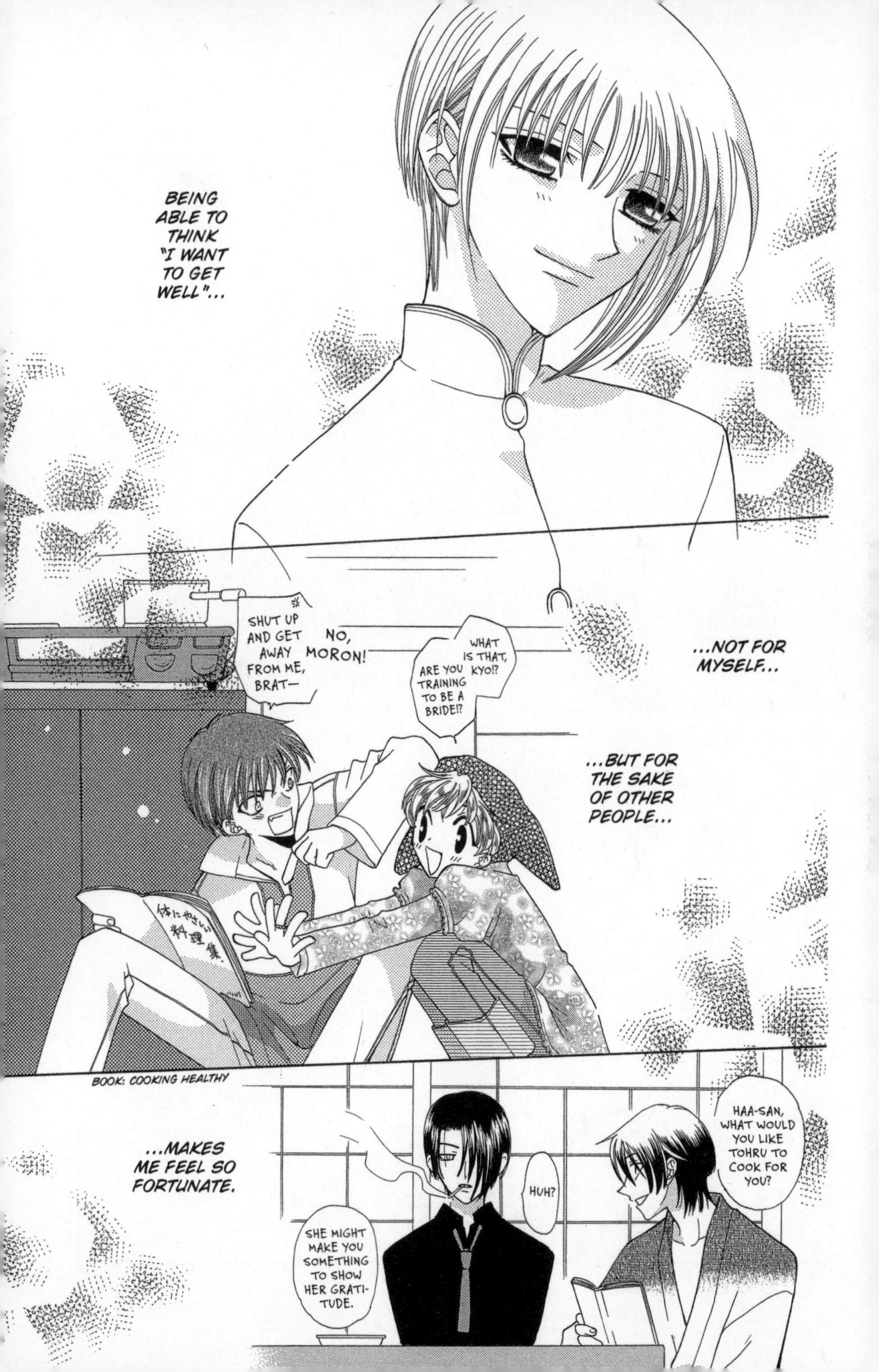
BEING ABLE TO THINK "I WANT TO GET WELL"...
...NOT FOR MYSELF...
...BUT FOR THE SAKE OF OTHER PEOPLE...
WHAT IS THAT, KYO!? ARE YOU TRAINING TO BE A BRIDE!?
NO, MORON!
SHUT UP AND GET AWAY FROM ME, BRAT—
体にやさしい料理集
BOOK: COOKING HEALTHY
HAA-SAN, WHAT WOULD YOU LIKE TOHRU TO COOK FOR YOU?
HUH?
SHE MIGHT MAKE YOU SOMETHING TO SHOW HER GRATITUDE.
...MAKES ME FEEL SO FORTUNATE.

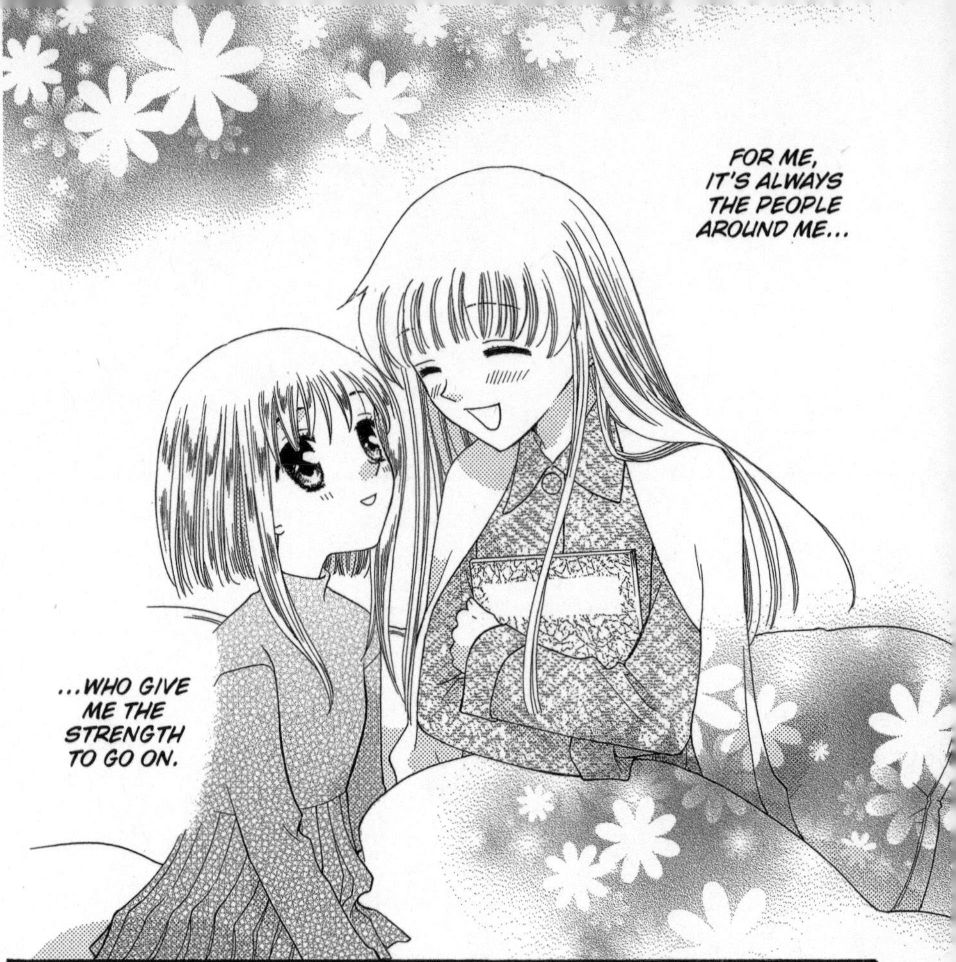
FOR ME, IT'S ALWAYS THE PEOPLE AROUND ME...
...WHO GIVE ME THE STRENGTH TO GO ON.

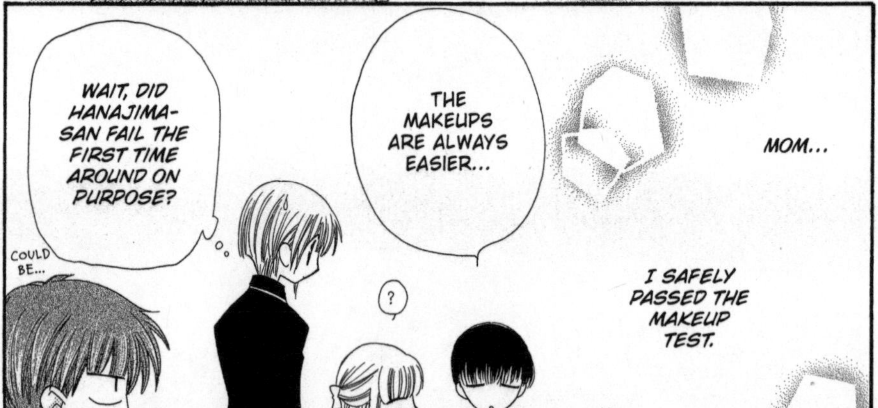
MOM...
I SAFELY PASSED THE MAKEUP TEST.
THE MAKEUPS ARE ALWAYS EASIER...
?
WAIT, DID HANAJIMA-SAN FAIL THE FIRST TIME AROUND ON PURPOSE?
COULD BE...

COLLECTOR'S EDITION

Fruits Basket

COLLECTOR'S EDITION

Fruits Basket

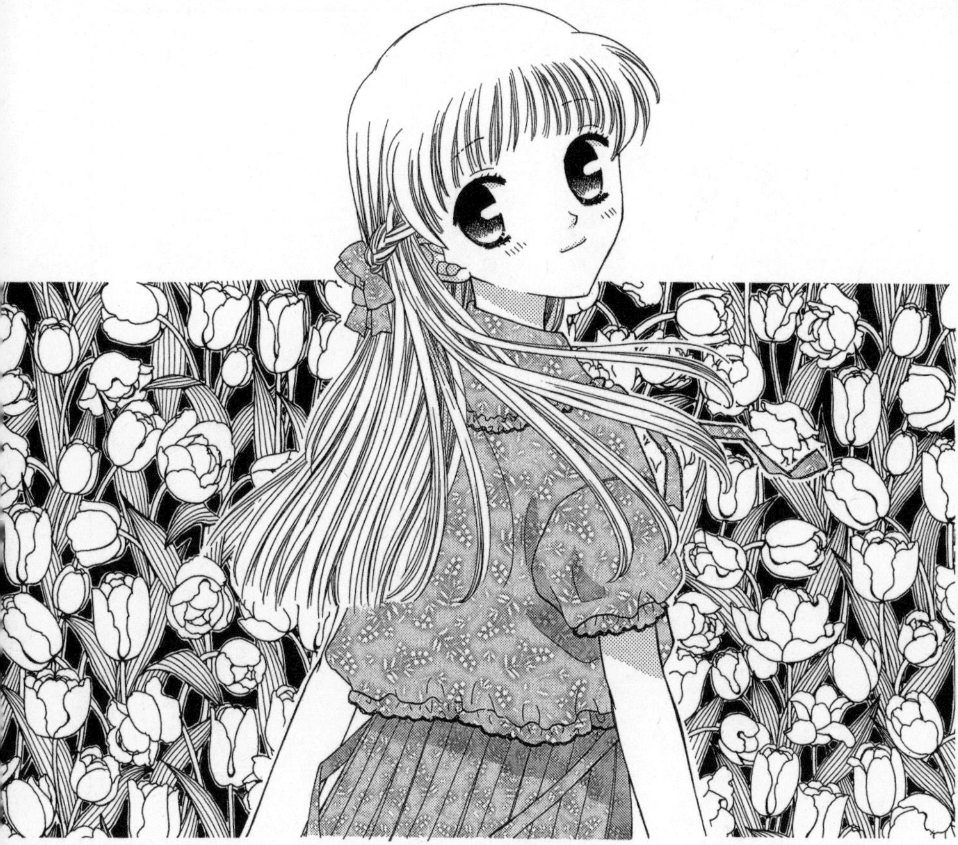

Chapter 31

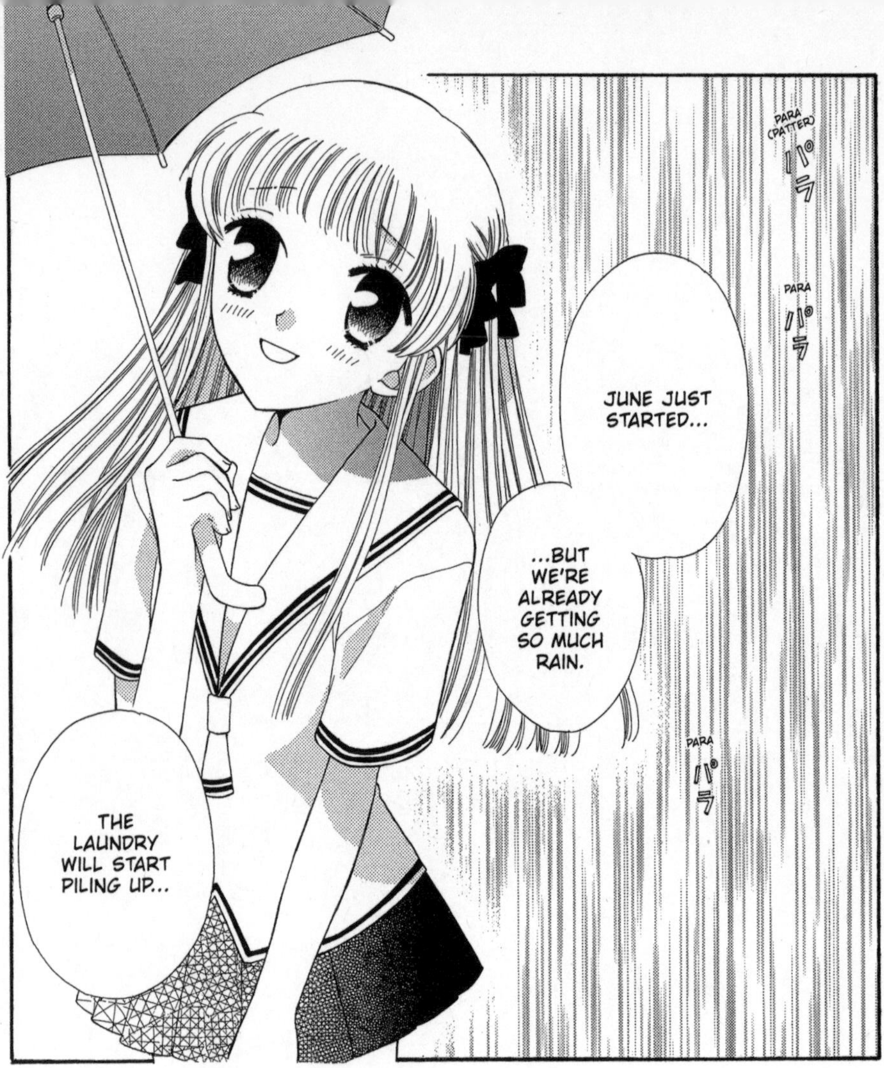
PARA (PATTER) パラ
PARA パラ
JUNE JUST STARTED...
...BUT WE'RE ALREADY GETTING SO MUCH RAIN.
PARA パラ
THE LAUNDRY WILL START PILING UP...

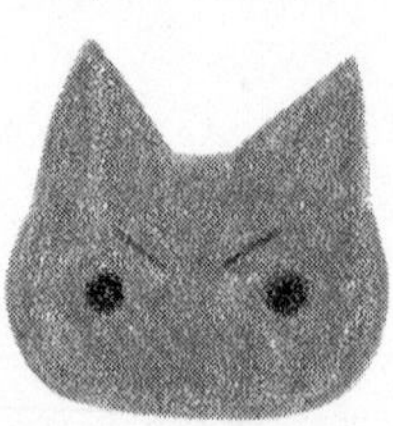

CAT

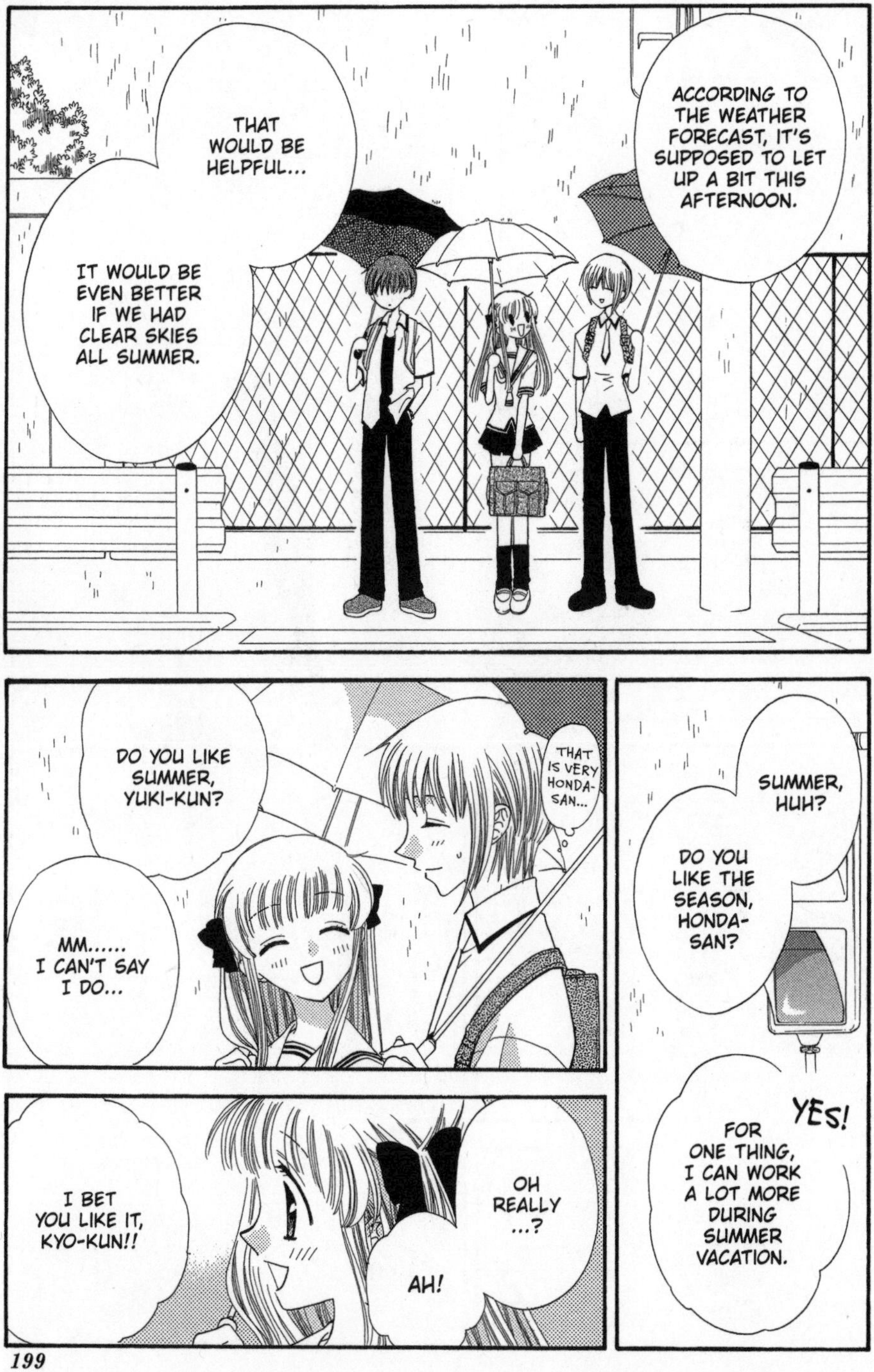
ACCORDING TO THE WEATHER FORECAST, IT'S SUPPOSED TO LET UP A BIT THIS AFTERNOON.
THAT WOULD BE HELPFUL...
IT WOULD BE EVEN BETTER IF WE HAD CLEAR SKIES ALL SUMMER.
SUMMER, HUH?
DO YOU LIKE THE SEASON, HONDA-SAN?
YES!
FOR ONE THING, I CAN WORK A LOT MORE DURING SUMMER VACATION.
THAT IS VERY HONDA-SAN...
DO YOU LIKE SUMMER, YUKI-KUN?
MM...... I CAN'T SAY I DO...
OH REALLY ...?
AH!
I BET YOU LIKE IT, KYO-KUN!!

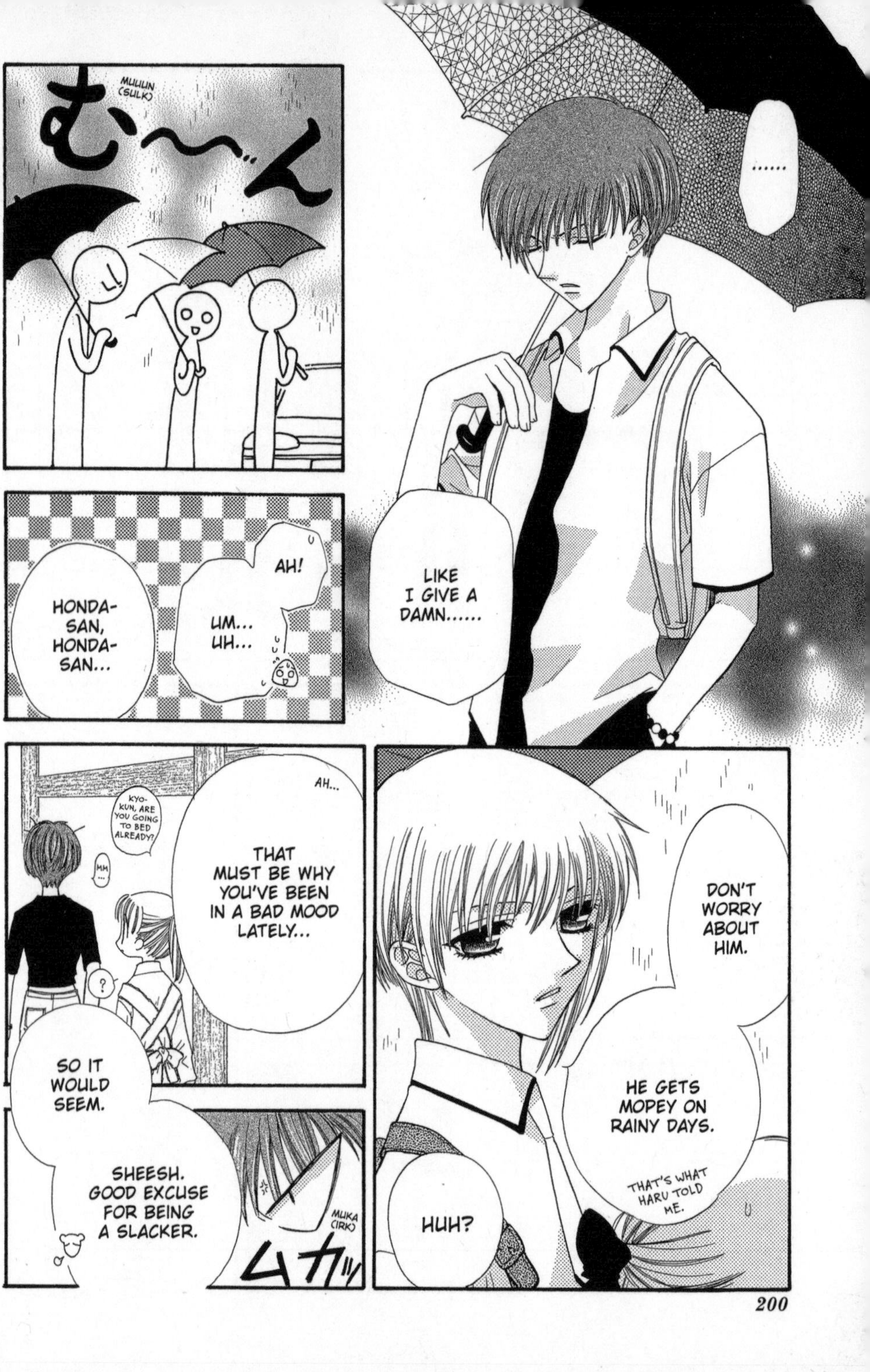
......
LIKE I GIVE A DAMN......
MUUUN (SULK)
む〜〜ん
AH!
UM... UH...
HONDA-SAN, HONDA-SAN...
DON'T WORRY ABOUT HIM.
HE GETS MOPEY ON RAINY DAYS.
THAT'S WHAT HARU TOLD ME.
HUH?
AH...
THAT MUST BE WHY YOU'VE BEEN IN A BAD MOOD LATELY...
KYO-KUN, ARE YOU GOING TO BED ALREADY?
MM...
?
SO IT WOULD SEEM.
SHEESH. GOOD EXCUSE FOR BEING A SLACKER.
MUKA (IRK)
ムカッ

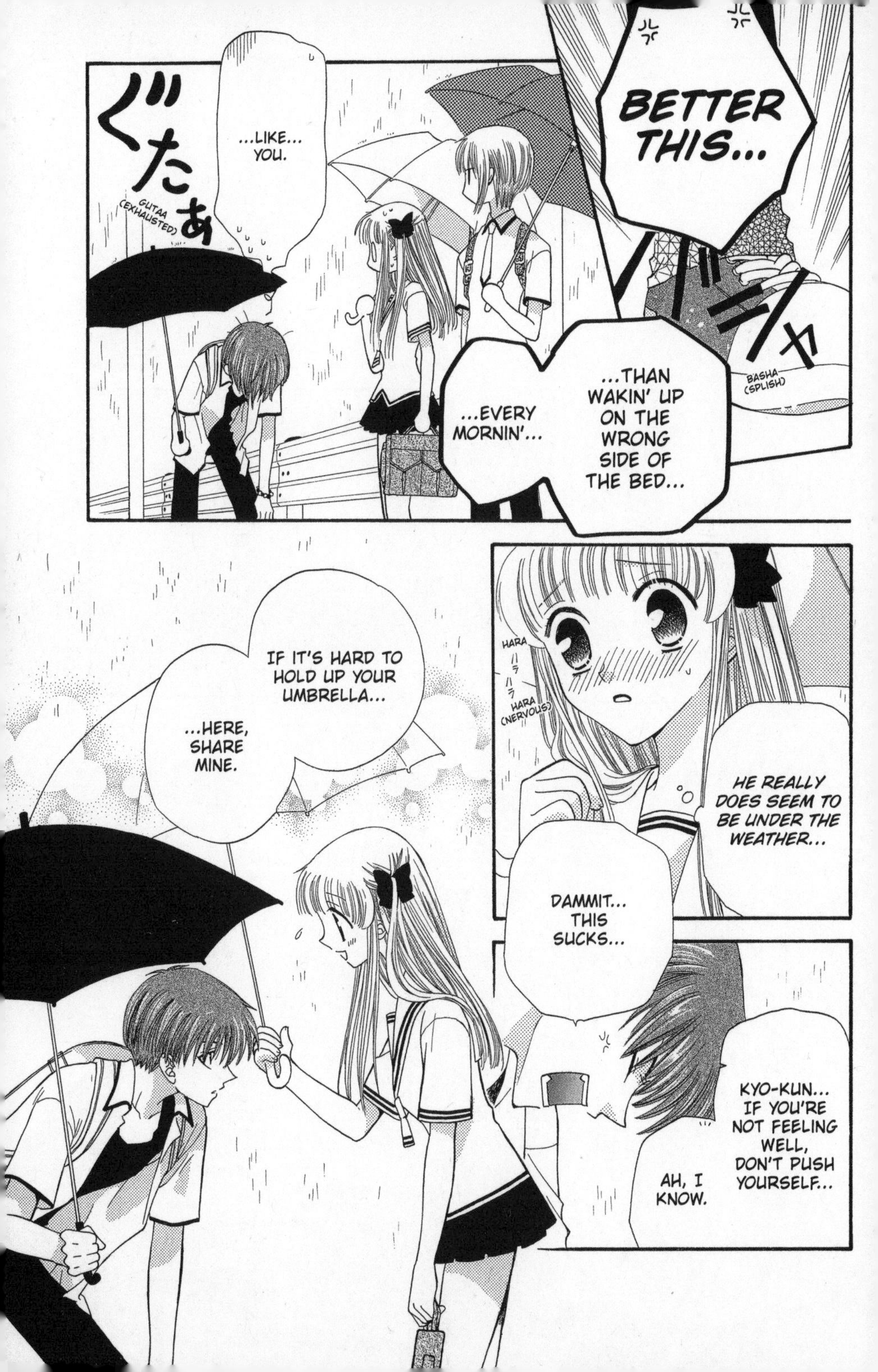

BETTER THIS...
BASHA (SPLISH)
...THAN WAKIN' UP ON THE WRONG SIDE OF THE BED...
...EVERY MORNIN'...
...LIKE... YOU.
GUTAA (EXHAUSTED)
HARA HARA (NERVOUS)
HE REALLY DOES SEEM TO BE UNDER THE WEATHER...
DAMMIT... THIS SUCKS...
KYO-KUN... IF YOU'RE NOT FEELING WELL, DON'T PUSH YOURSELF...
AH, I KNOW.
IF IT'S HARD TO HOLD UP YOUR UMBRELLA...
...HERE, SHARE MINE.

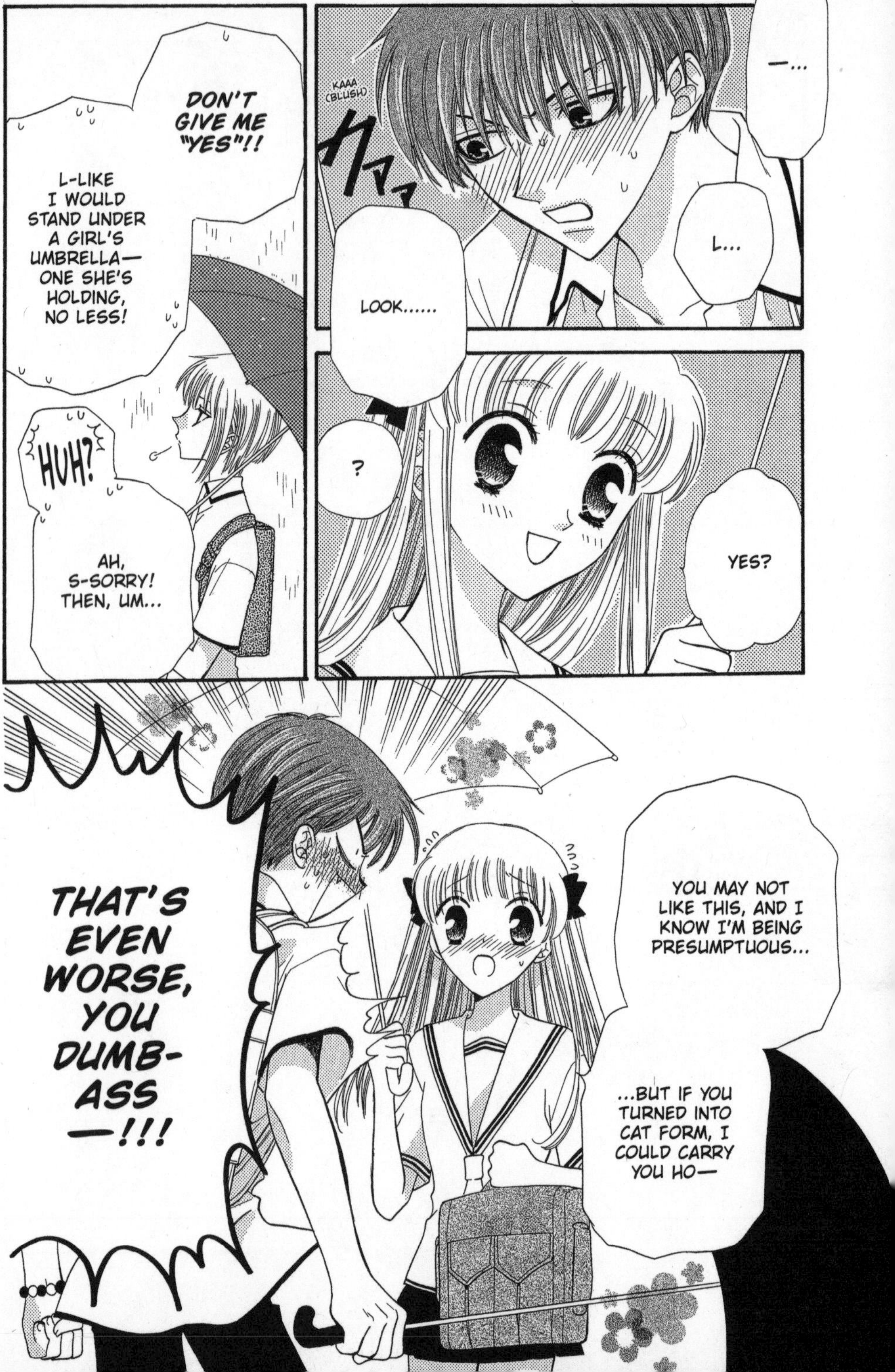
—...
KAAA (BLUSH)
L...
LOOK......
YES?
?
DON'T GIVE ME "YES"!!
L-LIKE I WOULD STAND UNDER A GIRL'S UMBRELLA— ONE SHE'S HOLDING, NO LESS!
HUH?
AH, S-SORRY! THEN, UM...
YOU MAY NOT LIKE THIS, AND I KNOW I'M BEING PRESUMPTUOUS...
...BUT IF YOU TURNED INTO CAT FORM, I COULD CARRY YOU HO—
THAT'S EVEN WORSE, YOU DUMB-ASS—!!!

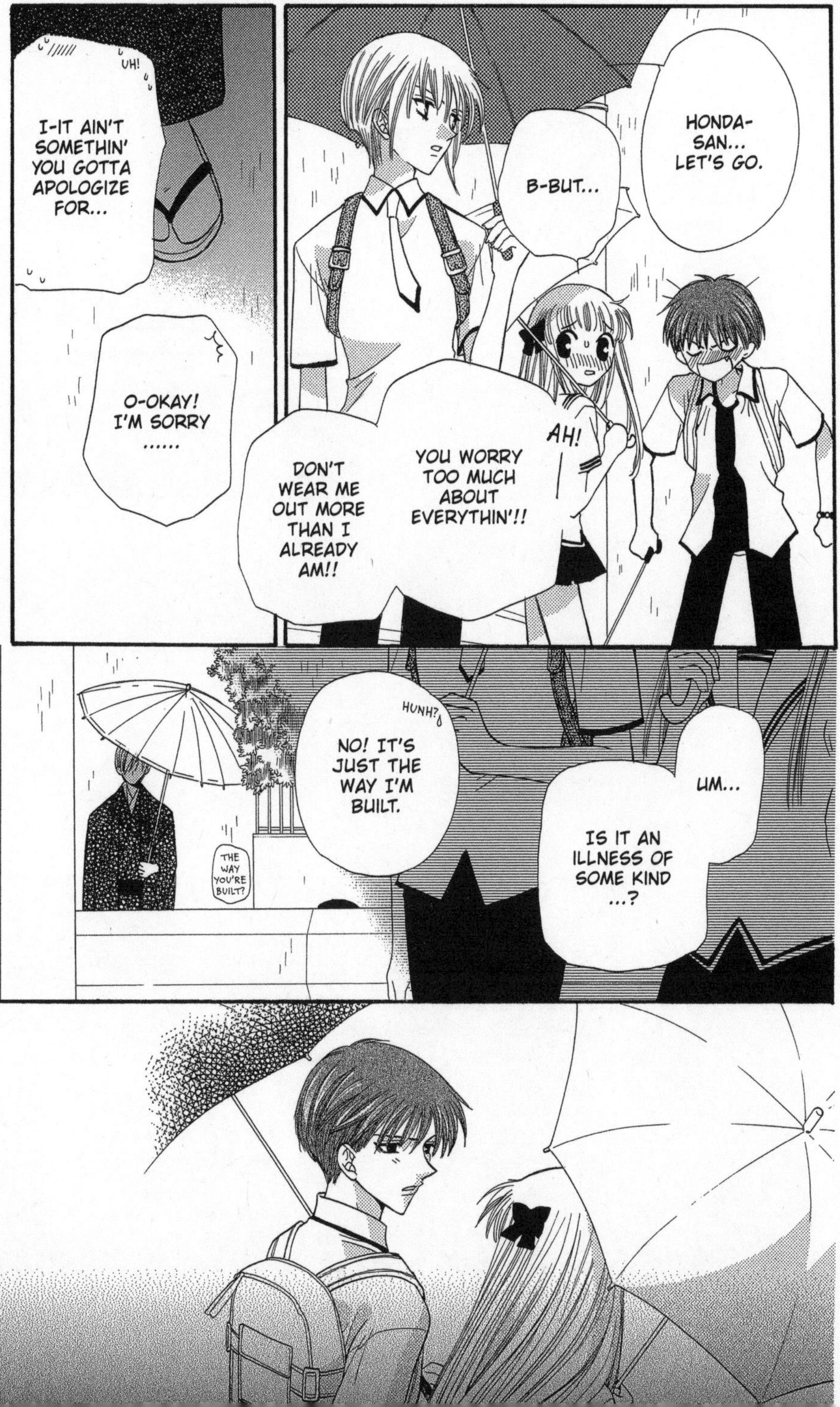
HONDA-SAN... LET'S GO.
B-BUT...
AH!
YOU WORRY TOO MUCH ABOUT EVERYTHIN'!!
DON'T WEAR ME OUT MORE THAN I ALREADY AM!!
UH!
I-IT AIN'T SOMETHIN' YOU GOTTA APOLOGIZE FOR...
O-OKAY! I'M SORRY ......
UM...
IS IT AN ILLNESS OF SOME KIND ...?
HUNH?
NO! IT'S JUST THE WAY I'M BUILT.
THE WAY YOU'RE BUILT?

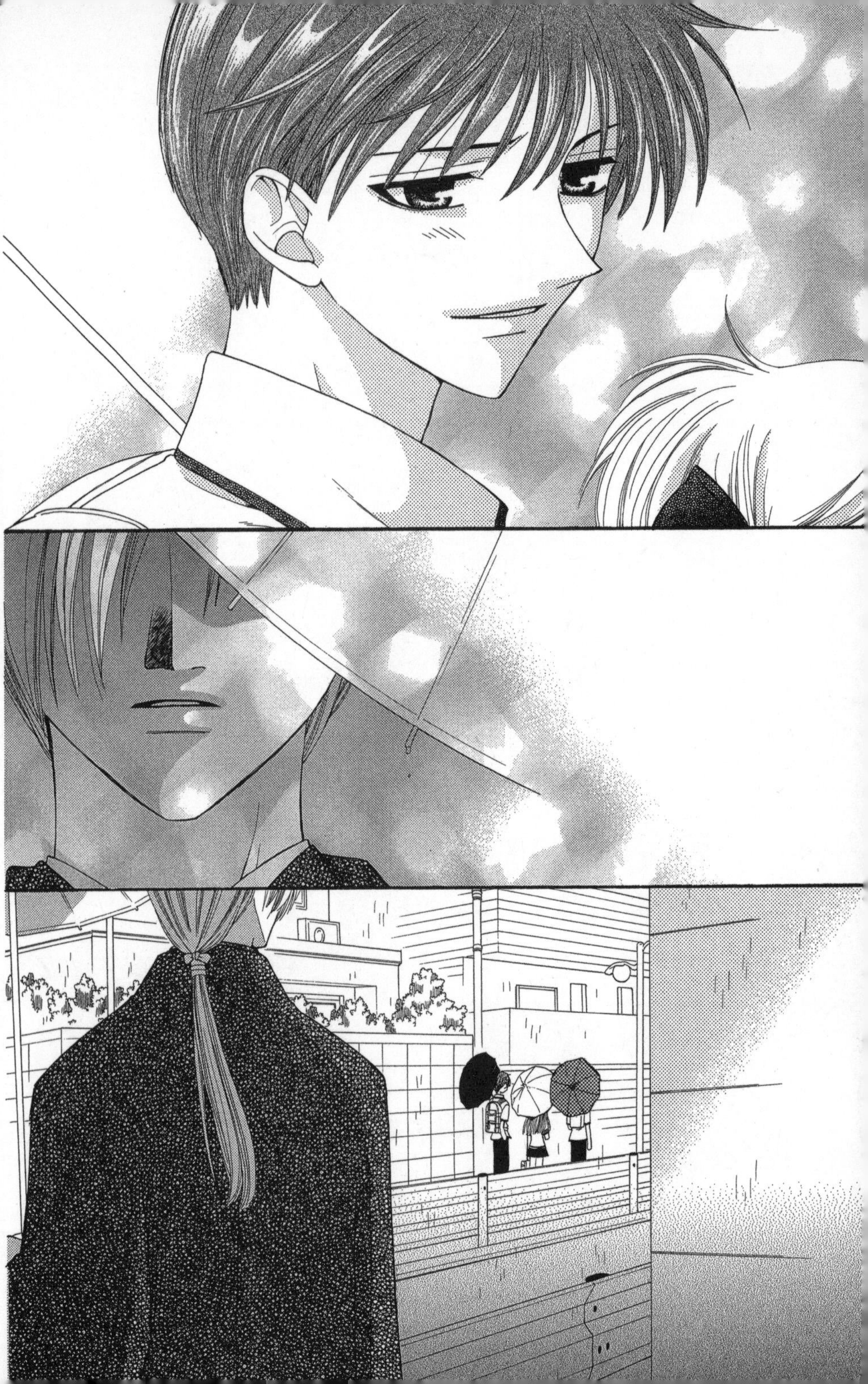

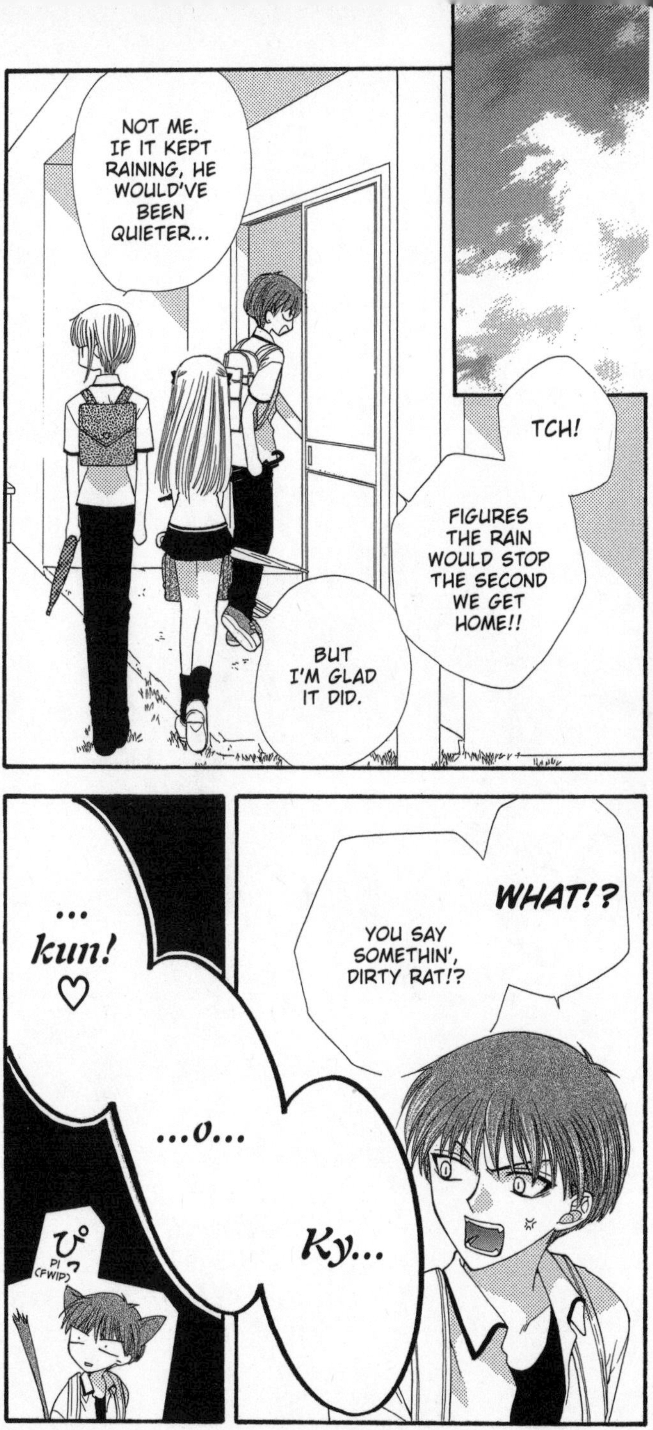
TCH!
FIGURES THE RAIN WOULD STOP THE SECOND WE GET HOME!!
BUT I'M GLAD IT DID.
NOT ME. IF IT KEPT RAINING, HE WOULD'VE BEEN QUIETER...
WHAT!?
YOU SAY SOMETHIN', DIRTY RAT!?
Ky...
...o...
... kun! ♡
ぴっ
PI (FWIP)

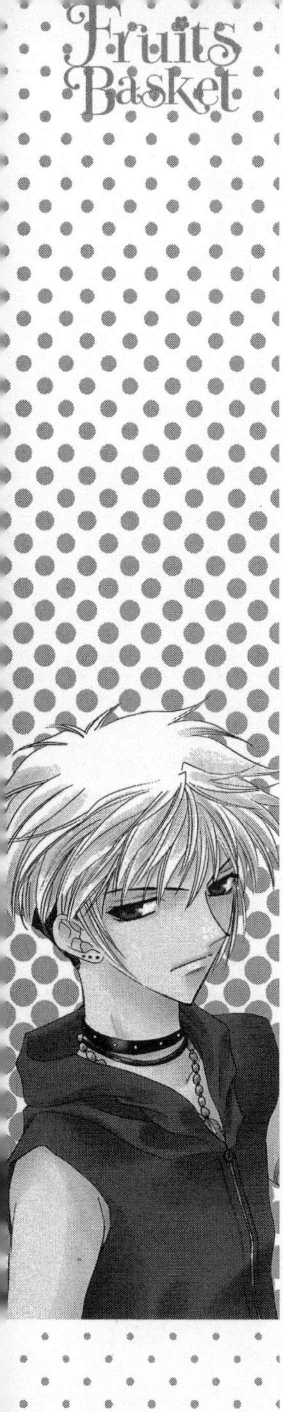
Fruits Basket

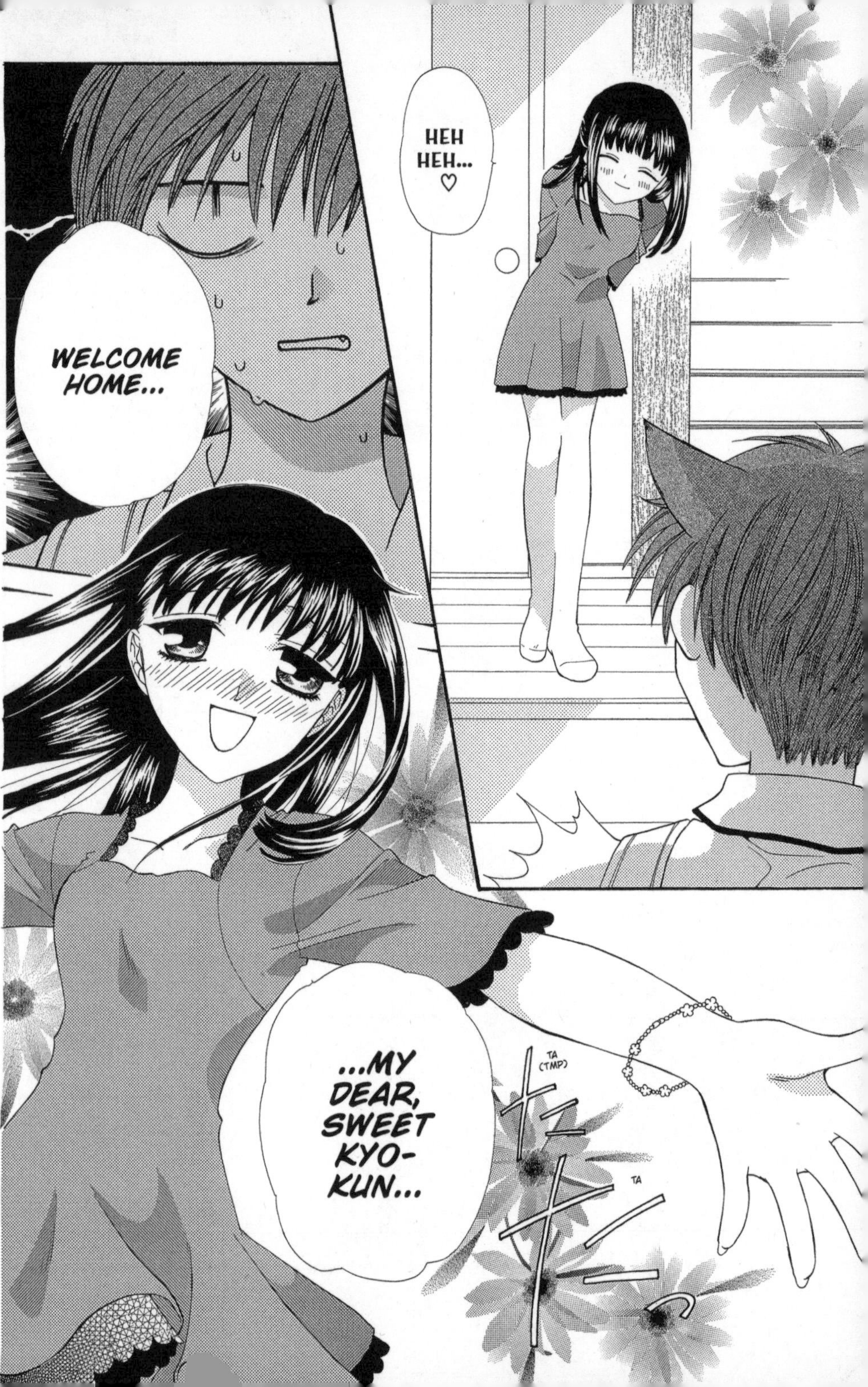
HEH HEH... ♡
WELCOME HOME...
...MY DEAR, SWEET KYO-KUN...
TA (TMP)
TA

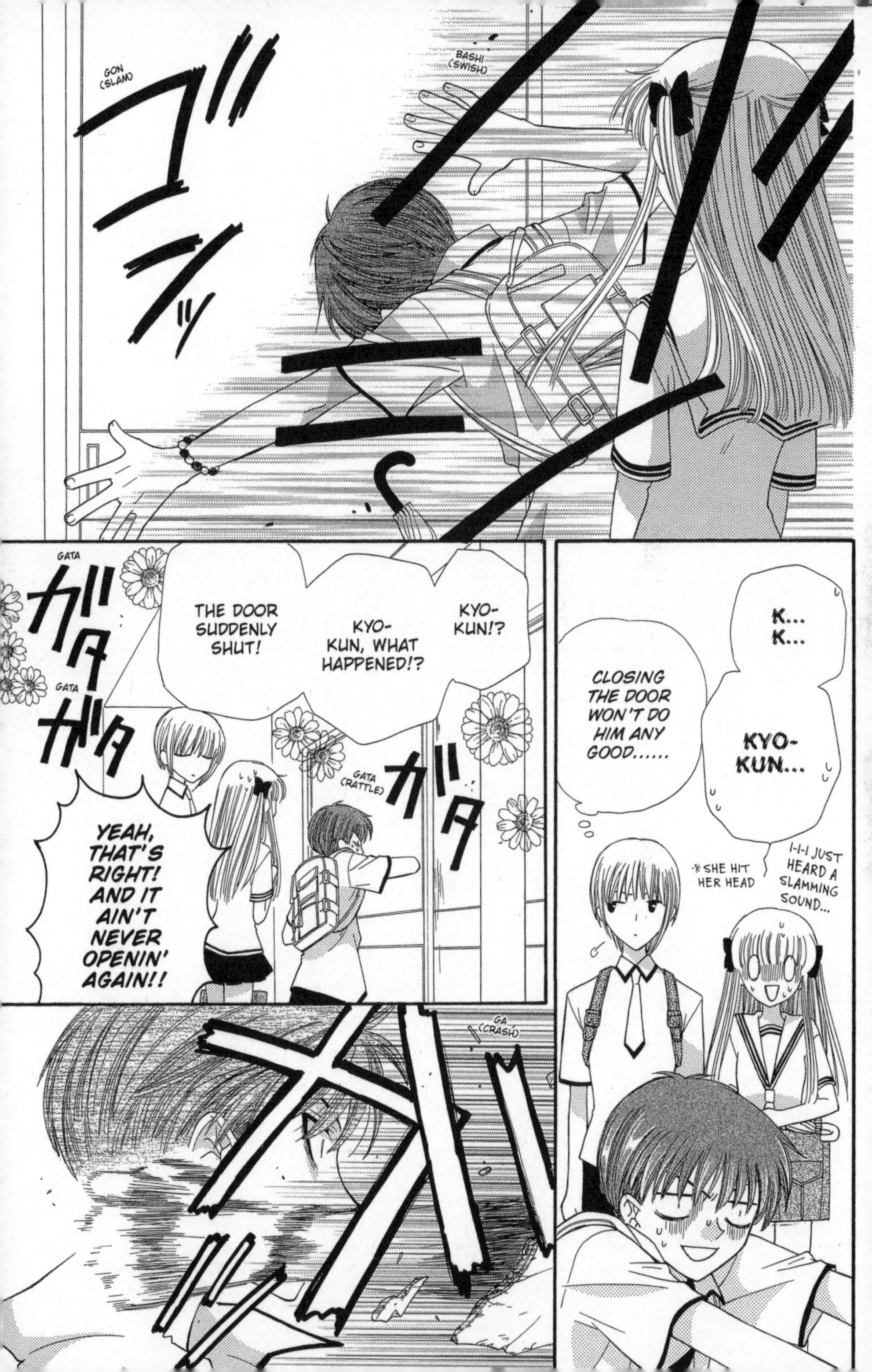
BASHI (SWISH)
GON (SLAM)
K... K...
KYO-KUN...
CLOSING THE DOOR WON'T DO HIM ANY GOOD......
I-I-I JUST HEARD A SLAMMING SOUND...
*SHE HIT HER HEAD
KYO-KUN!?
KYO-KUN, WHAT HAPPENED!?
THE DOOR SUDDENLY SHUT!
GATA
GATA
GATA (RATTLE)
YEAH, THAT'S RIGHT! AND IT AIN'T NEVER OPENIN' AGAIN!!
GA (CRASH)

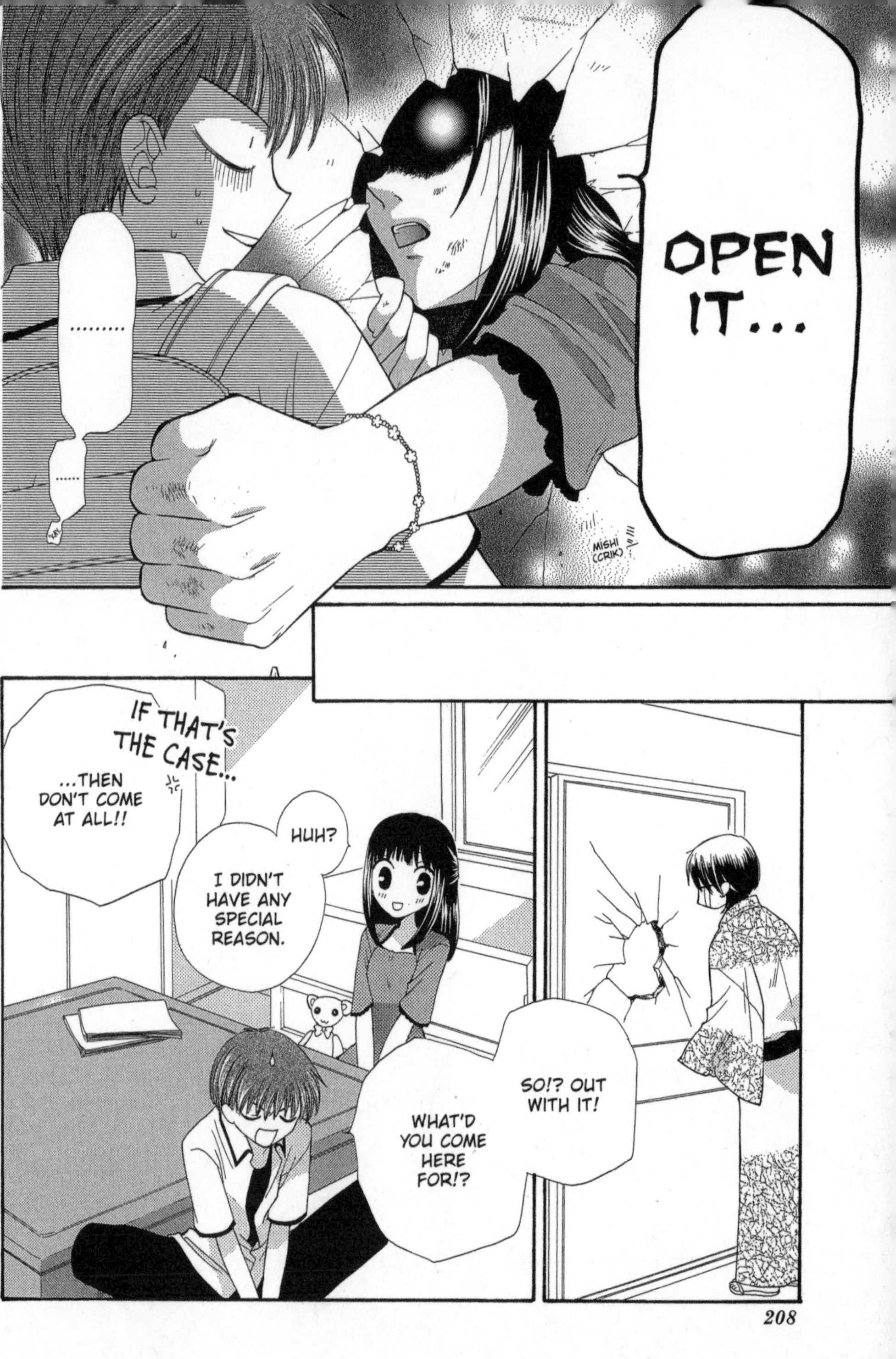
OPEN IT...
MISHI (CRIK)
....
......
SO!? OUT WITH IT!
WHAT'D YOU COME HERE FOR!?
HUH?
I DIDN'T HAVE ANY SPECIAL REASON.
IF THAT'S THE CASE...
...THEN DON'T COME AT ALL!!

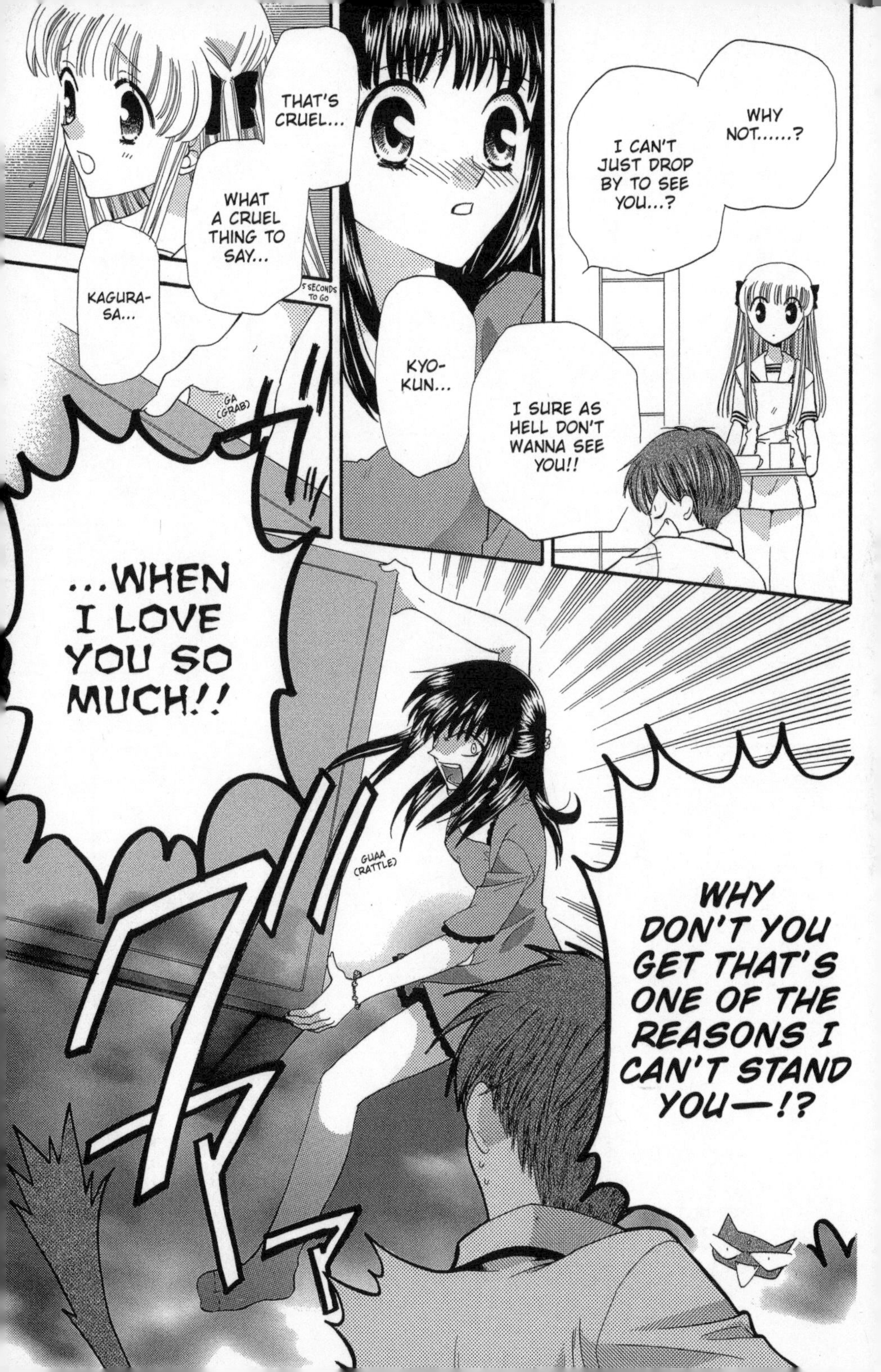
WHY NOT......?
I CAN'T JUST DROP BY TO SEE YOU...?
I SURE AS HELL DON'T WANNA SEE YOU!!
KYO-KUN...
THAT'S CRUEL...
WHAT A CRUEL THING TO SAY...
5 SECONDS TO GO
KAGURA-SA...
GA (GRAB)
...WHEN I LOVE YOU SO MUCH!!
GUAA (RATTLE)
WHY DON'T YOU GET THAT'S ONE OF THE REASONS I CAN'T STAND YOU—!?

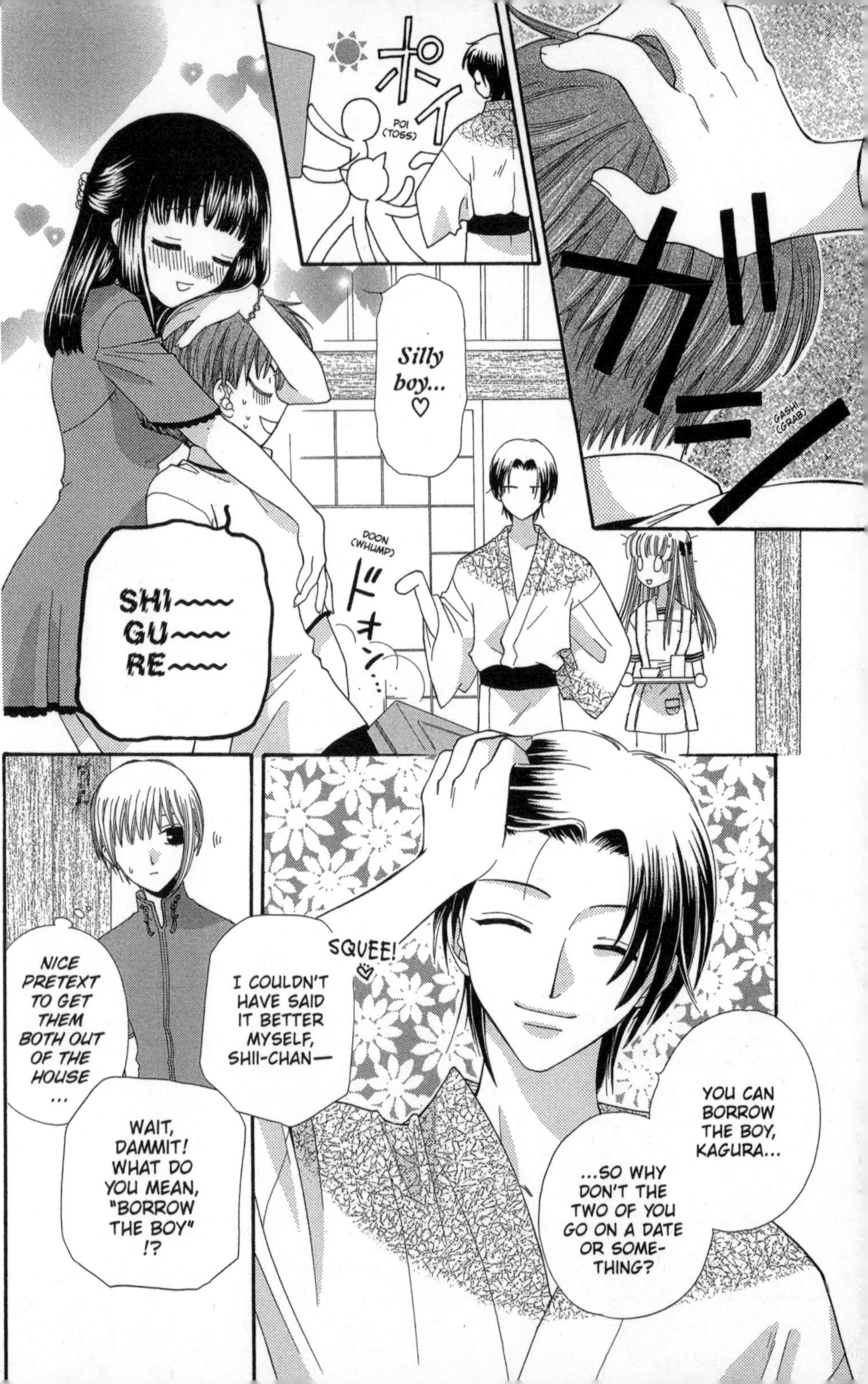
GASHI (GRAB)
ポイ
POI (TOSS)
Silly boy... ♡
DOON (WHUMP)
SHI~~~ GU~~~ RE~~~
YOU CAN BORROW THE BOY, KAGURA...
...SO WHY DON'T THE TWO OF YOU GO ON A DATE OR SOME-THING?
SQUEE!
I COULDN'T HAVE SAID IT BETTER MYSELF, SHII-CHAN—
WAIT, DAMMIT! WHAT DO YOU MEAN, "BORROW THE BOY" !?
NICE PRETEXT TO GET THEM BOTH OUT OF THE HOUSE ...

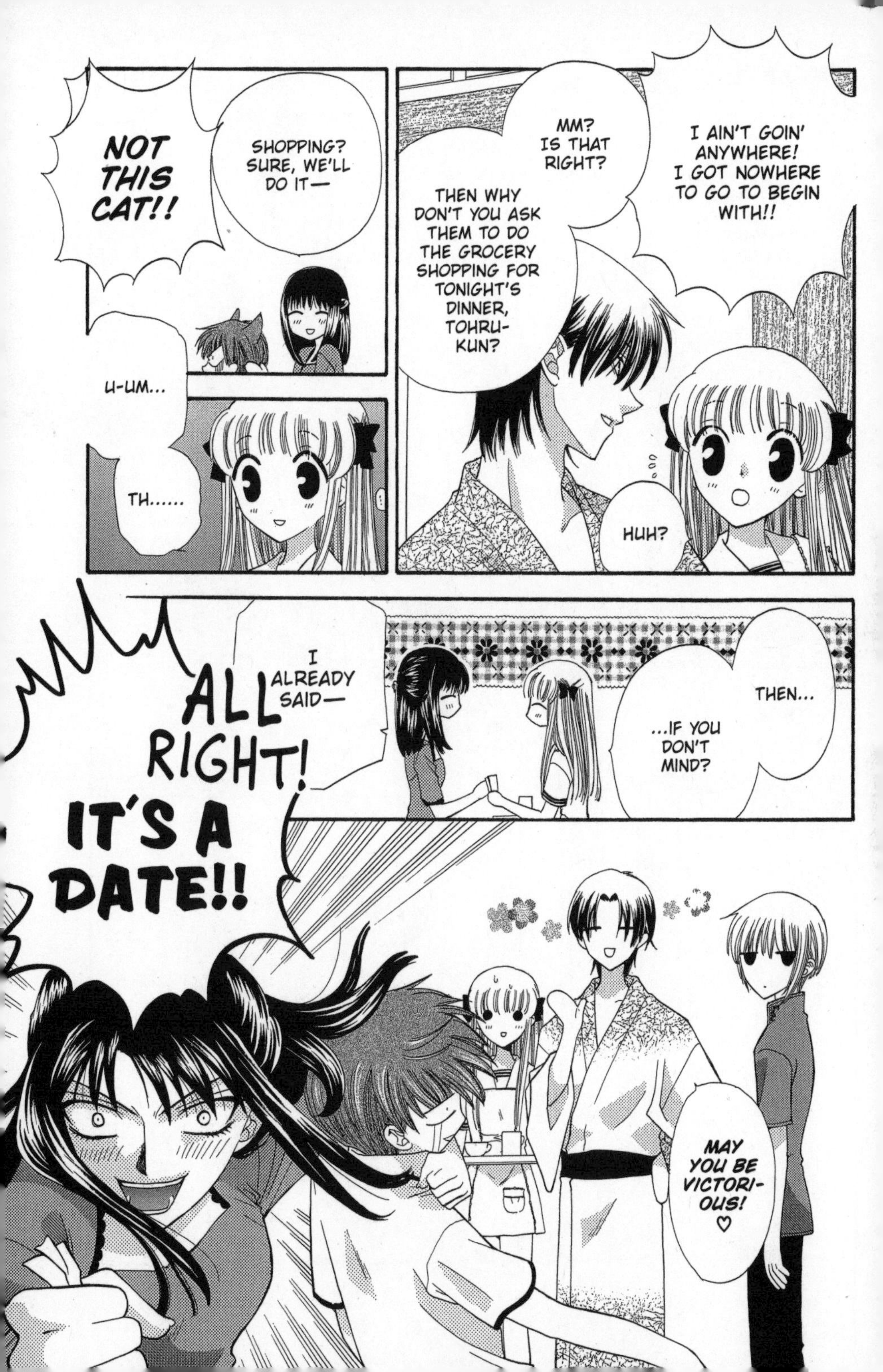
I AIN'T GOIN' ANYWHERE! I GOT NOWHERE TO GO TO BEGIN WITH!!
MM? IS THAT RIGHT?
THEN WHY DON'T YOU ASK THEM TO DO THE GROCERY SHOPPING FOR TONIGHT'S DINNER, TOHRU-KUN?
HUH?
SHOPPING? SURE, WE'LL DO IT—
NOT THIS CAT!!
U-UM...
TH......
THEN...
...IF YOU DON'T MIND?
I ALREADY SAID—
ALL RIGHT! IT'S A DATE!!
MAY YOU BE VICTORI-OUS! ♡

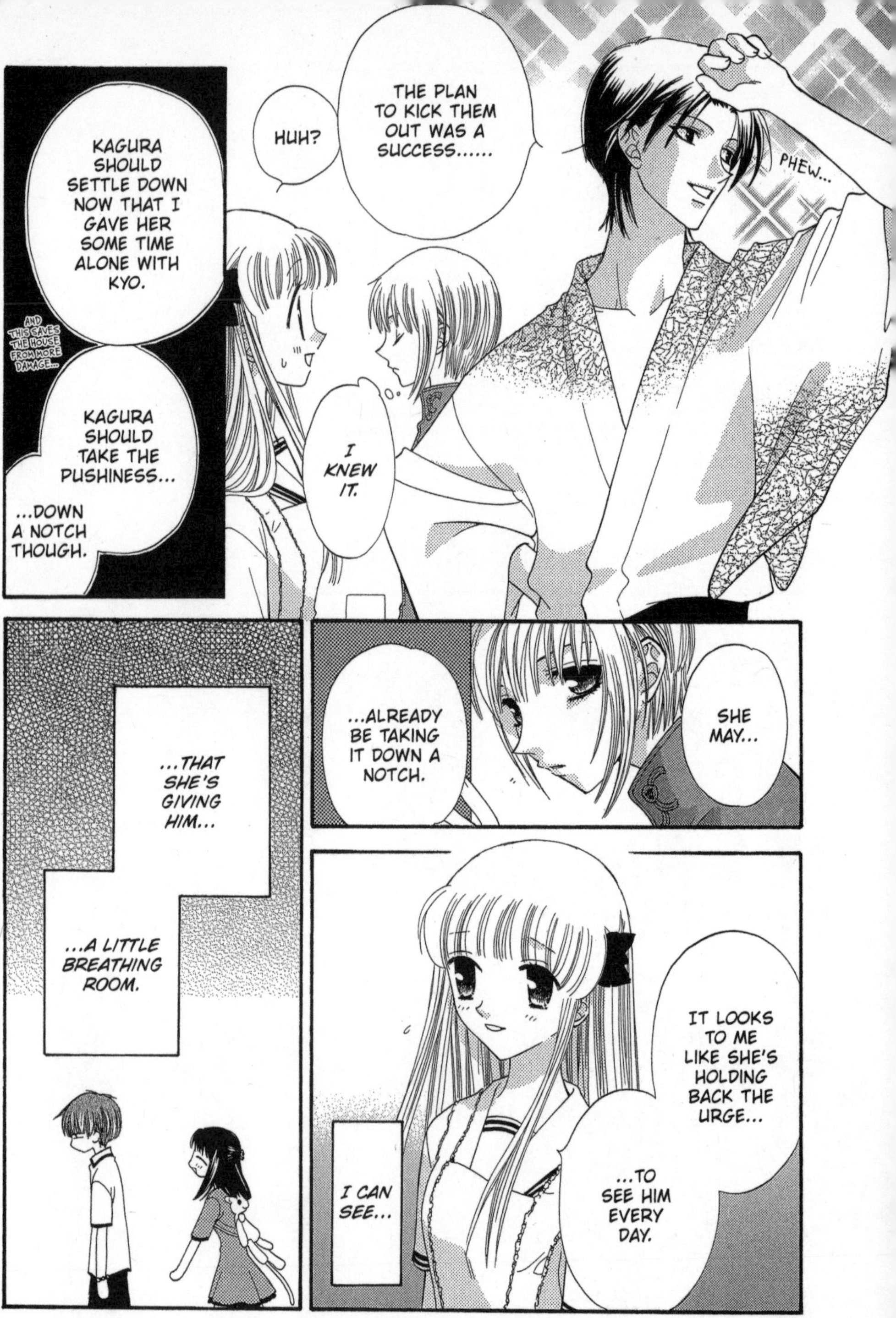
PHEW...
THE PLAN TO KICK THEM OUT WAS A SUCCESS......
HUH?
I KNEW IT.
KAGURA SHOULD SETTLE DOWN NOW THAT I GAVE HER SOME TIME ALONE WITH KYO.
AND THIS SAVES THE HOUSE FROM MORE DAMAGE...
KAGURA SHOULD TAKE THE PUSHINESS...
...DOWN A NOTCH THOUGH.
SHE MAY...
...ALREADY BE TAKING IT DOWN A NOTCH.
IT LOOKS TO ME LIKE SHE'S HOLDING BACK THE URGE...
...TO SEE HIM EVERY DAY.
I CAN SEE...
...THAT SHE'S GIVING HIM...
...A LITTLE BREATHING ROOM.

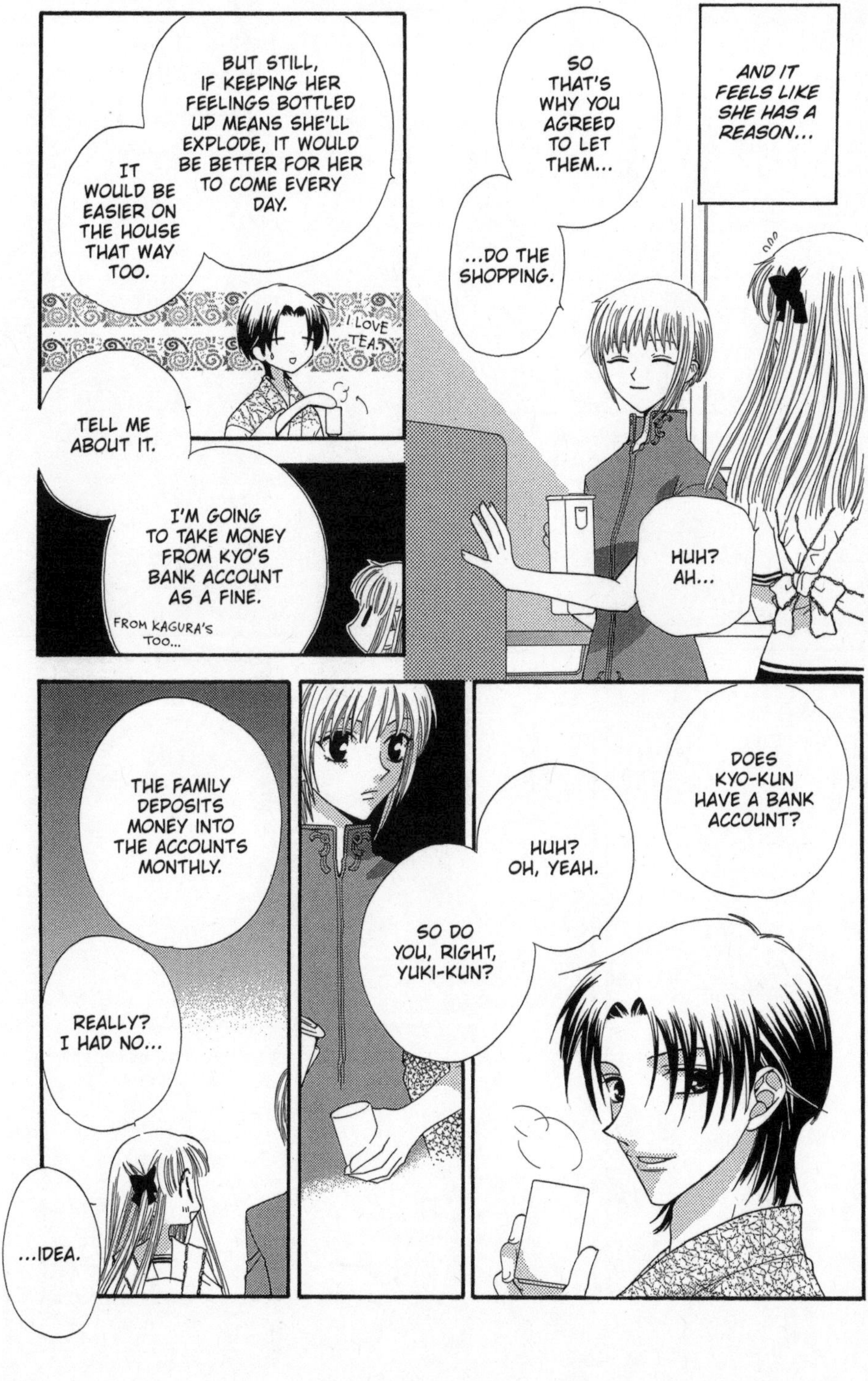
AND IT FEELS LIKE SHE HAS A REASON…
SO THAT'S WHY YOU AGREED TO LET THEM…
…DO THE SHOPPING.
HUH? AH…
BUT STILL, IF KEEPING HER FEELINGS BOTTLED UP MEANS SHE'LL EXPLODE, IT WOULD BE BETTER FOR HER TO COME EVERY DAY.
IT WOULD BE EASIER ON THE HOUSE THAT WAY TOO.
I LOVE TEA.
TELL ME ABOUT IT.
I'M GOING TO TAKE MONEY FROM KYO'S BANK ACCOUNT AS A FINE.
FROM KAGURA'S TOO…
DOES KYO-KUN HAVE A BANK ACCOUNT?
HUH? OH, YEAH.
SO DO YOU, RIGHT, YUKI-KUN?
THE FAMILY DEPOSITS MONEY INTO THE ACCOUNTS MONTHLY.
REALLY? I HAD NO…
…IDEA.

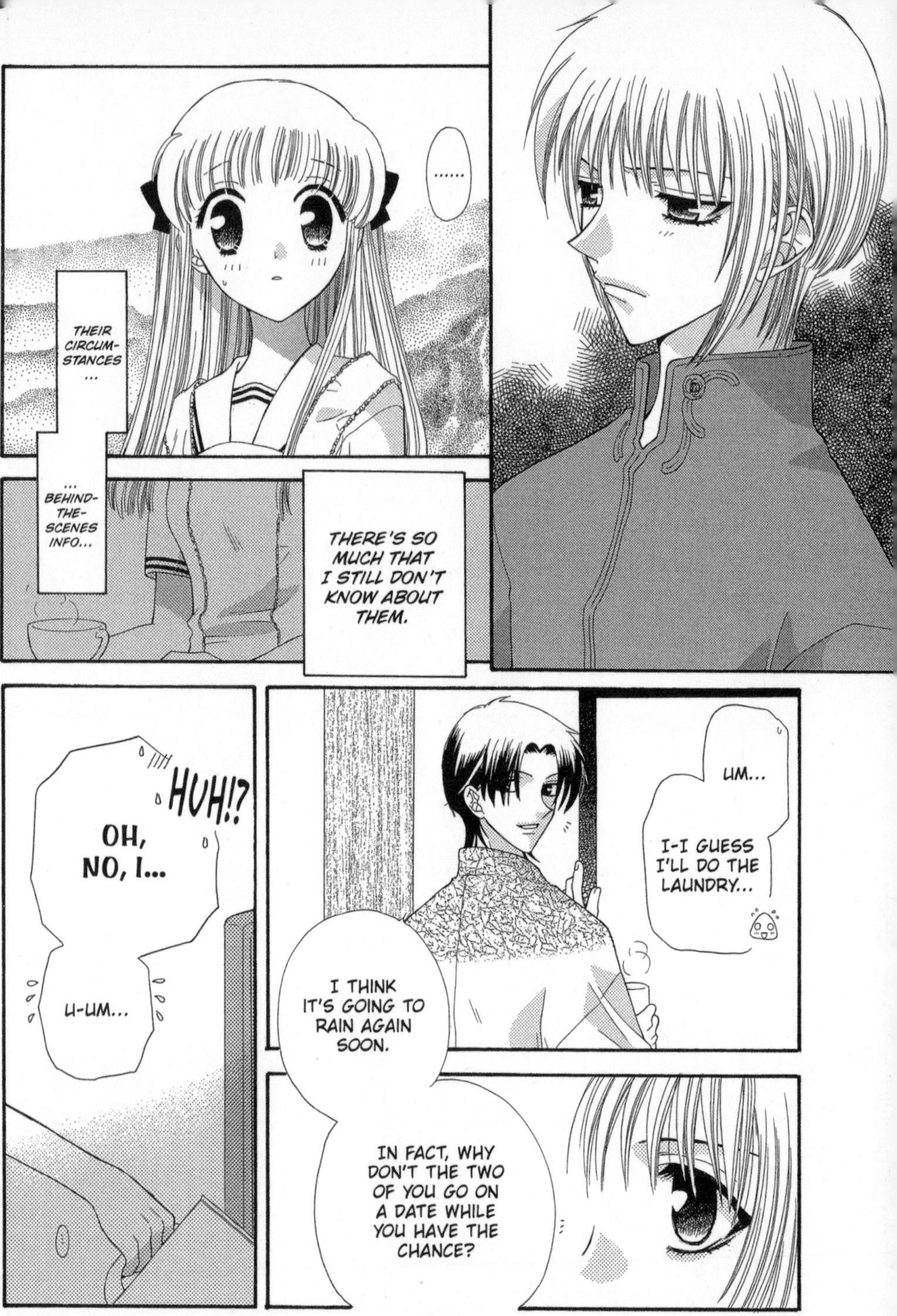
......
THEIR CIRCUM-STANCES...
...BEHIND-THE-SCENES INFO...
THERE'S SO MUCH THAT I STILL DON'T KNOW ABOUT THEM.
UM...
I-I GUESS I'LL DO THE LAUNDRY...
I THINK IT'S GOING TO RAIN AGAIN SOON.
IN FACT, WHY DON'T THE TWO OF YOU GO ON A DATE WHILE YOU HAVE THE CHANCE?
HUH!?
OH, NO, I...
U-UM...

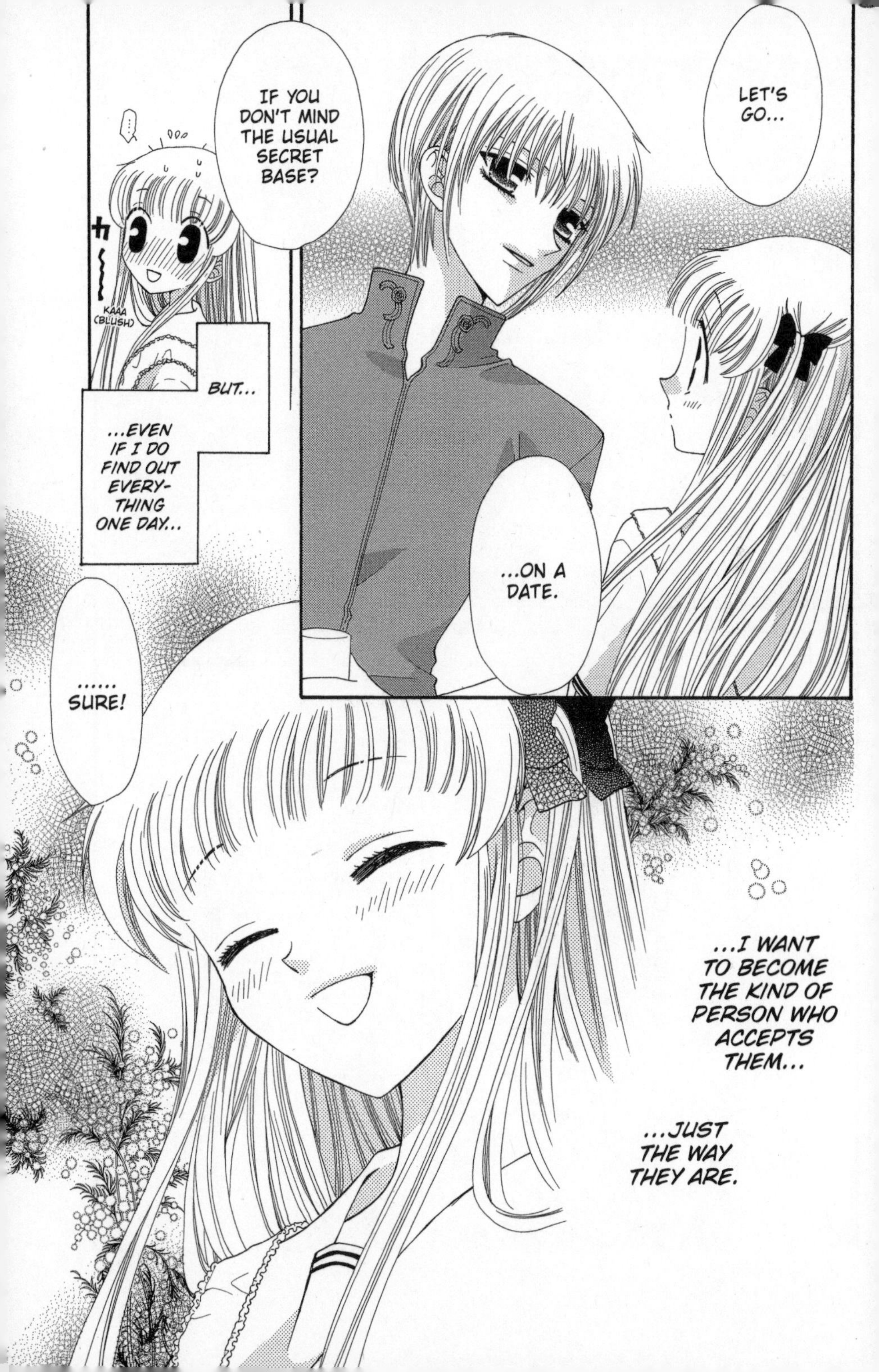
LET'S GO...
...ON A DATE.
IF YOU DON'T MIND THE USUAL SECRET BASE?
...
KAAA (BLUSH)
BUT...
...EVEN IF I DO FIND OUT EVERYTHING ONE DAY...
...... SURE!
...I WANT TO BECOME THE KIND OF PERSON WHO ACCEPTS THEM...
...JUST THE WAY THEY ARE.

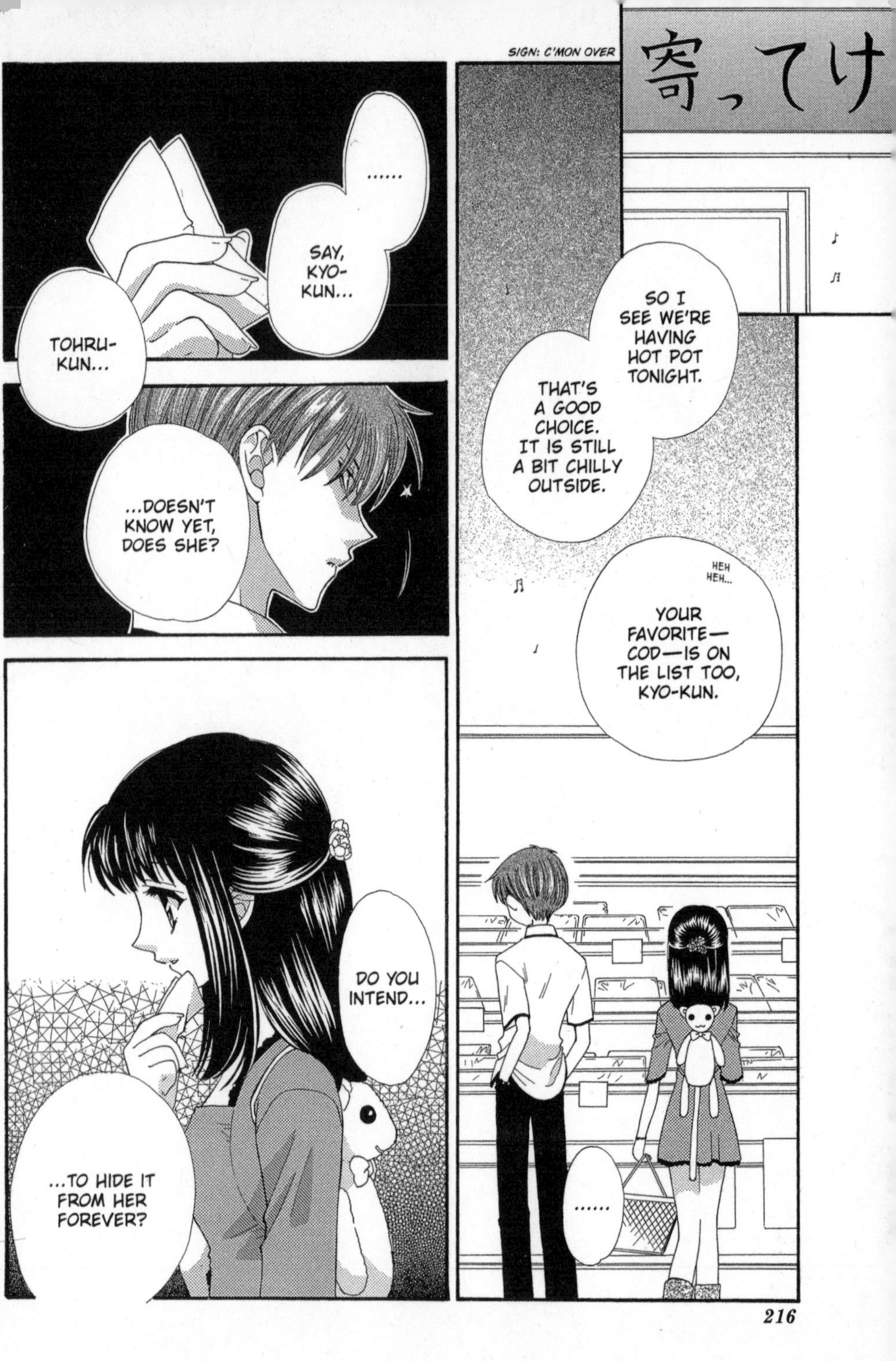
SIGN: C'MON OVER
寄ってけ
SO I SEE WE'RE HAVING HOT POT TONIGHT.
THAT'S A GOOD CHOICE. IT IS STILL A BIT CHILLY OUTSIDE.
HEH HEH...
YOUR FAVORITE—COD—IS ON THE LIST TOO, KYO-KUN.
......
......
SAY, KYO-KUN...
TOHRU-KUN...
...DOESN'T KNOW YET, DOES SHE?
DO YOU INTEND...
...TO HIDE IT FROM HER FOREVER?

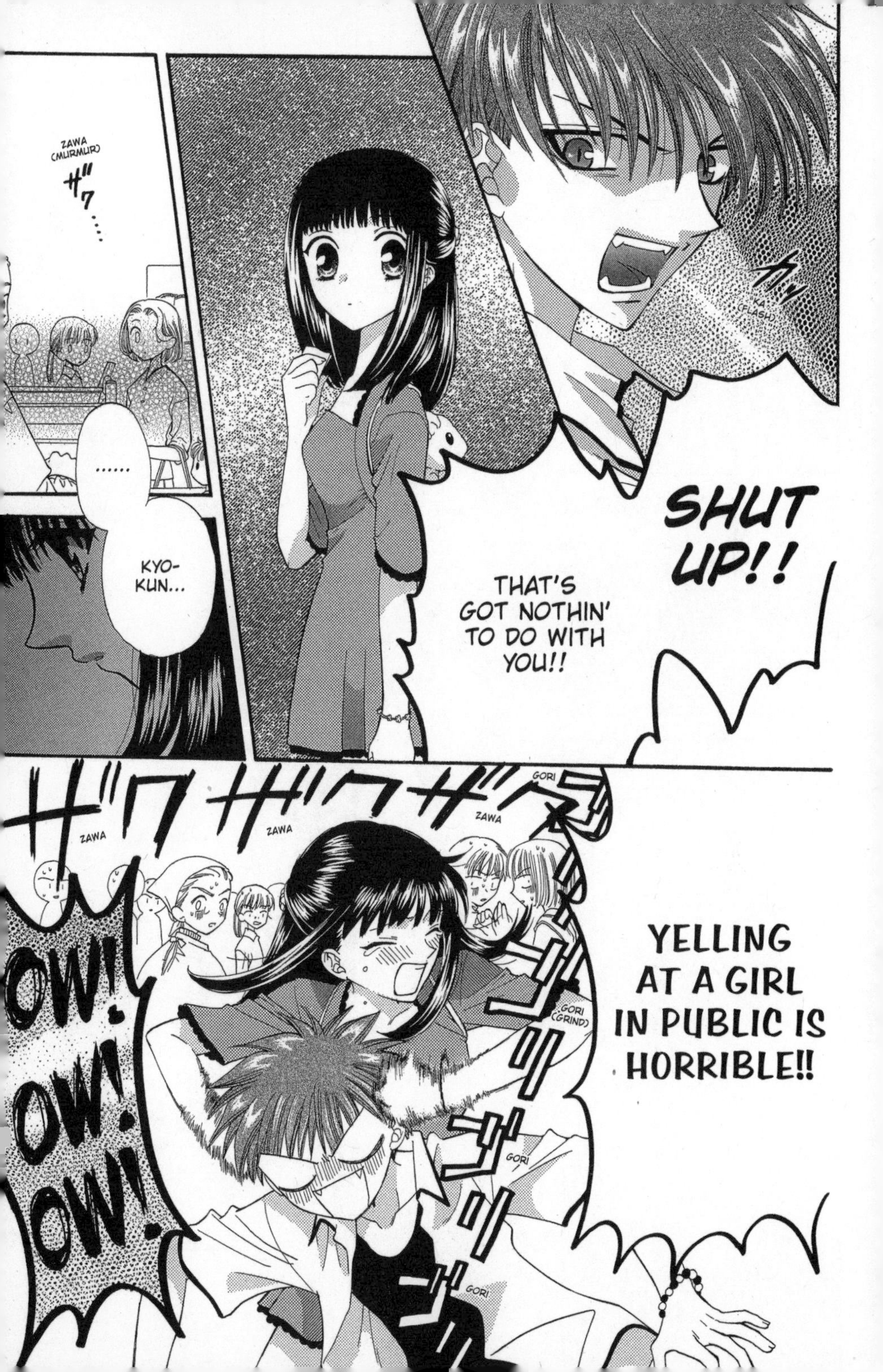

KA (FLASH)
SHUT UP!!
THAT'S GOT NOTHIN' TO DO WITH YOU!!
ZAWA (MURMUR)
......
KYO-KUN...
ZAWA
ZAWA
ZAWA
GORI
GORI (GRIND)
GORI
GORI
YELLING AT A GIRL IN PUBLIC IS HORRIBLE!!
OW! OW! OW! OW!

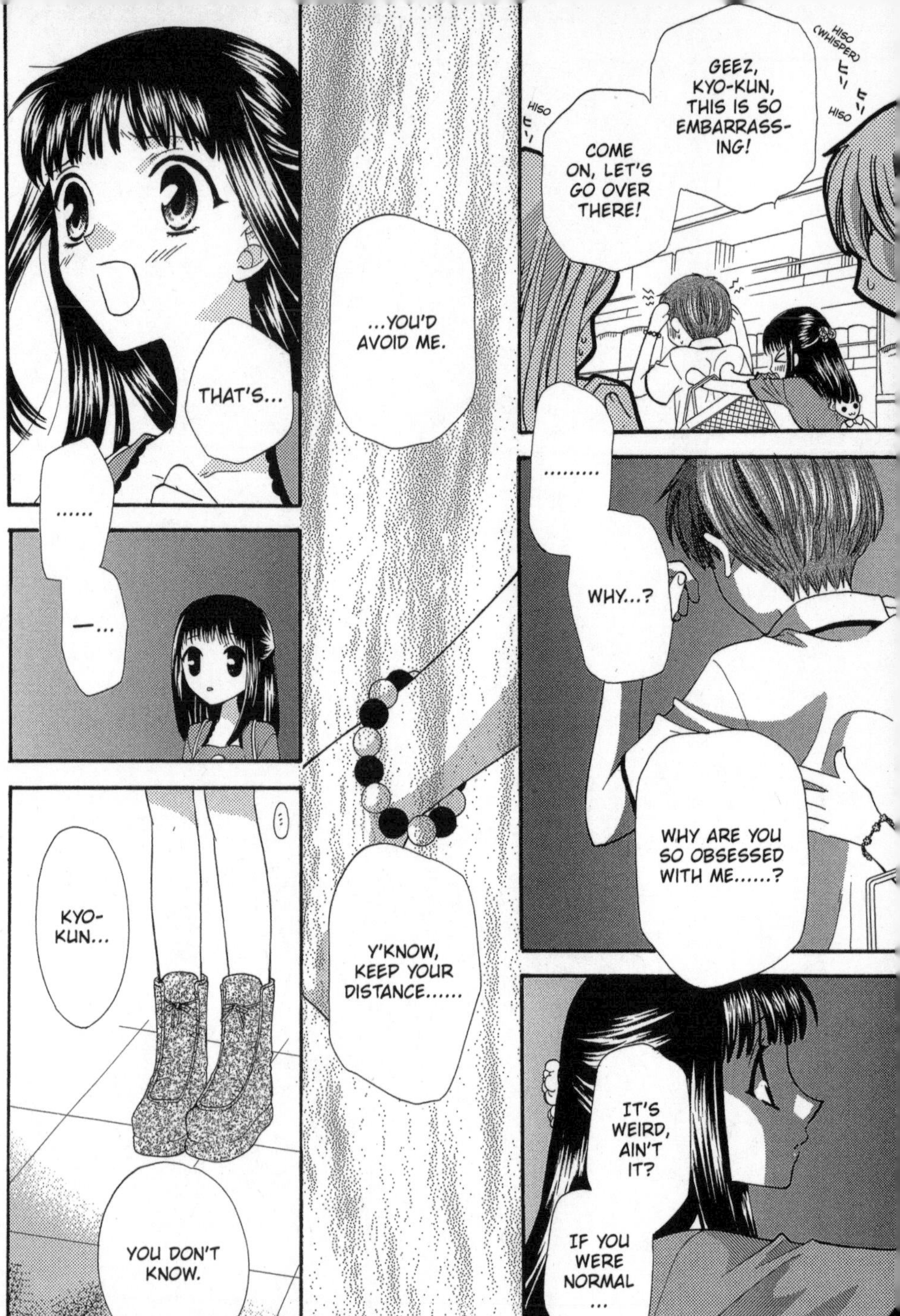
HISO
HISO (WHISPER)
HISO
GEEZ, KYO-KUN, THIS IS SO EMBARRASS-ING!
COME ON, LET'S GO OVER THERE!
....
WHY...?
WHY ARE YOU SO OBSESSED WITH ME......?
IT'S WEIRD, AIN'T IT?
IF YOU WERE NORMAL ...
...YOU'D AVOID ME.
Y'KNOW, KEEP YOUR DISTANCE......
THAT'S...
......
—...
KYO-KUN...
YOU DON'T KNOW.

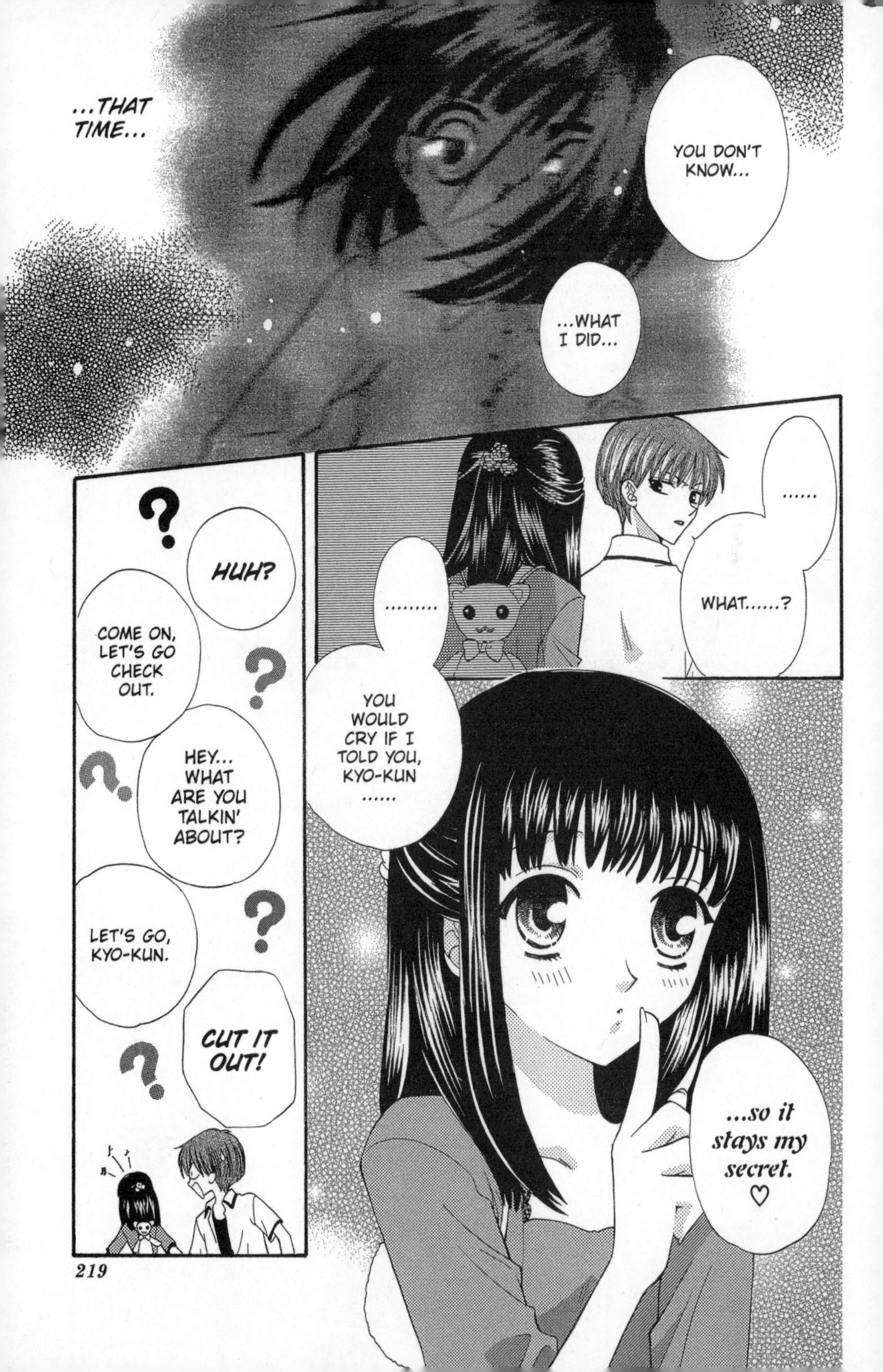
YOU DON'T KNOW...
...WHAT I DID...
...THAT TIME...
......
WHAT......?
....
YOU WOULD CRY IF I TOLD YOU, KYO-KUN ......
...so it stays my secret. ♡
HUH?
COME ON, LET'S GO CHECK OUT.
HEY... WHAT ARE YOU TALKIN' ABOUT?
LET'S GO, KYO-KUN.
CUT IT OUT!

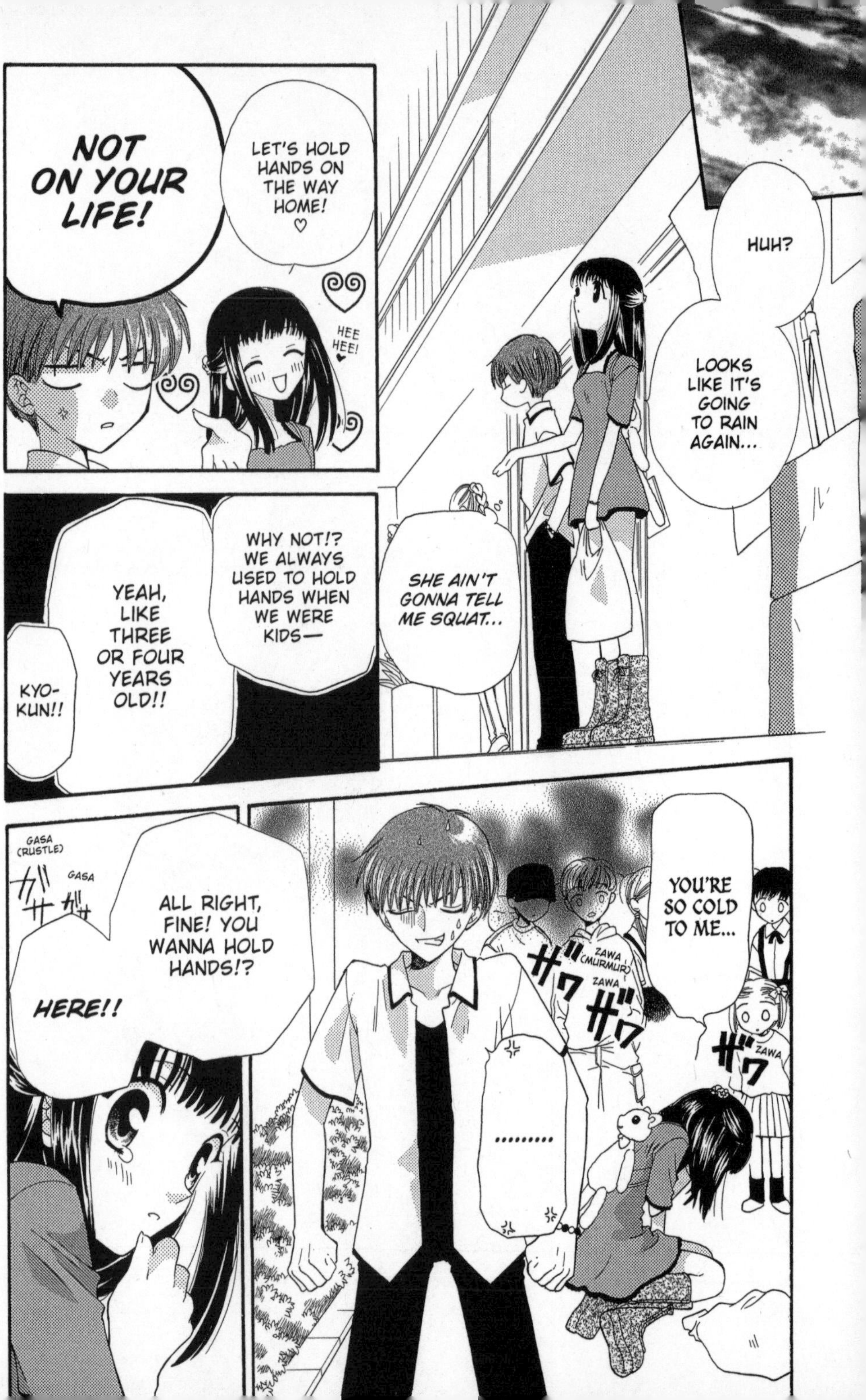
HUH?
LOOKS LIKE IT'S GOING TO RAIN AGAIN...
SHE AIN'T GONNA TELL ME SQUAT...
LET'S HOLD HANDS ON THE WAY HOME! ♡
NOT ON YOUR LIFE!
HEE HEE! ♥
WHY NOT!? WE ALWAYS USED TO HOLD HANDS WHEN WE WERE KIDS—
YEAH, LIKE THREE OR FOUR YEARS OLD!!
KYO-KUN!!
YOU'RE SO COLD TO ME...
ZAWA (MURMUR) ZAWA
ザワ ザワ
ZAWA
ザワ
....
GASA (RUSTLE)
GASA
ガサ ガサ
ALL RIGHT, FINE! YOU WANNA HOLD HANDS!?
HERE!!

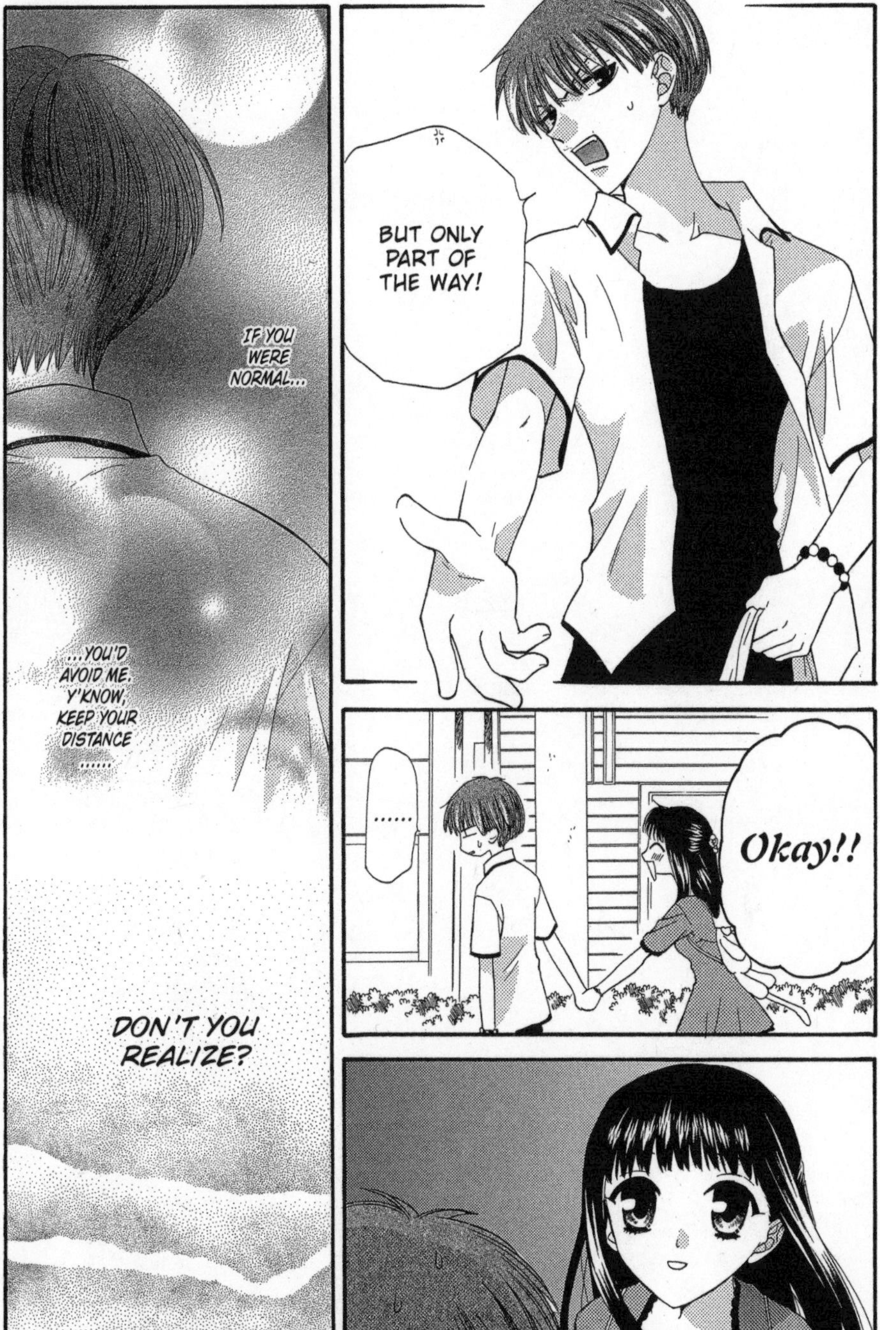
BUT ONLY PART OF THE WAY!
Okay!!
......
IF YOU WERE NORMAL...
...YOU'D AVOID ME. Y'KNOW, KEEP YOUR DISTANCE ......
DON'T YOU REALIZE?

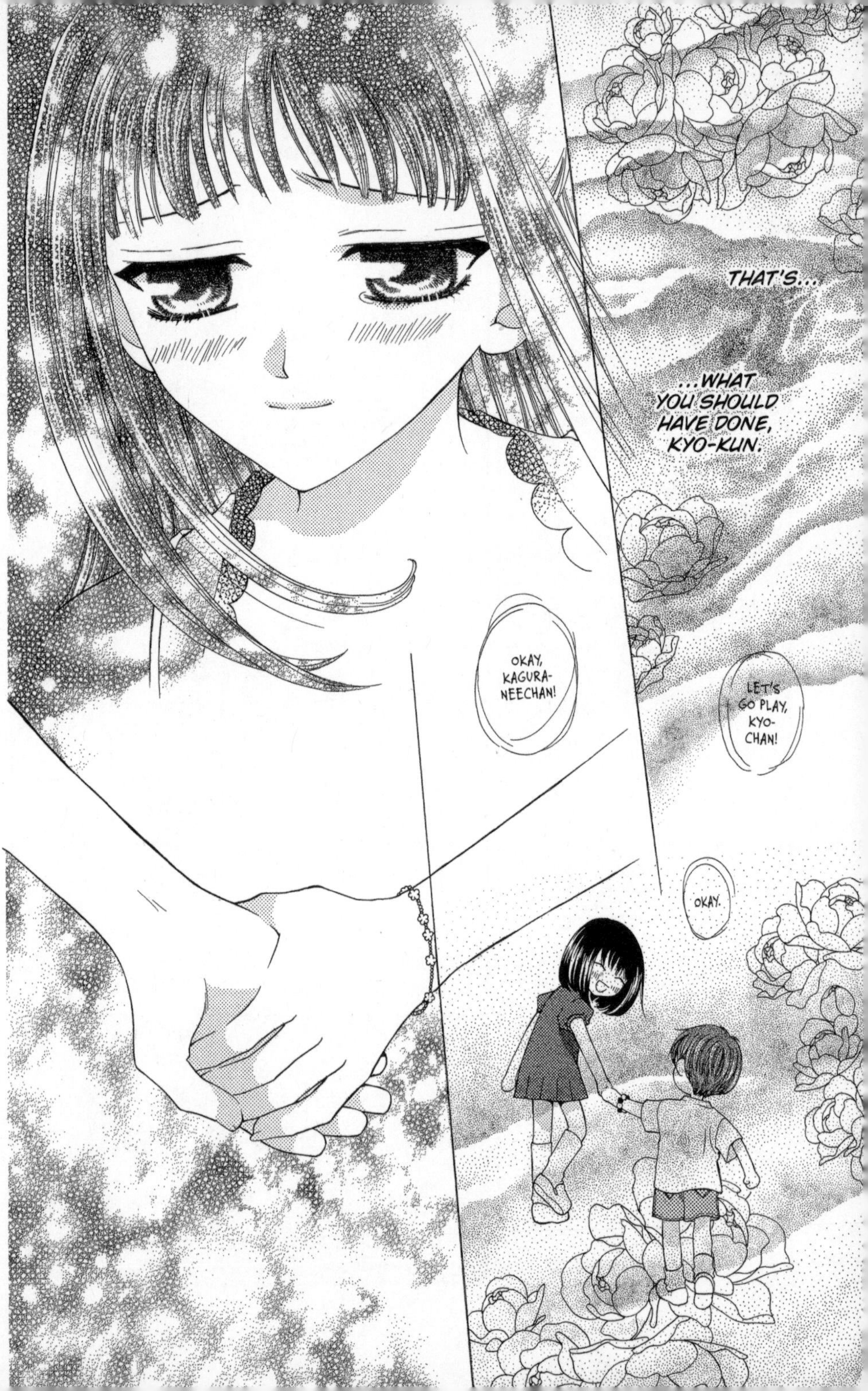
THAT'S...
...WHAT YOU SHOULD HAVE DONE, KYO-KUN.
LET'S GO PLAY, KYO-CHAN!
OKAY.
OKAY, KAGURA-NEECHAN!

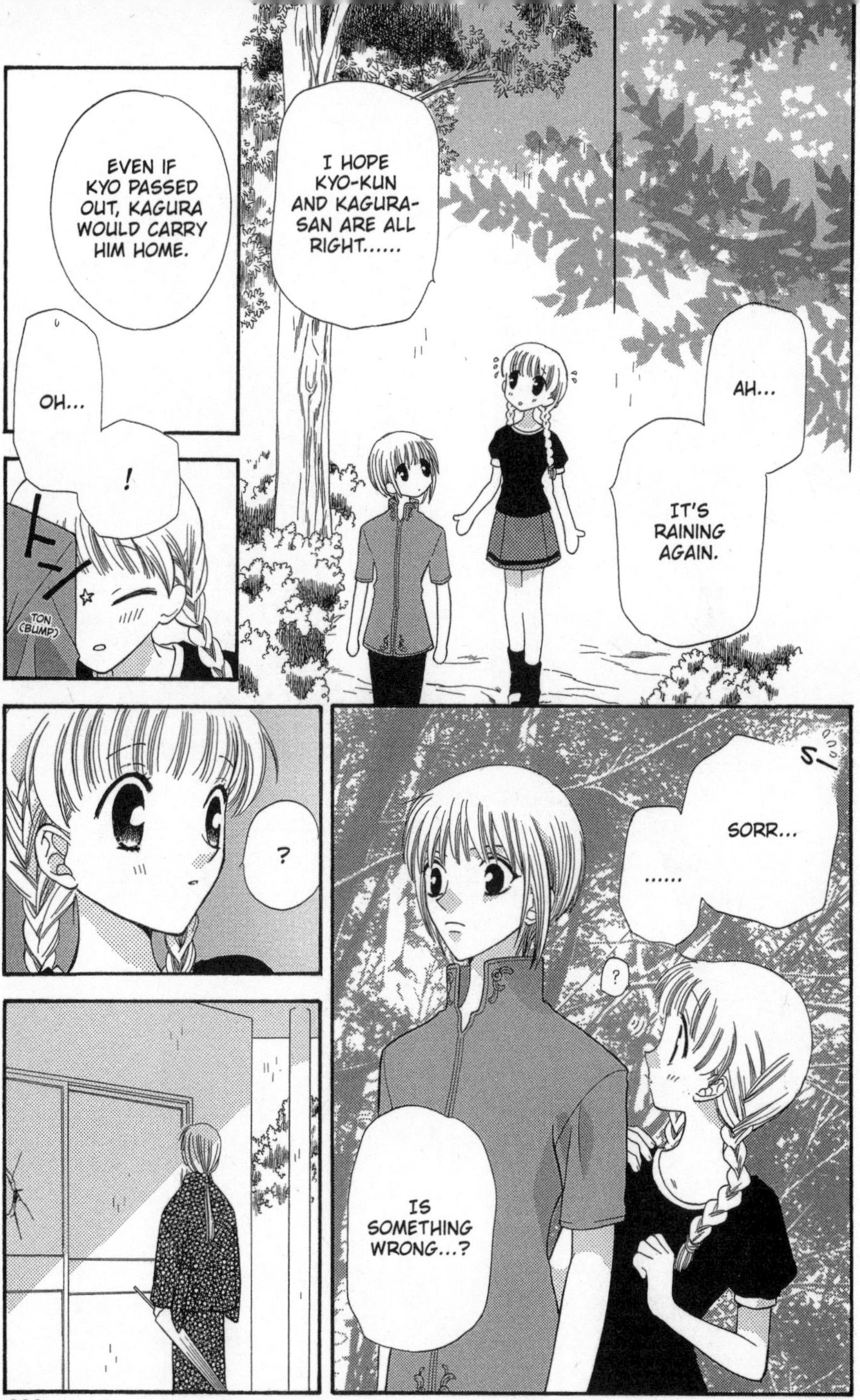
AH...
IT'S RAINING AGAIN.
I HOPE KYO-KUN AND KAGURA-SAN ARE ALL RIGHT......
EVEN IF KYO PASSED OUT, KAGURA WOULD CARRY HIM HOME.
OH...
!
TON (BUMP)
SORR...
......
?
IS SOMETHING WRONG...?
?

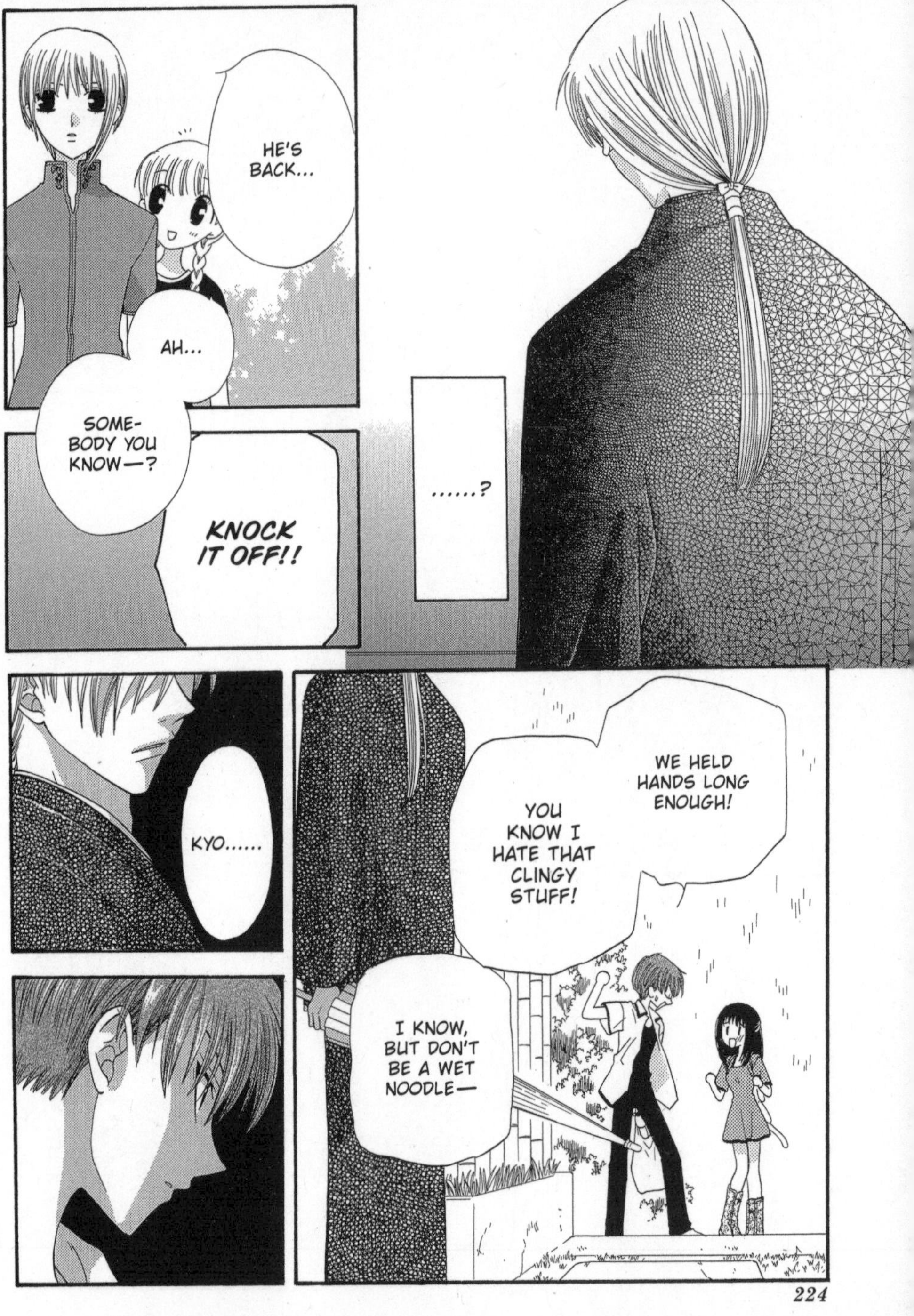
......?
HE'S BACK...
AH...
SOME-BODY YOU KNOW—?
KNOCK IT OFF!!
WE HELD HANDS LONG ENOUGH!
YOU KNOW I HATE THAT CLINGY STUFF!
I KNOW, BUT DON'T BE A WET NOODLE—
KYO......

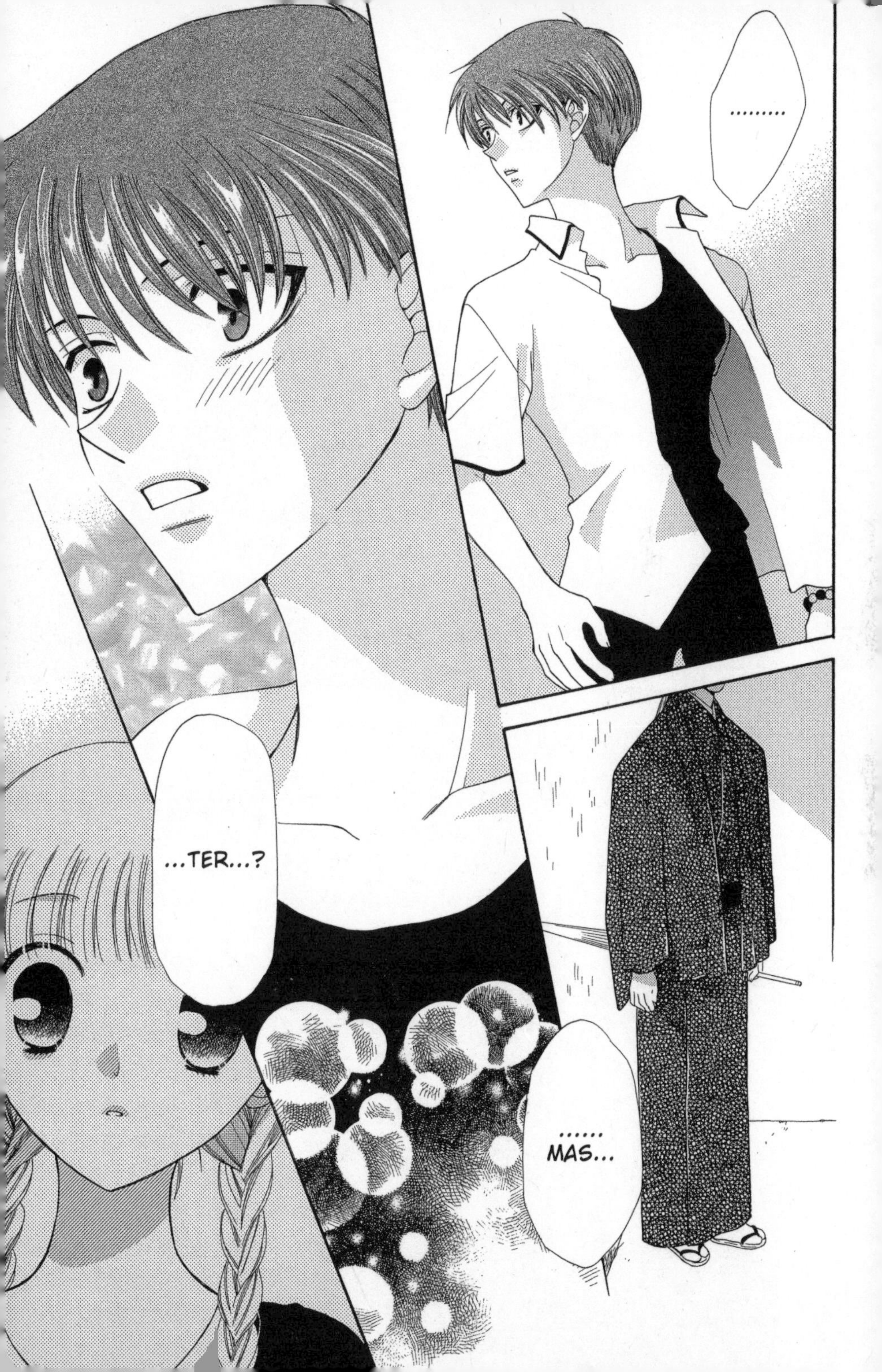
....
......
MAS...
...TER...?

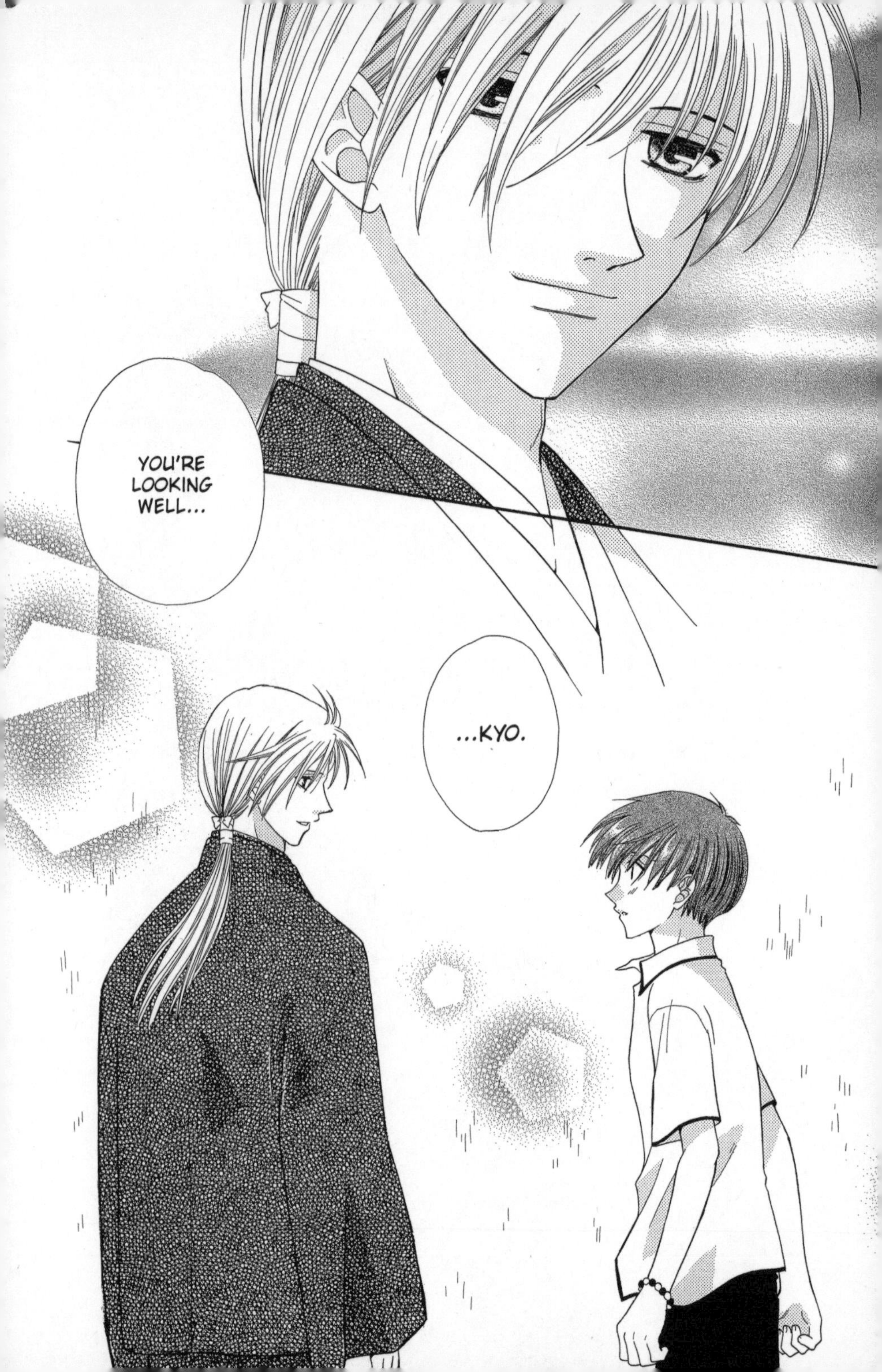
YOU'RE LOOKING WELL...
...KYO.

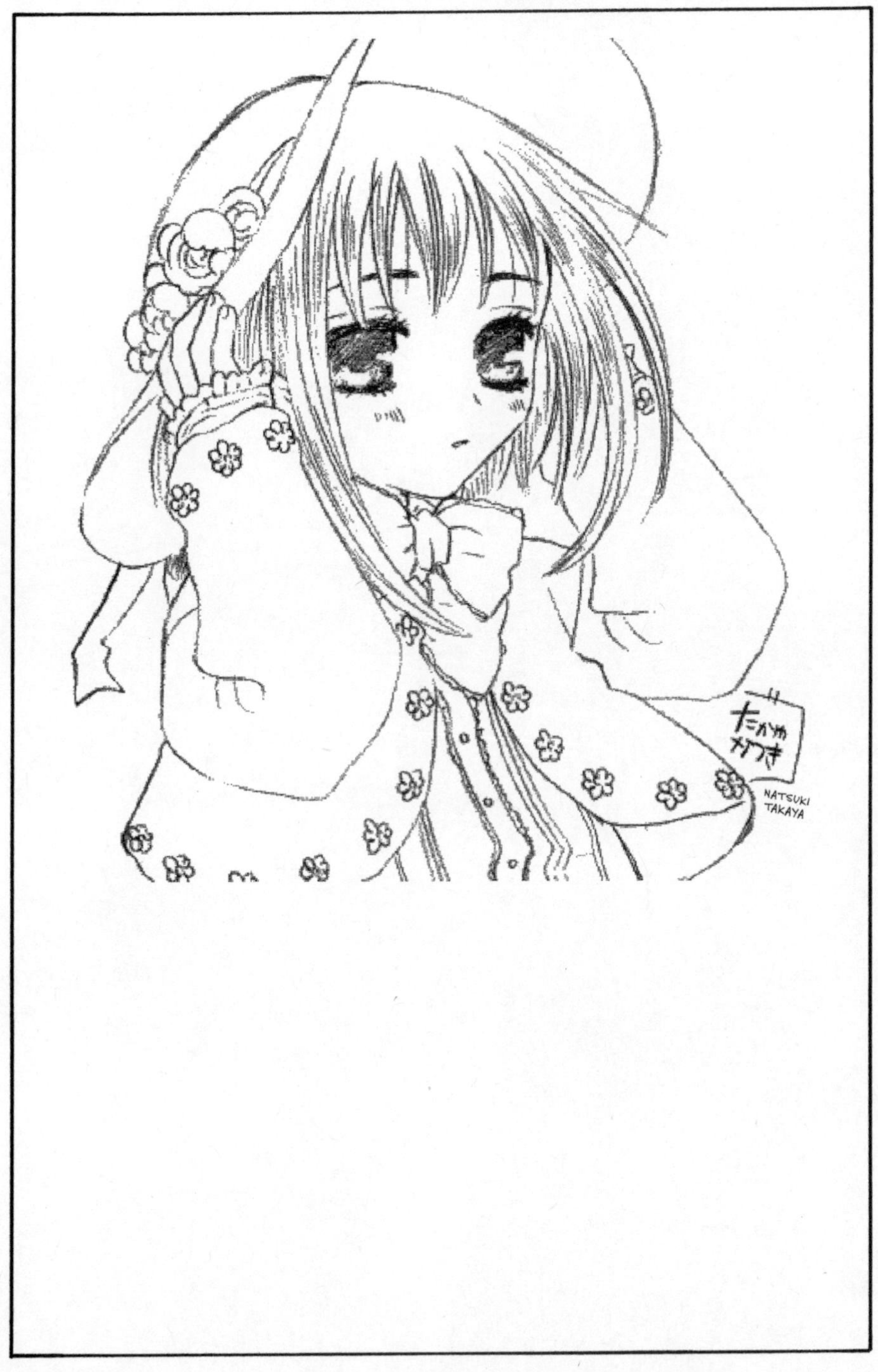
たかや
なつき
NATSUKI TAKAYA

Chapter 32

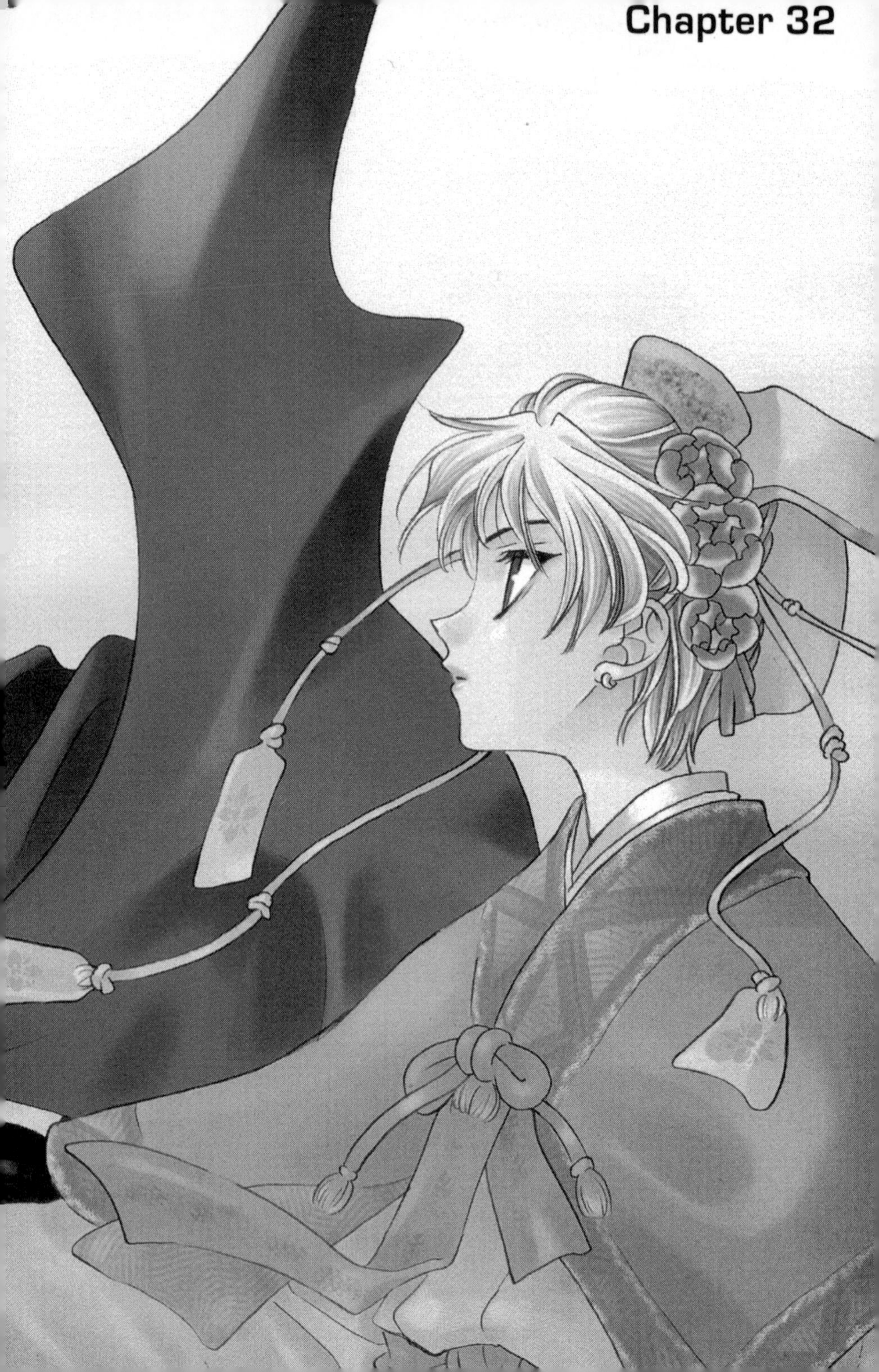

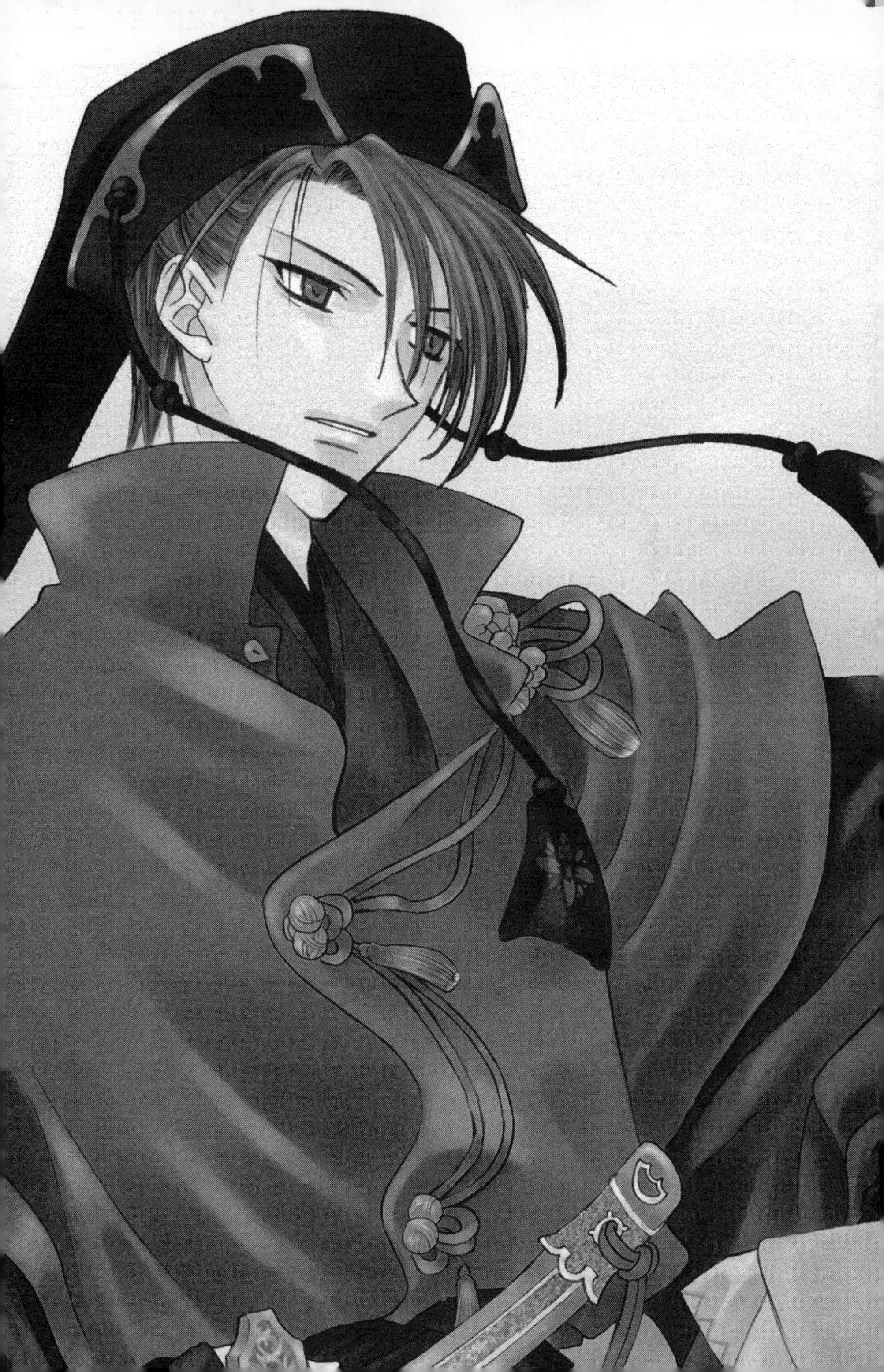

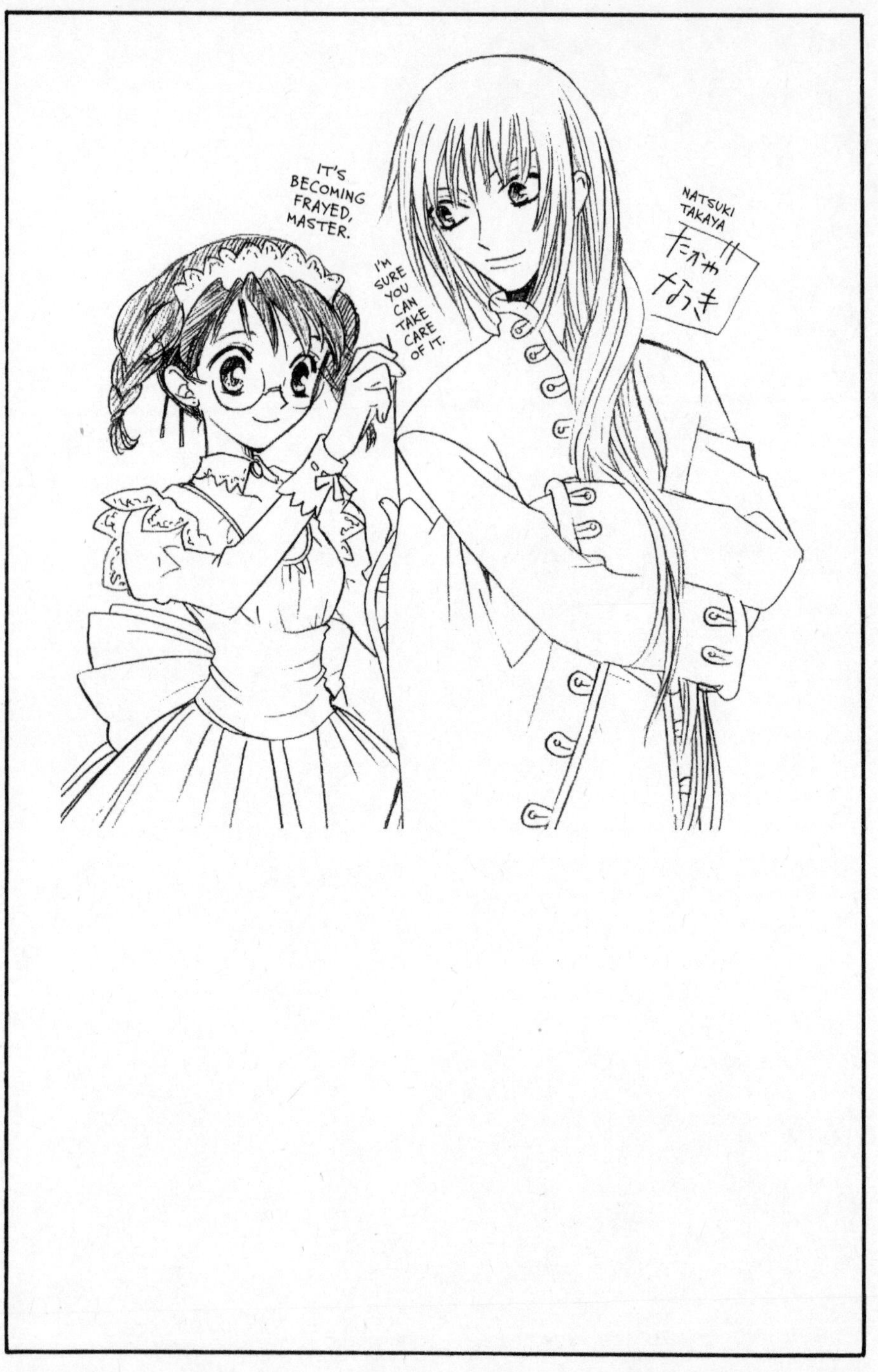
NATSUKI TAKAYA
たかや なつき
IT'S BECOMING FRAYED, MASTER.
I'M SURE YOU CAN TAKE CARE OF IT.

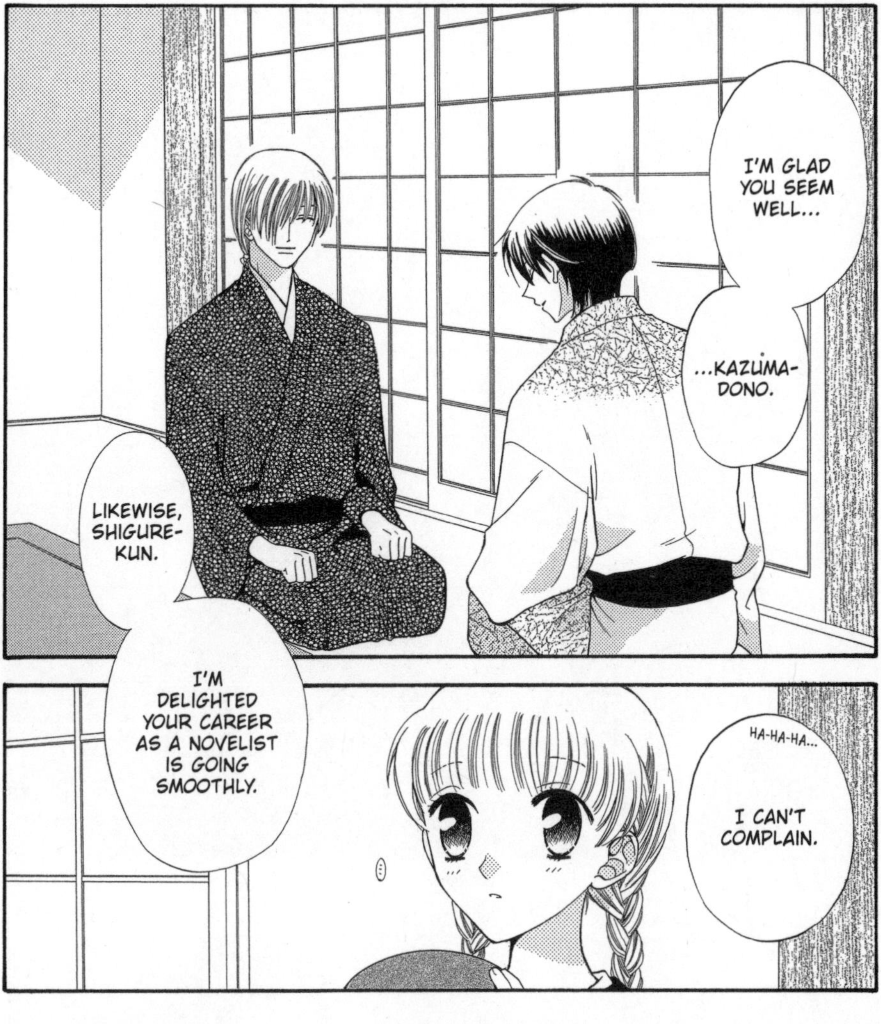
I'M GLAD YOU SEEM WELL...
...KAZUMA-DONO.
LIKEWISE, SHIGURE-KUN.
I'M DELIGHTED YOUR CAREER AS A NOVELIST IS GOING SMOOTHLY.
HA-HA-HA...
I CAN'T COMPLAIN.

yuki

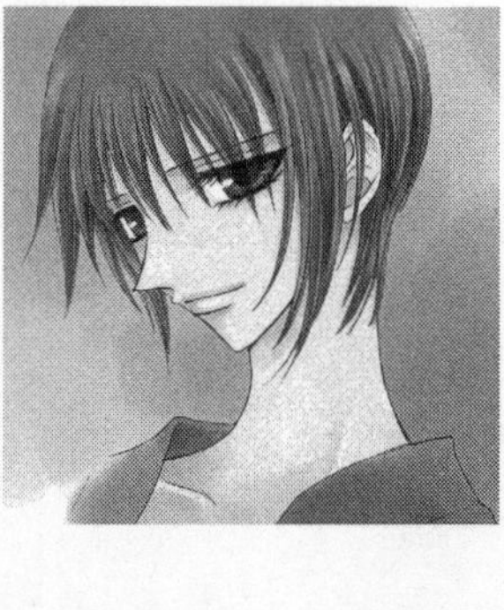

tohru

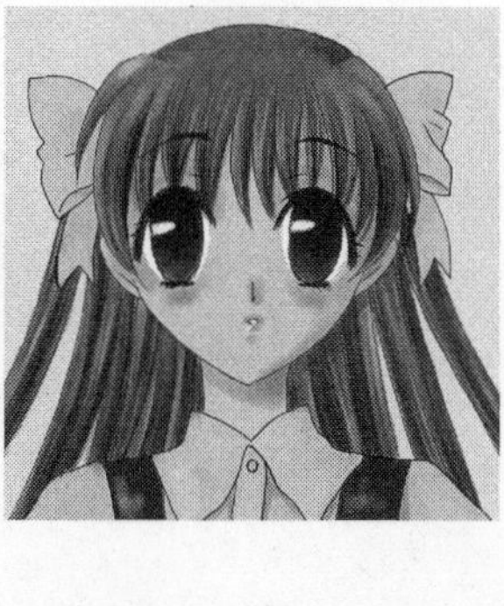

kyo

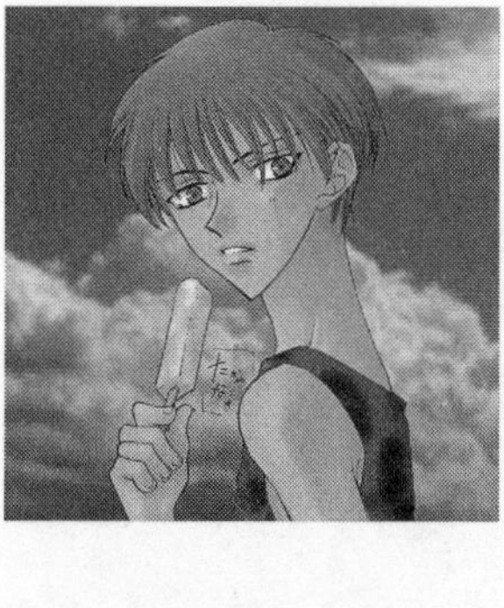

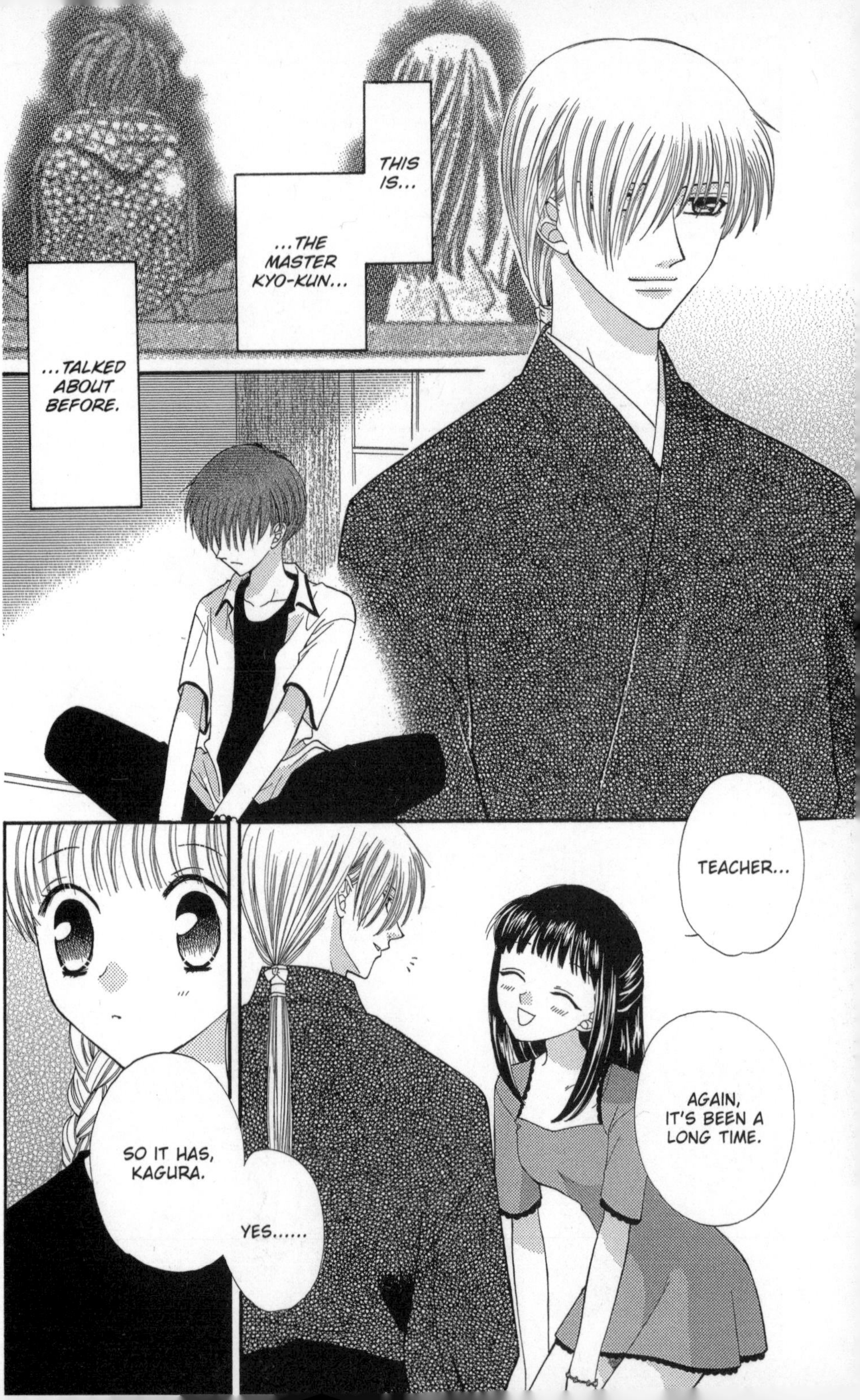
THIS IS...
...THE MASTER KYO-KUN...
...TALKED ABOUT BEFORE.
TEACHER...
AGAIN, IT'S BEEN A LONG TIME.
SO IT HAS, KAGURA.
YES......

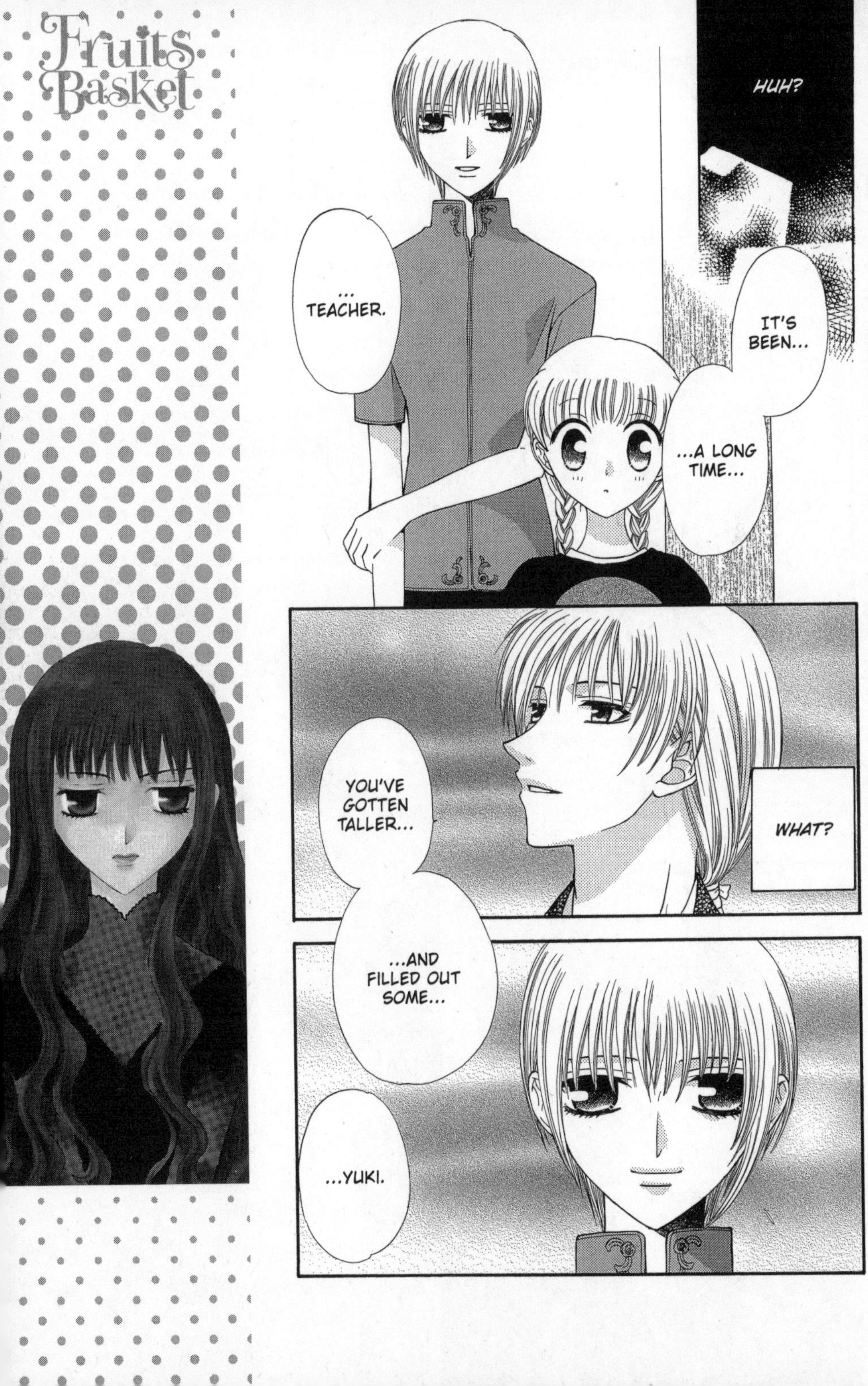
Fruits Basket
HUH?
IT'S BEEN...
...A LONG TIME...
...TEACHER.
WHAT?
YOU'VE GOTTEN TALLER...
...AND FILLED OUT SOME...
...YUKI.

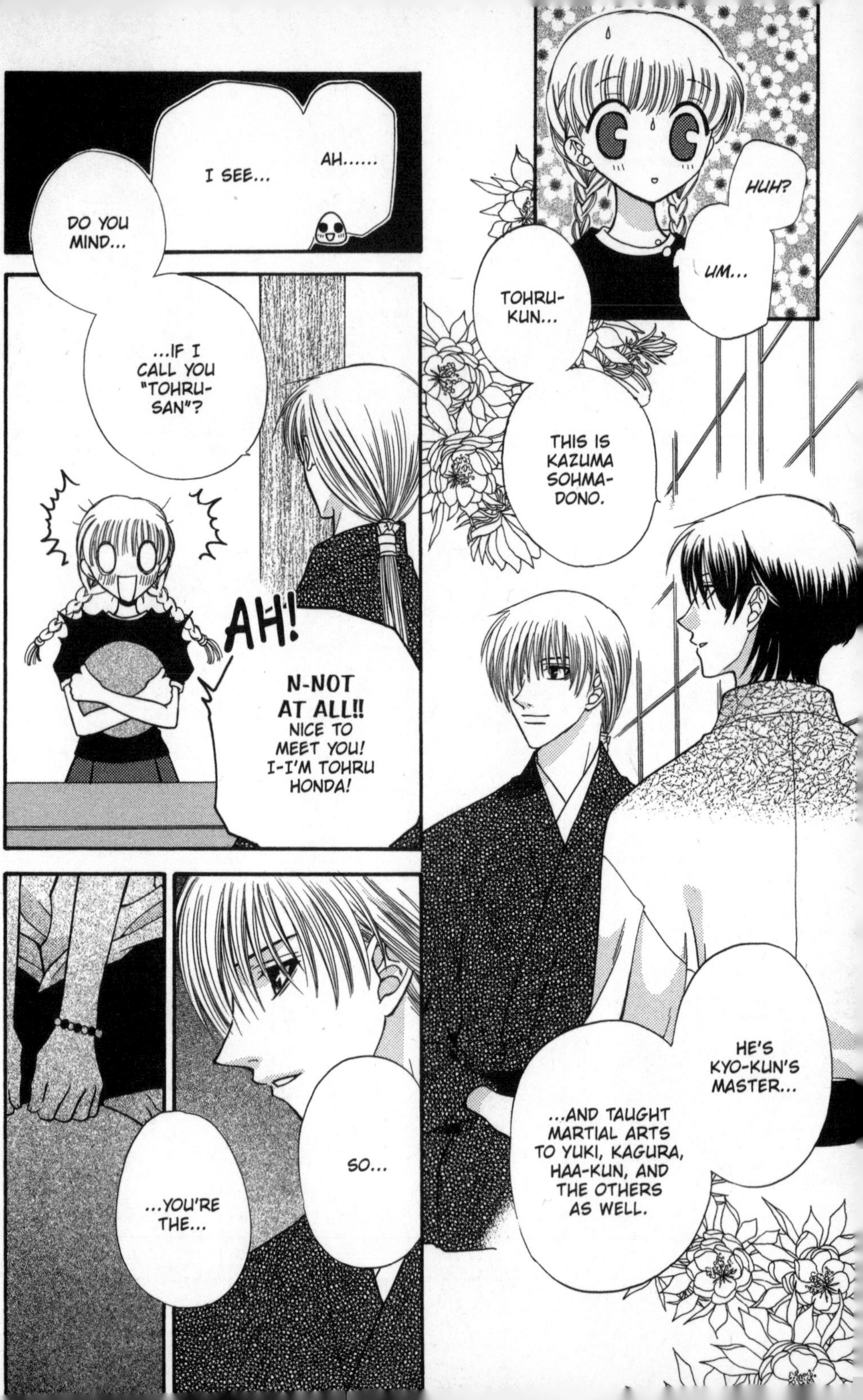
HUH?
UM...
TOHRU-KUN...
THIS IS KAZUMA SOHMA-DONO.
HE'S KYO-KUN'S MASTER...
...AND TAUGHT MARTIAL ARTS TO YUKI, KAGURA, HAA-KUN, AND THE OTHERS AS WELL.
AH......
I SEE...
DO YOU MIND...
...IF I CALL YOU "TOHRU-SAN"?
AH!
N-NOT AT ALL!! NICE TO MEET YOU! I-I'M TOHRU HONDA!
SO...
...YOU'RE THE...

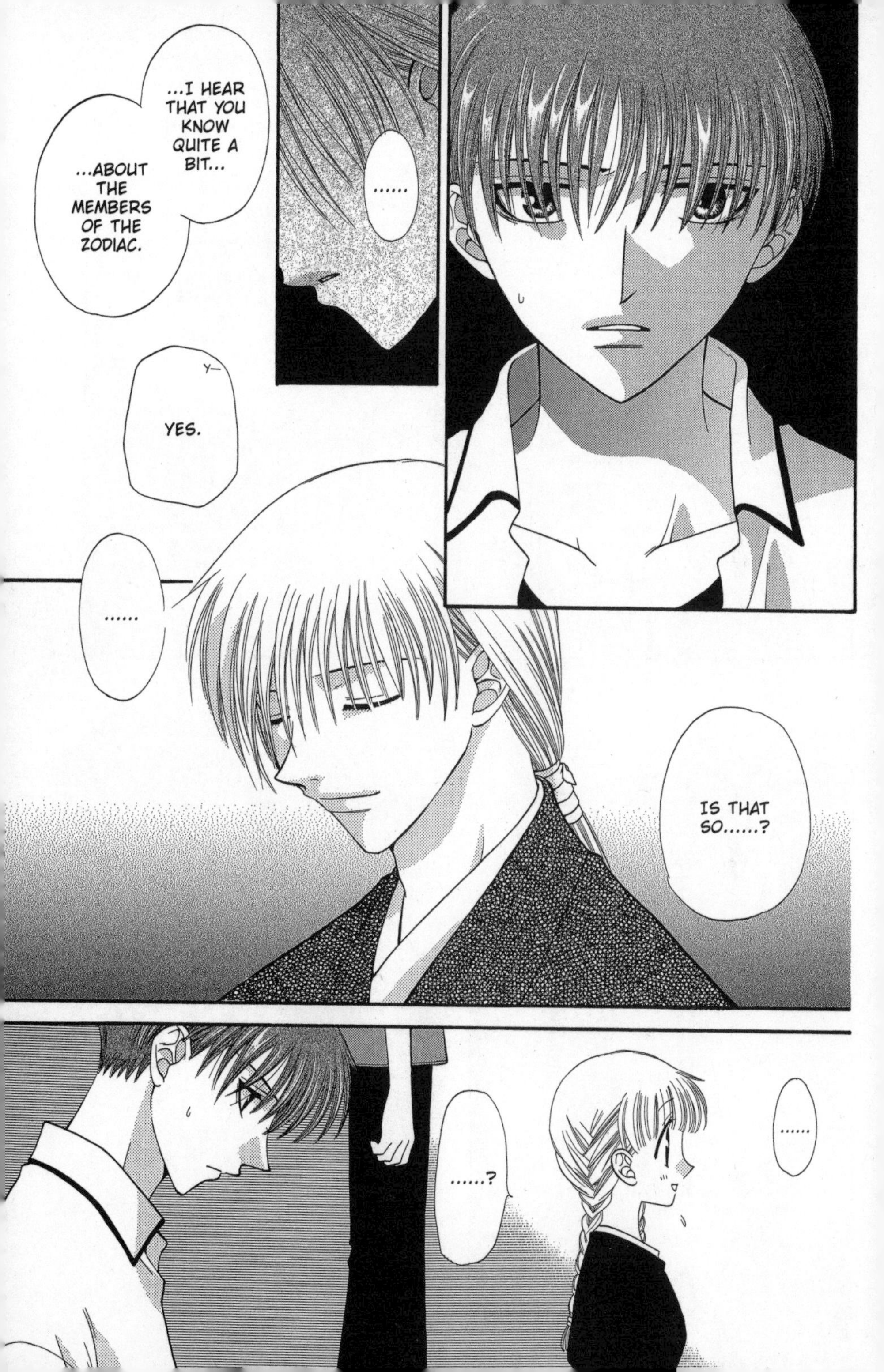
......
...I HEAR THAT YOU KNOW QUITE A BIT...
...ABOUT THE MEMBERS OF THE ZODIAC.
Y— YES.
IS THAT SO......?
......
......
......?

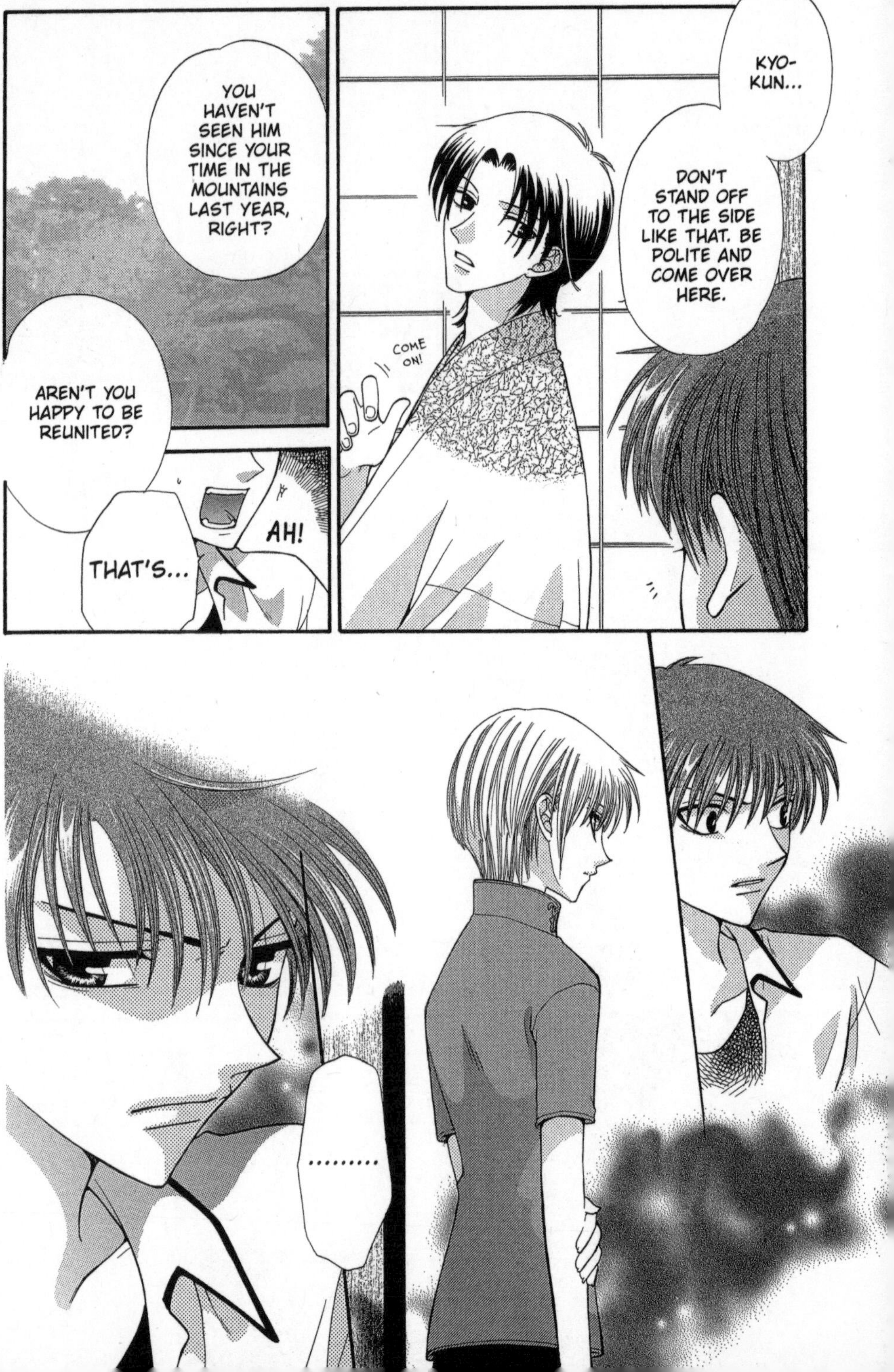
KYO-KUN...
DON'T STAND OFF TO THE SIDE LIKE THAT. BE POLITE AND COME OVER HERE.
COME ON!
YOU HAVEN'T SEEN HIM SINCE YOUR TIME IN THE MOUNTAINS LAST YEAR, RIGHT?
AREN'T YOU HAPPY TO BE REUNITED?
AH!
THAT'S...
....

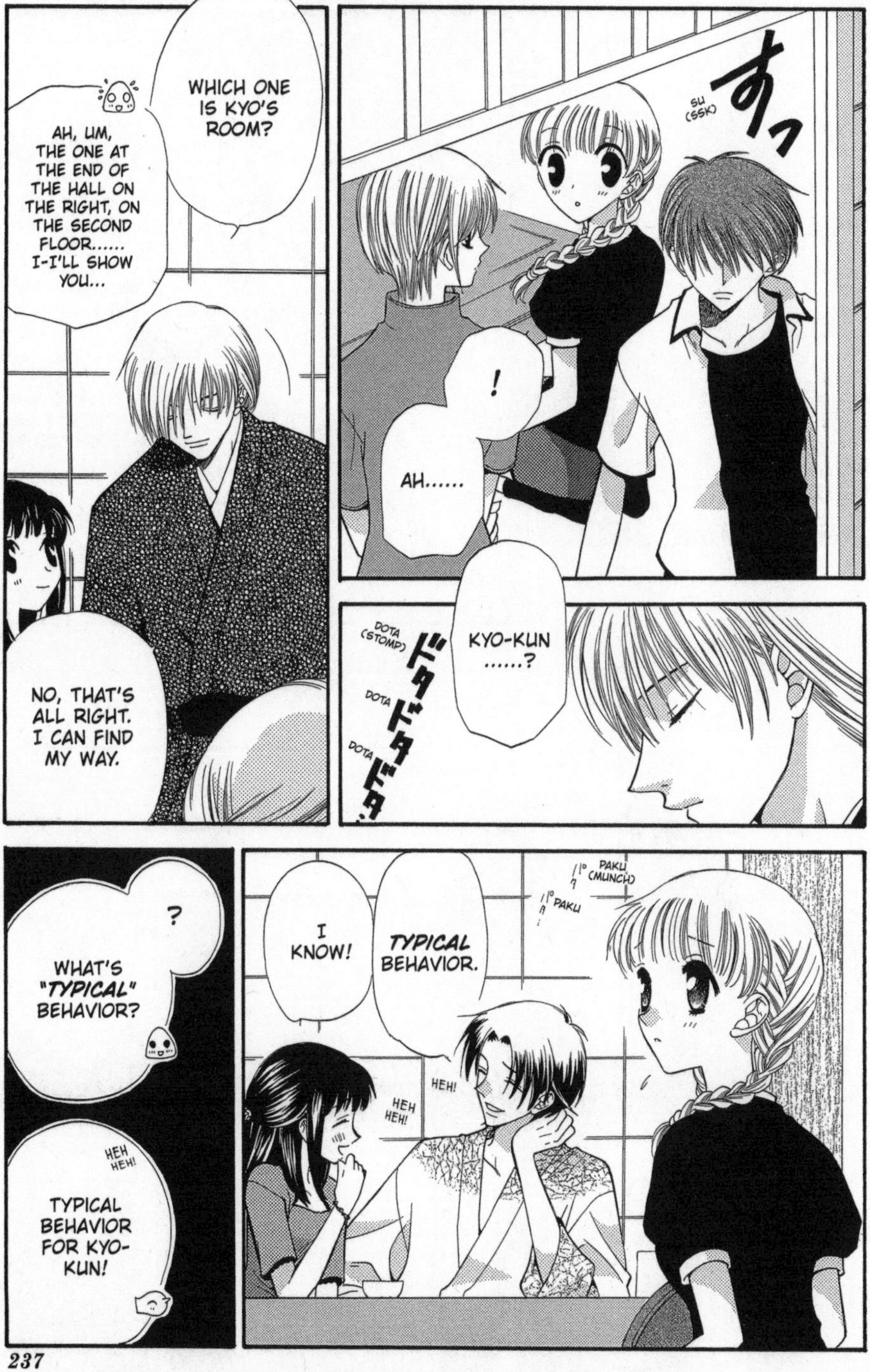
SU (SSK)
すっ
!
AH......
DOTA (STOMP)
ドタ
DOTA
ドタ
DOTA
ドタ
KYO-KUN ......?
WHICH ONE IS KYO'S ROOM?
AH, UM, THE ONE AT THE END OF THE HALL ON THE RIGHT, ON THE SECOND FLOOR...... I-I'LL SHOW YOU...
NO, THAT'S ALL RIGHT. I CAN FIND MY WAY.
PAKU (MUNCH)
PAKU
TYPICAL BEHAVIOR.
I KNOW!
HEH!
HEH HEH!
?
WHAT'S "*TYPICAL*" BEHAVIOR?
HEH HEH!
TYPICAL BEHAVIOR FOR KYO-KUN!

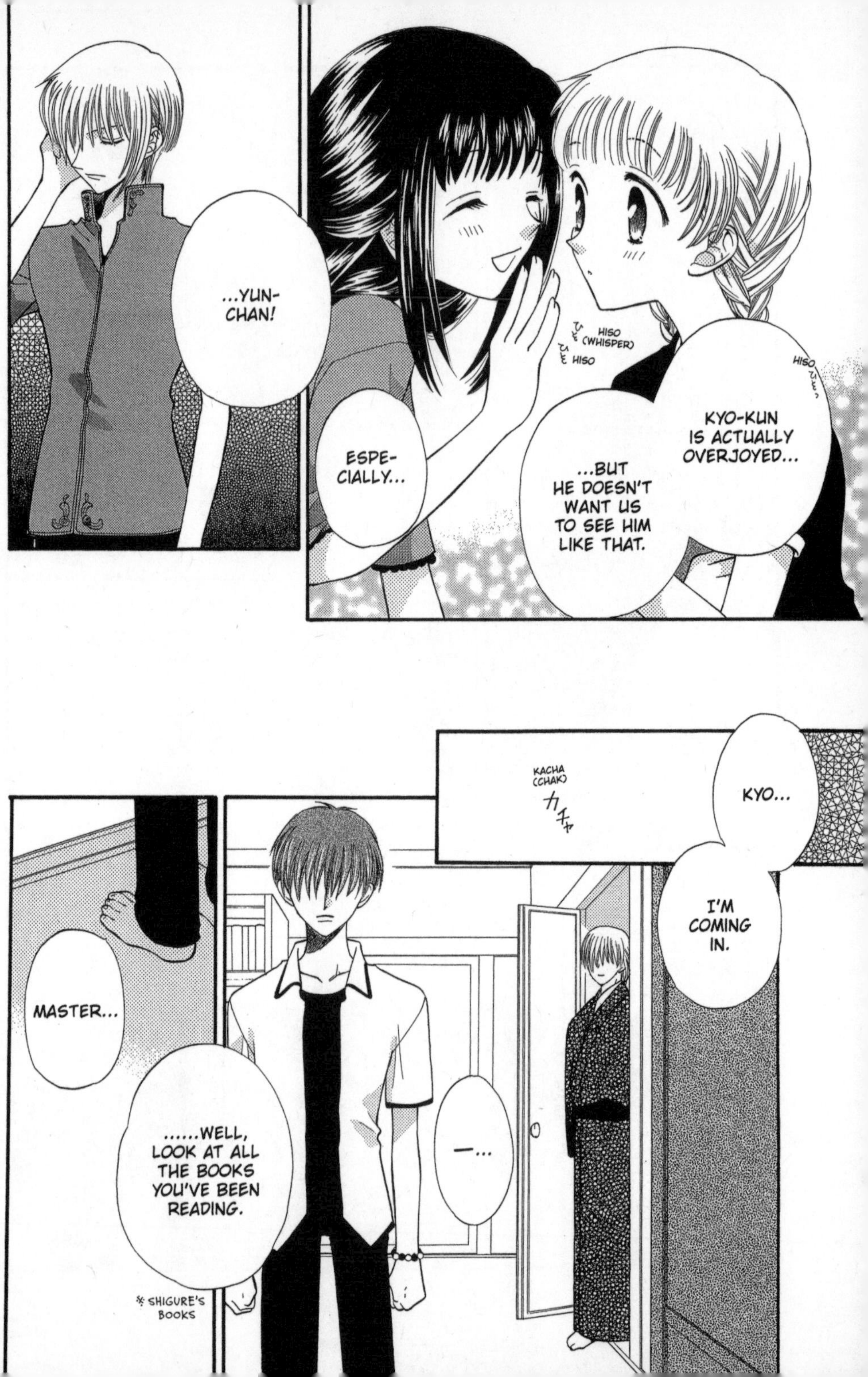
HISO
ひそ
KYO-KUN IS ACTUALLY OVERJOYED...
...BUT HE DOESN'T WANT US TO SEE HIM LIKE THAT.
HISO (WHISPER)
ひそ
HISO
ひそ
ESPE-CIALLY...
...YUN-CHAN!
KACHA (CHAK)
カチャ
KYO...
I'M COMING IN.
—...
......WELL, LOOK AT ALL THE BOOKS YOU'VE BEEN READING.
MASTER...
* SHIGURE'S BOOKS

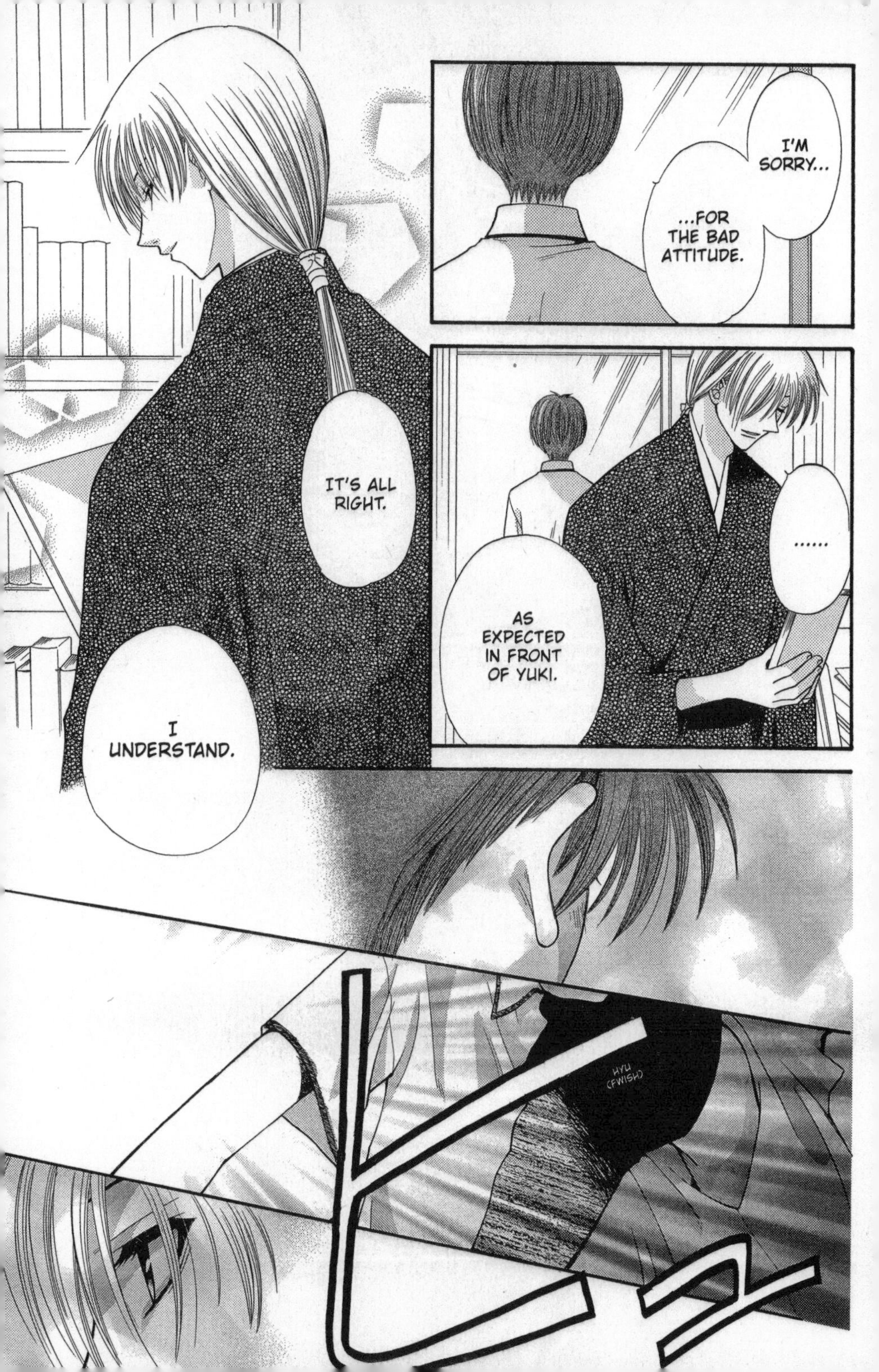
I'M SORRY...
...FOR THE BAD ATTITUDE.
......
AS EXPECTED IN FRONT OF YUKI.
IT'S ALL RIGHT.
I UNDERSTAND.
HYU (FWISH)

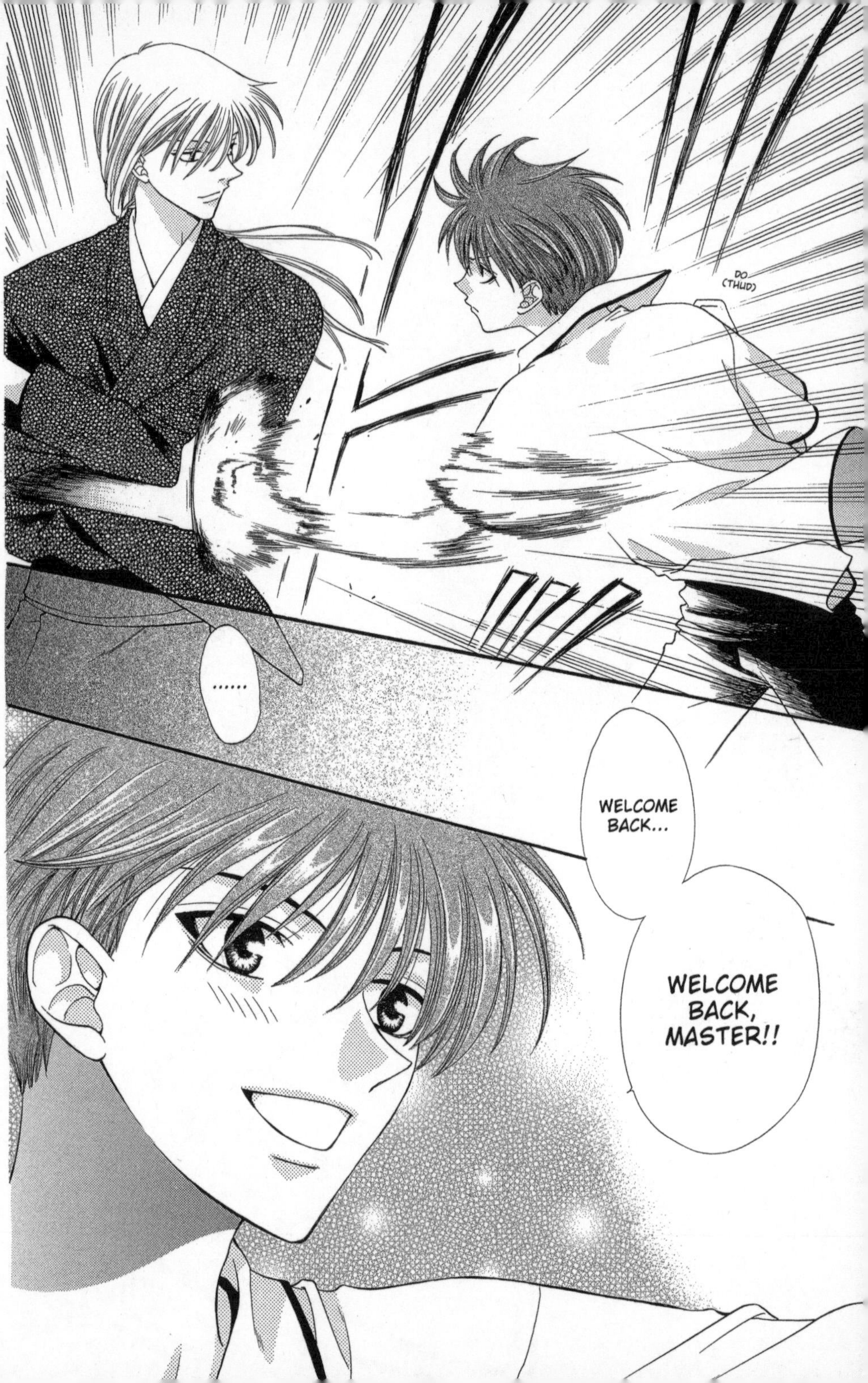
DO (THUD)
......
WELCOME BACK...
WELCOME BACK, MASTER!!

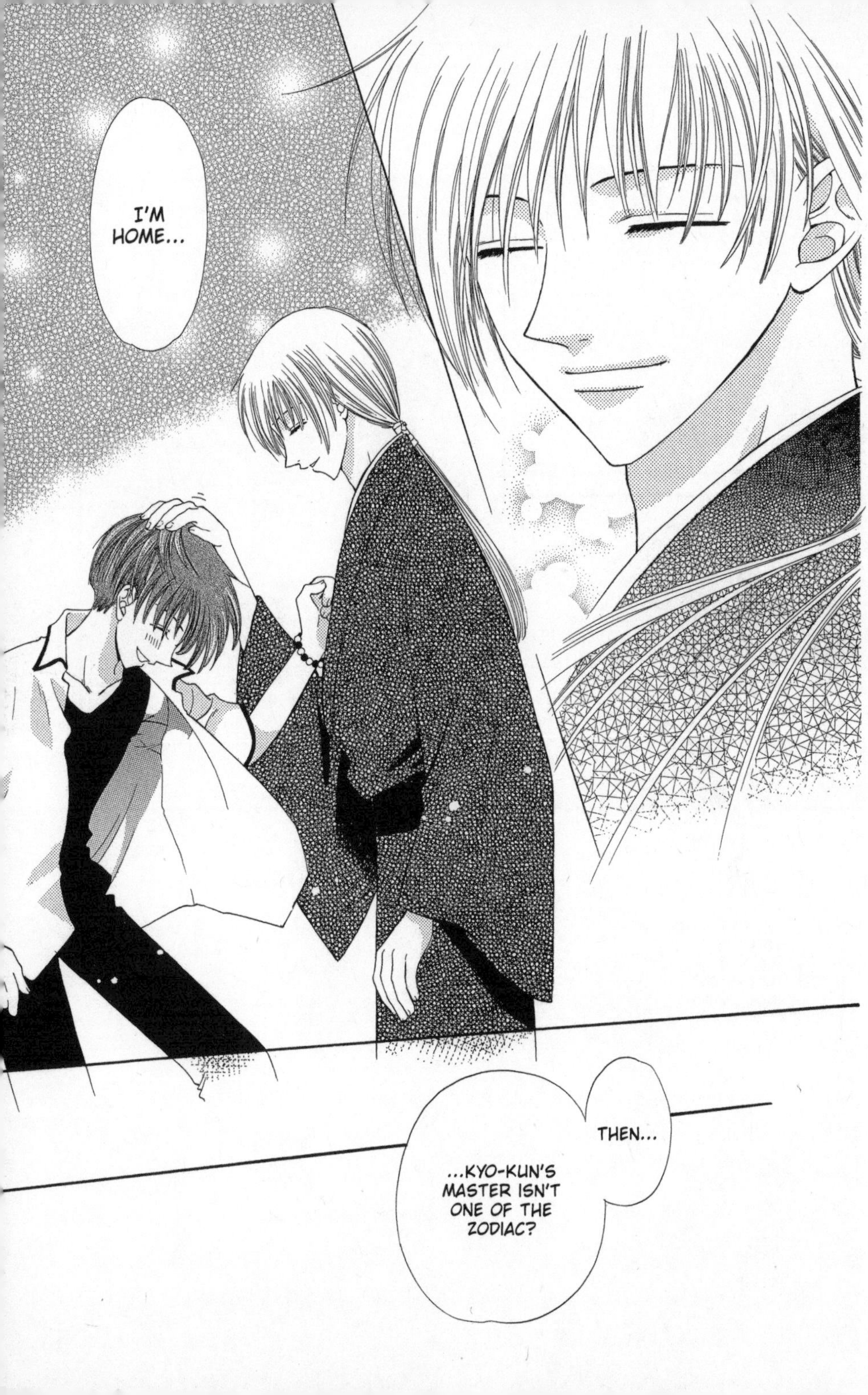
I'M HOME...
THEN...
...KYO-KUN'S MASTER ISN'T ONE OF THE ZODIAC?

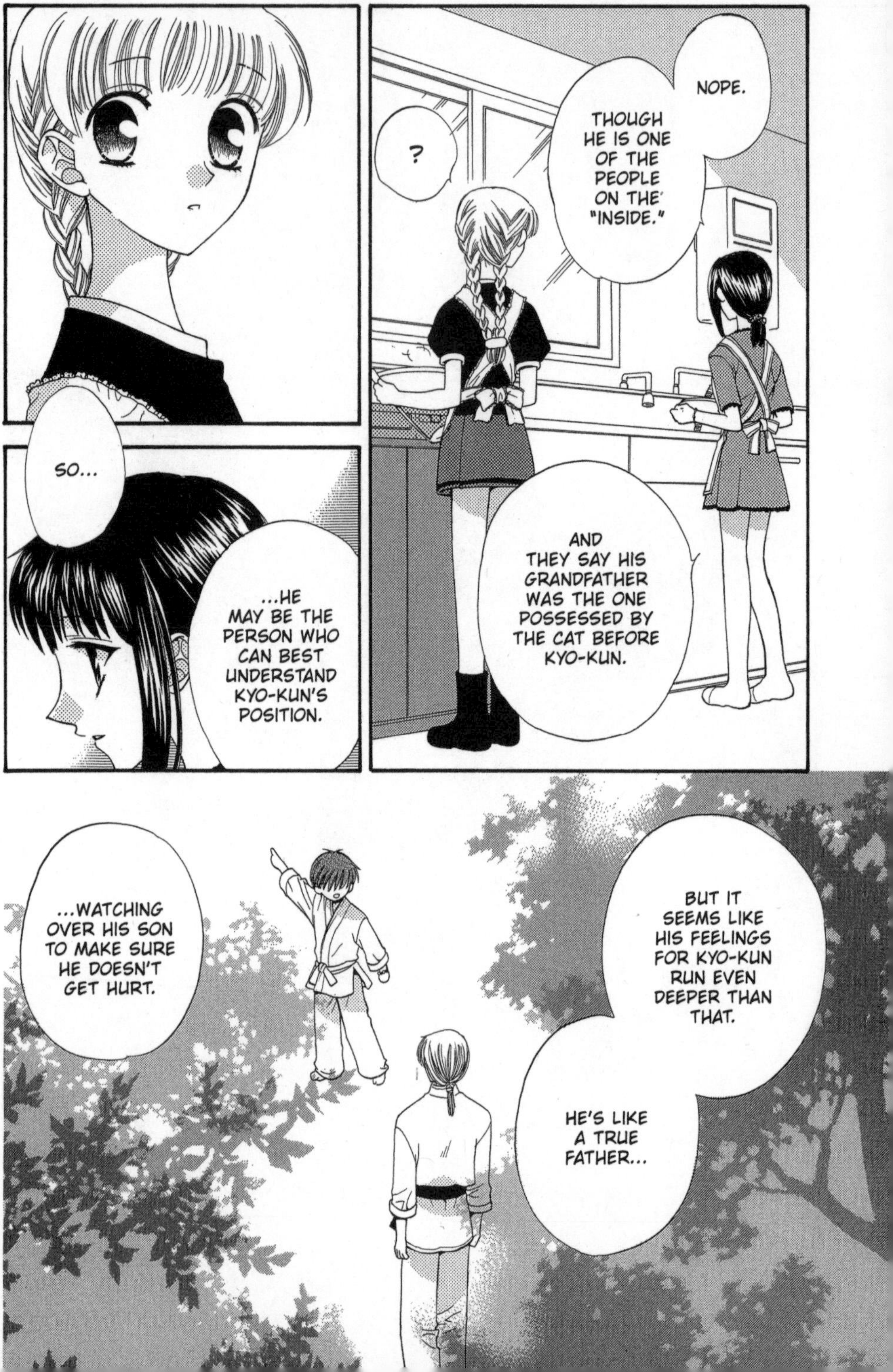
NOPE.
THOUGH HE IS ONE OF THE PEOPLE ON THE "INSIDE."
?
AND THEY SAY HIS GRANDFATHER WAS THE ONE POSSESSED BY THE CAT BEFORE KYO-KUN.
SO...
...HE MAY BE THE PERSON WHO CAN BEST UNDERSTAND KYO-KUN'S POSITION.
BUT IT SEEMS LIKE HIS FEELINGS FOR KYO-KUN RUN EVEN DEEPER THAN THAT.
HE'S LIKE A TRUE FATHER...
...WATCHING OVER HIS SON TO MAKE SURE HE DOESN'T GET HURT.

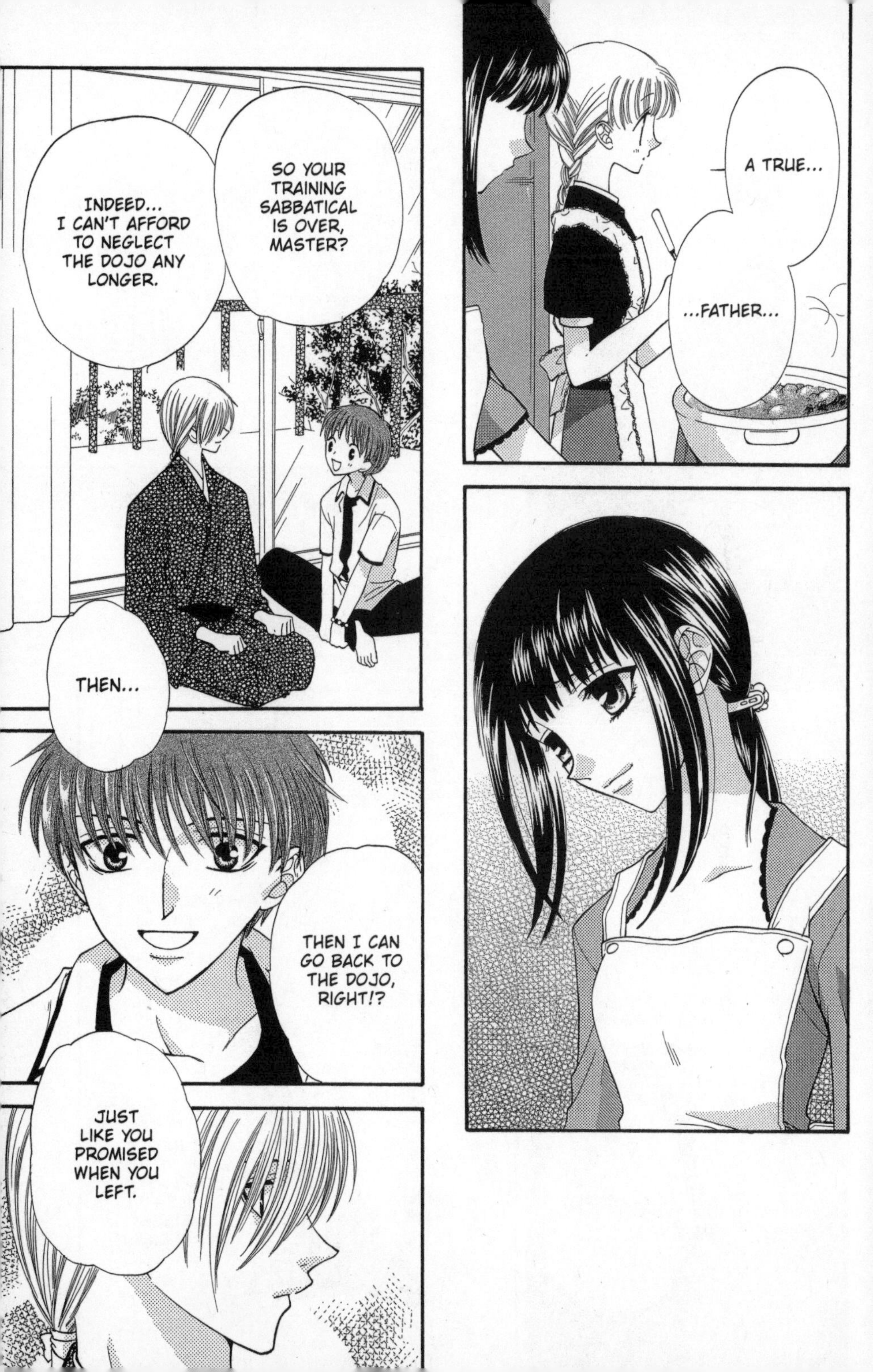
A TRUE...
...FATHER...
SO YOUR TRAINING SABBATICAL IS OVER, MASTER?
INDEED... I CAN'T AFFORD TO NEGLECT THE DOJO ANY LONGER.
THEN...
THEN I CAN GO BACK TO THE DOJO, RIGHT!?
JUST LIKE YOU PROMISED WHEN YOU LEFT.

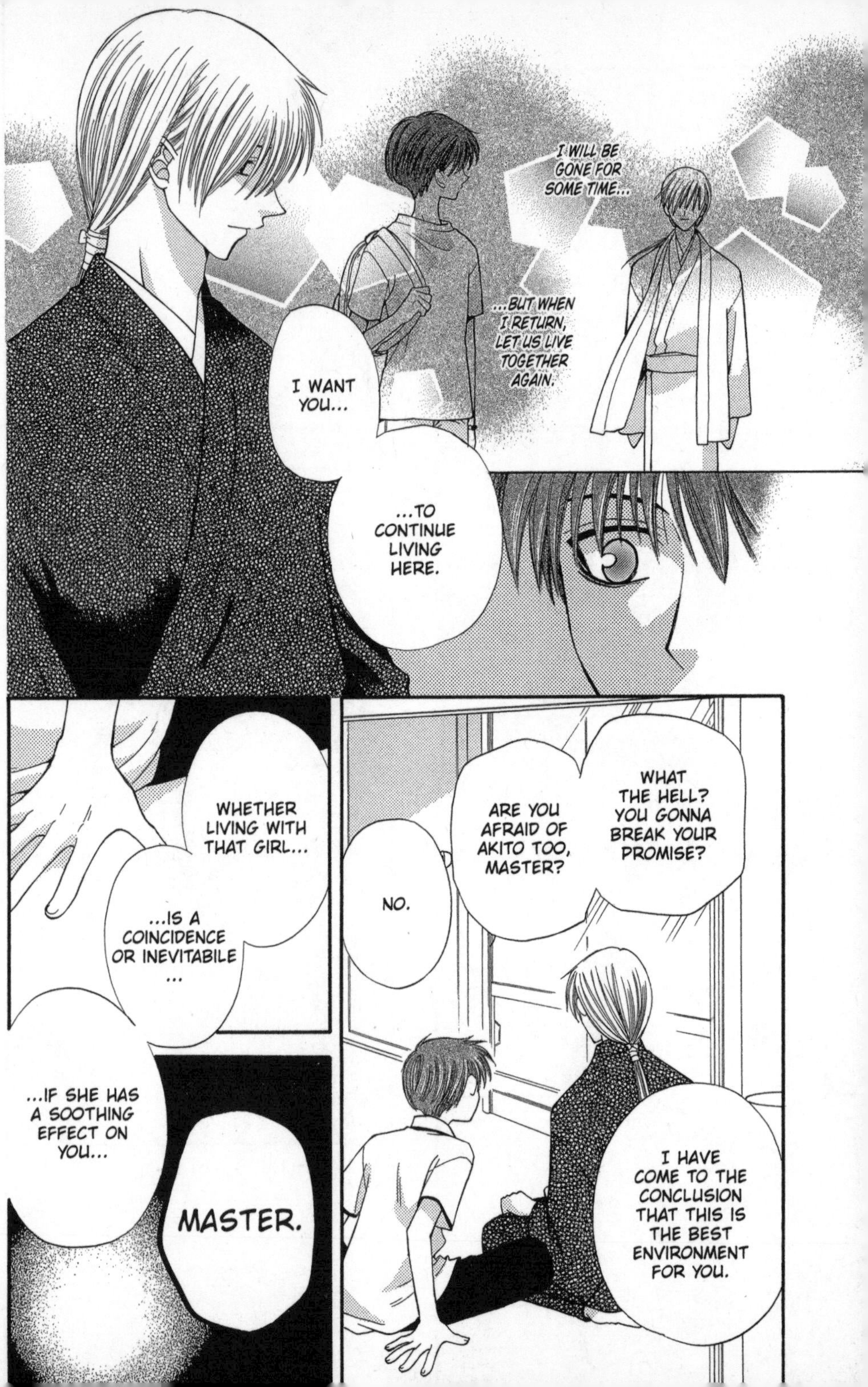
I WILL BE GONE FOR SOME TIME...
...BUT WHEN I RETURN, LET US LIVE TOGETHER AGAIN.
I WANT YOU...
...TO CONTINUE LIVING HERE.
WHAT THE HELL? YOU GONNA BREAK YOUR PROMISE?
ARE YOU AFRAID OF AKITO TOO, MASTER?
NO.
I HAVE COME TO THE CONCLUSION THAT THIS IS THE BEST ENVIRONMENT FOR YOU.
WHETHER LIVING WITH THAT GIRL...
...IS A COINCIDENCE OR INEVITABILE ...
...IF SHE HAS A SOOTHING EFFECT ON YOU...
MASTER.

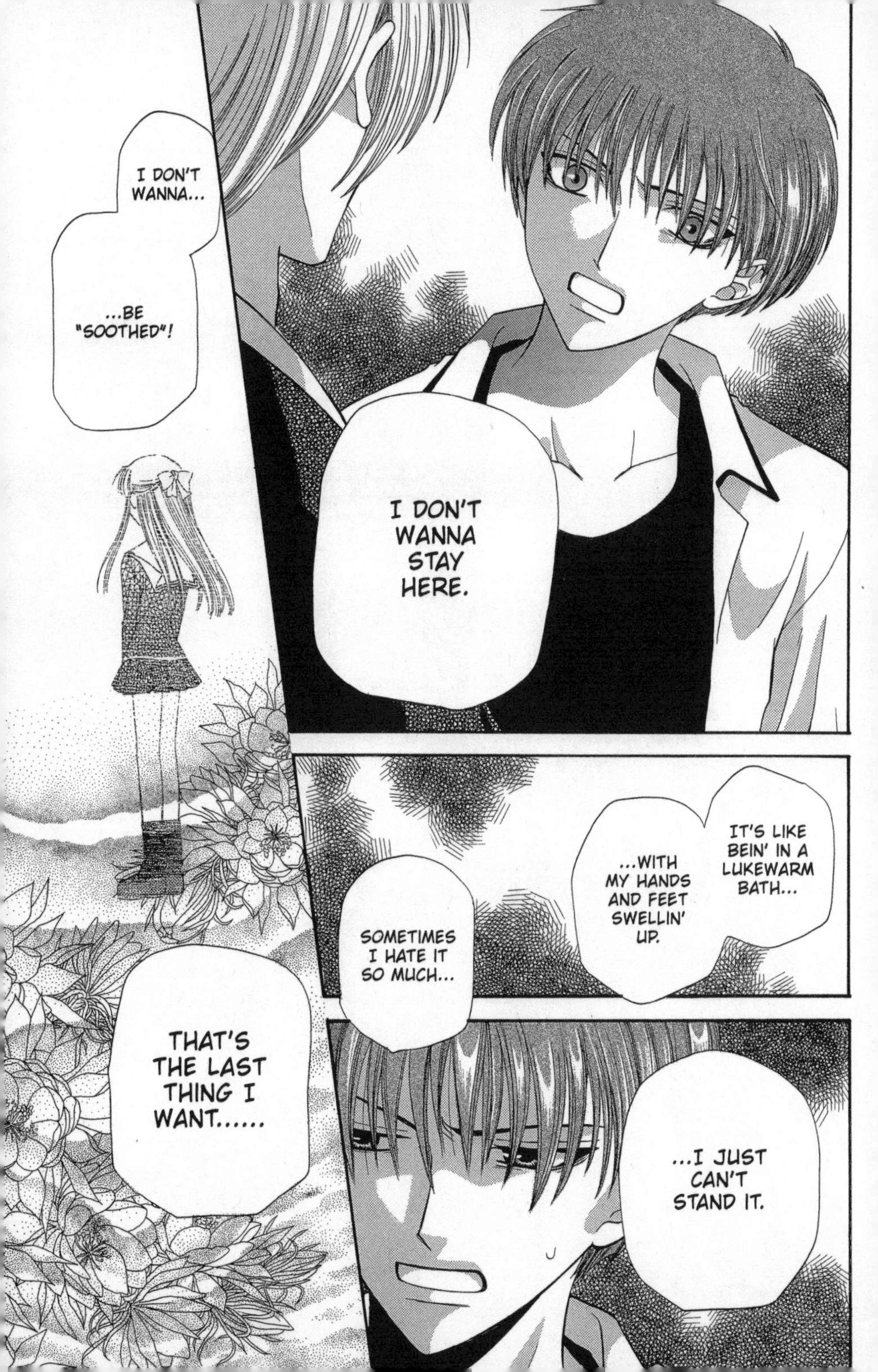
I DON'T WANNA STAY HERE.
IT'S LIKE BEIN' IN A LUKEWARM BATH...
...WITH MY HANDS AND FEET SWELLIN' UP.
SOMETIMES I HATE IT SO MUCH...
...I JUST CAN'T STAND IT.
I DON'T WANNA...
...BE "SOOTHED"!
THAT'S THE LAST THING I WANT......

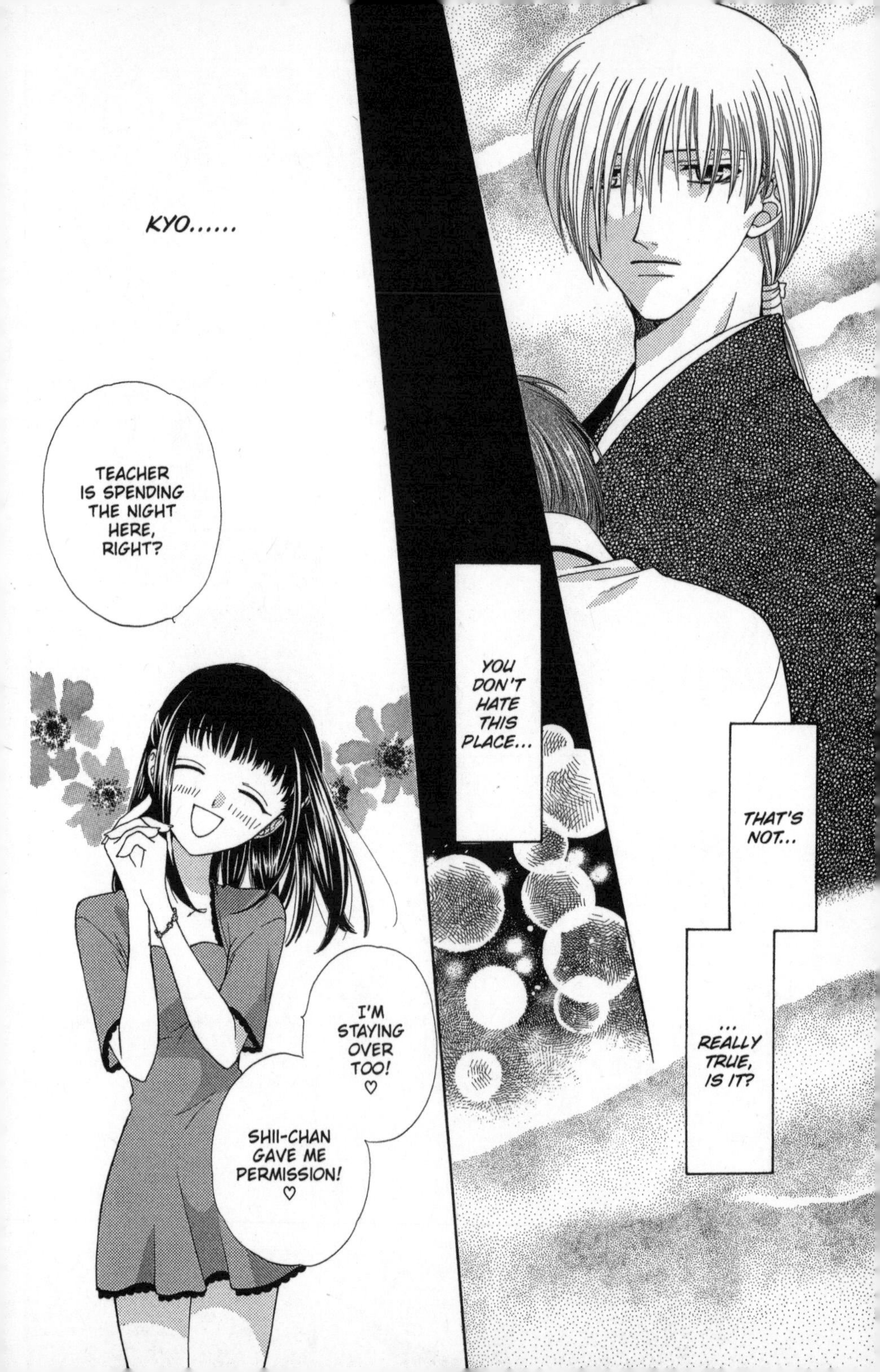
YOU DON'T HATE THIS PLACE...
THAT'S NOT...
...REALLY TRUE, IS IT?
KYO......
TEACHER IS SPENDING THE NIGHT HERE, RIGHT?
I'M STAYING OVER TOO! ♡
SHII-CHAN GAVE ME PERMISSION! ♡

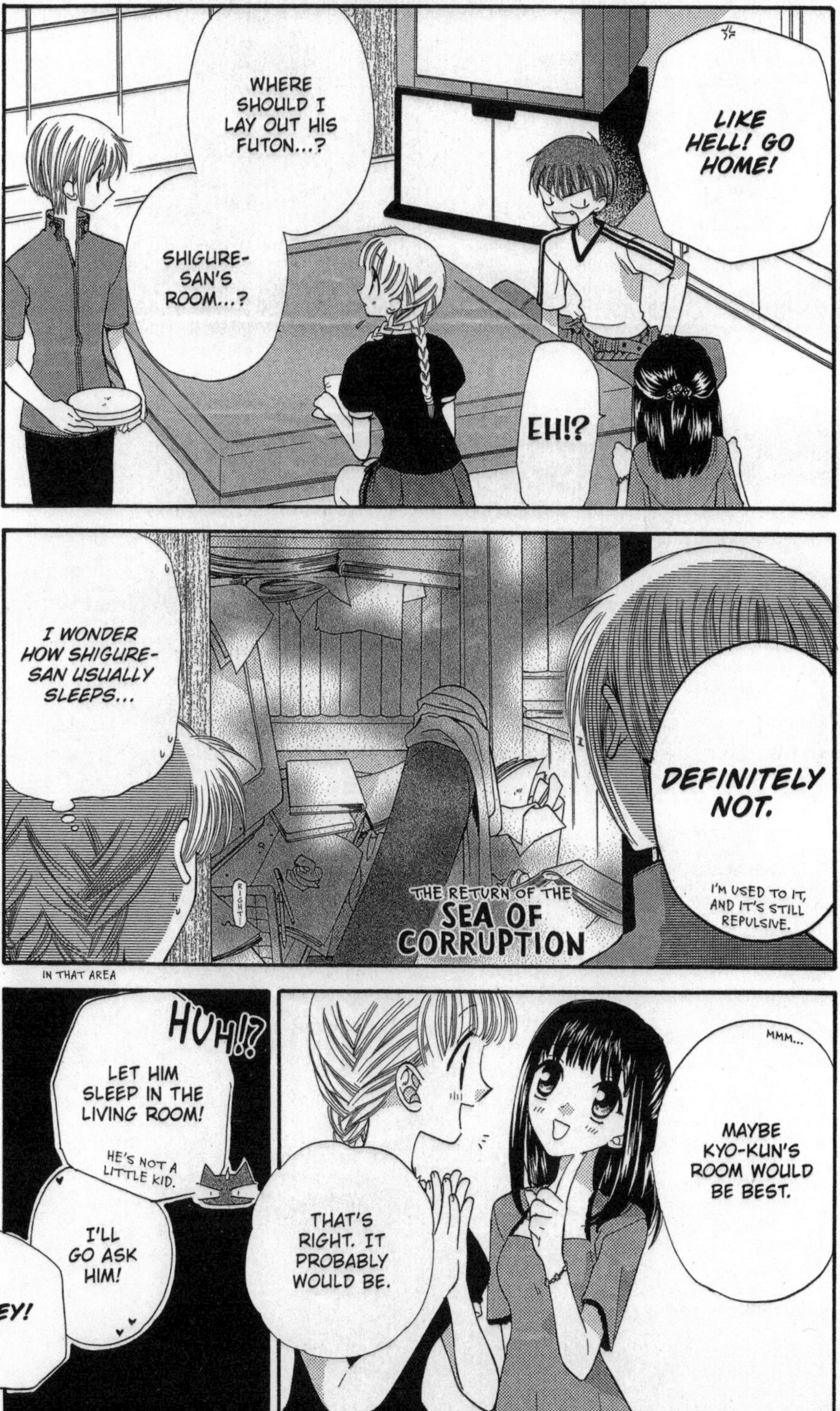
LIKE HELL! GO HOME!
WHERE SHOULD I LAY OUT HIS FUTON...?
SHIGURE-SAN'S ROOM...?
EH!?
DEFINITELY NOT.
I'M USED TO IT, AND IT'S STILL REPULSIVE.
I WONDER HOW SHIGURE-SAN USUALLY SLEEPS...
THE RETURN OF THE SEA OF CORRUPTION
RIGHT...
IN THAT AREA
MMM...
MAYBE KYO-KUN'S ROOM WOULD BE BEST.
THAT'S RIGHT. IT PROBABLY WOULD BE.
HUH!?
LET HIM SLEEP IN THE LIVING ROOM!
HE'S NOT A LITTLE KID.
I'LL GO ASK HIM!
HEY!

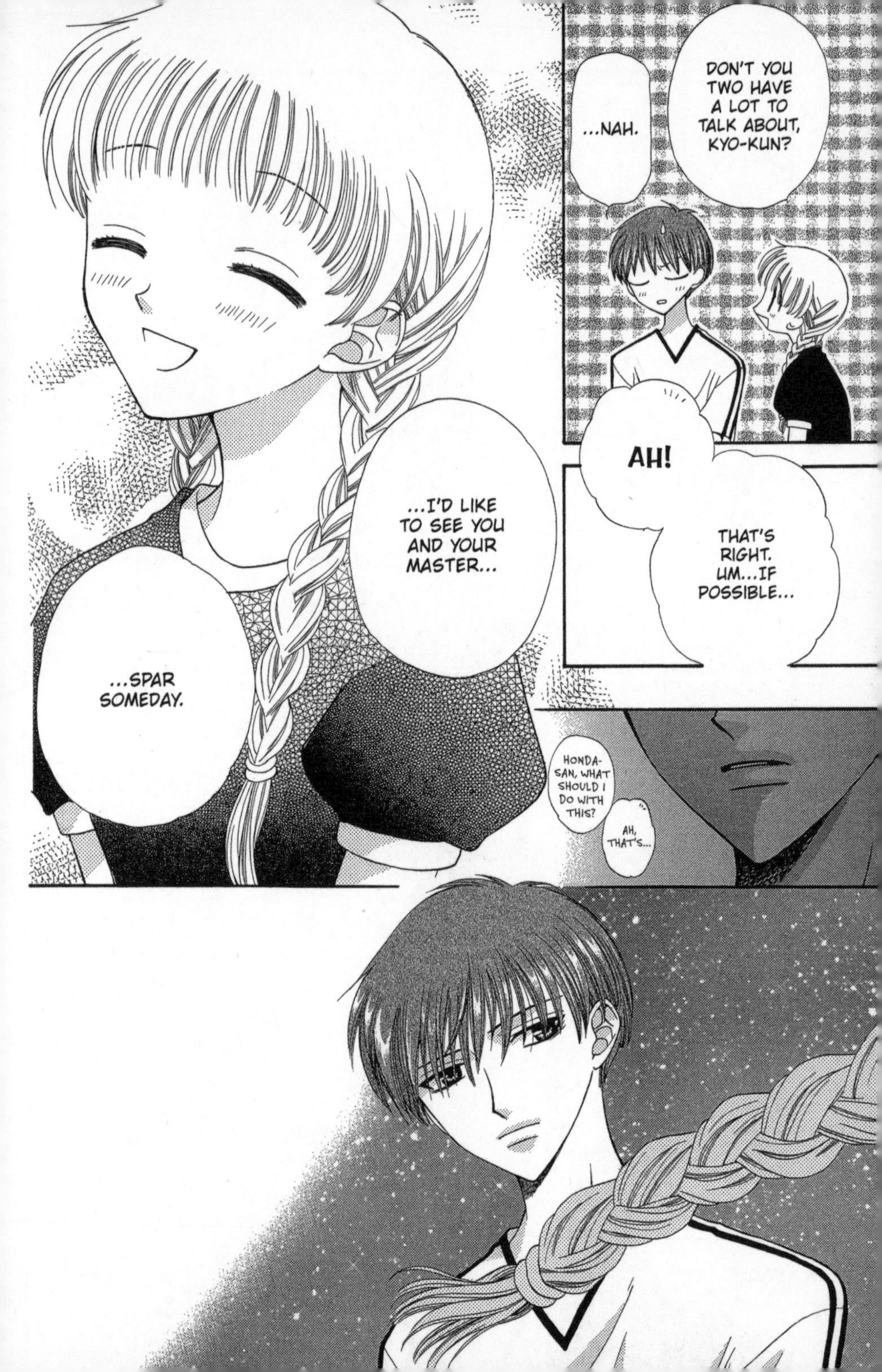
DON'T YOU TWO HAVE A LOT TO TALK ABOUT, KYO-KUN?
...NAH.
AH!
THAT'S RIGHT. UM...IF POSSIBLE...
HONDA-SAN, WHAT SHOULD I DO WITH THIS?
AH, THAT'S...
...I'D LIKE TO SEE YOU AND YOUR MASTER...
...SPAR SOMEDAY.

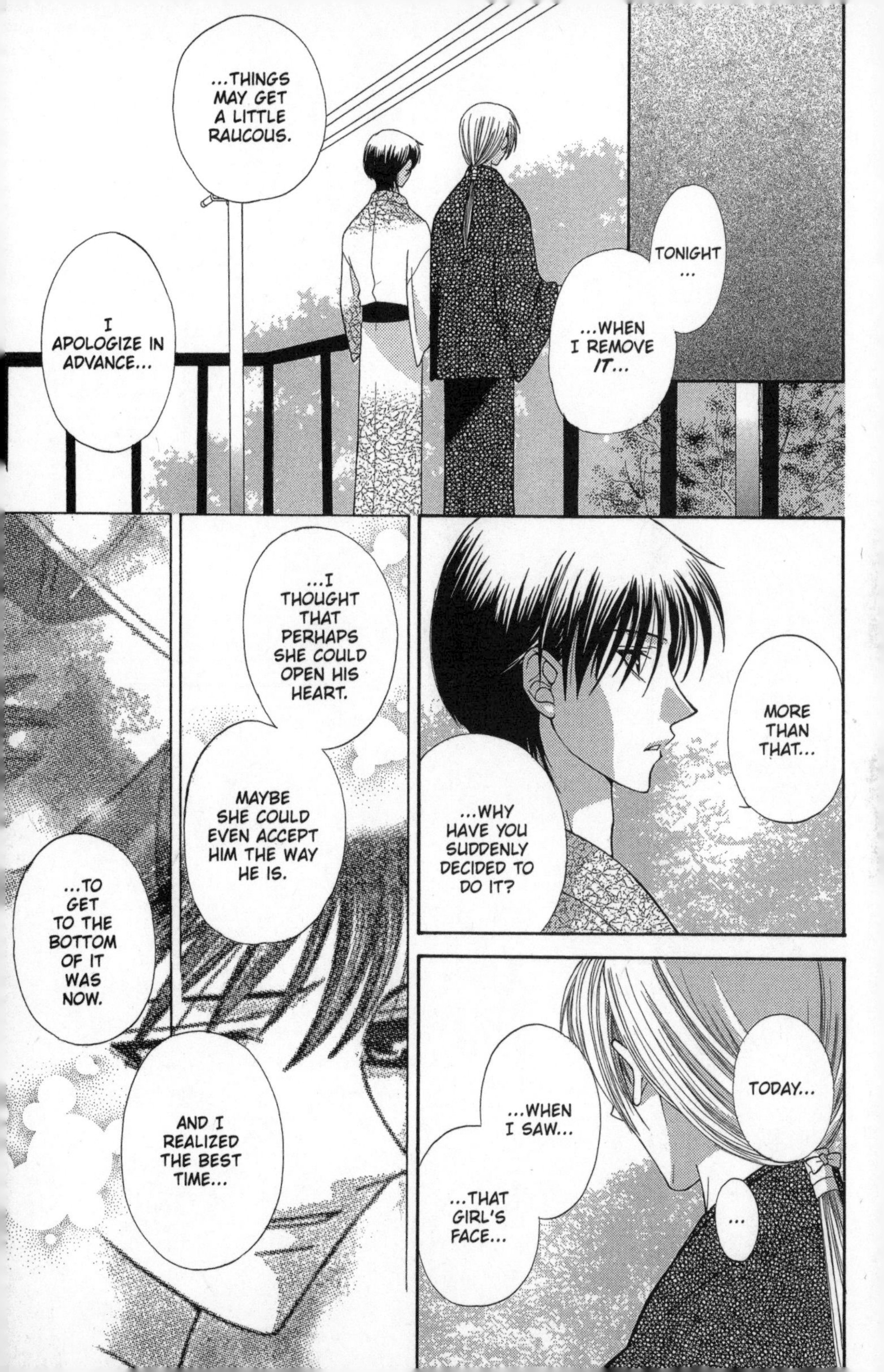
TONIGHT ...
...WHEN I REMOVE *IT*...
...THINGS MAY GET A LITTLE RAUCOUS.
I APOLOGIZE IN ADVANCE...
MORE THAN THAT...
...WHY HAVE YOU SUDDENLY DECIDED TO DO IT?
TODAY...
...
...WHEN I SAW...
...THAT GIRL'S FACE...
...I THOUGHT THAT PERHAPS SHE COULD OPEN HIS HEART.
MAYBE SHE COULD EVEN ACCEPT HIM THE WAY HE IS.
AND I REALIZED THE BEST TIME...
...TO GET TO THE BOTTOM OF IT WAS NOW.

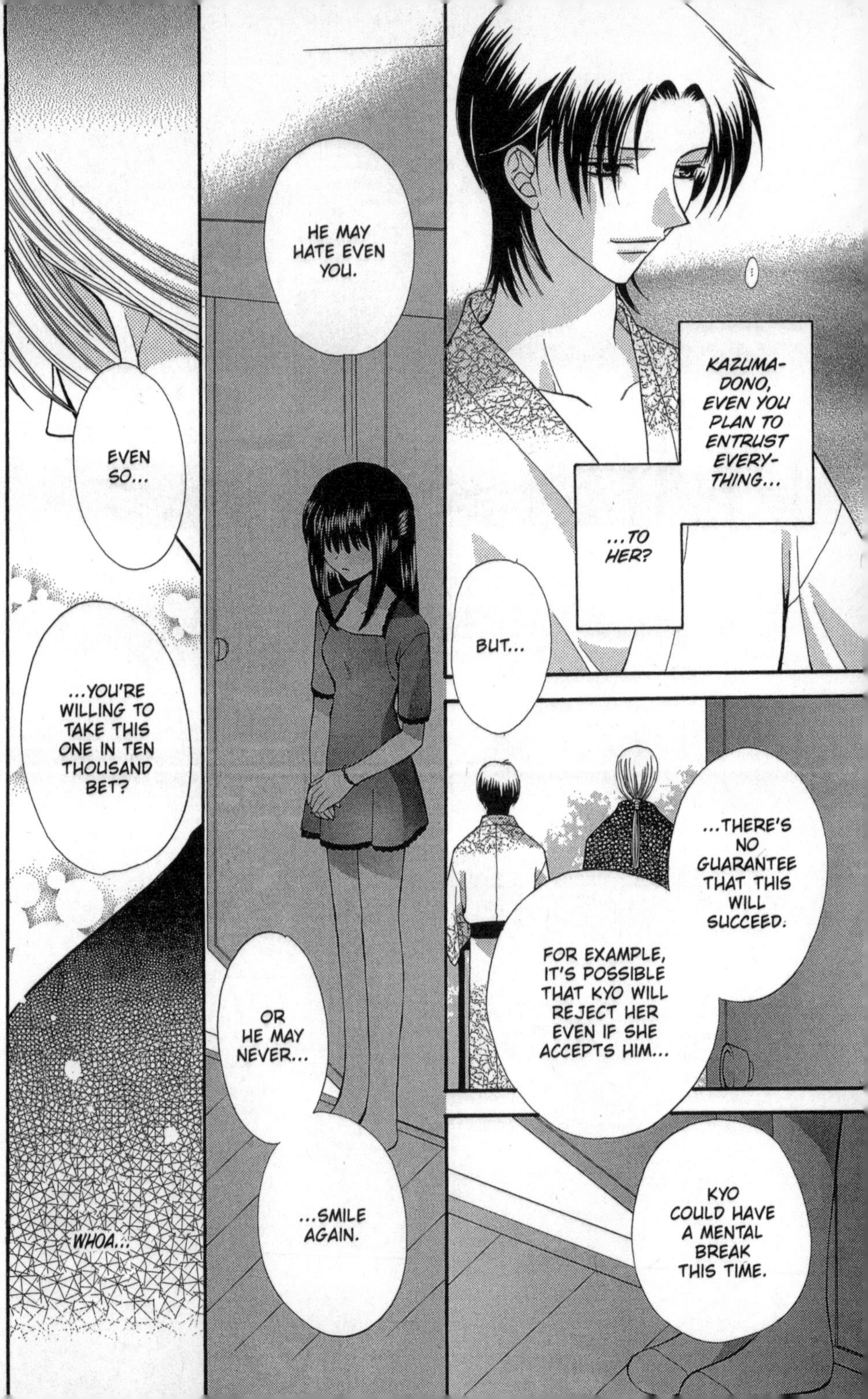
...
KAZUMA-DONO, EVEN YOU PLAN TO ENTRUST EVERYTHING...
...TO HER?
BUT...
...THERE'S NO GUARANTEE THAT THIS WILL SUCCEED.
FOR EXAMPLE, IT'S POSSIBLE THAT KYO WILL REJECT HER EVEN IF SHE ACCEPTS HIM...
KYO COULD HAVE A MENTAL BREAK THIS TIME.
HE MAY HATE EVEN YOU.
OR HE MAY NEVER...
...SMILE AGAIN.
EVEN SO...
...YOU'RE WILLING TO TAKE THIS ONE IN TEN THOUSAND BET?
WHOA...

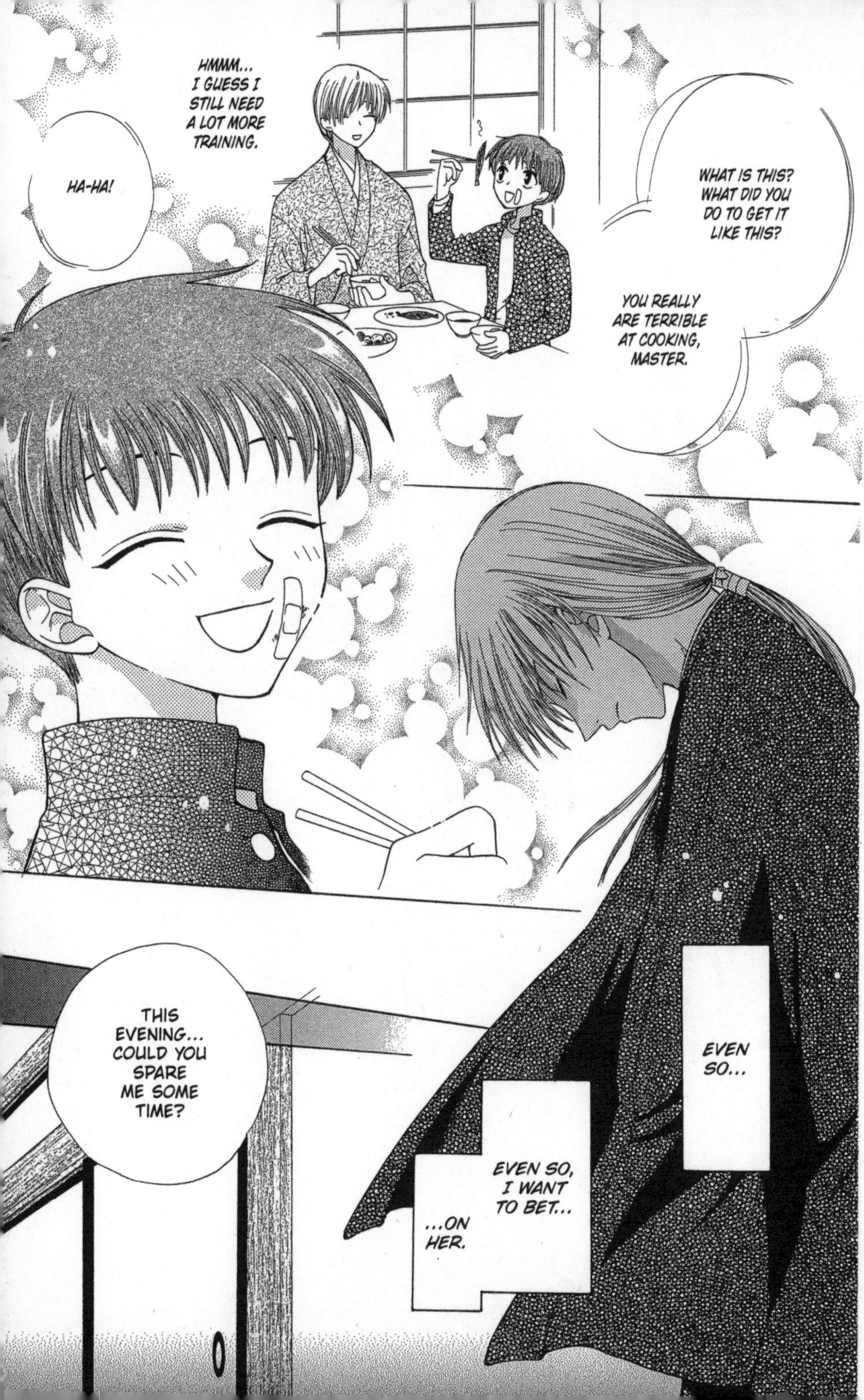
WHAT IS THIS? WHAT DID YOU DO TO GET IT LIKE THIS?
YOU REALLY ARE TERRIBLE AT COOKING, MASTER.
HMMM... I GUESS I STILL NEED A LOT MORE TRAINING.
HA-HA!
EVEN SO...
EVEN SO, I WANT TO BET...
...ON HER.
THIS EVENING... COULD YOU SPARE ME SOME TIME?

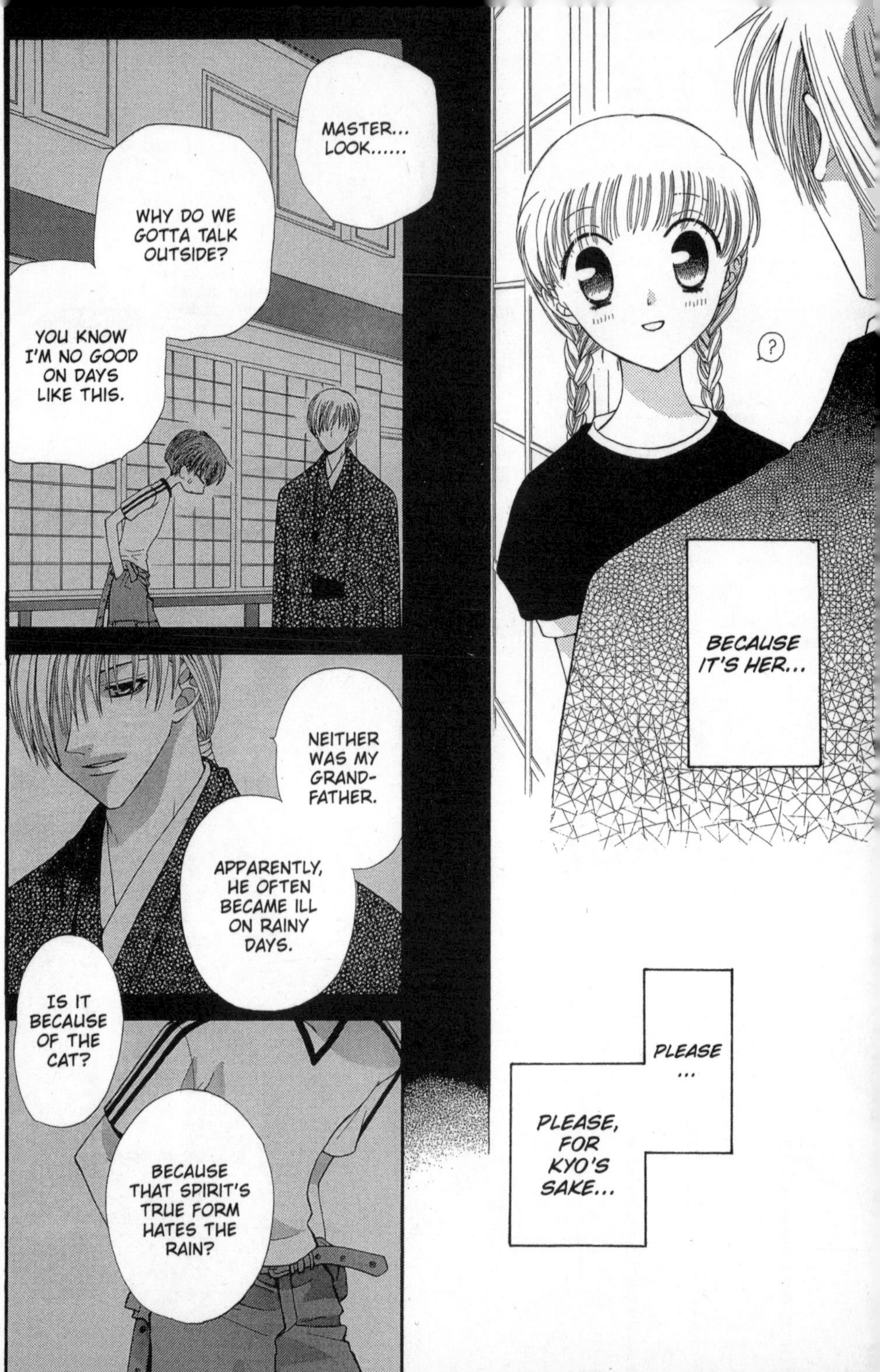
?
BECAUSE IT'S HER...
PLEASE...
PLEASE, FOR KYO'S SAKE...
MASTER... LOOK......
WHY DO WE GOTTA TALK OUTSIDE?
YOU KNOW I'M NO GOOD ON DAYS LIKE THIS.
NEITHER WAS MY GRAND-FATHER.
APPARENTLY, HE OFTEN BECAME ILL ON RAINY DAYS.
IS IT BECAUSE OF THE CAT?
BECAUSE THAT SPIRIT'S TRUE FORM HATES THE RAIN?

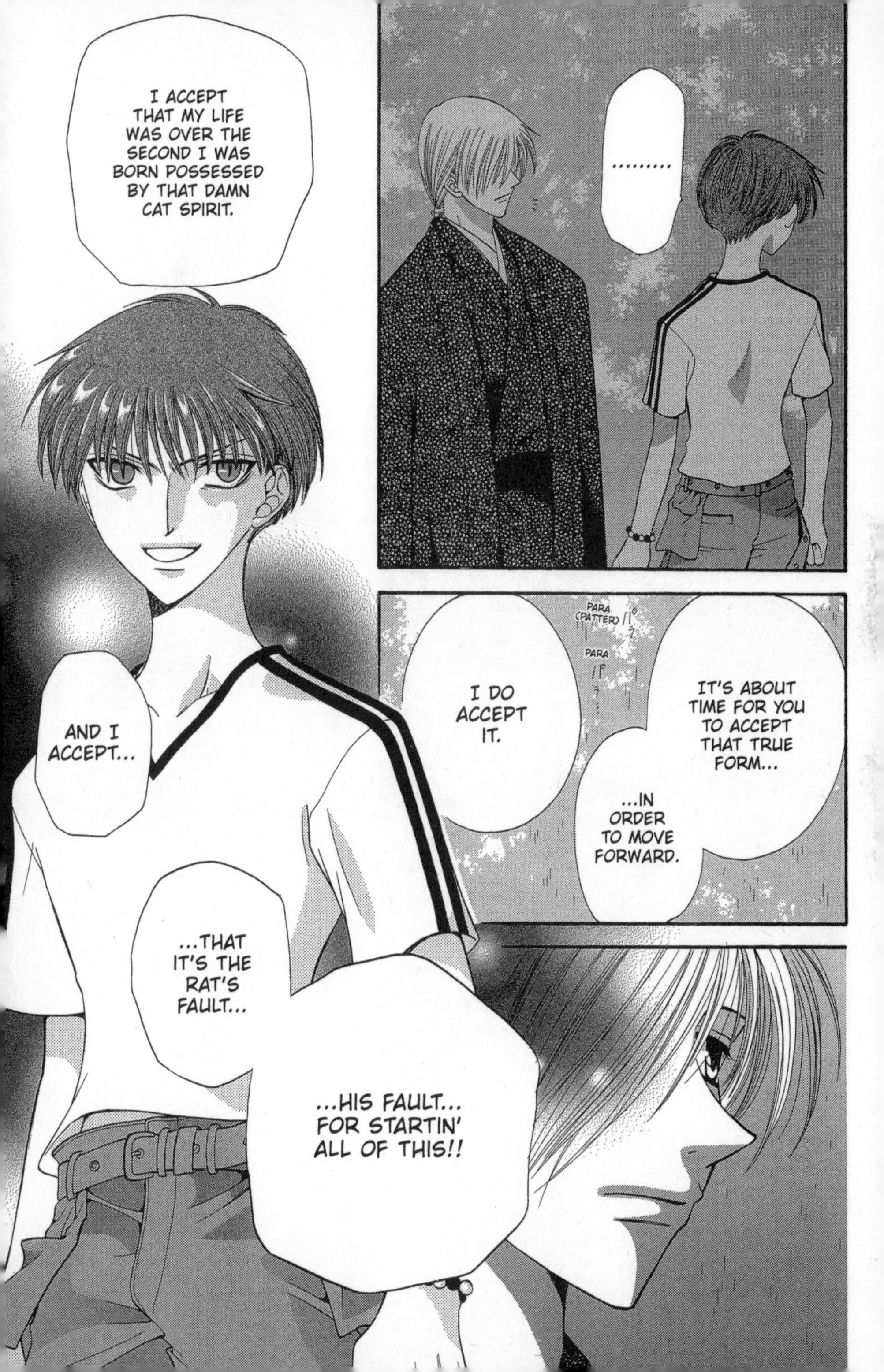
....
IT'S ABOUT TIME FOR YOU TO ACCEPT THAT TRUE FORM...
...IN ORDER TO MOVE FORWARD.
PARA. (PATTER)
PARA
I DO ACCEPT IT.
I ACCEPT THAT MY LIFE WAS OVER THE SECOND I WAS BORN POSSESSED BY THAT DAMN CAT SPIRIT.
AND I ACCEPT...
...THAT IT'S THE RAT'S FAULT...
...HIS FAULT... FOR STARTIN' ALL OF THIS!!

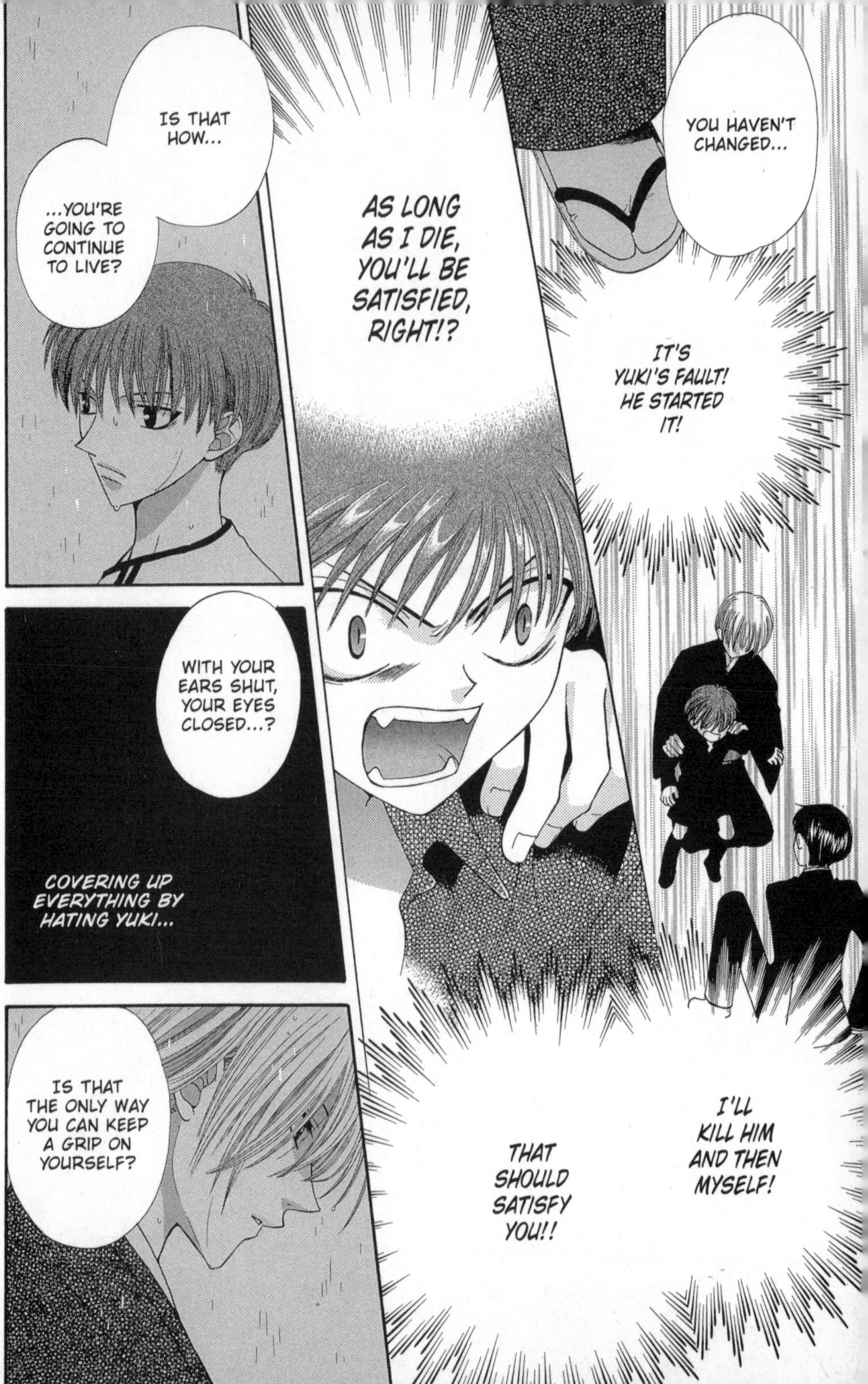

YOU HAVEN'T CHANGED...
IT'S YUKI'S FAULT! HE STARTED IT!
I'LL KILL HIM AND THEN MYSELF!
THAT SHOULD SATISFY YOU!!
AS LONG AS I DIE, YOU'LL BE SATISFIED, RIGHT!?
IS THAT HOW...
...YOU'RE GOING TO CONTINUE TO LIVE?
WITH YOUR EARS SHUT, YOUR EYES CLOSED...?
COVERING UP EVERYTHING BY HATING YUKI...
IS THAT THE ONLY WAY YOU CAN KEEP A GRIP ON YOURSELF?

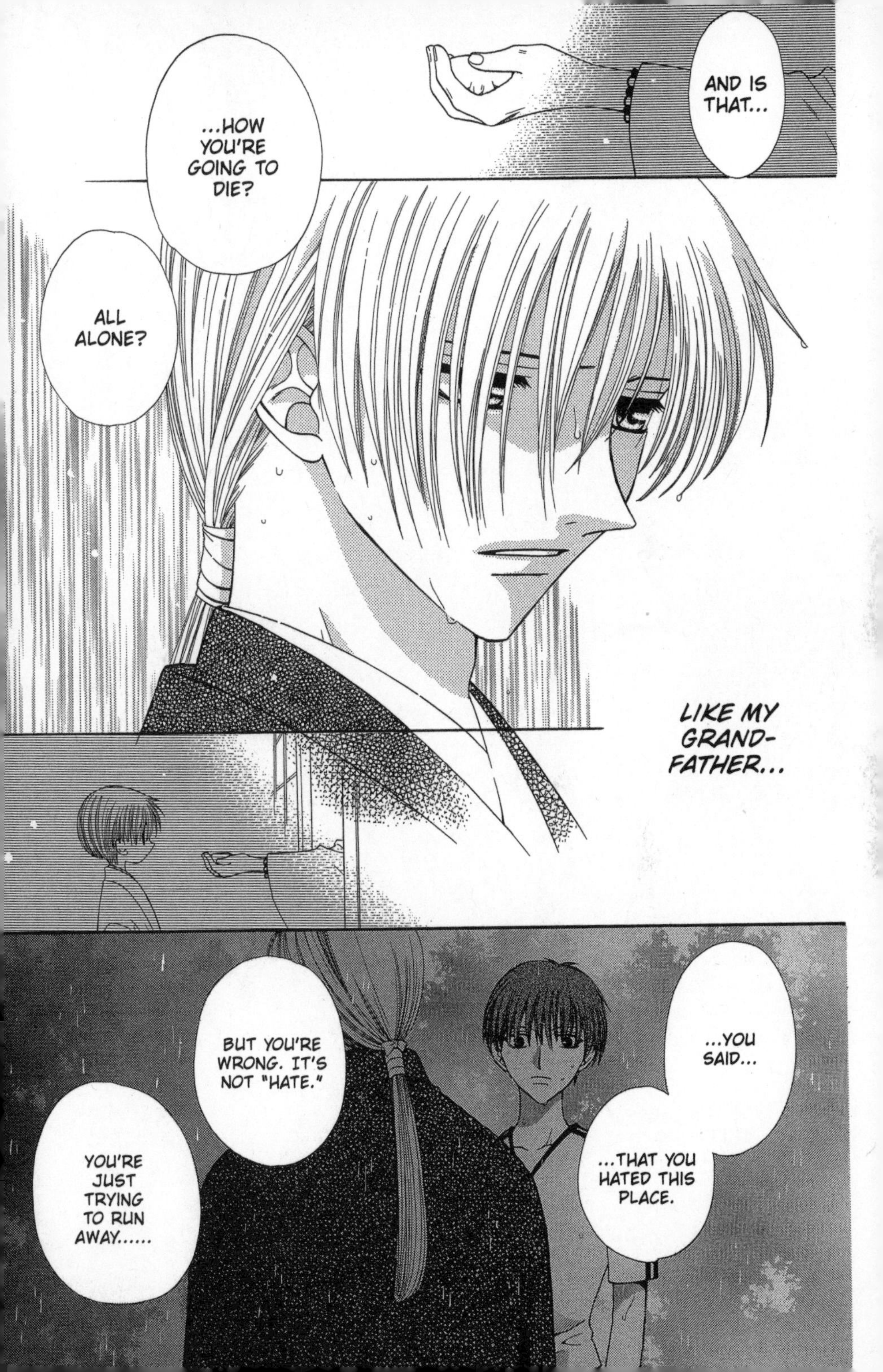
AND IS THAT...
...HOW YOU'RE GOING TO DIE?
ALL ALONE?
LIKE MY GRAND-FATHER...
...YOU SAID...
...THAT YOU HATED THIS PLACE.
BUT YOU'RE WRONG. IT'S NOT "HATE."
YOU'RE JUST TRYING TO RUN AWAY......

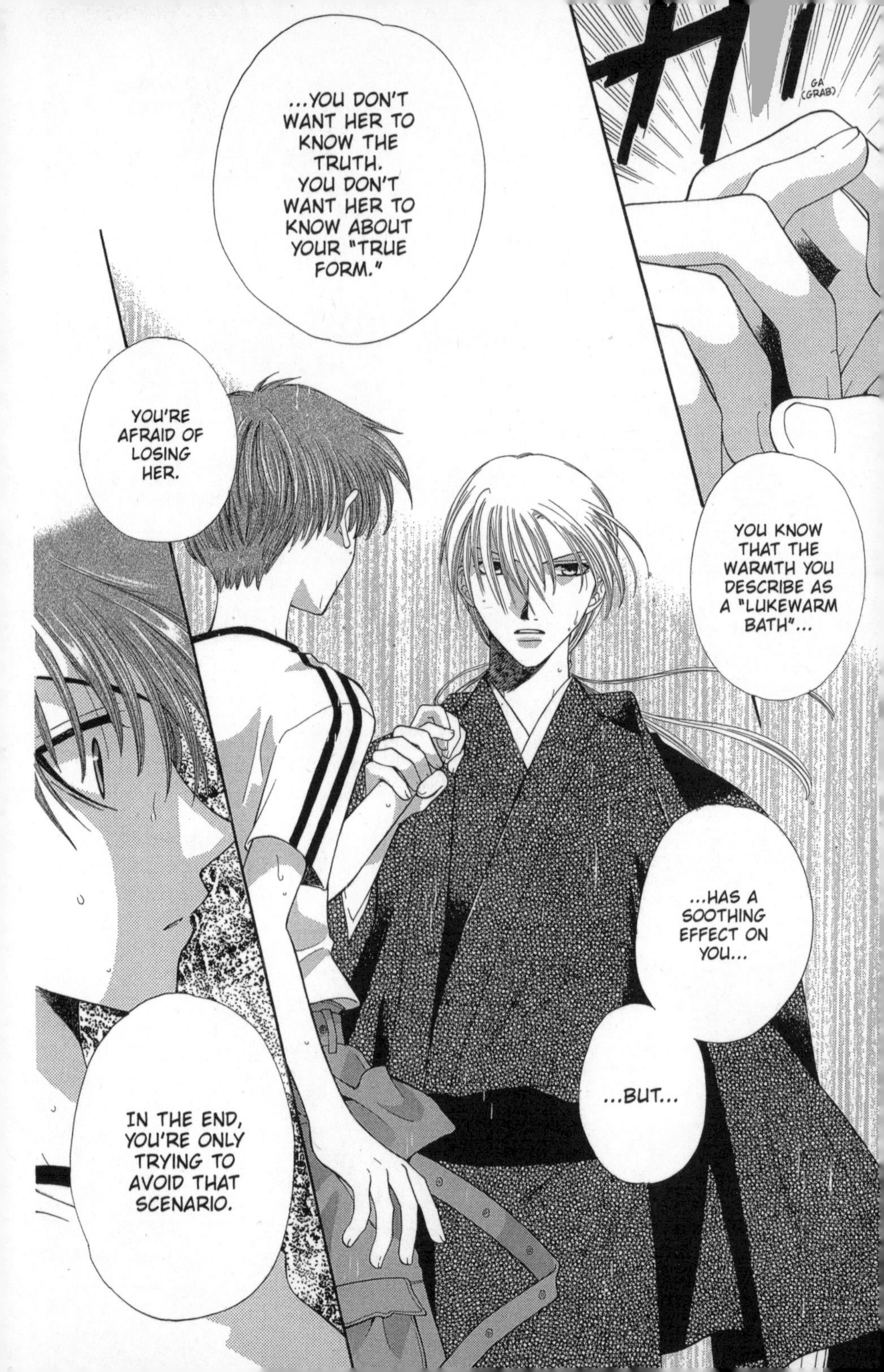
GA (GRAB)
YOU KNOW THAT THE WARMTH YOU DESCRIBE AS A "LUKEWARM BATH"...
...HAS A SOOTHING EFFECT ON YOU...
...BUT...
...YOU DON'T WANT HER TO KNOW THE TRUTH. YOU DON'T WANT HER TO KNOW ABOUT YOUR "TRUE FORM."
YOU'RE AFRAID OF LOSING HER.
IN THE END, YOU'RE ONLY TRYING TO AVOID THAT SCENARIO.

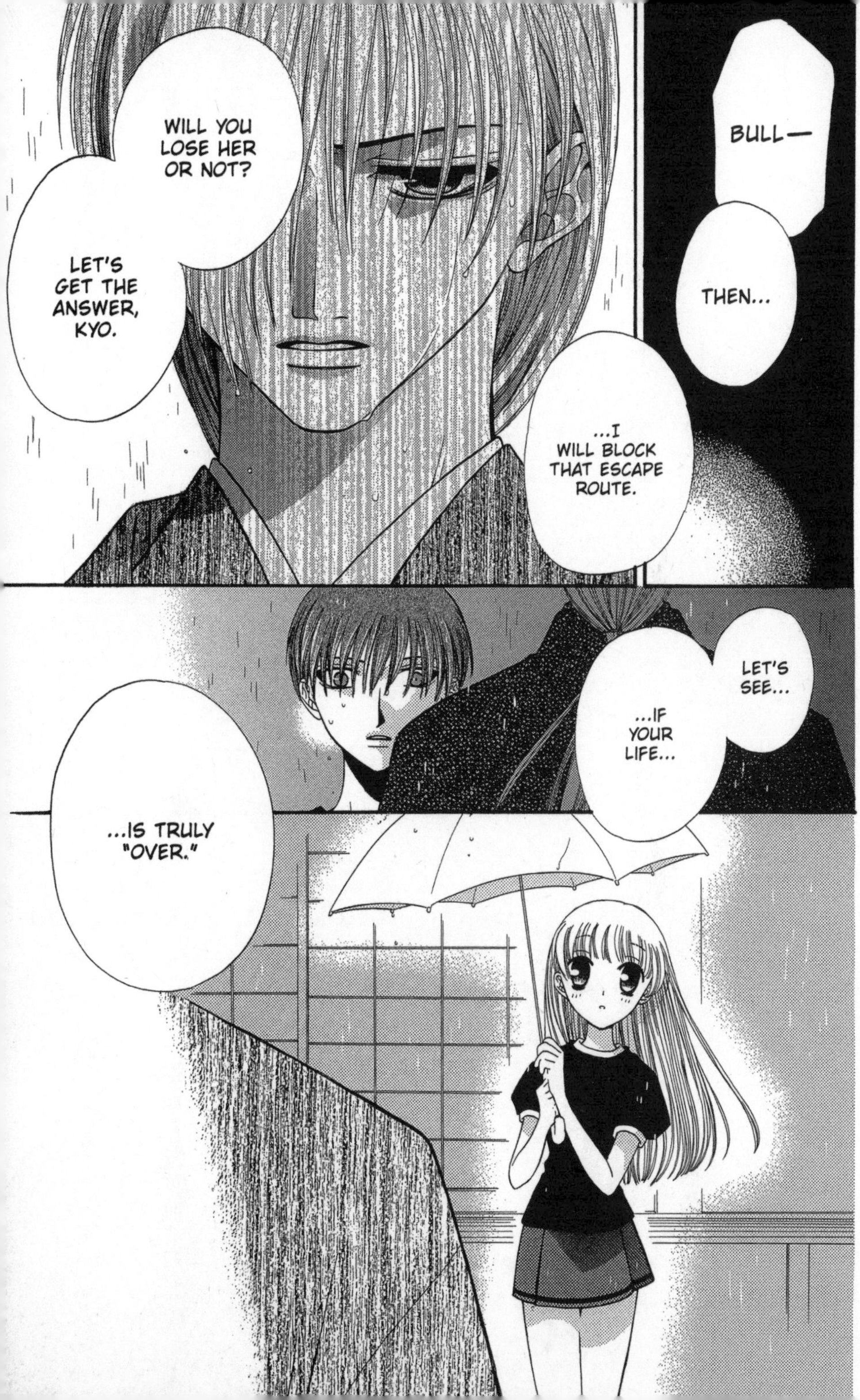
BULL—
THEN...
...I WILL BLOCK THAT ESCAPE ROUTE.
WILL YOU LOSE HER OR NOT?
LET'S GET THE ANSWER, KYO.
LET'S SEE...
...IF YOUR LIFE...
...IS TRULY "OVER."

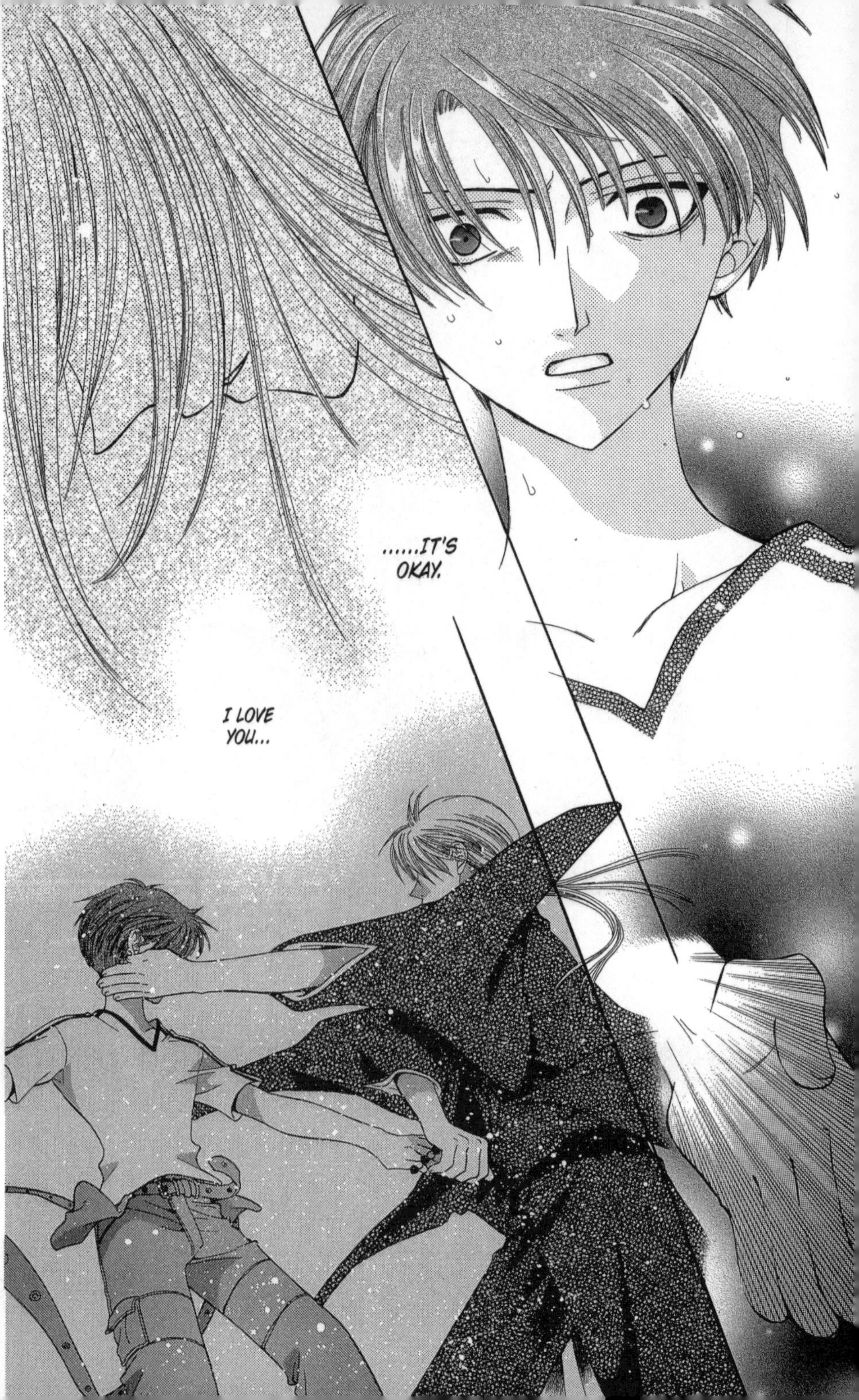
......IT'S OKAY.
I LOVE YOU...

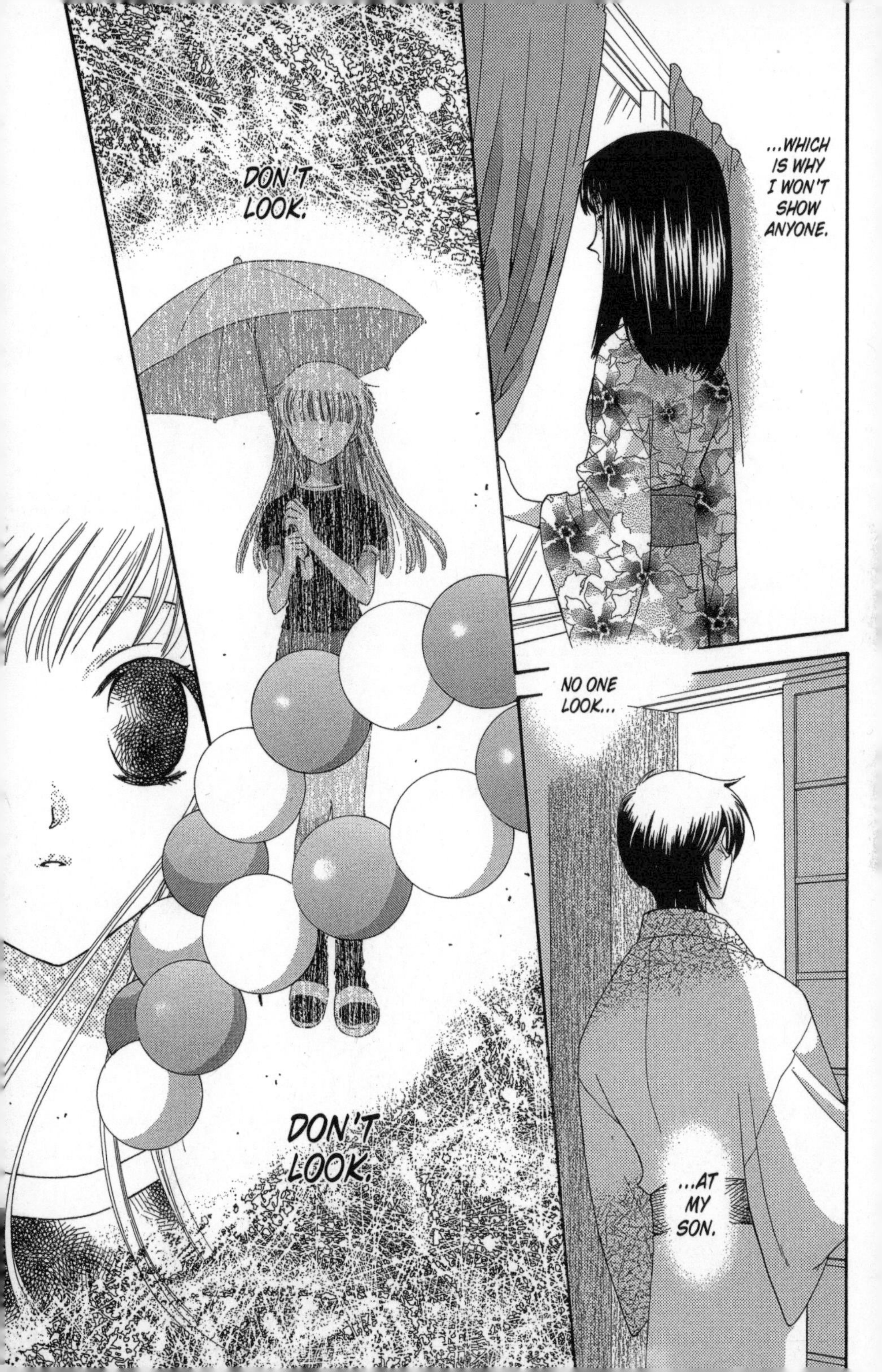
...WHICH IS WHY I WON'T SHOW ANYONE.
NO ONE LOOK...
...AT MY SON.
DON'T LOOK.
DON'T LOOK.

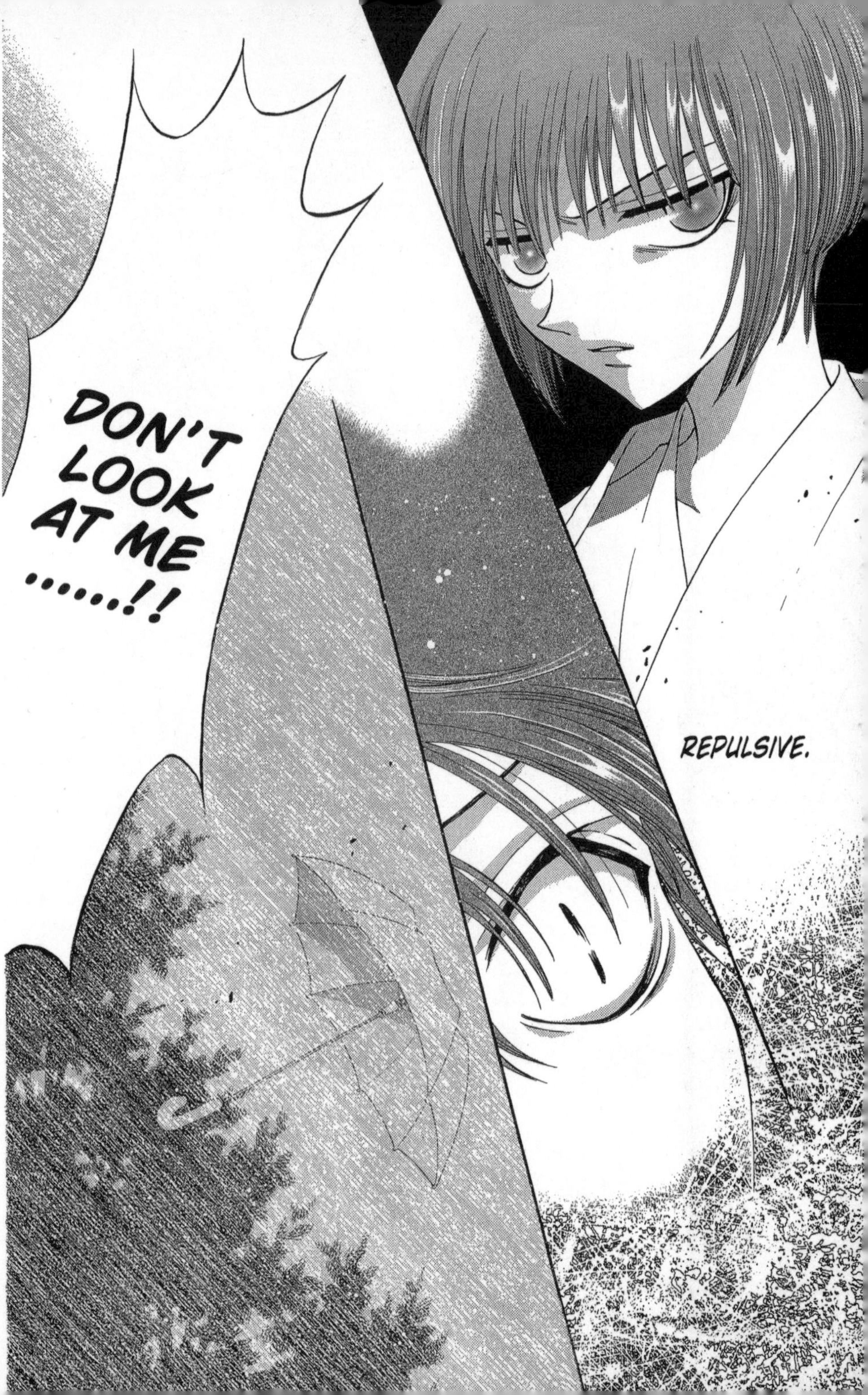
REPULSIVE.
DON'T LOOK AT ME ......!!

Chapter 33

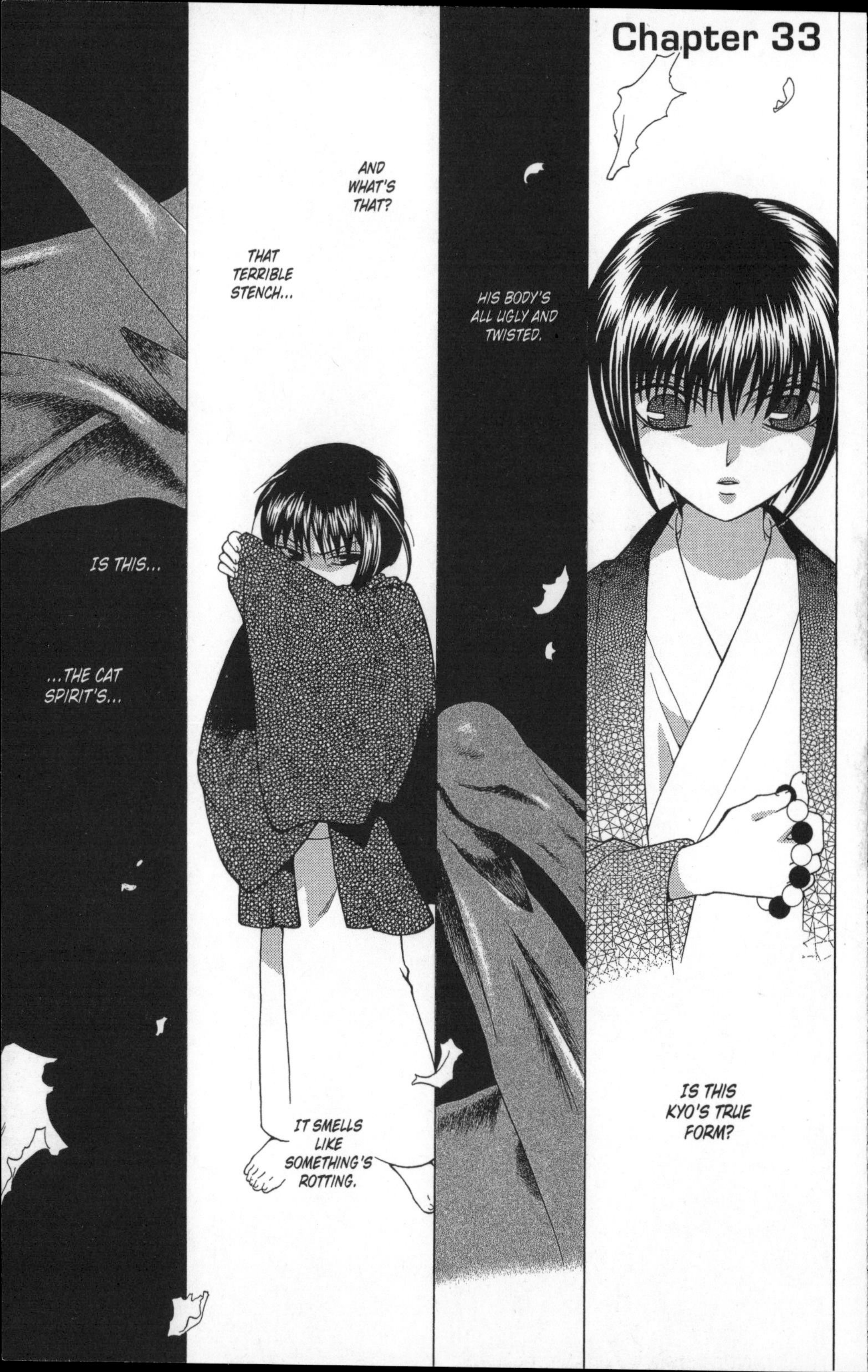
IS THIS KYO'S TRUE FORM?
HIS BODY'S ALL UGLY AND TWISTED.
AND WHAT'S THAT?
THAT TERRIBLE STENCH...
IT SMELLS LIKE SOMETHING'S ROTTING.
IS THIS...
...THE CAT SPIRIT'S...

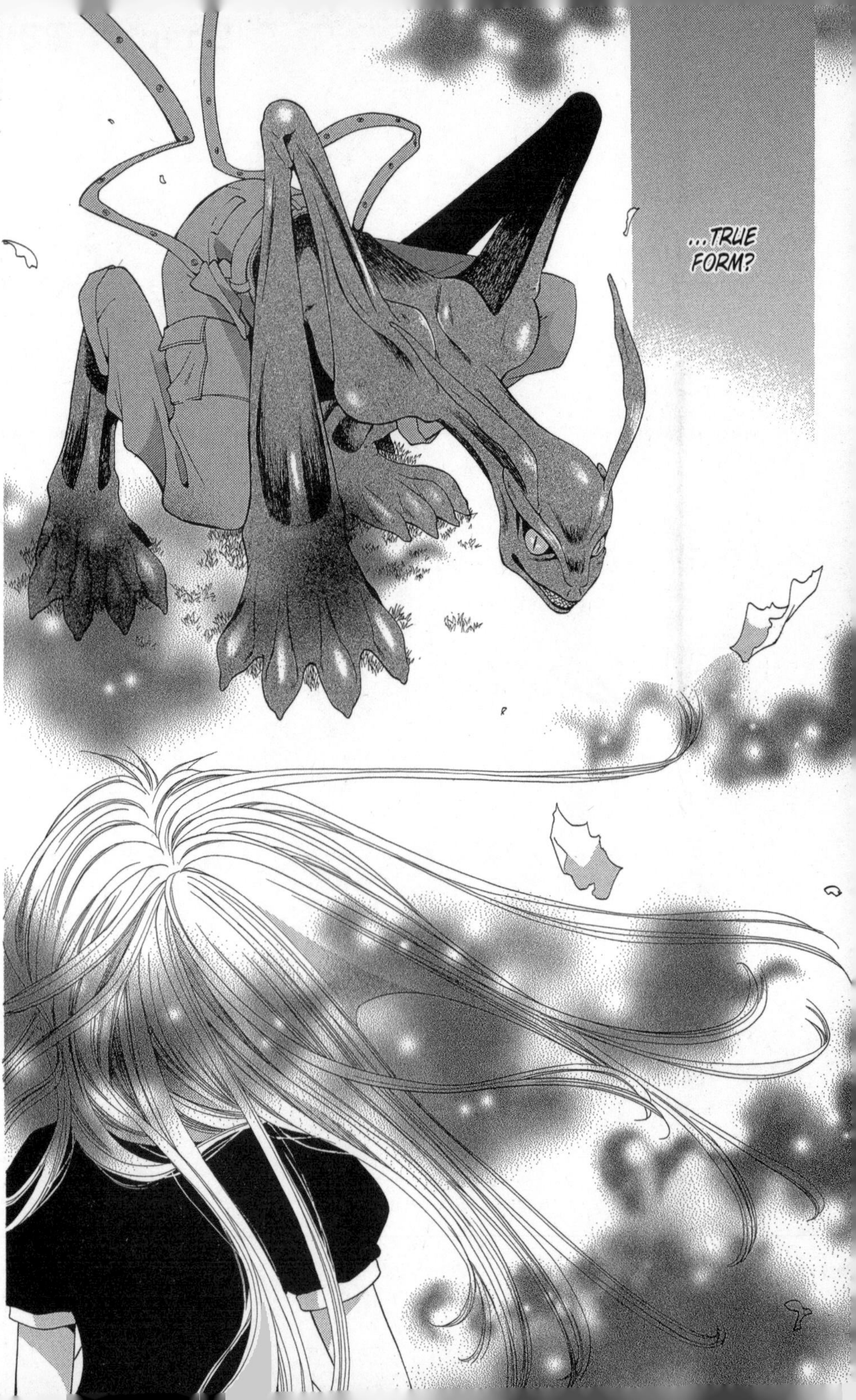
...TRUE FORM?

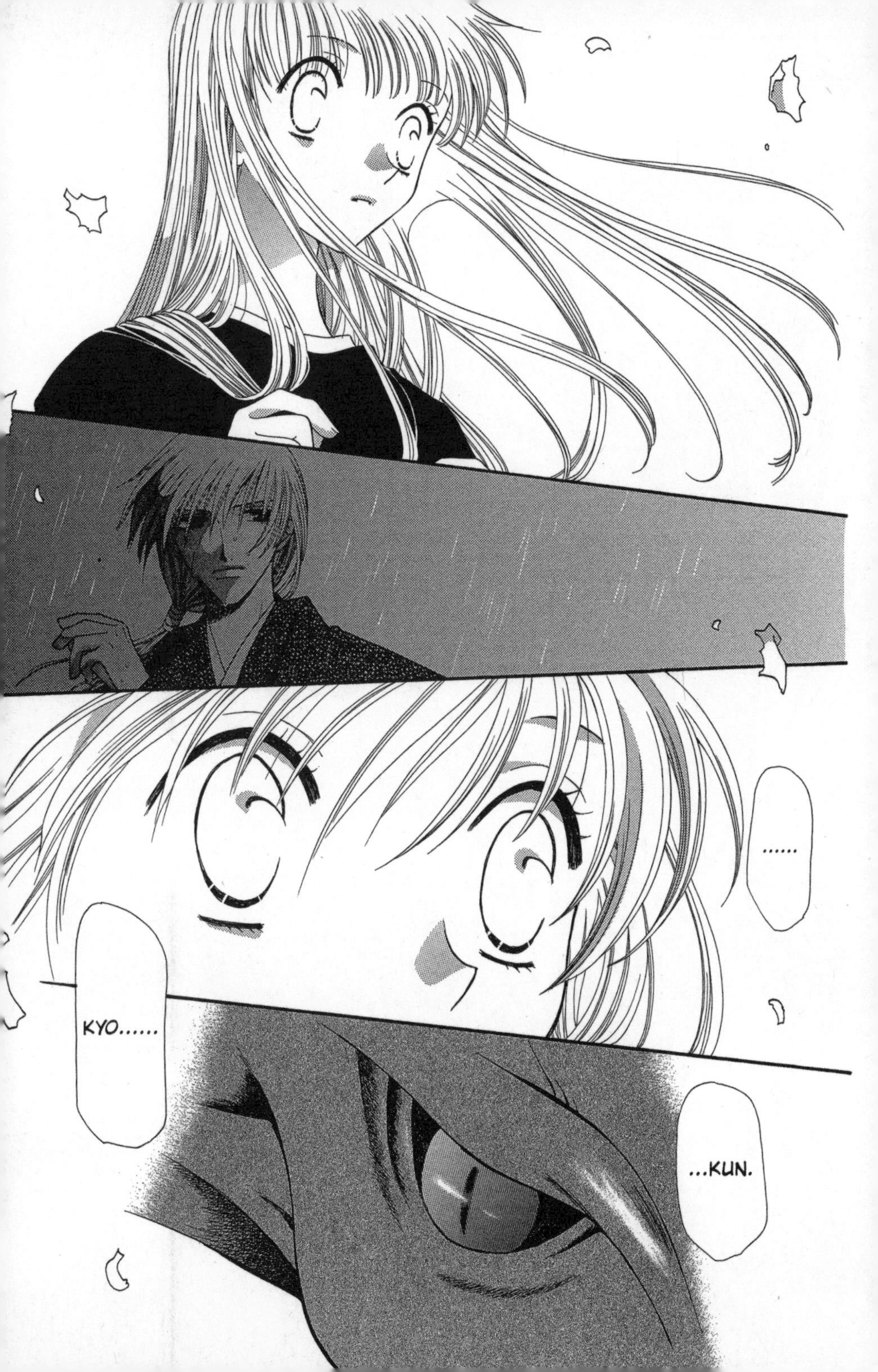
......
KYO......
...KUN.

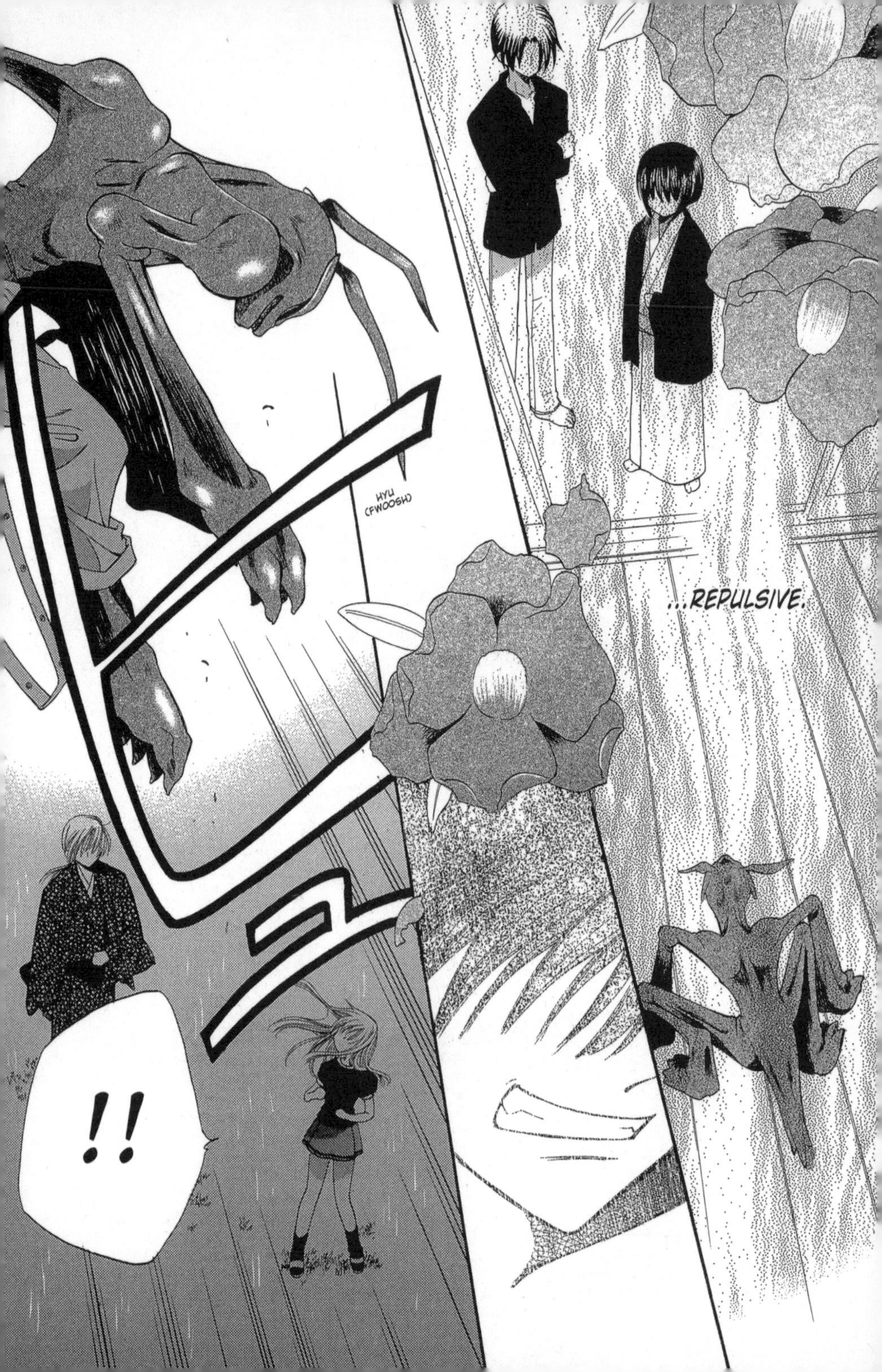
...REPULSIVE.
HYU
(FWOOSH)
!!

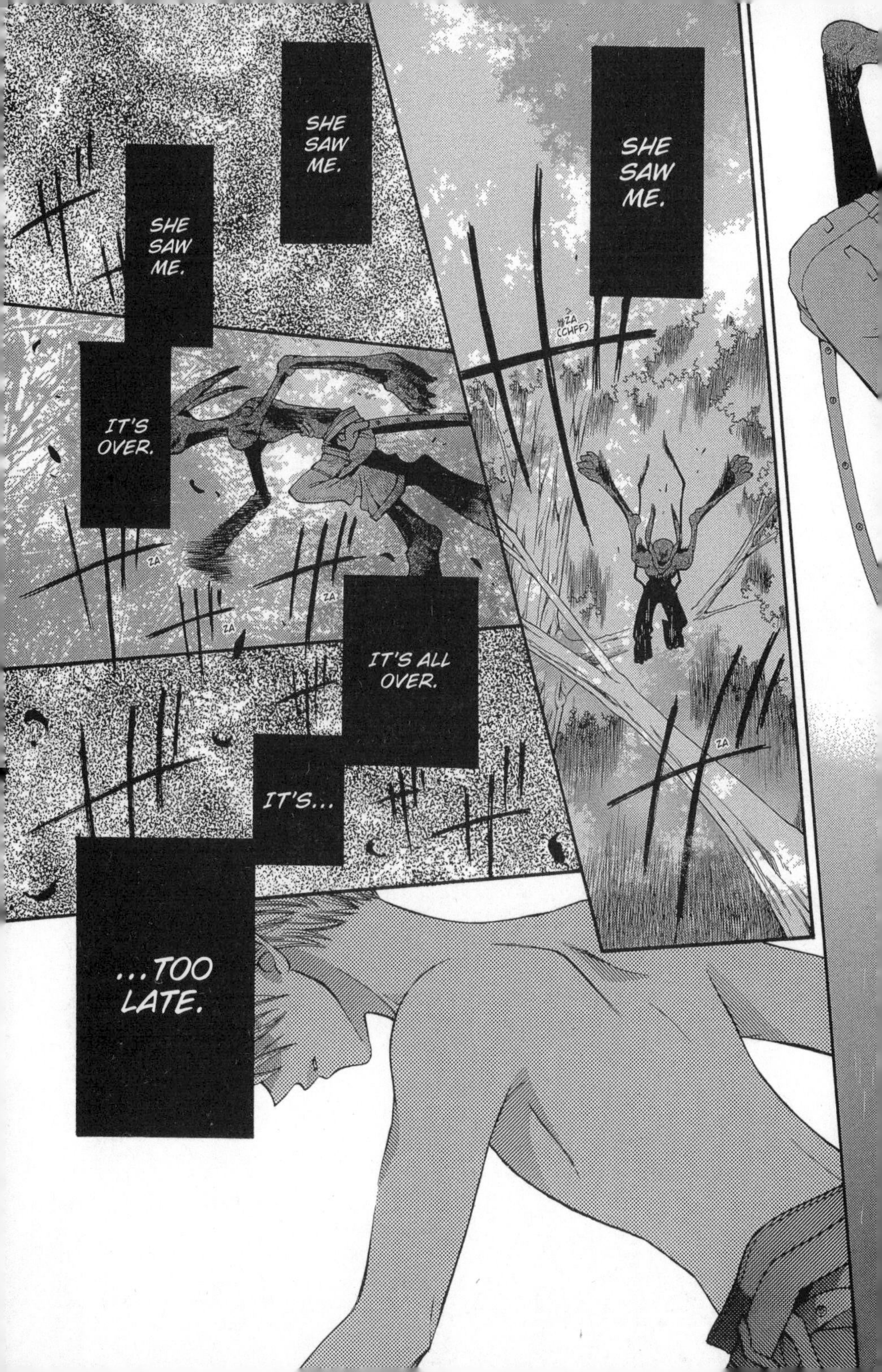
SHE SAW ME.
ZA (CHFF)
ZA
SHE SAW ME.
SHE SAW ME.
ZA
IT'S OVER.
ZA
ZA
ZA
IT'S ALL OVER.
IT'S...
ZA
...TOO LATE.

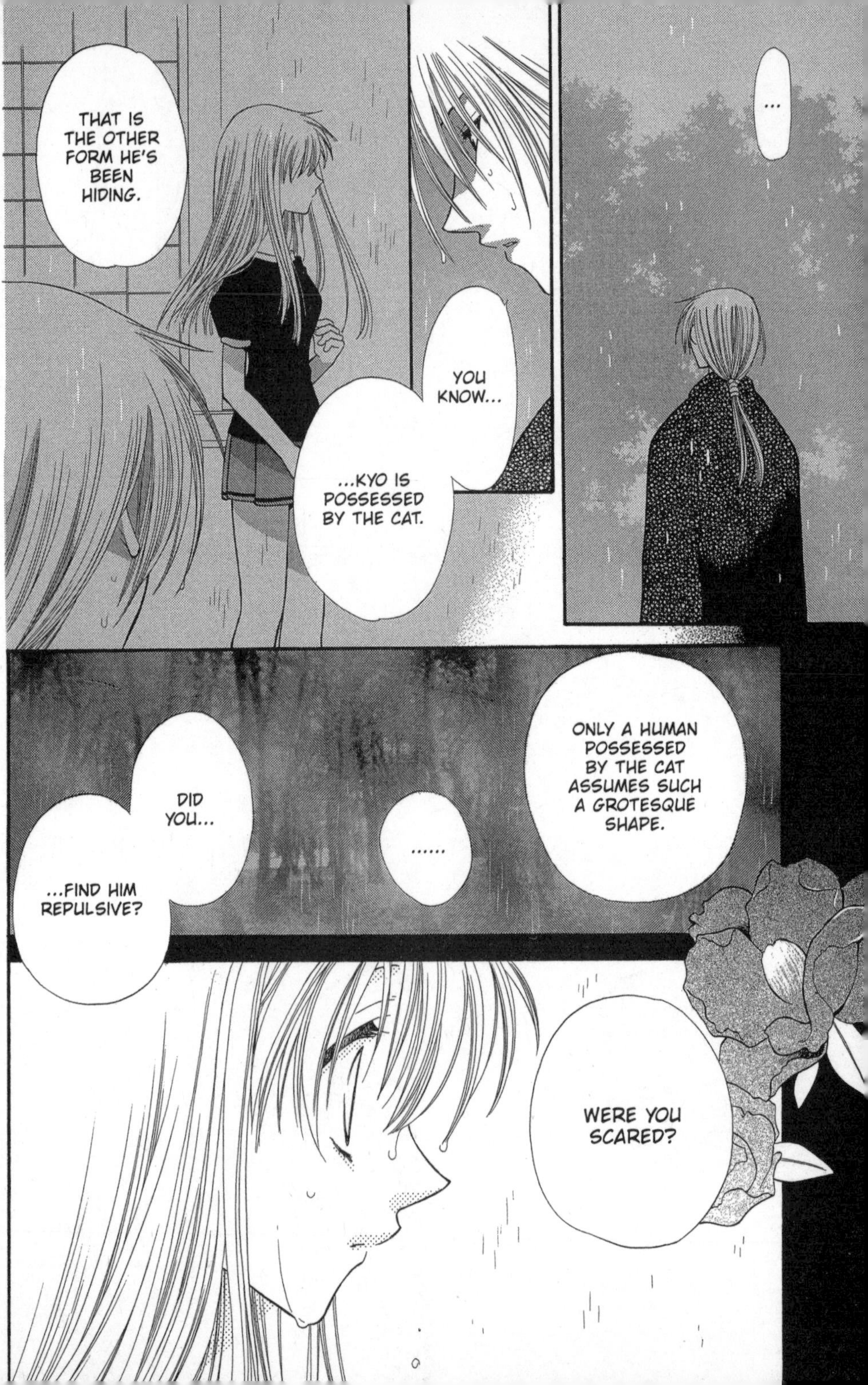
...
YOU KNOW...
...KYO IS POSSESSED BY THE CAT.
THAT IS THE OTHER FORM HE'S BEEN HIDING.
ONLY A HUMAN POSSESSED BY THE CAT ASSUMES SUCH A GROTESQUE SHAPE.
......
DID YOU...
...FIND HIM REPULSIVE?
WERE YOU SCARED?

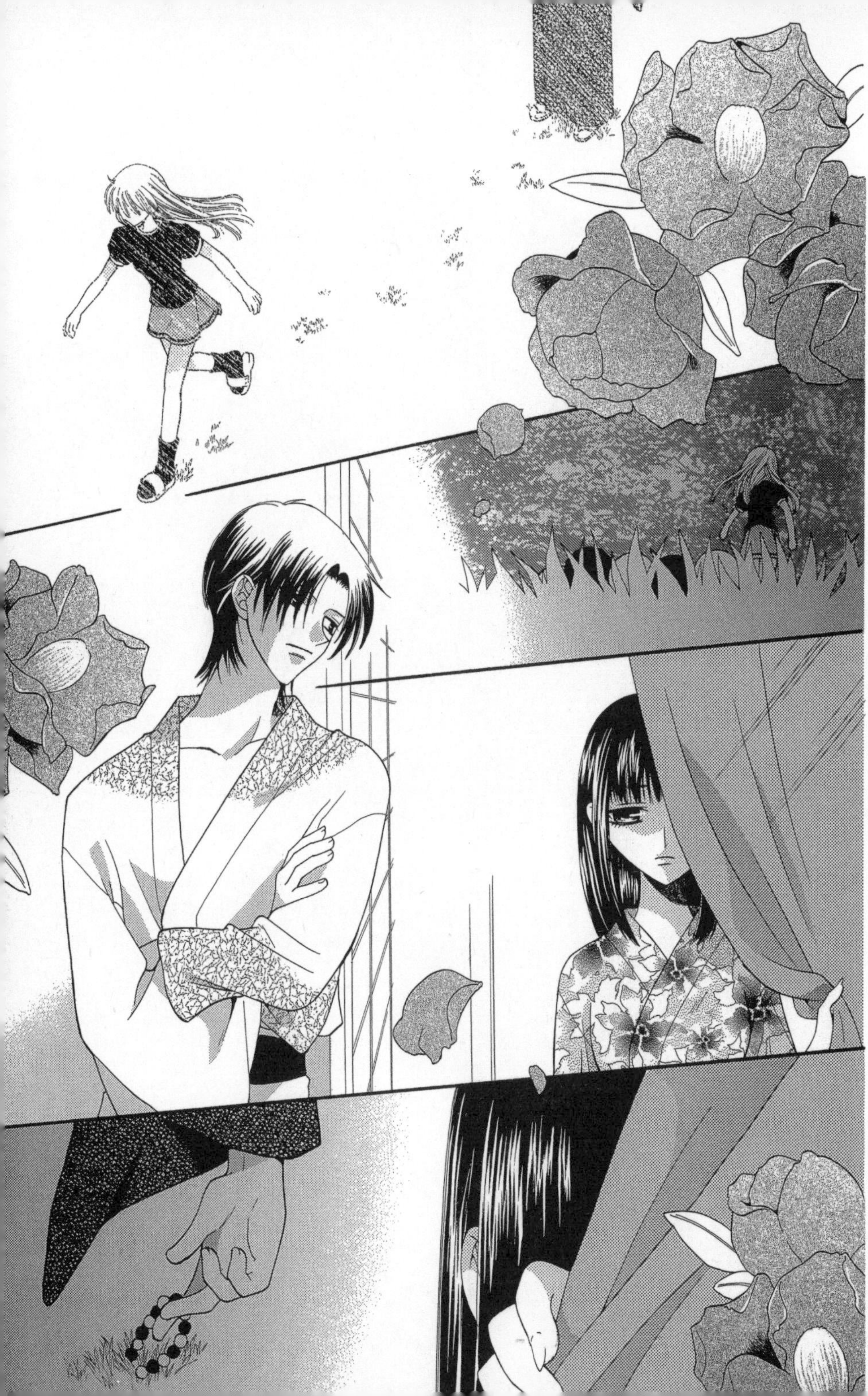

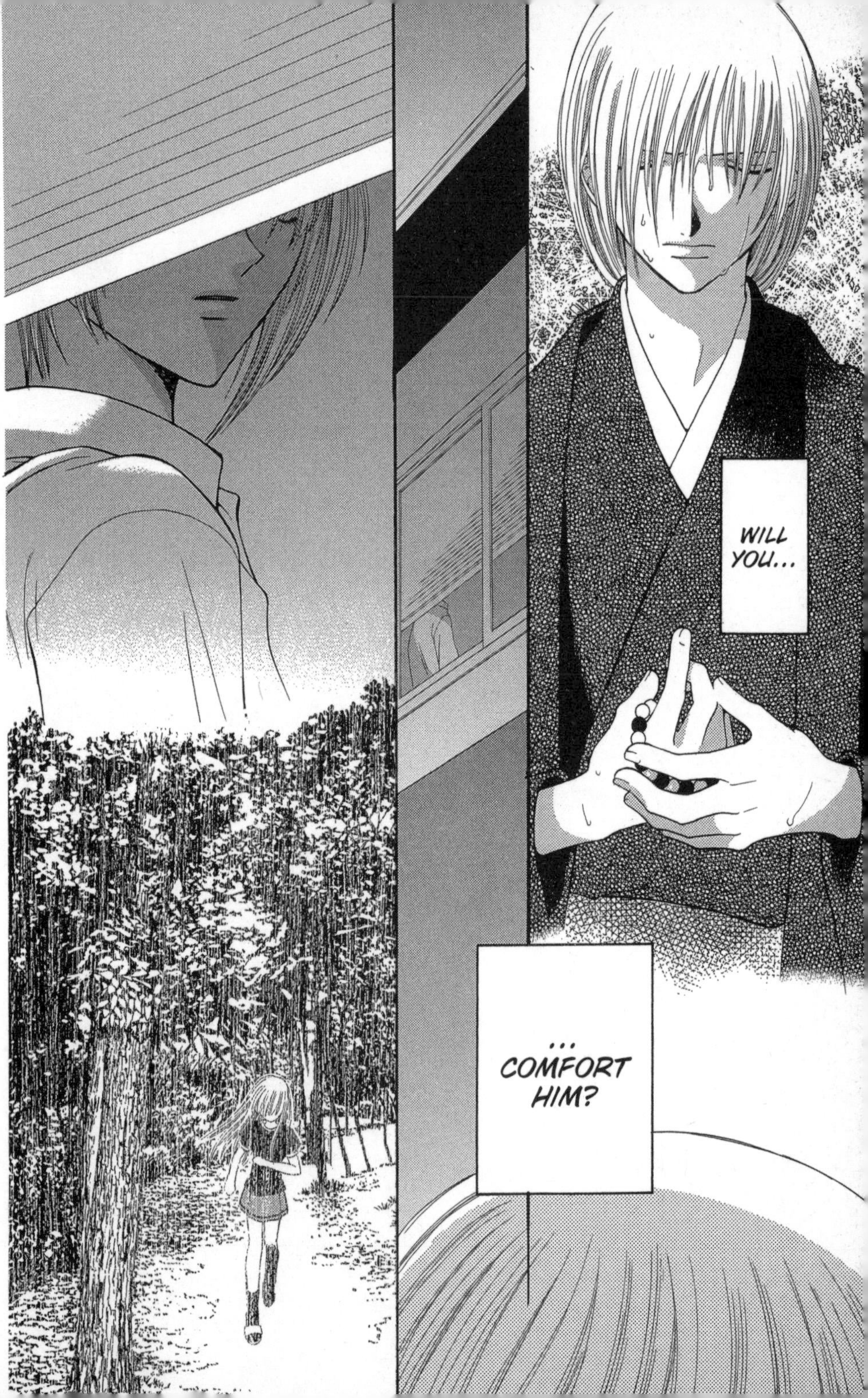
WILL YOU...
... COMFORT HIM?

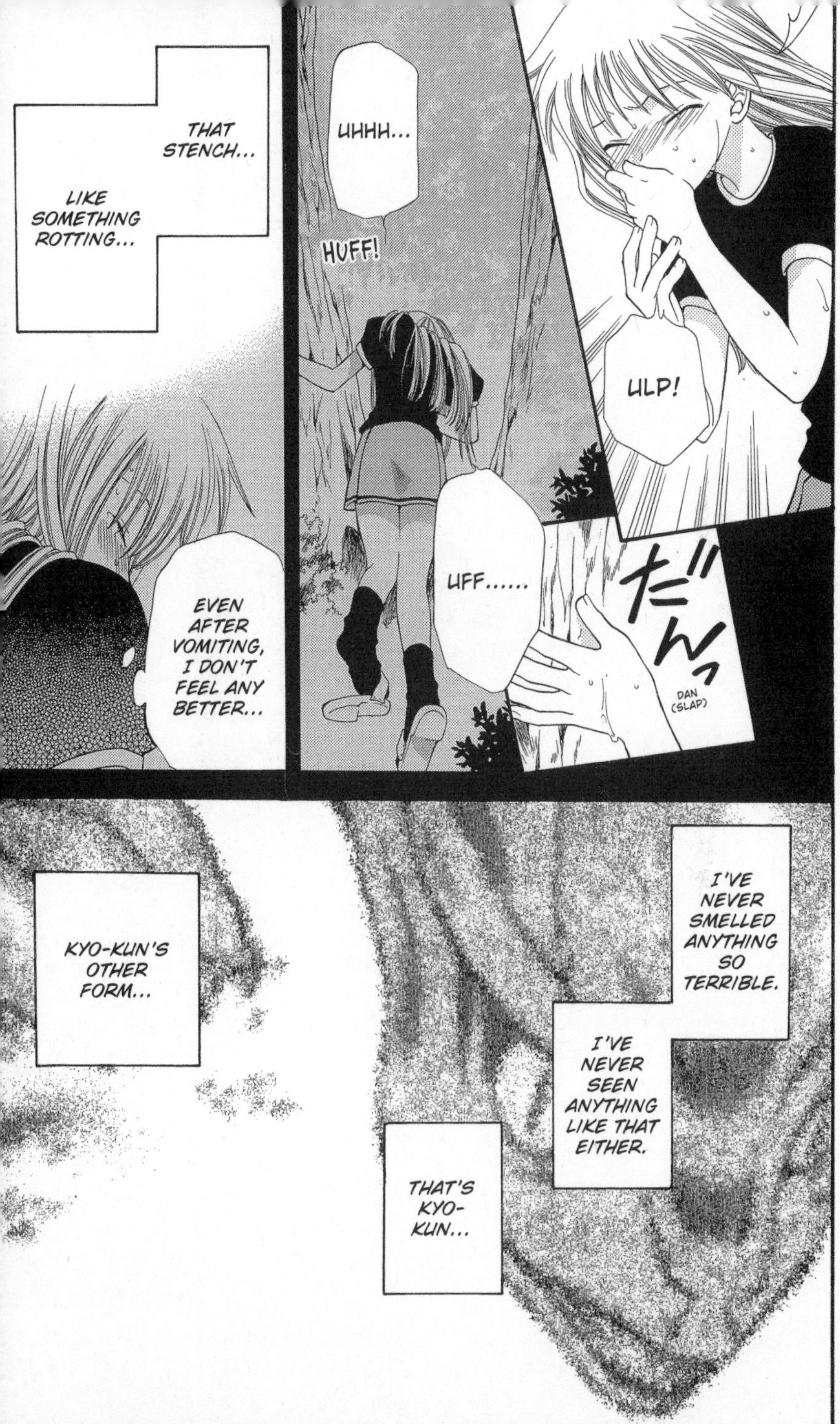
ULP!
だんっ
DAN (SLAP)
UHHH...
HUFF!
UFF......
THAT STENCH...
LIKE SOMETHING ROTTING...
EVEN AFTER VOMITING, I DON'T FEEL ANY BETTER...
I'VE NEVER SMELLED ANYTHING SO TERRIBLE.
I'VE NEVER SEEN ANYTHING LIKE THAT EITHER.
THAT'S KYO-KUN...
KYO-KUN'S OTHER FORM...

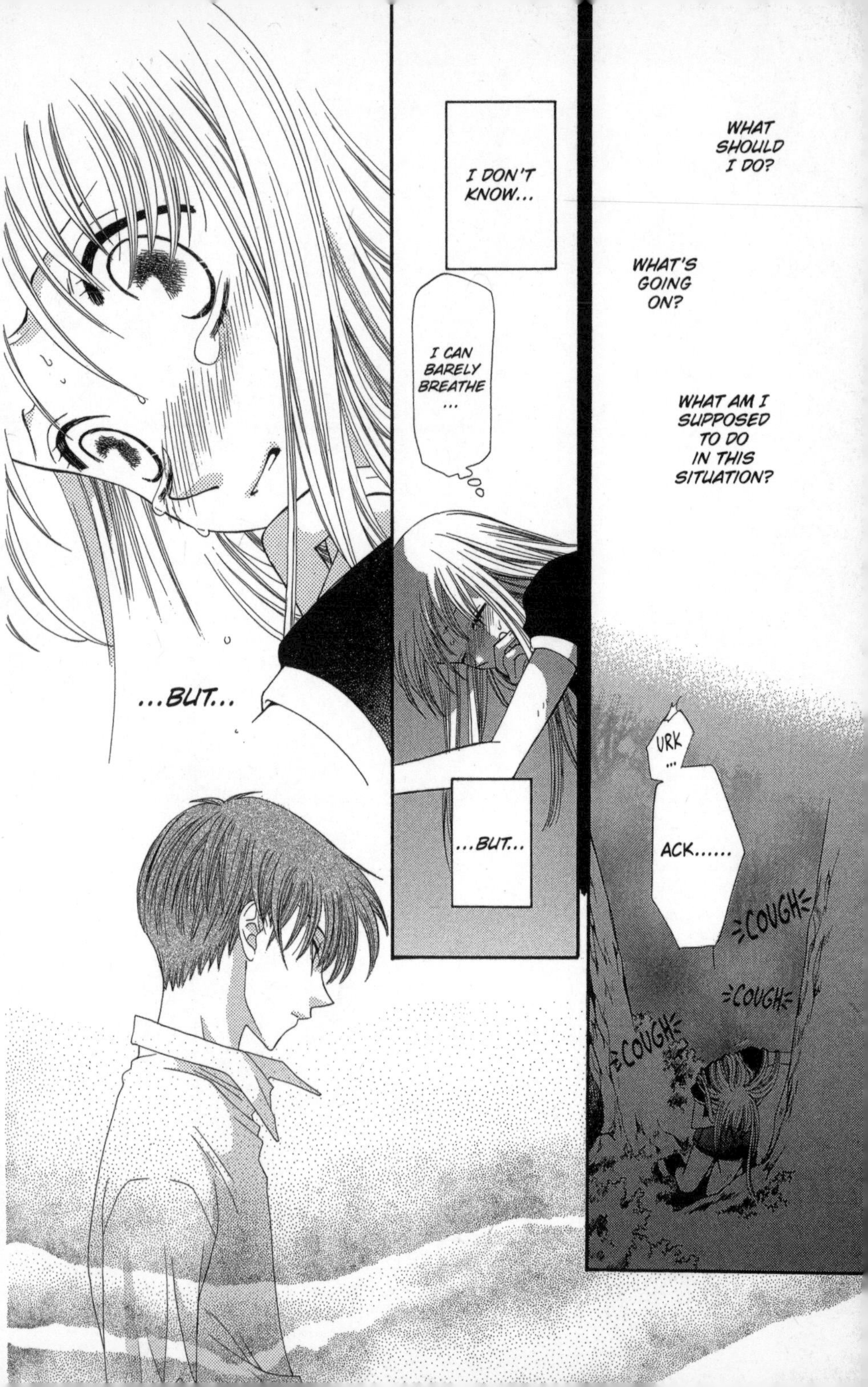
WHAT SHOULD I DO?
WHAT'S GOING ON?
WHAT AM I SUPPOSED TO DO IN THIS SITUATION?
URK ...
ACK......
COUGH
COUGH
COUGH
I DON'T KNOW...
I CAN BARELY BREATHE ...
...BUT...
...BUT...

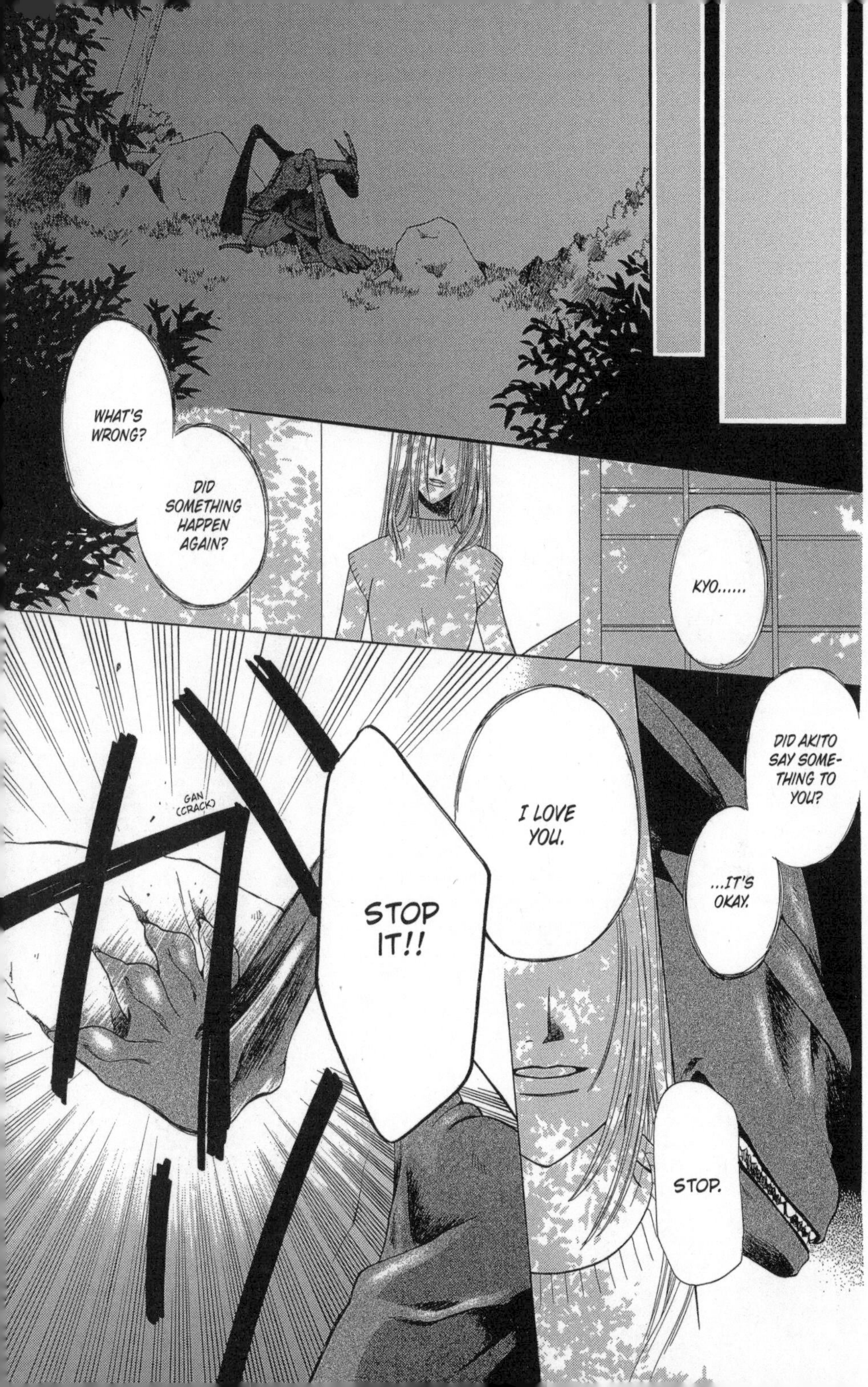
KYO......
WHAT'S WRONG?
DID SOMETHING HAPPEN AGAIN?
DID AKITO SAY SOME-THING TO YOU?
...IT'S OKAY.
I LOVE YOU.
STOP.
STOP IT!!
GAN (CRACK)

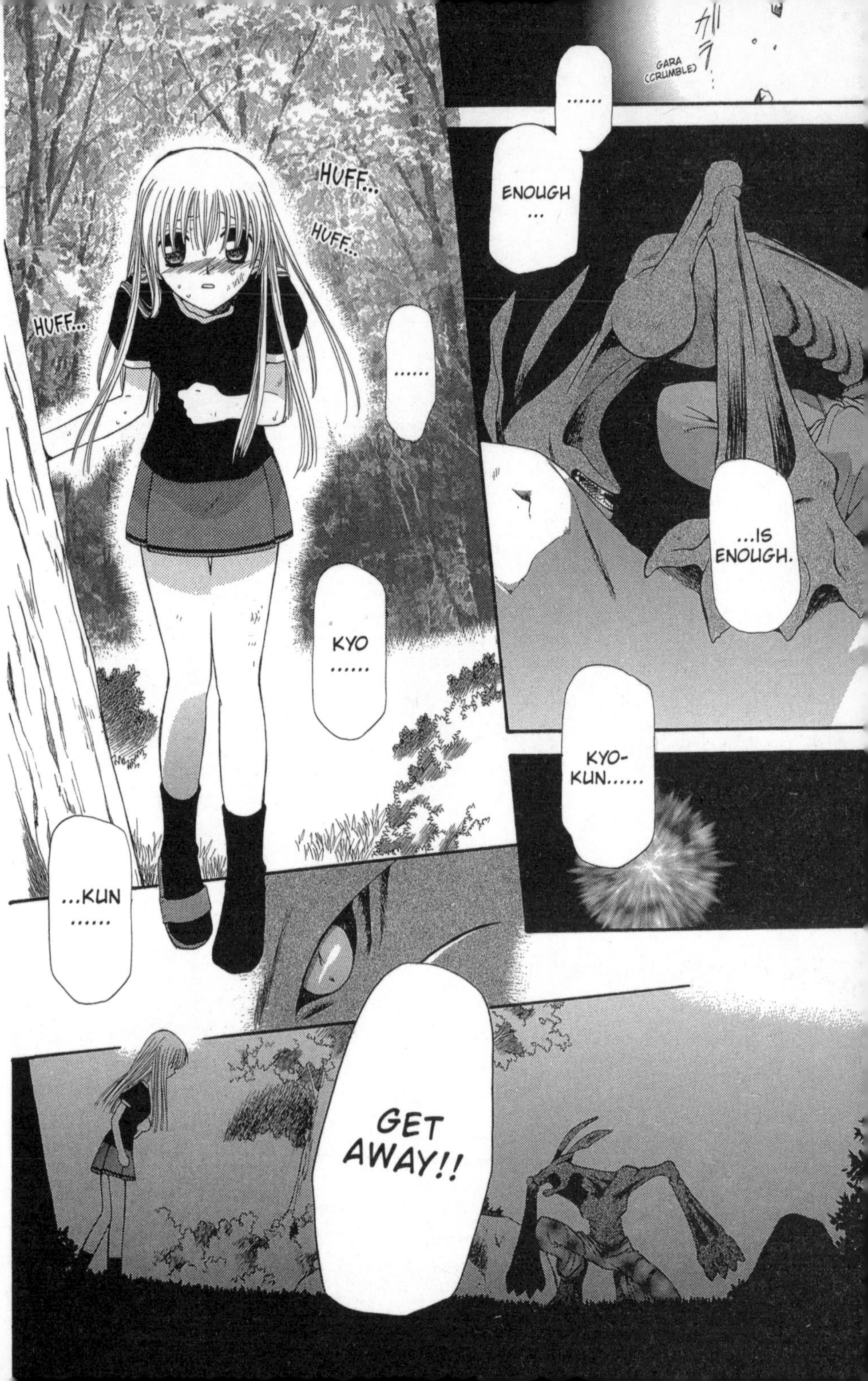
GARA (CRUMBLE)
......
ENOUGH ...
...IS ENOUGH.
KYO-KUN......
HUFF...
HUFF...
HUFF...
......
KYO ......
...KUN ......
GET AWAY!!

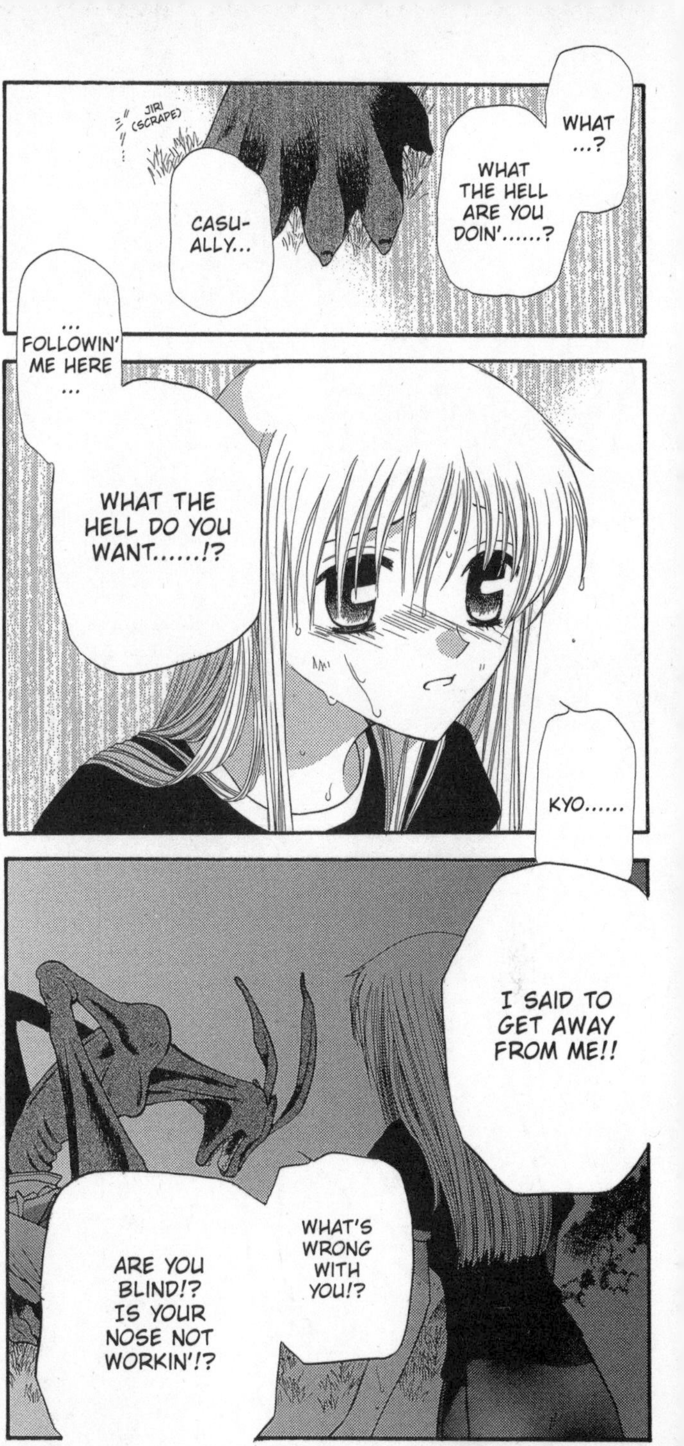
WHAT ...?
WHAT THE HELL ARE YOU DOIN'......?
JIRI (SCRAPE)
CASU-ALLY...
... FOLLOWIN' ME HERE ...
WHAT THE HELL DO YOU WANT......!?
KYO......
I SAID TO GET AWAY FROM ME!!
WHAT'S WRONG WITH YOU!?
ARE YOU BLIND!? IS YOUR NOSE NOT WORKIN'!?
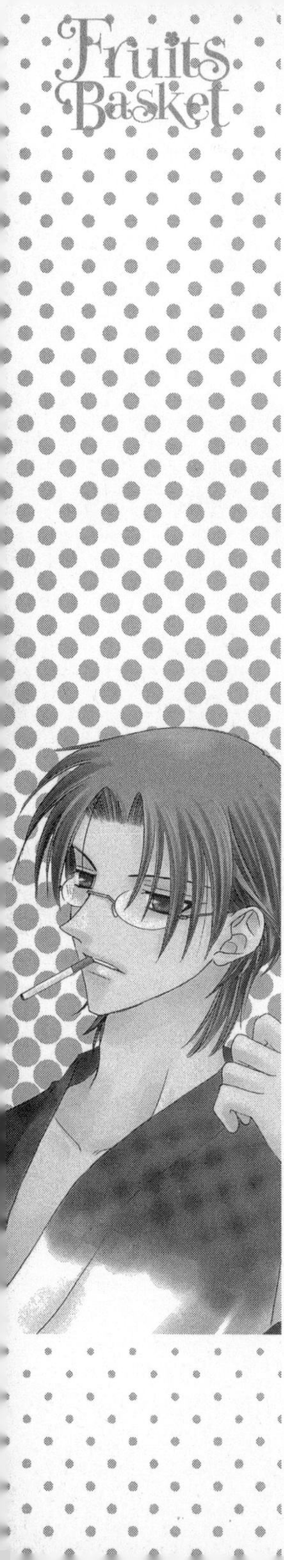
Fruits Basket

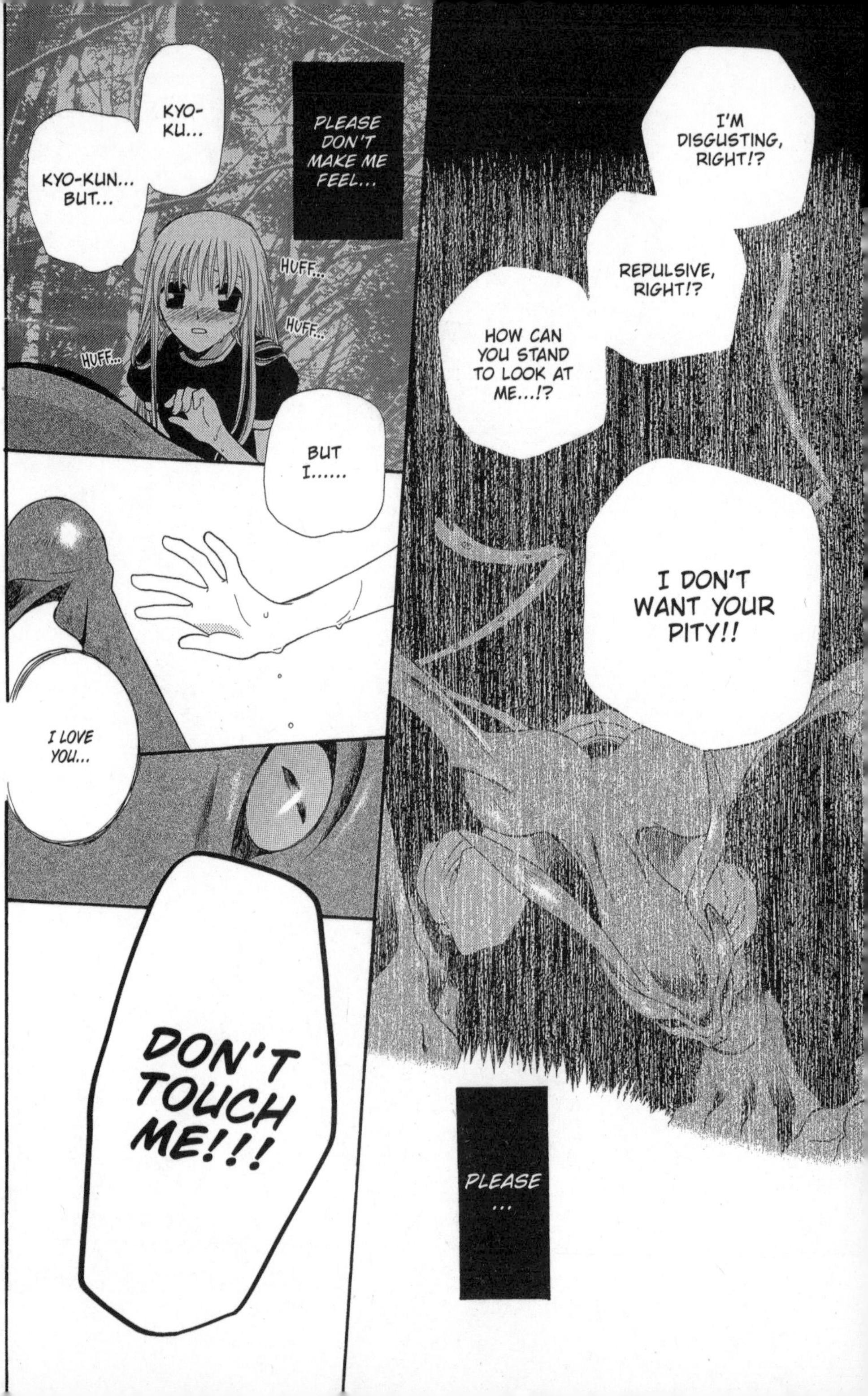
I'M DISGUSTING, RIGHT!?
REPULSIVE, RIGHT!?
HOW CAN YOU STAND TO LOOK AT ME...!?
I DON'T WANT YOUR PITY!!
PLEASE DON'T MAKE ME FEEL...
KYO-KU...
KYO-KUN... BUT...
HUFF...
HUFF...
HUFF...
BUT I......
I LOVE YOU...
DON'T TOUCH ME!!!
PLEASE ...

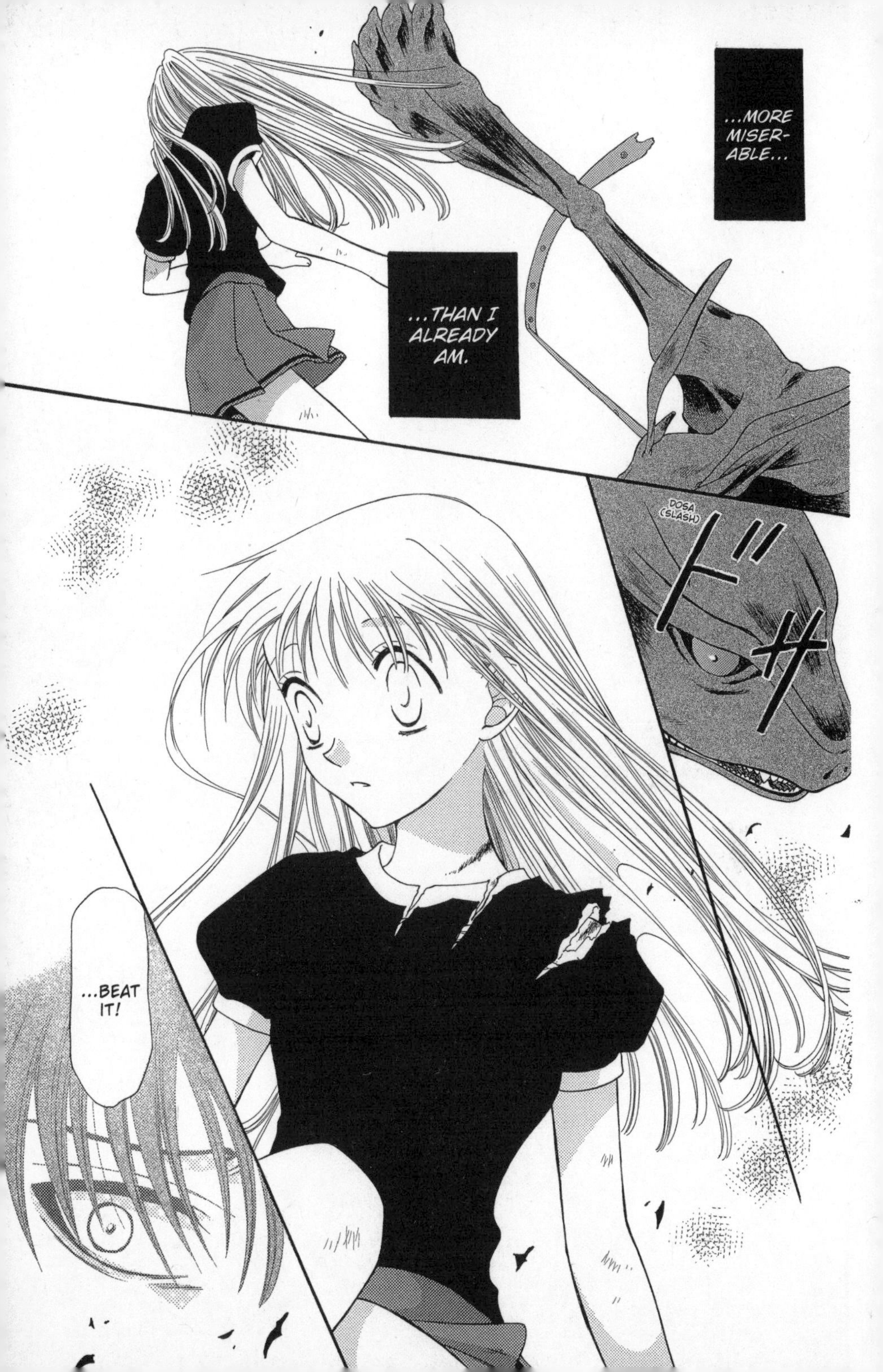
...MORE MISER-ABLE...
...THAN I ALREADY AM.
DOSA (SLASH)
ドサ
...BEAT IT!

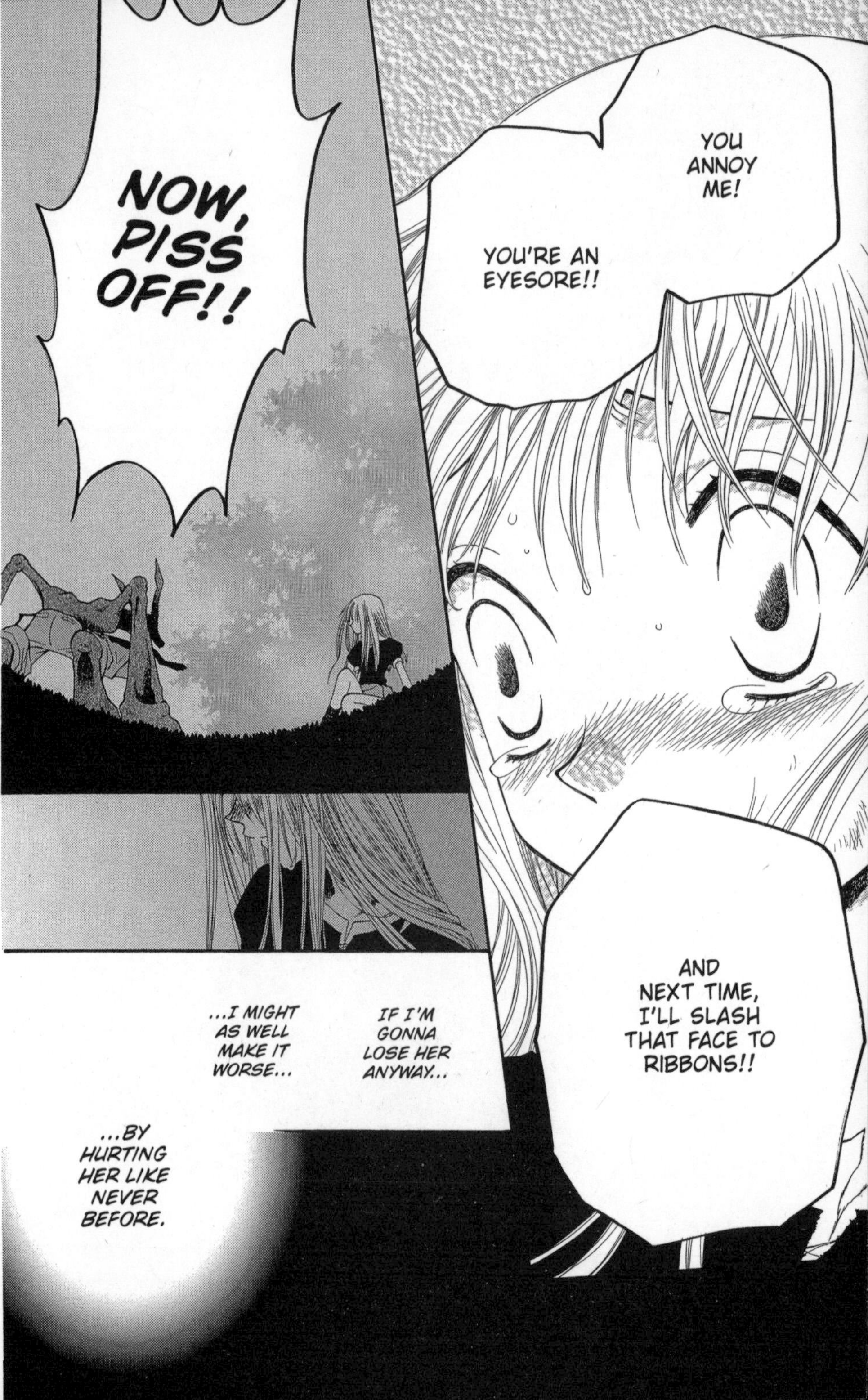
YOU ANNOY ME!
YOU'RE AN EYESORE!!
AND NEXT TIME, I'LL SLASH THAT FACE TO RIBBONS!!
NOW, PISS OFF!!
IF I'M GONNA LOSE HER ANYWAY...
...I MIGHT AS WELL MAKE IT WORSE...
...BY HURTING HER LIKE NEVER BEFORE.

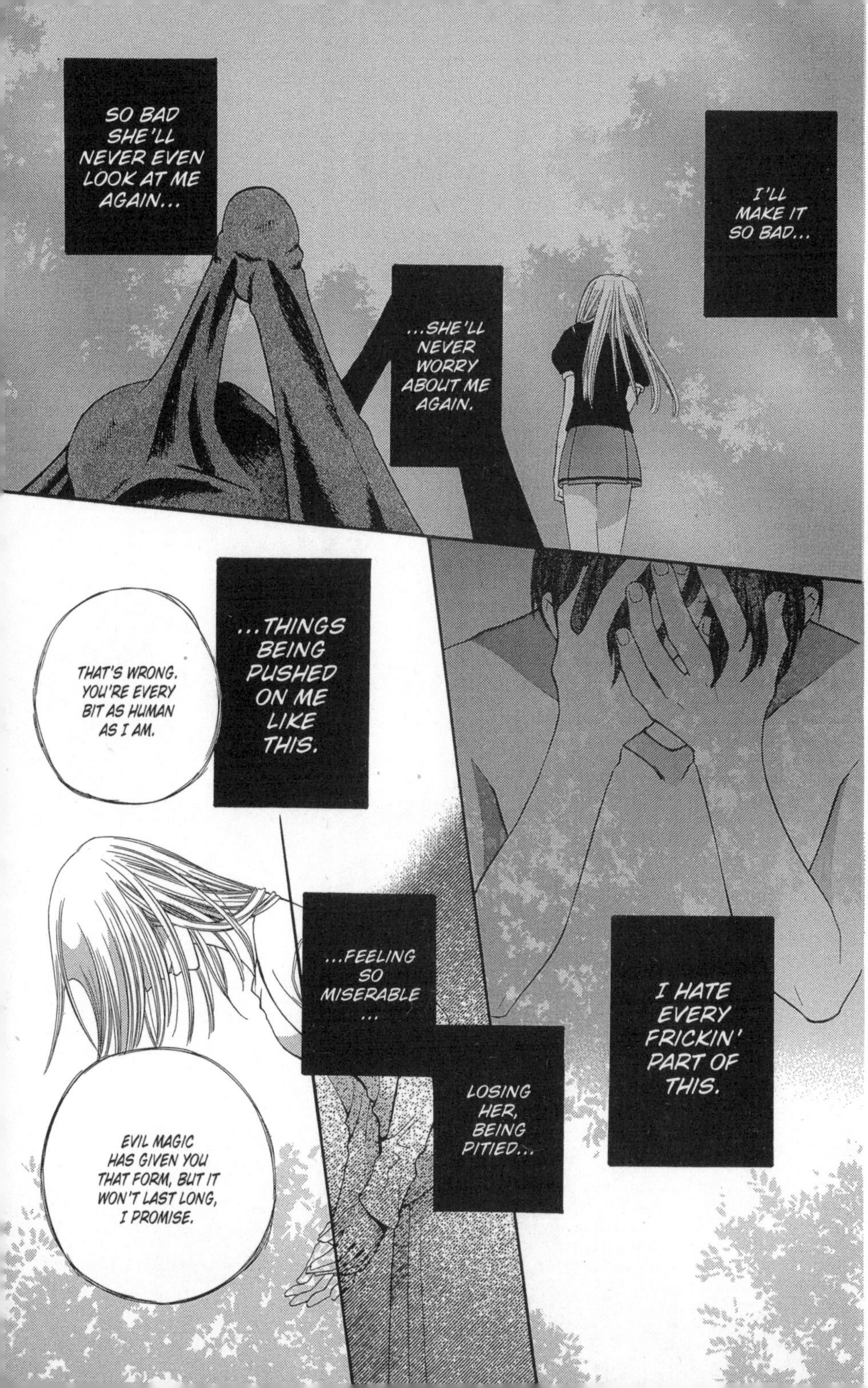
I'LL MAKE IT SO BAD...
SO BAD SHE'LL NEVER EVEN LOOK AT ME AGAIN...
...SHE'LL NEVER WORRY ABOUT ME AGAIN.
I HATE EVERY FRICKIN' PART OF THIS.
...THINGS BEING PUSHED ON ME LIKE THIS.
THAT'S WRONG. YOU'RE EVERY BIT AS HUMAN AS I AM.
...FEELING SO MISERABLE...
LOSING HER, BEING PITIED...
EVIL MAGIC HAS GIVEN YOU THAT FORM, BUT IT WON'T LAST LONG, I PROMISE.

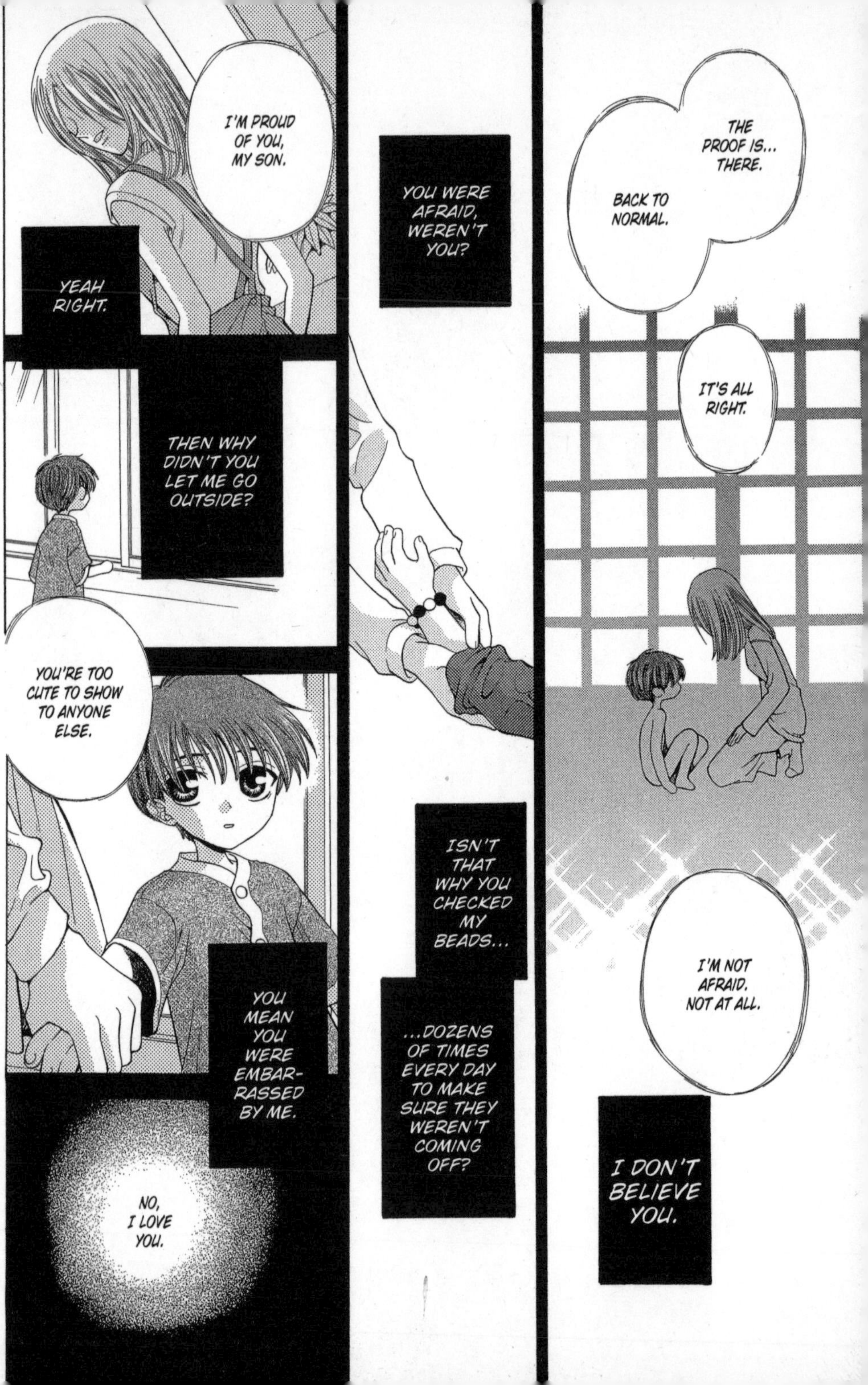
BACK TO NORMAL.
THE PROOF IS... THERE.
IT'S ALL RIGHT.
I'M NOT AFRAID. NOT AT ALL.
I DON'T BELIEVE YOU.
YOU WERE AFRAID, WEREN'T YOU?
ISN'T THAT WHY YOU CHECKED MY BEADS...
...DOZENS OF TIMES EVERY DAY TO MAKE SURE THEY WEREN'T COMING OFF?
I'M PROUD OF YOU, MY SON.
YEAH RIGHT.
THEN WHY DIDN'T YOU LET ME GO OUTSIDE?
YOU'RE TOO CUTE TO SHOW TO ANYONE ELSE.
YOU MEAN YOU WERE EMBARRASSED BY ME.
NO, I LOVE YOU.

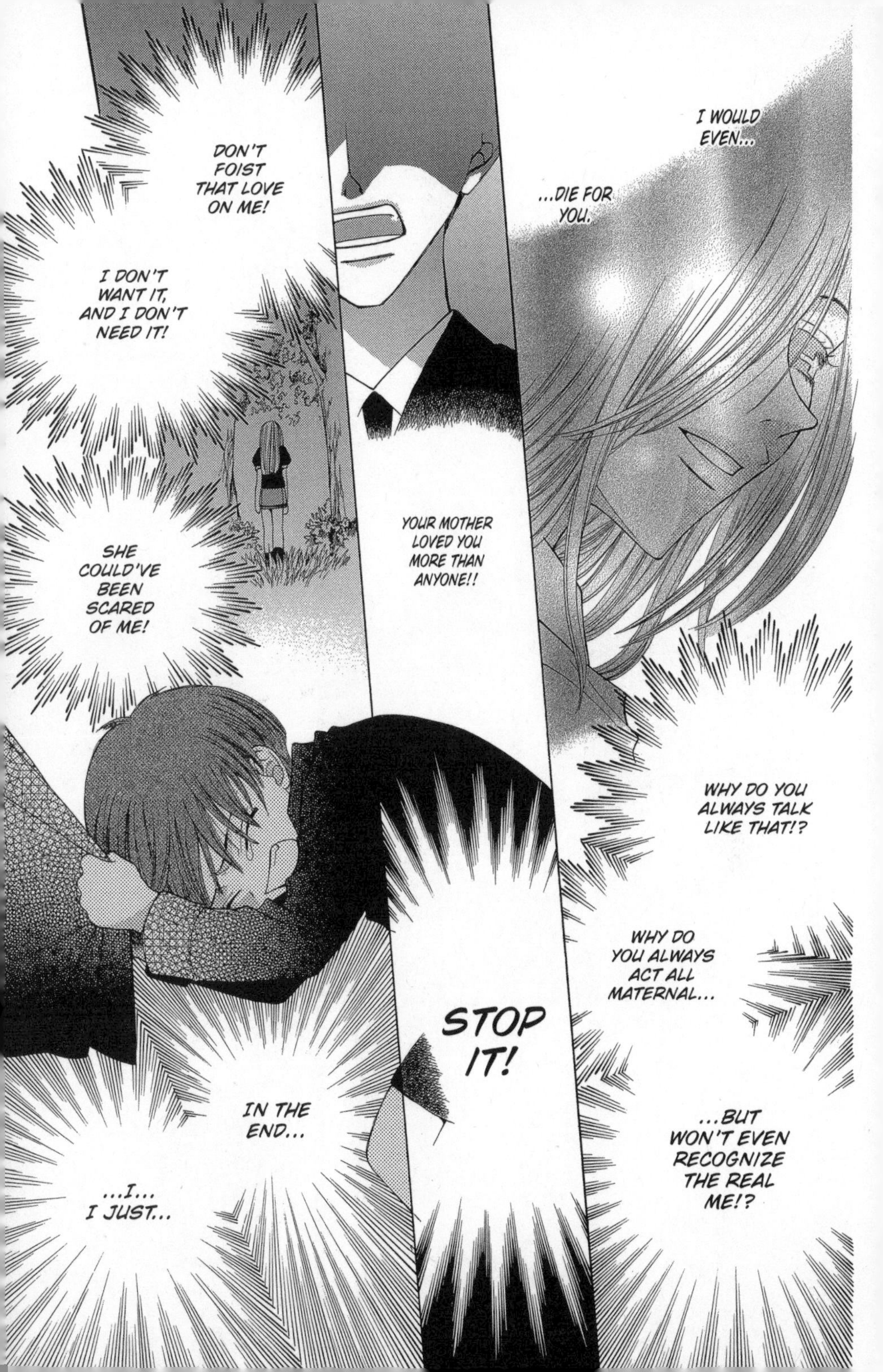
I WOULD EVEN...
...DIE FOR YOU.
YOUR MOTHER LOVED YOU MORE THAN ANYONE!!
DON'T FOIST THAT LOVE ON ME!
I DON'T WANT IT, AND I DON'T NEED IT!
SHE COULD'VE BEEN SCARED OF ME!
WHY DO YOU ALWAYS TALK LIKE THAT!?
WHY DO YOU ALWAYS ACT ALL MATERNAL...
...BUT WON'T EVEN RECOGNIZE THE REAL ME!?
STOP IT!
IN THE END...
...I... I JUST...

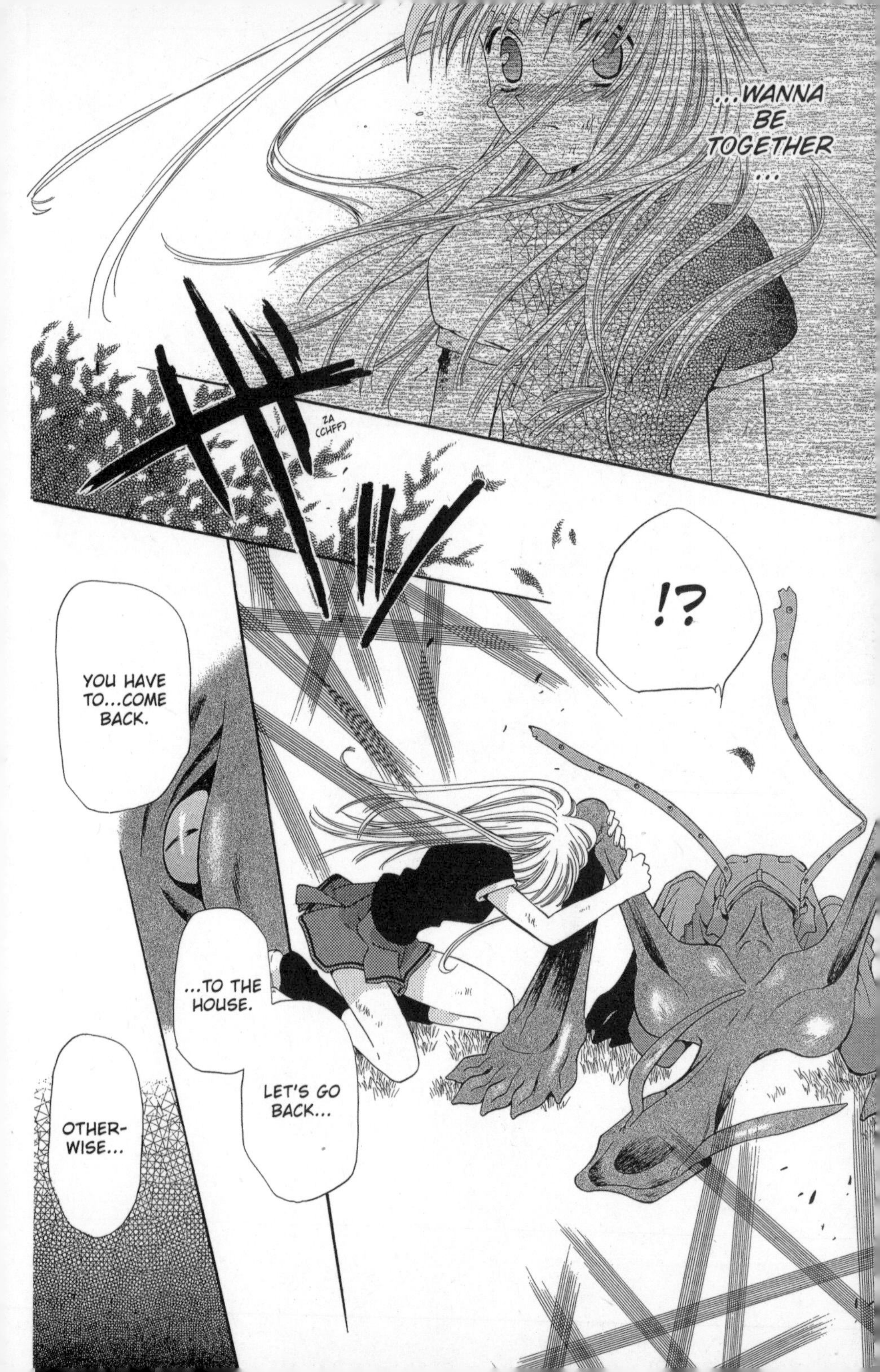
...WANNA BE TOGETHER...
ZA (CHFF)
!?
YOU HAVE TO...COME BACK.
...TO THE HOUSE.
LET'S GO BACK...
OTHER-WISE...

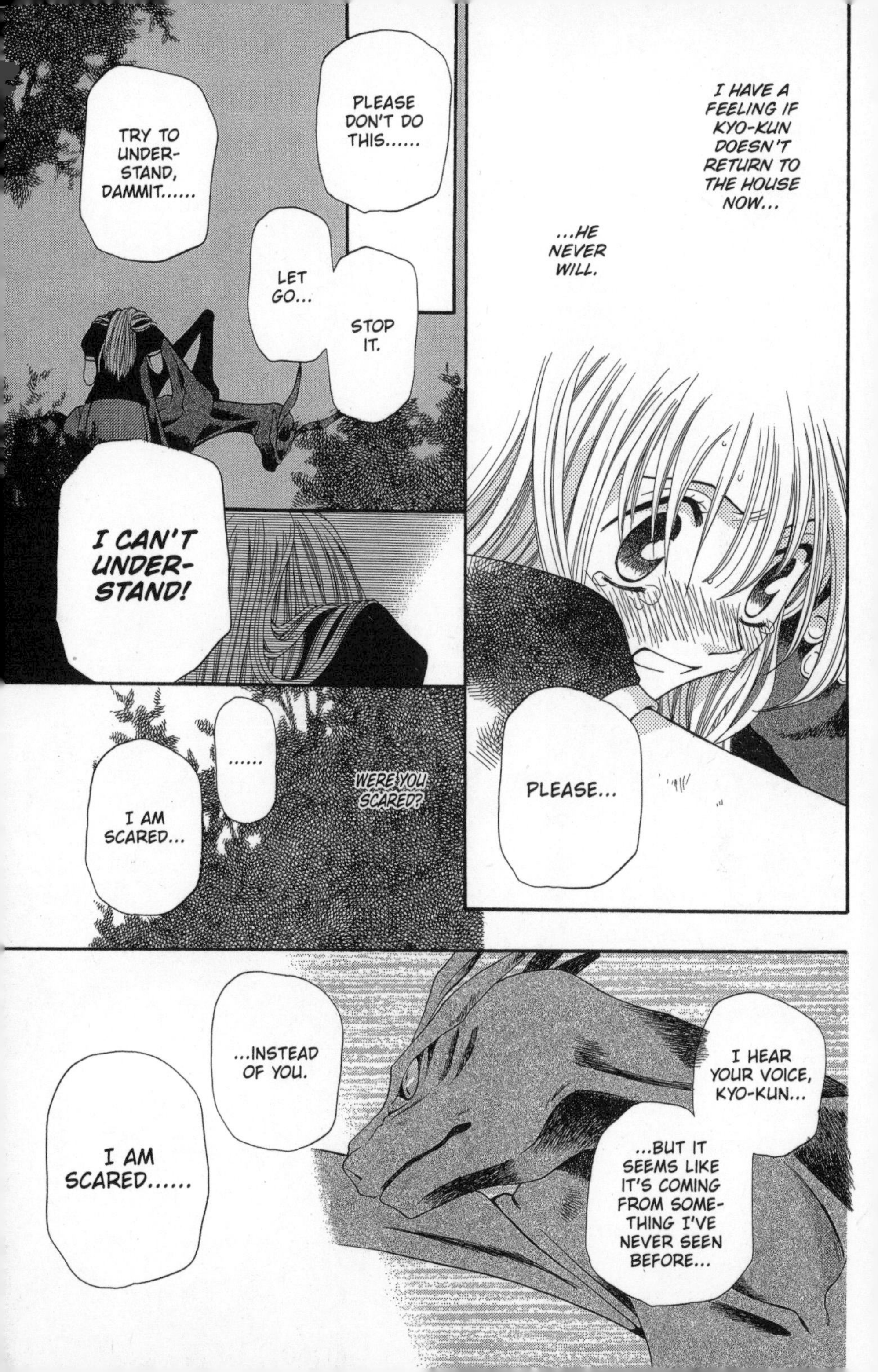
I HAVE A FEELING IF KYO-KUN DOESN'T RETURN TO THE HOUSE NOW...
...HE NEVER WILL.
PLEASE...
PLEASE DON'T DO THIS......
TRY TO UNDER-STAND, DAMMIT......
LET GO...
STOP IT.
I CAN'T UNDER-STAND!
WERE YOU SCARED?
......
I AM SCARED...
I HEAR YOUR VOICE, KYO-KUN...
...BUT IT SEEMS LIKE IT'S COMING FROM SOME-THING I'VE NEVER SEEN BEFORE...
...INSTEAD OF YOU.
I AM SCARED......

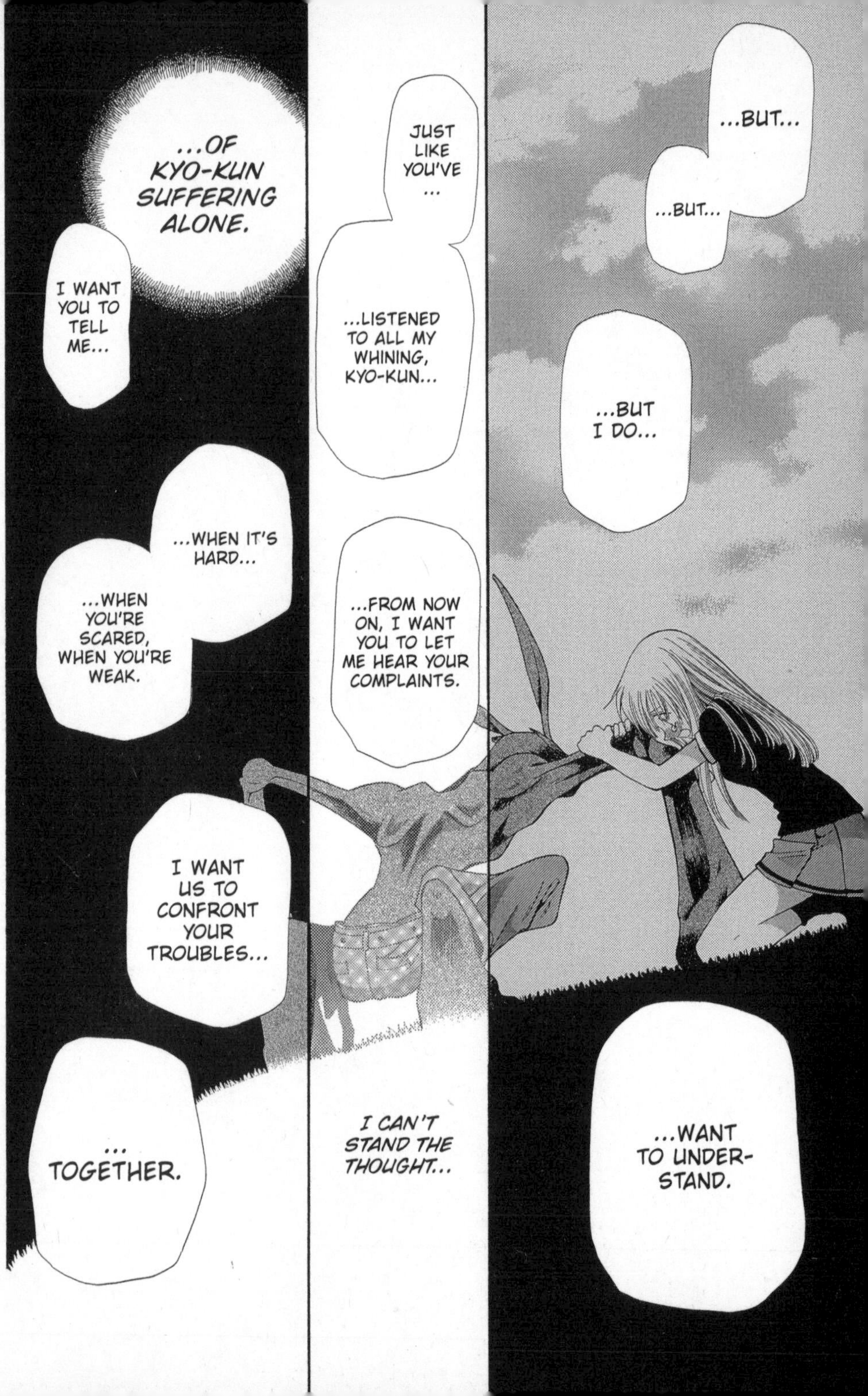
...BUT...
...BUT...
...BUT I DO...
...WANT TO UNDER-STAND.
JUST LIKE YOU'VE ...
...LISTENED TO ALL MY WHINING, KYO-KUN...
...FROM NOW ON, I WANT YOU TO LET ME HEAR YOUR COMPLAINTS.
I CAN'T STAND THE THOUGHT...
...OF KYO-KUN SUFFERING ALONE.
I WANT YOU TO TELL ME...
...WHEN IT'S HARD...
...WHEN YOU'RE SCARED, WHEN YOU'RE WEAK.
I WANT US TO CONFRONT YOUR TROUBLES...
... TOGETHER.

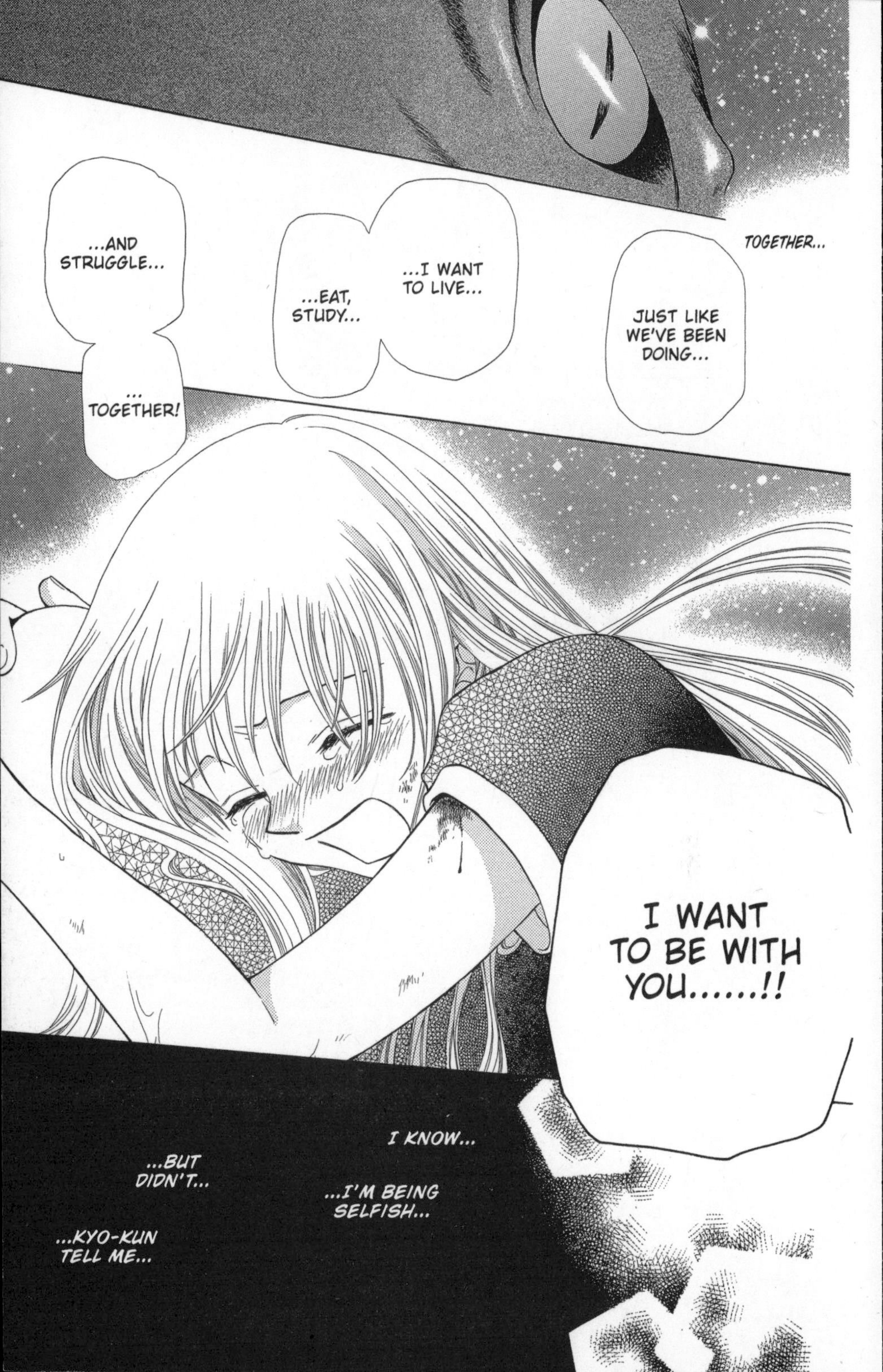
TOGETHER...
JUST LIKE WE'VE BEEN DOING...
...I WANT TO LIVE...
...EAT, STUDY...
...AND STRUGGLE...
... TOGETHER!
I WANT TO BE WITH YOU......!!
I KNOW...
...I'M BEING SELFISH...
...BUT DIDN'T...
...KYO-KUN TELL ME...

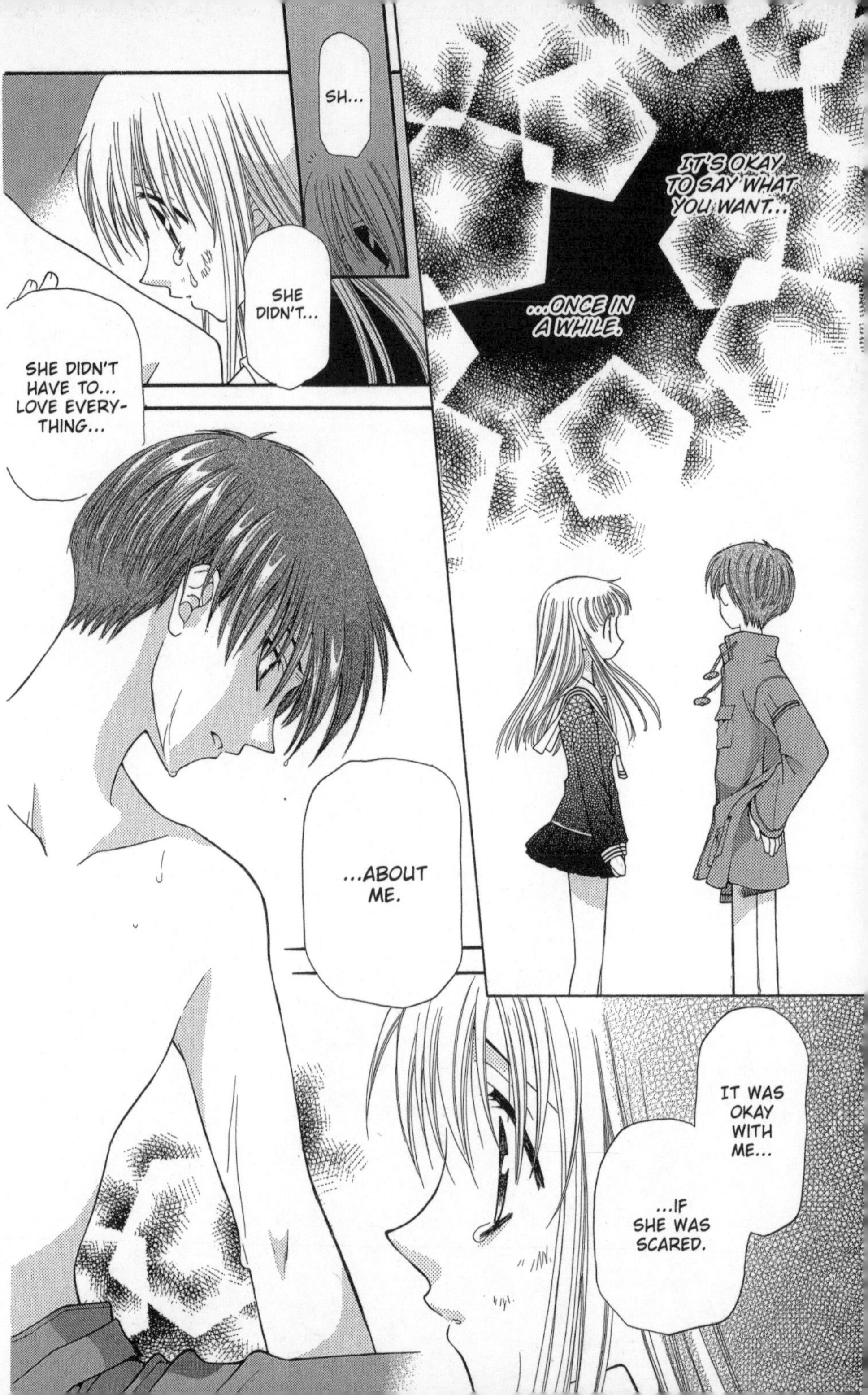
IT'S OKAY TO SAY WHAT YOU WANT...
...ONCE IN A WHILE.
SH...
SHE DIDN'T...
SHE DIDN'T HAVE TO... LOVE EVERYTHING...
...ABOUT ME.
IT WAS OKAY WITH ME...
...IF SHE WAS SCARED.

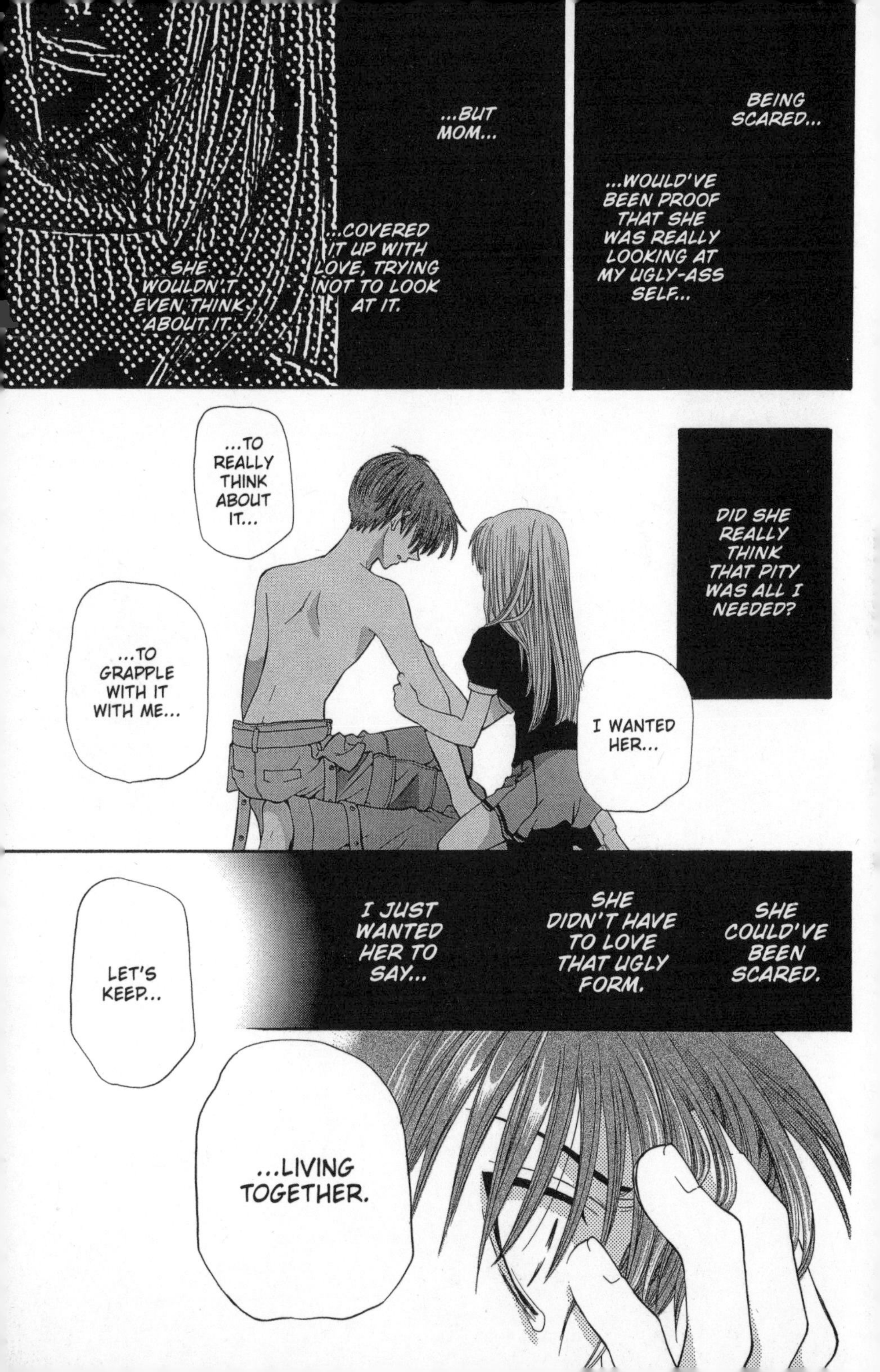
BEING SCARED...
...WOULD'VE BEEN PROOF THAT SHE WAS REALLY LOOKING AT MY UGLY-ASS SELF...
...BUT MOM...
...COVERED IT UP WITH LOVE, TRYING NOT TO LOOK AT IT.
SHE WOULDN'T EVEN THINK ABOUT IT.
DID SHE REALLY THINK THAT PITY WAS ALL I NEEDED?
I WANTED HER...
...TO REALLY THINK ABOUT IT...
...TO GRAPPLE WITH IT WITH ME...
SHE COULD'VE BEEN SCARED.
SHE DIDN'T HAVE TO LOVE THAT UGLY FORM.
I JUST WANTED HER TO SAY...
LET'S KEEP...
...LIVING TOGETHER.

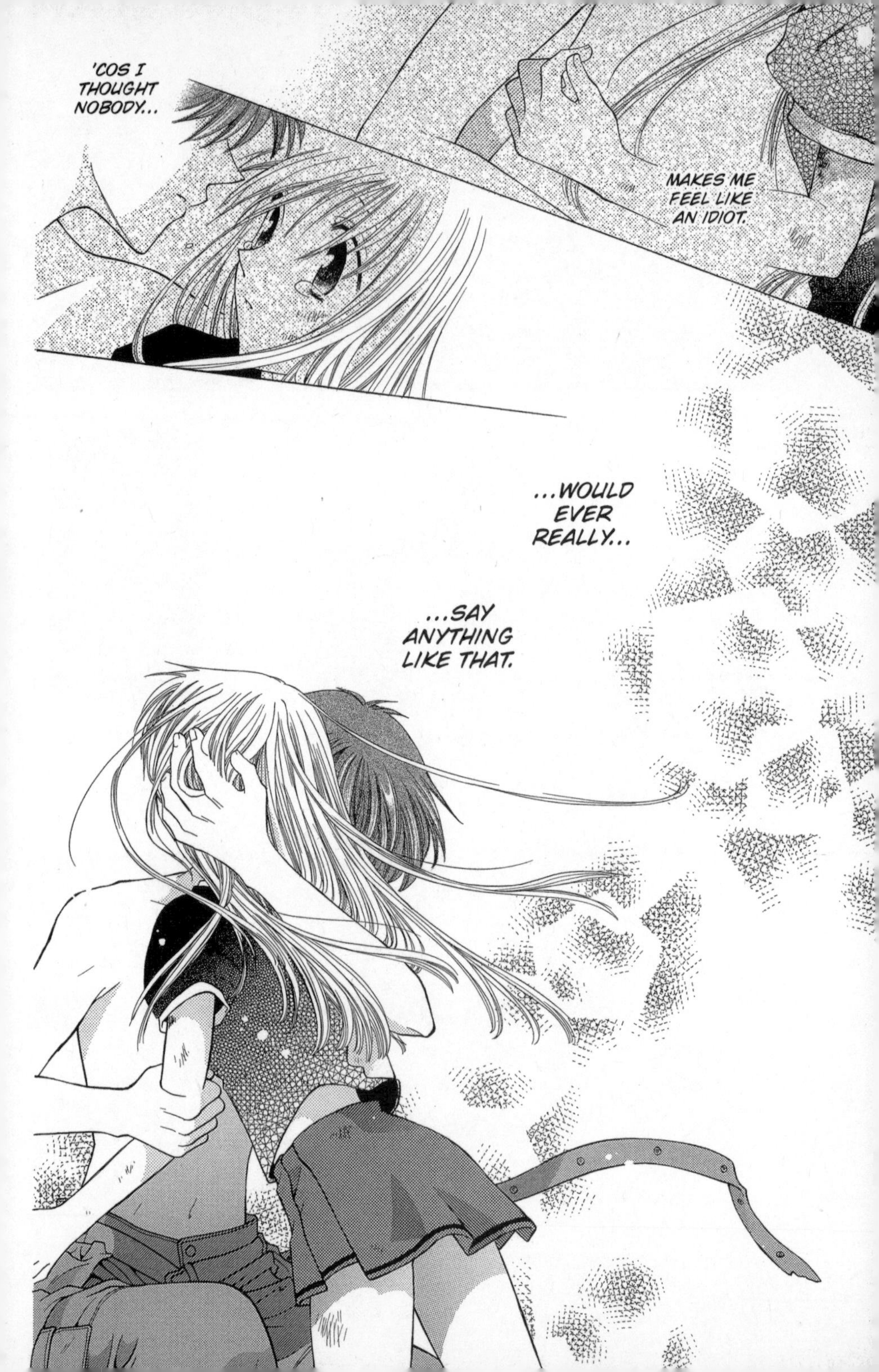
MAKES ME FEEL LIKE AN IDIOT.
'COS I THOUGHT NOBODY...
...WOULD EVER REALLY...
...SAY ANYTHING LIKE THAT.

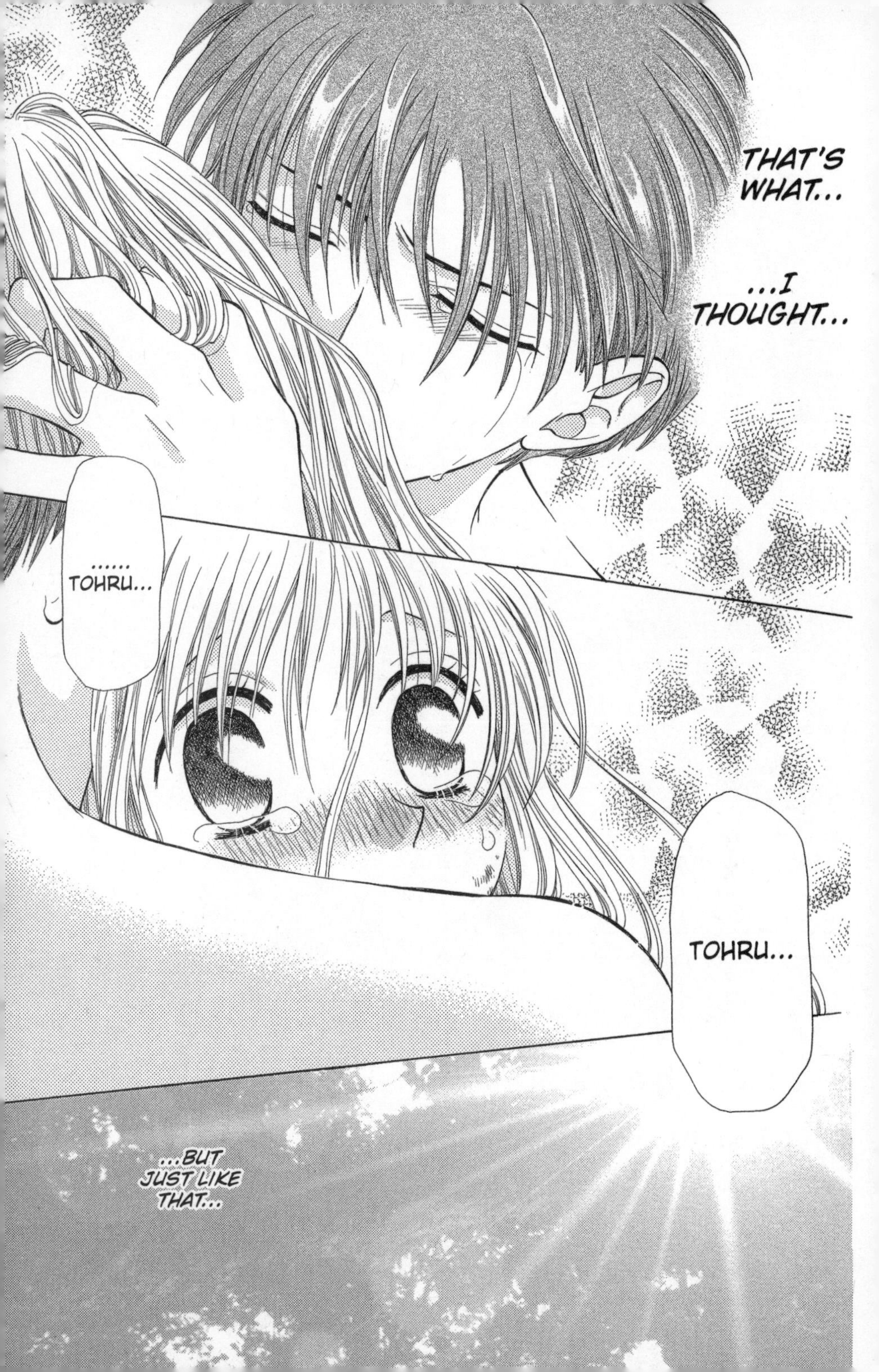
THAT'S WHAT...
...I THOUGHT...
......TOHRU...
TOHRU...
...BUT JUST LIKE THAT...

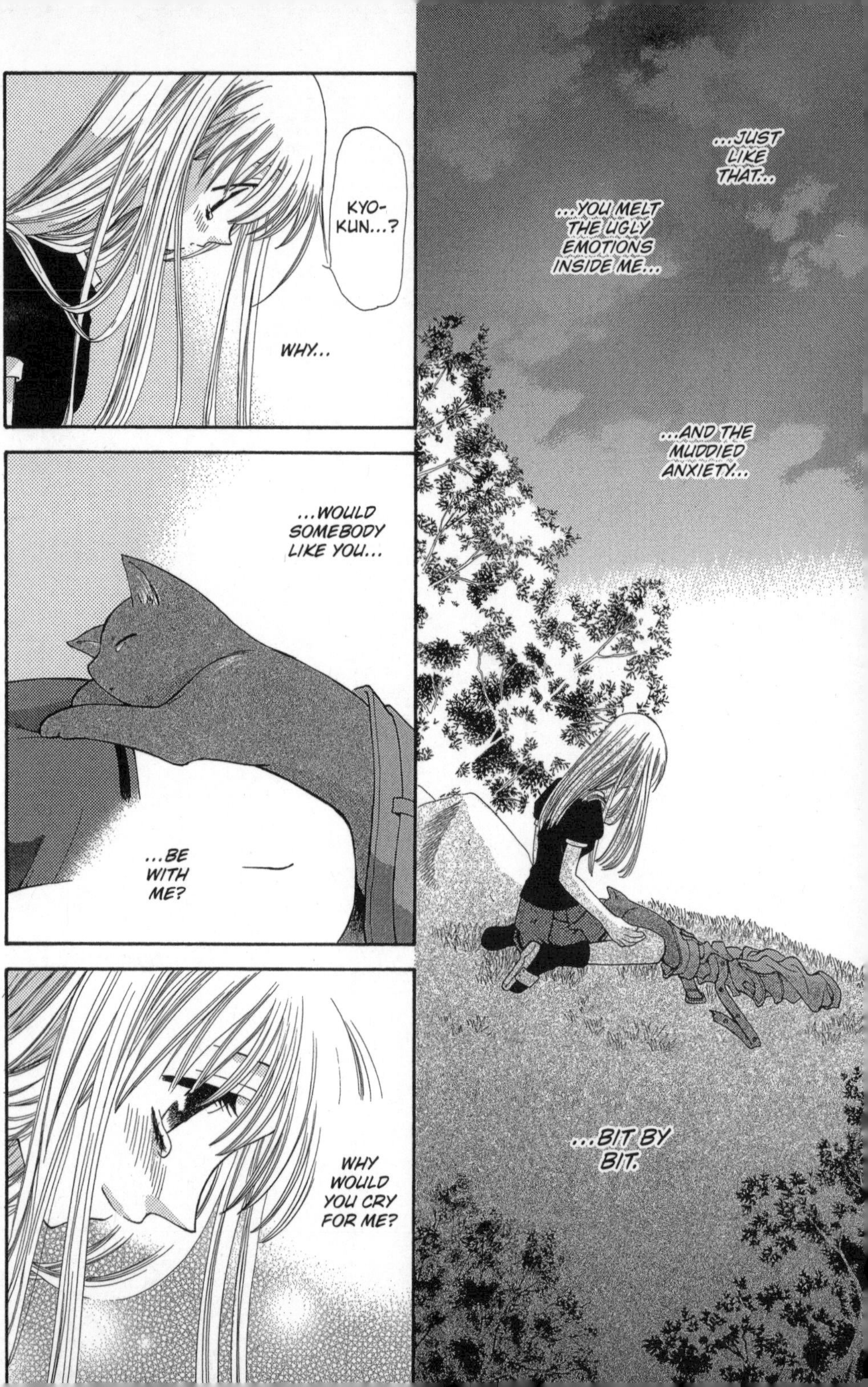
KYO-KUN...?
WHY...
...WOULD SOMEBODY LIKE YOU...
...BE WITH ME?
WHY WOULD YOU CRY FOR ME?
...JUST LIKE THAT...
...YOU MELT THE UGLY EMOTIONS INSIDE ME...
...AND THE MUDDIED ANXIETY...
...BIT BY BIT.

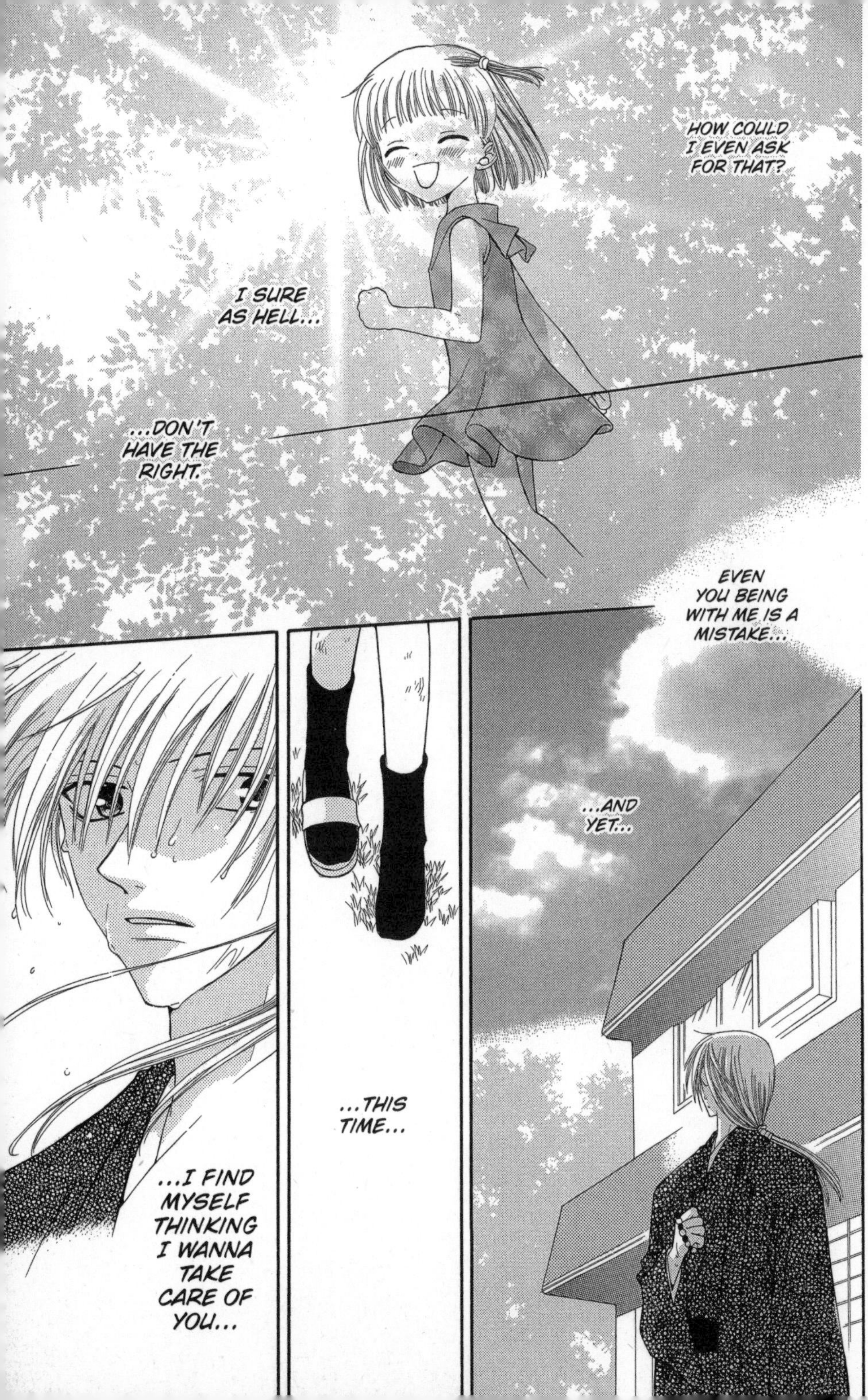
HOW COULD I EVEN ASK FOR THAT?
I SURE AS HELL...
...DON'T HAVE THE RIGHT.
EVEN YOU BEING WITH ME IS A MISTAKE...
...AND YET...
...THIS TIME...
...I FIND MYSELF THINKING I WANNA TAKE CARE OF YOU...

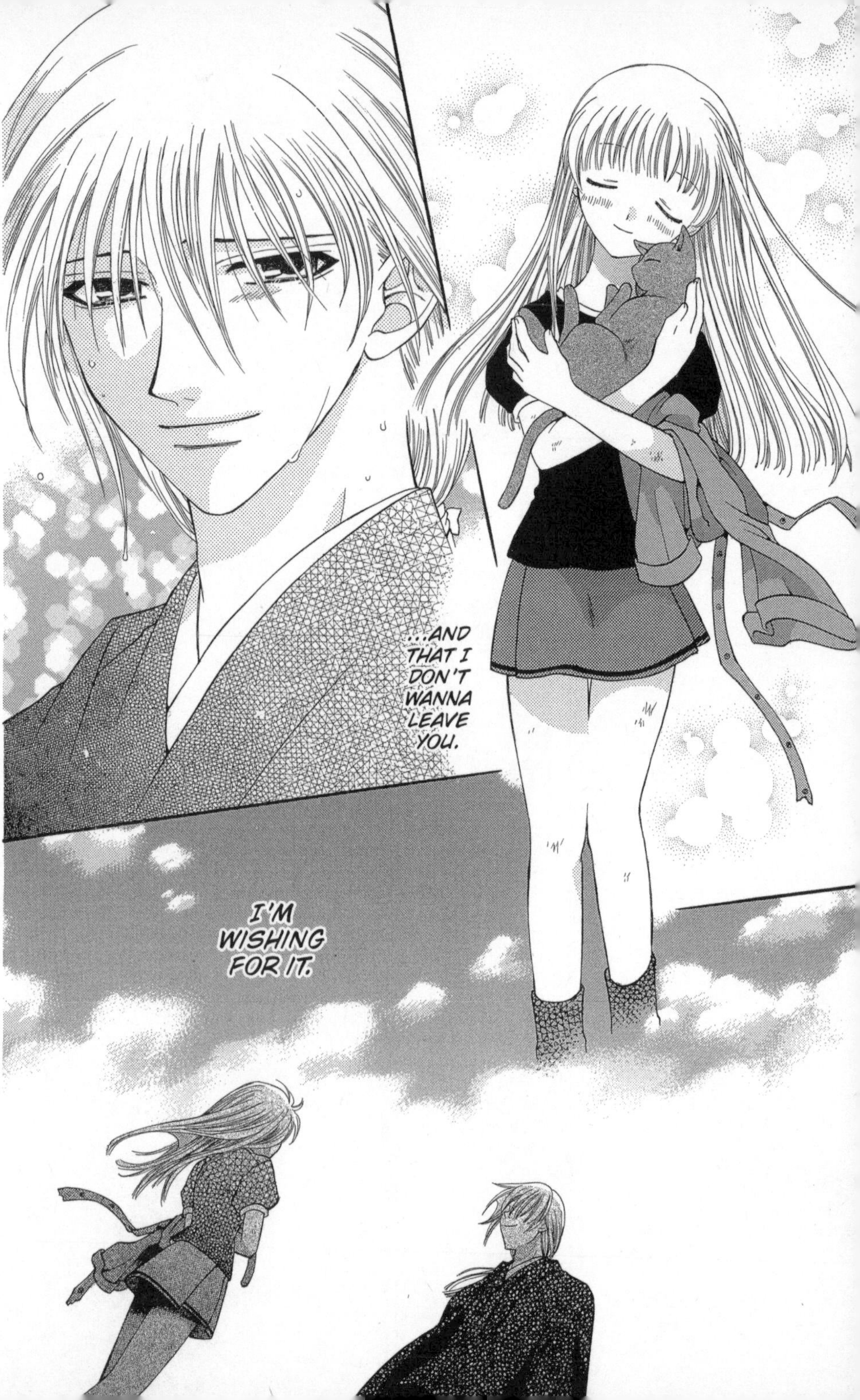
...AND THAT I DON'T WANNA LEAVE YOU.
I'M WISHING FOR IT.

COLLECTOR'S EDITION

Fruits Basket

COLLECTOR'S EDITION

Fruits Basket

Chapter 34

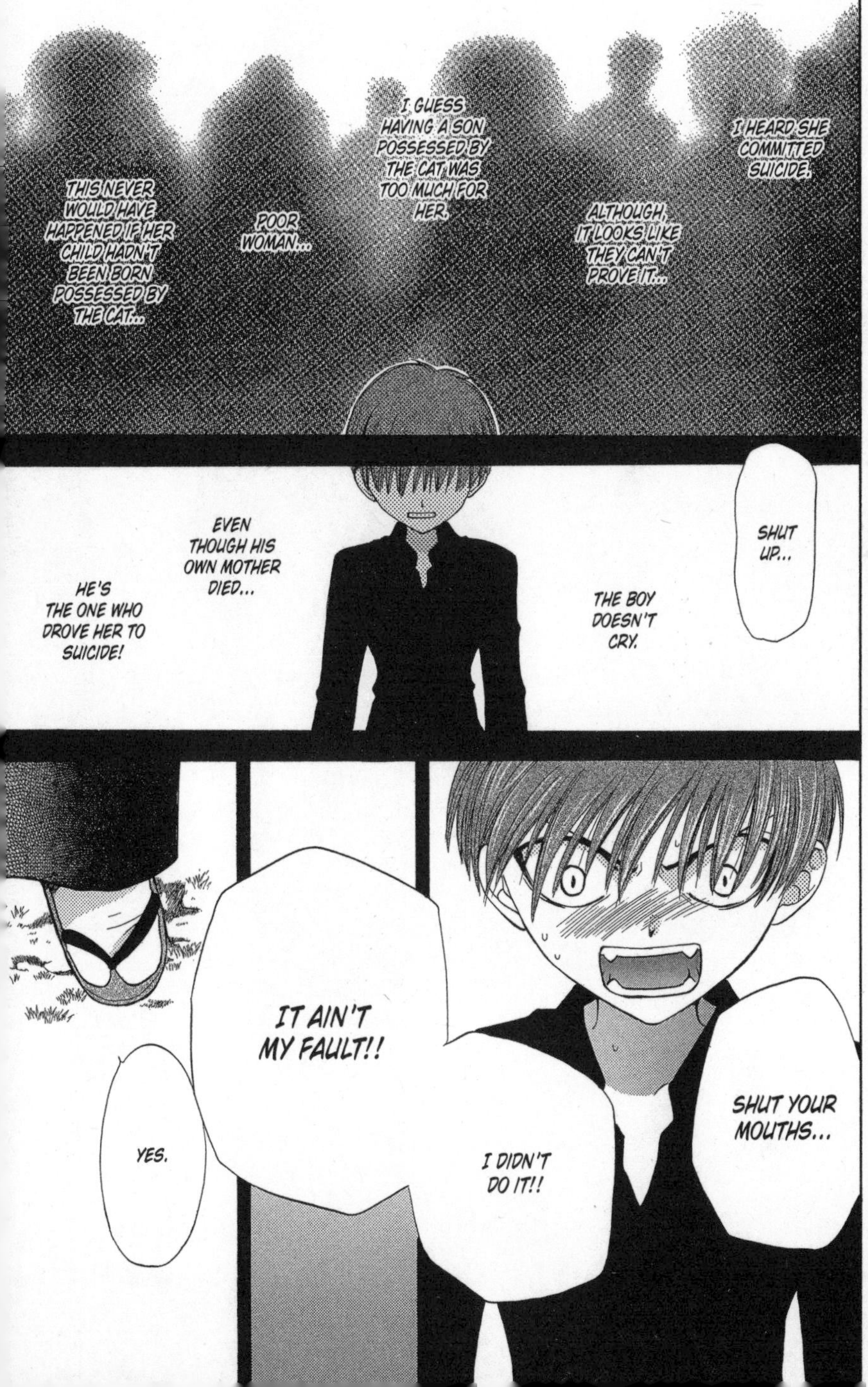
I HEARD SHE COMMITTED SUICIDE.
ALTHOUGH, IT LOOKS LIKE THEY CAN'T PROVE IT...
I GUESS HAVING A SON POSSESSED BY THE CAT WAS TOO MUCH FOR HER.
POOR WOMAN...
THIS NEVER WOULD HAVE HAPPENED IF HER CHILD HADN'T BEEN BORN POSSESSED BY THE CAT...
SHUT UP...
THE BOY DOESN'T CRY.
EVEN THOUGH HIS OWN MOTHER DIED...
HE'S THE ONE WHO DROVE HER TO SUICIDE!
SHUT YOUR MOUTHS...
IT AIN'T MY FAULT!!
I DIDN'T DO IT!!
YES.

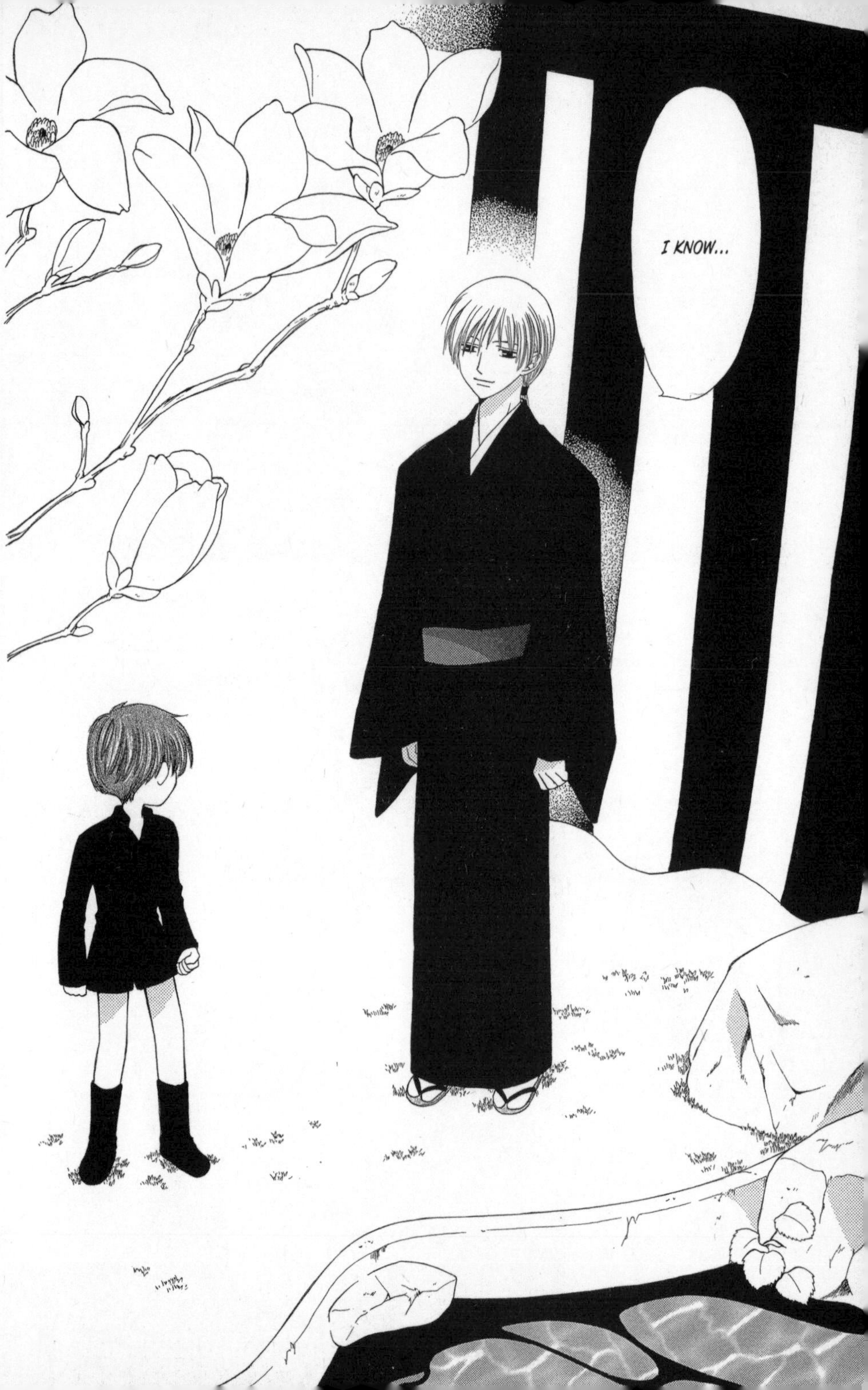
I KNOW...

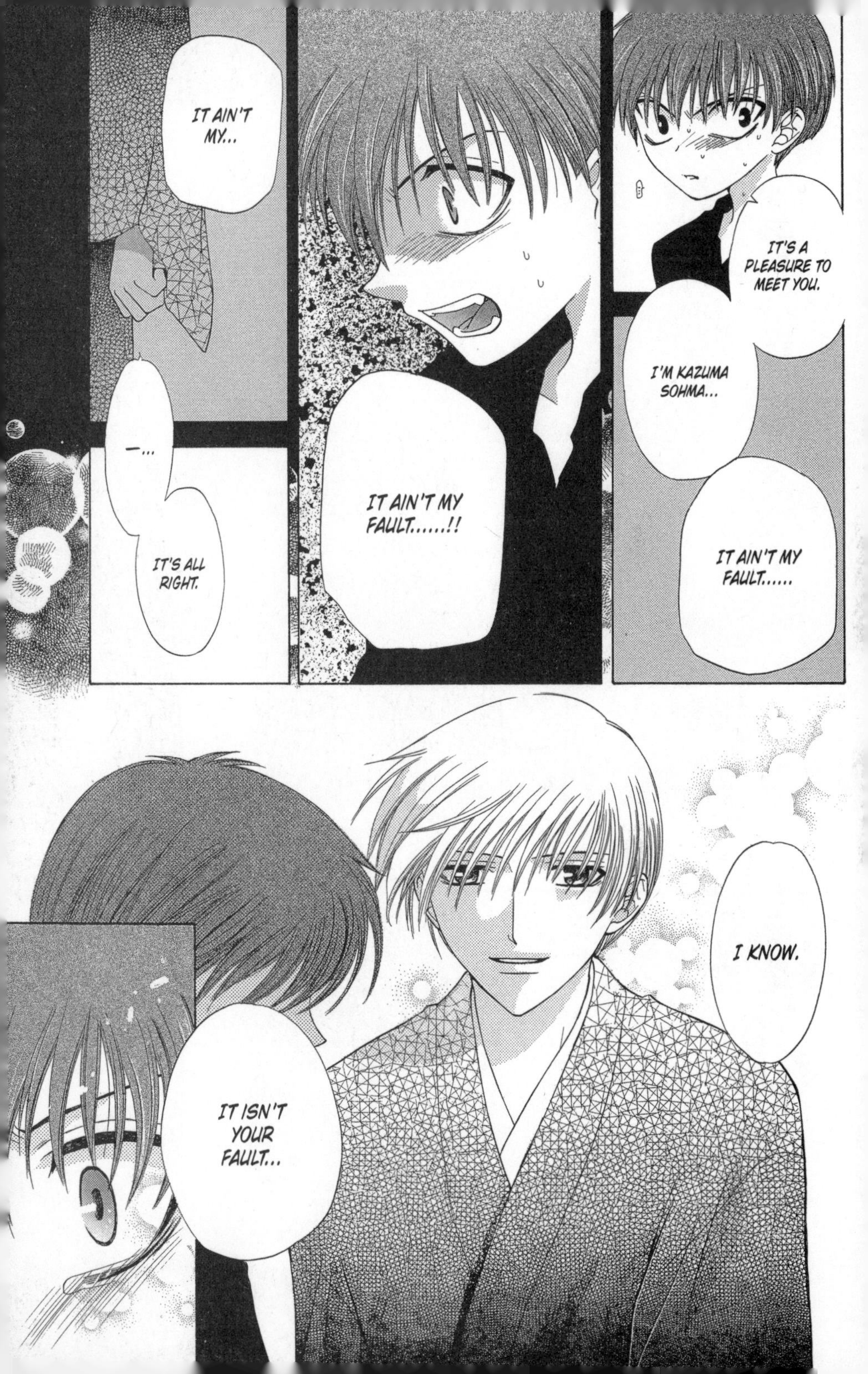
IT'S A PLEASURE TO MEET YOU.
I'M KAZUMA SOHMA...
IT AIN'T MY FAULT......
IT AIN'T MY FAULT......!!
IT AIN'T MY...
—...
IT'S ALL RIGHT.
I KNOW.
IT ISN'T YOUR FAULT...

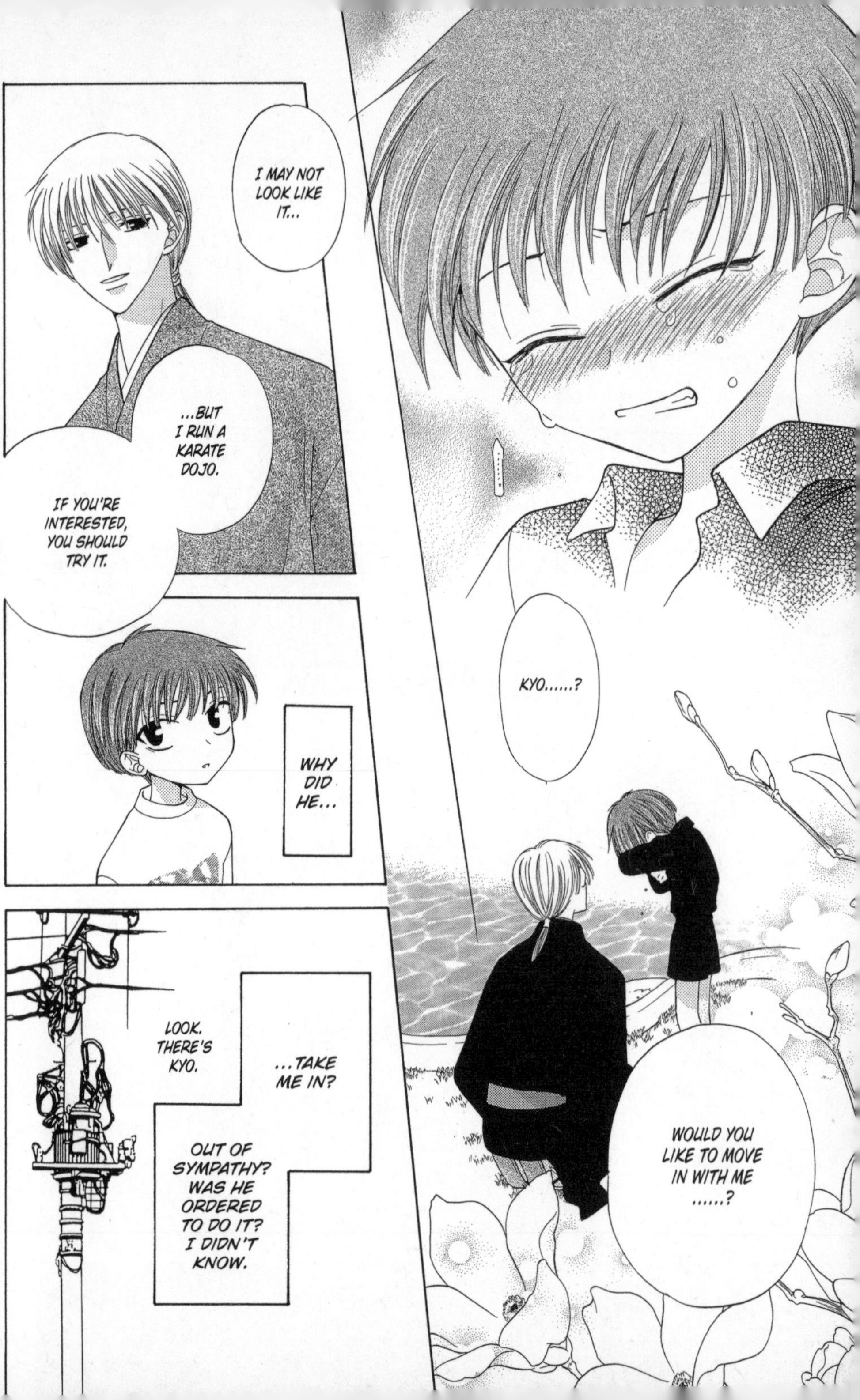
KYO......?
WOULD YOU LIKE TO MOVE IN WITH ME ......?
I MAY NOT LOOK LIKE IT...
...BUT I RUN A KARATE DOJO.
IF YOU'RE INTERESTED, YOU SHOULD TRY IT.
WHY DID HE...
...TAKE ME IN?
LOOK. THERE'S KYO.
OUT OF SYMPATHY? WAS HE ORDERED TO DO IT? I DIDN'T KNOW.

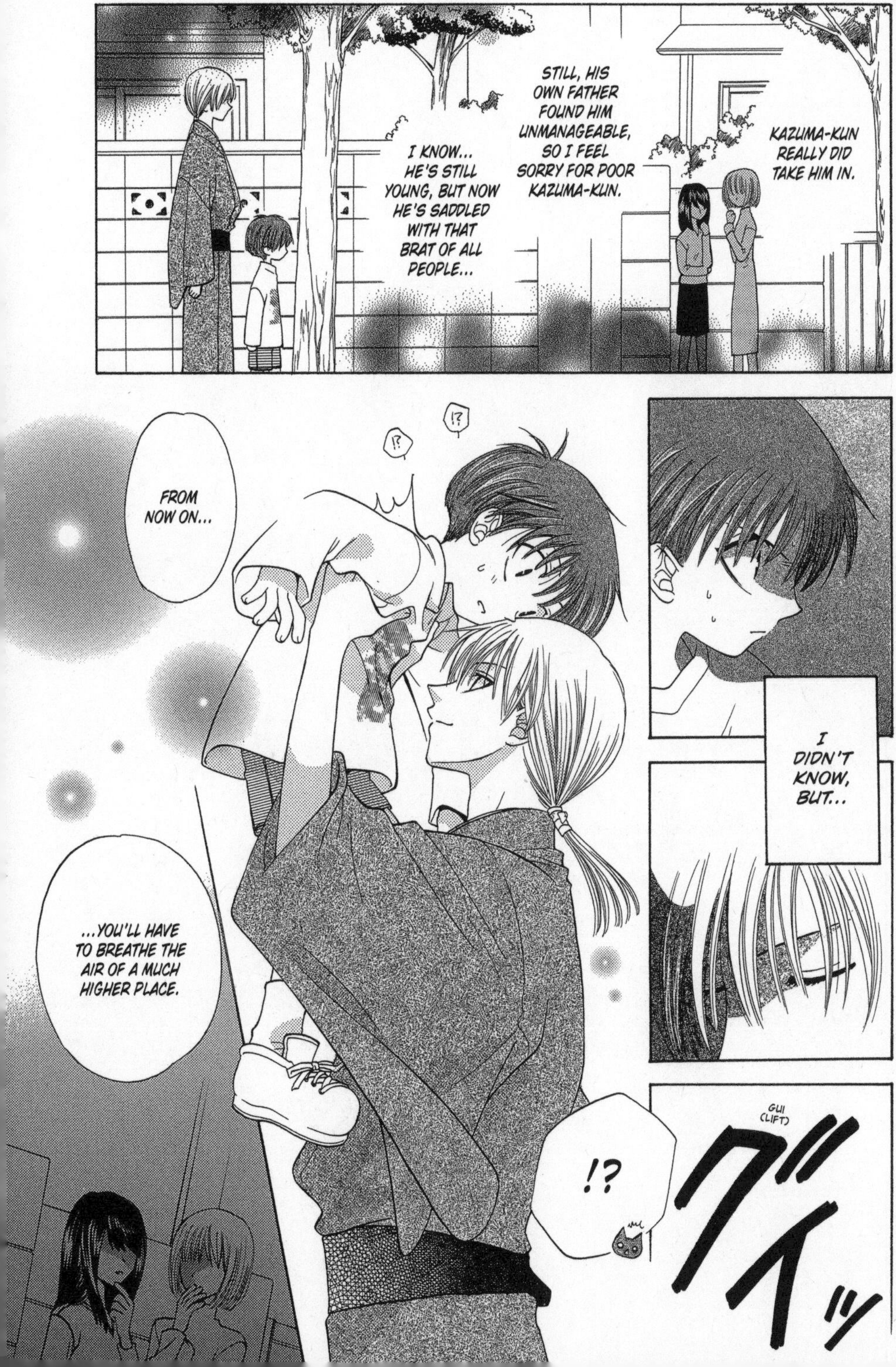
KAZUMA-KUN REALLY DID TAKE HIM IN.
STILL, HIS OWN FATHER FOUND HIM UNMANAGEABLE, SO I FEEL SORRY FOR POOR KAZUMA-KUN.
I KNOW... HE'S STILL YOUNG, BUT NOW HE'S SADDLED WITH THAT BRAT OF ALL PEOPLE...
I DIDN'T KNOW, BUT...
GUI (LIFT)
グイッ
!?
!?
!?
FROM NOW ON...
...YOU'LL HAVE TO BREATHE THE AIR OF A MUCH HIGHER PLACE.

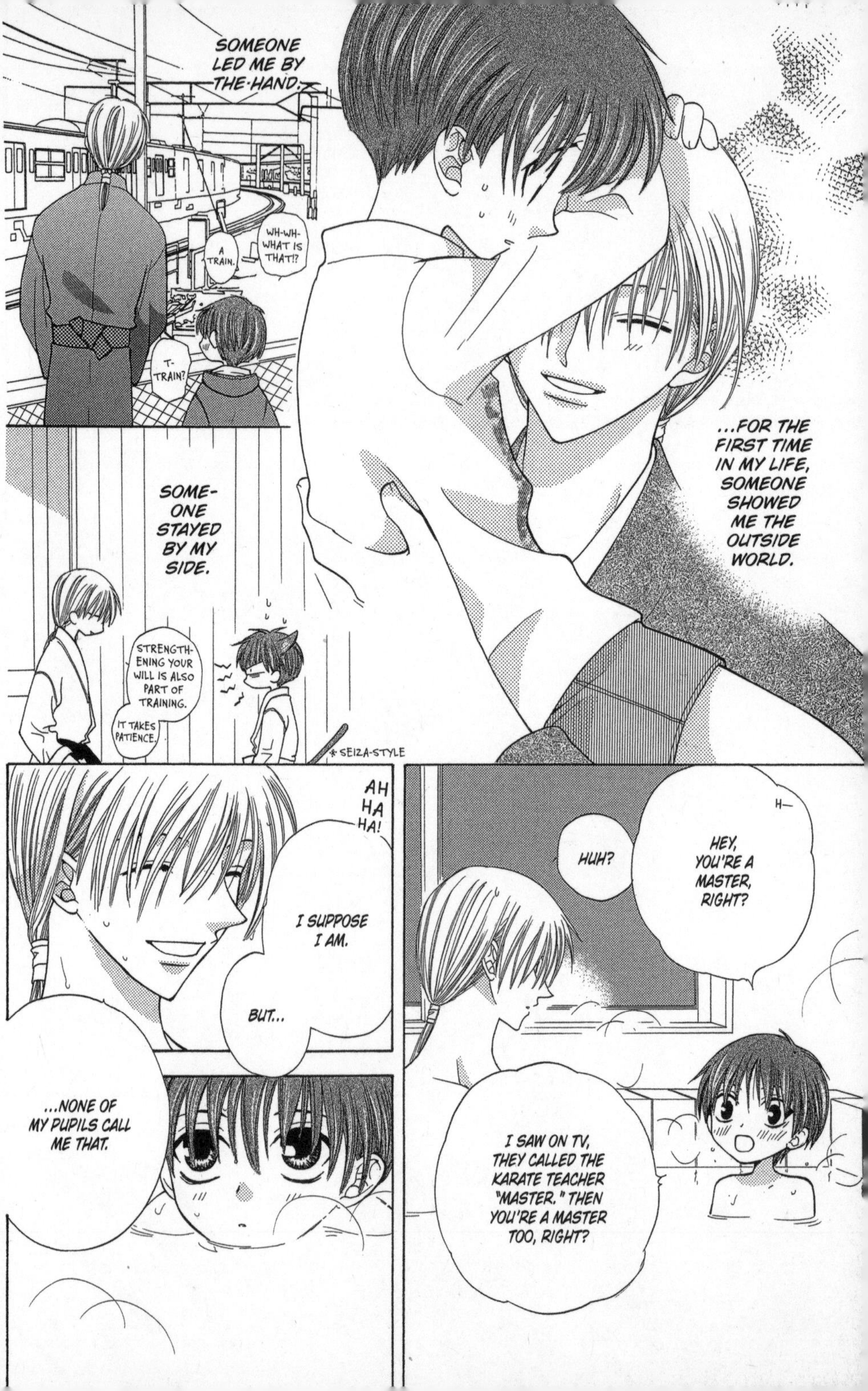
...FOR THE FIRST TIME IN MY LIFE, SOMEONE SHOWED ME THE OUTSIDE WORLD.
SOMEONE LED ME BY THE HAND.
WH-WH- WHAT IS THAT!?
A TRAIN.
T- TRAIN?
SOME- ONE STAYED BY MY SIDE.
STRENGTH- ENING YOUR WILL IS ALSO PART OF TRAINING.
IT TAKES PATIENCE.
* SEIZA-STYLE
H—
HEY, YOU'RE A MASTER, RIGHT?
HUH?
I SAW ON TV, THEY CALLED THE KARATE TEACHER "MASTER." THEN YOU'RE A MASTER TOO, RIGHT?
AH HA HA!
I SUPPOSE I AM.
BUT...
...NONE OF MY PUPILS CALL ME THAT.

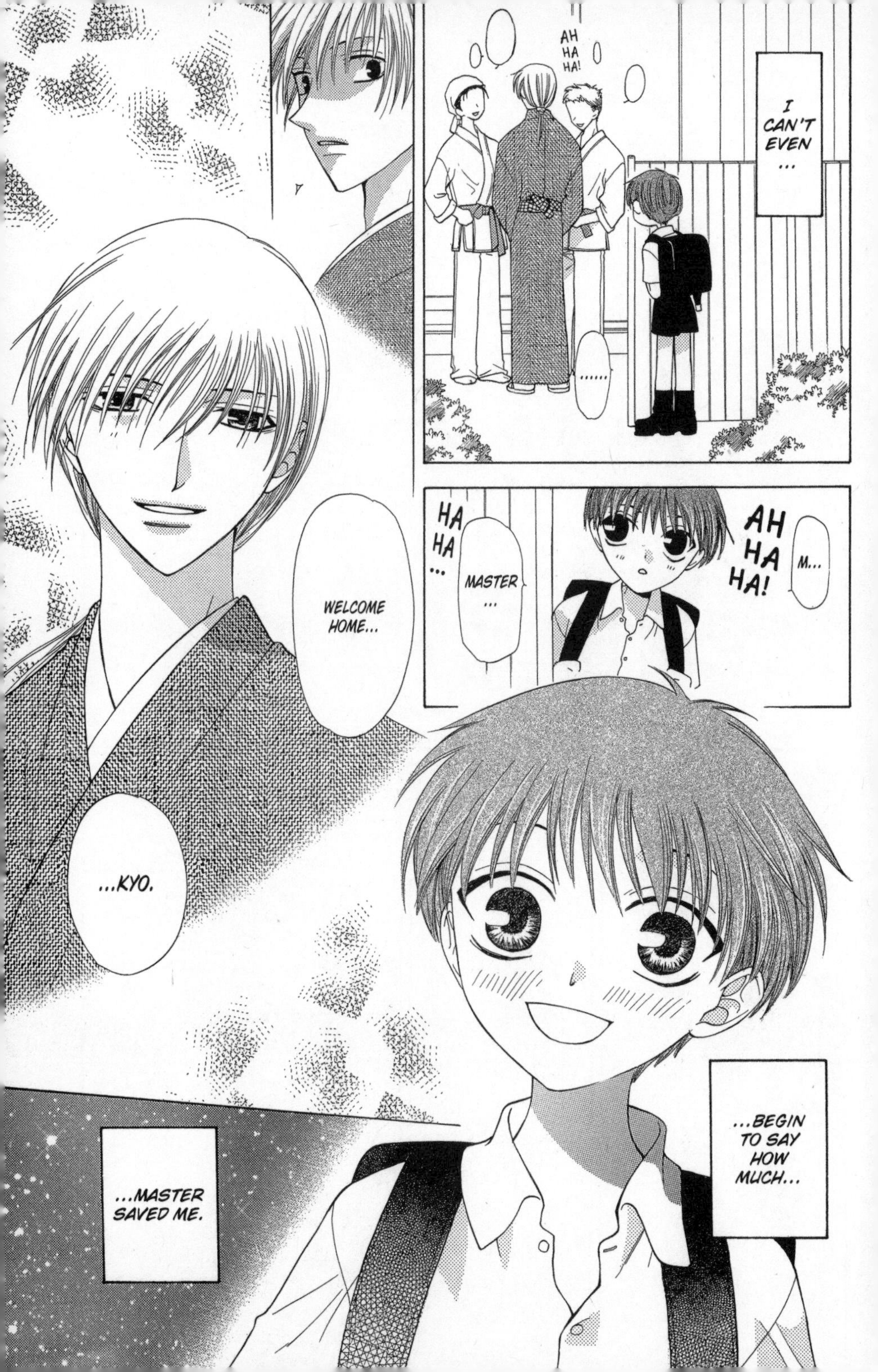
I CAN'T EVEN ...
AH HA HA!
......
AH HA HA!
M...
MASTER ...
HA HA ...
WELCOME HOME...
...KYO.
...BEGIN TO SAY HOW MUCH...
...MASTER SAVED ME.

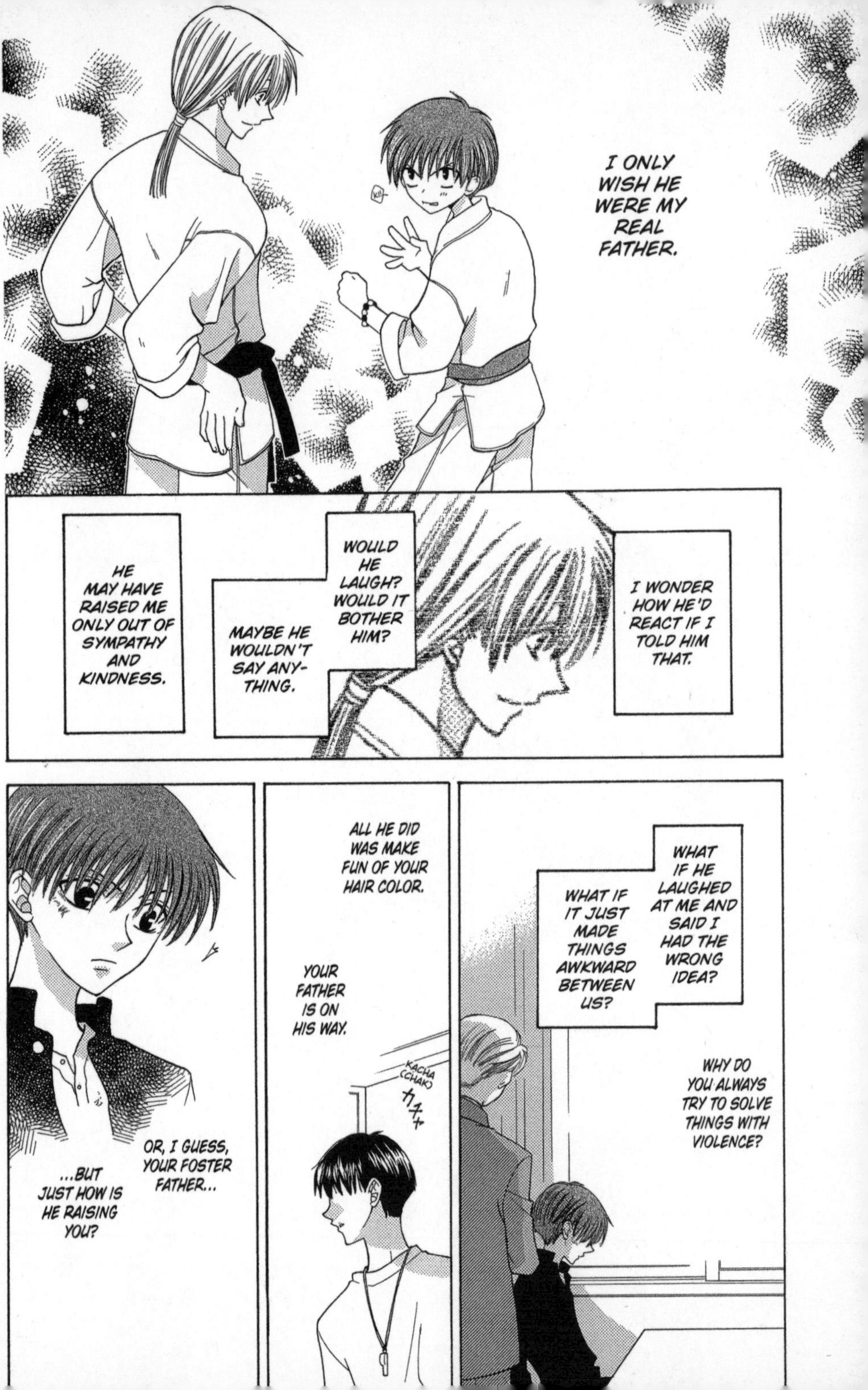
I ONLY WISH HE WERE MY REAL FATHER.
I WONDER HOW HE'D REACT IF I TOLD HIM THAT.
WOULD HE LAUGH? WOULD IT BOTHER HIM?
MAYBE HE WOULDN'T SAY ANY-THING.
HE MAY HAVE RAISED ME ONLY OUT OF SYMPATHY AND KINDNESS.
WHAT IF HE LAUGHED AT ME AND SAID I HAD THE WRONG IDEA?
WHAT IF IT JUST MADE THINGS AWKWARD BETWEEN US?
WHY DO YOU ALWAYS TRY TO SOLVE THINGS WITH VIOLENCE?
ALL HE DID WAS MAKE FUN OF YOUR HAIR COLOR.
YOUR FATHER IS ON HIS WAY.
KACHA (CHAK)
カチャ
OR, I GUESS, YOUR FOSTER FATHER...
...BUT JUST HOW IS HE RAISING YOU?

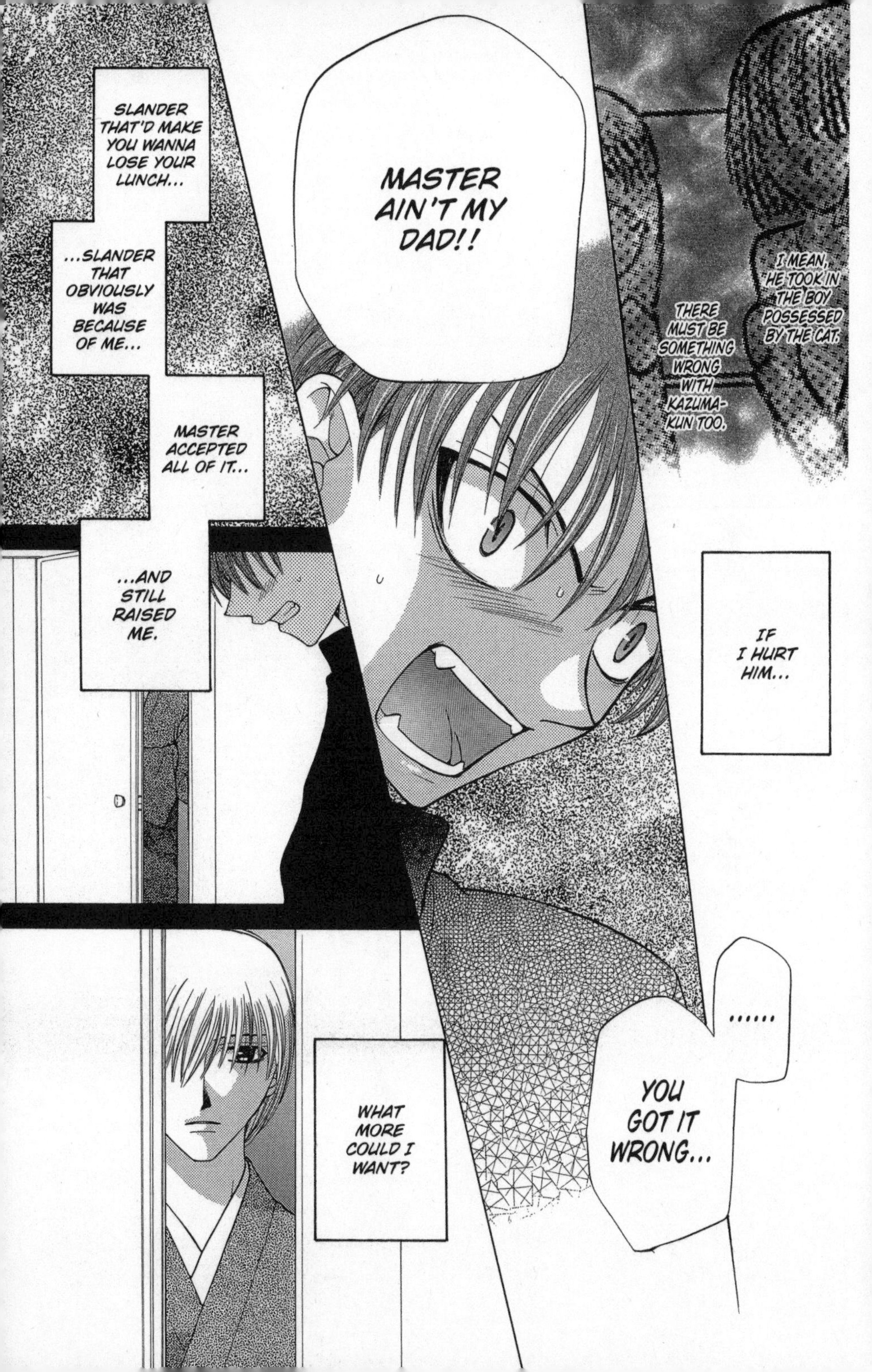
I MEAN, HE TOOK IN THE BOY POSSESSED BY THE CAT.
THERE MUST BE SOMETHING WRONG WITH KAZUMA-KUN TOO.
MASTER AIN'T MY DAD!!
SLANDER THAT'D MAKE YOU WANNA LOSE YOUR LUNCH...
...SLANDER THAT OBVIOUSLY WAS BECAUSE OF ME...
MASTER ACCEPTED ALL OF IT...
...AND STILL RAISED ME.
IF I HURT HIM...
......
YOU GOT IT WRONG...
WHAT MORE COULD I WANT?

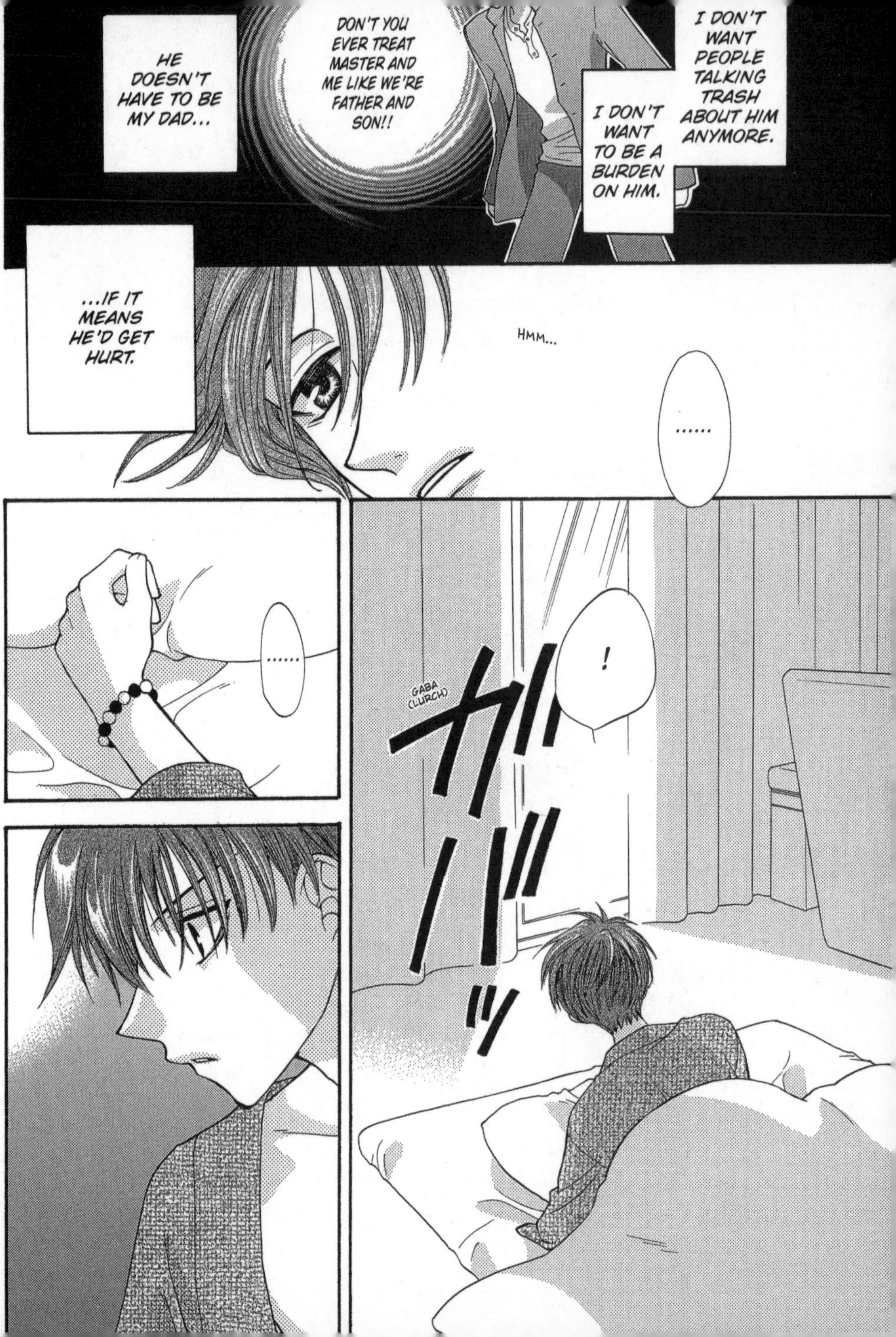
I DON'T WANT PEOPLE TALKING TRASH ABOUT HIM ANYMORE.
I DON'T WANT TO BE A BURDEN ON HIM.
DON'T YOU EVER TREAT MASTER AND ME LIKE WE'RE FATHER AND SON!!
HE DOESN'T HAVE TO BE MY DAD...
...IF IT MEANS HE'D GET HURT.
HMM...
......
!
ガバッ
GABA (LURCH)
......

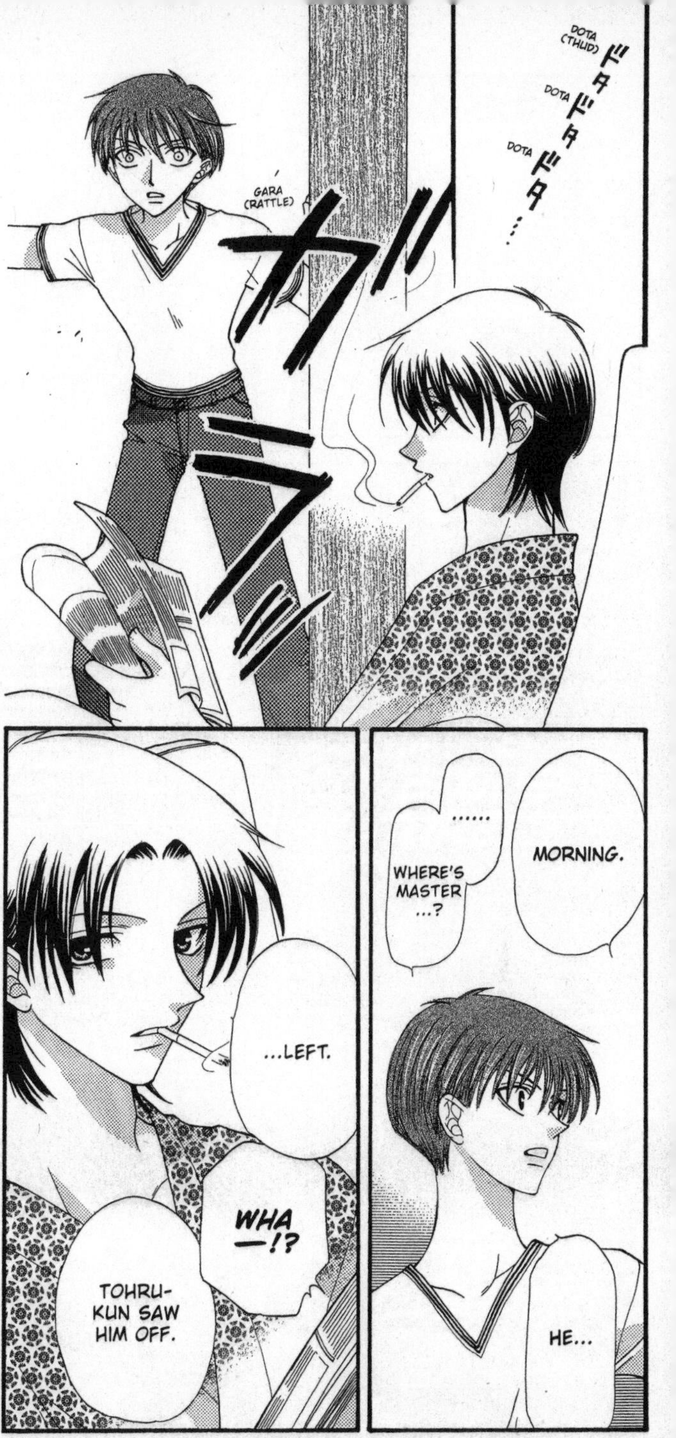
DOTA (THUD) ドタ
DOTA ドタ
DOTA ドタ...
GARA (RATTLE) ガラ
MORNING.
......
WHERE'S MASTER ...?
HE...
...LEFT.
WHA—!?
TOHRU-KUN SAW HIM OFF.

Fruits Basket

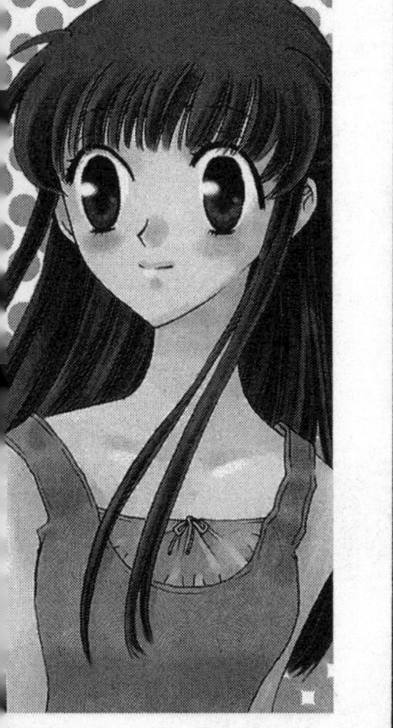

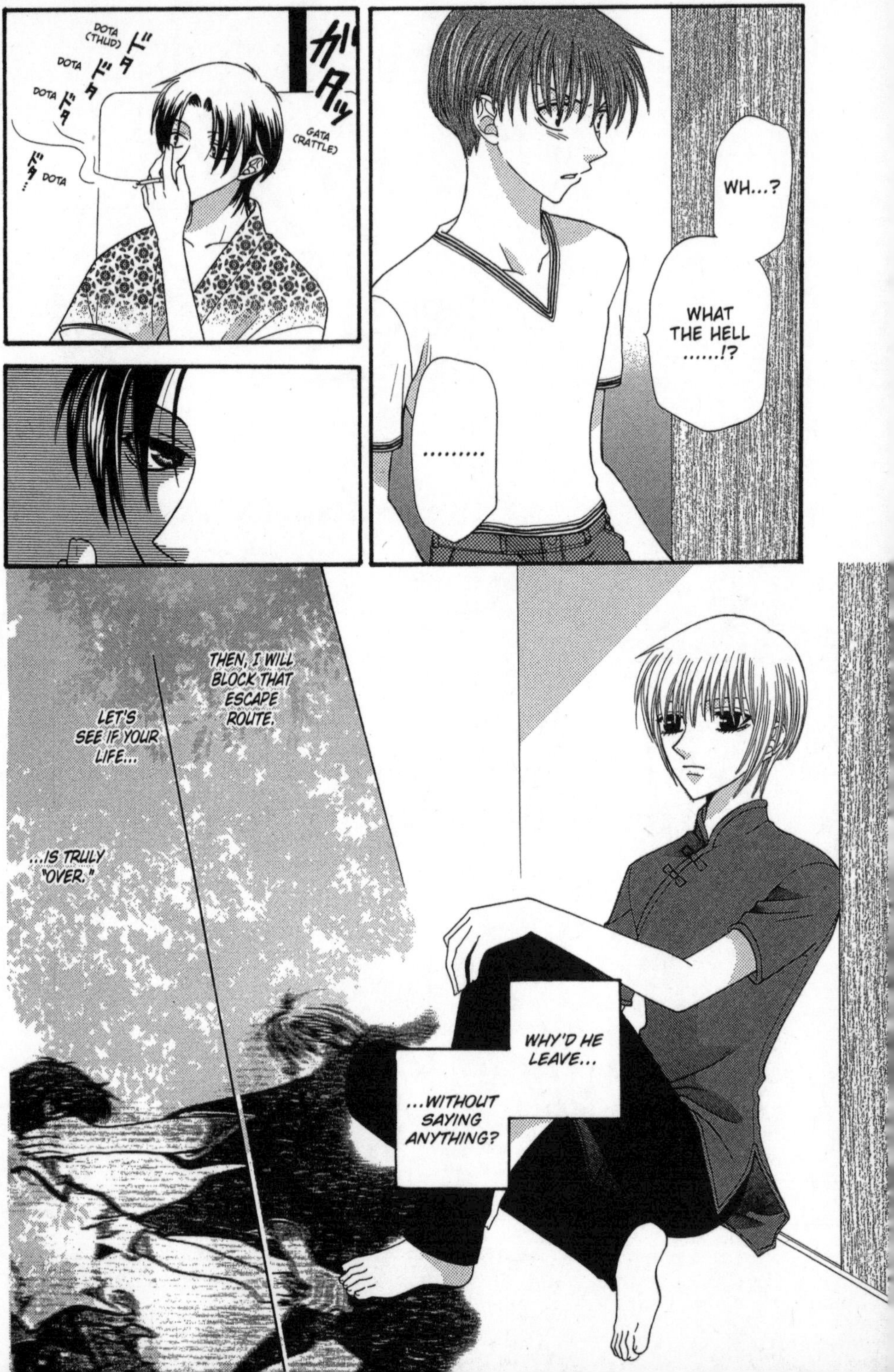
WH...?
WHAT THE HELL ......!?
....
ガタッ
GATA (RATTLE)
ドタ
DOTA (THUD)
ドタ
DOTA
ドタ
DOTA
ドタ...
DOTA
WHY'D HE LEAVE...
...WITHOUT SAYING ANYTHING?
THEN, I WILL BLOCK THAT ESCAPE ROUTE.
LET'S SEE IF YOUR LIFE...
...IS TRULY "OVER."

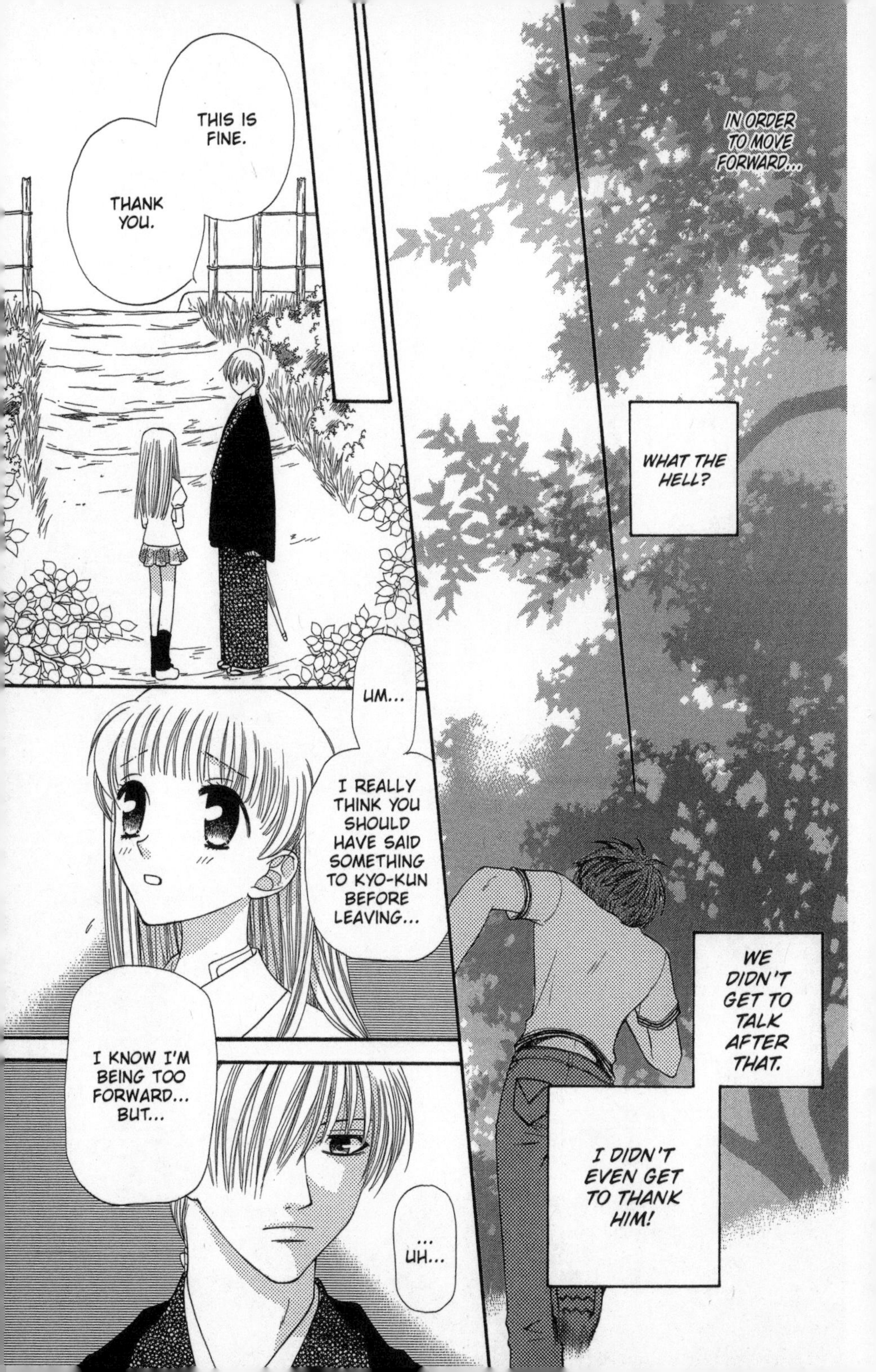
IN ORDER TO MOVE FORWARD...
WHAT THE HELL?
WE DIDN'T GET TO TALK AFTER THAT.
I DIDN'T EVEN GET TO THANK HIM!
THIS IS FINE.
THANK YOU.
UM...
I REALLY THINK YOU SHOULD HAVE SAID SOMETHING TO KYO-KUN BEFORE LEAVING...
I KNOW I'M BEING TOO FORWARD... BUT...
... UH...

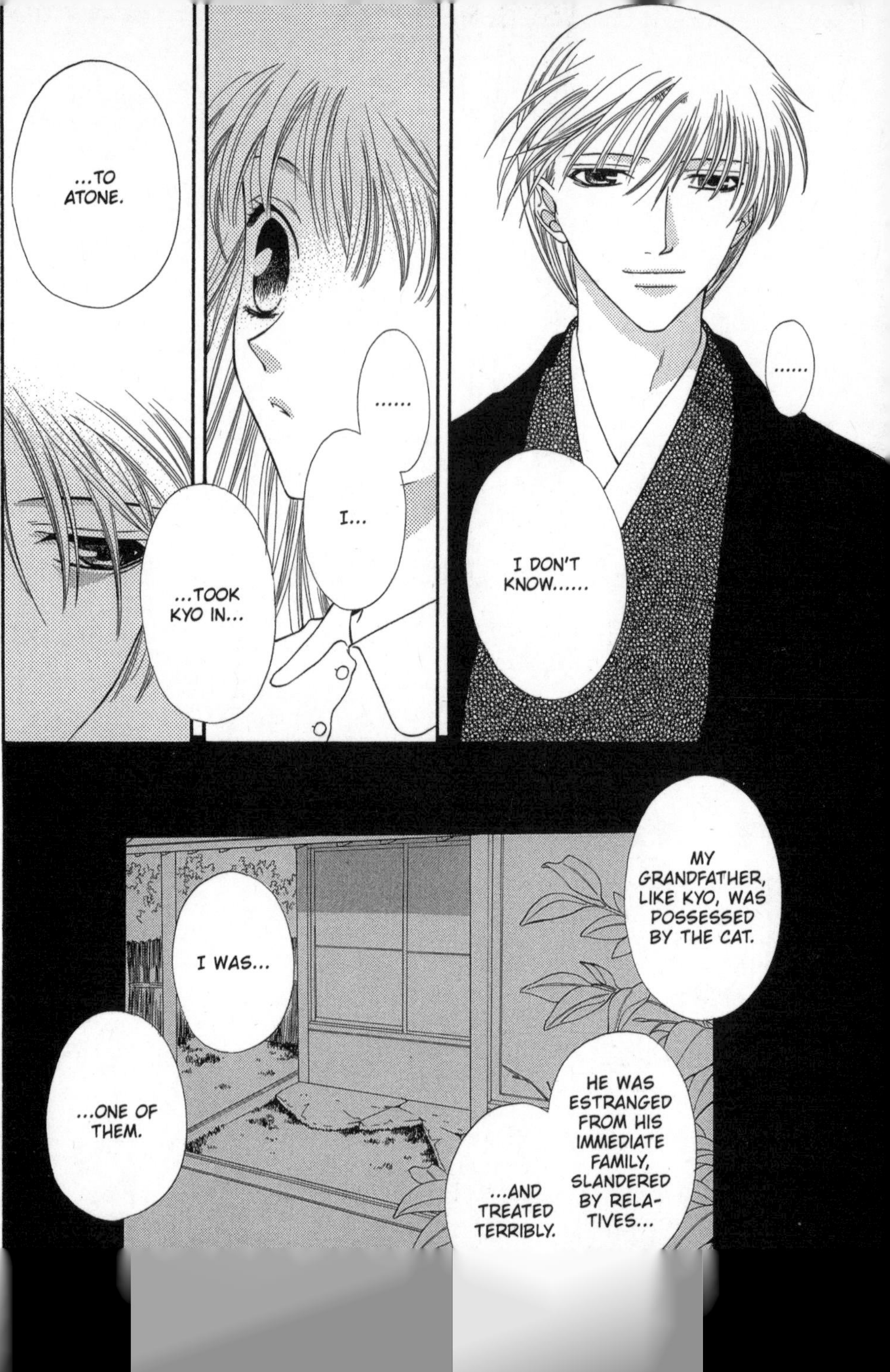
......
I DON'T KNOW......
......
I...
...TOOK KYO IN...
...TO ATONE.
MY GRANDFATHER, LIKE KYO, WAS POSSESSED BY THE CAT.
HE WAS ESTRANGED FROM HIS IMMEDIATE FAMILY, SLANDERED BY RELA-TIVES...
...AND TREATED TERRIBLY.
I WAS...
...ONE OF THEM.

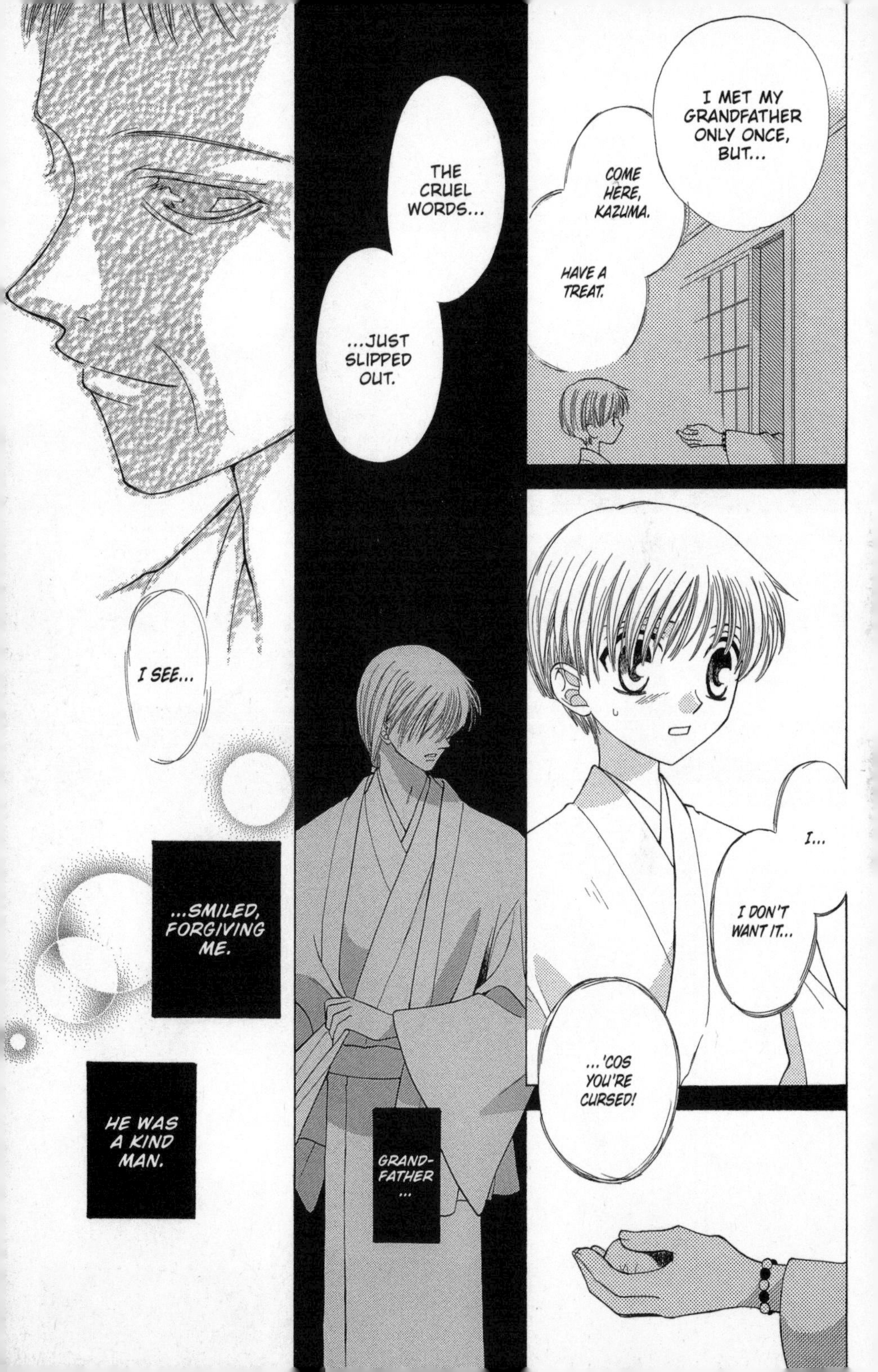
I MET MY GRANDFATHER ONLY ONCE, BUT...
COME HERE, KAZUMA.
HAVE A TREAT.
I...
I DON'T WANT IT...
...'COS YOU'RE CURSED!
THE CRUEL WORDS...
...JUST SLIPPED OUT.
GRAND-FATHER ...
I SEE...
...SMILED, FORGIVING ME.
HE WAS A KIND MAN.

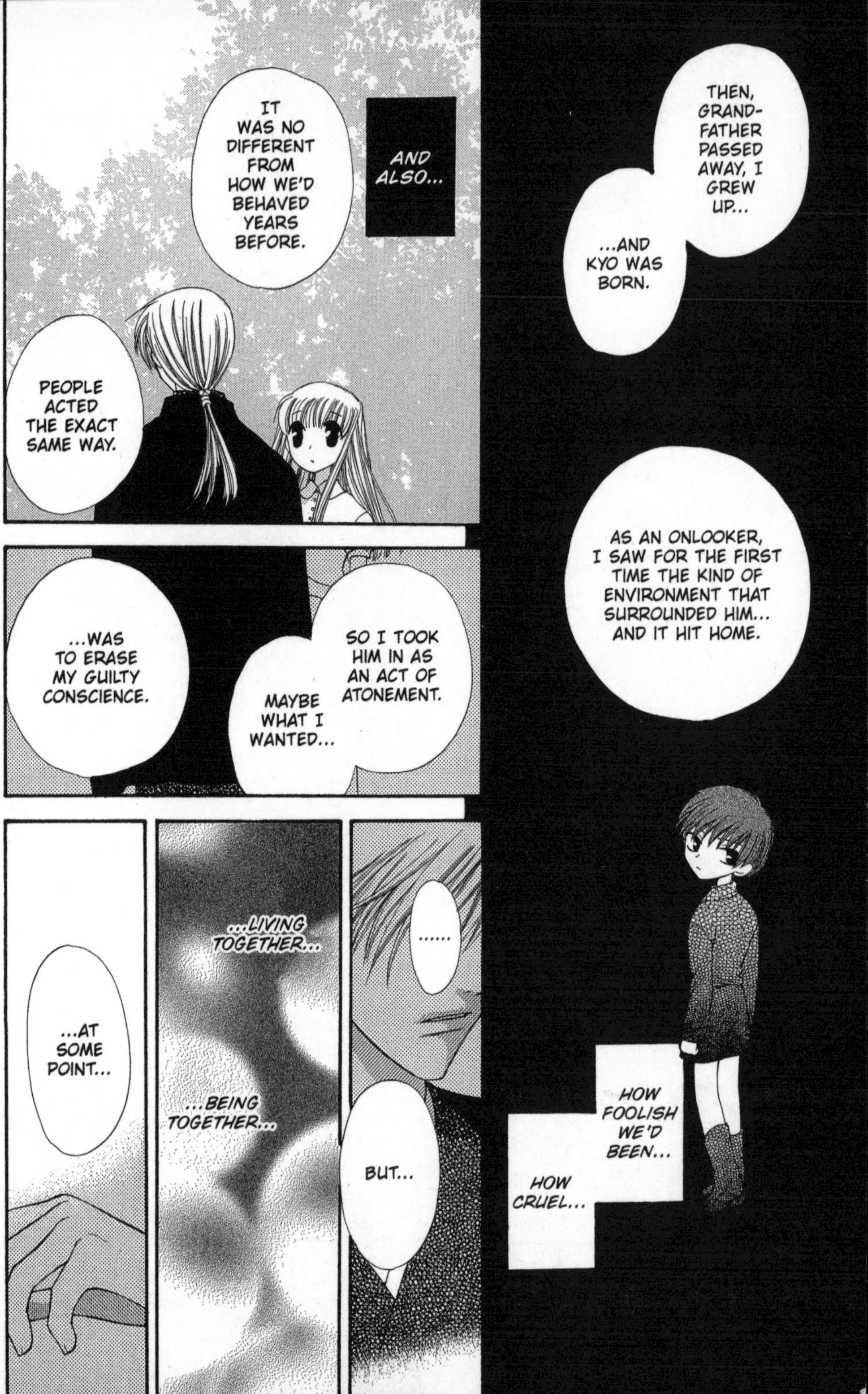
THEN, GRAND-FATHER PASSED AWAY, I GREW UP...
...AND KYO WAS BORN.
AS AN ONLOOKER, I SAW FOR THE FIRST TIME THE KIND OF ENVIRONMENT THAT SURROUNDED HIM... AND IT HIT HOME.
HOW FOOLISH WE'D BEEN...
HOW CRUEL...
AND ALSO...
IT WAS NO DIFFERENT FROM HOW WE'D BEHAVED YEARS BEFORE.
PEOPLE ACTED THE EXACT SAME WAY.
SO I TOOK HIM IN AS AN ACT OF ATONEMENT.
MAYBE WHAT I WANTED...
...WAS TO ERASE MY GUILTY CONSCIENCE.
......
BUT...
...LIVING TOGETHER...
...BEING TOGETHER...
...AT SOME POINT...

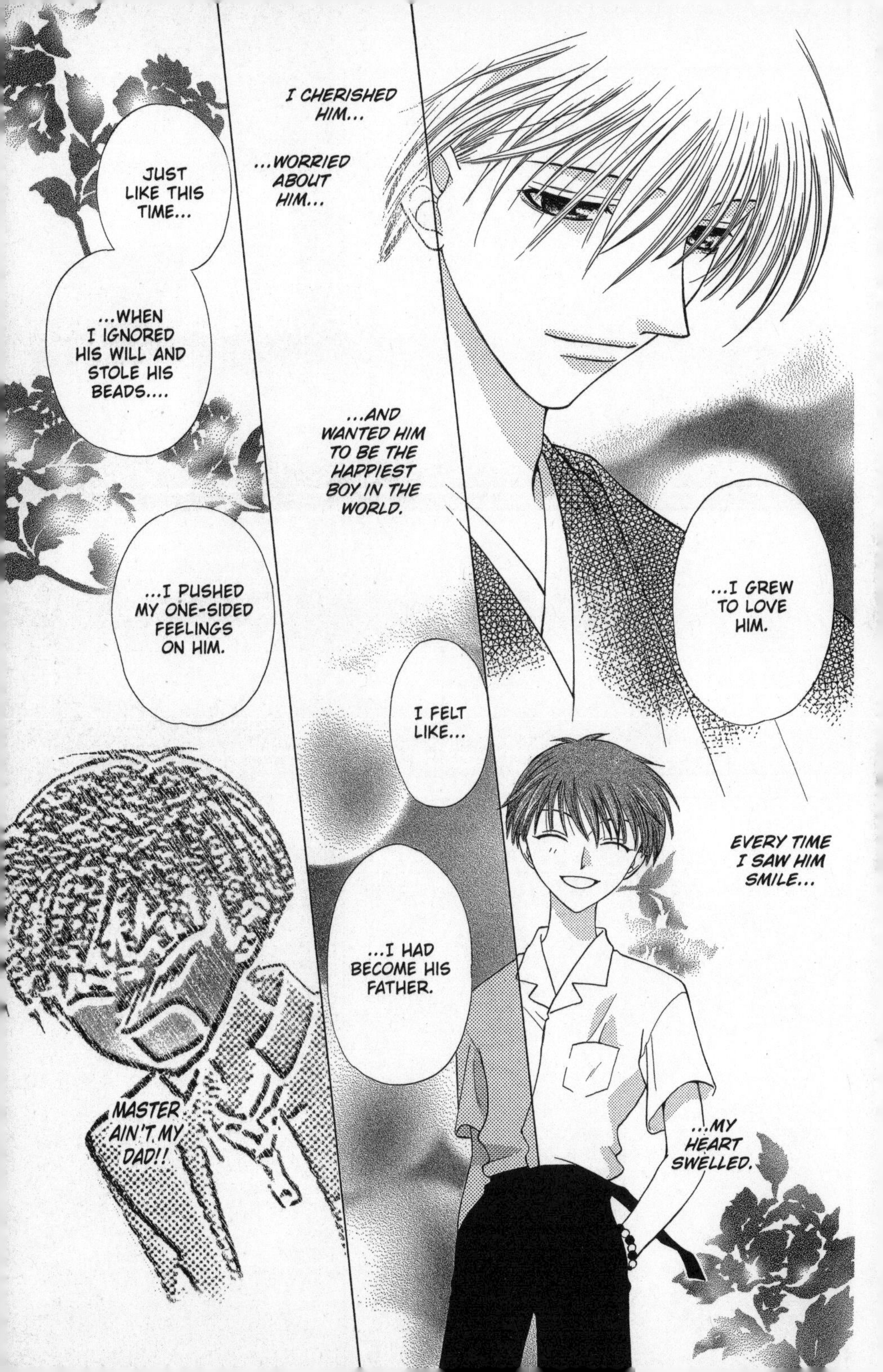
I CHERISHED HIM...
...WORRIED ABOUT HIM...
...AND WANTED HIM TO BE THE HAPPIEST BOY IN THE WORLD.
...I GREW TO LOVE HIM.
EVERY TIME I SAW HIM SMILE...
...MY HEART SWELLED.
I FELT LIKE...
...I HAD BECOME HIS FATHER.
JUST LIKE THIS TIME...
...WHEN I IGNORED HIS WILL AND STOLE HIS BEADS....
...I PUSHED MY ONE-SIDED FEELINGS ON HIM.
MASTER AIN'T MY DAD!!

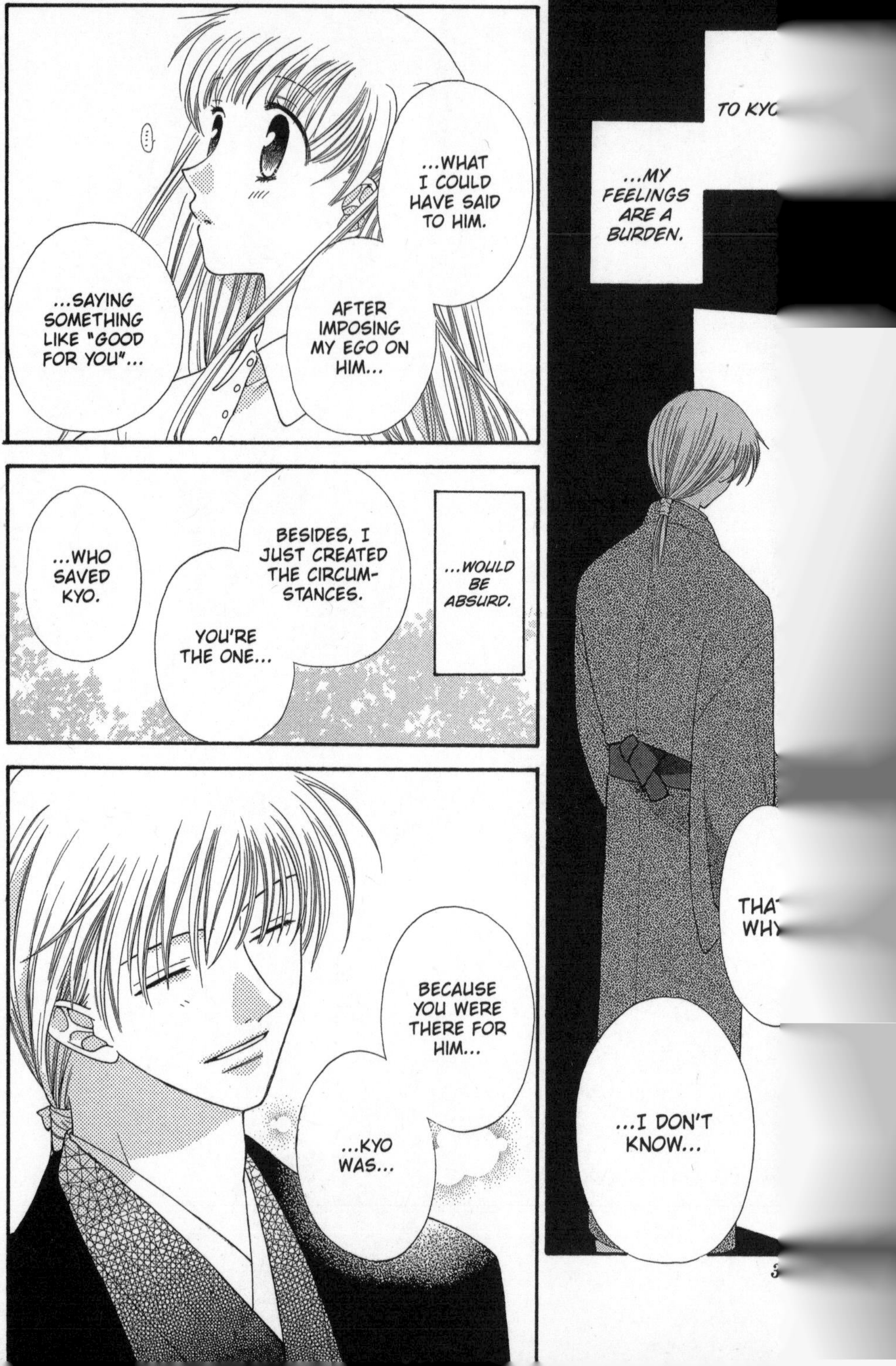
...MY FEELINGS ARE A BURDEN.
...I DON'T KNOW...
...WHAT I COULD HAVE SAID TO HIM.
AFTER IMPOSING MY EGO ON HIM...
...SAYING SOMETHING LIKE "GOOD FOR YOU"...
...WOULD BE ABSURD.
BESIDES, I JUST CREATED THE CIRCUM-STANCES.
YOU'RE THE ONE...
...WHO SAVED KYO.
BECAUSE YOU WERE THERE FOR HIM...
...KYO WAS...

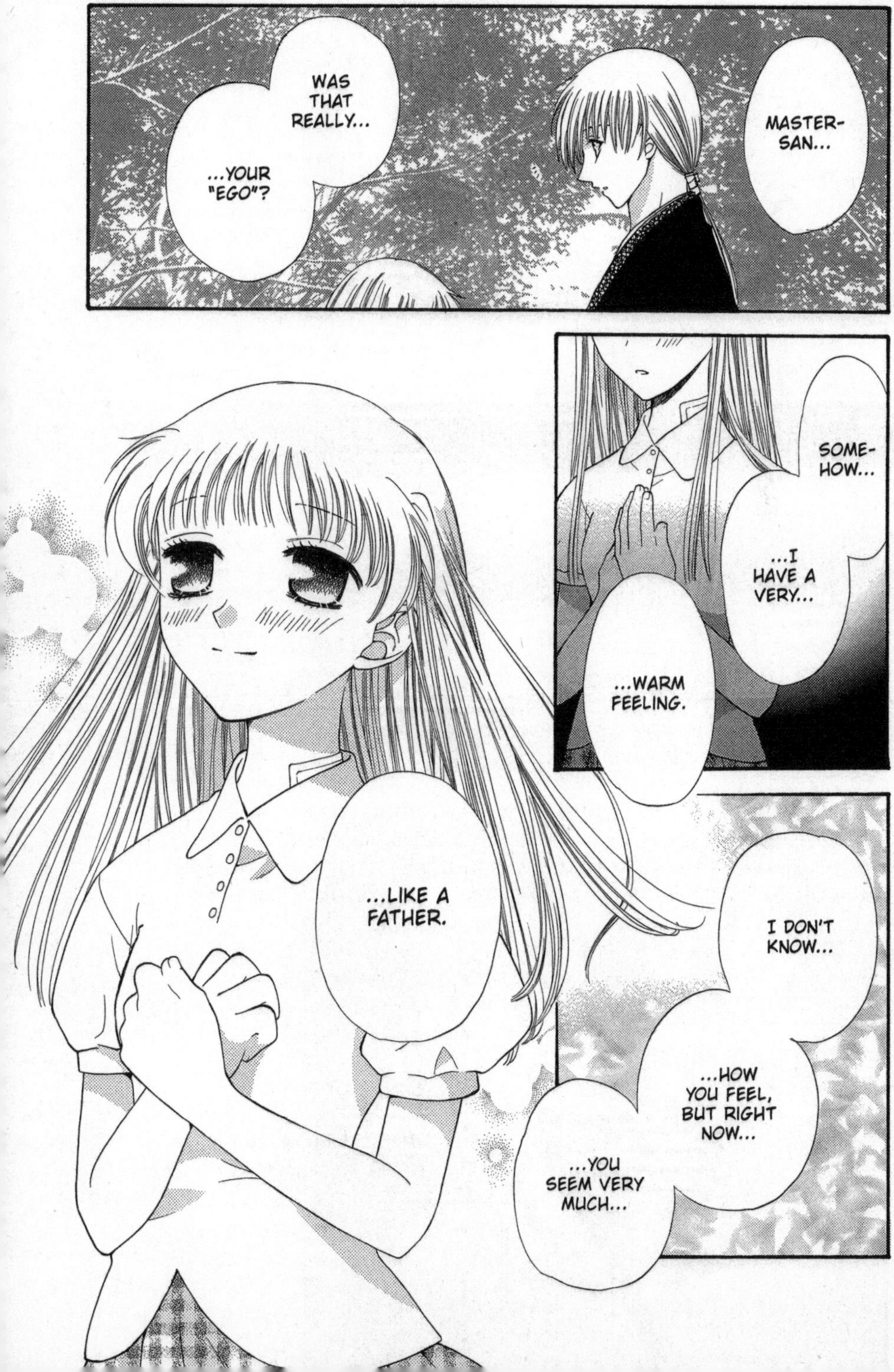
MASTER-SAN...
WAS THAT REALLY...
...YOUR "EGO"?
SOME-HOW...
...I HAVE A VERY...
...WARM FEELING.
I DON'T KNOW...
...HOW YOU FEEL, BUT RIGHT NOW...
...YOU SEEM VERY MUCH...
...LIKE A FATHER.

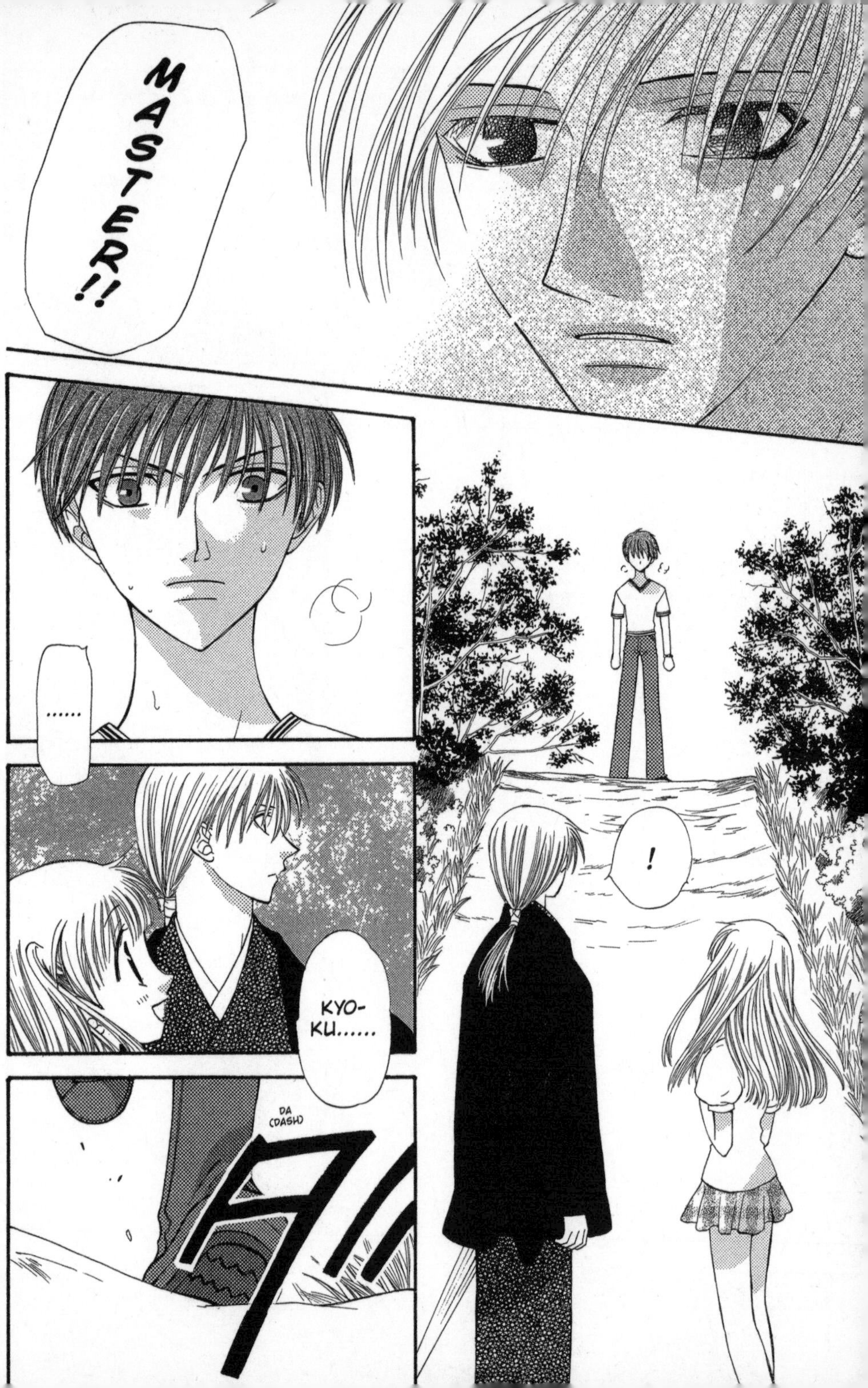
MASTER!!
!
......
KYO-KU......
DA (DASH)

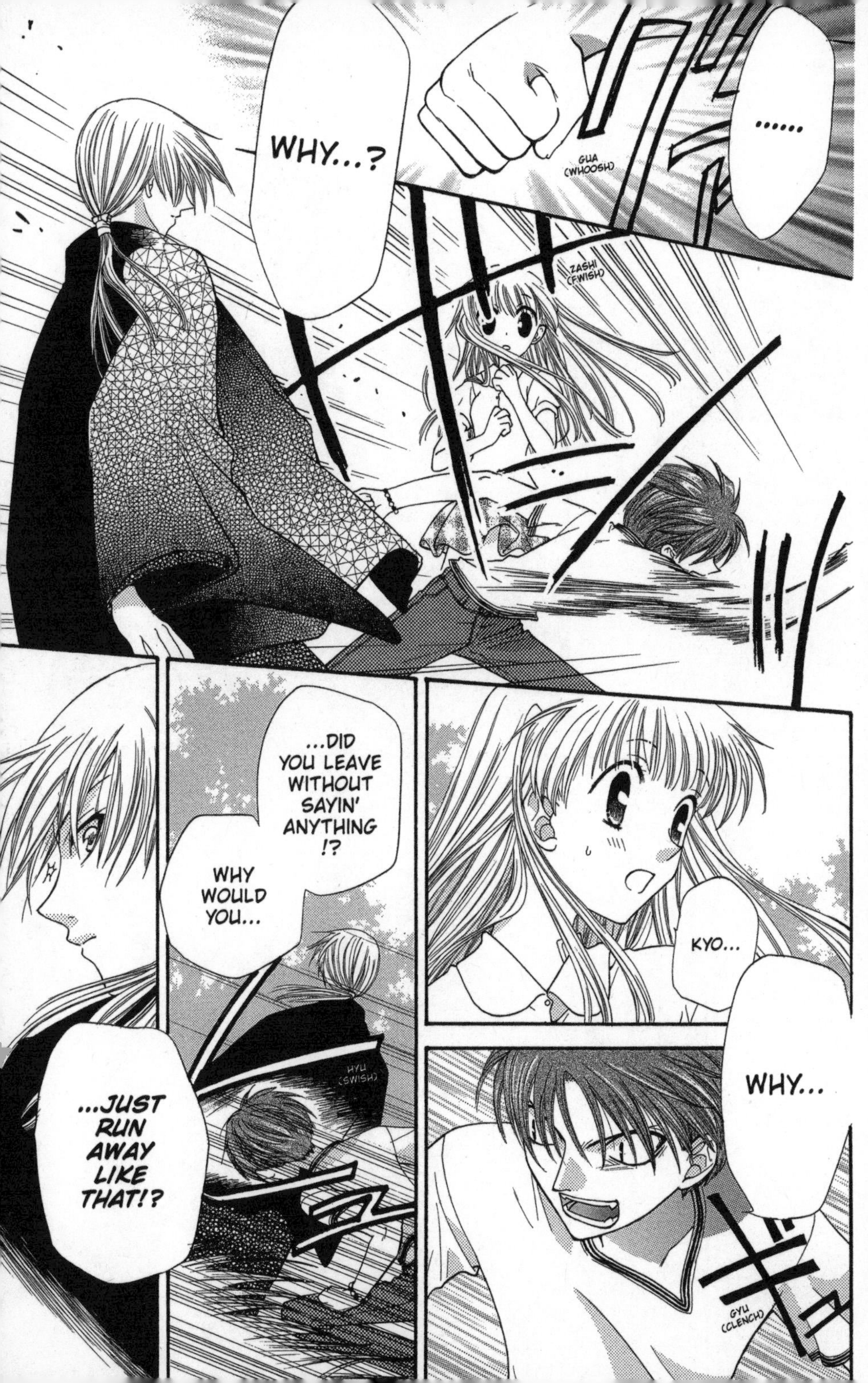
......
GUA (WHOOSH)
WHY...?
ZASHI (FWISH)
KYO...
WHY...
GYU (CLENCH)
...DID YOU LEAVE WITHOUT SAYIN' ANYTHING!?
WHY WOULD YOU...
HYU (SWISH)
...JUST RUN AWAY LIKE THAT!?

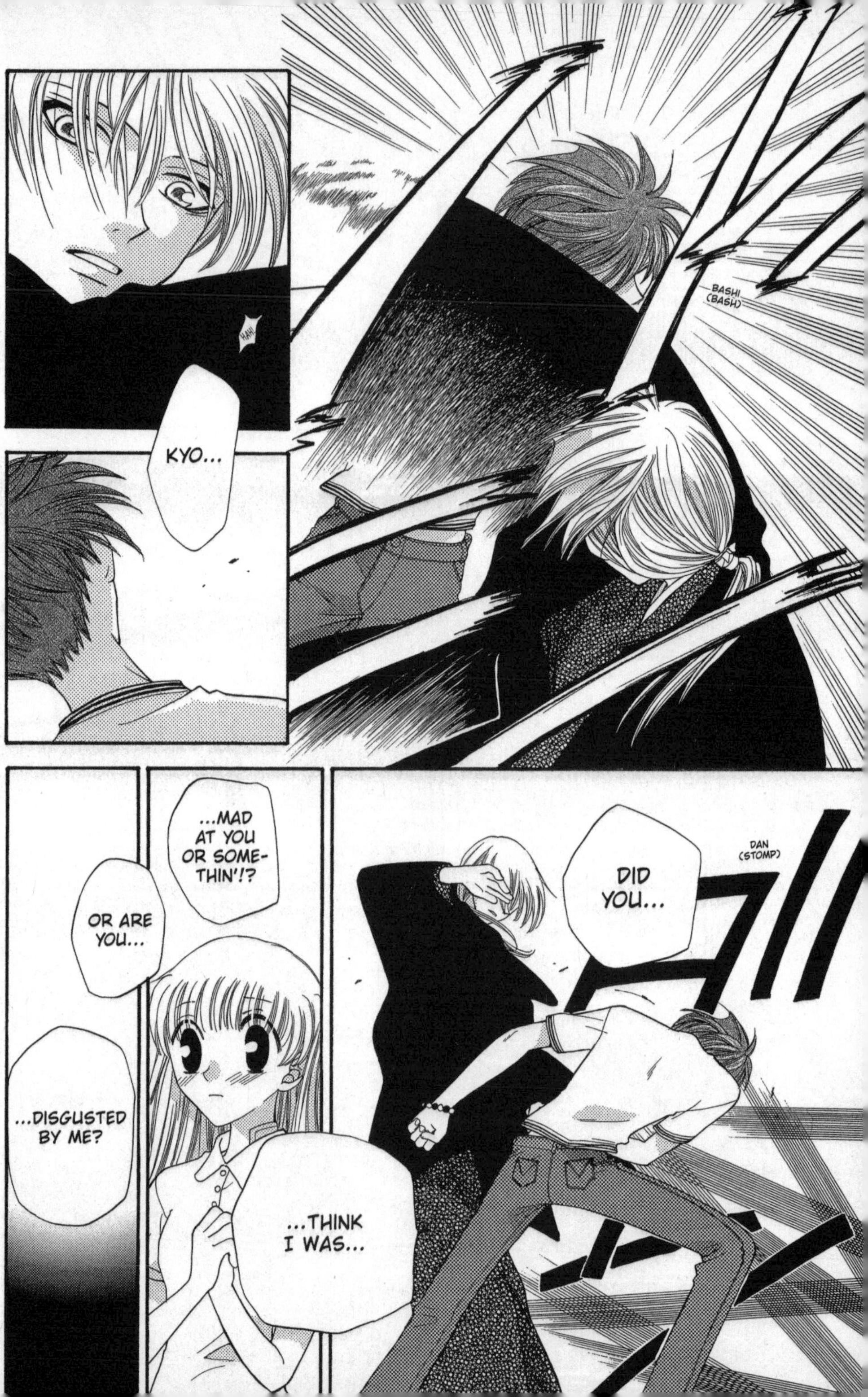
BASHI (BASH)
HAH!
KYO...
DAN (STOMP)
DID YOU...
...THINK I WAS...
...MAD AT YOU OR SOME-THIN'!?
OR ARE YOU...
...DISGUSTED BY ME?

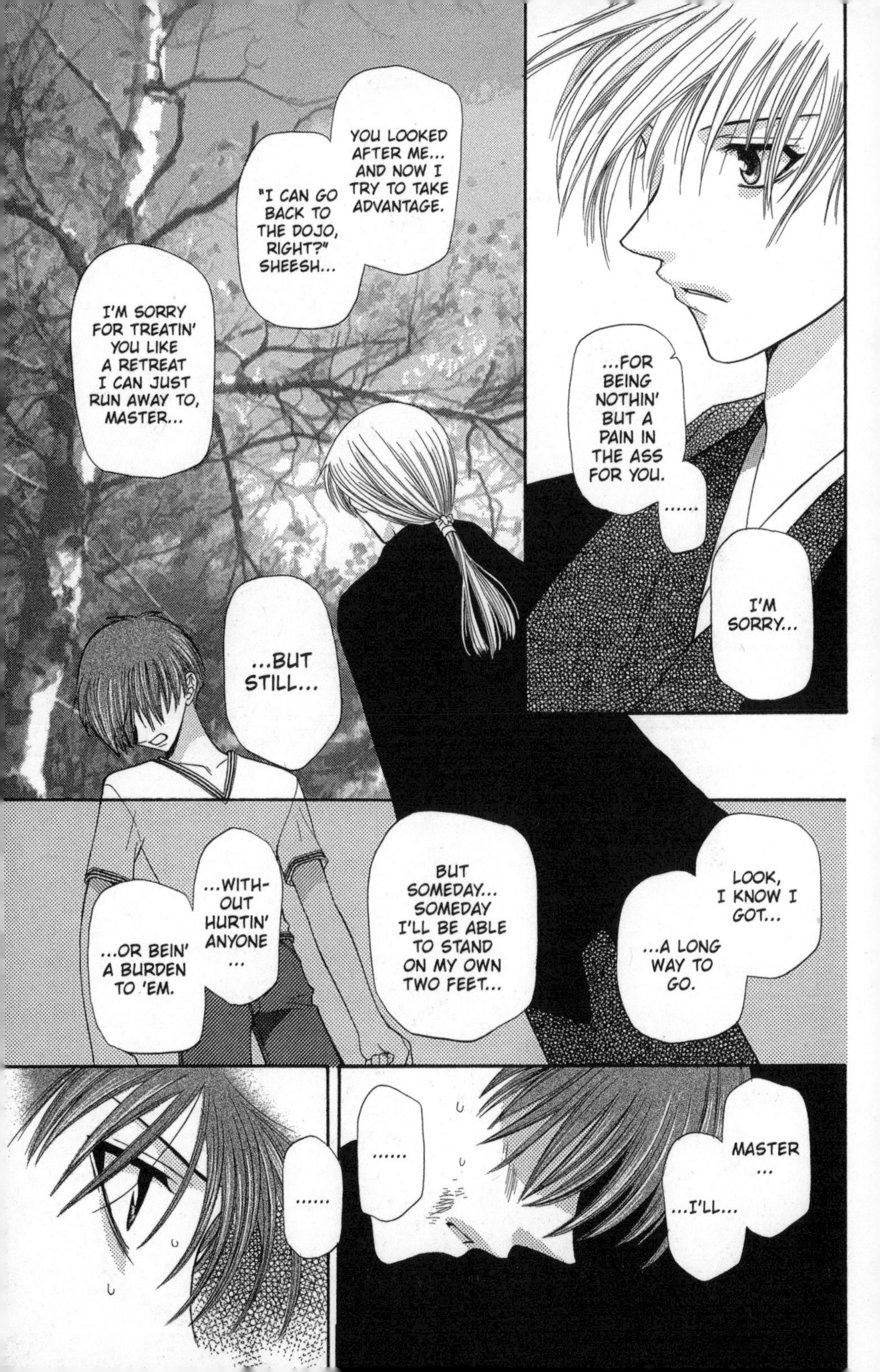
...FOR BEING NOTHIN' BUT A PAIN IN THE ASS FOR YOU.
......
I'M SORRY...
YOU LOOKED AFTER ME... AND NOW I TRY TO TAKE ADVANTAGE.
"I CAN GO BACK TO THE DOJO, RIGHT?" SHEESH...
I'M SORRY FOR TREATIN' YOU LIKE A RETREAT I CAN JUST RUN AWAY TO, MASTER...
...BUT STILL...
LOOK, I KNOW I GOT...
...A LONG WAY TO GO.
BUT SOMEDAY... SOMEDAY I'LL BE ABLE TO STAND ON MY OWN TWO FEET...
...WITH-OUT HURTIN' ANYONE ...
...OR BEIN' A BURDEN TO 'EM.
MASTER ...
...I'LL...
......
......

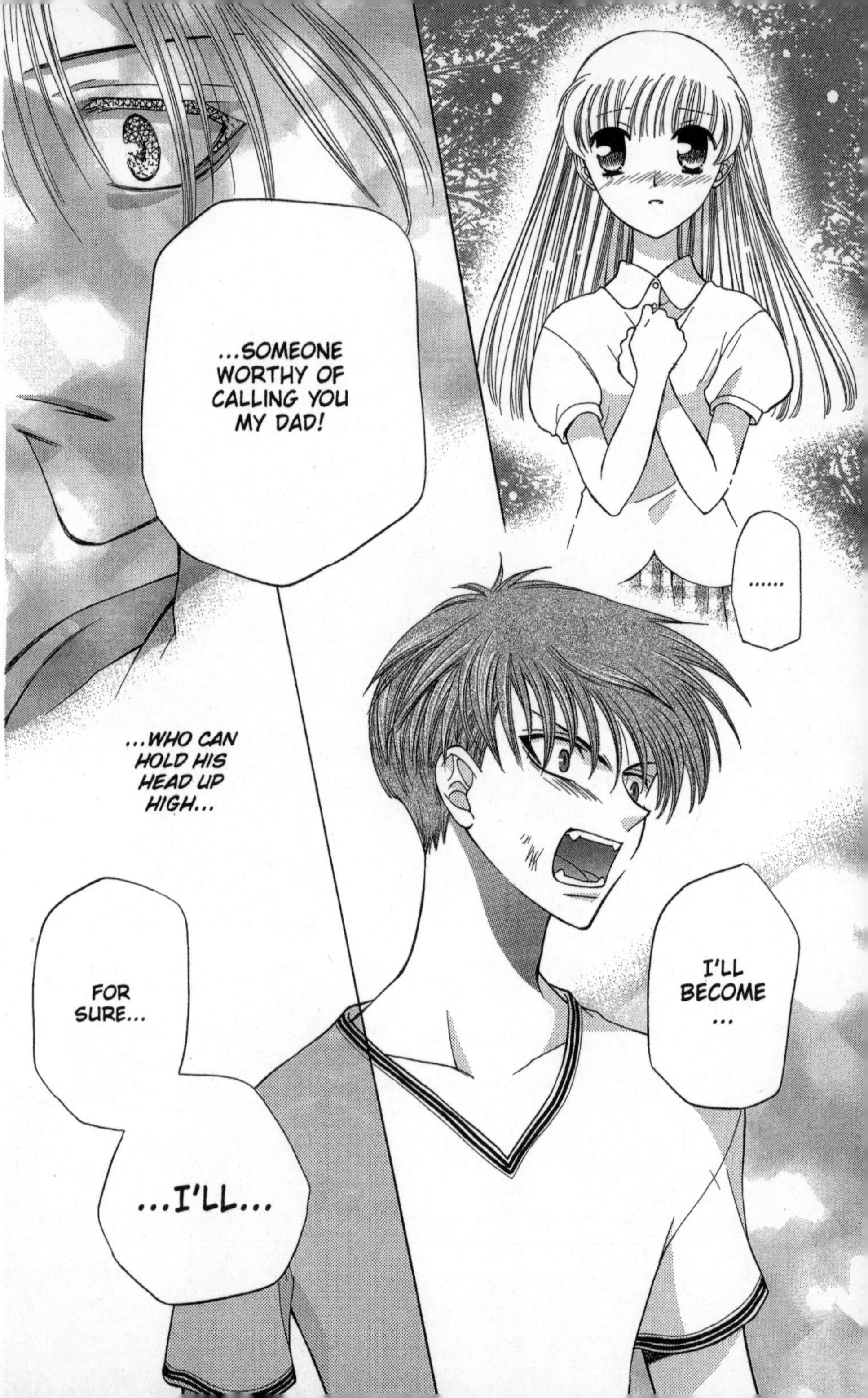
......
FOR SURE... ...I'LL...
I'LL BECOME ...
...WHO CAN HOLD HIS HEAD UP HIGH...
...SOMEONE WORTHY OF CALLING YOU MY DAD!

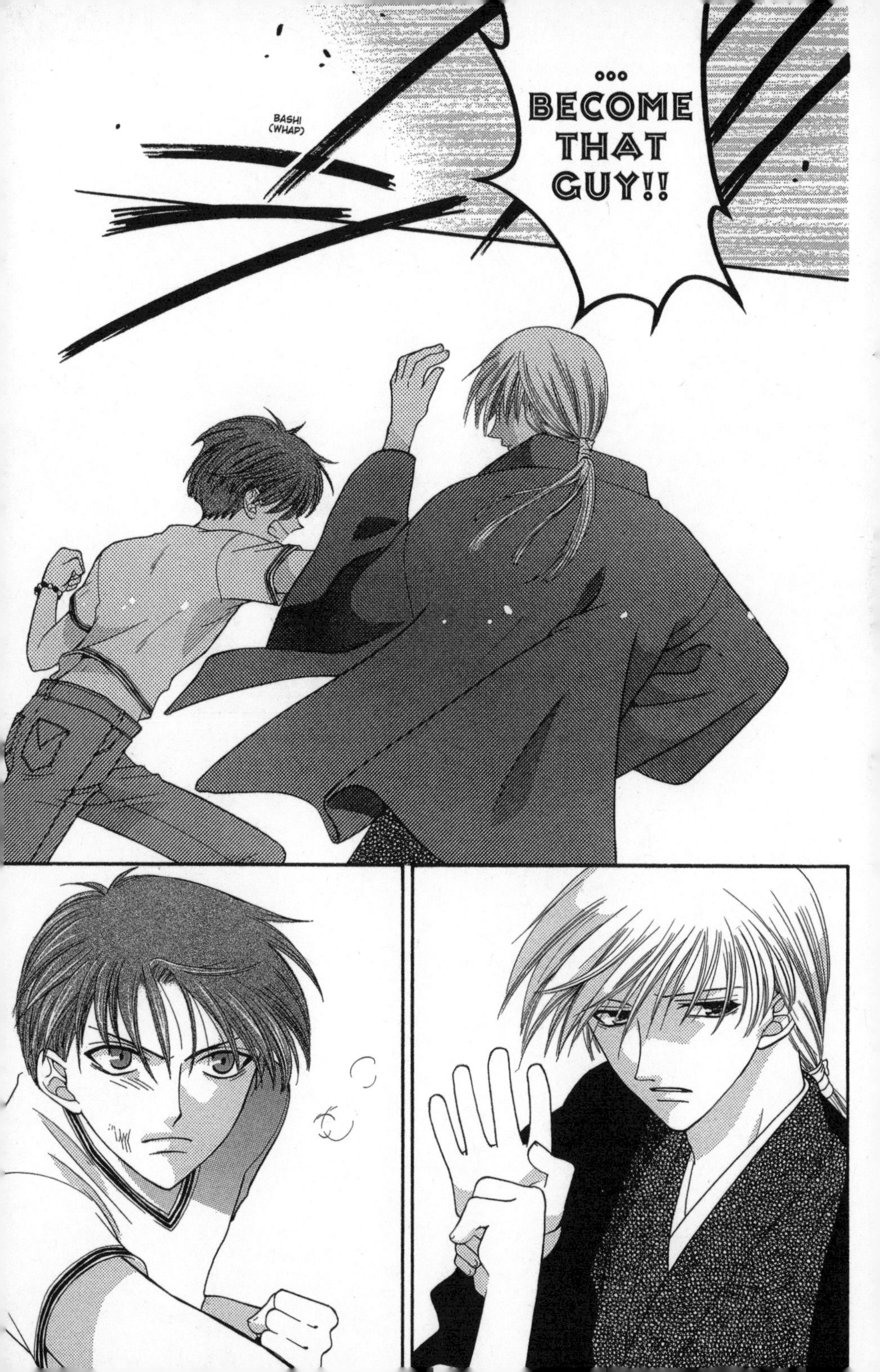
...BECOME THAT GUY!!
BASHI (WHAP)

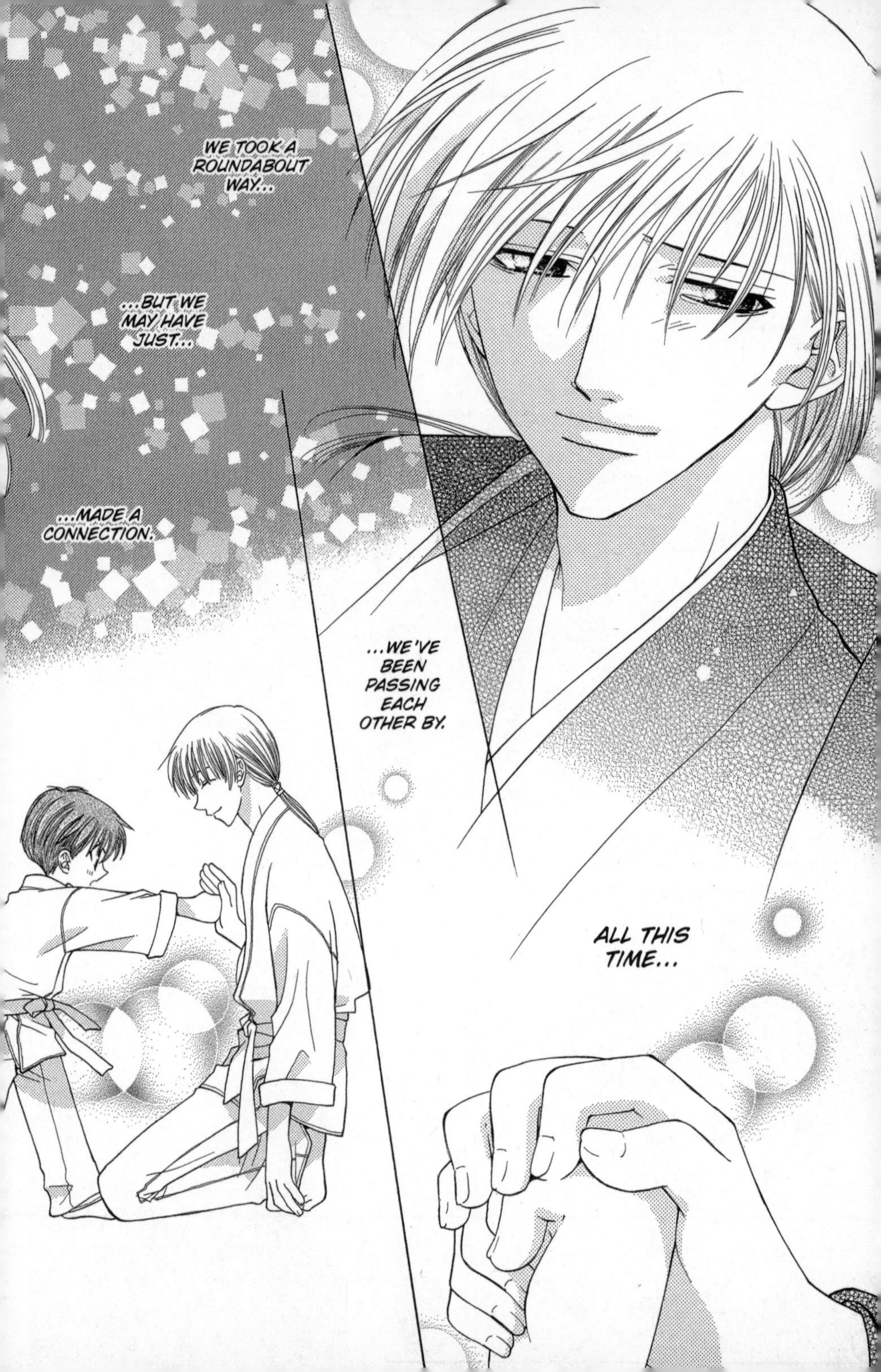
ALL THIS TIME...
...WE'VE BEEN PASSING EACH OTHER BY.
WE TOOK A ROUNDABOUT WAY...
...BUT WE MAY HAVE JUST...
...MADE A CONNECTION.

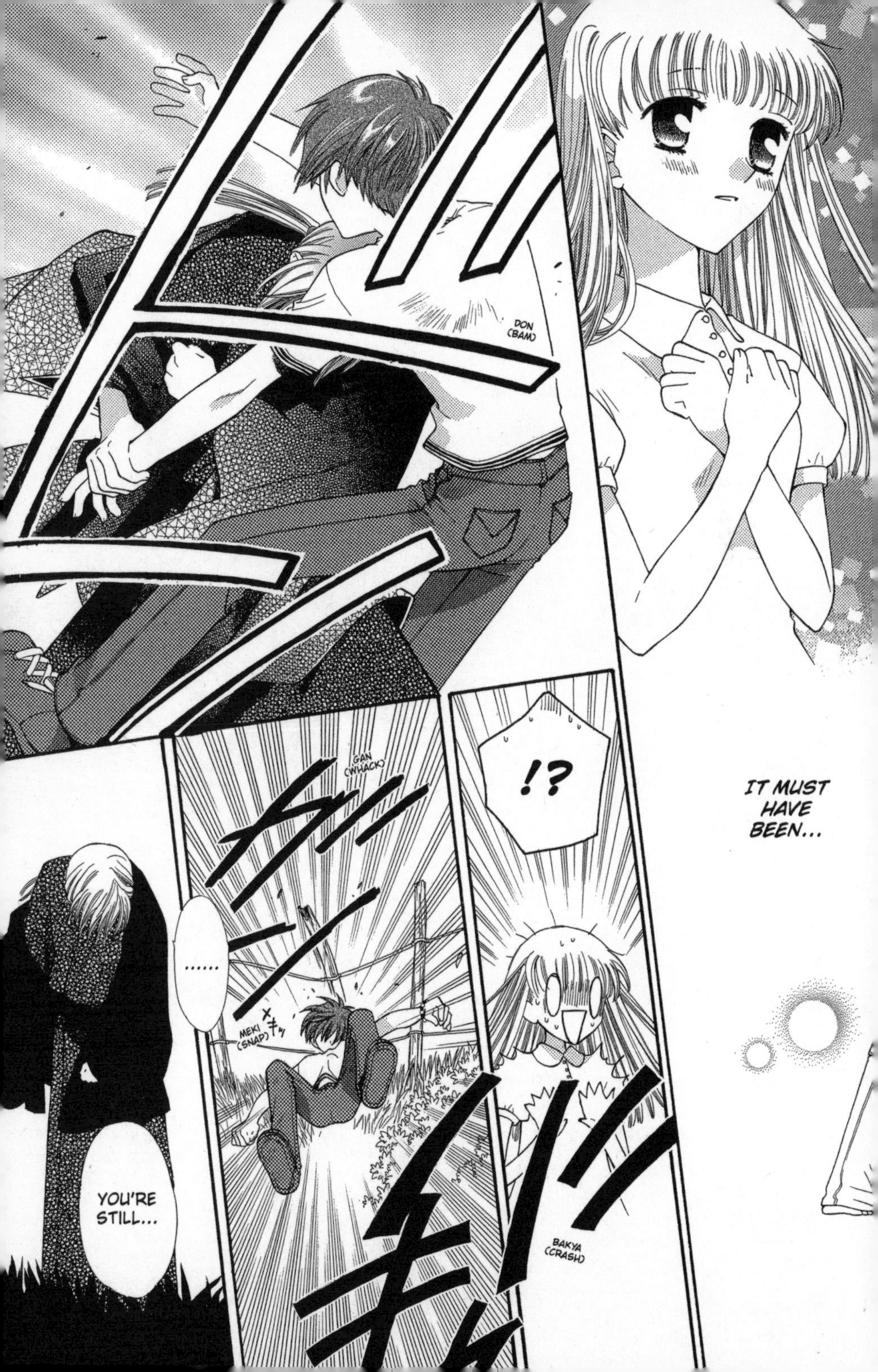
IT MUST HAVE BEEN...
DON (BAM)
!?
BAKYA (CRASH)
GAN (WHACK)
MEKI (SNAP)
......
YOU'RE STILL...

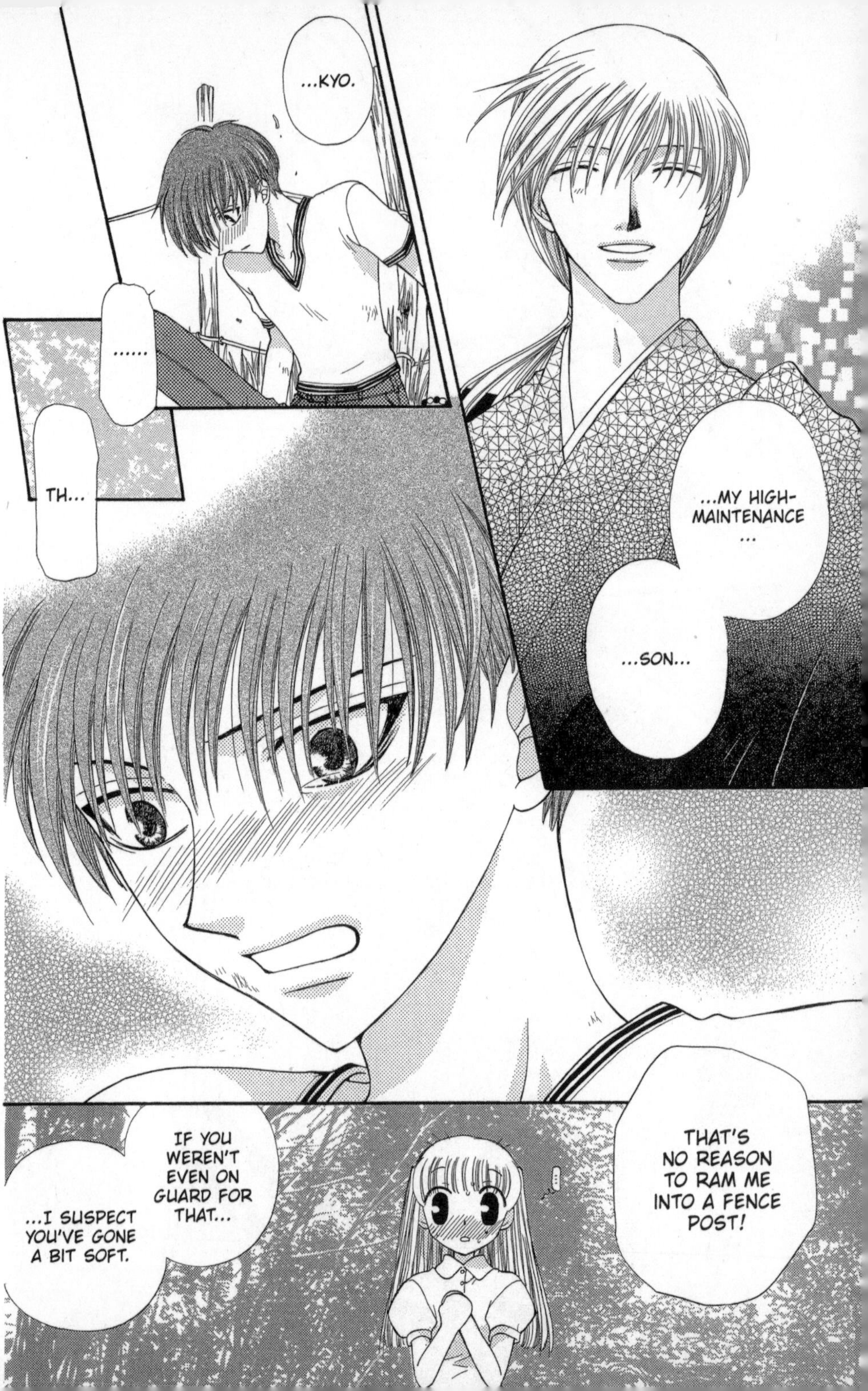
...MY HIGH-MAINTENANCE ...
...SON...
...KYO.
......
TH...
THAT'S NO REASON TO RAM ME INTO A FENCE POST!
IF YOU WEREN'T EVEN ON GUARD FOR THAT...
...I SUSPECT YOU'VE GONE A BIT SOFT.

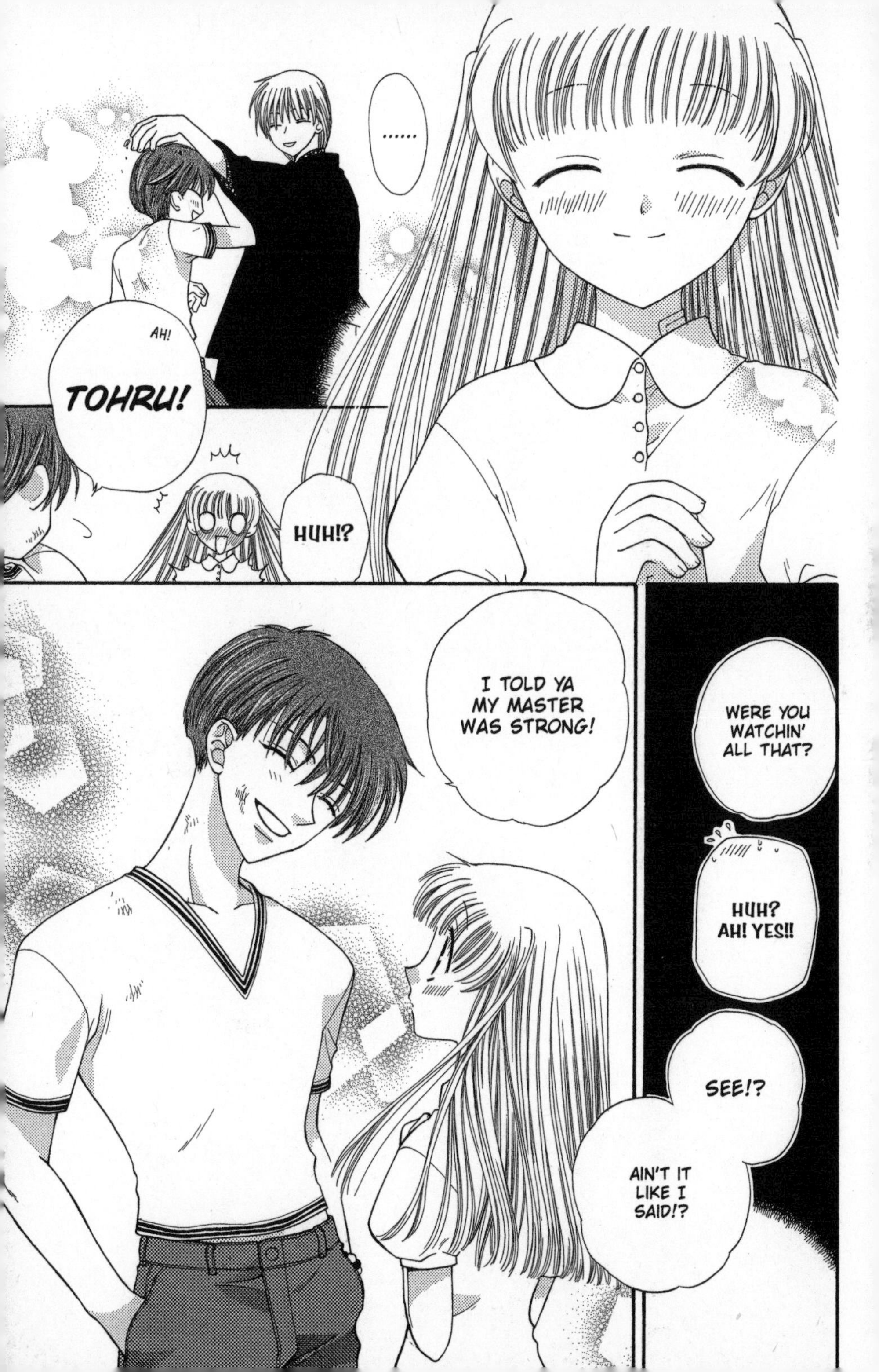
......
AH!
TOHRU!
HUH!?
WERE YOU WATCHIN' ALL THAT?
HUH? AH! YES!!
SEE!?
AIN'T IT LIKE I SAID!?
I TOLD YA MY MASTER WAS STRONG!

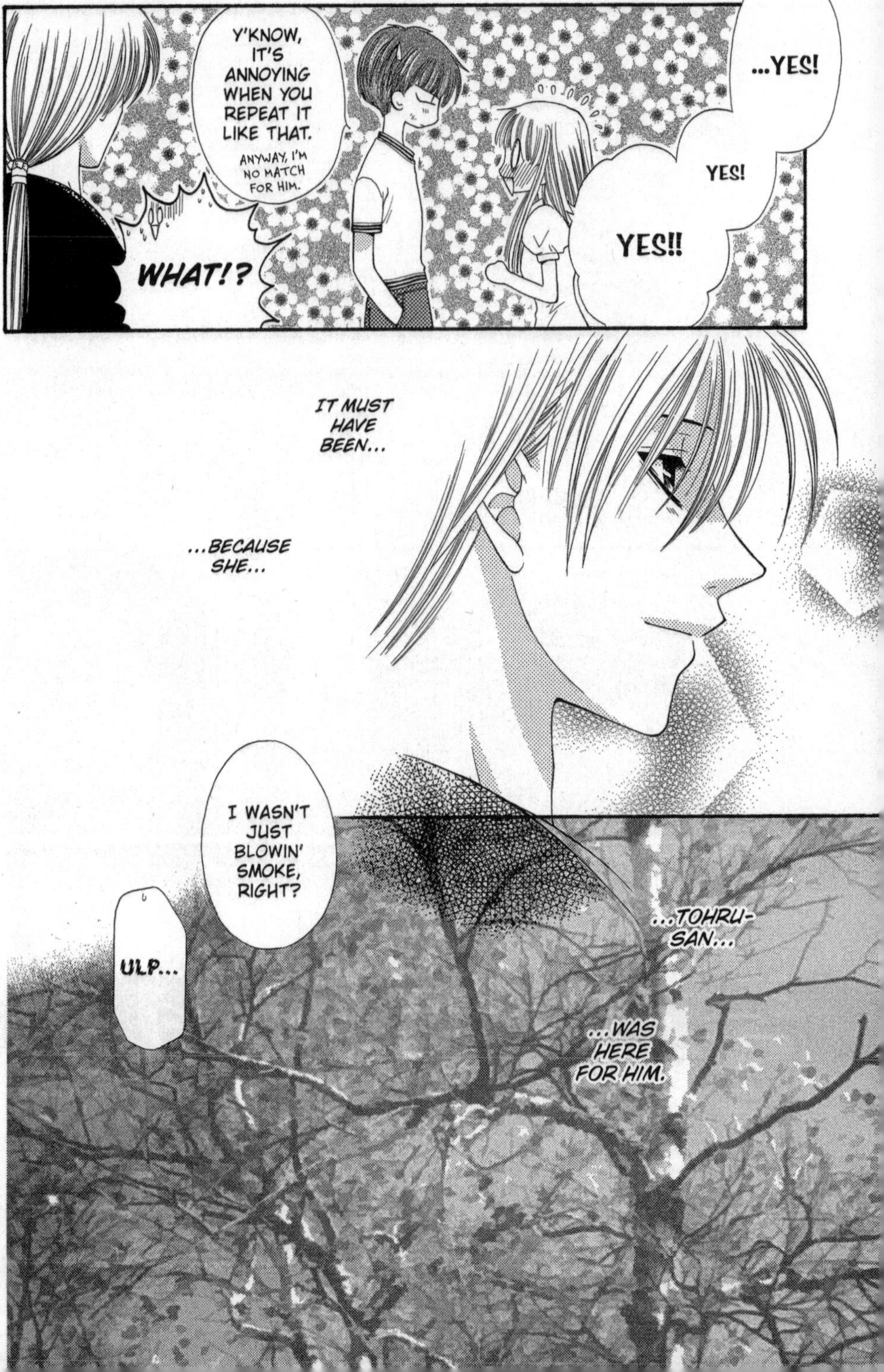
...YES!
YES!
YES!!
Y'KNOW, IT'S ANNOYING WHEN YOU REPEAT IT LIKE THAT.
ANYWAY, I'M NO MATCH FOR HIM.
WHAT!?
IT MUST HAVE BEEN...
...BECAUSE SHE...
...TOHRU-SAN...
...WAS HERE FOR HIM.
I WASN'T JUST BLOWIN' SMOKE, RIGHT?
ULP...

Chapter 35

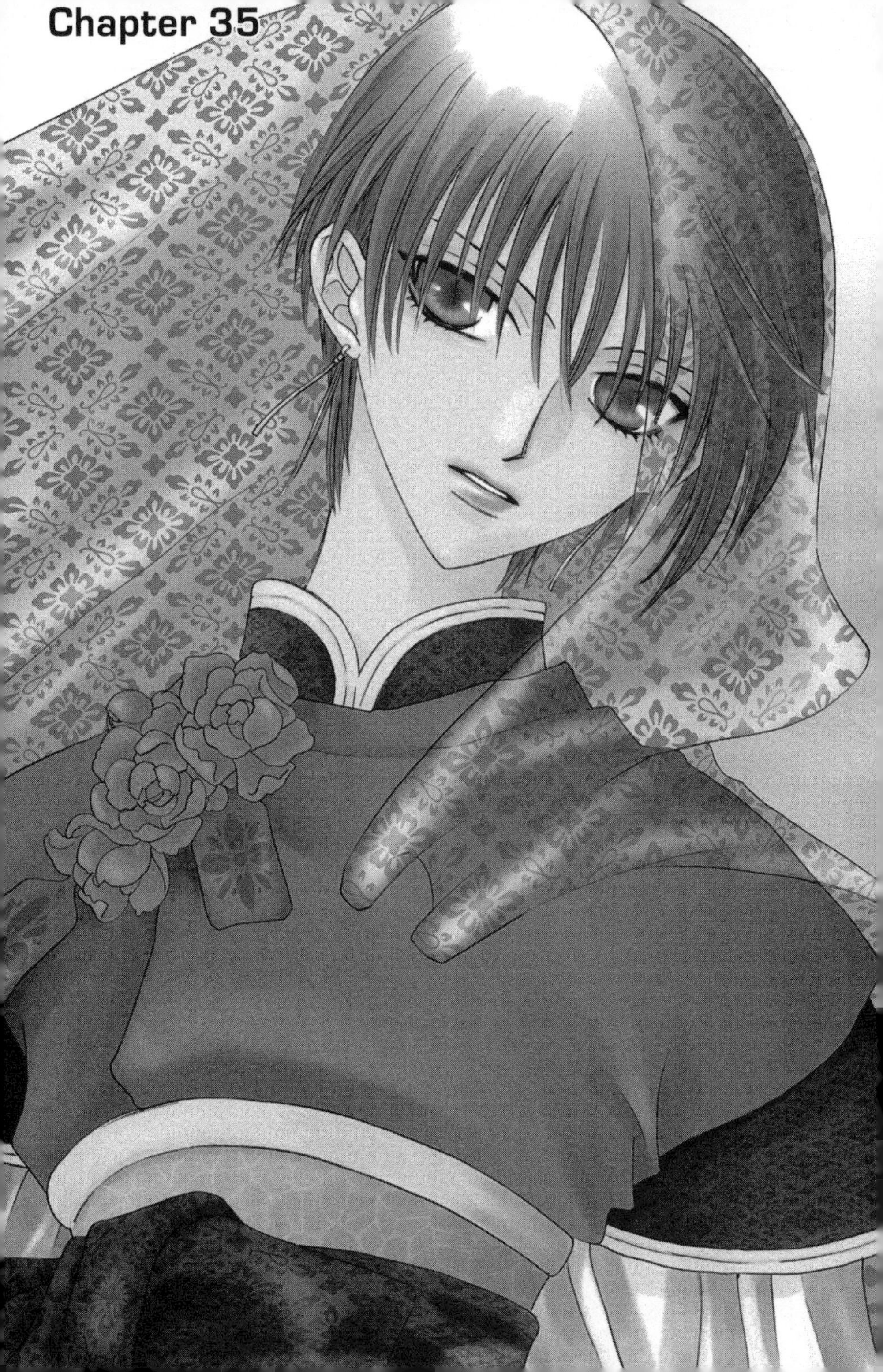

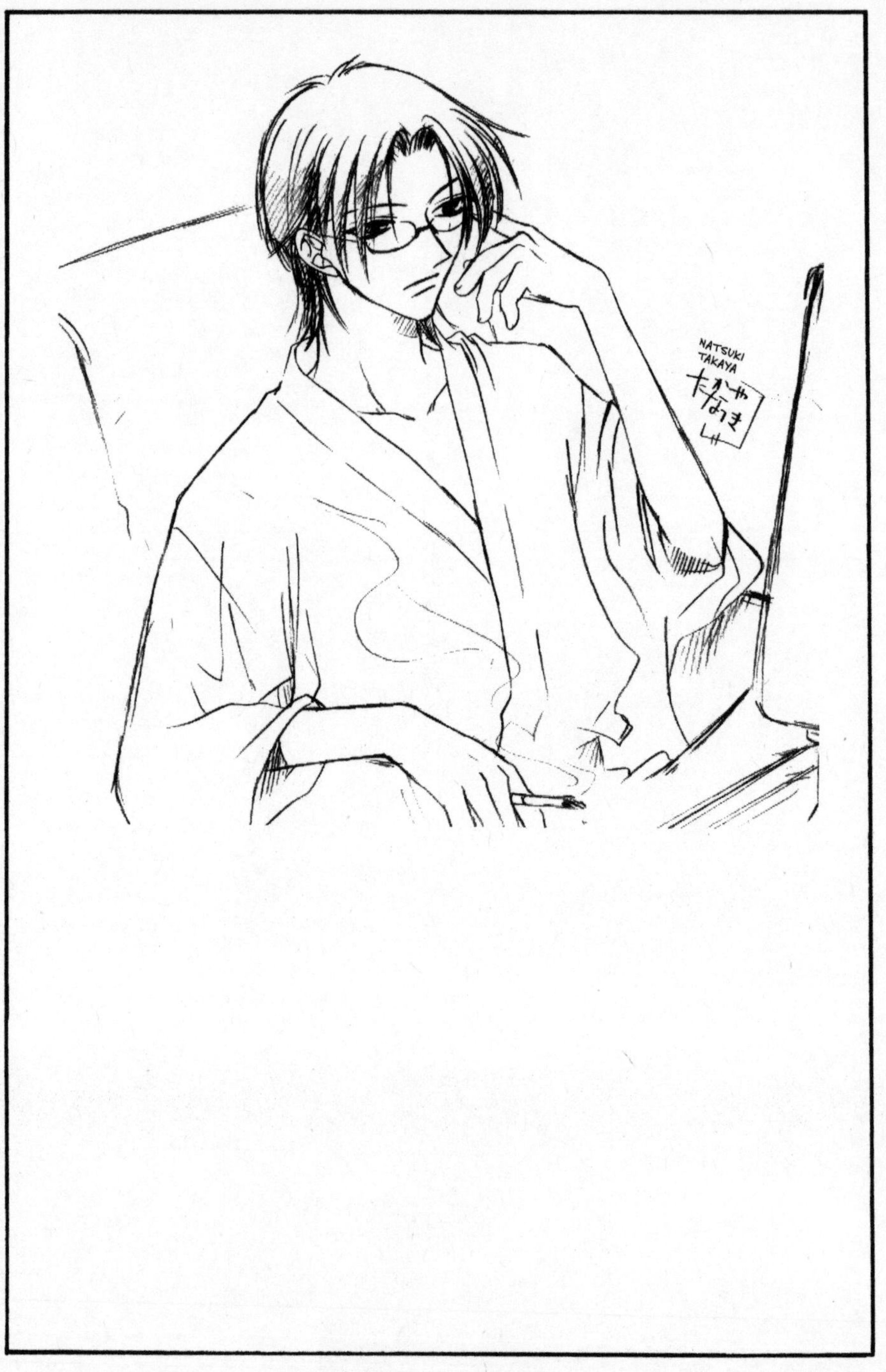
NATSUKI
TAKAYA

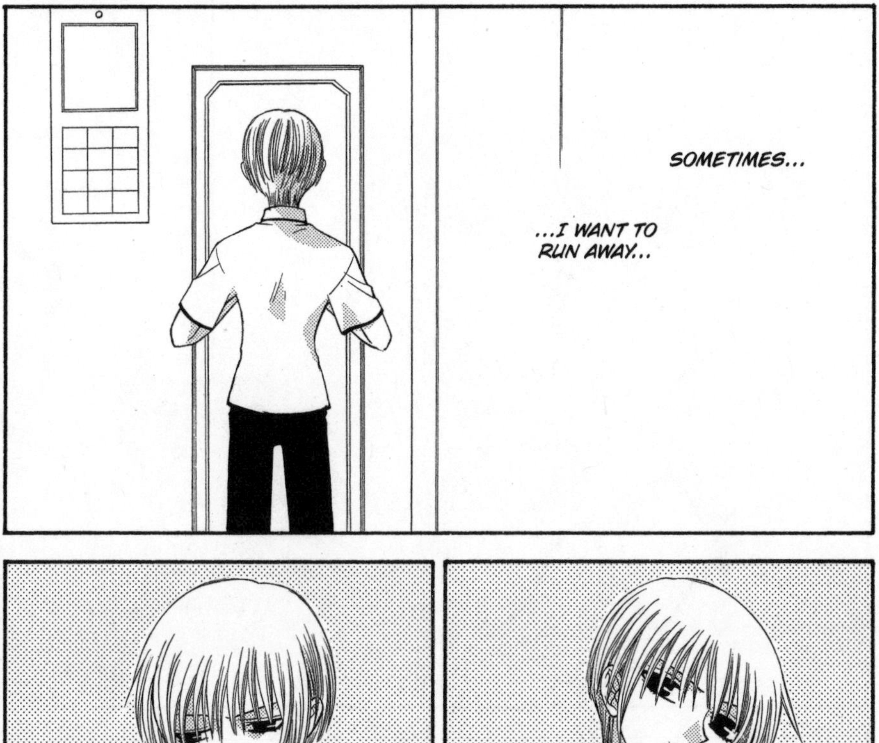
SOMETIMES...
...I WANT TO RUN AWAY...

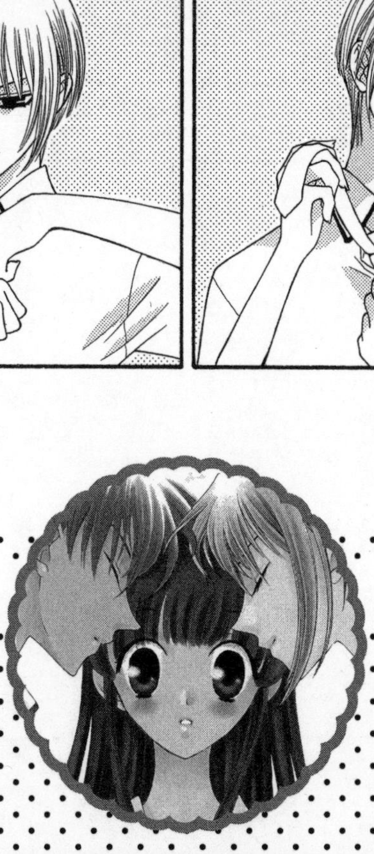

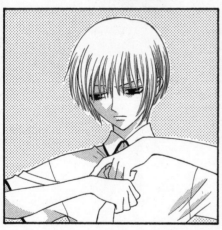

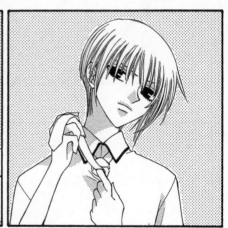

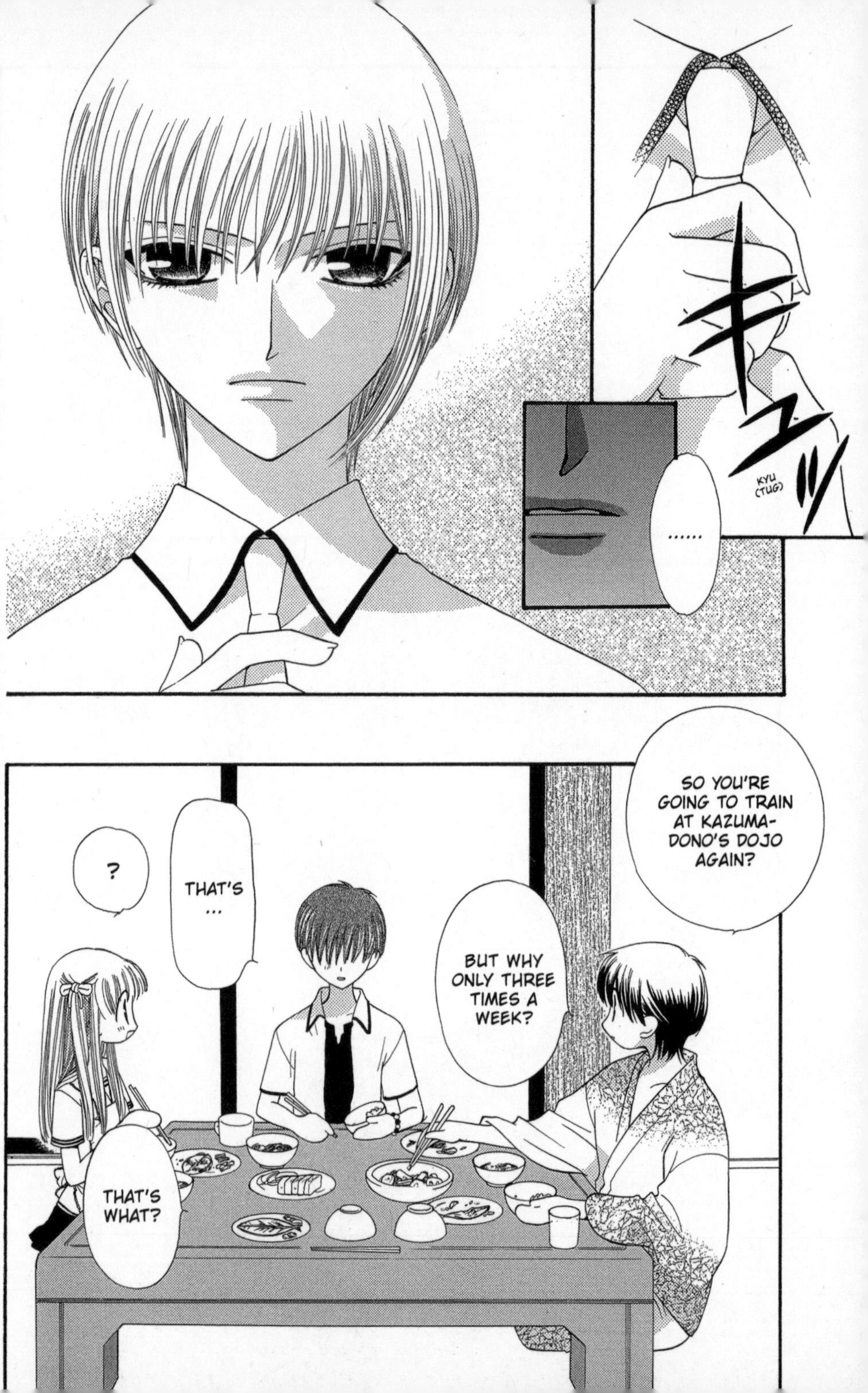
KYU
(TUG)
......
SO YOU'RE GOING TO TRAIN AT KAZUMA-DONO'S DOJO AGAIN?
BUT WHY ONLY THREE TIMES A WEEK?
THAT'S ...
?
THAT'S WHAT?

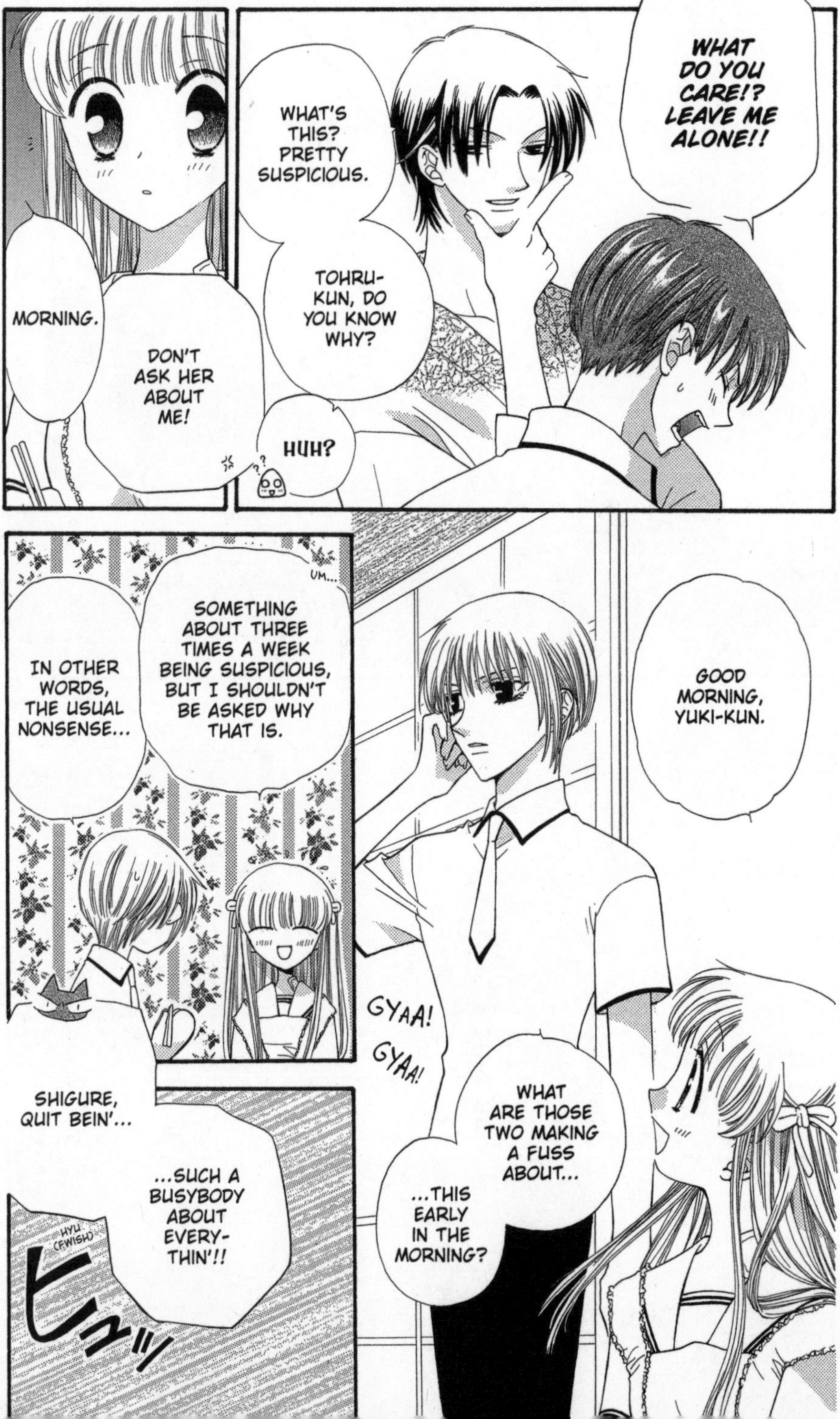
WHAT DO YOU CARE!? LEAVE ME ALONE!!
WHAT'S THIS? PRETTY SUSPICIOUS.
TOHRU-KUN, DO YOU KNOW WHY?
HUH?
DON'T ASK HER ABOUT ME!
MORNING.
GOOD MORNING, YUKI-KUN.
GYAA!
GYAA!
WHAT ARE THOSE TWO MAKING A FUSS ABOUT...
...THIS EARLY IN THE MORNING?
UM...
SOMETHING ABOUT THREE TIMES A WEEK BEING SUSPICIOUS, BUT I SHOULDN'T BE ASKED WHY THAT IS.
IN OTHER WORDS, THE USUAL NONSENSE...
SHIGURE, QUIT BEIN'...
...SUCH A BUSYBODY ABOUT EVERY-THIN'!!
HYU (FWISH)
ヒュッ

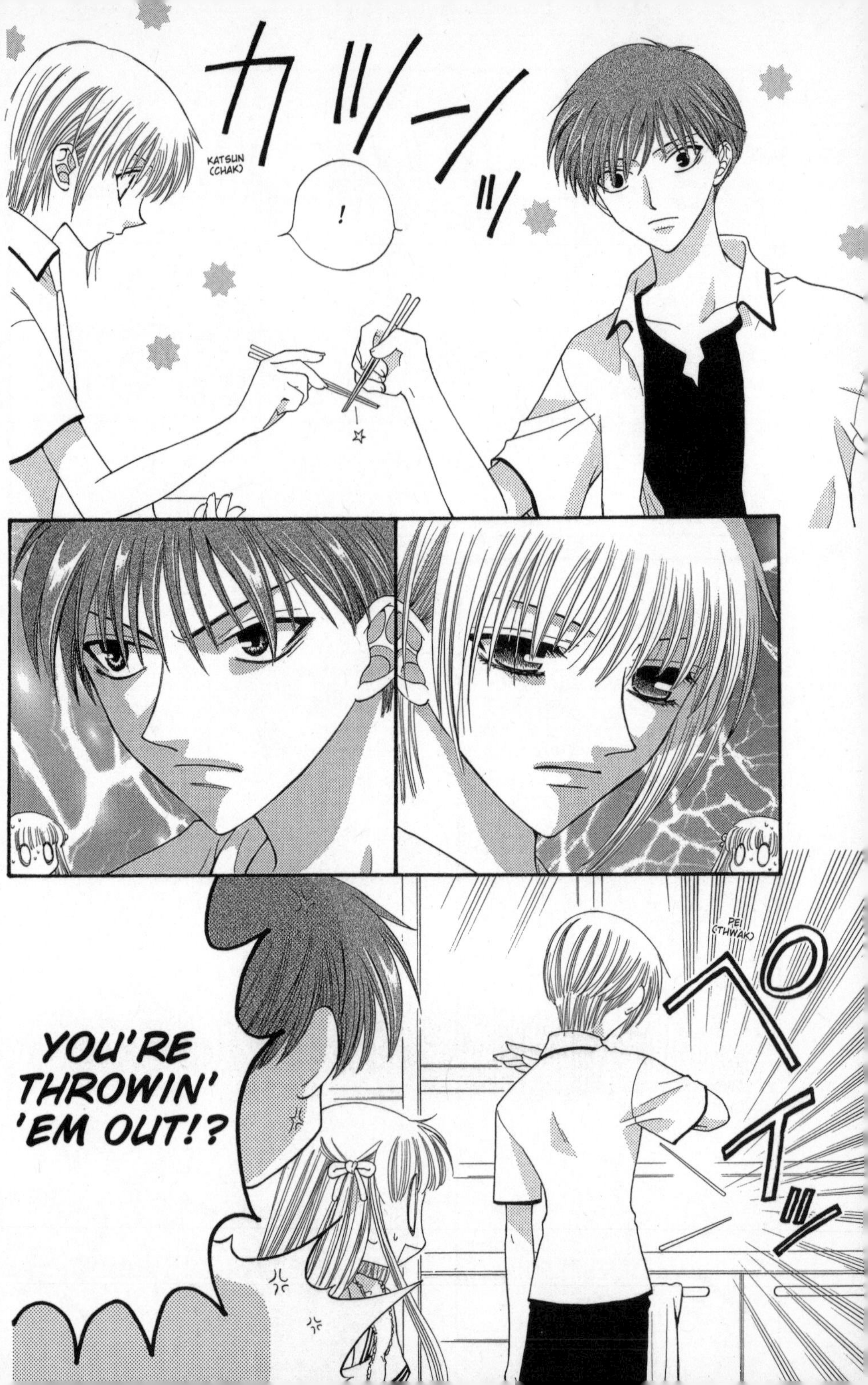
KATSUN
(CHAK)
!
PEI
(THWAK)
YOU'RE THROWIN' 'EM OUT!?

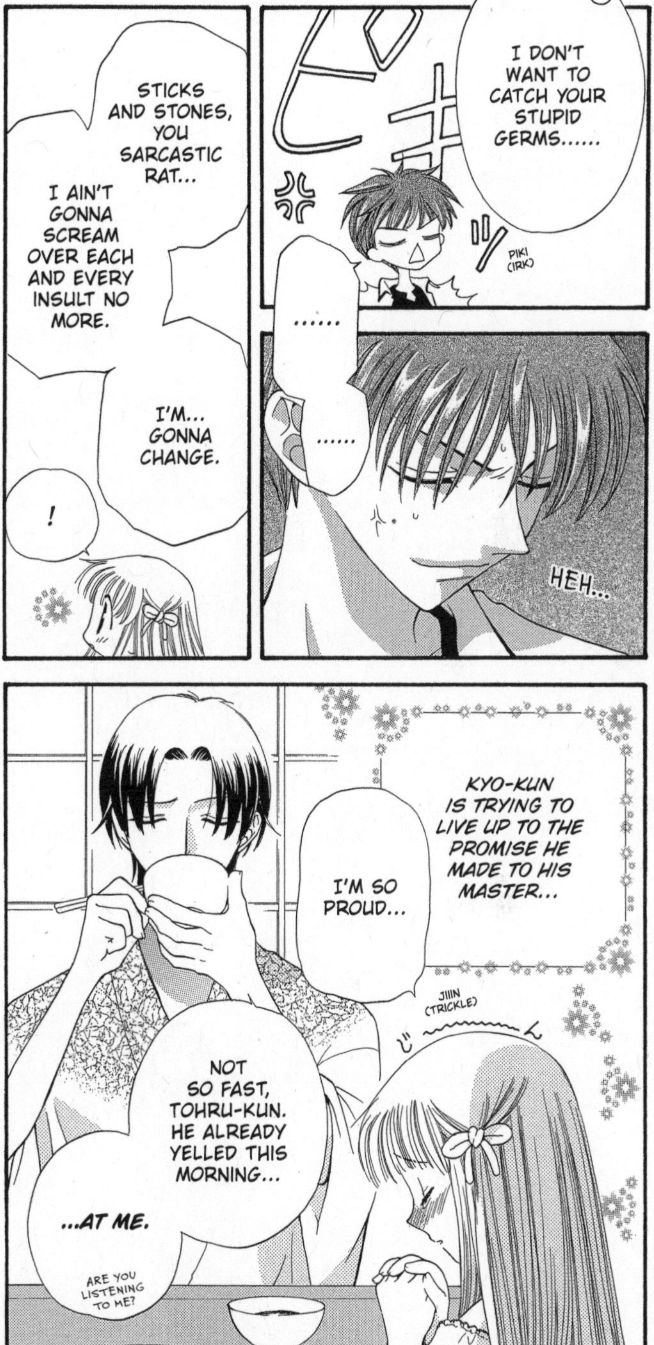
I DON'T WANT TO CATCH YOUR STUPID GERMS......
PIKI (IRK)
......
......
HEH...
STICKS AND STONES, YOU SARCASTIC RAT...
I AIN'T GONNA SCREAM OVER EACH AND EVERY INSULT NO MORE.
I'M... GONNA CHANGE.
!
KYO-KUN IS TRYING TO LIVE UP TO THE PROMISE HE MADE TO HIS MASTER...
I'M SO PROUD...
JIIN (TRICKLE)
NOT SO FAST, TOHRU-KUN. HE ALREADY YELLED THIS MORNING...
...AT ME.
ARE YOU LISTENING TO ME?

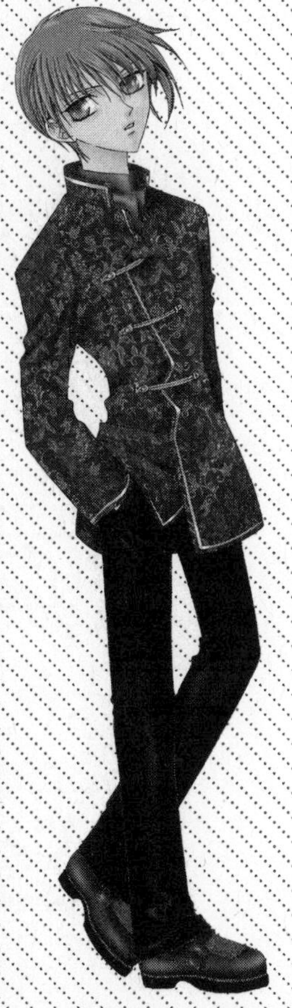

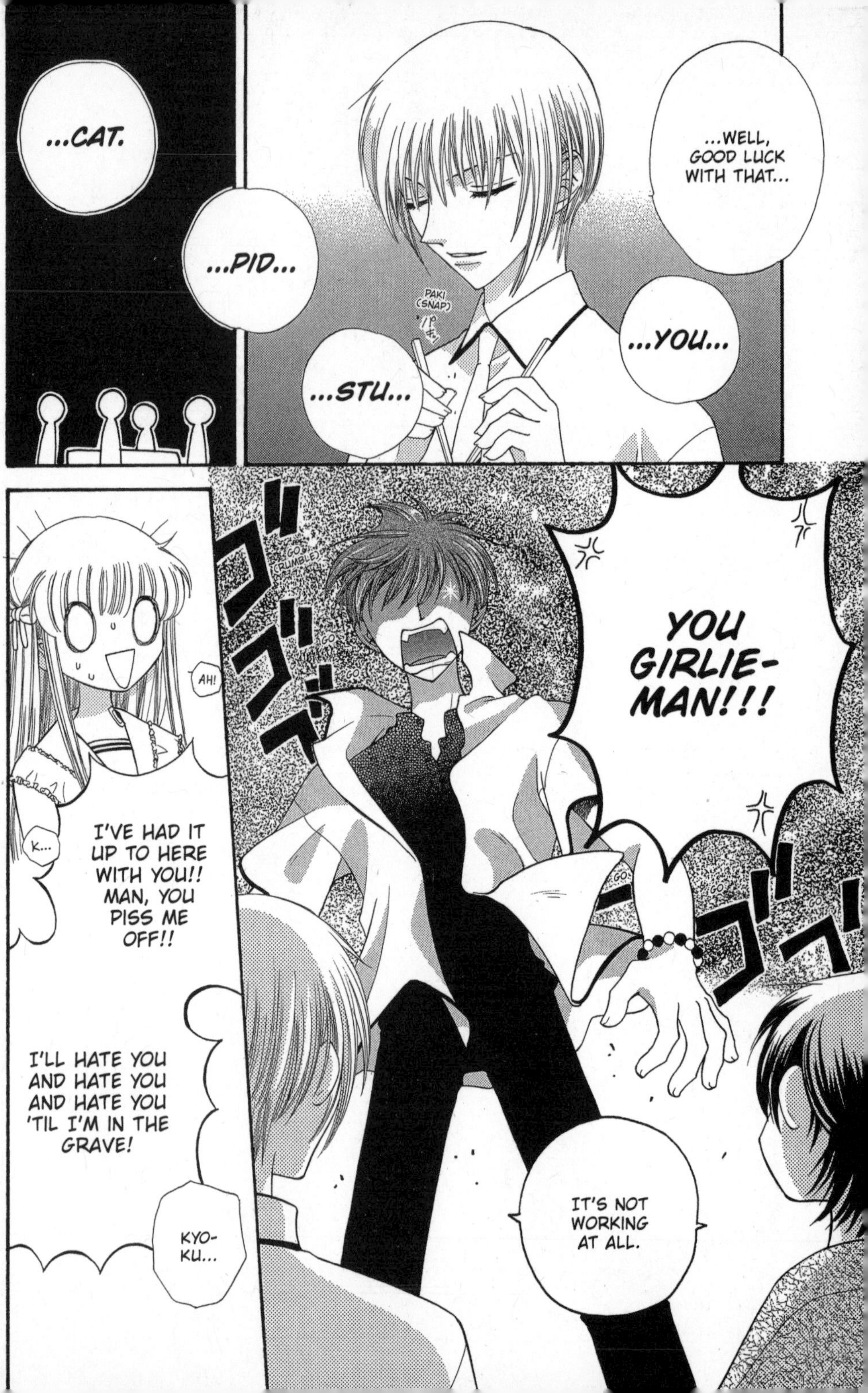
...WELL, GOOD LUCK WITH THAT...
...YOU...
PAKI (SNAP)
...STU...
...PID...
...CAT.
GO (RUMBLE)
YOU GIRLIE-MAN!!!
GO GO
GO GO
IT'S NOT WORKING AT ALL.
AH!
K...
I'VE HAD IT UP TO HERE WITH YOU!! MAN, YOU PISS ME OFF!!
I'LL HATE YOU AND HATE YOU AND HATE YOU 'TIL I'M IN THE GRAVE!
KYO-KU...

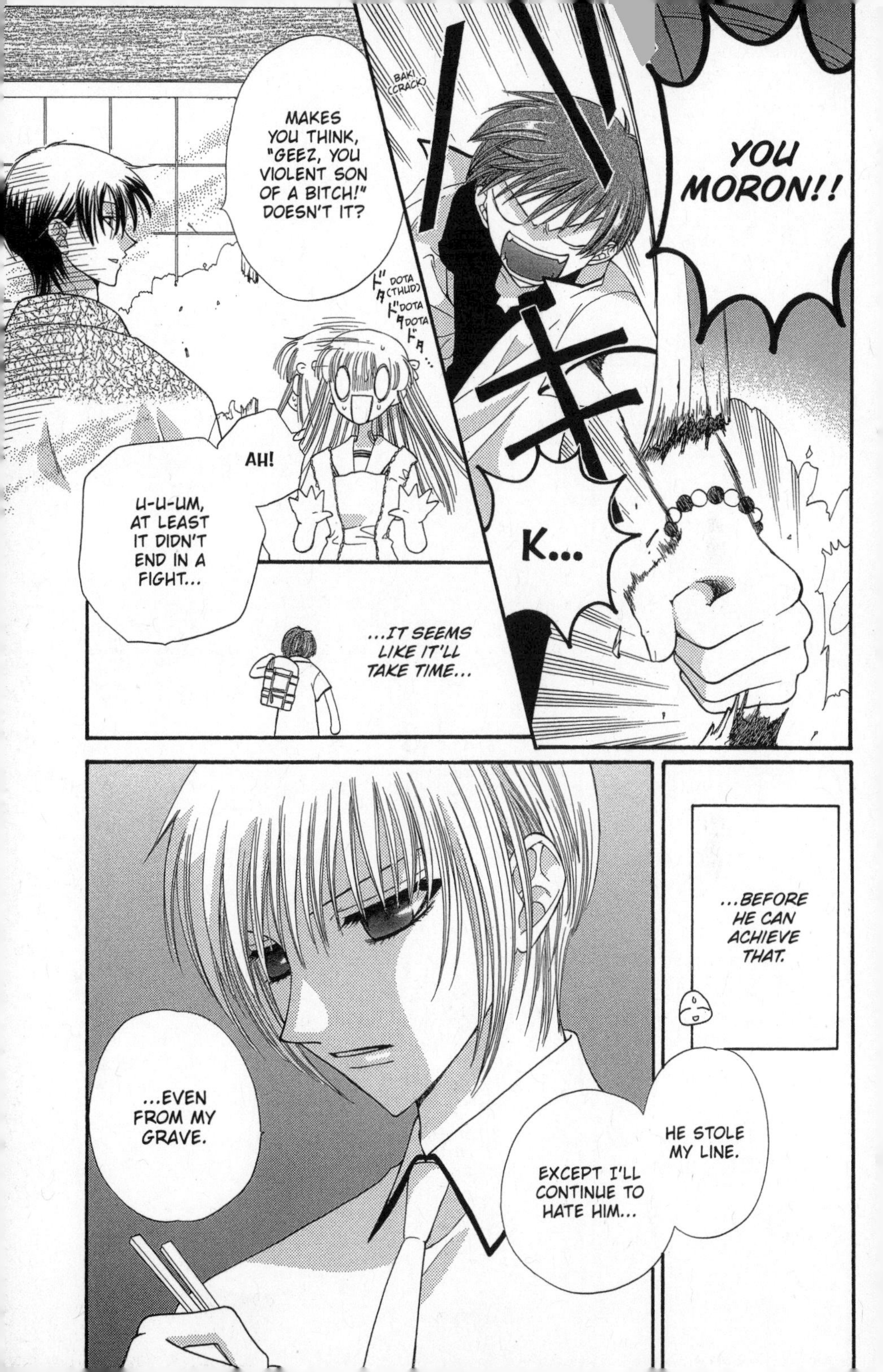
YOU MORON!!
BAKI (CRACK)
K...
MAKES YOU THINK, "GEEZ, YOU VIOLENT SON OF A BITCH!" DOESN'T IT?
DOTA (THUD) DOTA DOTA
AH!
U-U-UM, AT LEAST IT DIDN'T END IN A FIGHT...
...IT SEEMS LIKE IT'LL TAKE TIME...
...BEFORE HE CAN ACHIEVE THAT.
HE STOLE MY LINE.
EXCEPT I'LL CONTINUE TO HATE HIM...
...EVEN FROM MY GRAVE.

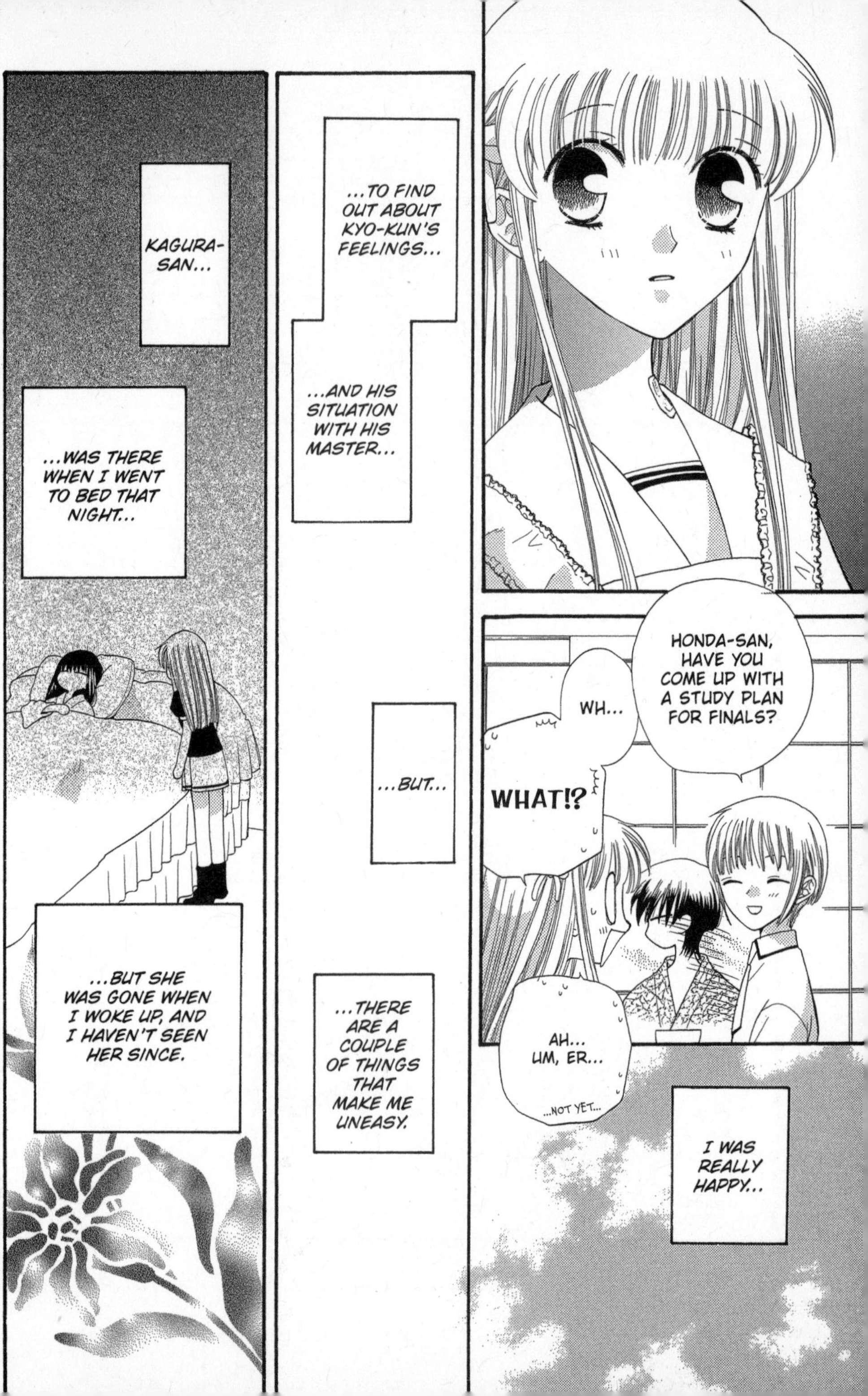
HONDA-SAN, HAVE YOU COME UP WITH A STUDY PLAN FOR FINALS?
WH...
WHAT!?
AH... UM, ER...
...NOT YET...
I WAS REALLY HAPPY...
...TO FIND OUT ABOUT KYO-KUN'S FEELINGS...
...AND HIS SITUATION WITH HIS MASTER...
...BUT...
...THERE ARE A COUPLE OF THINGS THAT MAKE ME UNEASY.
KAGURA-SAN...
...WAS THERE WHEN I WENT TO BED THAT NIGHT...
...BUT SHE WAS GONE WHEN I WOKE UP, AND I HAVEN'T SEEN HER SINCE.

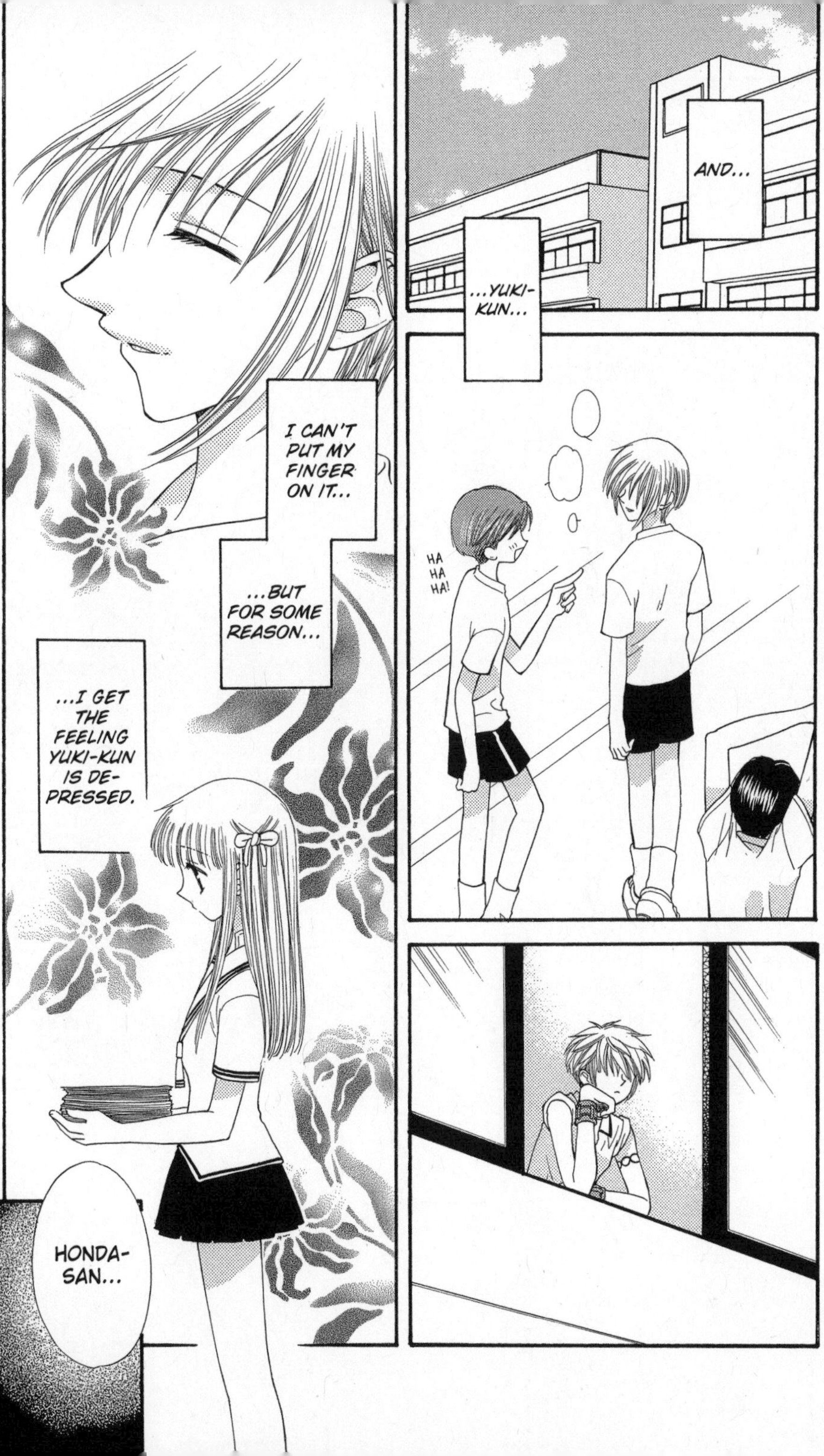
AND...
...YUKI-KUN...
HA HA HA!
I CAN'T PUT MY FINGER ON IT...
...BUT FOR SOME REASON...
...I GET THE FEELING YUKI-KUN IS DE-PRESSED.
HONDA-SAN...

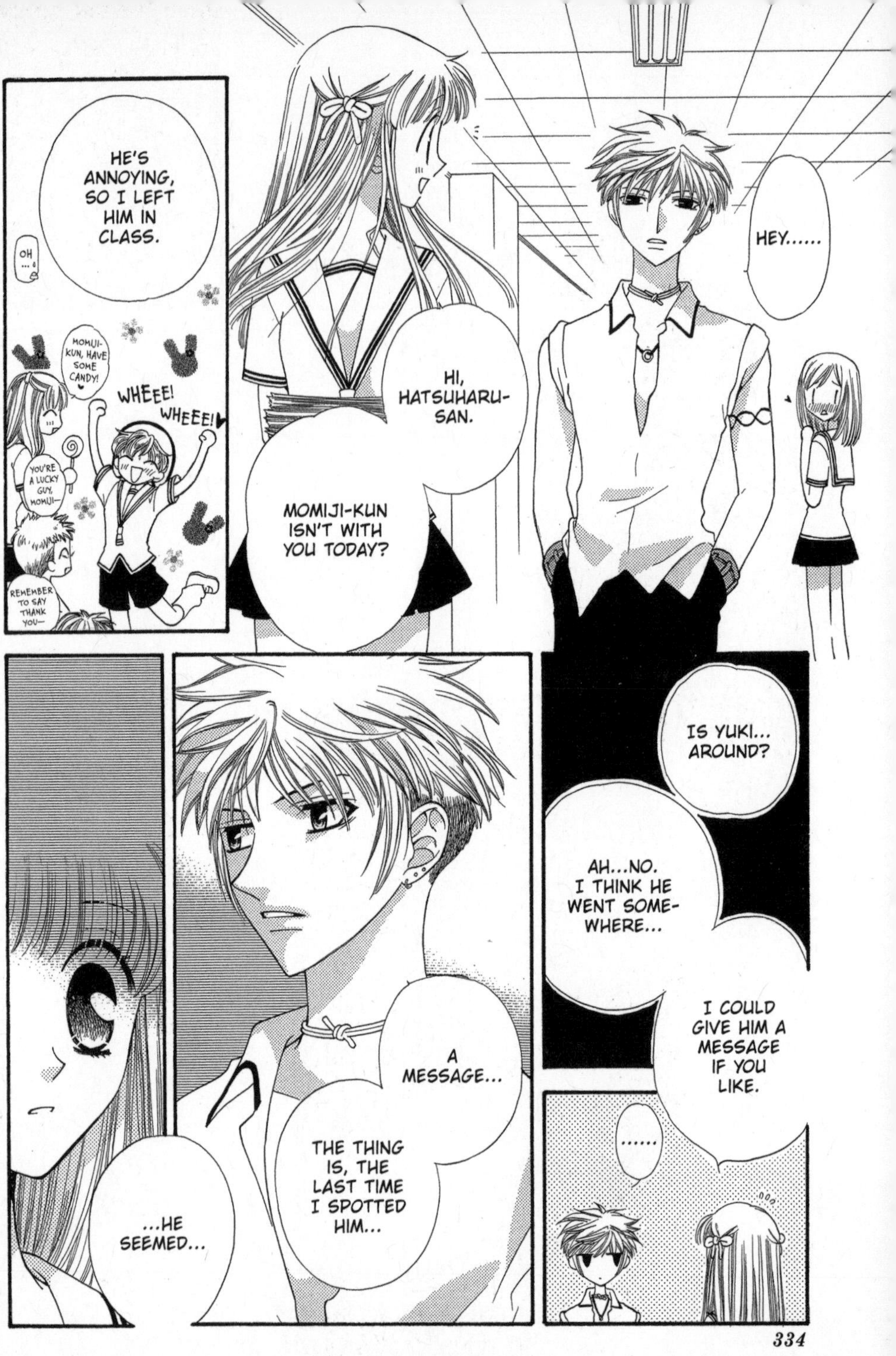
HEY......
HI, HATSUHARU-SAN.
MOMIJI-KUN ISN'T WITH YOU TODAY?
HE'S ANNOYING, SO I LEFT HIM IN CLASS.
OH...
MOMIJI-KUN, HAVE SOME CANDY!
WHEEE! WHEEE!
YOU'RE A LUCKY GUY, MOMIJI—
REMEMBER TO SAY THANK YOU—
IS YUKI... AROUND?
AH...NO. I THINK HE WENT SOME-WHERE...
I COULD GIVE HIM A MESSAGE IF YOU LIKE.
......
A MESSAGE...
THE THING IS, THE LAST TIME I SPOTTED HIM...
...HE SEEMED...

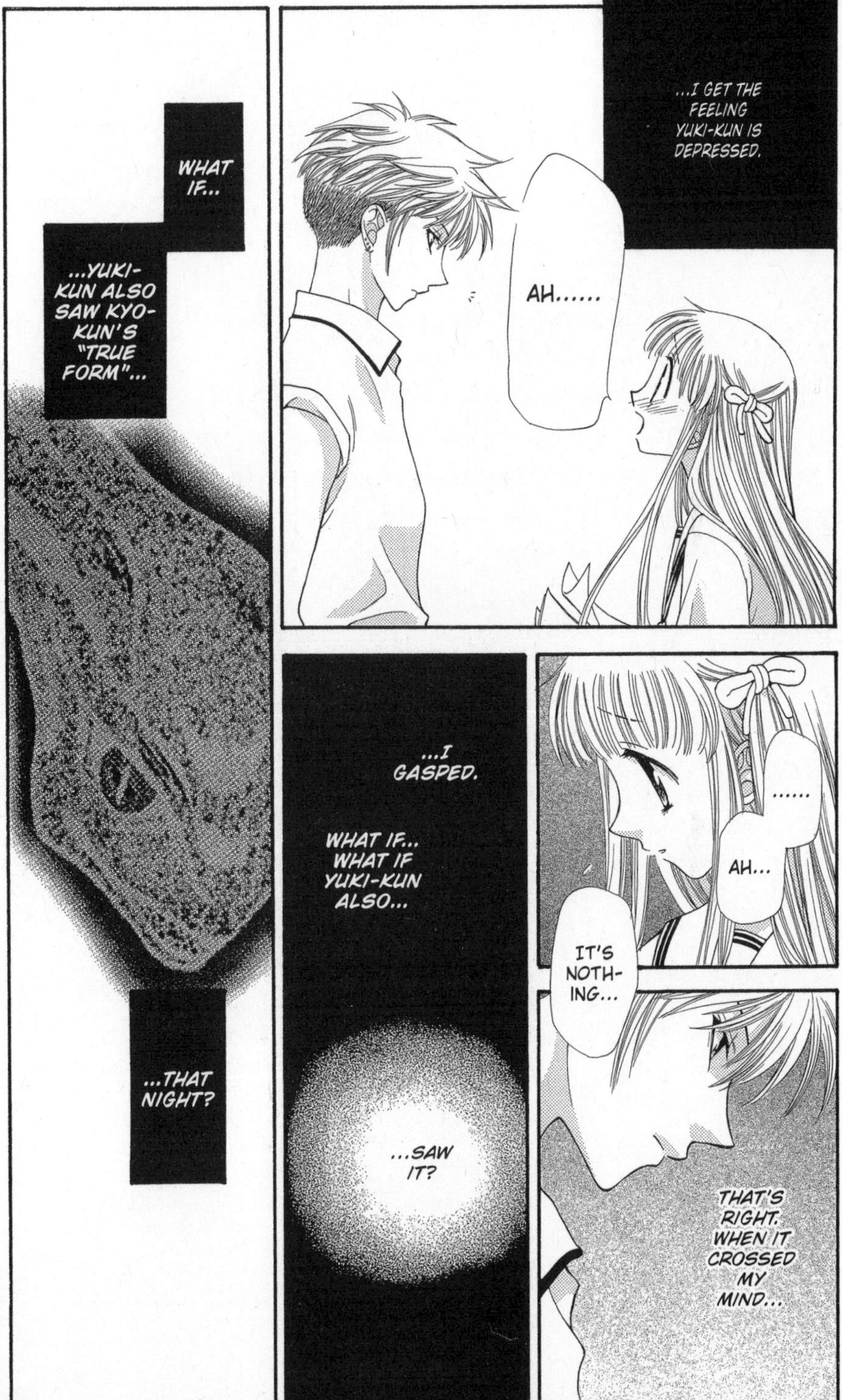
...I GET THE FEELING YUKI-KUN IS DEPRESSED.
AH......
......
AH...
IT'S NOTHING...
THAT'S RIGHT. WHEN IT CROSSED MY MIND...
...I GASPED.
WHAT IF... WHAT IF YUKI-KUN ALSO...
...SAW IT?
WHAT IF...
...YUKI-KUN ALSO SAW KYO-KUN'S "TRUE FORM"...
...THAT NIGHT?

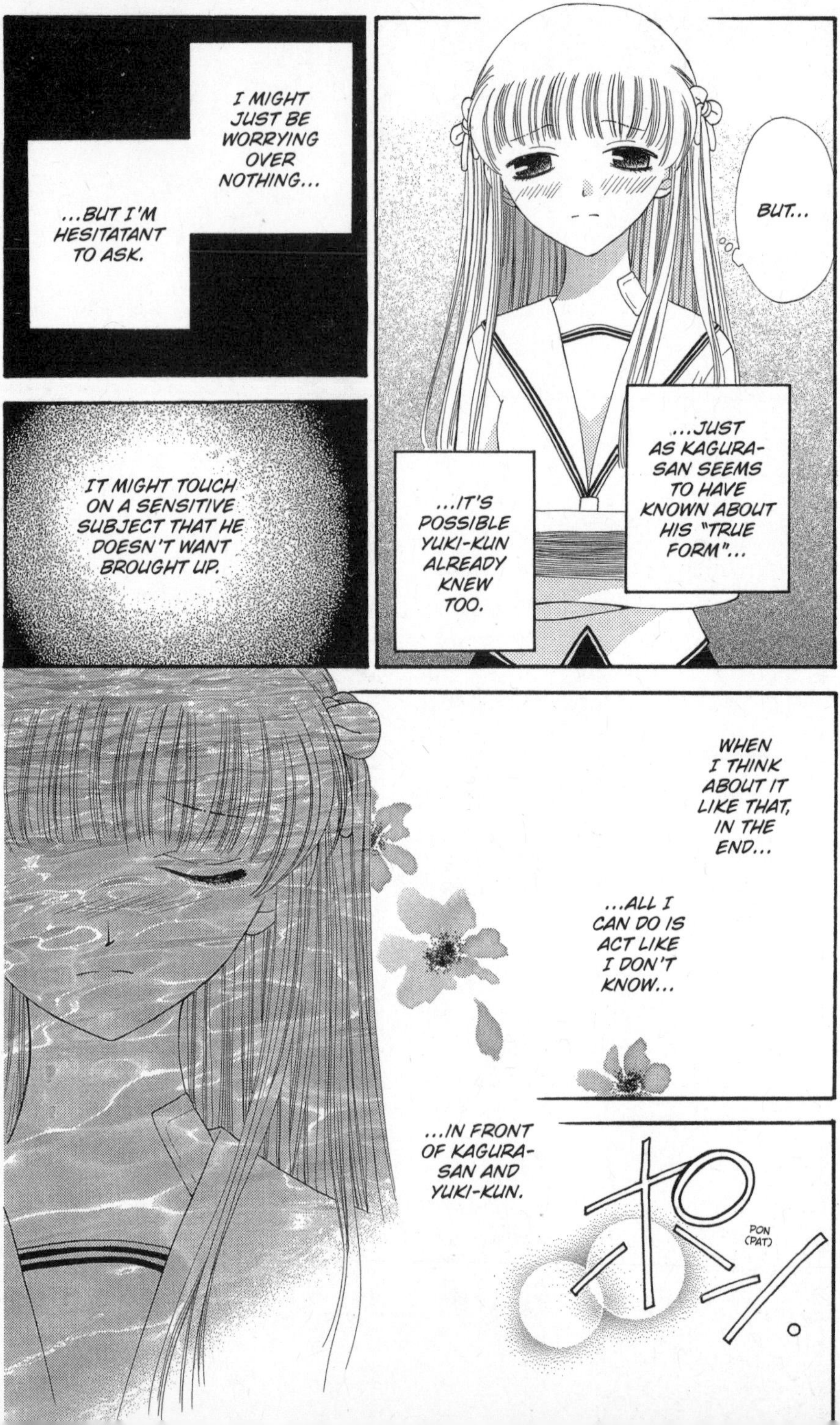
BUT...
...JUST AS KAGURA-SAN SEEMS TO HAVE KNOWN ABOUT HIS "TRUE FORM"...
...IT'S POSSIBLE YUKI-KUN ALREADY KNEW TOO.
I MIGHT JUST BE WORRYING OVER NOTHING...
...BUT I'M HESITATANT TO ASK.
IT MIGHT TOUCH ON A SENSITIVE SUBJECT THAT HE DOESN'T WANT BROUGHT UP.
WHEN I THINK ABOUT IT LIKE THAT, IN THE END...
...ALL I CAN DO IS ACT LIKE I DON'T KNOW...
...IN FRONT OF KAGURA-SAN AND YUKI-KUN.
PON (PAT)

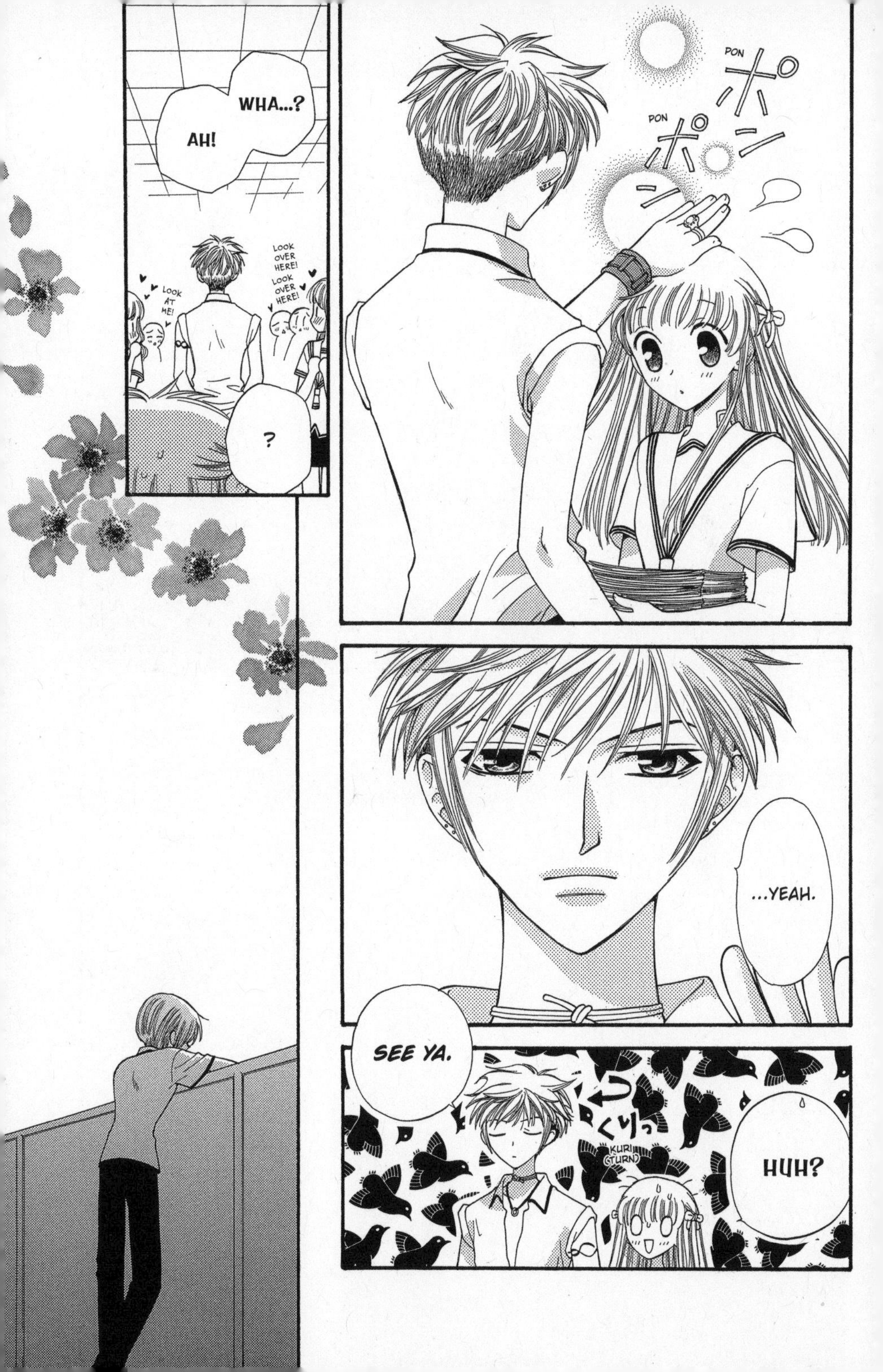
PON
PON
WHA...?
AH!
LOOK OVER HERE!
LOOK OVER HERE!
LOOK AT ME!
?
...YEAH.
SEE YA.
くりっ
KURI (TURN)
HUH?

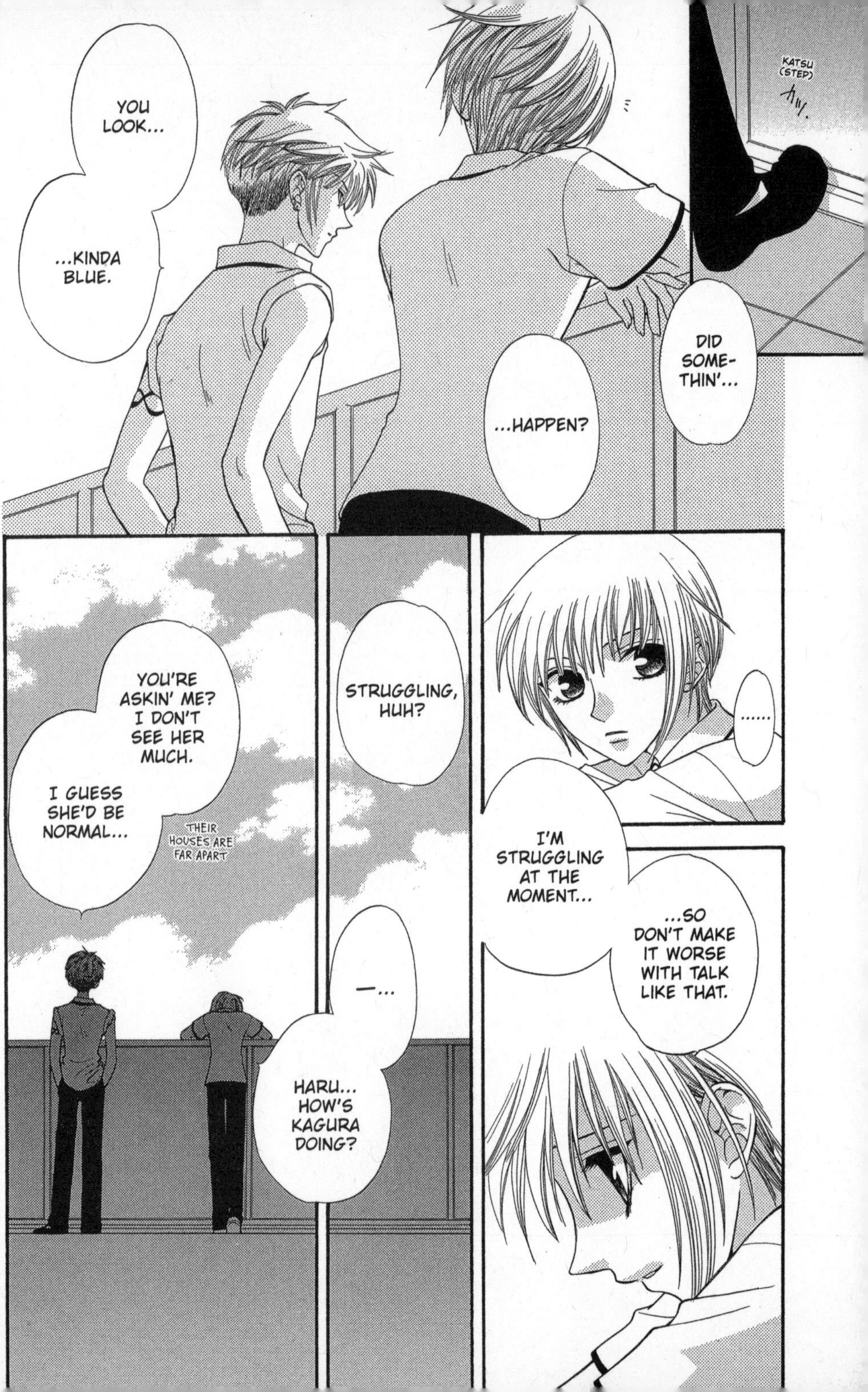
KATSU (STEP)
カッ
DID SOMETHIN'...
...HAPPEN?
YOU LOOK...
...KINDA BLUE.
......
I'M STRUGGLING AT THE MOMENT...
...SO DON'T MAKE IT WORSE WITH TALK LIKE THAT.
STRUGGLING, HUH?
—...
HARU... HOW'S KAGURA DOING?
YOU'RE ASKIN' ME? I DON'T SEE HER MUCH.
I GUESS SHE'D BE NORMAL...
THEIR HOUSES ARE FAR APART

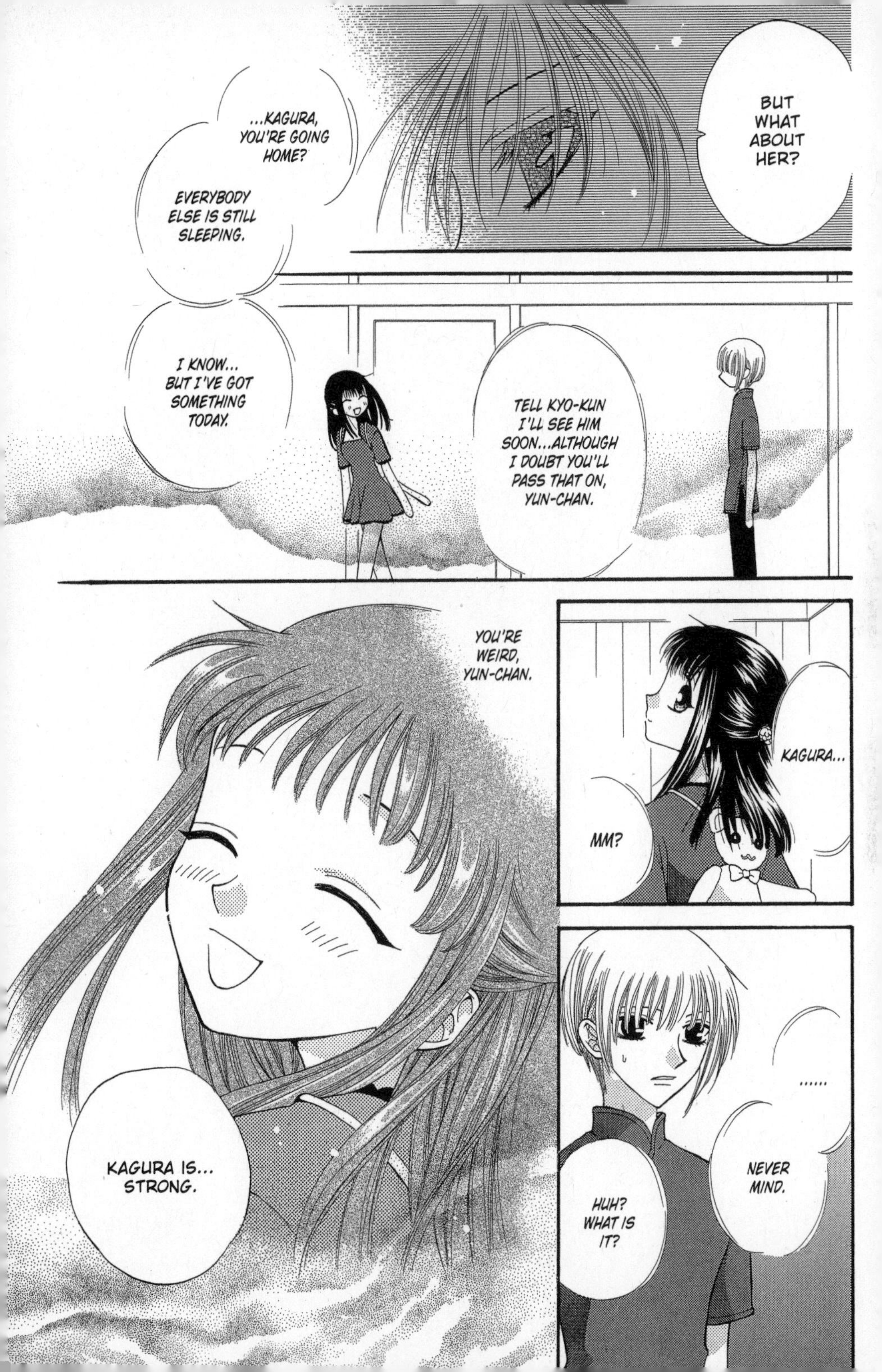
BUT WHAT ABOUT HER?
...KAGURA, YOU'RE GOING HOME?
EVERYBODY ELSE IS STILL SLEEPING.
I KNOW... BUT I'VE GOT SOMETHING TODAY.
TELL KYO-KUN I'LL SEE HIM SOON...ALTHOUGH I DOUBT YOU'LL PASS THAT ON, YUN-CHAN.
KAGURA...
MM?
......
NEVER MIND.
HUH? WHAT IS IT?
YOU'RE WEIRD, YUN-CHAN.
KAGURA IS... STRONG.

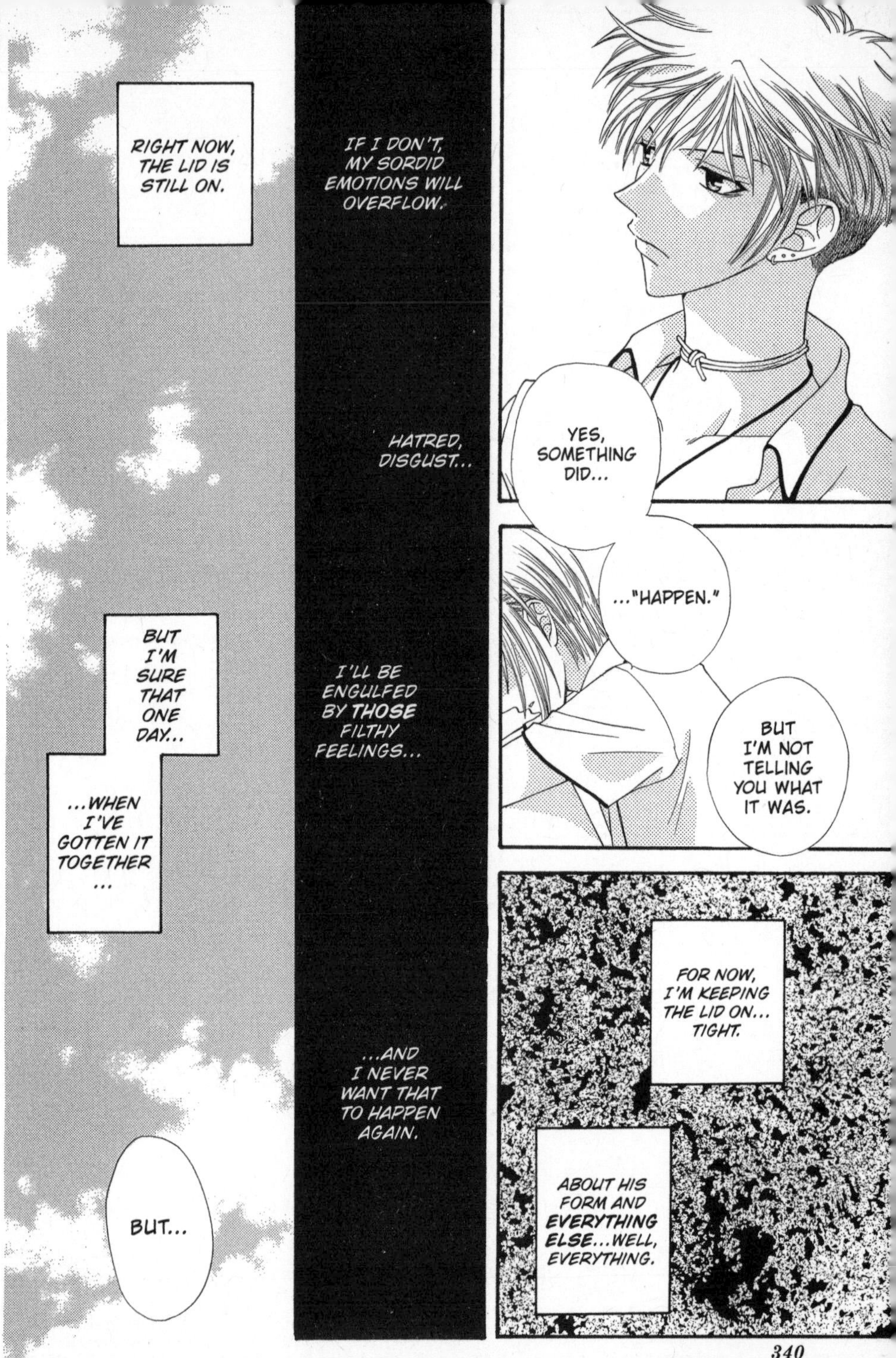
YES, SOMETHING DID...
..."HAPPEN."
BUT I'M NOT TELLING YOU WHAT IT WAS.
FOR NOW, I'M KEEPING THE LID ON... TIGHT.
ABOUT HIS FORM AND EVERYTHING ELSE...WELL, EVERYTHING.
IF I DON'T, MY SORDID EMOTIONS WILL OVERFLOW.
HATRED, DISGUST...
I'LL BE ENGULFED BY THOSE FILTHY FEELINGS...
...AND I NEVER WANT THAT TO HAPPEN AGAIN.
RIGHT NOW, THE LID IS STILL ON.
BUT I'M SURE THAT ONE DAY...
...WHEN I'VE GOTTEN IT TOGETHER...
BUT...

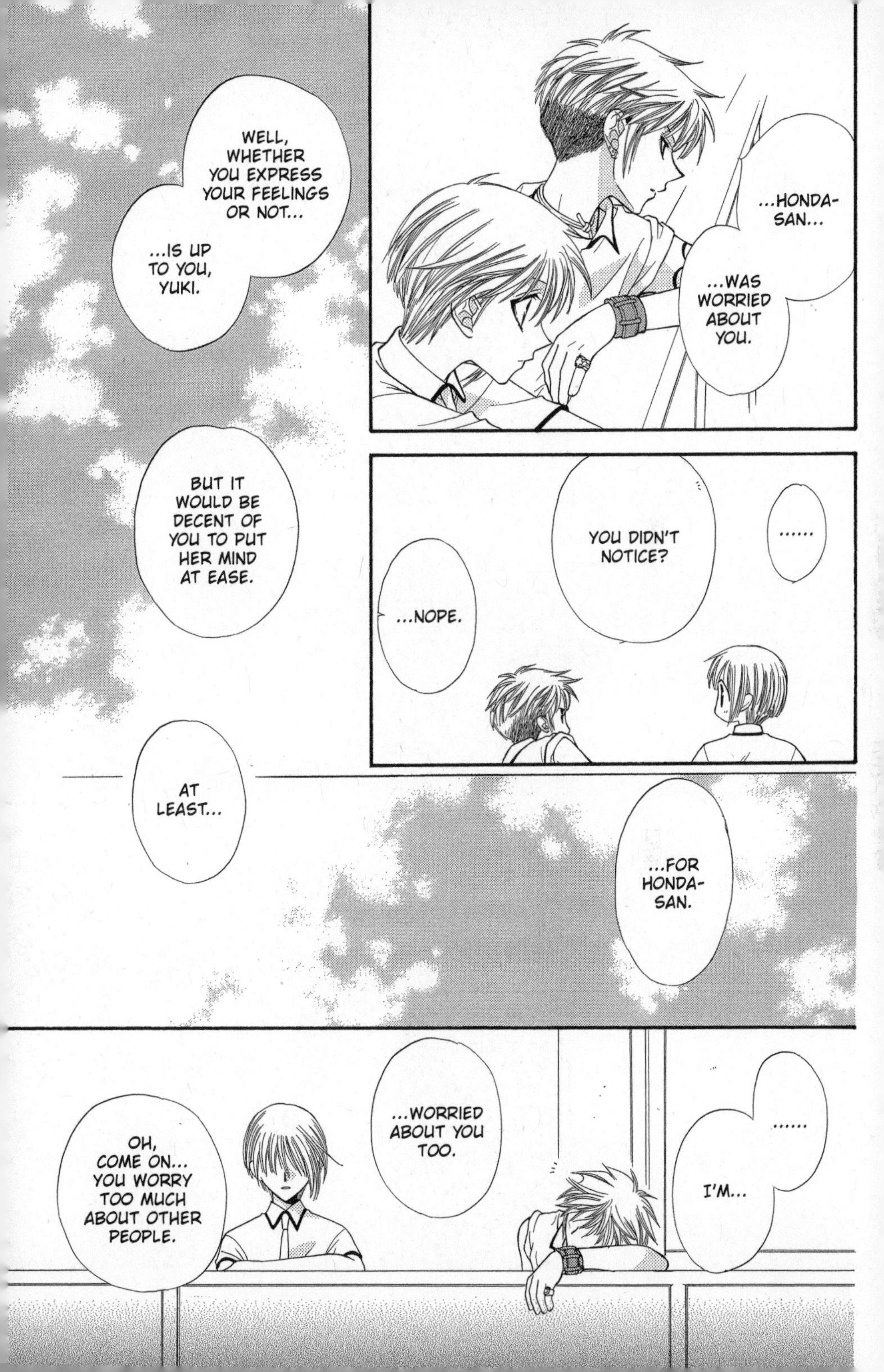
...HONDA-SAN...
...WAS WORRIED ABOUT YOU.
......
YOU DIDN'T NOTICE?
...NOPE.
WELL, WHETHER YOU EXPRESS YOUR FEELINGS OR NOT...
...IS UP TO YOU, YUKI.
BUT IT WOULD BE DECENT OF YOU TO PUT HER MIND AT EASE.
AT LEAST...
...FOR HONDA-SAN.
......
I'M...
...WORRIED ABOUT YOU TOO.
OH, COME ON... YOU WORRY TOO MUCH ABOUT OTHER PEOPLE.

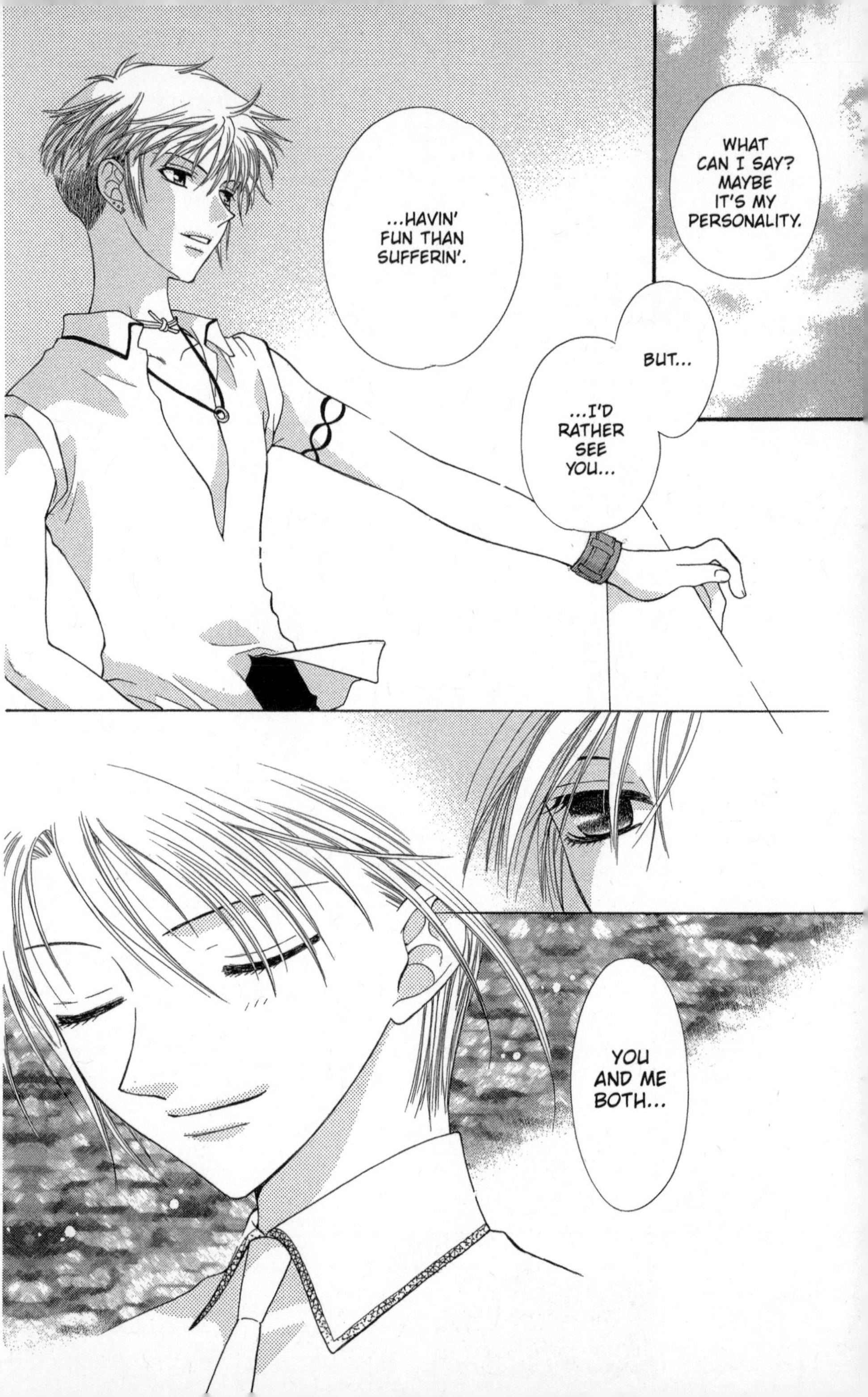
WHAT CAN I SAY? MAYBE IT'S MY PERSONALITY.
BUT...
...I'D RATHER SEE YOU...
...HAVIN' FUN THAN SUFFERIN'.
YOU AND ME BOTH...

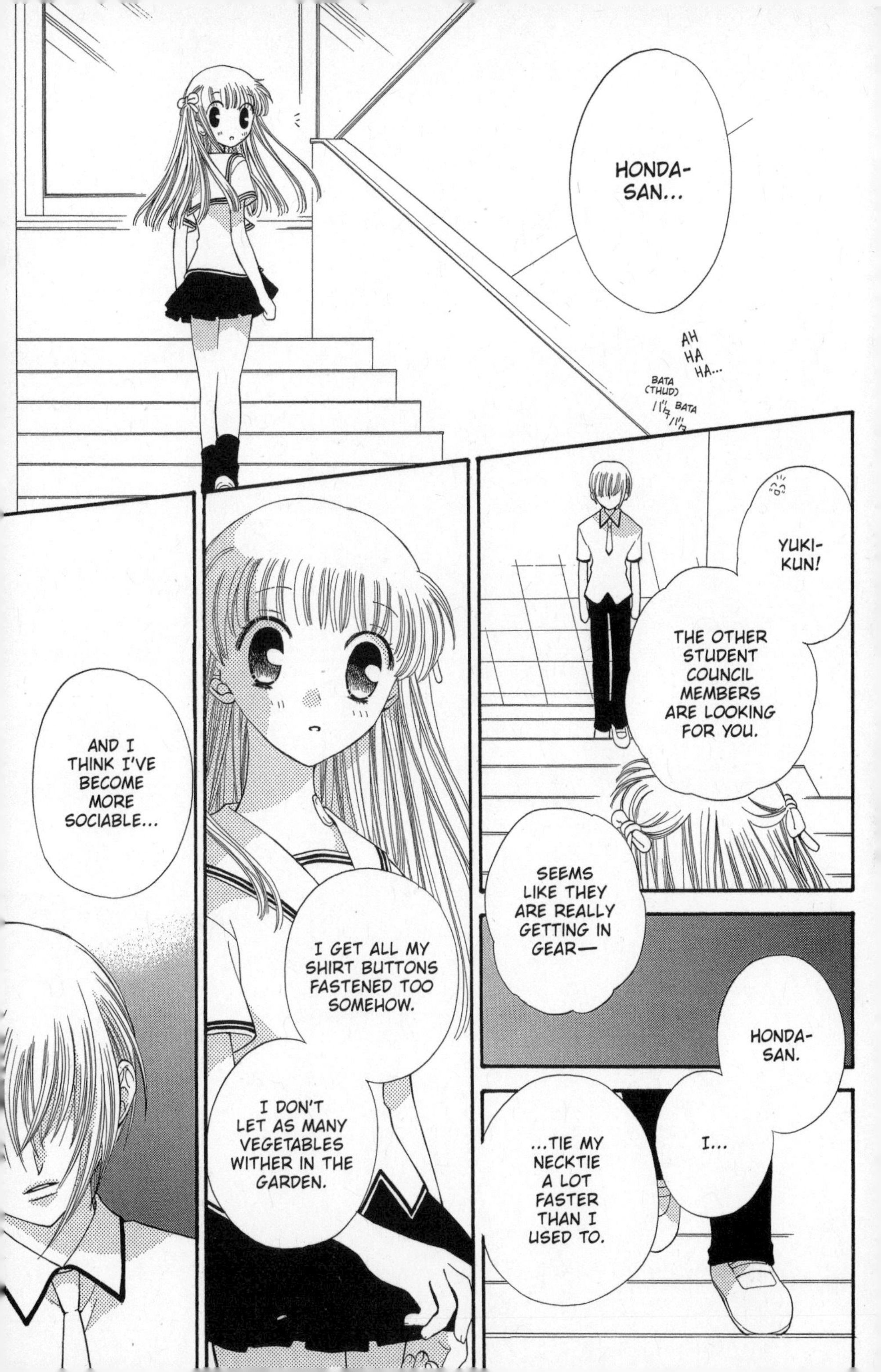
HONDA-SAN...
AH HA HA...
BATA (THUD) BATA
YUKI-KUN!
THE OTHER STUDENT COUNCIL MEMBERS ARE LOOKING FOR YOU.
SEEMS LIKE THEY ARE REALLY GETTING IN GEAR—
HONDA-SAN.
I...
...TIE MY NECKTIE A LOT FASTER THAN I USED TO.
I GET ALL MY SHIRT BUTTONS FASTENED TOO SOMEHOW.
I DON'T LET AS MANY VEGETABLES WITHER IN THE GARDEN.
AND I THINK I'VE BECOME MORE SOCIABLE...

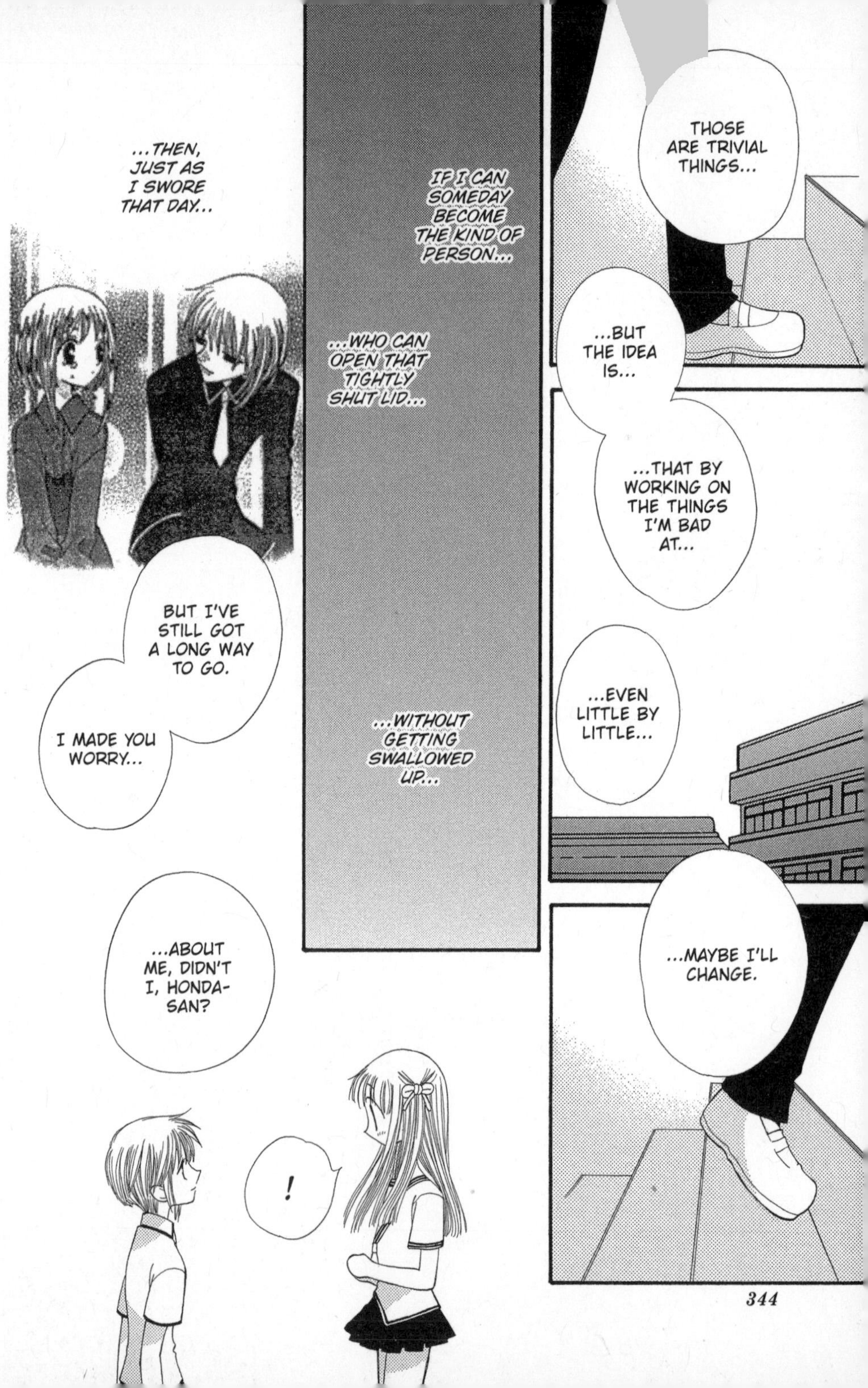
THOSE ARE TRIVIAL THINGS...
...BUT THE IDEA IS...
...THAT BY WORKING ON THE THINGS I'M BAD AT...
...EVEN LITTLE BY LITTLE...
...MAYBE I'LL CHANGE.
IF I CAN SOMEDAY BECOME THE KIND OF PERSON...
...WHO CAN OPEN THAT TIGHTLY SHUT LID...
...WITHOUT GETTING SWALLOWED UP...
...THEN, JUST AS I SWORE THAT DAY...
BUT I'VE STILL GOT A LONG WAY TO GO.
I MADE YOU WORRY...
...ABOUT ME, DIDN'T I, HONDA-SAN?
!

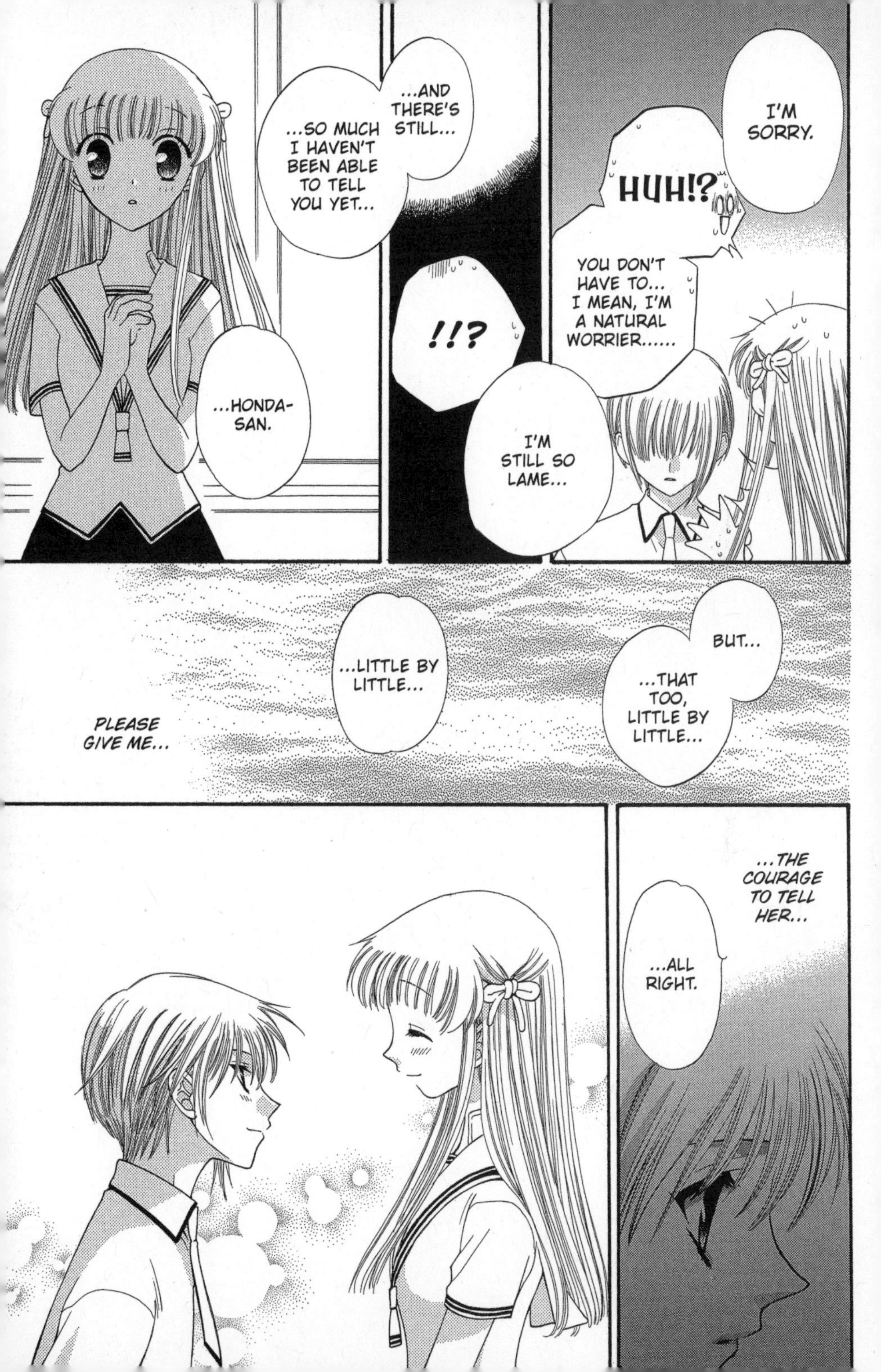
I'M SORRY.
HUH!?
YOU DON'T HAVE TO... I MEAN, I'M A NATURAL WORRIER......
!!?
I'M STILL SO LAME...
...AND THERE'S STILL...
...SO MUCH I HAVEN'T BEEN ABLE TO TELL YOU YET...
...HONDA-SAN.
BUT...
...THAT TOO, LITTLE BY LITTLE...
...LITTLE BY LITTLE...
PLEASE GIVE ME...
...THE COURAGE TO TELL HER...
...ALL RIGHT.

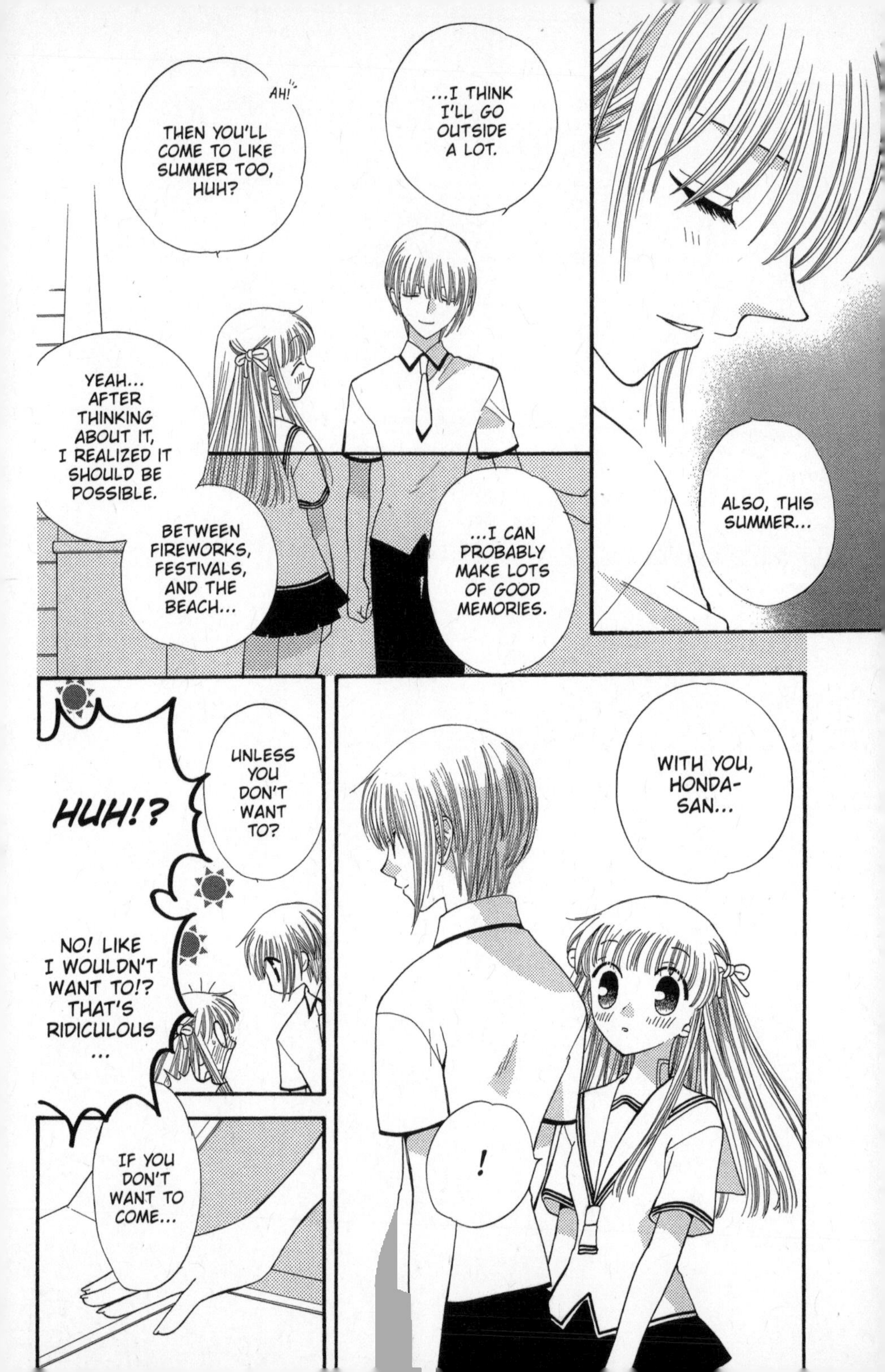
...I THINK I'LL GO OUTSIDE A LOT.
AH! THEN YOU'LL COME TO LIKE SUMMER TOO, HUH?
YEAH... AFTER THINKING ABOUT IT, I REALIZED IT SHOULD BE POSSIBLE.
BETWEEN FIREWORKS, FESTIVALS, AND THE BEACH...
ALSO, THIS SUMMER...
...I CAN PROBABLY MAKE LOTS OF GOOD MEMORIES.
WITH YOU, HONDA-SAN...
!
UNLESS YOU DON'T WANT TO?
HUH!?
NO! LIKE I WOULDN'T WANT TO!? THAT'S RIDICULOUS...
IF YOU DON'T WANT TO COME...

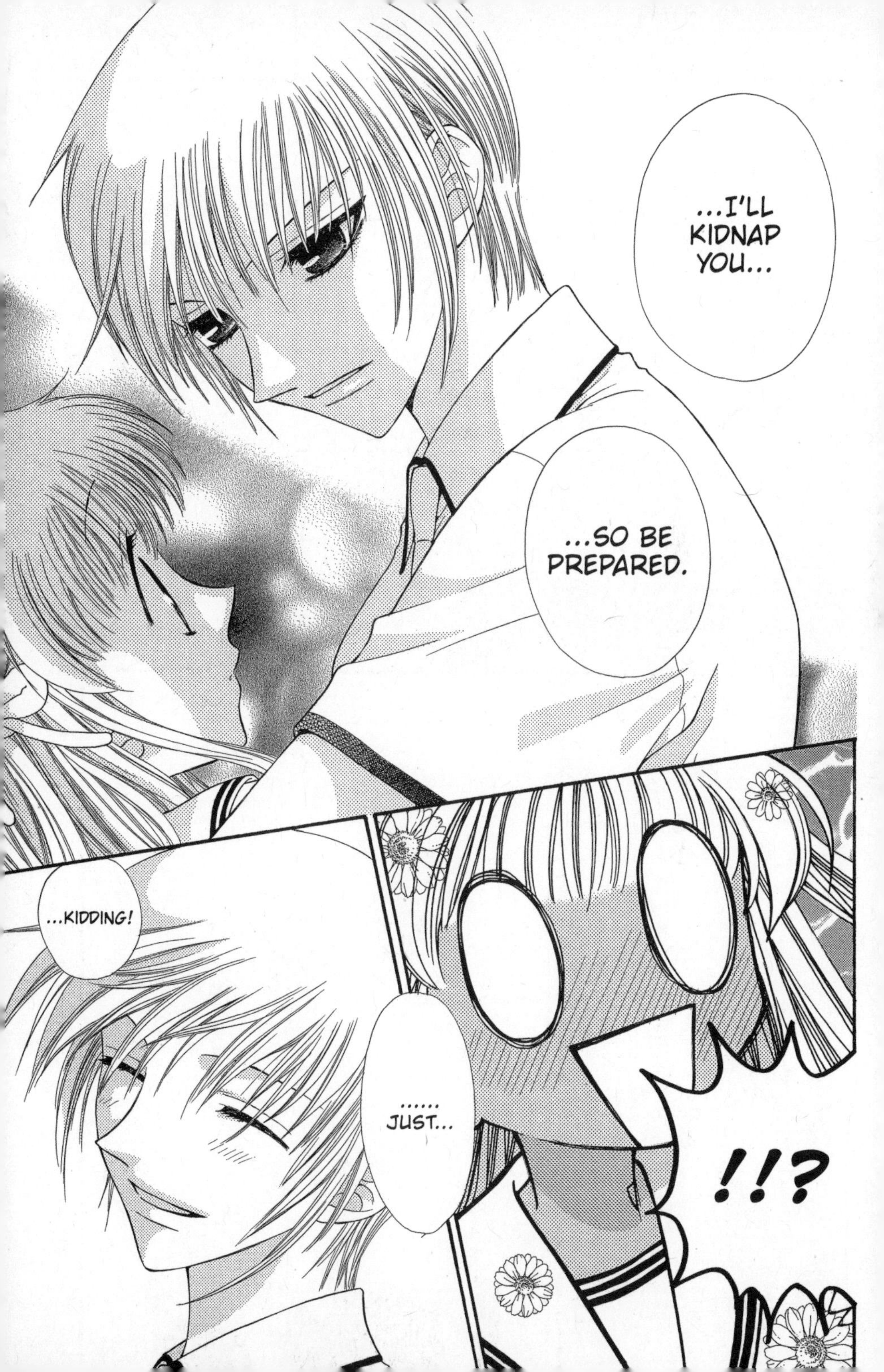
...I'LL KIDNAP YOU...
...SO BE PREPARED.
!!?
......JUST...
...KIDDING!

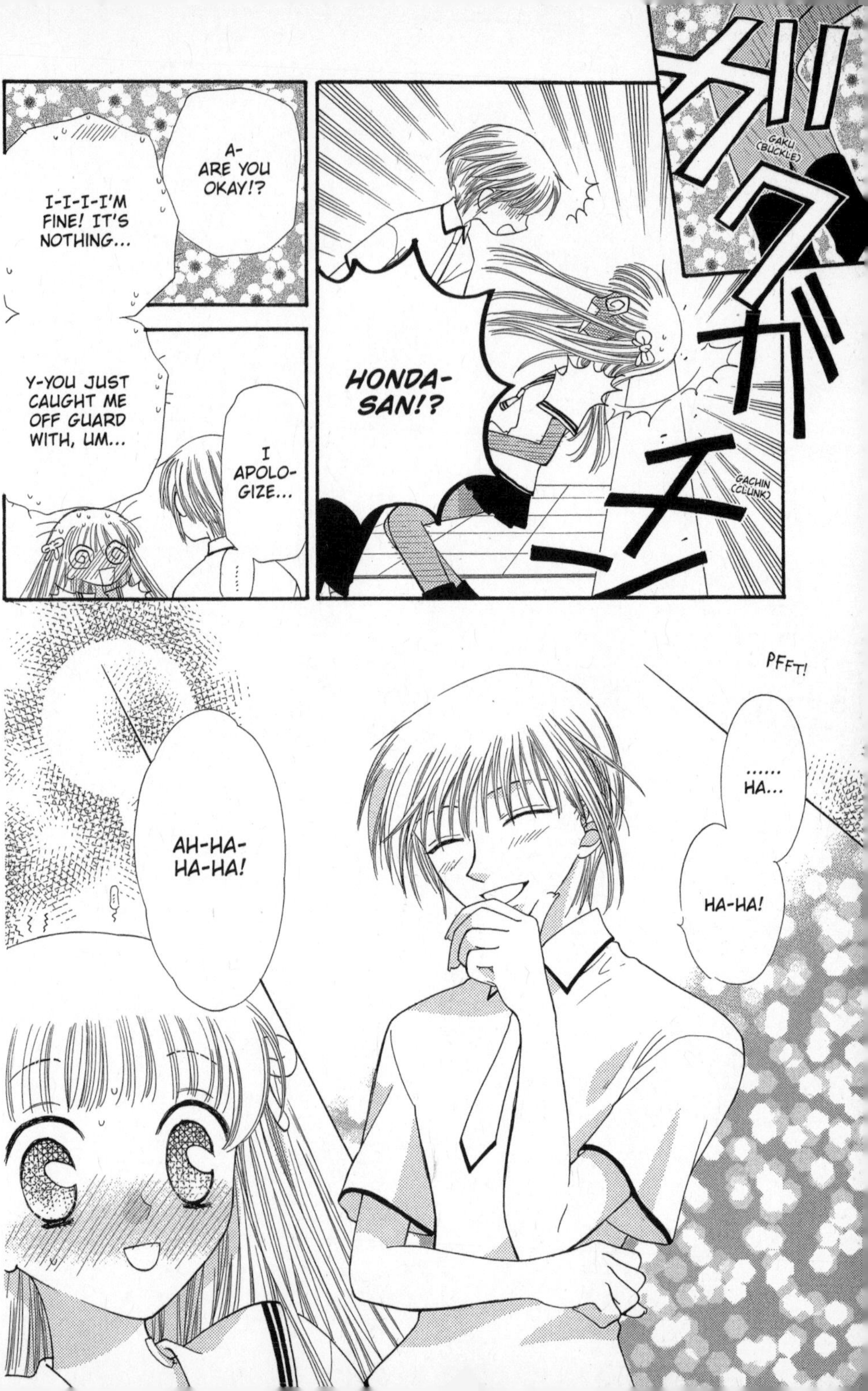
GAKU (BUCKLE)
GACHIN (CLUNK)
HONDA-SAN!?
A- ARE YOU OKAY!?
I-I-I-I'M FINE! IT'S NOTHING...
I APOLOGIZE...
Y-YOU JUST CAUGHT ME OFF GUARD WITH, UM...
PFFT!
......HA...
HA-HA!
AH-HA-HA-HA!

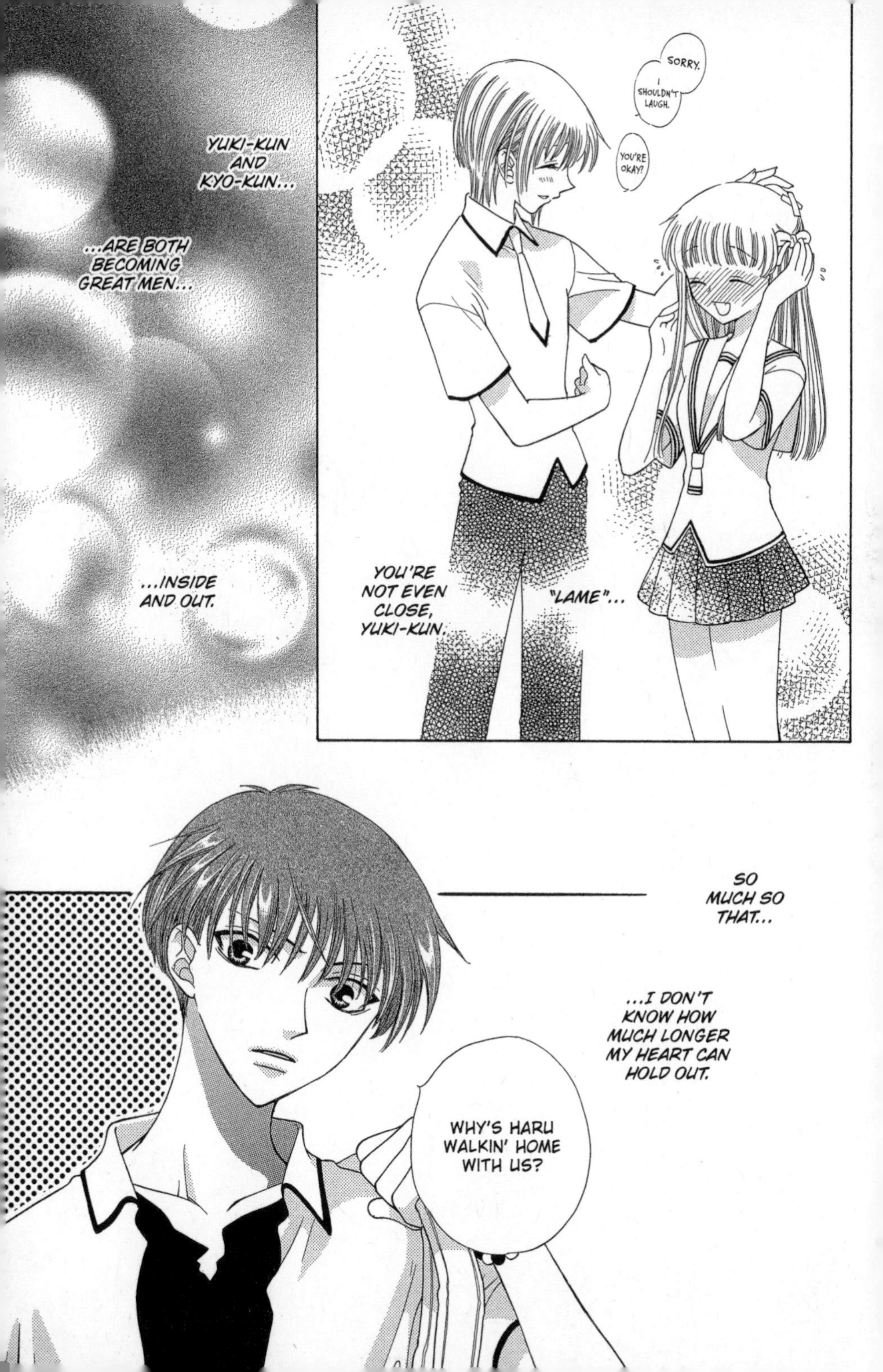
SORRY.
I SHOULDN'T LAUGH.
YOU'RE OKAY?
"LAME"...
YOU'RE NOT EVEN CLOSE, YUKI-KUN.
YUKI-KUN AND KYO-KUN...
...ARE BOTH BECOMING GREAT MEN...
...INSIDE AND OUT.
SO MUCH SO THAT...
...I DON'T KNOW HOW MUCH LONGER MY HEART CAN HOLD OUT.
WHY'S HARU WALKIN' HOME WITH US?

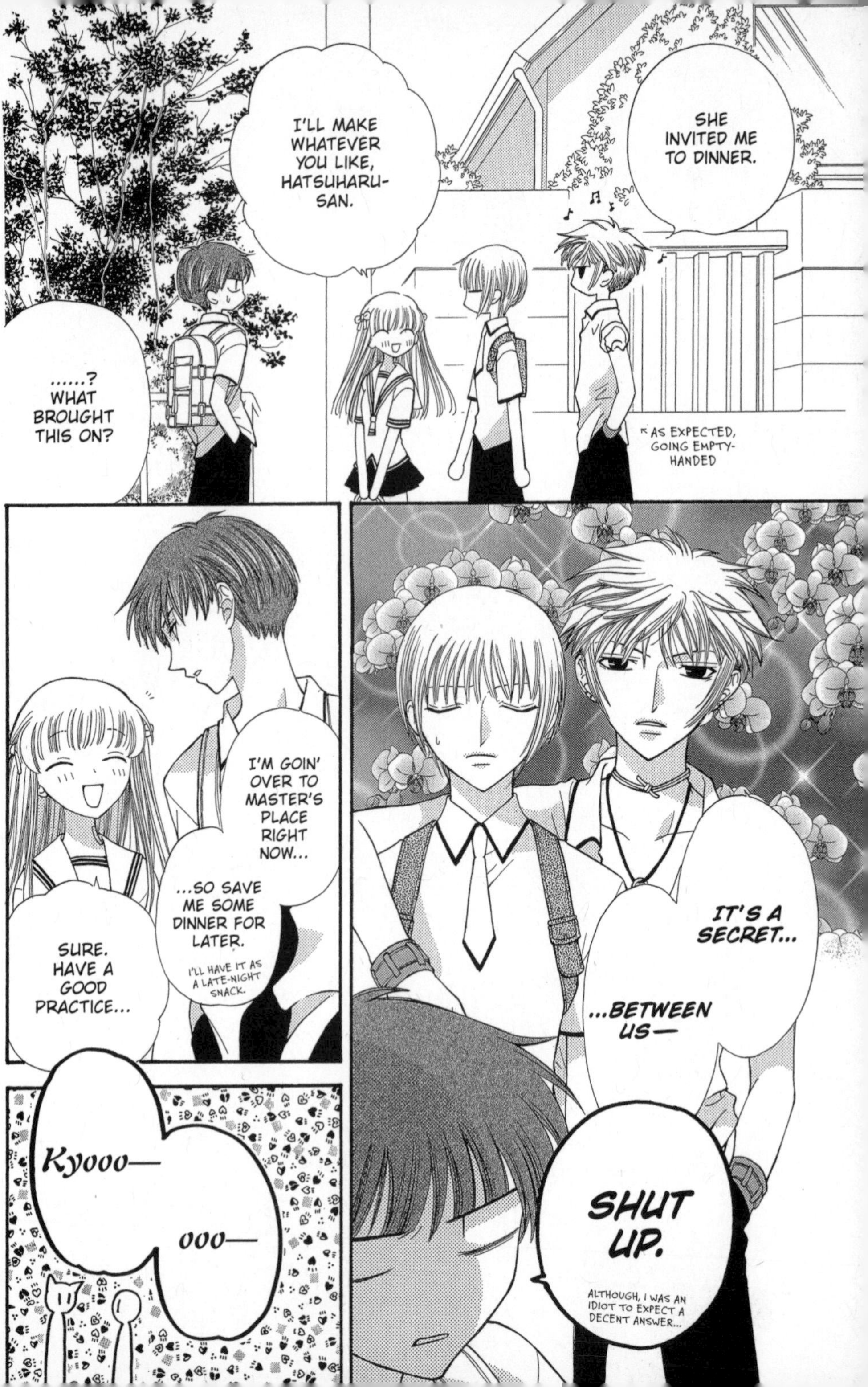
SHE INVITED ME TO DINNER.
I'LL MAKE WHATEVER YOU LIKE, HATSUHARU-SAN.
......? WHAT BROUGHT THIS ON?
AS EXPECTED, GOING EMPTY-HANDED
IT'S A SECRET...
...BETWEEN US—
SHUT UP.
ALTHOUGH, I WAS AN IDIOT TO EXPECT A DECENT ANSWER...
I'M GOIN' OVER TO MASTER'S PLACE RIGHT NOW...
...SO SAVE ME SOME DINNER FOR LATER.
I'LL HAVE IT AS A LATE-NIGHT SNACK.
SURE. HAVE A GOOD PRACTICE...
Kyooo—
ooo—

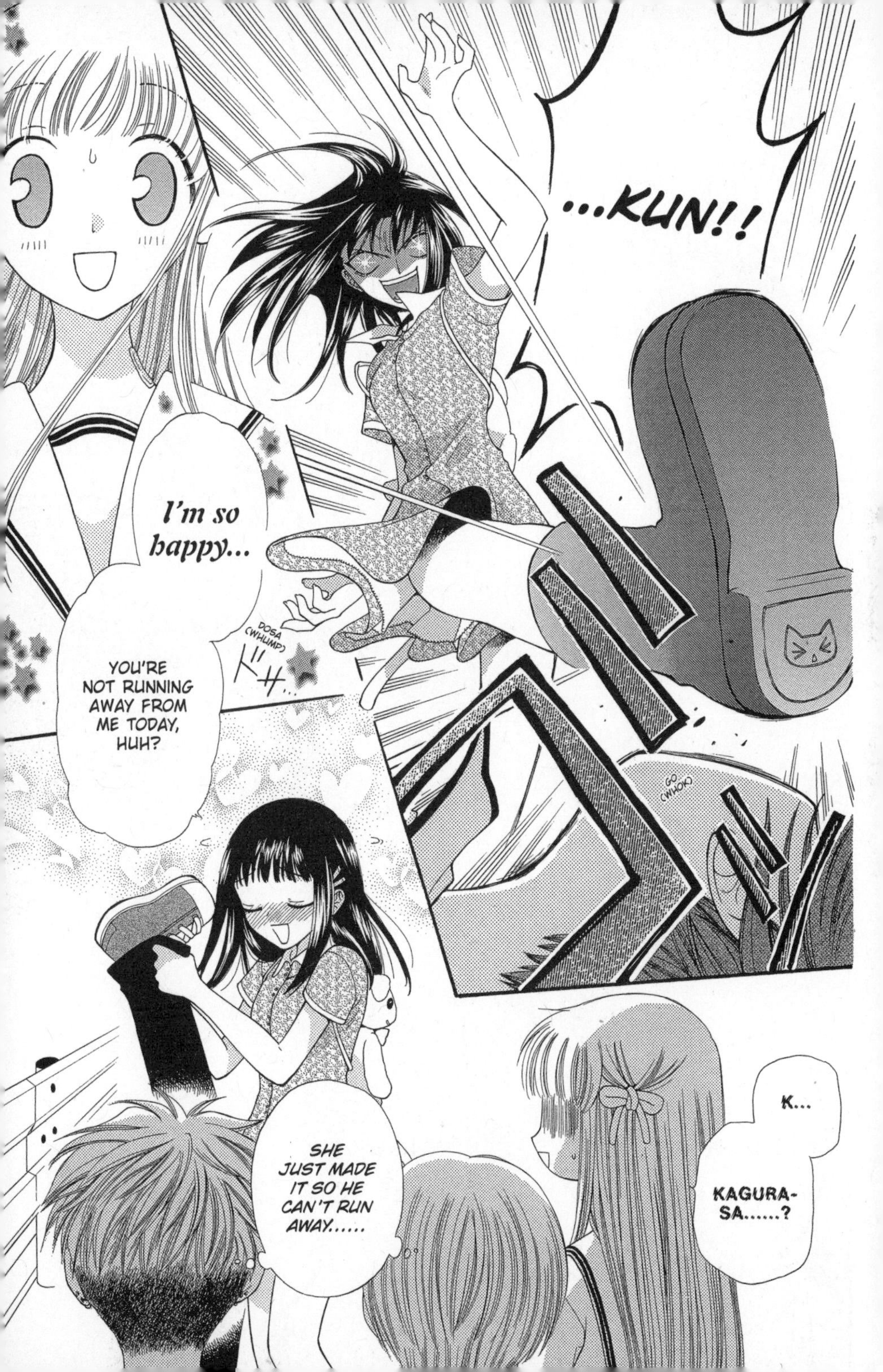
...KUN!!
GO (WHOK)
I'm so happy...
DOSA (WHUMP)
YOU'RE NOT RUNNING AWAY FROM ME TODAY, HUH?
K...
KAGURA-SA......?
SHE JUST MADE IT SO HE CAN'T RUN AWAY......

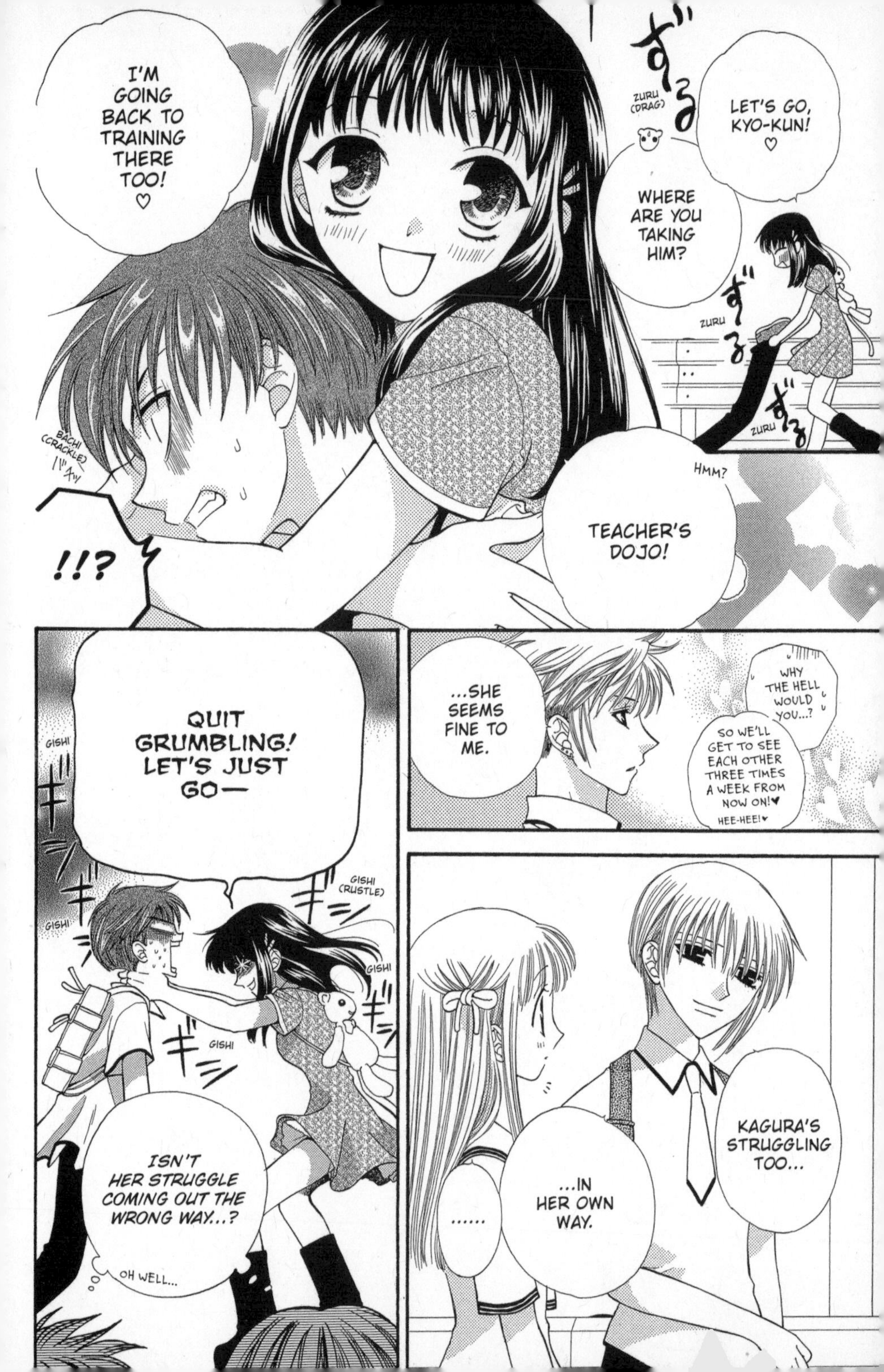

LET'S GO, KYO-KUN! ♡
ZURU (DRAG)
WHERE ARE YOU TAKING HIM?
ZURU
ZURU
HMM?
TEACHER'S DOJO!
I'M GOING BACK TO TRAINING THERE TOO! ♡
BACHI (CRACKLE)
!!?
WHY THE HELL WOULD YOU...?
SO WE'LL GET TO SEE EACH OTHER THREE TIMES A WEEK FROM NOW ON!♥
HEE-HEE!♥
...SHE SEEMS FINE TO ME.
KAGURA'S STRUGGLING TOO...
...IN HER OWN WAY.
......
QUIT GRUMBLING! LET'S JUST GO—
GISHI (RUSTLE)
GISHI
GISHI
GISHI
ISN'T HER STRUGGLE COMING OUT THE WRONG WAY...?
OH WELL...

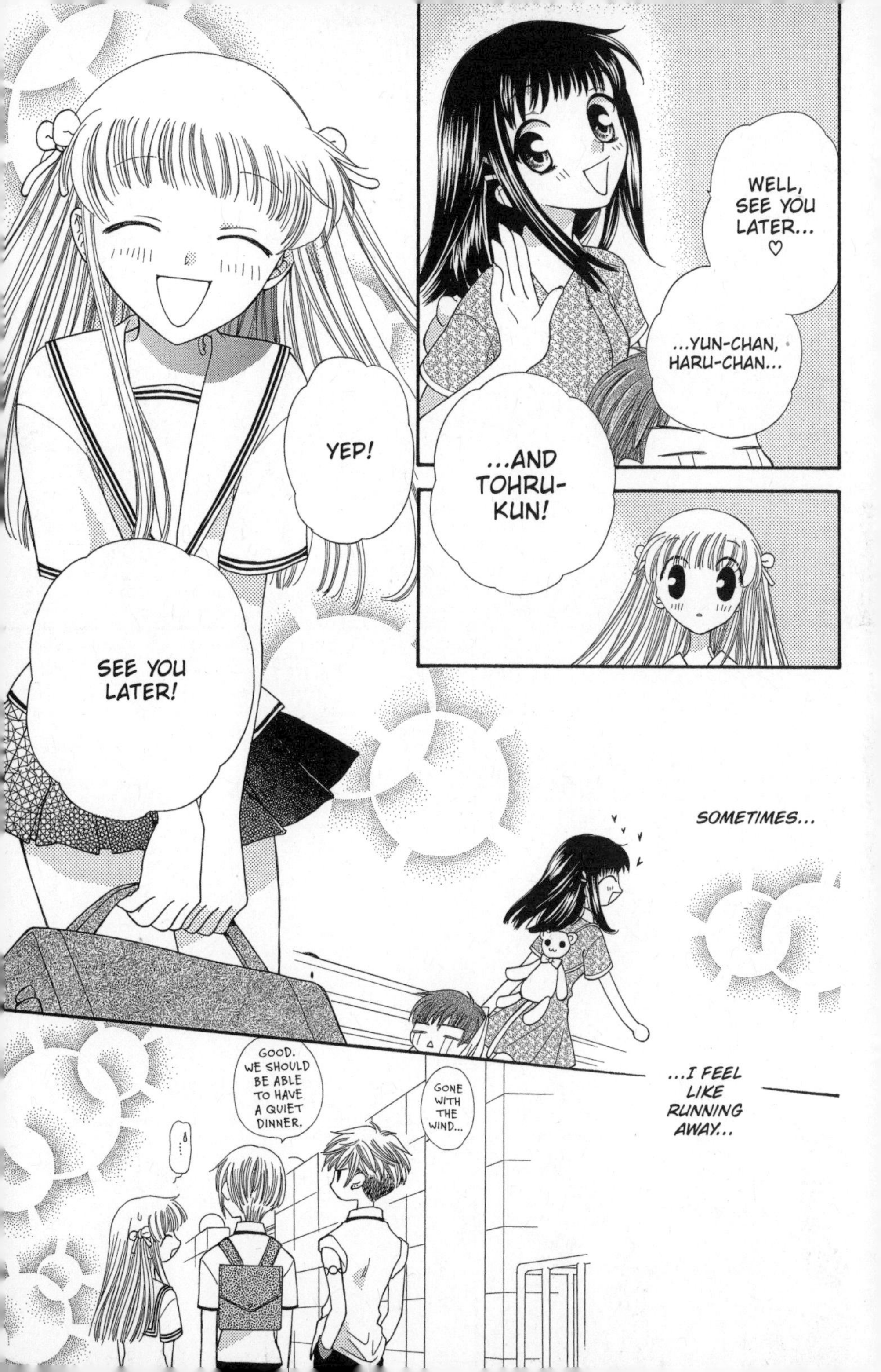
WELL, SEE YOU LATER... ♡
...YUN-CHAN, HARU-CHAN...
...AND TOHRU-KUN!
YEP!
SEE YOU LATER!
SOMETIMES...
...I FEEL LIKE RUNNING AWAY...
GONE WITH THE WIND...
GOOD. WE SHOULD BE ABLE TO HAVE A QUIET DINNER.
...

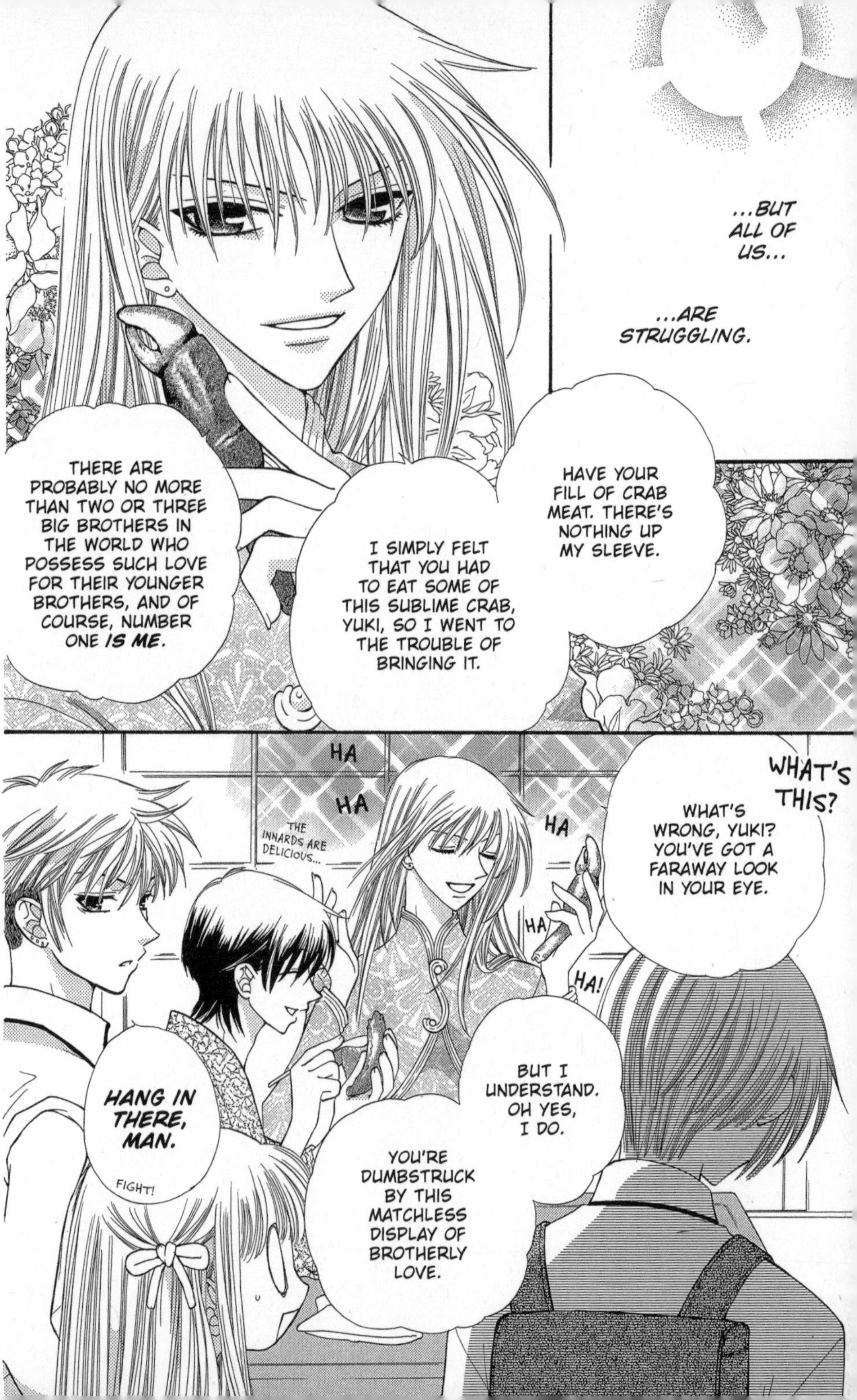
...BUT ALL OF US...
...ARE STRUGGLING.
HAVE YOUR FILL OF CRAB MEAT. THERE'S NOTHING UP MY SLEEVE.
I SIMPLY FELT THAT YOU HAD TO EAT SOME OF THIS SUBLIME CRAB, YUKI, SO I WENT TO THE TROUBLE OF BRINGING IT.
THERE ARE PROBABLY NO MORE THAN TWO OR THREE BIG BROTHERS IN THE WORLD WHO POSSESS SUCH LOVE FOR THEIR YOUNGER BROTHERS, AND OF COURSE, NUMBER ONE *IS ME*.
WHAT'S THIS?
WHAT'S WRONG, YUKI? YOU'VE GOT A FARAWAY LOOK IN YOUR EYE.
HA HA HA HA HA!
THE INNARDS ARE DELICIOUS...
BUT I UNDERSTAND. OH YES, I DO.
YOU'RE DUMBSTRUCK BY THIS MATCHLESS DISPLAY OF BROTHERLY LOVE.
HANG IN THERE, MAN.
FIGHT!

Chapter 36

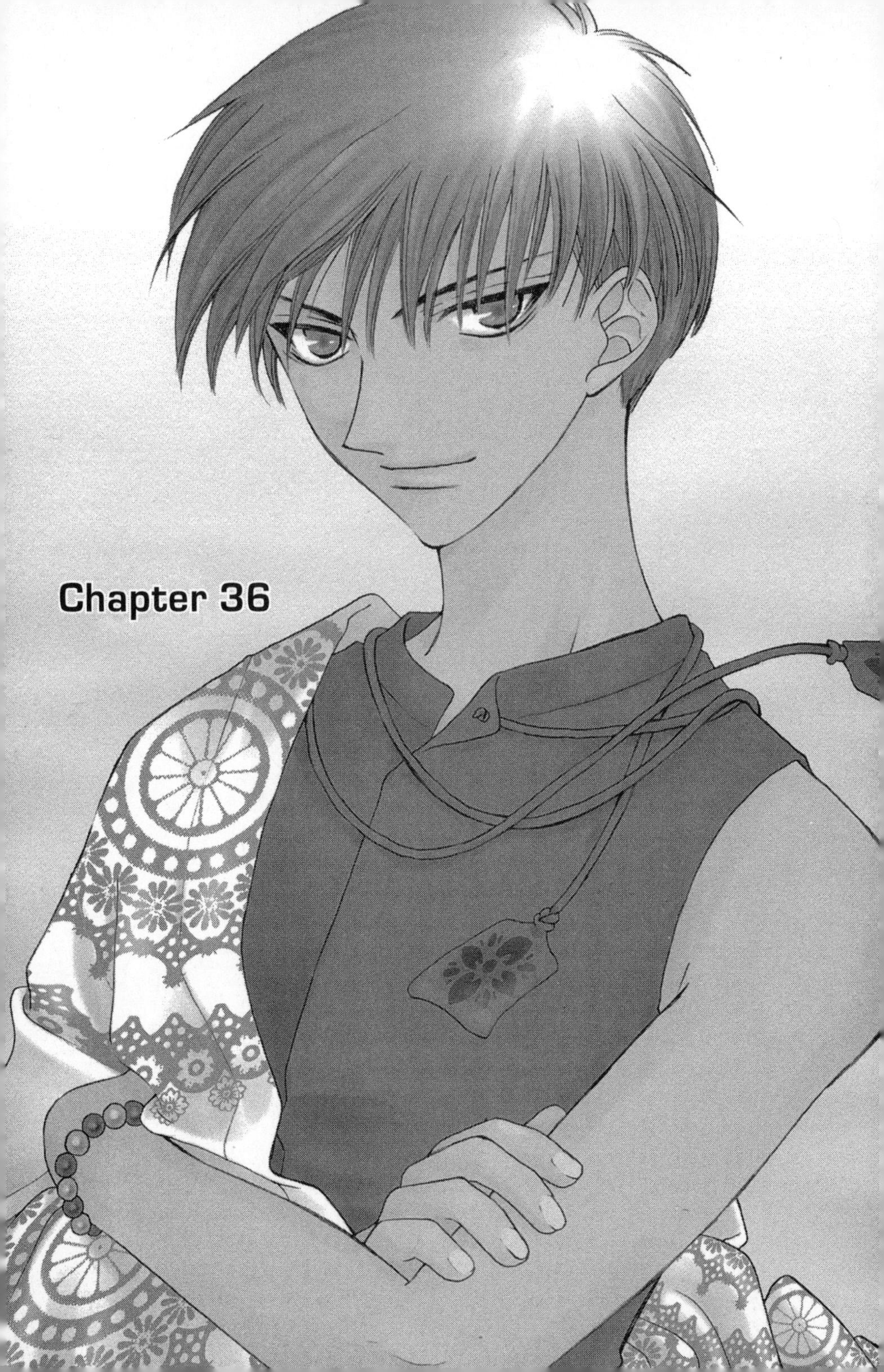

COLLECTOR'S EDITION

Fruits Basket

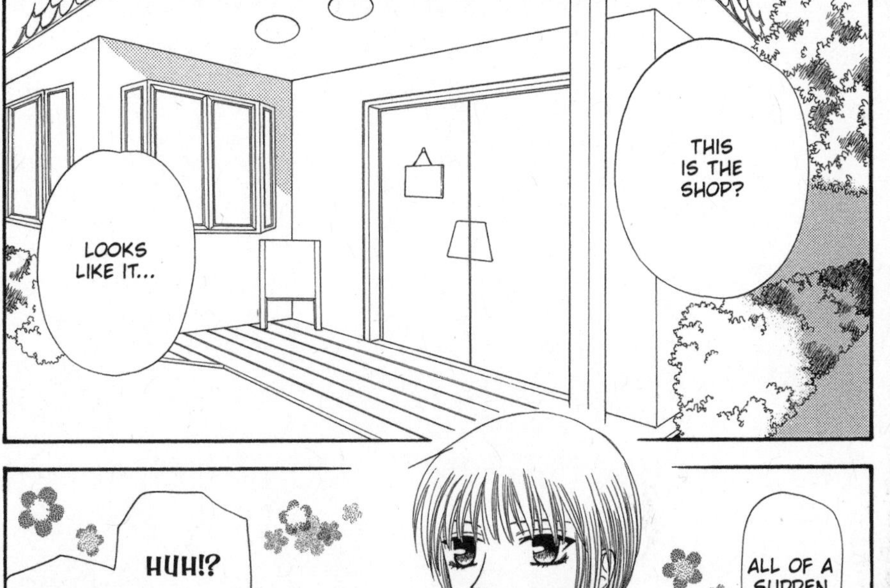
THIS IS THE SHOP?
LOOKS LIKE IT...
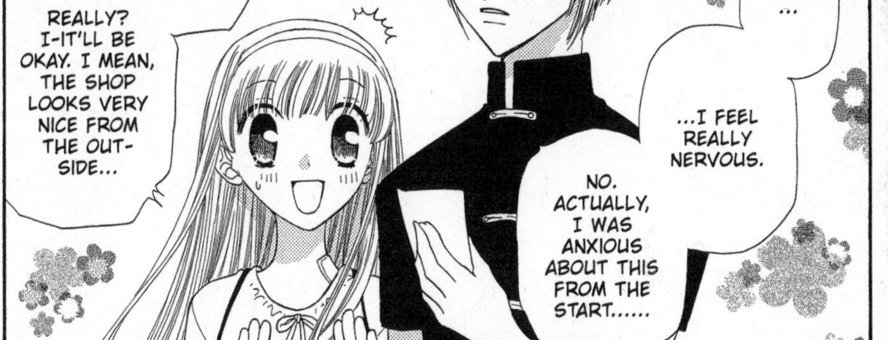
ALL OF A SUDDEN ...
...I FEEL REALLY NERVOUS.
NO. ACTUALLY, I WAS ANXIOUS ABOUT THIS FROM THE START......
HUH!?
REALLY? I-IT'LL BE OKAY. I MEAN, THE SHOP LOOKS VERY NICE FROM THE OUT-SIDE...
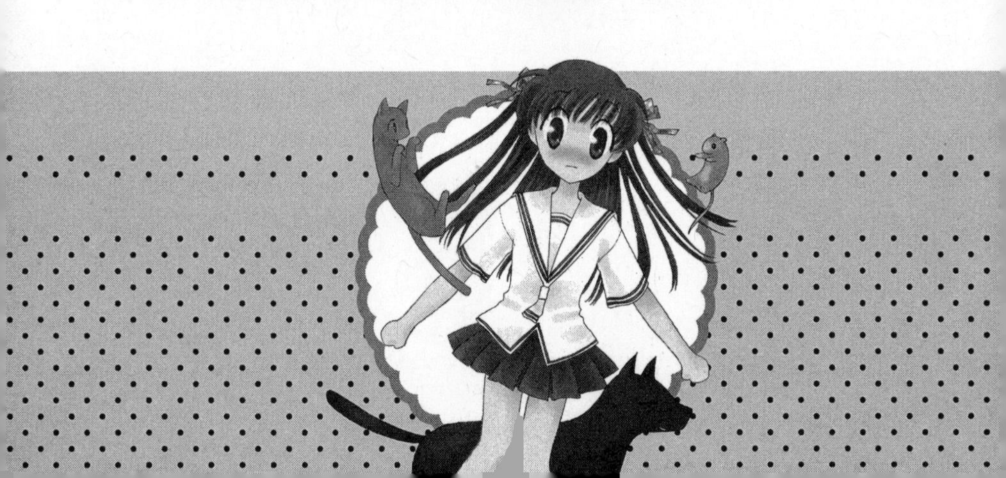

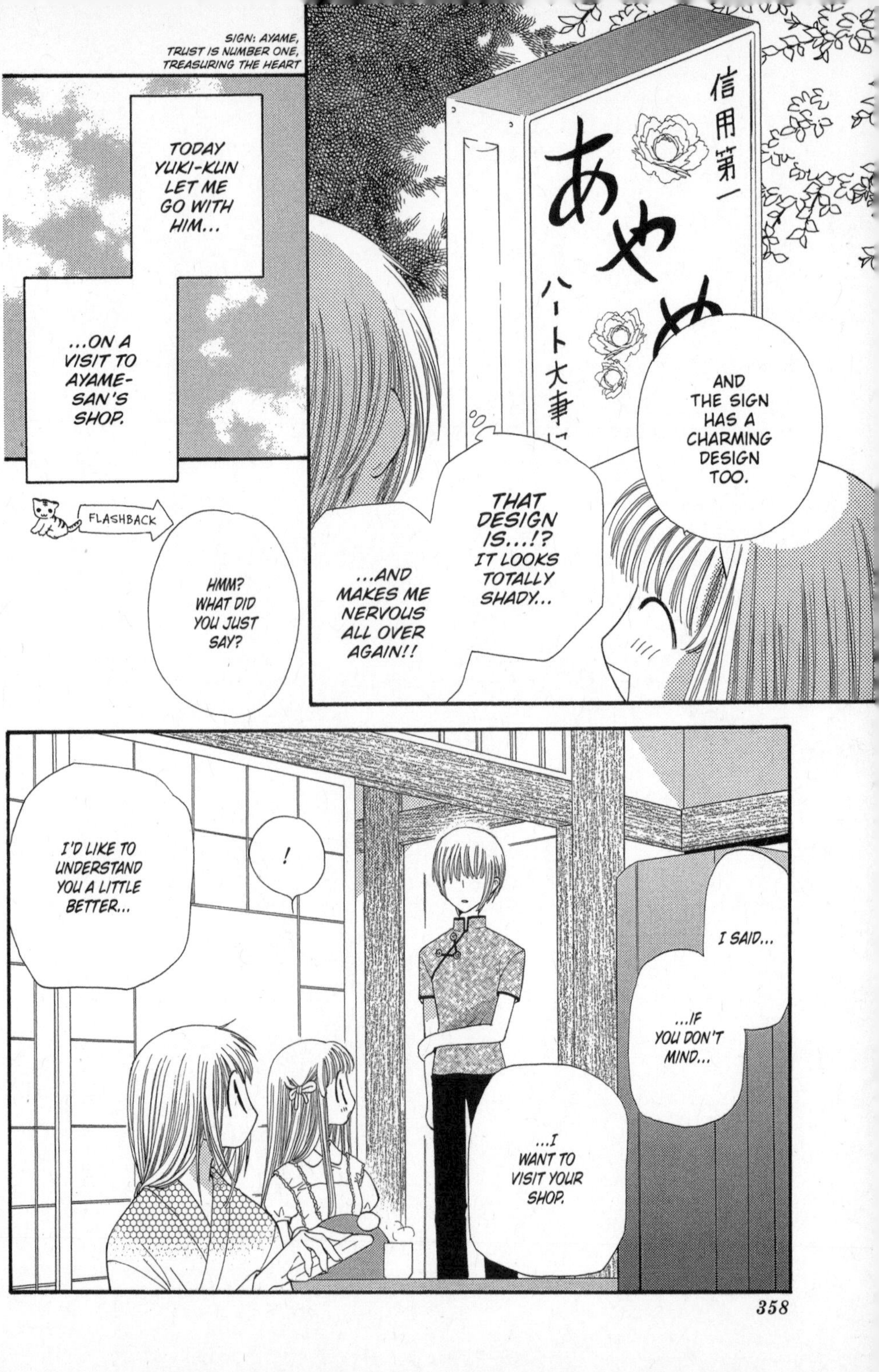
SIGN: AYAME, TRUST IS NUMBER ONE, TREASURING THE HEART
信用第一
あやめ
ハート大事に
AND THE SIGN HAS A CHARMING DESIGN TOO.
THAT DESIGN IS...!? IT LOOKS TOTALLY SHADY...
...AND MAKES ME NERVOUS ALL OVER AGAIN!!
TODAY YUKI-KUN LET ME GO WITH HIM...
...ON A VISIT TO AYAME-SAN'S SHOP.
FLASHBACK
HMM? WHAT DID YOU JUST SAY?
I SAID...
...IF YOU DON'T MIND...
...I WANT TO VISIT YOUR SHOP.
!
I'D LIKE TO UNDERSTAND YOU A LITTLE BETTER...

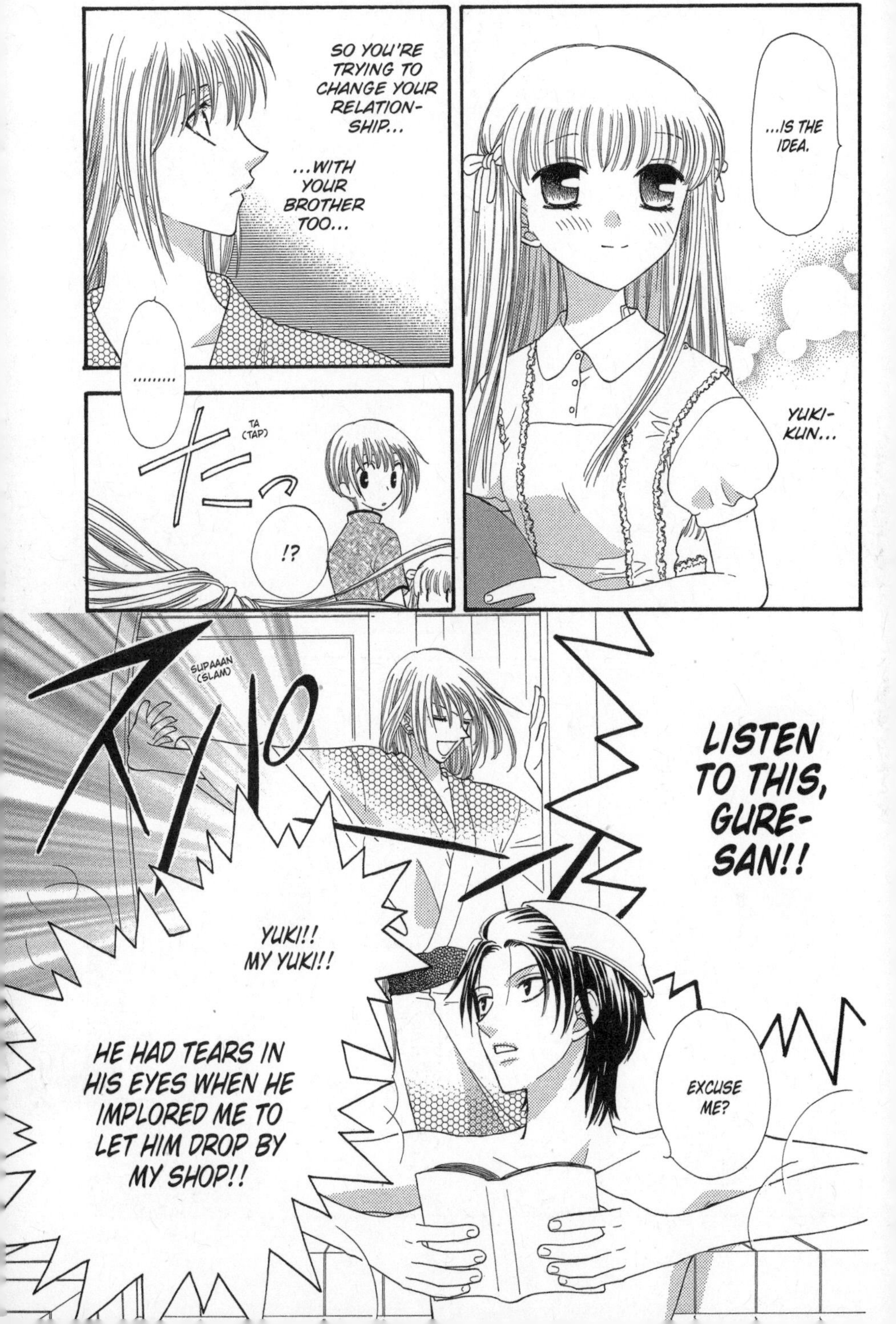
...IS THE IDEA.
YUKI-KUN...
SO YOU'RE TRYING TO CHANGE YOUR RELATION-SHIP...
...WITH YOUR BROTHER TOO...
....
TA (TAP)
!?
SUPAAAN (SLAM)
LISTEN TO THIS, GURE-SAN!!
YUKI!! MY YUKI!!
HE HAD TEARS IN HIS EYES WHEN HE IMPLORED ME TO LET HIM DROP BY MY SHOP!!
EXCUSE ME?

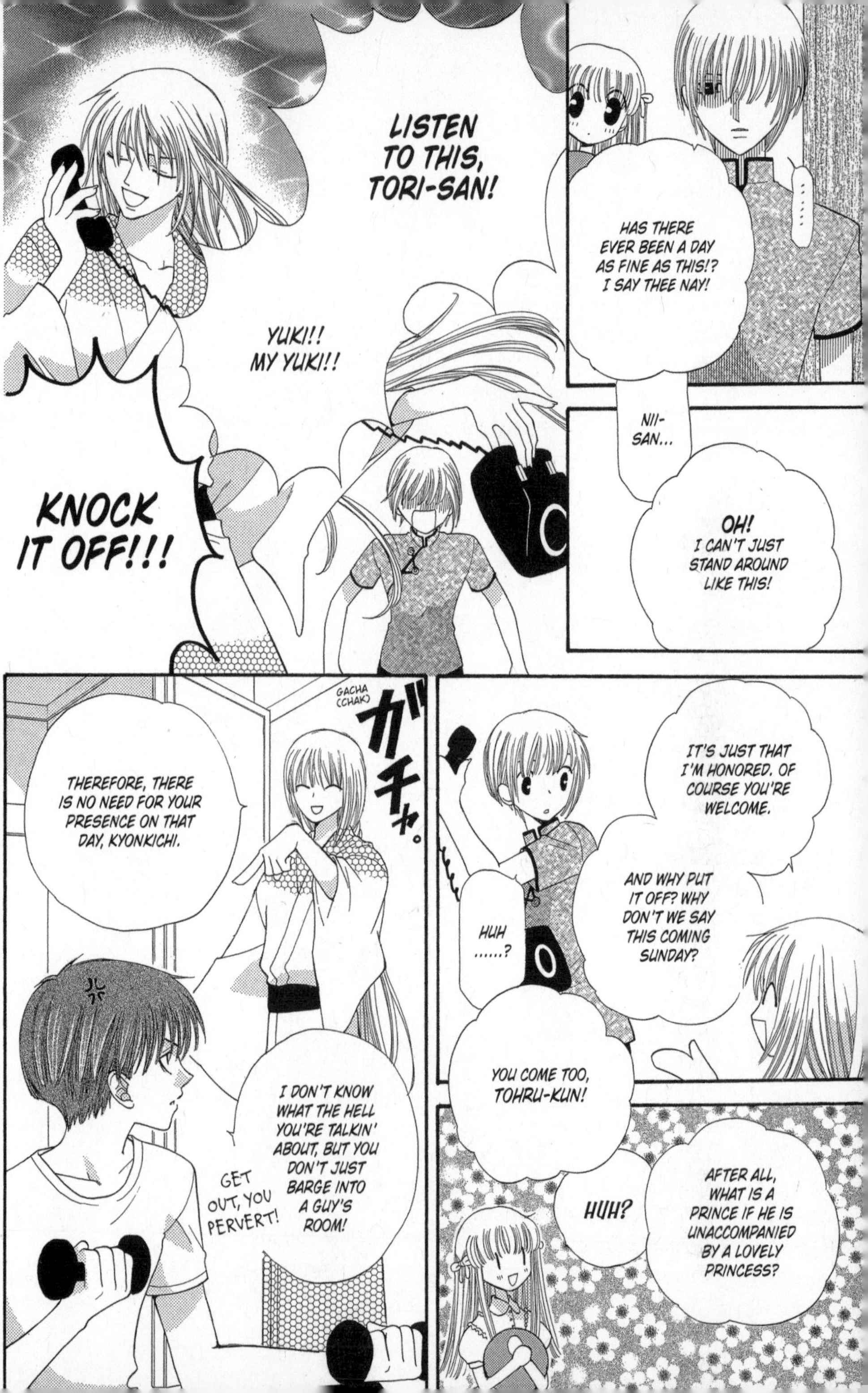
HAS THERE EVER BEEN A DAY AS FINE AS THIS!? I SAY THEE NAY!
......
NII-SAN...
OH! I CAN'T JUST STAND AROUND LIKE THIS!
LISTEN TO THIS, TORI-SAN!
YUKI!! MY YUKI!!
KNOCK IT OFF!!!
IT'S JUST THAT I'M HONORED. OF COURSE YOU'RE WELCOME.
AND WHY PUT IT OFF? WHY DON'T WE SAY THIS COMING SUNDAY?
HUH ......?
YOU COME TOO, TOHRU-KUN!
AFTER ALL, WHAT IS A PRINCE IF HE IS UNACCOMPANIED BY A LOVELY PRINCESS?
HUH?
GACHA (CHAK)
ガチャ。
THEREFORE, THERE IS NO NEED FOR YOUR PRESENCE ON THAT DAY, KYONKICHI.
I DON'T KNOW WHAT THE HELL YOU'RE TALKIN' ABOUT, BUT YOU DON'T JUST BARGE INTO A GUY'S ROOM!
GET OUT, YOU PERVERT!

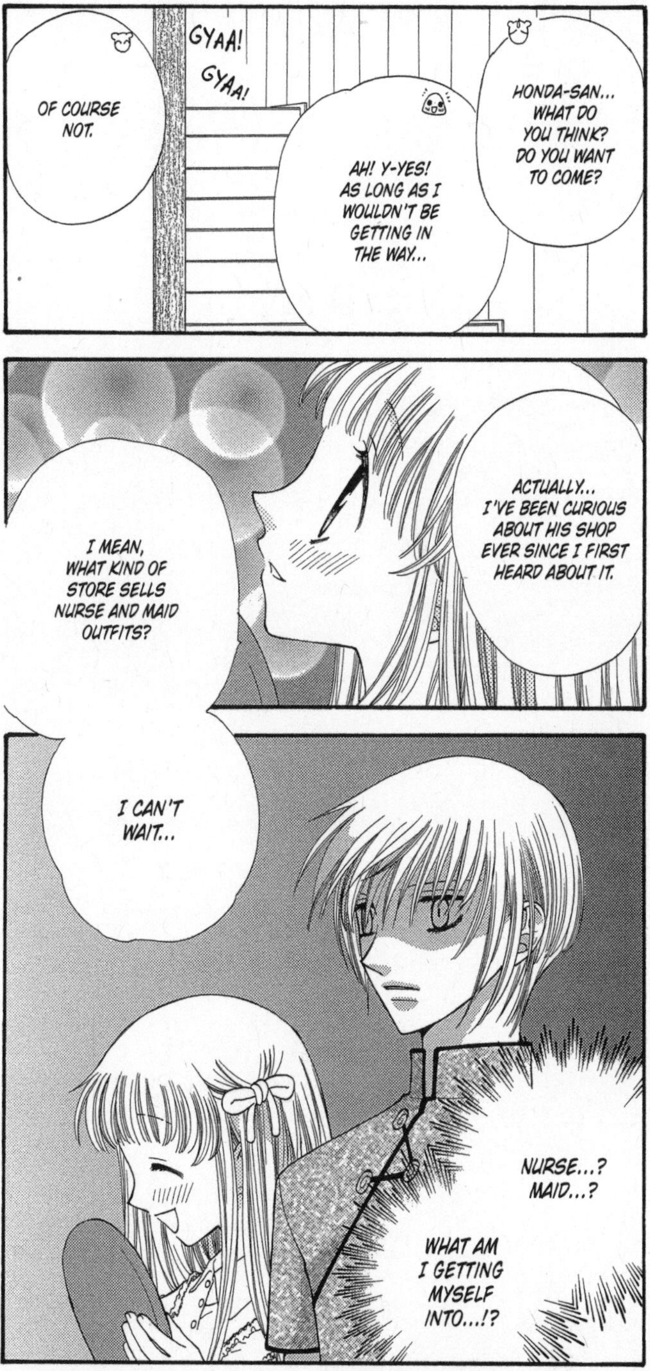
HONDA-SAN... WHAT DO YOU THINK? DO YOU WANT TO COME?
AH! Y-YES! AS LONG AS I WOULDN'T BE GETTING IN THE WAY...
GYAA! GYAA!
OF COURSE NOT.
ACTUALLY... I'VE BEEN CURIOUS ABOUT HIS SHOP EVER SINCE I FIRST HEARD ABOUT IT.
I MEAN, WHAT KIND OF STORE SELLS NURSE AND MAID OUTFITS?
I CAN'T WAIT...
NURSE...? MAID...?
WHAT AM I GETTING MYSELF INTO...!?

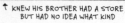

↑ KNEW HIS BROTHER HAD A STORE BUT HAD NO IDEA WHAT KIND

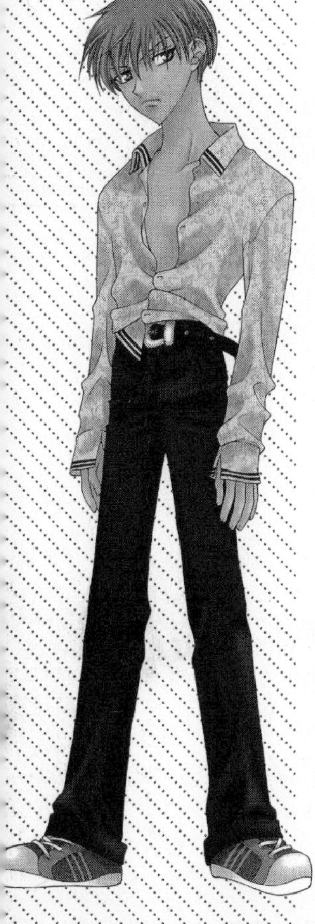

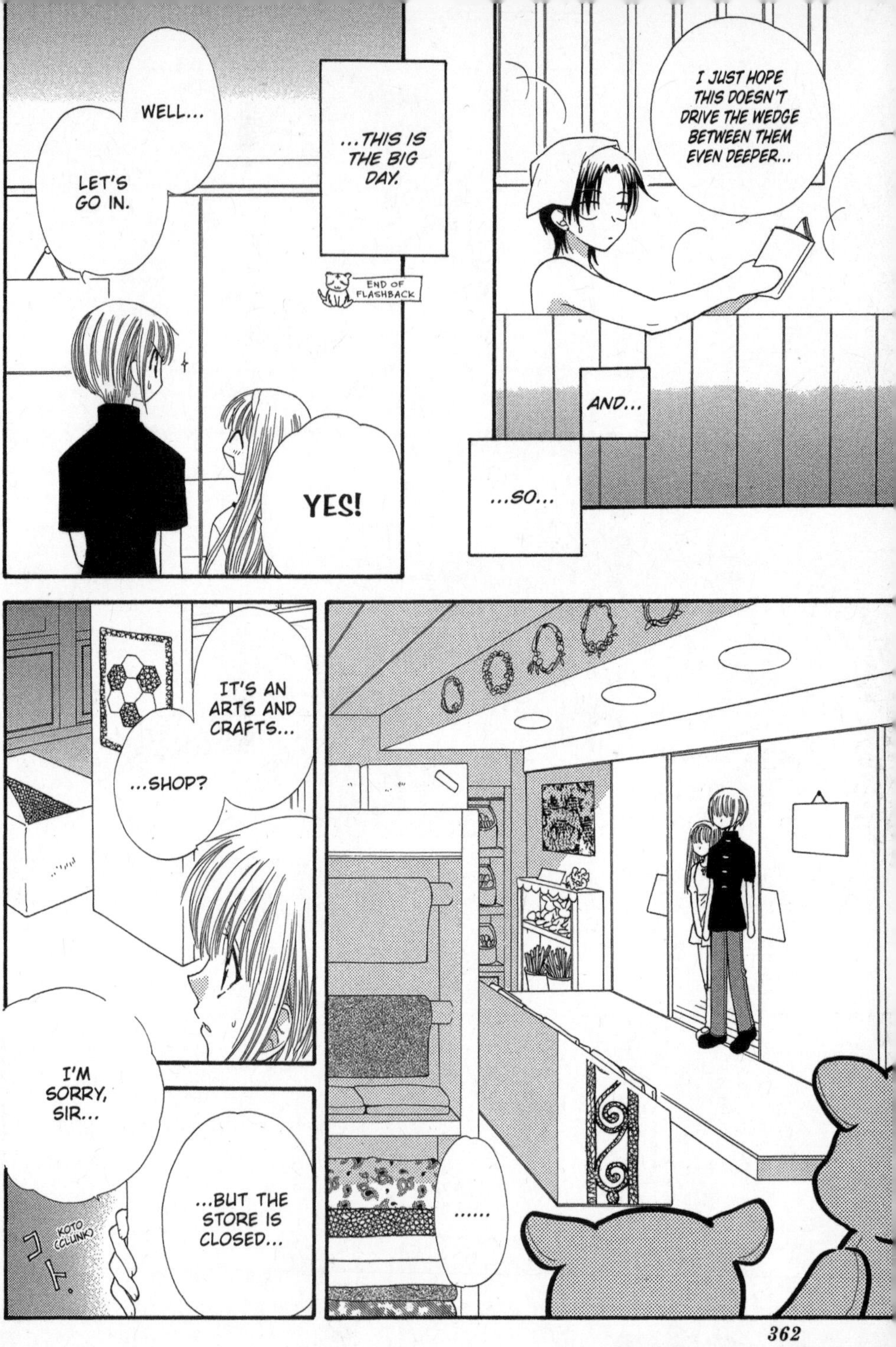
I JUST HOPE THIS DOESN'T DRIVE THE WEDGE BETWEEN THEM EVEN DEEPER...
AND...
...SO...
...THIS IS THE BIG DAY.
END OF FLASHBACK
WELL...
LET'S GO IN.
YES!
......
IT'S AN ARTS AND CRAFTS...
...SHOP?
I'M SORRY, SIR...
...BUT THE STORE IS CLOSED...
KOTO (CLUNK)
コト。

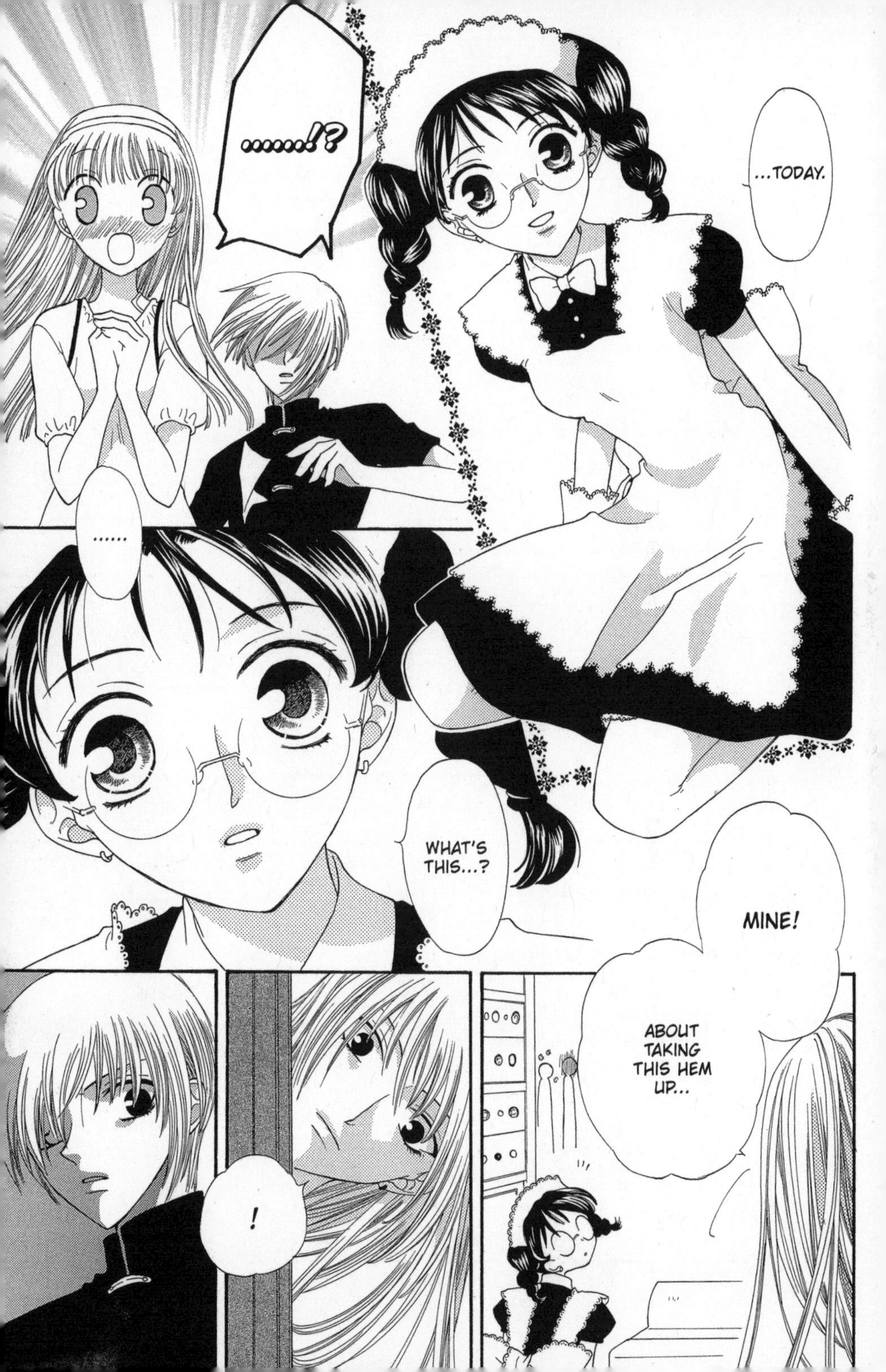
...TODAY.
......!?
......
WHAT'S THIS...?
MINE!
ABOUT TAKING THIS HEM UP...
!

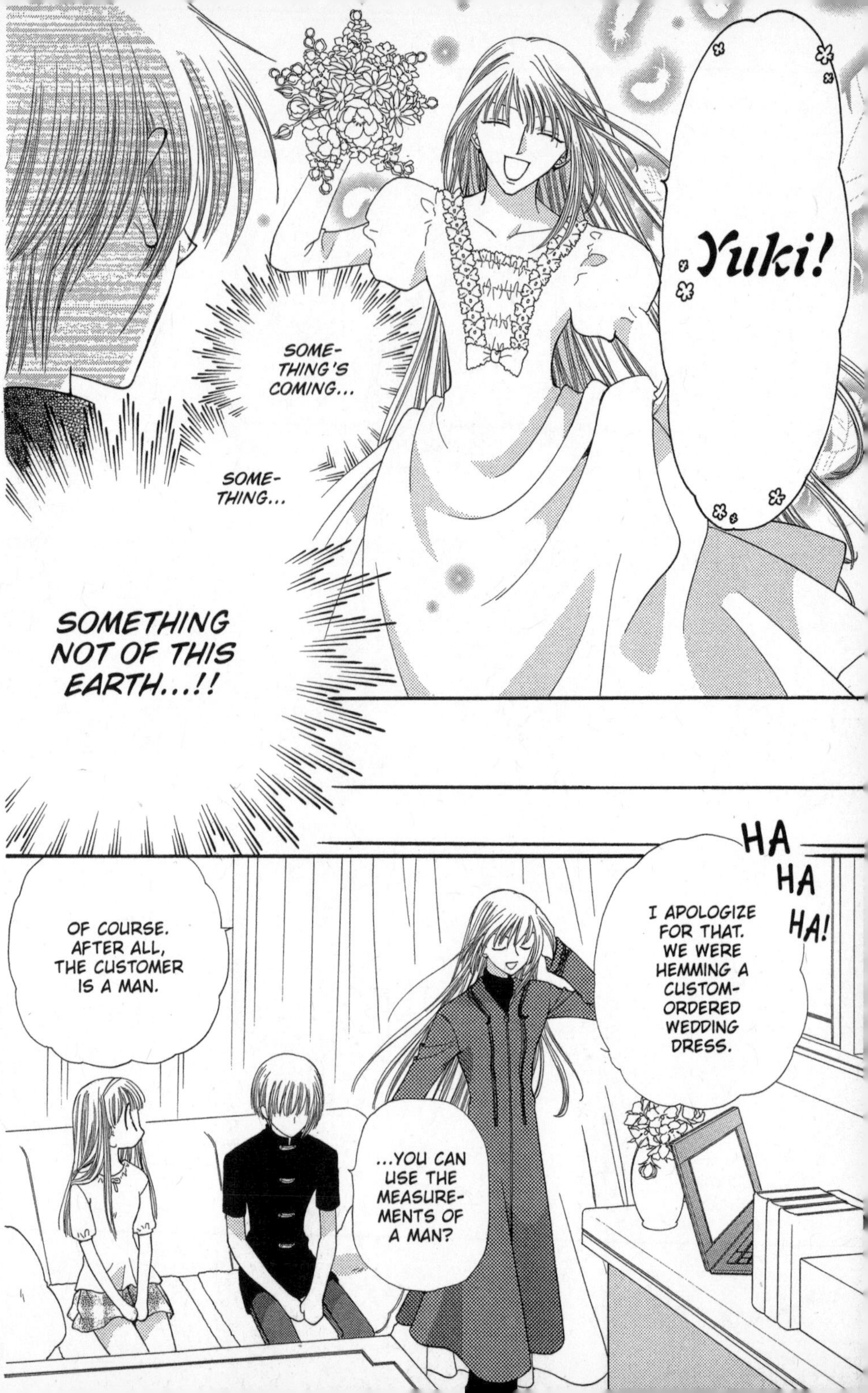
Yuki!
SOME-THING'S COMING...
SOME-THING...
SOMETHING NOT OF THIS EARTH...!!
HA HA HA!
I APOLOGIZE FOR THAT. WE WERE HEMMING A CUSTOM-ORDERED WEDDING DRESS.
...YOU CAN USE THE MEASURE-MENTS OF A MAN?
OF COURSE. AFTER ALL, THE CUSTOMER IS A MAN.

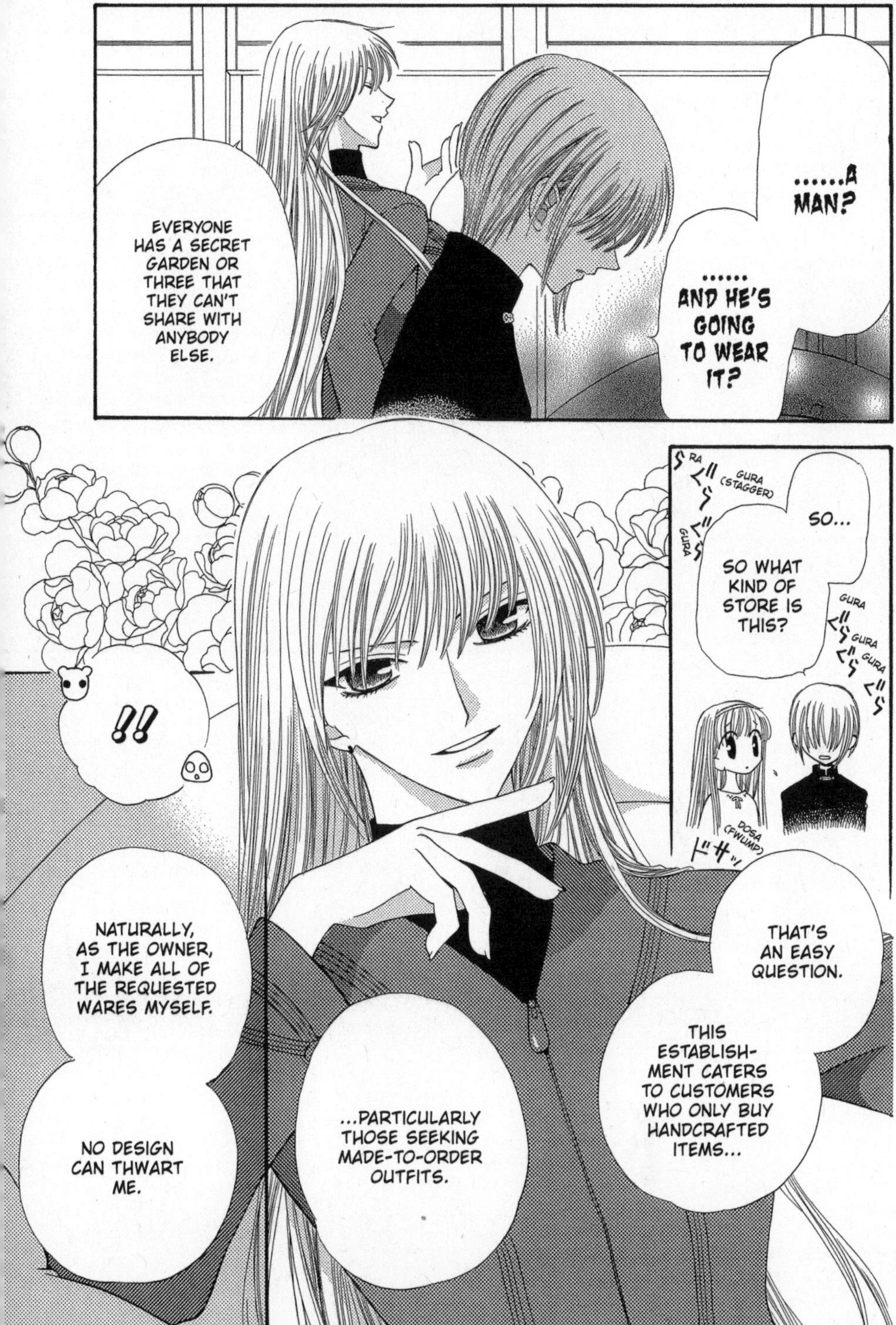
......A MAN?
...... AND HE'S GOING TO WEAR IT?
EVERYONE HAS A SECRET GARDEN OR THREE THAT THEY CAN'T SHARE WITH ANYBODY ELSE.
RA
GURA (STAGGER)
GURA
SO...
SO WHAT KIND OF STORE IS THIS?
GURA
GURA
GURA
DOSA (FWLUMP)
ドサッ
!!
THAT'S AN EASY QUESTION.
THIS ESTABLISHMENT CATERS TO CUSTOMERS WHO ONLY BUY HANDCRAFTED ITEMS...
...PARTICULARLY THOSE SEEKING MADE-TO-ORDER OUTFITS.
NATURALLY, AS THE OWNER, I MAKE ALL OF THE REQUESTED WARES MYSELF.
NO DESIGN CAN THWART ME.

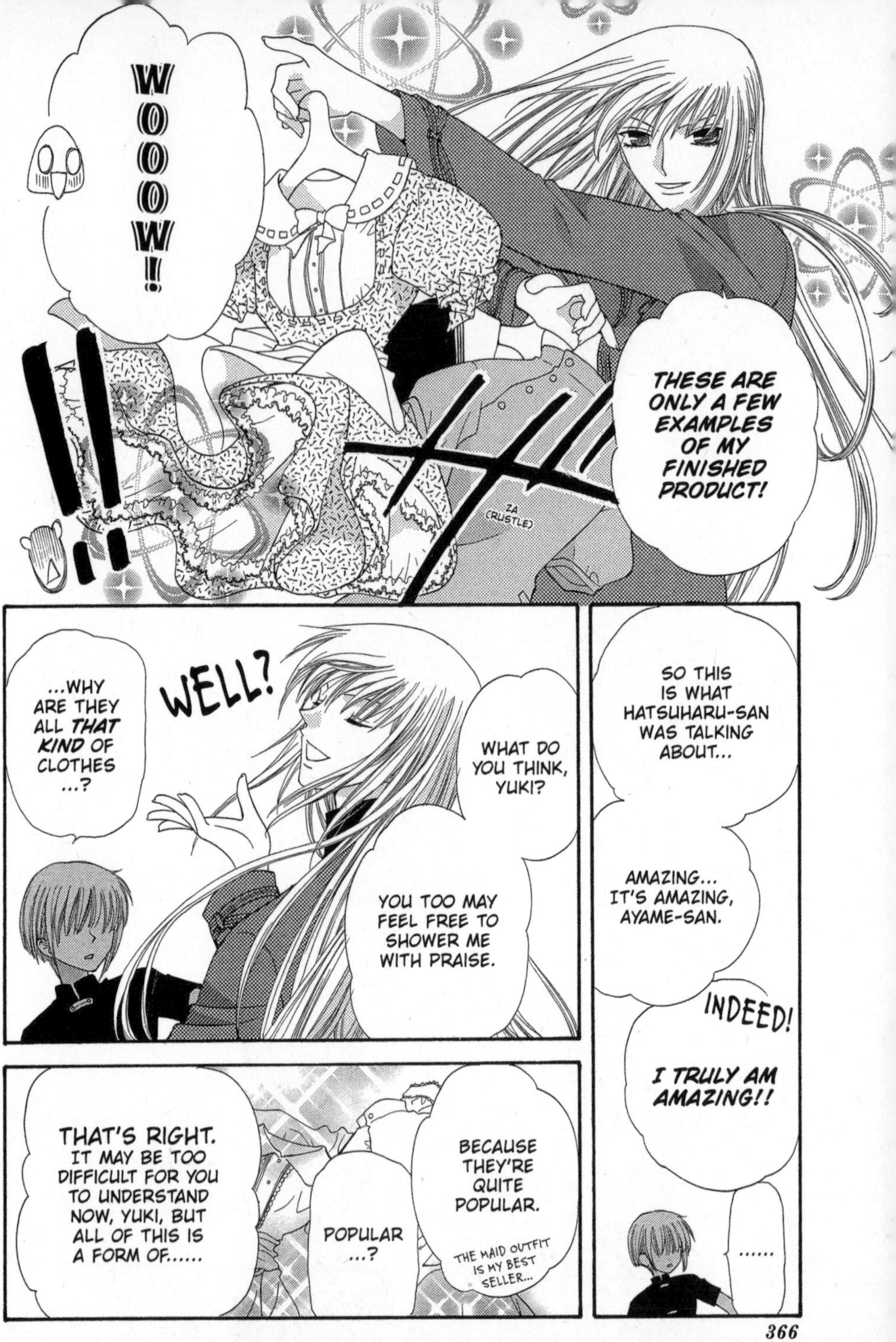
THESE ARE ONLY A FEW EXAMPLES OF MY FINISHED PRODUCT!
ZA (RUSTLE)
WOOOOW!
!!
SO THIS IS WHAT HATSUHARU-SAN WAS TALKING ABOUT...
AMAZING... IT'S AMAZING, AYAME-SAN.
INDEED!
I TRULY AM AMAZING!!
......
WHAT DO YOU THINK, YUKI?
WELL?
YOU TOO MAY FEEL FREE TO SHOWER ME WITH PRAISE.
...WHY ARE THEY ALL THAT KIND OF CLOTHES ...?
BECAUSE THEY'RE QUITE POPULAR.
THE MAID OUTFIT IS MY BEST SELLER...
POPULAR ...?
THAT'S RIGHT. IT MAY BE TOO DIFFICULT FOR YOU TO UNDERSTAND NOW, YUKI, BUT ALL OF THIS IS A FORM OF......

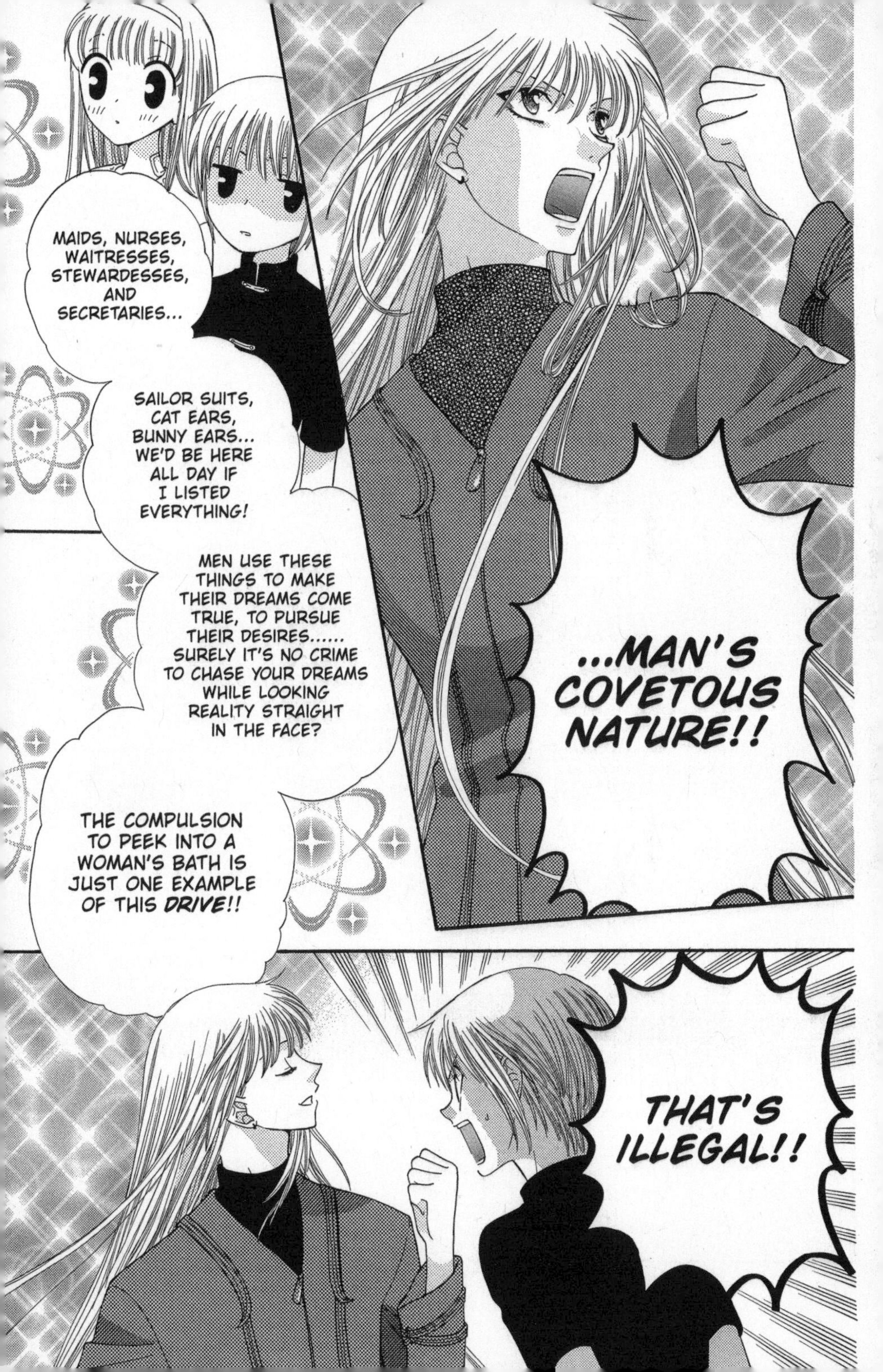
MAIDS, NURSES, WAITRESSES, STEWARDESSES, AND SECRETARIES...
SAILOR SUITS, CAT EARS, BUNNY EARS... WE'D BE HERE ALL DAY IF I LISTED EVERYTHING!
MEN USE THESE THINGS TO MAKE THEIR DREAMS COME TRUE, TO PURSUE THEIR DESIRES...... SURELY IT'S NO CRIME TO CHASE YOUR DREAMS WHILE LOOKING REALITY STRAIGHT IN THE FACE?
THE COMPULSION TO PEEK INTO A WOMAN'S BATH IS JUST ONE EXAMPLE OF THIS DRIVE!!
...MAN'S COVETOUS NATURE!!
THAT'S ILLEGAL!!

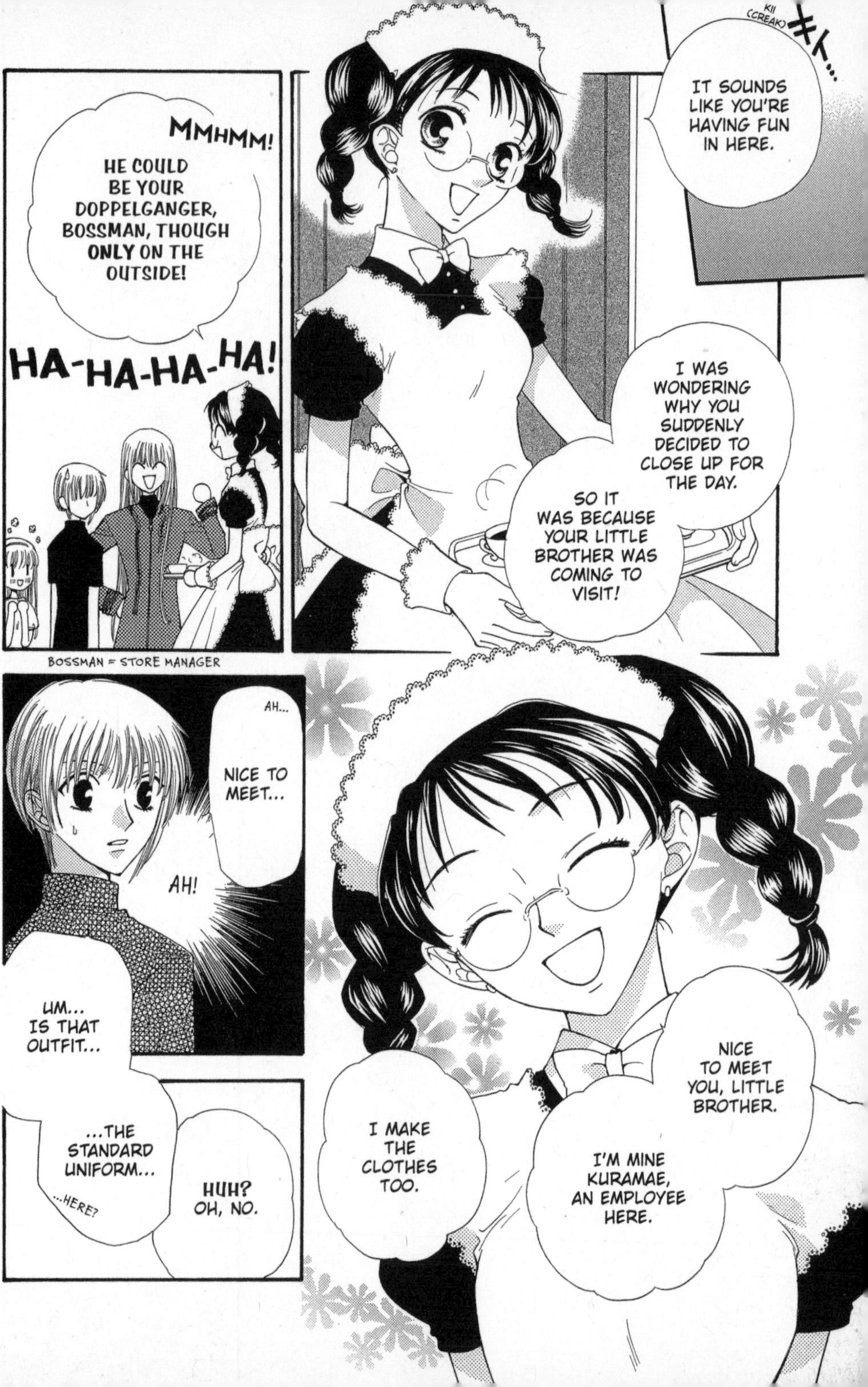
KII (CREAK)
IT SOUNDS LIKE YOU'RE HAVING FUN IN HERE.
I WAS WONDERING WHY YOU SUDDENLY DECIDED TO CLOSE UP FOR THE DAY.
SO IT WAS BECAUSE YOUR LITTLE BROTHER WAS COMING TO VISIT!
MMHMM!
HE COULD BE YOUR DOPPELGANGER, BOSSMAN, THOUGH ONLY ON THE OUTSIDE!
HA-HA-HA-HA!
BOSSMAN = STORE MANAGER
AH...
NICE TO MEET...
AH!
NICE TO MEET YOU, LITTLE BROTHER.
I'M MINE KURAMAE, AN EMPLOYEE HERE.
UM... IS THAT OUTFIT...
...THE STANDARD UNIFORM...
...HERE?
HUH? OH, NO.
I MAKE THE CLOTHES TOO.

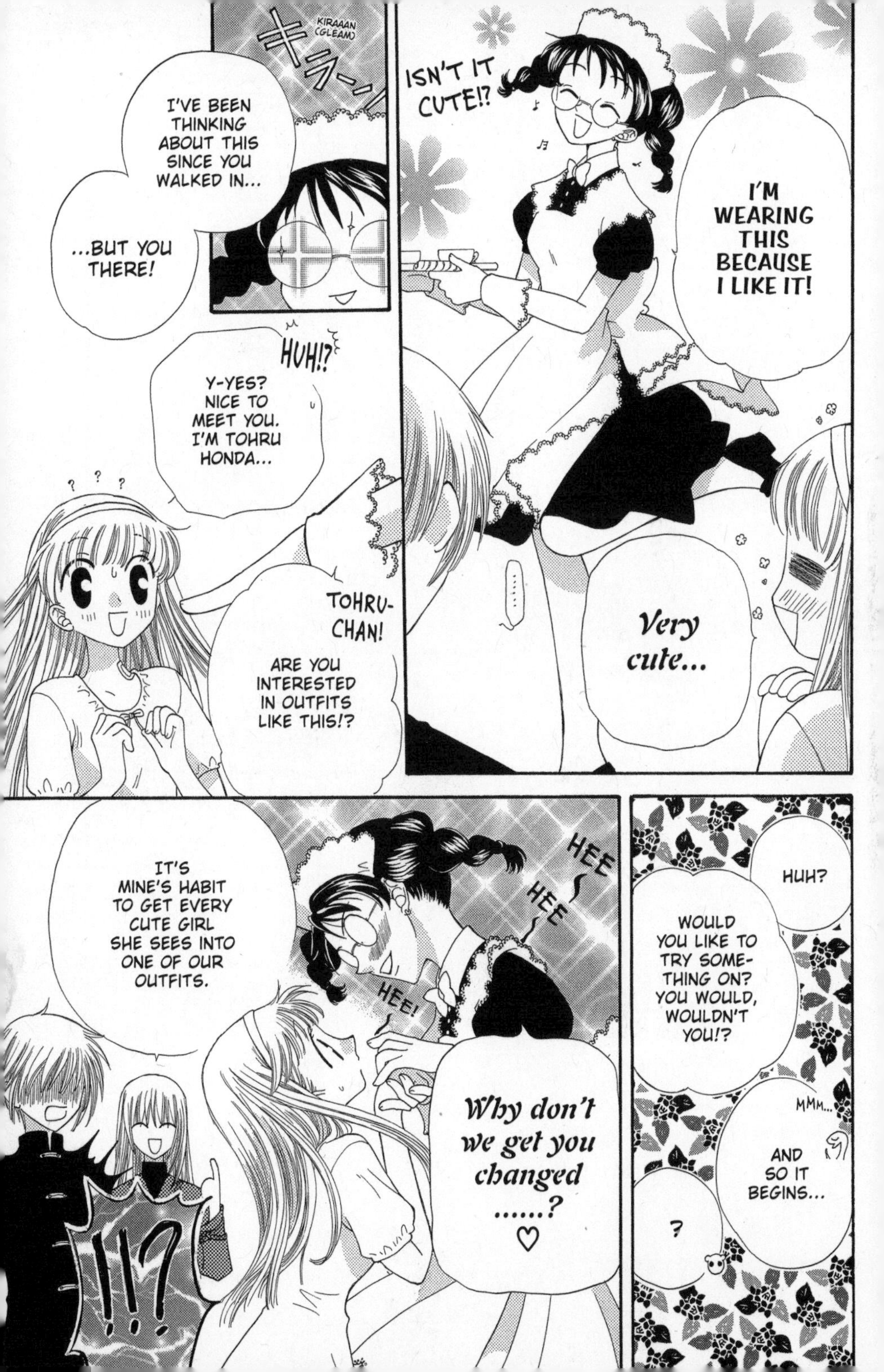
ISN'T IT CUTE!?
I'M WEARING THIS BECAUSE I LIKE IT!
......
Very cute...
KIRAAAN (GLEAM)
I'VE BEEN THINKING ABOUT THIS SINCE YOU WALKED IN...
...BUT YOU THERE!
HUH!?
Y-YES? NICE TO MEET YOU. I'M TOHRU HONDA...
TOHRU-CHAN!
ARE YOU INTERESTED IN OUTFITS LIKE THIS!?
HUH?
WOULD YOU LIKE TO TRY SOME-THING ON? YOU WOULD, WOULDN'T YOU!?
MMM...
AND SO IT BEGINS...
?
HEE HEE
HEE!
Why don't we get you changed ......? ♡
IT'S MINE'S HABIT TO GET EVERY CUTE GIRL SHE SEES INTO ONE OF OUR OUTFITS.
!!?

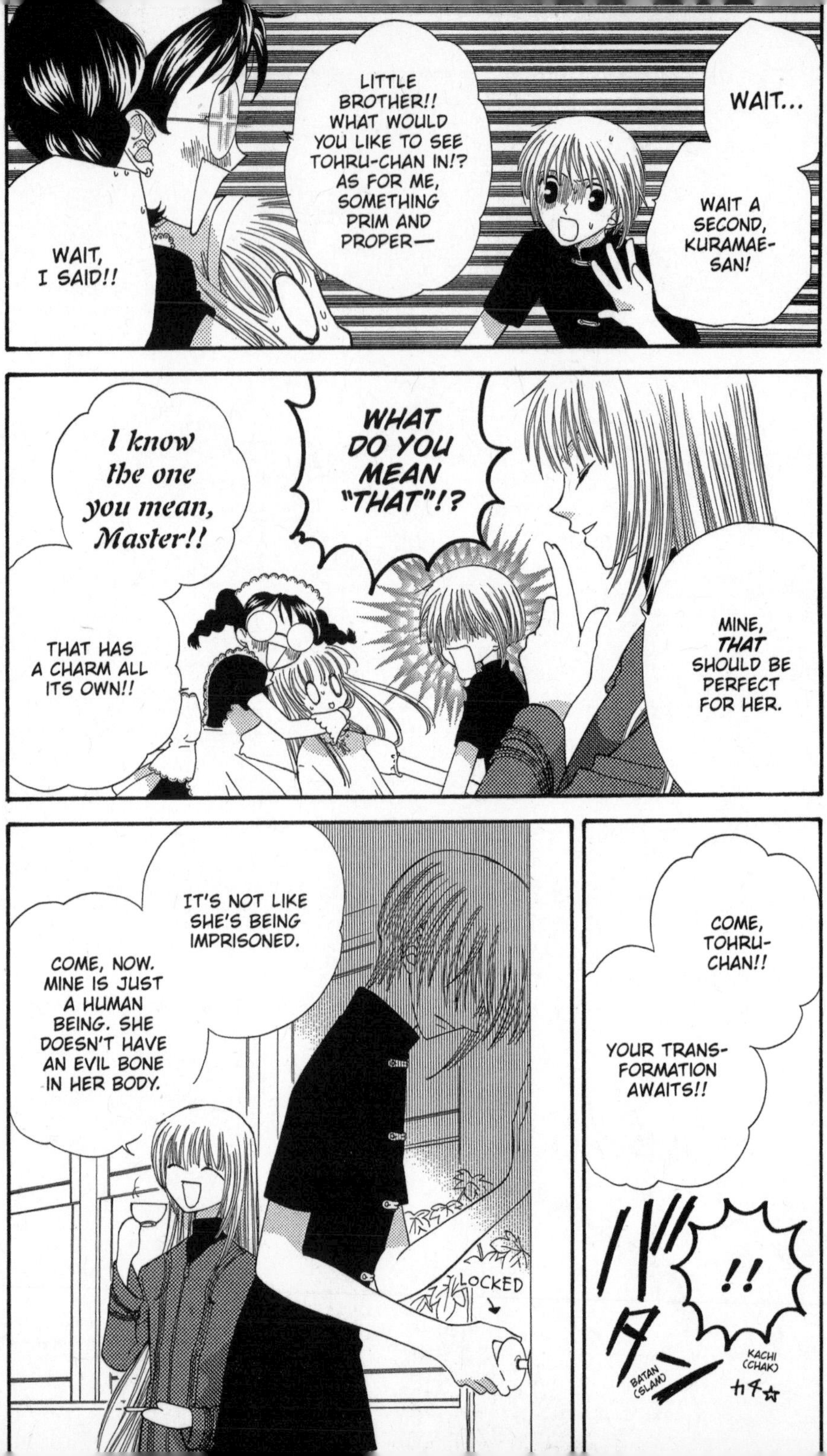
WAIT...
WAIT A SECOND, KURAMAE-SAN!
LITTLE BROTHER!! WHAT WOULD YOU LIKE TO SEE TOHRU-CHAN IN!? AS FOR ME, SOMETHING PRIM AND PROPER—
WAIT, I SAID!!
MINE, *THAT* SHOULD BE PERFECT FOR HER.
WHAT DO YOU MEAN "THAT"!?
I know the one you mean, Master!!
THAT HAS A CHARM ALL ITS OWN!!
COME, TOHRU-CHAN!!
YOUR TRANSFORMATION AWAITS!!
!!
バタン
BATAN (SLAM)
カチ☆
KACHI (CHAK)
IT'S NOT LIKE SHE'S BEING IMPRISONED.
COME, NOW. MINE IS JUST A HUMAN BEING. SHE DOESN'T HAVE AN EVIL BONE IN HER BODY.
LOCKED

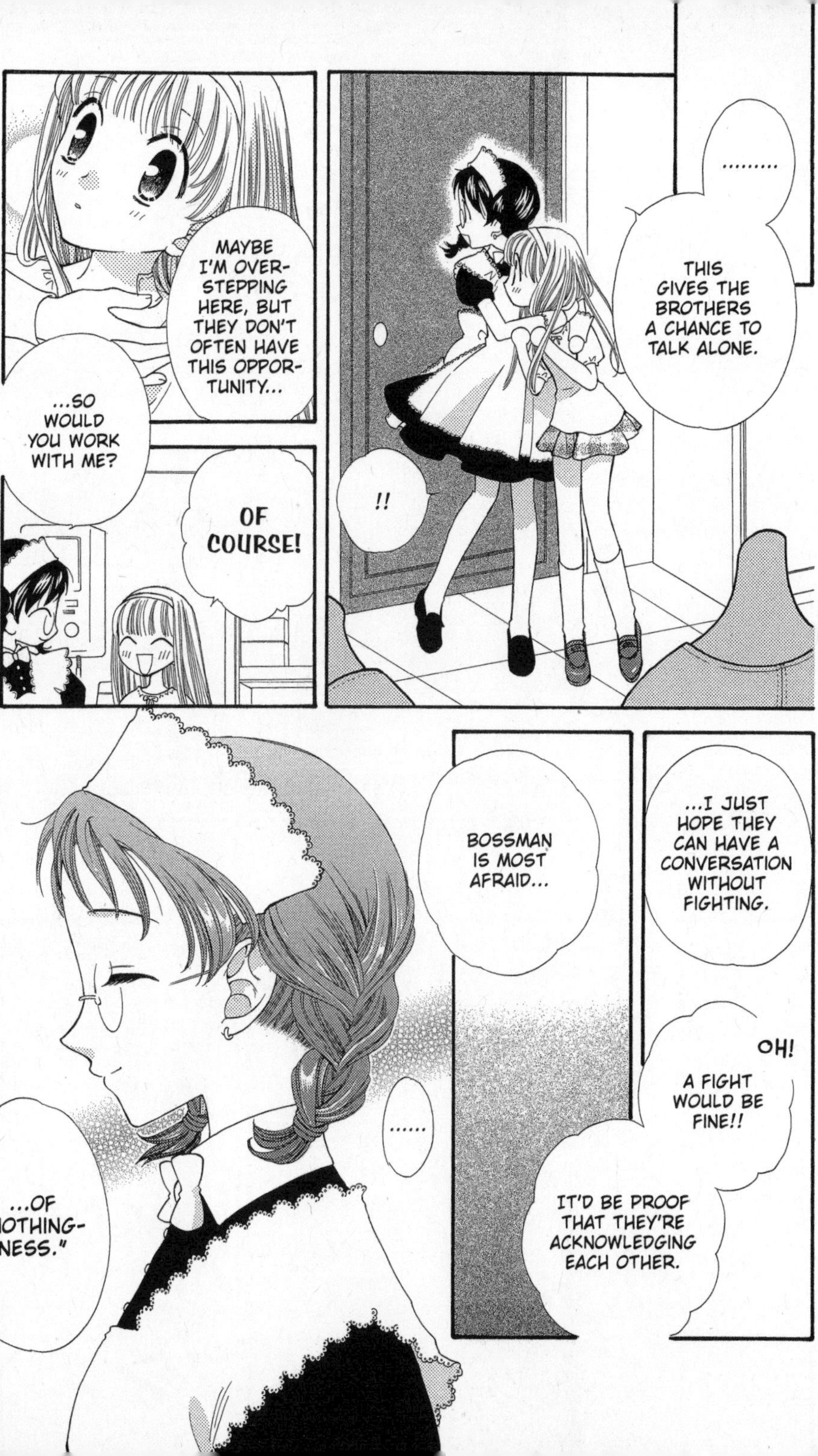
....
THIS GIVES THE BROTHERS A CHANCE TO TALK ALONE.
!!
MAYBE I'M OVER-STEPPING HERE, BUT THEY DON'T OFTEN HAVE THIS OPPOR-TUNITY...
...SO WOULD YOU WORK WITH ME?
OF COURSE!
...I JUST HOPE THEY CAN HAVE A CONVERSATION WITHOUT FIGHTING.
OH!
A FIGHT WOULD BE FINE!!
IT'D BE PROOF THAT THEY'RE ACKNOWLEDGING EACH OTHER.
BOSSMAN IS MOST AFRAID...
......
...OF "NOTHING-NESS."

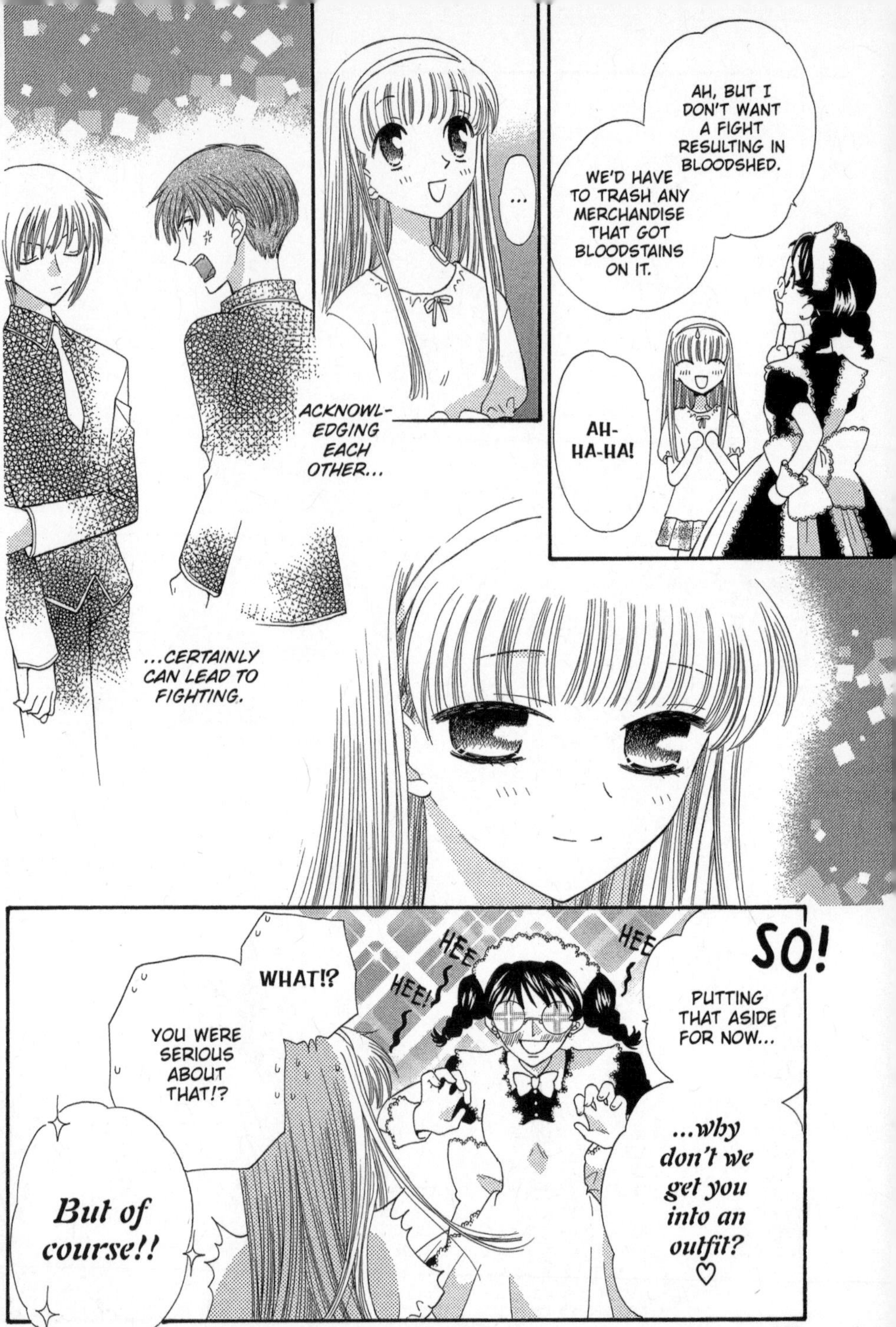
AH, BUT I DON'T WANT A FIGHT RESULTING IN BLOODSHED.
WE'D HAVE TO TRASH ANY MERCHANDISE THAT GOT BLOODSTAINS ON IT.
AH-HA-HA!
...
ACKNOWL-EDGING EACH OTHER...
...CERTAINLY CAN LEAD TO FIGHTING.
SO!
PUTTING THAT ASIDE FOR NOW...
...why don't we get you into an outfit? ♡
HEE HEE HEE!
WHAT!?
YOU WERE SERIOUS ABOUT THAT!?
But of course!!

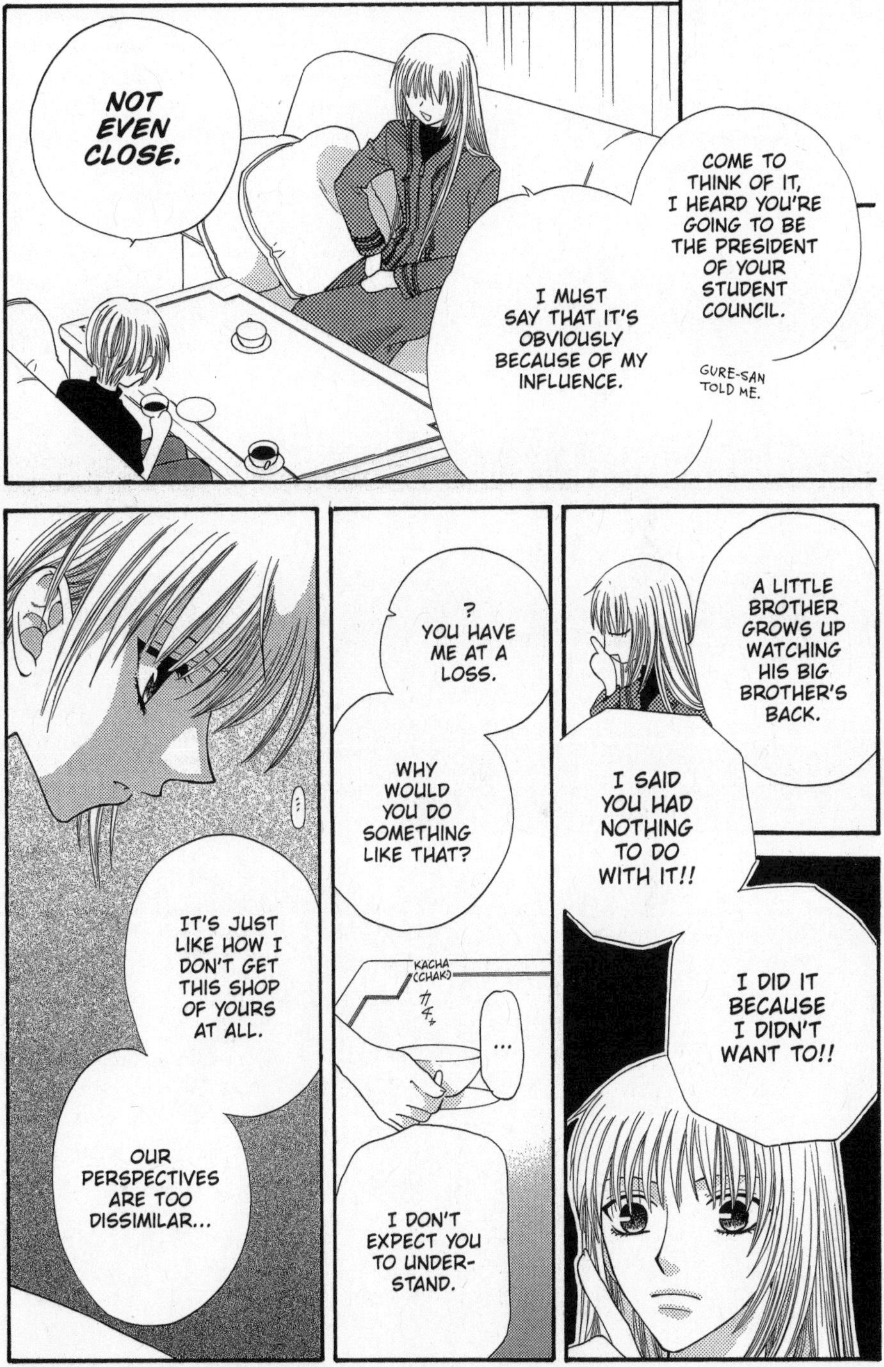
COME TO THINK OF IT, I HEARD YOU'RE GOING TO BE THE PRESIDENT OF YOUR STUDENT COUNCIL.
GURE-SAN TOLD ME.
I MUST SAY THAT IT'S OBVIOUSLY BECAUSE OF MY INFLUENCE.
NOT EVEN CLOSE.
A LITTLE BROTHER GROWS UP WATCHING HIS BIG BROTHER'S BACK.
I SAID YOU HAD NOTHING TO DO WITH IT!!
I DID IT BECAUSE I DIDN'T WANT TO!!
? YOU HAVE ME AT A LOSS.
WHY WOULD YOU DO SOMETHING LIKE THAT?
KACHA (CHAK)
...
I DON'T EXPECT YOU TO UNDER-STAND.
...
IT'S JUST LIKE HOW I DON'T GET THIS SHOP OF YOURS AT ALL.
OUR PERSPECTIVES ARE TOO DISSIMILAR...

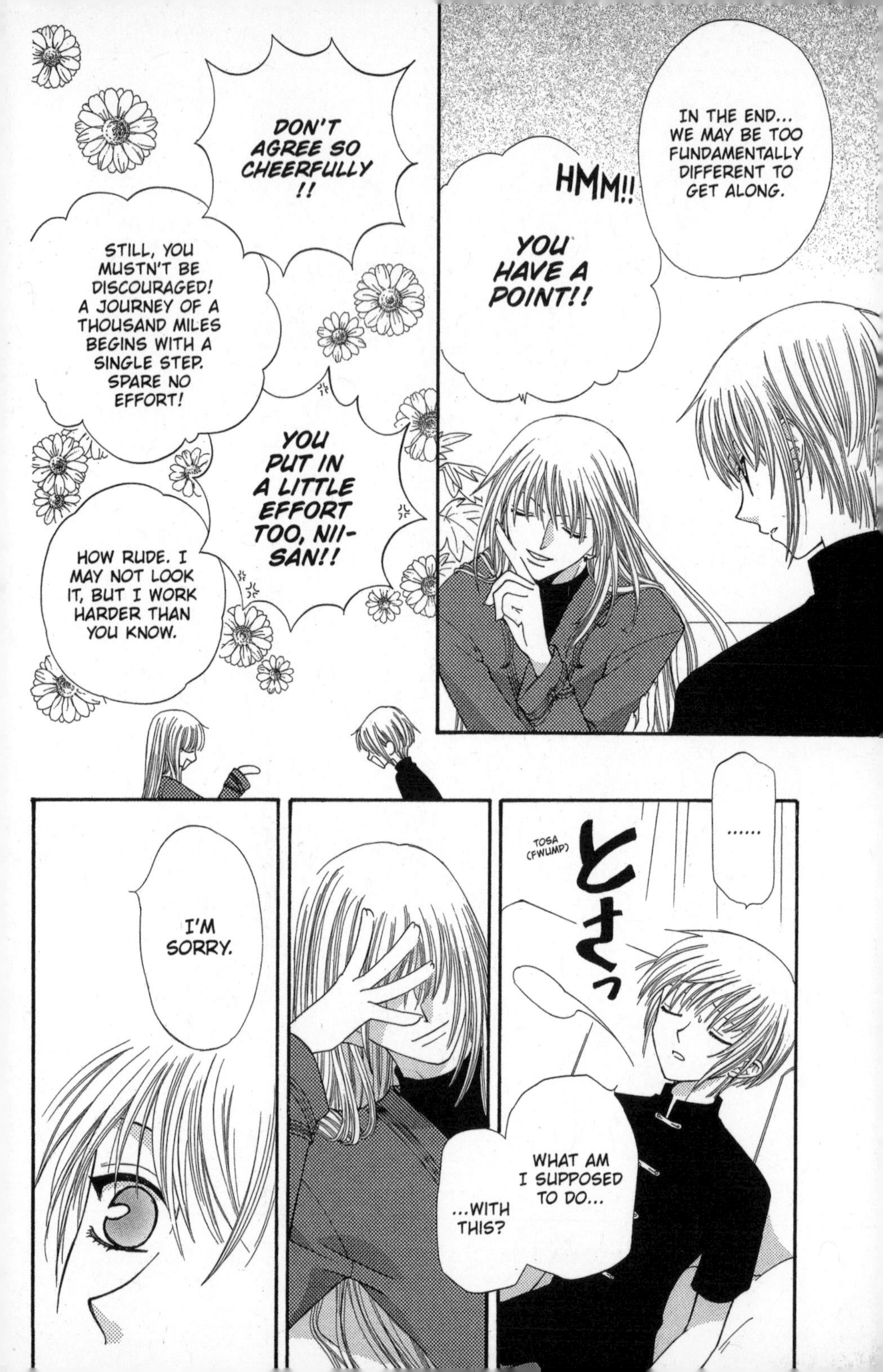
IN THE END... WE MAY BE TOO FUNDAMENTALLY DIFFERENT TO GET ALONG.
HMM!!
YOU HAVE A POINT!!
DON'T AGREE SO CHEERFULLY!!
STILL, YOU MUSTN'T BE DISCOURAGED! A JOURNEY OF A THOUSAND MILES BEGINS WITH A SINGLE STEP. SPARE NO EFFORT!
YOU PUT IN A LITTLE EFFORT TOO, NII-SAN!!
HOW RUDE. I MAY NOT LOOK IT, BUT I WORK HARDER THAN YOU KNOW.
......
TOSA (FWUMP)
とさっ
WHAT AM I SUPPOSED TO DO...
...WITH THIS?
I'M SORRY.

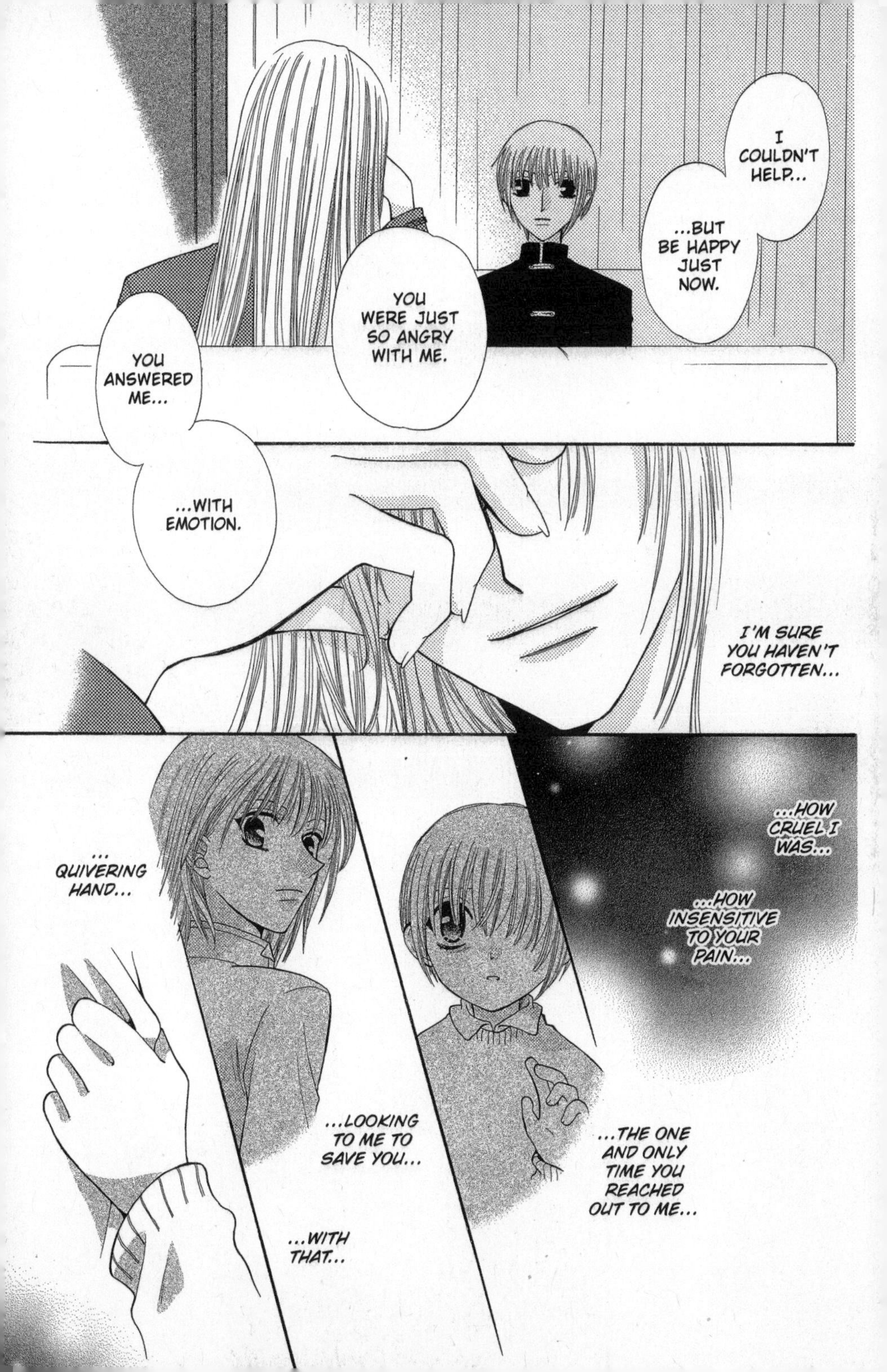
I COULDN'T HELP...
...BUT BE HAPPY JUST NOW.
YOU WERE JUST SO ANGRY WITH ME.
YOU ANSWERED ME...
...WITH EMOTION.
I'M SURE YOU HAVEN'T FORGOTTEN...
...HOW CRUEL I WAS...
...HOW INSENSITIVE TO YOUR PAIN...
...THE ONE AND ONLY TIME YOU REACHED OUT TO ME...
...LOOKING TO ME TO SAVE YOU...
...WITH THAT...
...QUIVERING HAND...

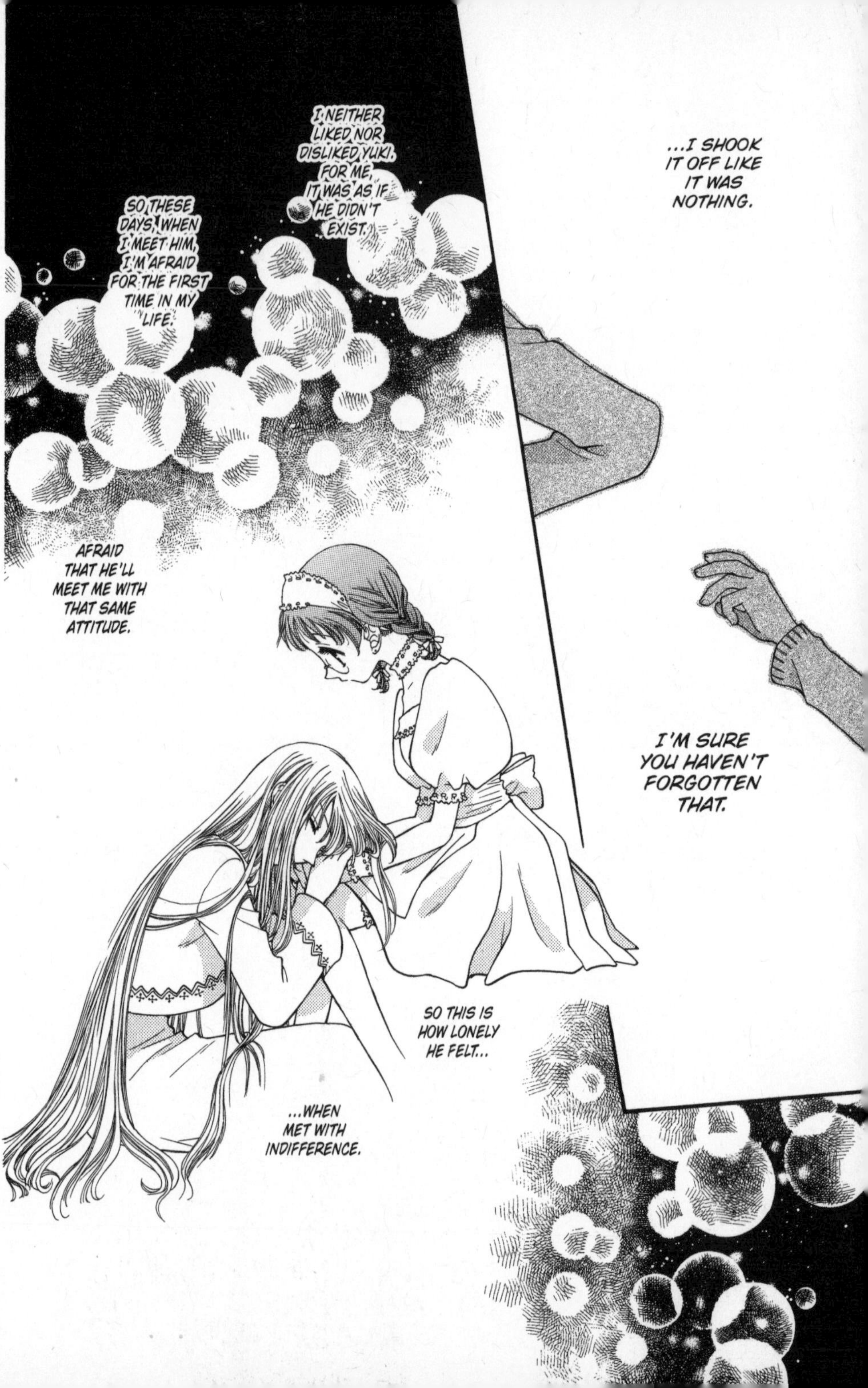
...I SHOOK IT OFF LIKE IT WAS NOTHING.
I'M SURE YOU HAVEN'T FORGOTTEN THAT.
I NEITHER LIKED NOR DISLIKED YUKI. FOR ME, IT WAS AS IF HE DIDN'T EXIST.
SO THESE DAYS, WHEN I MEET HIM, I'M AFRAID FOR THE FIRST TIME IN MY LIFE.
AFRAID THAT HE'LL MEET ME WITH THAT SAME ATTITUDE.
SO THIS IS HOW LONELY HE FELT...
...WHEN MET WITH INDIFFERENCE.

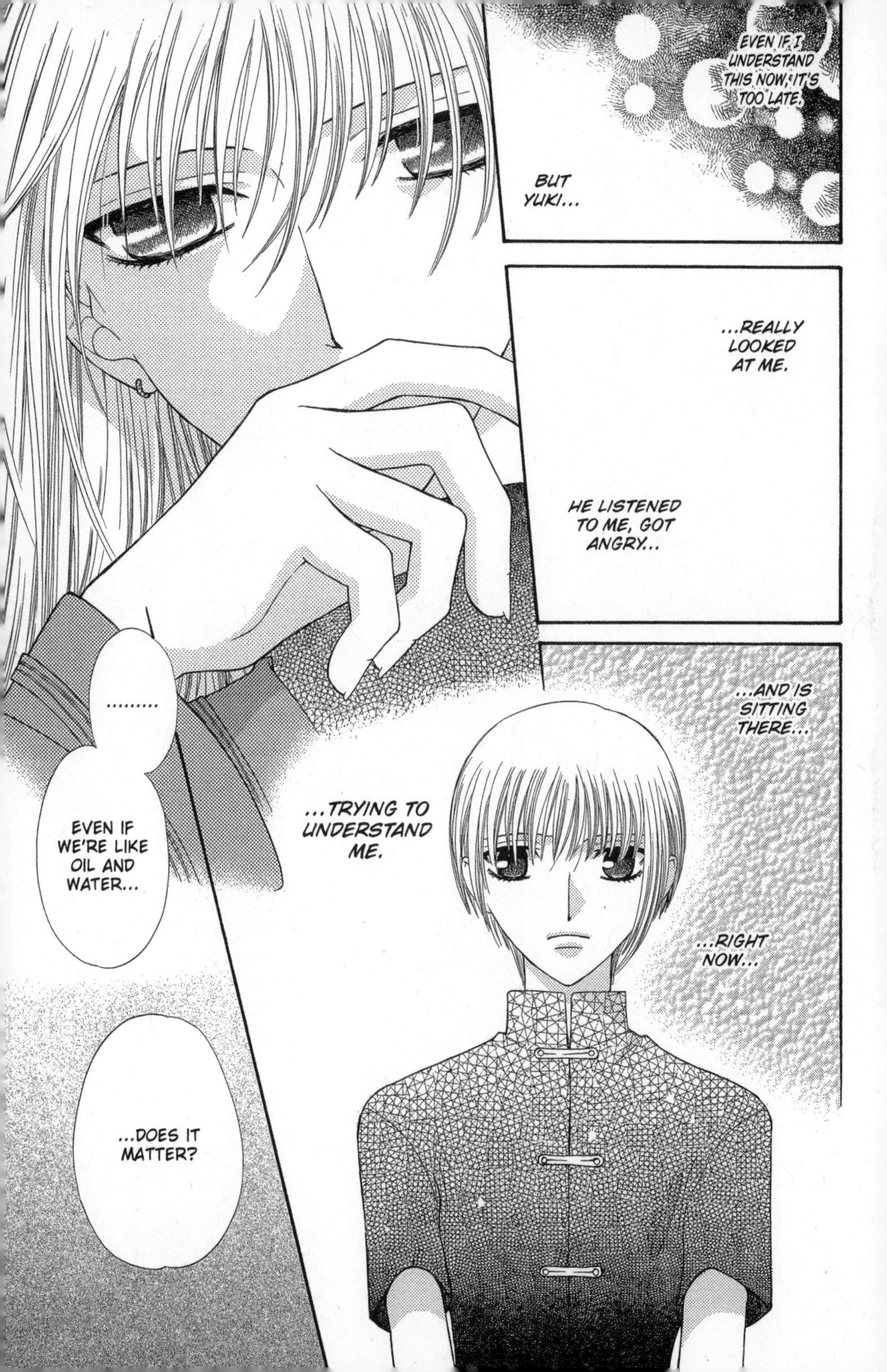
EVEN IF I UNDERSTAND THIS NOW, IT'S TOO LATE.
BUT YUKI...
...REALLY LOOKED AT ME.
HE LISTENED TO ME, GOT ANGRY...
...AND IS SITTING THERE...
...TRYING TO UNDERSTAND ME.
...RIGHT NOW...
....
EVEN IF WE'RE LIKE OIL AND WATER...
...DOES IT MATTER?

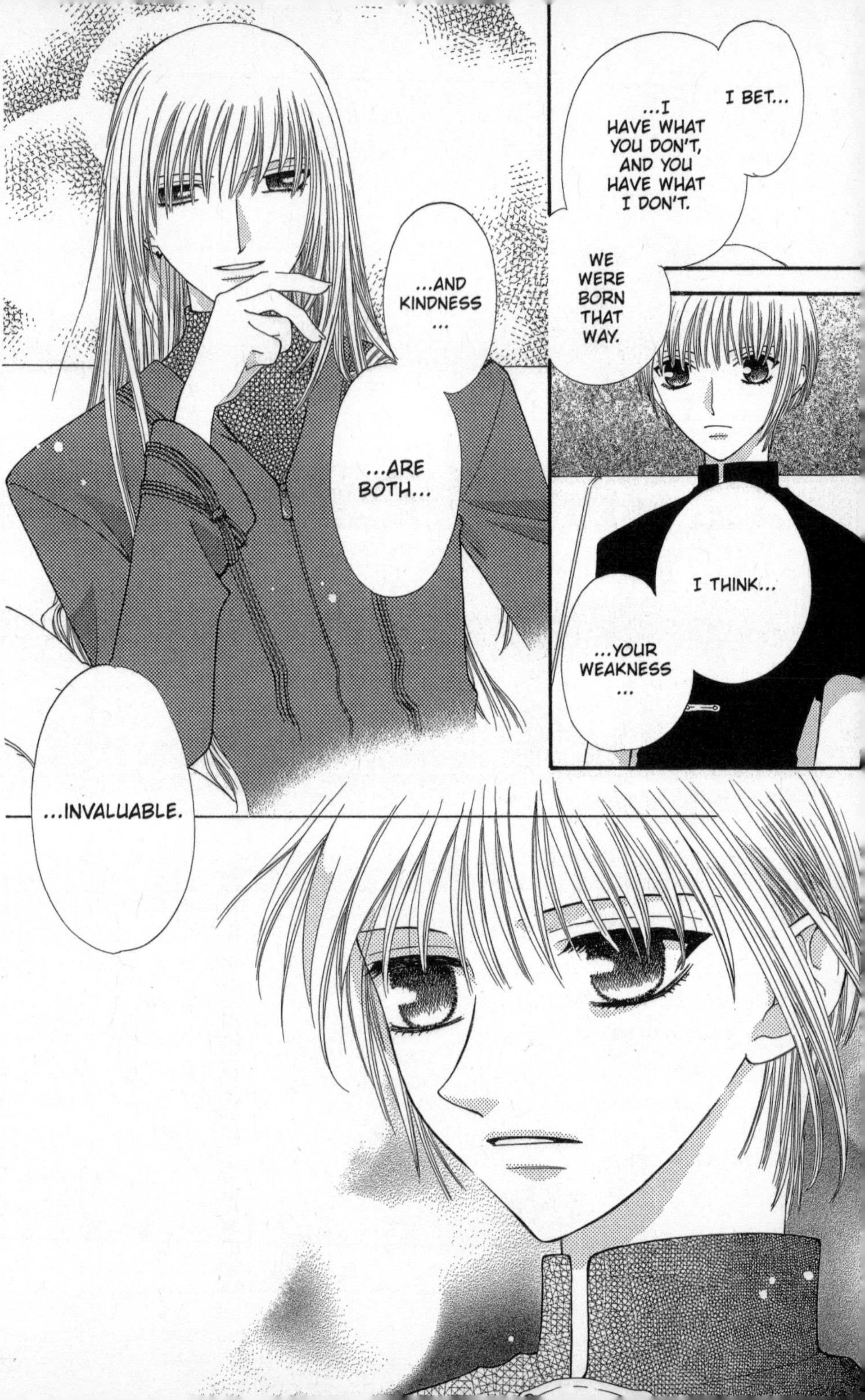
I BET...
...I HAVE WHAT YOU DON'T, AND YOU HAVE WHAT I DON'T.
WE WERE BORN THAT WAY.
I THINK...
...YOUR WEAKNESS...
...AND KINDNESS...
...ARE BOTH...
...INVALUABLE.

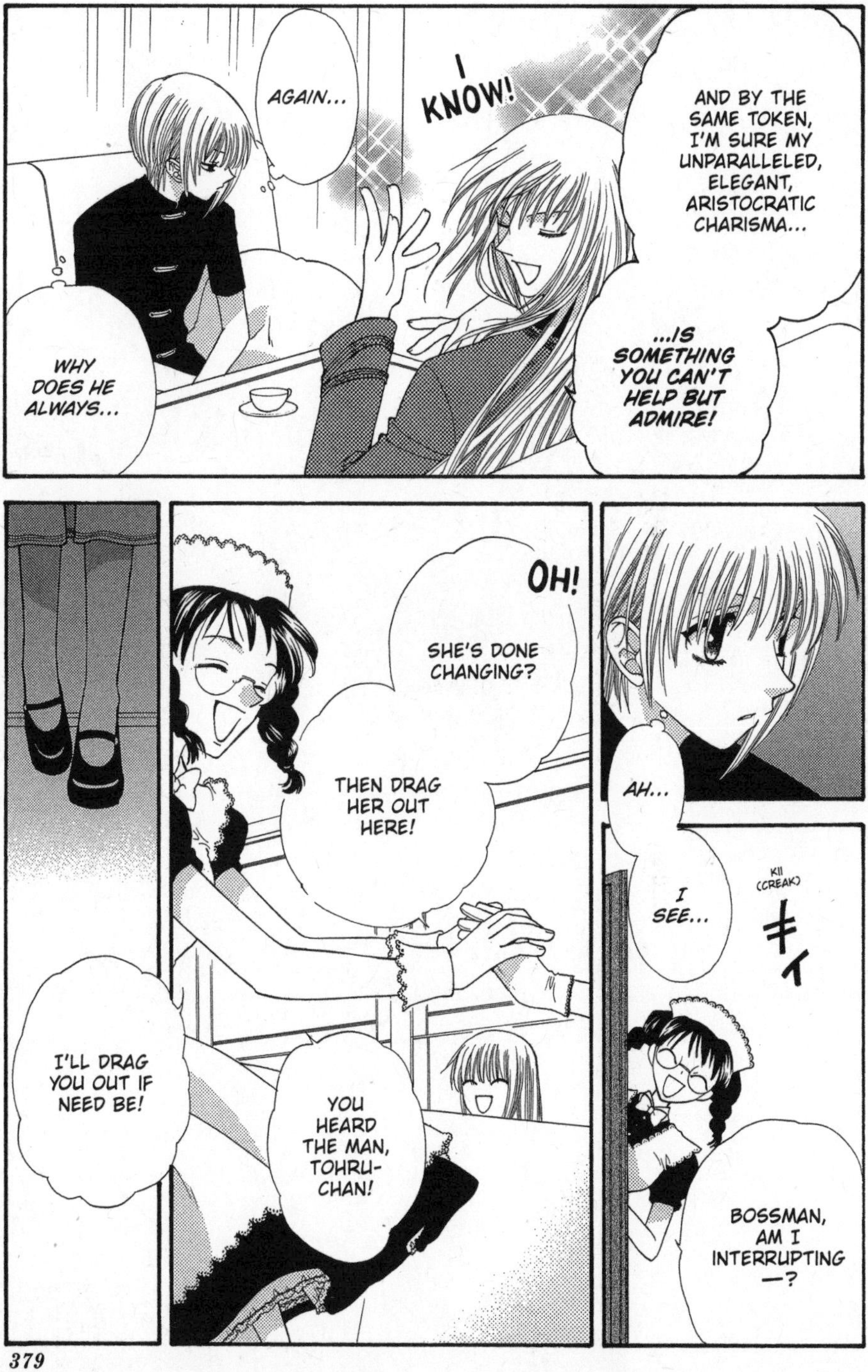
I KNOW!
AND BY THE SAME TOKEN, I'M SURE MY UNPARALLELED, ELEGANT, ARISTOCRATIC CHARISMA...
...IS SOMETHING YOU CAN'T HELP BUT ADMIRE!
WHY DOES HE ALWAYS...
AGAIN...
AH...
I SEE...
KII (CREAK)
キイ
BOSSMAN, AM I INTERRUPTING—?
OH!
SHE'S DONE CHANGING?
THEN DRAG HER OUT HERE!
YOU HEARD THE MAN, TOHRU-CHAN!
I'LL DRAG YOU OUT IF NEED BE!

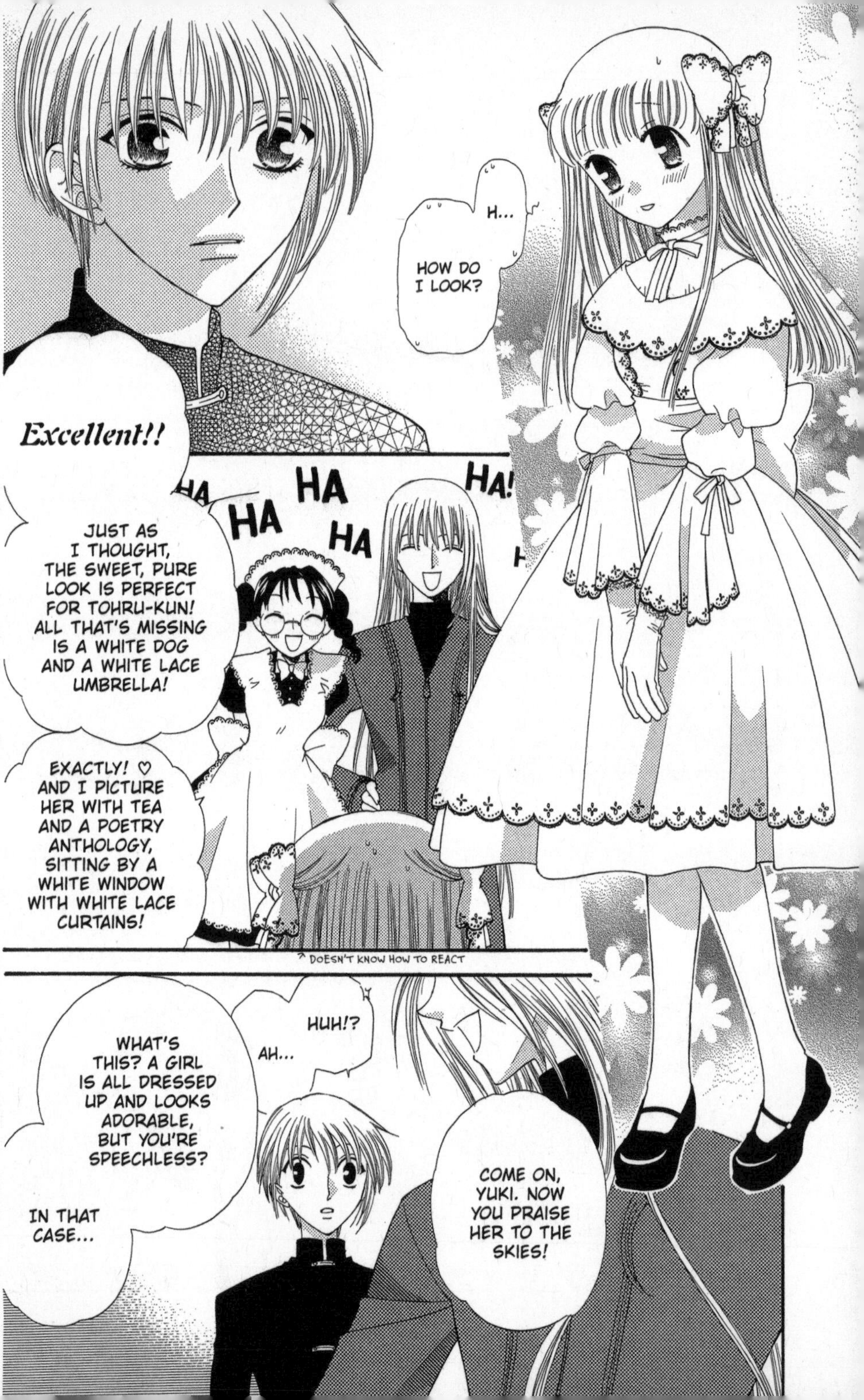

H...
HOW DO I LOOK?
Excellent!!
HA! HA HA HA HA HA
JUST AS I THOUGHT, THE SWEET, PURE LOOK IS PERFECT FOR TOHRU-KUN! ALL THAT'S MISSING IS A WHITE DOG AND A WHITE LACE UMBRELLA!
EXACTLY! ♡ AND I PICTURE HER WITH TEA AND A POETRY ANTHOLOGY, SITTING BY A WHITE WINDOW WITH WHITE LACE CURTAINS!
DOESN'T KNOW HOW TO REACT
COME ON, YUKI. NOW YOU PRAISE HER TO THE SKIES!
HUH!?
AH...
WHAT'S THIS? A GIRL IS ALL DRESSED UP AND LOOKS ADORABLE, BUT YOU'RE SPEECHLESS?
IN THAT CASE...

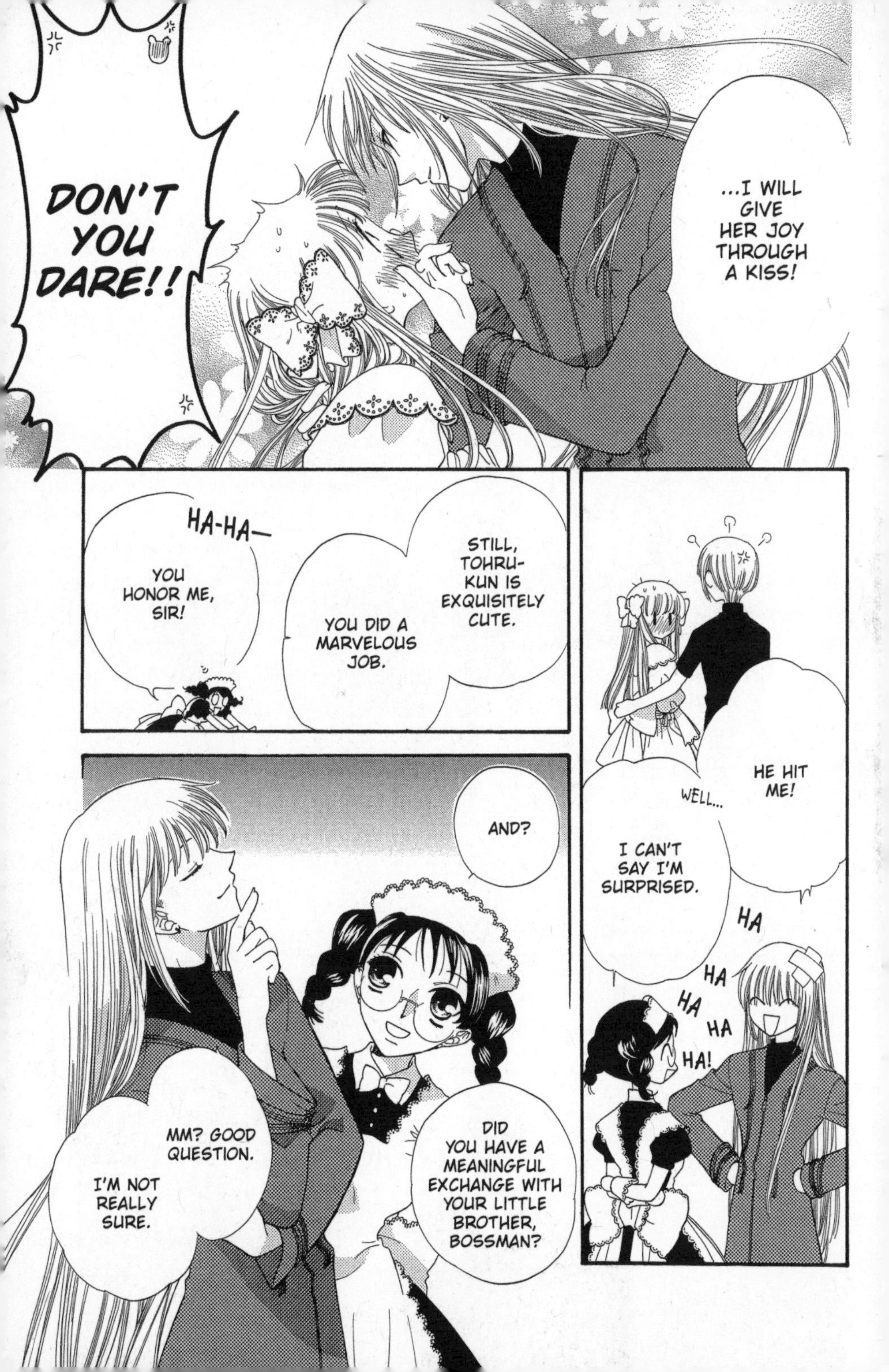
...I WILL GIVE HER JOY THROUGH A KISS!
DON'T YOU DARE!!
HE HIT ME!
WELL...
I CAN'T SAY I'M SURPRISED.
HA HA HA HA HA!
STILL, TOHRU-KUN IS EXQUISITELY CUTE.
YOU DID A MARVELOUS JOB.
HA-HA—
YOU HONOR ME, SIR!
AND?
DID YOU HAVE A MEANINGFUL EXCHANGE WITH YOUR LITTLE BROTHER, BOSSMAN?
MM? GOOD QUESTION.
I'M NOT REALLY SURE.

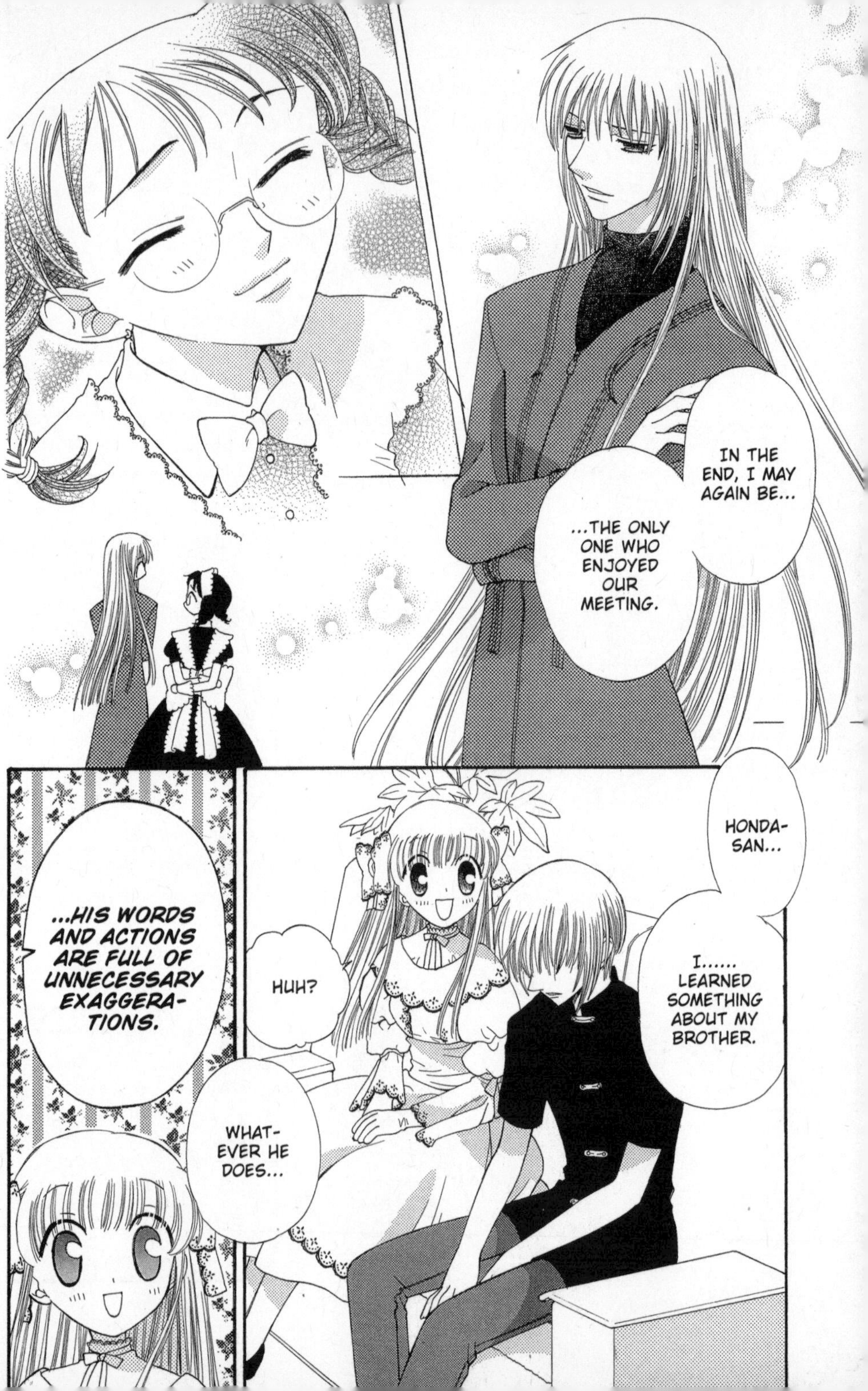
IN THE END, I MAY AGAIN BE...
...THE ONLY ONE WHO ENJOYED OUR MEETING.
HONDA-SAN...
I...... LEARNED SOMETHING ABOUT MY BROTHER.
HUH?
WHAT-EVER HE DOES...
...HIS WORDS AND ACTIONS ARE FULL OF UNNECESSARY EXAGGERA-TIONS.

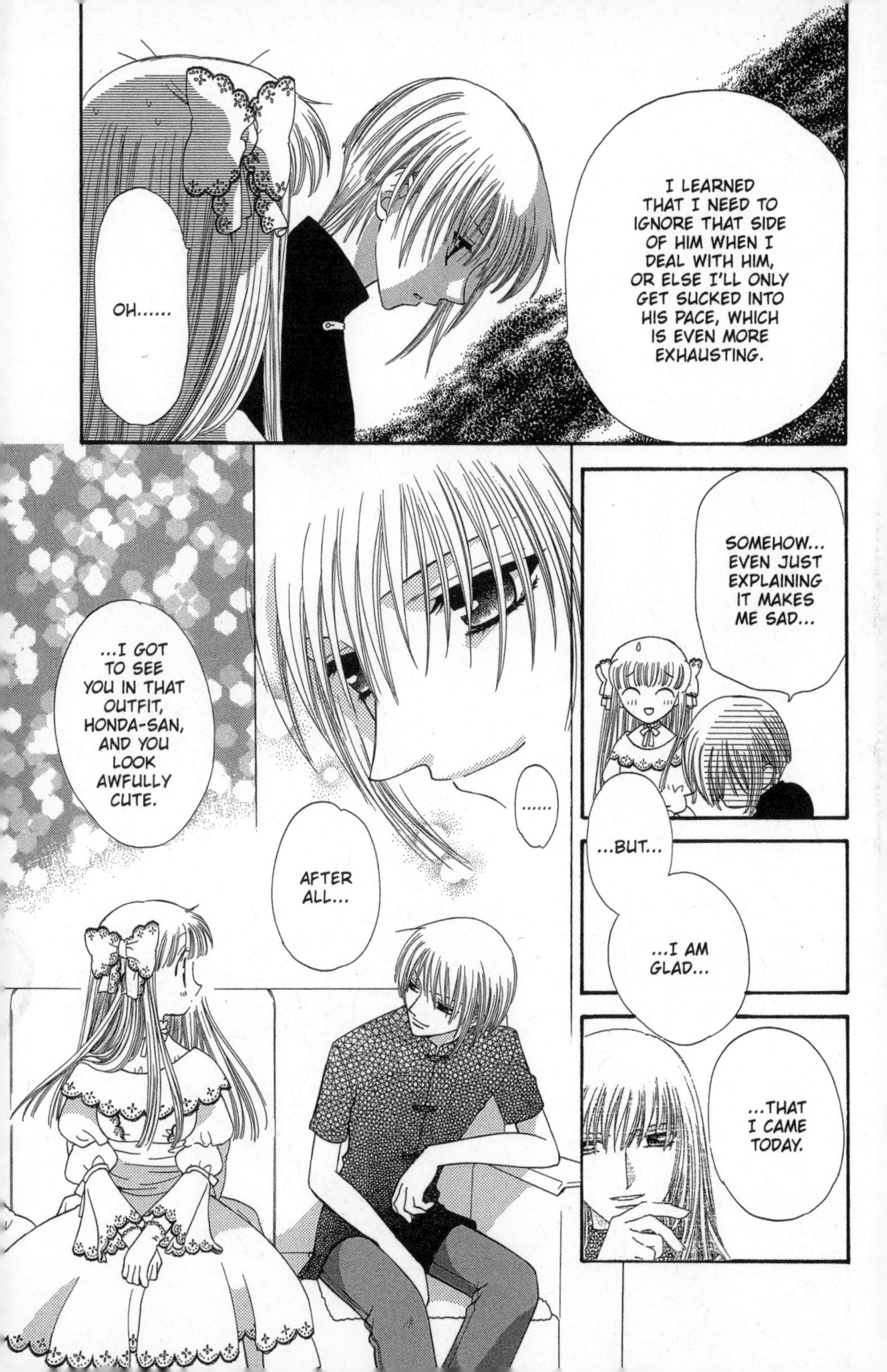
I LEARNED THAT I NEED TO IGNORE THAT SIDE OF HIM WHEN I DEAL WITH HIM, OR ELSE I'LL ONLY GET SUCKED INTO HIS PACE, WHICH IS EVEN MORE EXHAUSTING.
OH......
SOMEHOW... EVEN JUST EXPLAINING IT MAKES ME SAD...
...BUT...
...I AM GLAD...
...THAT I CAME TODAY.
......
AFTER ALL...
...I GOT TO SEE YOU IN THAT OUTFIT, HONDA-SAN, AND YOU LOOK AWFULLY CUTE.

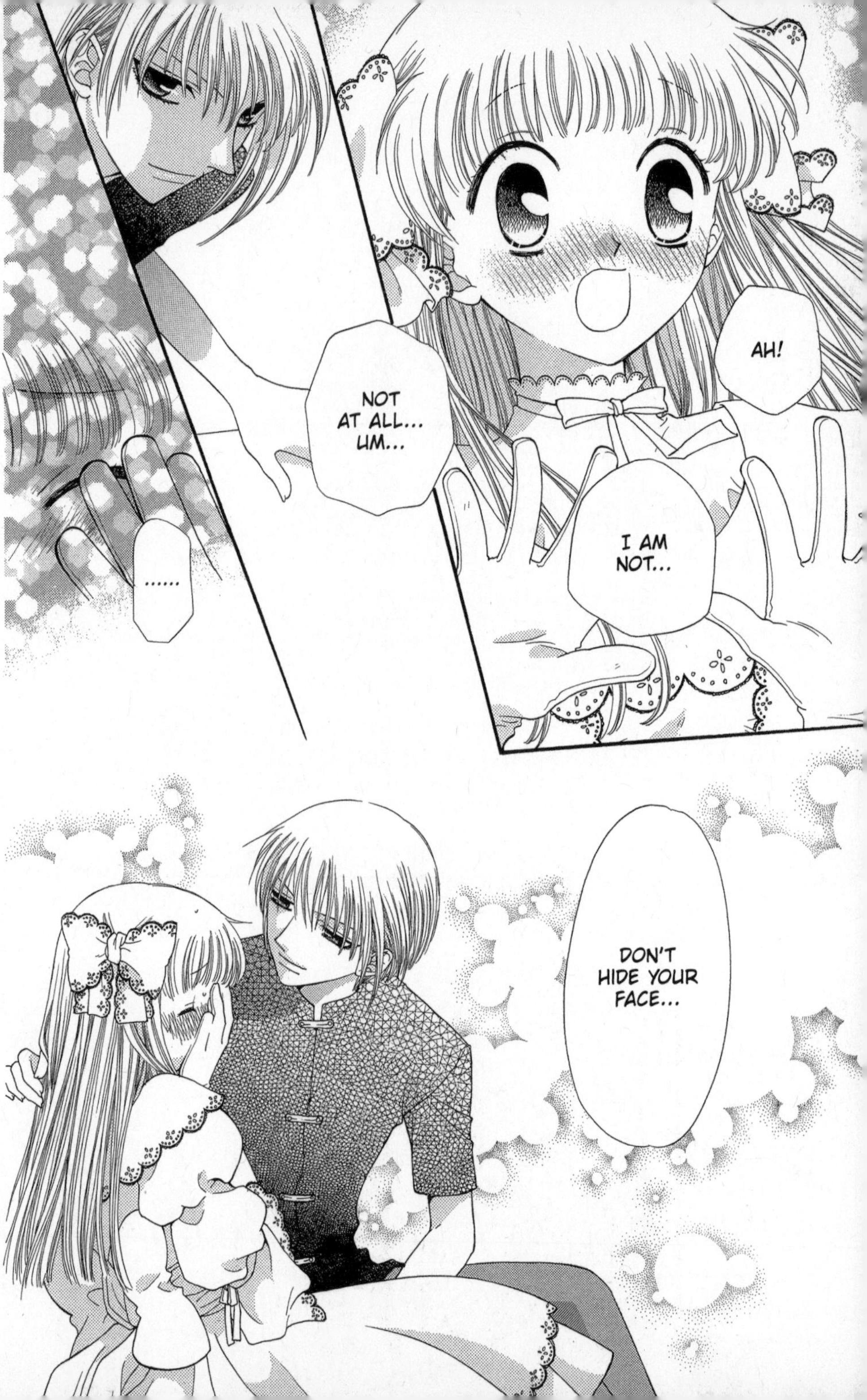
AH!
NOT AT ALL... UM...
I AM NOT...
......
DON'T HIDE YOUR FACE...

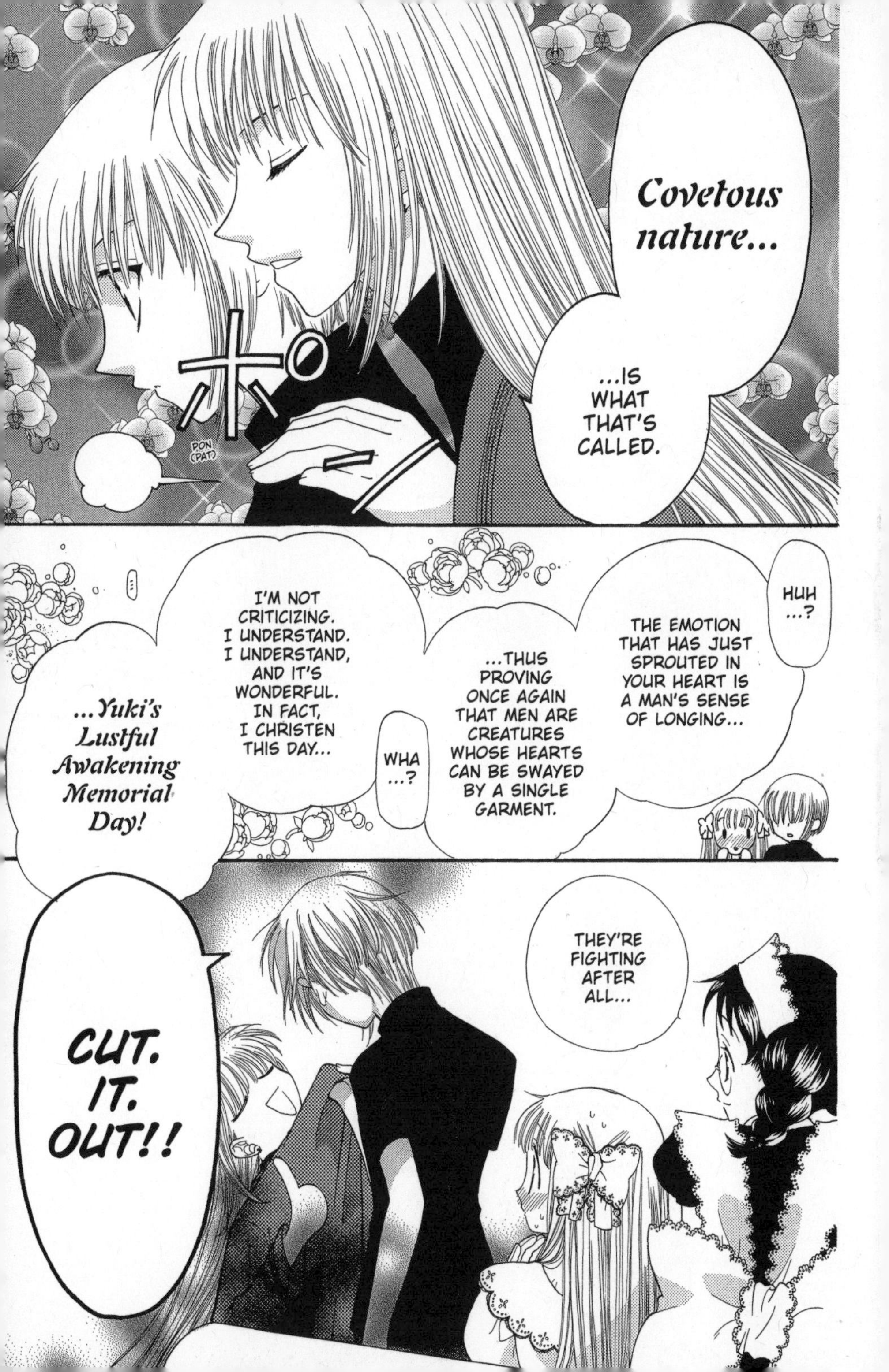
Covetous nature...
...IS WHAT THAT'S CALLED.
ポ
PON (PAT)
HUH ...?
THE EMOTION THAT HAS JUST SPROUTED IN YOUR HEART IS A MAN'S SENSE OF LONGING...
...THUS PROVING ONCE AGAIN THAT MEN ARE CREATURES WHOSE HEARTS CAN BE SWAYED BY A SINGLE GARMENT.
WHA ...?
I'M NOT CRITICIZING. I UNDERSTAND. I UNDERSTAND, AND IT'S WONDERFUL. IN FACT, I CHRISTEN THIS DAY...
...Yuki's Lustful Awakening Memorial Day!
...
THEY'RE FIGHTING AFTER ALL...
CUT. IT. OUT!!

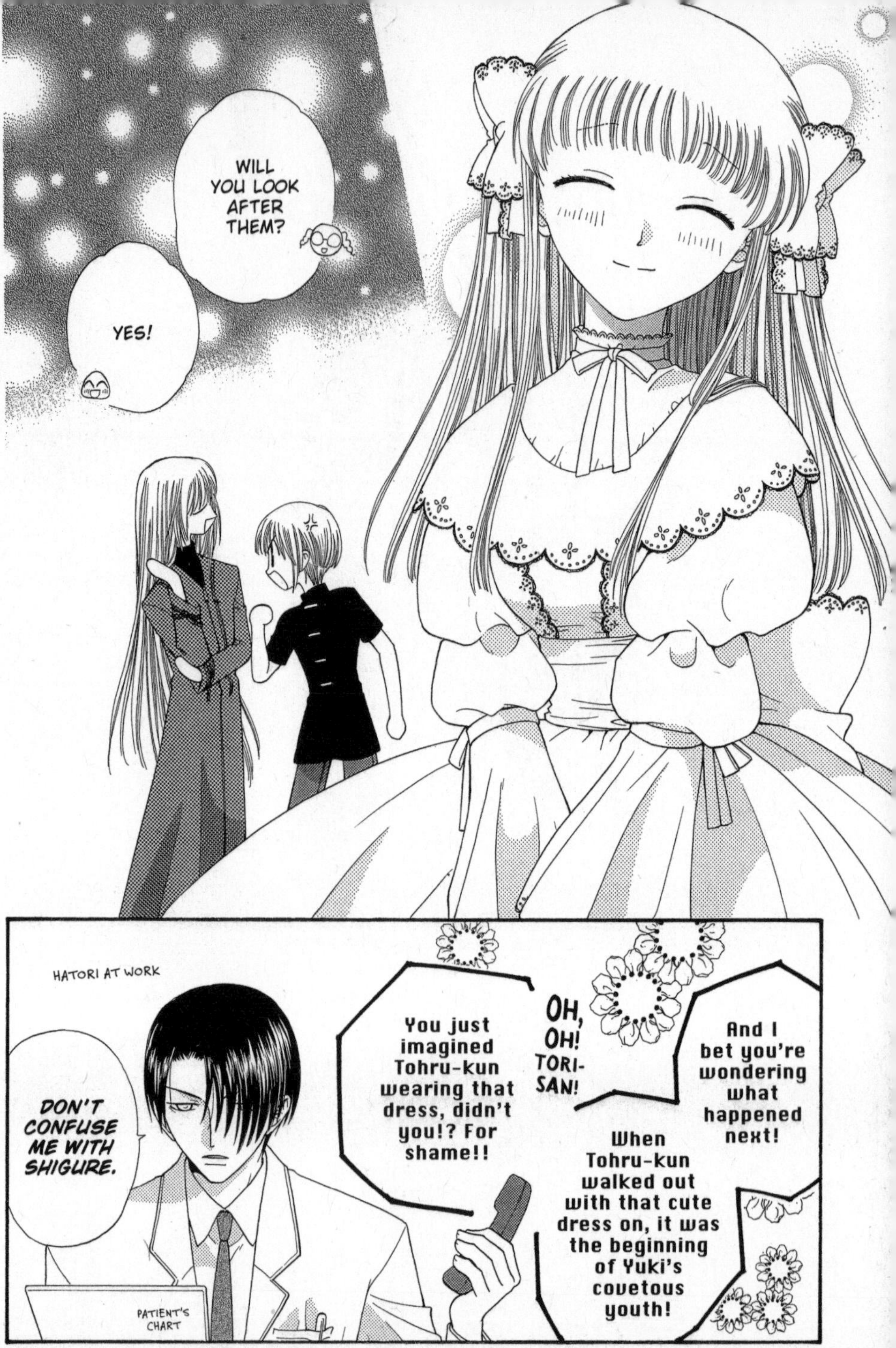
WILL YOU LOOK AFTER THEM?
YES!
And I bet you're wondering what happened next!
When Tohru-kun walked out with that cute dress on, it was the beginning of Yuki's covetous youth!
OH, OH! TORI-SAN!
You just imagined Tohru-kun wearing that dress, didn't you!? For shame!!
HATORI AT WORK
DON'T CONFUSE ME WITH SHIGURE.
PATIENT'S CHART

FEELING OF GRATITUDE

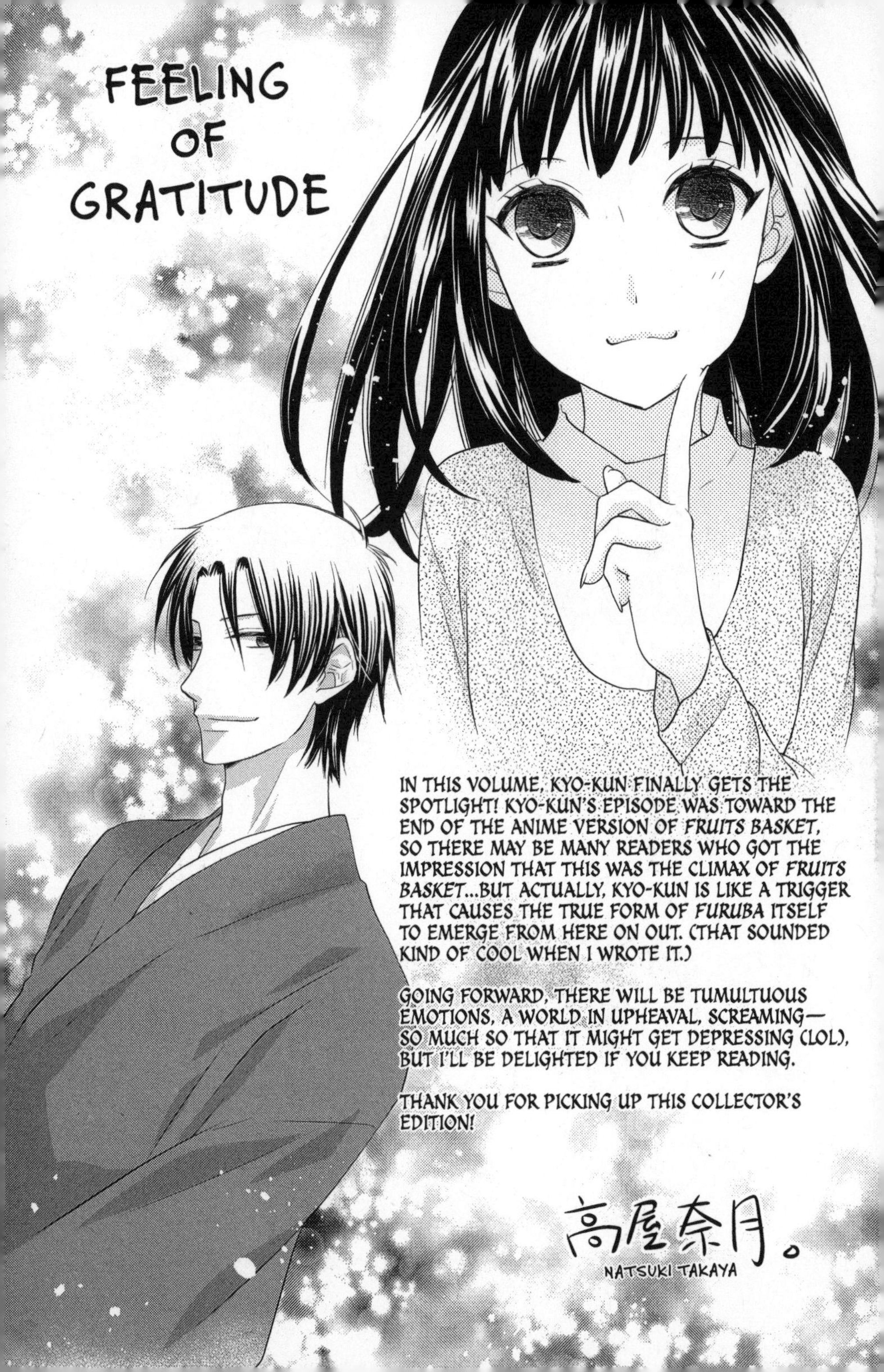

IN THIS VOLUME, KYO-KUN FINALLY GETS THE SPOTLIGHT! KYO-KUN'S EPISODE WAS TOWARD THE END OF THE ANIME VERSION OF *FRUITS BASKET*, SO THERE MAY BE MANY READERS WHO GOT THE IMPRESSION THAT THIS WAS THE CLIMAX OF *FRUITS BASKET*...BUT ACTUALLY, KYO-KUN IS LIKE A TRIGGER THAT CAUSES THE TRUE FORM OF *FURUBA* ITSELF TO EMERGE FROM HERE ON OUT. (THAT SOUNDED KIND OF COOL WHEN I WROTE IT.)

GOING FORWARD, THERE WILL BE TUMULTUOUS EMOTIONS, A WORLD IN UPHEAVAL, SCREAMING—SO MUCH SO THAT IT MIGHT GET DEPRESSING (LOL), BUT I'LL BE DELIGHTED IF YOU KEEP READING.

THANK YOU FOR PICKING UP THIS COLLECTOR'S EDITION!

高屋奈月。

NATSUKI TAKAYA

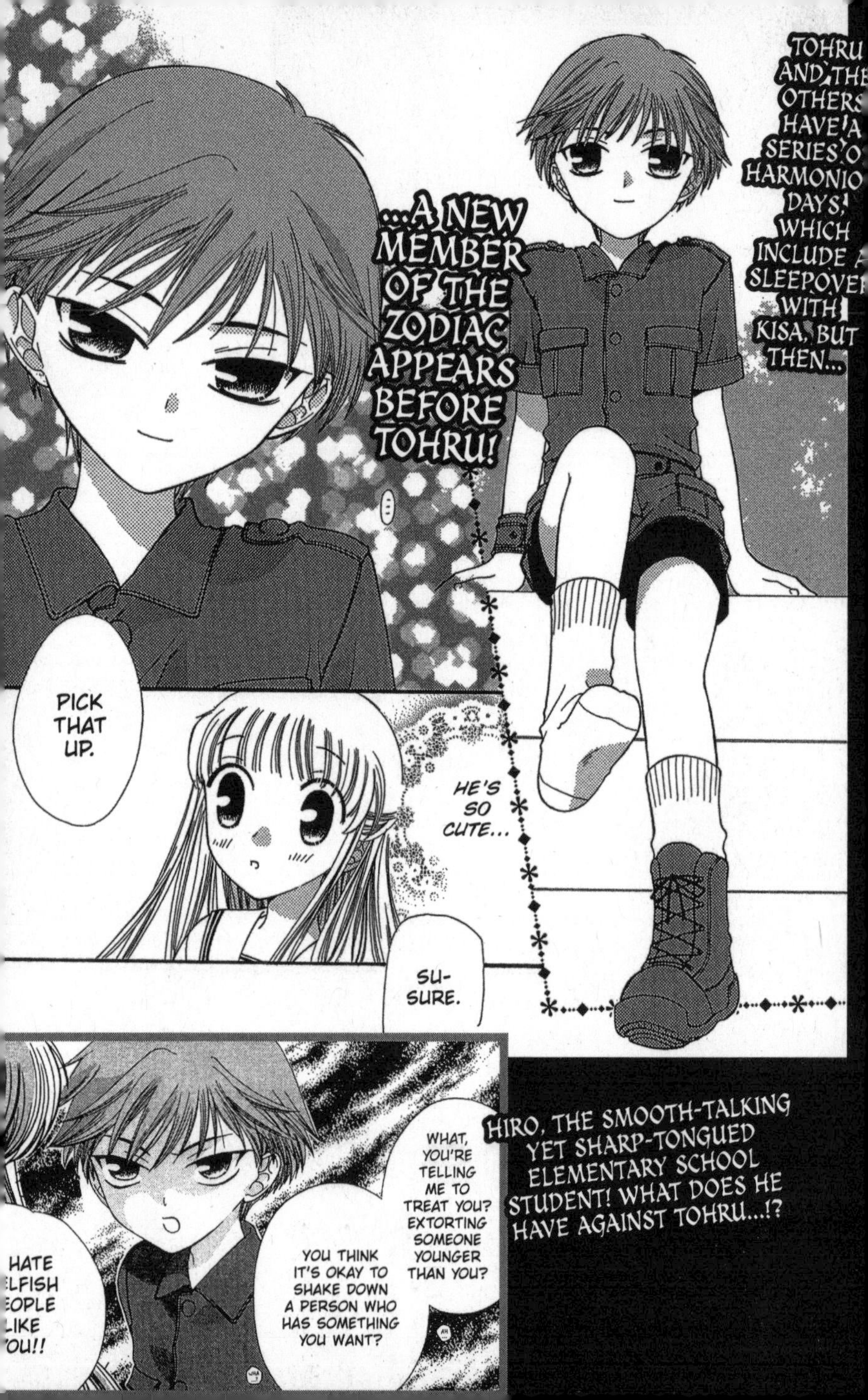
TOHRU AND THE OTHERS HAVE A SERIES O HARMONIO DAYS, WHICH INCLUDE A SLEEPOVE WITH KISA, BUT THEN...
...A NEW MEMBER OF THE ZODIAC APPEARS BEFORE TOHRU!
PICK THAT UP.
HE'S SO CUTE...
SU- SURE.
HIRO, THE SMOOTH-TALKING YET SHARP-TONGUED ELEMENTARY SCHOOL STUDENT! WHAT DOES HE HAVE AGAINST TOHRU...!?
WHAT, YOU'RE TELLING ME TO TREAT YOU? EXTORTING SOMEONE YOUNGER THAN YOU?
YOU THINK IT'S OKAY TO SHAKE DOWN A PERSON WHO HAS SOMETHING YOU WANT?
HATE ELFISH EOPLE LIKE OU!!

AND WE GET THE WHOLE STORY OF HOW TOHRU MET UO-CHAN BACK IN MIDDLE SCHOOL...

HUH...!?

P-PRESENT...

...YOU SAID!?

...BECAUSE I'VE GOT TOHRU.

I CAN LAUGH IN THIS "RESPECT-ABLE WORLD"...

HOW DID TWO PEOPLE SO DIFFERENT BECOME FRIENDS?

NAH, UM... I'M GOIN' HOME.

WHY? EAT BEFORE YOU GO.

TOHRU'S A GOOD COOK—

I'M NOT THAT GOOD...

BY THE WAY, WHAT ARE WE HAVING TONIGHT—?

PLUS, HATSUHARU GOES BERSERK IN CLASS!?

AND RITSU, THE SON OF THE HOT-SPRING INN HOSTESS, SHOWS UP TOO!?

THE BOTTO...

THE BOTTOM OF THE PAPER BAG...

Fruits Basket 4

COLLECTOR'S EDITION

IN STORES AUGUST 2016!!

TRANSLATION NOTES

COMMON HONORIFICS

no honorific: Indicates familiarity or closeness; if used without permission or reason, addressing someone in this manner would constitute an insult.

-san: The Japanese equivalent of Mr./Mrs./Miss. If a situation calls for politeness, this is the fail-safe honorific.

-sama: Conveys great respect; may also indicate that the social status of the speaker is lower than that of the addressee.

-dono: A very polite honorific, more formal (and sometimes distant) than *-san*.

-kun: Used most often when referring to boys, this indicates affection or familiarity. Occasionally used by older men among their peers, but it may also be used by anyone referring to a person of lower standing.

-chan: An affectionate honorific indicating familiarity used mostly in reference to girls; also used in reference to cute persons or animals of either gender.

-senpai: A suffix used to address upperclassmen or more experienced coworkers.

-kouhai: A suffix used to address underclassmen or less experienced coworkers.

-sensei: A respectful term for teachers, artists, or high-level professionals.

Page 10
Jason: This is a reference to the character Jason Voorhees in the *Friday the 13th* film series. The hockey mask–wearing, undead serial killer is best known for murdering young people in remote cabins by a lake.

Page 15
Golden Week: Golden Week is the popular spring holiday in Japan, typically running from the end of April through the beginning of May. Many workers can take off during this period, which is actually four national holidays rounded out to a week: Shouwa Day (April 29), which honors the birthday of the Shouwa emperor, Hirohito, who reigned from 1926–1989; Constitution Memorial Day (May 3), which celebrates the founding of the Constitution of Japan in 1947; Greenery Day (May 4), for the appreciation of nature; and Children's Day (May 5), in celebration of children.

Page 45
Je t'aime, mon ami—bon voyage!: This is French for "I love you, my friend—I hope you have a safe and enjoyable journey!"

Page 45
Annyeong hashimnikka: This is a very formal way to say "How are you?" in Korean. Both Ayame's line and this one are, of course, jokey non sequiturs.

Page 46
Kinpachi-*sensei*: The main character of the eponymous, long-running TV drama, Kinpachi-sensei is the teacher of a third-year middle school class and is known for handing out life lessons, as well as tackling teen issues of the day, such as bullying, homophobia, teen pregnancy, and shut-ins.

Page 46
The character for "person": The kanji for "person" is read as *hito* and consists of two lines leaning toward each other and meeting at the top, a fine metaphor for people connecting with and supporting one another.

Page 57
The Graduate: This is a reference to the ending of the 1967 film *The Graduate*, when the main character interrupts the wedding of his on-again, off-again girlfriend and runs off with her.

Page 80
-*nii*: Like the term *nii-san*, this means "big brother," albeit more colloquially.

Page 108
Ladder lottery: *Amidakuji* in Japanese, this lottery is named after the way the paper is folded into a fan shape resembling the halo of the celestial Buddha Amida. It creates random pairings between two sets and is often used to distribute things fairly to people (for example, prizes or chores).

Page 127
Onee-chan: This is a familiar form of address for an older sister or a young adult female. Kisa looks up to Tohru as a kind of "big sister" and so naturally uses this form.

Page 133
Waves, curses: The kanji in the background (meaning "waves" and "curses") are a reference to the Hanajima siblings' paranormal abilities. Saki can send out stunning "electric waves" and can also read "waves," kind of like mind reading. Megumi can't sense waves like Saki, but he is able to cast powerful curses.

Page 191
Oji-chan: This is a fond term for an uncle or an avuncular middle-aged man.

Page 298
Seiza: A traditional Japanese style of sitting, this involves kneeling while sitting on the soles of one's feet.

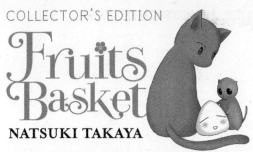

COLLECTOR'S EDITION

Fruits Basket

NATSUKI TAKAYA

Translation: Sheldon Drzka   •   Lettering: Lys Blakeslee

Fruits Basket Collector's Edition, Vol. 3 by Natsuki Takaya
© 2015 by Natsuki Takaya
All rights reserved.
First published in Japan in 2015 by HAKUSENSHA, INC., Tokyo.
English language translation rights in U.S.A., Canada and U.K. arranged with
HAKUSENSHA, INC., Tokyo through Tuttle-Mori Agency, Inc., Tokyo.

English Translation © 2016 by Yen Press, LLC

Yen Press
1290 Avenue of the Americas
New York, NY 10104

Visit us at yenpress.com
facebook.com/yenpress
twitter.com/yenpress
yenpress.tumblr.com

First Yen Press Edition: July 2016

Yen Press is an imprint of Yen Press, LLC.
The Yen Press name and logo are trademarks of Yen Press, LLC.

The publisher is not responsible for websites (or their content) that are not owned by the publisher.

Library of Congress Control Number: 2016932692

ISBN: 978-0-316-36064-7

10 9 8 7 6 5 4 3 2 1

BVG

Printed in the United States of America